The Way It Was:
The Jewish World of Rural Hesse

Mathilda W. Stein

FrederickMax Publications
Atlanta, Georgia

Printed in Canada by Friesens through Four Colour Imports, Louisville, Kentucky, United States

Edited by Maureen MacLaughlin, Mitzvah Publications, Atlanta, Georgia

Cover by Lead Free Studios, Atlanta, Georgia

ISBN 0-9673282-0-9

To obtain copies of and pricing information for this book write:
FrederickMax Publications
430 Montevallo Drive
Atlanta, Georgia   30342
United States

Table of Contents

Acknowledgements

The following people gave of their time and expertise to promote this project:

Hans Gliss, municipal town officer of Lauterbach
Frau Jakob, officer of *Gemeinde Schwalmtal*
Roy Johnson
Maureen MacLaughlin
Ellen Kierr Stein
Dr. Jason Stein
Dr. Kenneth W. Stein
Max K. Stein
Dr. Ursula Miriam Wippich
Mr. Ziegler, municipal officer of Alsfeld

Dedication

*In memory of my dear parents, Berta Lamm Wertheim
and Frederick Wertheim, and my beloved husband,
Max K. Stein*

*U*nless yesterday is understood, the anguish of today is distorted. The advent of Adolf Hitler was merely an impelling force that legalized harsher persecution of Jews in Germany and culminated in the Holocaust. For centuries in Europe, the churches and other formidable forces had painstakingly laid the groundwork for Goebbel's anti-semitic propaganda to fall on fertile soil and contributed to the willing execution of Hitler's mandate of the 'Final Solution' by ordinary Germans. Since the churches have been so powerful and authoritative from the Middle Ages to the present, a major responsibility for the Holocaust must fall on the Christian ecclesiastical institutions in Europe.

[3

JEWS IN THE ROMAN EMPIRE

CONSTANTINE THE GREAT (306-337) was the first Roman Emperor who radically limited the rights of Jews as citizens of the Roman Empire, a privilege that had been conferred upon them by Caracalla in 211. As Christianity grew in power in the Roman Empire, it influenced the emperors to limit further the civil and political rights of the Jews. Most of the imperial laws that dealt with Jews since the days of Constantine are found in the *Codex Theodosianus* (438) and in the Latin and Greek code of Justinian (534). These legal charters were important in furthering the ongoing decline of Jewish rights. The Roman law regarding Jews was the basis for later Christian and Moslem legal rulings. The Justinian body of law established the second-class status of the Jew in the Middle Ages, and the medieval Church assigned Jews to an even lower status by giving religious sanction to their legal disadvantages.

JEWS IN THE GERMAN LANDS

THE FIRST JEWS TO ARRIVE in Germany (which was then part of the Roman Empire) were tradesmen who accompanied the Roman legions. These Jews settled in towns such as Cologne, Mainz, Speyer, and Trier in the region of the Rhine River. Not only did these newcomers have a history of nearly two thousand years behind them, but they also carried their recorded history with them in a book held sacred by their faith and their tradition. These Jews were filled with the awareness that they had been chosen for a difficult life and the fulfillment of laws for the sake of a covenant between them and their God.[1] However, in Europe, during the turmoil of the fall of the Roman Empire and the mass migrations of the fourth and fifth centuries as well as the forced conversions of the heathens, most Jewish communities perished.

A continuously documented history of Jews in Germany exists only since the ninth and tenth centuries. During this time, the most important trade routes led through German lands and Jewish merchants continued to travel and settle in the centers of commerce and trade.[2] For a while, Jews were protected as merchants, traders, and importers of oriental products. Immigrants are always well received as long as they fill an existing void in the economy better than the members of the local population.[3]

In 1084, when Rüdiger von Speyer wanted to elevate his rural diocese into a town bishop's see, he granted the Jews privileges which were more favorable than

Preface

rights promised to Jews in other cities. At that time, the bishop declared that he had prevailed upon the Jews to settle in Speyer "in order to increase honor in our city." Six years later, the rights of the Jews of Speyer were confirmed and broadened by Emperor Heinrich IV (1050-1106). Under his protection, Jews were to be free from persecutions in their professional and religious lives. Furthermore, it was forbidden to take away from Jews property such as real estate, gardens, vineyards, fields, and slaves. Forced baptism and torture for exacting confessions were prohibited. The killing of Jews called for severe penalties, which invites speculation as to why this explicit regulation was needed.

JEWS AND THE
CRUSADES

IN 1096, AT THE BEGINNING of the first Crusade, the Jews of Speyer were warned by their persecuted co-religionists in Rouen and Metz in France. The Jews of Speyer did not heed the warning and on May 3, 1096, Christian hordes attacked them on a Sabbath. Bishop John quickly took decisive action and the Jewish community of Speyer lost only ten or eleven members of their congregation. The destiny of the Jews of Worms was less favorable because the strong central power of a bishop was missing. Part of the Jewish community of Worms fled to the bishop's fortification while others remained in their homes. The latter group was attacked first and killed one-by-one, and then the Christian hordes looted the victims' homes and the synagogue. A week later, the mob returned with reinforcements and attacked the bishop's bastion. As the Jews witnessed the fate of their brethren, they killed themselves while reciting "Hear, O Israel: the Lord our God, the Lord is One." The mob stripped their remains and profaned the corpses. Very few of the Jews of Worms were saved by their Christian friends or spared by converting to Christianity. The death count in Worms amounted to eight hundred souls.[4]

During the Crusades in 1146, the monk Radulph prevailed upon the crusaders to avenge themselves on "those who had crucified Jesus." In 1198, Pope Innocent III ordered that, during the absence of the crusaders, no interest should be chargeable on debts Christians had entered into with Jews and any interest already received should be returned. However, the spiritual leader of the second Crusade, Bernard of Clairvaux, forbade excesses against Jews, who were neither to be killed nor expelled. Although persecution of Jews was thereafter less extensive, many Jews had already been murdered by the time the Clairvaux directive was announced.[5]

ANTI-SEMITISM

THROUGHOUT THE MIDDLE AGES, the Church often clashed with worldly powers and, as a result, it endeavored to strengthen its spiritual supremacy by waging a battle against Jews.[6] During the Middle Ages and well into modern times, the self-directing way of life of Jews was construed by Christians as an obstinate denial of Jesus as the Messiah. Regardless of the Church's effort to turn them from their 'faithlessness,' Jews remained tenacious and unbending. That continual refusal unsettled Christians and underscored its steadfastness in its own tenets. Therefore,

Christianity chose to attack Judaism and Jews, whose sorry plight would bear testimony to the supposedly infallible authority of the Church.[7] The primary issues were Christ as the Messiah, the Trinity, the Incarnation of Christ, and the Blessed Virgin. The struggle climaxed with the accusation that Jews had killed Christ: an accusation that lasted well into the twentieth century and only became obsolete with the arrival of Vatican II.

I also encountered the accusation of having killed Christ. As a child of seven, I was attending public school in the predominantly Lutheran town of Lauterbach, Hesse, my birthplace. Betty, who played ball with me during recess, announced one day that she could no longer have a good time with me because I had murdered Christ, her Lord. I assured her that I had done no such thing and explained that my hands were neither big nor strong enough for such an act. Although Betty agreed about my physical limitations for killing someone, she declared that her aunt had directed her not to play with me, because I was Jewish and all Jews had murdered Christ.

The Jewish population in German lands increased after the tenth century, especially in the large cities where they inhabited densely-crammed Jewish quarters. Because contact was no longer restricted to marginal interaction with Jewish traveling merchants, anti-Jewish notions intensified. Nevertheless, Jews were always a small minority, even in German cities, where they barely amounted to more than five percent.[8]

The widely-held view of the Church fathers was to suffer the presence of the Jews because of Christian love for one's fellow man. According to Christian authorities, Jews would survive until the Last Judgment, at which time they would bear witness to the divinity of Christ. As a consequence of this doctrine of brotherly love, the popes took the Jews under their protection from oppression. At least until the thirteenth century, attempts at proselytizing Jews were usually effected without force. However, in provincial regions ecclesiastical personnel and institutions often actively participated in the persecution of Jews, where official church doctrine did not penetrate.

Since ancient days, the common people had held onto superstitious notions of the Jew as anti-Christ, sorcerer, personification of the devil, devil worshipper, mixer of poison, practitioner of black magic, and medical man who used his skill to the detriment of Christians. Lack of understanding of Jewish rituals and the allegation that Jews had murdered Christ gave rise to a mentality that was widespread and effective in furthering modern anti-semitism, which added a biological basis to the idea that all Jews were enemies of mankind.[9]

In Lauterbach and in Alsfeld, where I attended school, educational authorities and teachers proclaimed daily in class that all Jews belonged to an underclass of the human race. For the most part, I do not believe that teachers intended to demean Jewish students personally, but the effect of their assertions on Jewish youngsters was, of course, immeasurably harmful. Any prejudice against Jews taught and caught at home by parents was well-reinforced at school.

Furthermore, hatred of Jews was closely tied to economic causes. The economic circumstances of Jews in German lands were rigidly restricted by the guilds. For all practical purposes, only cattle dealing and itinerant selling of small items were left for supporting a Jewish family in an area where the villagers, too, endured oppressive burdens imposed by the feudal lords.

Jews were also money lenders, because Christian biblical canon prohibited moneylending for interest. Jews dealing in unsecured loans frequently charged fifty to one hundred percent interest because of the high risk involved. During the late Middle Ages, hostility and ill will toward Jews escalated because the lower aristocracy, craftsmen, and peasants were indebted to Jews. Hatred of Jews led to numerous forcible cancellations of debts in which the clergy, sovereigns, and the upper classes in cities cooperated only too readily.

JEWS AND THE RULERS OF GERMAN LANDS

JEWS, LIKE OTHER MERCHANTS, benefited from the protection of the German king or emperor. A profitable franchise that might originally have been granted to an individual Jewish merchant would often be extended to embrace a Jewish community. Protection of Jews was placed directly under the German king or emperor, and was therefore solidly established in the criminal law.[10] Jews who held letters of protection in the Holy Roman Empire from 1236 on were called *Schutzjuden* (protected Jews) and they were regarded as 'serfs of the chamber' (*servi camerae regis*). When the emperor needed funds, he granted his right over the Jews to territorial feudal lords and free cities. They in turn charged a regular fee for letters of protection to the Jews living within their domain. As a result, Jews became the subjects of the local feudal lords and free cities, which furnished either a personal or communal letter of protection (*Schutzbrief*). Letters of protection had to be renewed periodically for a fee set by the sovereign and they generated a good income. In Hesse, the feudal lords who 'kept Jews' turned into potentates with a passion for baroque castles.[11] Many a palace in that region was built with money exacted from Jews who paid excessively for the privilege of living under wretched conditions at the pleasure of the sovereign.

During the seventh century, the Anglo-Saxon Benedictine monk, St. Boniface (672-754), converted the Germanic tribes of the Frisians, Thuringians, and Hessians to Christianity and founded the Monastery at Fulda (seven miles from Lauterbach). The remains of the martyred St. Boniface were laid to rest in the Fulda Cathedral. Also in Fulda, the first accusation in Germany of a ritual murder by Jews took place in 1235. A grist mill went up in flames and two children were burned to death while their parents attended church on Christmas Eve. No one considered that the children may have been playing with fire during their parents' absence. Instead, the citizens of Fulda accused the local Jews of wanting to obtain a mysterious medicine from the blood of these children. Immediately, the Fulda townsmen killed thirty-two Jews. The citizenry sent the poorly-preserved remains of the children to King Frederick II (1194-1250), who advised that the children should be buried. He also ordered a careful investigation of the incident because he was determined to apply common sense in combating dangerous superstitions. Theologians and jurists rendered an innocent verdict based on the fact that devout Jews were strictly forbidden to have any connection with blood and especially the partaking of human blood.[12]

JEWS AND THE CHURCH

GREGORY IX (1227-1241) also intervened in favor of the persecuted Jews and forbade that Jews be robbed, killed, or forcibly baptized. On July 5, 1247, Innocent IV (1243-1254) emphatically opposed the accusation of ritual murders. Although that papal outlook remained the basis pertaining to the accusation of ritual murder, royal directives and papal announcements could not prevent ritual blood accusations from being frequently propagated locally within the sphere of 'folk piety.'

During the thirteenth century, Jews were accused of profaning Christ by desecrating the sacred wafers. These accusations were spread by Franciscan and Dominican preachers as well as by converts from Judaism. The official Church issued additional restrictive measures to avoid close contact and sexual relations between Jews and Christians. In 1265, Pope Clement IV decreed that Jews could no longer dwell among Christians but had to take up quarters in a segregated part of a town or a village, which was to be separated from the living quarters of Christians by a fence, a wall, or a trench. This ordinance turned into the standard for the future ghettos.[13] The Fourth Lateran Council in 1215 decreed that Jews had to wear special clothing (a pointed hat with pommel) and a 'Jew ring.' Seven centuries later, the Nazis used this decree as a model for their regulation of Jews wearing the yellow star and the compulsory addition of the names of Sara and Israel.

In 1259, a synod in Fritzlar (in Hesse) directed that on Good Friday no Jew was to be seen looking out of a window of his home, standing in a doorway, or moving about in the streets.[14] This dictum lasted well into the twentieth century in Lauterbach, even before Hitler officially seized power. My mother emphasized to her children that for a Jew, Good Friday was no day to play outdoors.

THE BLACK DEATH AND POGROMS

IN THE EARLY PART of the fourteenth century, accusations of ritual murders and charges of violating the sanctity of the Host by Jews continued to bear heavily on the Jewish population, especially in the west, southwest, and south of Germany. In 1349, the Black Death broke out in German lands. Returning Crusaders spread this epidemic, which is estimated to have killed three-quarters of the population of Europe and Asia. At that time, no one knew that this disease was spread by fleas carried in the coat of rats, and since no explanation for this affliction could be found, Jews were accused of having poisoned the wells. The Church, which had a virtual monopoly on education, did nothing to refute the allegation, even though Jews died along with Christians.[15]

An intense wave of Jewish persecution started in Chillon, Savoy, which at that time belonged to Germany. The Jew Belanvingus after being tortured (I saw the chambers in the basement of the Chillon castle), confessed that he and other Jews had plotted to spread the plague all over Europe. Although totally innocent of these charges, he ultimately succumbed to the torture: he was forced to admit that the Jews (contrary to actual fact) had prepared large quantities of a decoction of spiders, frogs, hearts of Christians, and consecrated wafers. This poison had been distributed to all Jews, who in turn had poisoned the wells. Thereupon, all Jews of Chillon were slaughtered.[16]

The brunt of this wave of persecution in German lands reached Fulda with a slaughter of Jews by the end of March 1349. On July 24, 1349, the Jews of Frankfurt am Main were destroyed by murder and by suicide from fire.[17] By 135l, after the Black Death had abated in German regions, two hundred ten Jewish communities had been annihilated and their members killed; synagogues were destroyed; the sacred scrolls of the *Torah* were reduced to ashes; tombstones were thrown down and graves were broken into in search of hidden treasures.[18] In Hesse, the Jewish communities of Frankfurt am Main, Fulda, Friedberg, and other small communities were completely destroyed, though some Jews succeeded in fleeing.[19]

In the fifteenth century, the battle against the Jews remained on the agenda of the Catholic orders. The Pope could not assert himself too much because the orders rendered dedicated service to the Church. For instance, John of Capistrano (1386-1456) of the Franciscan order, spread horror and fear against the Jews. As a consequence of his homiletics, hundreds of Jews lost their lives in Silesia.[20] From the seventeenth century on, blood libel accusations spread to Eastern Europe. Only in 1965 did the Church repudiate the blood libel of Trent (1475).[21]

MARTIN LUTHER
AND THE JEWS

AT FIRST, THE GERMAN religious reformer Martin Luther (1483-1546) had high hopes for converting Jews. However, when the Jews remained steadfast in their beliefs, he turned vehemently against them. In addition to his fulminations against the Jews, Luther formulated harsh words toward all those whom he considered his enemies—princes, bishops, and the Pope. In the case of the Jews he suggested forced labor and deportation, which were precursors to the 'Final Solution' in Hitler's gas chambers. Luther's notions were steadily inculcated by German Protestantism that endured as a strong power in German life.

Martin Luther's hostility toward Jews was also exacerbated by his friend, Martin Bucer (1491-1551) from Strassburg, a former Dominican brother and religious reformer. When Landgrave Philip of Hesse (1504-1567) wanted to give an exact status to the Jews in his territories, he appointed Martin Bucer and six clergymen of his realm to offer a written opinion. The panel declared that on principle Jews were to be exiled. Toleration of Jews was possible, but only if prior regulations set up by devout Catholic bishops were expanded by additional provisos with stipulations asserting that Jews, as long as they persisted in their religion, should be restricted to the lowest social status. Also, they were to desist from studying the *Talmud* and to show no irreverence to Christ and Christians. Furthermore, Jews were not to exchange views on religion with Christians except for discussions with specially-designated clergymen, and their wives and children were to attend Christian sermons.[22] Nevertheless, in Hesse there were Catholic enclaves where Jews were better tolerated because Catholics in Hesse had also tasted the bitter cup of being a religious minority, so some of their earlier ardor for persecuting Jews lessened while they were occupied with keeping their own adversaries at bay.

THE ENLIGHTENMENT

AS LONG AS CHRISTIANITY was dominant, Jews were outside the pale of social life in German lands. However, with the advent of the Enlightenment in the eighteenth century, Christianity lost ground to more secular views of the world. In 1791, when the French revolutionaries emancipated their Jews they declared: "To the man, everything; to the Jew, nothing." As a citizen the Jew was to gain full freedom, as a Jew he was to be regarded as a naught. Nevertheless, Voltaire (1694-1778), a French Enlightenment philosopher and writer, maintained that Jewish traits were immutable. Jews were ignorant by nature and it was not possible to assimilate them into modern society even if they were deprived of their religion. Voltaire declared that the degenerated Christian-Jewish-Oriental turn of mind had afflicted the dignity and liberty of the European intellect like a plague. Voltaire's postulates on Jews came to be the fundamental elements of racial anti-semitism.

While a leading German intellectual, Gotthold Ephraim Lessing (1729-1780), was advocating the full civic emancipation of Jews, the German Romantic poet and historian, Ernst Moritz Arndt (1769-1860), ascribed to the Jews their own 'national character,' which by its 'deviation' threatened the Teutonic race. Stories and tales by Arndt were assigned reading during my last two years in German literature classes in Lauterbach. The anti-Jewish theological elements of the German philosopher, Johann Gottlieb Fichte (1762-1814), as well as those of the German theologian, Friedrich Daniel Ernst Schleiermacher (1768-1834), completed the process of cleansing "positive Christianity from its negative Jewish traits."[23] In 1793, the German philosopher Fichte absolutely rejected the granting of civil rights to Jews because of the inherently evil Jewish character, which he believed could not be rooted out. These theorems were not lost on my teachers in Lauterbach and Alsfeld. To this day, I cringe when I recall their habitual pronouncements in class about the 'negative character of the inferior Jew' and the damage he inflicted on the inherently superior 'Aryan' race. I rarely had the privilege of acquiring knowledge without propaganda.

In 1811, the 'Christian German Dinner Society' counted among its members Fichte, Kleist (a poet and playwright), Brentano (a poet of the German Romantic era), and Savigny (a jurist). The statutes of the association included a stipulation that not only Jews, but also baptized former Jews and their descendants, were to be excluded from membership. The Berlin Jewish author, Saul Ascher, criticized the German Nationalists who had replaced traditional Christian enmity with a racial war of words in order to shut out Jews. The anti-semitic followers of Friedrich

Ludwig Jahn (the founder of sports education for German youth) descended on Ascher. Ascher's publication, *Germanomanie*, condemned the fanaticism of the German student associations that had burned his writings. In 1817, the German-Jewish poet Heinrich Heine (1797-1856) uttered a fateful prophecy: "This act has only been a prologue, where books are burned, in the end humans will also be reduced to ashes."[24]

THE HEP! HEP!
RIOTS

A NUMBER OF ANTI-JEWISH riots broke out in Germany in 1819, at which time the provocative "Hep! Hep!" cry was employed against Jews. This reprehensible hunting cry was probably first used for driving goats in Franconia and was chanted by the tormentors of Jews as early as the fourteenth century. It may also have originated from the initials of the crusaders' exclamation '*Hierosolyma est perdita*' ('Jerusalem is lost'). Konrad List, a bourgeois merchant of Lauterbach and the father of one of my playmates, used to shriek "Hep! Hep!" while his daughter and I were happily playing with dolls. Even as an eight year old, I sensed that this

Anti-Jewish riots in Frankfurt am Main, 1819

Hepp! Hepp!

scream was intended to embarrass and frighten me. I pretended that nothing had happened and continued to play as if the intended vexation of my playmate's father was meant for someone else. But in reality I quivered.

ANTI-SEMITISM IN
THE NINETEENTH
CENTURY

DURING THE FIRST HALF of the nineteenth century, public anti-semitism was not only customary, but socially acceptable. In Hesse, the military considered it fashionable to humiliate Jews in the streets. It was of little consolation to those affected that the official position in Darmstadt harshly censured these excesses in an era of so-called official Enlightenment and liberal views.

On January 1, 1824, Darmstadt lifted the special payment of taxes for Jews. Although the excessive fiscal burden was eliminated, the question of seeking social and human contacts for Jews in Hesse arose. In 1827, an association for the moral improvement of Jews in German lands as well as in the Grand Duchy of Hesse was founded. For this purpose and in keeping with a division of German lands into three parts, an executive committee was formed and headed by Dr. Levi, Dr. Weil, and Anton F. Mayer. The point at issue was to liberate from their plight "a helpless class of humans" by instilling love for Germany and while maintaining the faith of their fathers. With expressions appropriate to this historic moment, the executive committee inculcated the Jewish community elders with the nationalistic theme of the hour. Chairmen of rural district councils were contacted because doubts existed whether particular Jewish communities and their elders possessed the necessary understanding for this task. In late autumn of 1845, three clergymen, Heber from Offenbach, Helfrich from Dolgesheim, and Huth from Seeheim, as well as the secondary school teacher of classics, Dr. Hainebach from Giessen, founded an "association of the friends of Israel" in the Grand Duchy of Hesse. Higher authorities noted on a petition "do not proceed."

OTTO BÖCKEL
AND
POLITICAL
ANTI-SEMITISM

IN 1817, 1829, AND 1844, A SERIES of poor harvests occurred in German lands. During this agricultural crisis there was increasing resentment among the peasants, who were bitter about being exploited not only by the administrative powers and the lords, but also by the Jews. Such beliefs were promoted in the writings of the Hessian clergyman, Ludwig Rudolf Oeser. who considered Jews a leprosy that damaged the marrow and poisoned the body of the German people. Pastor Oeser's teachings germinated well on Hessian soil. In 1847, a year of poor harvest in the Kraich region in the Odenwald (a highland between the plain of the river Rhine and the river Main), a pamphlet was circulated which urged abolition of the aristocracy, assassination of civil servants, expulsion of Jews, and an era of persecution and attacks on Jews began. In Mannheim, bloodthirsty posters appeared with a human being swinging on a gallows and an executioner's ax bearing the inscription "Ten o'clock in the evening! Hep! Hep!" In spring of 1847, in the Tauber area (the Tauber flows into the Main at Wertheim), the Jews bolted their doors and left the lights on at night out of fear of looting.[25] In 1858, another minister, J. W. Urich from Gonterskirchen in the county of Giessen, complained passionately in the Gonterskirchen *Chronicle* that "many of its townspeople are in the predatory claws of the Jews."

On February 2, 1887, the rabid anti-Semite, Otto Böckel (1859-1923), was elected to the parliament in Germany. The Böckel movement was a development that flowed from the true sentiment of the population in Upper Hesse.[26] Böckel was hailed enthusiastically as a liberator and called the second Luther. On February 29,

1890, another anti-Semite, Oswald Zimmermann, received twenty-four percent of the votes in Lauterbach and won the election in Upper Hesse. On August 17, 1890, the German Reform Society for the election district of Alsfeld-Lauterbach-Schotten was founded and announced ruthless battle against Jews.

In a subsequent election in the spring of 1893, the anti-Semite Stöcker received no votes and Zimmermann obtained only twenty-six ballots.[27] Nevertheless, the *Reichstag* (German parliament) acquired seventeen anti-Semites in 1893 and fourteen in 1898.[28] In 1892, Böckel was indeed the 'German king of the peasants'- as he liked to hear himself characterized in the Marburg-Friedberg-Büdingen-Lauterbach area. From 1886 until 1890, Böckel did not encounter much opposition. He ultimately failed because of lack of organization.

Böckel's ideas had a pernicious influence on the lives of the Jews in Upper Hesse. Böckel's racial creed stemmed from his study of German mythology and his perception of the philosophical primitive religion of his people.[29] He wished to obtain basic religious feeling and the "German racial philosophy" directly through the utterances of the national spirit and national characteristics.[30] The relevance and priority ascribed to the primitive German racial philosophy permeated through most lessons during my years in school in Lauterbach and Alsfeld. The only two teachers in Lauterbach who did not subscribe to the German racial philosophy were my biology teacher, Mr. Maurer, and my French teacher, Mr. Benz. By the time I reached the *Oberrealschule* in Alsfeld in 1930, German racial philosophy had permeated every subject and was practiced by all my teachers, who stressed the inferiority and baseness of any culture and religion other than that of the Germanic 'Aryan' ideal.

1927/28 Lauterbach high school class.
Standing left to right:
Henrich Krocker
Heinrich Daum
Heinrich Hoffmann
Helmut Feldmann
Roberto Junkers
Erich Opel
Kurt Stöhr
Otto Euler
Heinrich Kleinschmidt
Lothar Schiff
Seated left to right:
Gertrud Hofstetter
Trudel List
Marie Jänicke
Marga Sommer
Anna Wagner
Mathilde Wertheim
Teacher: Karl Maurer

After the formation of the first German Reich in 1871, the anti-Semite, Heinrich von Treitschke (1834-1896), proclaimed "the Jews are our calamity." At that time, the Catholic Church was considered an adversary of the new Reich and was viewed as the embodiment of backwardness. The Pope took a defensive stand by making the 'godless Jewish press' responsible for the Church's plight. Consequently, the Catholic Church stigmatized Jews in general and charged them with being enemies of Christianity and propagators of materialism without religion.[31] That accusation, too, came to be the bane of my existence while growing up in Germany.

In 1881, the political economist, Eugen Dühring, in *The Jewish Question as a Racial, Moral and Cultural Issue*, painted a ghastly picture of Jewish iron rule in all spheres of civil life, including political parties, courts, town halls, theaters, and science laboratories. He condemned Schiller and Goethe because they had come under the influence of the 'Slavic Jew Lessing' and he also berated the 'Jew Nietzsche.' For Dühring, the word 'Jew' was an invective. He proclaimed: "Nordic man who has fully matured under the cool heavens, has the duty to exterminate parasitic bloodlines after the manner of poisonous snakes and wild beasts of prey."[32] Newspapers, my teachers, and others often voiced Dühring's views while I was growing up. These statements fired me with an ardor for an early departure from Germany, even if it meant leaving without my parents.

WORLD WAR I   IN 1914, AT THE OUTBREAK OF WORLD WAR I, nine hundred ninety-one of a group of one thousand one hundred Jewish university students volunteered for service in the armed forces. The youngest German volunteer toward the end of the war in 1918 was the thirteen-year-old Jew Joseph Zippes, who eventually lost both his legs. Of the ninety-six thousand Jewish servicemen who fought in the German army, the navy, and the fledgling air force ten thousand were volunteers. In all, twelve thousand German-Jewish soldiers were killed in action.[33] My mother's oldest brother, Siegfried Lamm of Kirtorf, was killed in action on October 12, 1915, at age twenty-five as a member of the Reserve-Infantry Regiment 81. My father's first cousin, Hugo Levi from Angenrod of Infantry Regiment 116, died as a prisoner-of-war on September 24, 1918, at age twenty-five. In the summer of 1959, my former high school classmate and erstwhile storm trooper, Helmut Stöppler of Maar, recounted cold-bloodedly that, when he rounded up Jews in Hessian towns and villages, German-Jewish servicemen of World War I were taken on the same cattle car transports as other German-Jewish victims headed for the 'Final Solution.'

Endnotes

1. Alex Bein, *Juden in Preussen* (Dortmund: Druckerei Hitzegard, 1981), p. 19.

2. Ismar Elbogen, *Geschichte der Juden in Deutschland* (Berlin: Erich Lichtenstein Verlag, 1935), p. 18.

3. Bein, *Juden in Preussen*, pp. 19, 20.

4. Elbogen, *Geschichte der Juden in Deutschland*, p. 30.

5. *Encyclopedia Judaica*, (Jerusalem, 1978), Vol. 5, p. 1139.

6. Elbogen, *Geschichte der Juden in Deutschland*, p. 59.

7. Uriel Tal, *Christians and Jews in Germany* (New York: Cornell University Press, 1975), pp. 15, 16.

8. Peter Herde, *Neunhundert Jahre Geschichte der Juden in Hessen* (Wiesbaden: Kommission für die Geschichte der Juden in Hessen, 1983), p. 2.

9. Herde, *Neunhundert Jahre Geschichte der Juden in Hessen*, pp. 2, 3.

10. Ibid, p. 3.

11. Dr. Walter Gunzert, *Hessische Heimat,* Number 14, July 14, 1965.

12. Leo Sievers, *Juden in Deutschland* (Hamburg: Verlag Gruner, 1977), pp. 41-43.

13. Elbogen, *Geschichte der Juden in Deutschland*, p. 60.

14. Ibid, p. 59.

15. Herde, *Neunhundert Jahre Geschichte der Juden in Hessen*, p. 9.

16. Sievers, *Juden in Deutschland,* p. 54.

17. Herde, *Neunhundert Jahre Geschichte der Juden in Hessen*, p. 10.

18. Sievers, *Juden in Deutschland,* p. 56.

19. Herde, *Neunhundert Jahre Geschichte der Juden in Hessen*, p. 11.

20. Elbogen, *Geschichte der Juden in Deutschland*, p. 90.

21. *Encyclopedia Judaica*, Volume 4, p. 1123.

22. Elbogen, *Geschichte der Juden in Deutschland,* pp. 115-116.

23. Herde, *Neunhundert Jahre Geschichte der Juden in Hessen*, pp. 13-15.

24. Alex Bein, *Juden in Preussen* (Dortmund: Druckerei Hitzegard, 1981), p. 27.

25. Gunzert, *Hessische Heimat*, Number 14, July 14, 1965.

26. Werner E. Mosse and Arnold Paucker, *Juden im Wilhemischen Deutschland 1890-1914* (Tübingen: Leo Baeck Institute, J.C.B. Mohr, Paul Siebeck, 1976), p. 160.

27. Karl Siegmar Baron von Galera, *Lauterbach in Hessen*, Vol. 3 (Neustadt an der Aisch: Verlag Degener and O., 1965), pp. 308-309.

28. Rüdiger Mack, *Neunhundert Jahre Geschichte der Juden in Hessen* (Wiesbaden: Kommission für die Geschichte der Juden in Hessen, 1983), p. 394.

29. Ibid, p. 383.

30. Ibid, pp. 380, 381, 384.

31. Elbogen, *Geschichte der Juden in Deutschland*, p. 279.

32. Sievers, *Juden in Deutschland*, p. 223.

33. Ibid, p. 235.

The History of Jews in German Lands
from the Thirteenth Century
to the Enlightenment

Upper Hesse region in the eighteenth century

The Way It Was: The Jewish World of Rural Hesse

JEWS IN GERMAN LANDS FROM THE THIRTEENTH CENTURY ON

*J*ews lived in German lands as early as the thirteenth century. From 1236 on, Jews in German lands were protected and taxed by the emperor. Later, the emperors transferred their rights over the Jews to free cities and territorial princes, who issued letters of protection (*Schutzbriefe*) for a periodic fee from the Jews living in their dominions. From the fourteenth century on, the existence of Jews in German lands and Upper Hesse depended upon protection of a lord or a town.

During the Black Death (1348-1350), which raged across continental Europe, Jews were massacred in German lands because they were accused of poisoning the wells, thereby causing the outbreak of bubonic, septicemic, and pneumonic plagues. In Alsfeld, nine hundred people fell victim to the Black Death.[1]

In the sixteenth century, the *Landjudenschaft*, a self-governing Jewish institution, was set up in the territories of the Holy Roman Empire. This organization wielded great influence within Jewish communities in German lands and represented Jewish communities before the sovereigns. During the eighteenth and the beginning of the nineteenth centuries, the *Landjudenschaft* of Upper Hesse met every three years in the village of Wieseck near Giessen. The organization was essentially an association of individuals, combining the functions and powers of a local community with those of an inter-communal body that acted both internally and externally. However, Jews who were under the sponsorship of local feudal lords could not participate in these conferences.[2] In 1685, in Hesse-Darmstadt, Jews were allowed to elect a chief rabbi and judge. The functions of the judge, however, were regulated by the sovereign in Hesse-Darmstadt.

In 1774, the Earldom of Darmstadt in Hesse ranked Jews below livestock on a list of household items.[3] In 1782, hunger and privation bore down upon the general population of Angenrod and ended in ill fortune, particularly for the twelve Jewish families. In 1819 "Hep! Hep!"—the derogatory rallying cry initiating persecution against the Jews-broke out in Angenrod and its environs.

COURT JEWS

SOME JEWS, HOWEVER, LIVED under somewhat more favorable circumstances. Elector William the Ninth of Hesse-Kassel entrusted a Jew, Mayer Amschel Rothschild (1744-1812), with his valuable coin collection when Napoleon's soldiers entered Frankfurt am Main. Amschel hid the coins in the catacombs of the Jewish quarter. Mayer Amschel Rothschild was one of the 'court Jews' who, during the seventeenth and eighteenth centuries, served the sovereigns of some German lands, as well as other European rulers, with their commercial and financial expertise. A court Jew enjoyed favor or fell into disgrace at the pleasure of his sovereign; but some were influential and led lives of luxury. However, at court they were isolated from their non-Jewish peers because of their religion, while at the same time their high position set them apart from their co-religionists. Later, William the Ninth commissioned Mayer Amschel's son, Nathan Mayer of London, to make large investments in English securities. These speculative ventures profited William the Ninth of Hesse-Kassel as well as the Rothschild family.

In 1870-71, Germany, without Austria, was united under Prussian leadership. William I of Prussia was declared German emperor by the German princes assembled in the Palace of Versailles. In 1883, Otto von Bismarck began instituting sweeping social reforms in Germany, such as laws providing for sickness, accident, and old-age insurance, limitations on the labor of women and children, and the establishment of maximum working hours.

THE PRIVATE LIVES OF JEWS

IN THE SECOND HALF of the eighteenth century, a human being could be acquired as if he were real estate or merchandise. One's life from cradle to grave was in the hands of the sovereign of the village and district. The majority of the villagers were serfs of the local noble. Without exception, Jews had the legal status of *villeins*. The term *villein* or *villeinage* connotes a state of semi-bondage or serfdom.

A non-Jewish family was allowed to have two children. All progeny beyond two became the property of the sovereign. This restriction led to a folk science in birth control. In the event that one of the two offspring died, a family could bring another child into the world. The objective was to have no more than two children in order to prevent a child from being born a serf of the feudal lord. Skillful application of rosemary and other strong herbs were used for birth control. After the termination of serfdom, the secrets of that technique expired with the experts who had known them.[4] During this era, Jews did not practice birth control because of their religious beliefs. If birth control had been permitted, then perhaps the recurrent fates of the Jews through history might have led ultimately to their extinction. People who are not allowed to own land or real estate, and who constantly live under threat of annihilation are likely to die out if they have only two children. At that time, Jewish parents were not free and none of their children were freeborn.

Under Frederick the Great, King of Prussia from 1740-1786, protection was inheritable for only one child of a family. A new petition for protection (*Schutzbrief*) had to be filed for any additional children. Because sovereigns generally did not wish to 'hold' many Jews, a young couple was forced to defer marriage until a place could be found in their town, village, or hamlet.[5] Maybe the prevailing statutes in Prussia regarding Jews influenced the Angenrod authorities to keep special registration books of their Jews.

ASHKENAZIC AND SEPHARDIC JEWS IN GERMAN LANDS

THE ASHKENAZIC JEWS in the Angenrod area had been forced to flee to Poland and Russia around 1349 at the time of the bubonic plague. They took east with them from Germany a style of dressing in caftans, wigs, and black coats. Also in the east, most Jews were forced to live from hand to mouth. Contact with others outside of the Jewish settlement was limited. At that time the various dialects of Yiddish came into being, Chassidism evolved as a mystic philosophy of life, and orthodoxy emerged as a compensating factor.

Upon their return to regions of Upper Hesse, the Ashkenazic Jews kept up their Eastern Yiddish. Often their surnames were peculiar: *Blaumilch* (blue milk), *Nelkenstock* (carnation stem), *Wurm* (worm), or *Rubinstein* (stone of the ruby). These names recall an era when last names had to be purchased. Consequently, poor people were forced to acquire names of derisive meaning, whereas the wealthy received names of valuable connotation. The center of Yiddish-Chassidic families in the Angenrod region was in Schenklengsfeld, which is situated in the direction of Fulda, approximately nineteen miles from Angenrod. Marriages took place between Jews from Schenklengsfeld and Jews from Angenrod.[6]

Most Askkenazic Jews in German lands were self-assured. For almost nine hundred years they had maintained their position under dire conditions, and they had endured privations and sacrifices. The feudal lords had used the large sums extracted from those Jews for wars, pomp, splendor, and finery, as well as for patronage of arts and letters. The Jews rightfully surmised that most of what was beautiful and enduring had been financially sifted through them. Although those Jews certainly did not take kindly to their fate, they by-and-large survived unbroken.

Another variety of Jews in the Angenrod area were the Sephardic Jews. The Iberian peninsula was called '*Sepharad*' in Hebrew because of the name of a region mentioned in the Bible in *Obadiah 20*. The Sephardic group consisted mainly of Jews who, since the fifteenth century, had been driven out of Spain, Portugal, and France. Prior to their exile into Germany, the situation of the Sephardic Jews was different from that of the Ashkenazic Jews. The Sephardic Jews had been employed as scientists and diplomats and they were proficient in many languages. The highest honor that could be accorded someone in the Sephardic society was to be deemed learned, lettered, and cultured. Such values and attitudes encouraged an aristocracy of the educated: the chief goal of life was to be learned and always to continue one's studies. The descendants of that well-schooled group set high value on the study of Hebrew, *Torah*, Rashi, and Maimonides. The Sephardic Jews pursued their studies even if they found themselves in financially straightened circumstances.

However, in Hesse in the seventeenth and eighteenth centuries, Sephardic Jews were no longer needed as translators, diplomats, or scientists—hence they moved into a form of inner exile. Staying wherever they were granted permission to dwell, they made a living as best they could. Few members of the Sephardic group developed middle class ambitions, nor were they concerned about living in big cities. In the past they had been well acquainted with aristocracy, landed property, and estates and they felt comfortable with the policies of the feudal lords. Therefore, it was not accidental that the majority of Hessian Jews who were answerable to feudal lords came from the Sephardic areas of Spain, Portugal, and France. They were surrounded by non-Jews, and they were forced to earn a living primarily outside of the small Jewish community. However, even if more Jews had been permitted to live in the same village, the restrictive covenants for earning a livelihood would have made their economic self-sufficiency impossible.

CONVERSIONS   BECAUSE OF THE LIMITED contact between Jews and Christians there were few conversions. Nevertheless, in 1634, when a young Jewess converted to Christianity in Alsfeld, thirty sponsors volunteered to act as her godparents. Again in Alsfeld in 1670, a baptismal celebration was held, to which the entire Alsfeld populace was invited. A man, his wife, their four children, and a single male left Judaism. The converts were immediately accepted as citizens; they all received a *Guilder* (a unit of money) from each of their sponsors.[7] In 1747, Moses Jacob More, the schoolteacher in Alsfeld, forsook Judaism and was baptized.

SCHUTZJUDEN   JEWS WHO HELD LETTERS of protection in the Holy Roman Empire from 1236 on were called *Schutzjuden* (protected Jews). When the emperor needed funds, he granted his right over the Jews to territorial feudal lords and free cities. They in turn charged a regular fee for letters of protection to the Jews living within their domain. As a result, Jews became the subjects of the local feudal lords and free cities, which furnished either a personal or communal letter of protection (*Schutzbrief*). Letters of protection had to be renewed periodically for a fee set by the sovereign and they generated a good income. *Schutzjuden* were required to pay *Schutzgeld*, a fee for protection. However, *Schutz* (protection) did not mean real security. Rather, it was a form of blackmail, wherein payment protected the Jews against being abused. The specification of *Schutzjude* guarded, in some measure, against the hate and animosity toward Jews by those who feared the wrath of the sovereigns. The Jews of Angenrod appeared in the records as *Schutzjuden*. On the other hand, *Betteljuden* (beggar Jews), who could not afford to pay the required fee, could be subjected to mistreatment or immediate expulsion.

In 1667, the movement and abodes of the Vogelsberg region's *Schutzjuden* were highly restricted. In Alsfeld, *Schutzjuden* were allowed to live but not work in town.[8] It is recorded that letters of protection in Hesse-Darmstadt were individually granted to Jews in 1728 and 1737, subject to the verification of minimum wealth of six hundred *Gulden* and to the ability to read and write German. However, at that time the construction of new synagogues was forbidden.[9]

Schutzbrief of Michel Homburg

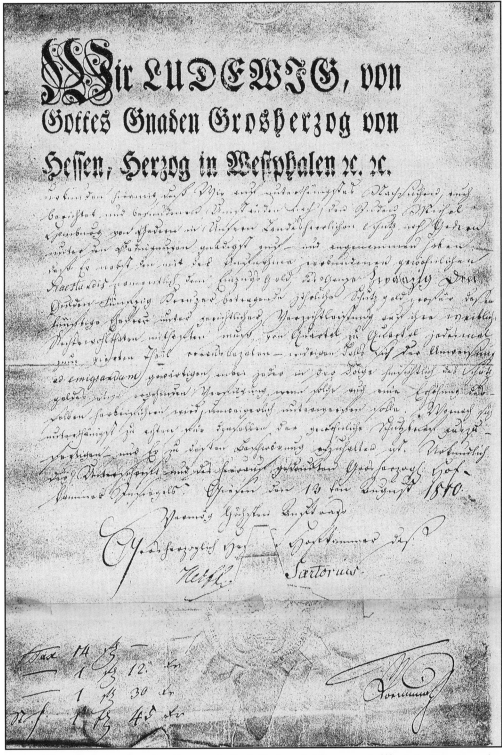

We, Ludwig, by the Grace of God Duke of Hesse and Westphalia, record herewith that we accept the Jew, Michel Homburg of Gedern, unto the protection of the sovereign for the yearly sum of twenty-three Gulden and fifty Kreuzer. However, his future wife must legally disclaim all rights for welfare. Furthermore, payments are due quarterly in advance even if a higher rate will be assessed.

Giessen, August 13, 1810

On behalf of the Duke—Sartorius

Under Frederick the Great (1740-1786), a more restrictive form of *Schutzjuden* allowed protection only during the lifetime of the individual Jew.[10] It is not clear whether a marriageable child of an Angenrod *Schutzjude* was permitted to settle in the village. The Jews barely eked out a minimal existence by peddling tobacco, wine, meat, and other small items. The *Schutzbrief* in Upper Hesse ordinarily limited residence to three years (as in Friedberg and Münzenberg)[a] or six years.

Renewal of a *Schutzbrief* was customary in the region of Hesse, but each case was handled individually at the discretion of the local feudal lord with whom the terms had to be continually renegotiated.[11] In 1728, a *Schutzbrief* for the benefit of the Jew Löw Praunheim in the Solms-Rödelheim area was valid for four years subject to certain conditions: Praunheim was obliged to practice an approved business, stay within the guidelines of *Schutz*, and pay in advance the yearly *Schutzgeld* of ten *Gulden*.[12]

THE JEWISH ENLIGHTENMENT (*HASKALAH*)

IN THE SEVENTEENTH CENTURY, Jewish culture in German lands was influenced by the *Derekh Erez* movement ('*Haskalah*' in Hebew), which literally translated means 'way of the world.' The term refers to the proper behavior of man toward his fellow man and includes rules of etiquette. The Jewish Enlightenment had its roots in the general Enlightenment movement in Europe. Rabbi Ezekiel Landau (1713-1793), Rabbi Moses Sofer (1762-1839), and the poet, Naphtali Herz (Hartwig), were the torchbearers in German lands of the *Derekh Erez* movement. These three intellectuals differed in their approach to this movement, but all agreed that *Derekh Erez* was always subordinate to *Torah*: *Torah* was unwavering, whereas *Derekh Erez* could be modified. Until emancipation, Jews applied *Derekh Erez* to their own milieu, whereas after the emancipation the task became to be Jewish in the outside world.[13]

In 1781, Immanuel Kant wrote the *Critique of Pure Reason*. In the same year, the Prussian private councilor, Christian Wilhelm Dohm, influenced by Moses Mendelssohn, demanded, in *About the Civic Improvement of Jews*, that Jewish separatism be abolished. Dohm's ideas inspired Emperor Joseph II of Austria, who viewed the Enlightenment as an instrument for strengthening his absolute power and for implementing his political goals. From 1782 to 1789, Joseph II released six directives for Jews in the Hapsburg region. Intended to change Jews into 'useful subjects,' the statutes decreed school reform, coercive measures for a controlled choice of vocation or profession, and compulsory military duty. In reality, Josef's mandate maintained numerous ordinances of exclusion for Jews, and he did not abolish discrimination against Jews. Nevertheless, the tenets of the so-called 'Edicts of Tolerance' were later used by the Prussians in order to emancipate their Jews.[14]

Moses Mendelssohn

---

[a] Münzenberg was the native town of Jüttel, the first wife of my paternal great-great grandfather, Raphael Wertheim of Angenrod. Münzenberg was also the home of a branch of the well-known Kalonymus family.

During the eighteenth century and the Enlightenment, Moses Mendelssohn (1729-1786) and Gotthold E. Lessing (1729-1780) were important intellectual figures. Lessing was one of the most influential figures of the Enlightenment. In addition to many other works, Lessing wrote *Nathan the Wise*, a drama inspired by Moses Mendelssohn. Mendelssohn is generally considered to be the originator of the *Haskalah* faction, which was the Hebrew term for the Enlightenment movement and ideology that began within Jewish society in the 1770s. Moses Mendelssohn prevailed upon his co-religionists to speak in the German language rather than Yiddish.

In 1783, Mendelssohn's translation of the Hebrew Bible was published. Originally, the emancipator had made the translation in order to instruct his own children, but it had also been intended to help Jews learn German. Mendelssohn was of the opinion that the mode of speech commonly used by Jews had contributed significantly to their backward conduct. Several esteemed rabbis in Germany, and especially Raphael Cohen of Hamburg, declared that reading the translated version of the Old Testament would constitute a danger for Judaism. They threatened to excommunicate members of their congregations for reading the Five Books of Moses in German. In those days, fear of straying from tradition was the dominating concern of many Jews; a closed doctrine of rabbinical rules controlled Jewish life and education in every respect.[15] In 1783, Mendelssohn issued his essay, *Jerusalem: Concerning Judaism and Religion*, in which he demanded not only that the restrictions imposed upon the Jews be dissolved, but also that this right be regarded as part of the general freedom of conscience.

Gabriel Riesser

In 1806, Gabriel Riesser, a champion of Jewish emancipation in Germany, was born in Hamburg. Riesser's grandfather, Raphael Cohen, had fled to Altona in northern Germany because of persecution of Jews in Poland. In Altona, he became a rabbi and an orthodox scholar. He disapproved of Mendelssohn's translation of the sacred scriptures into German. However, Gabriel's father, Lazarus Jakob Riesser, was an advocate of Mendelssohn's endeavors to connect Jewish faith with German culture and Gabriel Riesser was raised in that spirit.[16]

Gabriel grew up during a troubled era for Jews in German lands. After the War of Liberation (1813-1815), many Germans were displeased with their social standing and vented their anger on the Jews in the "Hep! Hep!" riots of 1819. After studying law in Kiel and Heidelberg, Riesser was denied the position of a lecturer in Heidelberg and in his native city, Hamburg. Because of his faith, he was also not allowed to practice law. The city of Hamburg, too, reverted the status of its Jews to their position in the early part of the eighteenth century.

Many Jews left German lands during those years. Paul Julius Reuter from Kassel founded Reuter's News Agency in London. Alfred Beit from Hamburg left for South Africa, where he developed the diamond mining industry. Later he donated two million *Mark* to his native city, Hamburg, for the erection of a university. Jacob Eberts, the Jewish composer from Cologne, went to Paris. He renamed himself Jacques Offenbach after his father's birthplace (Offenbach in Hesse) and became a successful composer of the French operetta.[17]

In 1840, Gabriel Riesser returned to Hamburg. Finally, his native city granted him civil rights and permitted him to practice law. In 1848, a revolution broke out in France and soon afterward, the revolt spread to Germany. The issues surrounding the revolution were elimination of censorship of the press, reorganization of the judiciary, and the creation of a federal government. When rioting began, the reigning governments tried to appease the masses by making minor concessions. When the German National Assembly convened on May 18, 1848, in the church of St. Paul in Frankfurt, five hundred sixty eight representatives negotiated for the people. Gabriel Riesser and ten other Jews were appointed delegates.[18] Riesser was one of the best speakers of the German National Assembly and eventually became its vice-president. On April 3, 1849, he was one of thirty-three delegates who called for the King of Prussia to become Emperor of Germany. Gabriel Riesser collaborated in creating the German Constitution, which was finished seventy years later by another Jew, Hugo Preuss.

Gabriel Riesser's plea for the equality of Jews was based not on forsaking Jewish identity, but on the idea of equal rights for all. That notion appealed even to orthodox Jewish communities that, until then, had feared loss of Jewish identity as a consequence of too much emancipation. Riesser was influential in replacing the word 'Jew' as terminology for prejudice and insult. Ultimately, the Jews of Switzerland were called 'Israelitic' congregations, the Jews of France were referred to as '*Israélites*,' and the Jews of Germany were designated as members of the 'Mosaic faith.'[19]

JEWISH WOMEN AND THE ENLIGHTENMENT

JEWISH WOMEN ALSO PLAYED an important part in the Enlightenment in the German lands. In 1847, Henrietta Herz (1764-1847), a society leader of Jewish birth, died in Berlin at the age of eighty-three. Her salon had been a focal point of Berlin's intellectual life. For forty years after the death of her husband, Marcus Herz, in 1803, Henrietta supported herself, her mother, and her sister by teaching languages. She taught the Hebrew alphabet to Wilhelm von Humboldt (1767-1835), German statesman and philologist, and she corresponded with him in Hebrew writing. In 1817, Henrietta Herz was baptized. Among her friends was Dorothea (Brendl) Schlegel (1763-1839), the oldest daughter of Moses Mendelssohn. Dorothea, a German author and translator, converted to Protestantism in 1802 and to Catholicism in 1808. She married the German philosopher, Friedrich von Schlegel. Rahel Levin (1771-1833), another Jewess from an orthodox home in Berlin, also established a salon for intellectuals. She married Karl August Varnhagen von Ense and converted to Protestantism.

Dorothea Schlegel

Rahel Levin

Henrietta Herz

The three close friends, Henrietta Herz, Dorothea Schlegel, and Rahel Levin were born at a time when women even of the upper and middle classes in German lands rarely left an impact upon the political, cultural, and social life. Yet these three women of Jewish birth and education were associated with poets and dramatists (Goethe, Schiller, and Heinrich von Kleist), philosophers (Kant and Hegel), naturalists and statesmen (the brothers Humboldt), as well as contemporary painters, musicians, and sculptors.[20] From his deep understanding of the Old Testament, Goethe fashioned the Faust segment, *Prologue in Heaven*, after the Book of Job. As a young man, Goethe had shown an unbiased attitude toward Jews by actively aiding in fighting a fire in the Frankfurt am Main ghetto.

JEWISH WRITERS AND ARTISTS

TWO JEWISH POETS of the school of late Romanticism in Germany, Ludwig Börne (1786-1856) and Heinrich Heine (1797-1856), also called for emancipation of all citizens, equal rights for women, liberation for Judaism, and freedom of literature, press, and theater, as well as limitations of the sovereigns through a constitution. Aside from Goethe, Heinrich Heine was the most significant German lyricist of the nineteenth century. The most famous German Jewish painter of the nineteenth century was Moritz Daniel Oppenheim (1801-1882). Born in Hanau near Frankfurt am Main, he painted Old and New Testament scenes. The Jewish genre paintings in which he specialized made him famous and some appeared in the United States in 1866 as *Family Scenes from Jewish Life of Former Days*.

EMANCIPATION OF JEWS IN GERMAN LANDS

FOR JEWS, THE PROCESS of becoming citizens varied considerably in German lands. The events of the French Revolution in 1789 initiated change for Jews in Frankfurt am Main and in Hamburg. Nevertheless, in small Jewish com-

Return of the Jewish volunteer from the War of Liberation (1813-1815) by
Moritz Daniel Oppenheim.

The Way It Was: The Jewish World of Rural Hesse

munities in Bavaria, the Grand Duchy of Baden, and the Grand Duchy of Hesse, living conditions for Jews lagged behind by decades.[21] In neighboring France, 1791 ushered in unrestricted equality of French Jews as full citizens. Ludwig the Tenth, the Landgrave of Darmstadt, was a friend and ally of Napoleon. Ludwig was later elevated to Grand Duke and he remained loyal to the Corsican even while Napoleon was in exile. Grand Duke Ludwig cared about his impoverished vassals and in order to understand more about their lives, he traveled anonymously among his subjects. He abolished serfdom and freed his people from double taxation.

However, in most German lands, governments delayed improving the legal and social status of their Jews. For twenty years, government departments and offices asked the heads of the Jewish communities for in-depth accounts and observations about individual projects. Results of these projects were summarized and on the basis of such surveys new studies were initiated, government committees were again consulted, and requests for additional reports were redirected to public offices. Those reports gave detailed evidence of the development of the emancipation discussions. But even as the papers concerning the emancipation of the Jews accumulated yearly, there was no definite decision with regard to the civil rights of Jews.[22]

After the Congress of Vienna (1815), two elements contributed considerably in delaying Jewish integration into German life. In the world of ideas, German Romanticism became a political creed that elevated the Christian-German notion of the Middle Ages to an ideal criterion for the present. From the beginning of my education in Germany, that ideology permeated every facet of my instruction. Even my German literature teachers in the United States in the 1960s, whether consciously or not, were strongly influenced by those concepts. The second consideration curbing Jewish integration in German lands after the Vienna Congress was that the economy had no room for former outsiders to become equal partners for the benefit of all.[23] After the Congress of Vienna, the Netherlands and France were the only European countries where Jews continued to possess full civil rights.

On January 1, 1824, Hesse terminated the special taxes that formerly had been levied on Jews.[24] No longer was any human being to be the property of another person. After many years of restrictions, Jews were allowed to own houses and other real estate and they were also directed to take surnames. Although the emancipation law for French Jews had been promulgated in 1791, in Germany a contrary mind-set had been dominant.

After 1830, if a Jew in Angenrod or Romrod wanted to become a citizen, he was obliged to swear on the *Torah* that money demanded and designated for initiation of citizenship was free of all encumbrance. Beginning in 1824, Jews were allowed to acquire real estate, but the transaction was subject to an independent appraisal and if Jews purchased land, they were required to cultivate it.

Moreover, in order for Jews to become citizens, they were required to live 'like Germans' and read and write in German.

The public mandate for change culminated in the opening of the Frankfurt Parliament on May 18, 1848, in the Church of St. Paul, where they proclaimed the 'Basic Rights of the German People.' This assembly was also charged with drafting a constitution for a new Germany. However, while the constitution was being debated, the sovereigns of the German lands recovered their authority. In reality, the ideals of the French Revolution did not remodel the human condition in Germany where idealistic momentum was followed by deep disillusionment. For many, immigration to the United States or other lands seemed the only hope for a meaningful life. Nevertheless, the Revolution of 1848 and the influence of the principles of liberalism advanced the progress of equality for Jews, which by and large was concluded in the 1860s.

Emancipation was intended to bring about social integration of Jews. Other than the several thousand bankers and wholesale merchants, Jews had been reduced primarily to a social underclass, where one third earned a livelihood by peddling. Although eliminating limitations on vocations, the new legislation did not abolish restrictions completely and consequently effected a certain distortion of the vocational structure of Jews. Moreover, emancipation was met with resistance by orthodox Jews, who feared the loss of Jewish identity, as well as by conservative politicians, who envisioned the principle of a Christian state to be in danger.

Public office and military positions remained closed for Jews. State-controlled universities did not employ Jews until World War I and equal rights were denied to Jews.[25] Full emancipation into all professions and social acceptance never existed during my days in Germany before Hitler. The law of 1869, which was intended to make the rights of citizenship "independent of religious adherence," was applied very unevenly. Saxony and Hesse-Darmstadt remained virtually untouched.[26]

In 1848, the Frankfurt Parliament proclaimed the 'Basic Rights of the German People.' But not until the 1860s did *de jure* emancipation of Jews in Hesse take place. In 1870, my grandfather, Herz Wertheim, served his country in the Franco-Prussian War, doubtless boosting the respect in which his Jewish and non-Jewish neighbors held him. In 1871, the German lands became a centralized confederacy headed by William I. Frederick III, who ruled for only ninety-nine days in 1888; William II became the next emperor of Germany until 1918. The activities of the rabid anti-semite Otto Böckel in Hesse between 1887 to 1894 did not affect my grandparents excessively. In the 1920s during the Weimar Republic (1918-1933), they nostalgically recalled the time of the Kaiser.

The years between 1870 and 1933 represented the highest pinnacle of assimilation of Jews in Germany. From 1905 until the Nazis took over in 1933, Jews achieved notably in the disciplines of medicine, physics, chemistry, literature, and the arts. Of thirty-eight Nobel Prize winners, eleven were German Jews, although Jews represented only less than one percent of the total population. In earlier days, Jews in Germany had had their talents crushed by unwritten laws that kept them out of the universities and many professions, and their children became exuberant over-achievers.

OCCUPATIONS OF JEWS IN GERMAN LANDS

Right: In Alsfeld, Wolf Spier (probably a descendant of Michel Spier from Merzhausen) advertised plain and printed cotton cloth in various colors and of several widths measured in *Ellen*. Prices are stated in *Kroner* and its particular smaller valuta. Wolf Spier's home was in the Baugasse.

THEORETICALLY, JEWS WERE PERMITTED to join guilds and serve apprenticeships, however, in practice this was hardly useful. Remuneration of an apprentice generally consisted of room-and-board in the home of his master. Moreover, Saturday was a craftsman's busiest day, but the holiness of the Sabbath forbade labor for the Jewish apprentice. But how could a Jew observe the kosher laws in his non-Jewish master's home for three years and strictly observe the Sabbath? Even when it became lawful in the Electorate of Hesse, it was a formidable task for an observant Jew to obtain and then to complete successfully an apprenticeship with a non-Jewish master. Even if a Jew completed the required apprenticeship, then he remained subject to admission by the guild of his craft to become a journeyman.

This advertisement for the opening of a shoe store in Alsfeld is by Adolph Levi, a relative of my paternal grandmother, Hannchen Levi Wertheim. The store was located at Mainzergasse 206 and offered a large selection of shoes of best quality and rendered excellent service.

In Angenrod, new ordinances were continuously promulgated pertaining to the killing of cattle and the selling of meat. Only one Jewish family in a community was allowed to kill cattle ritually (*schächten*) for kosher meat.[27] In view of the fact that many Jews in small villages in Upper Hesse earned their livelihood by butchering, this measure was probably contrived to visit hardship upon the Jews of Angenrod and its vicinity.

Jews were allowed to sell merchandise in an established store. However, if a Jew intended to engage in wholesale merchandising, he was obligated to prove that he possessed four thousand *Gulden*. How many Jews of Kestrich, Romrod, Grebenau, Storndorf, or Angenrod could realistically take advantage of these opportunities?

Jews were also required to possess 'sound moral attitudes.' This requirement is ironic since, in the 1980s, the inhabitants of Angenrod praised the Jews for their exemplary moral conduct. In 1832, in Hungen, Upper Hesse, twenty-nine miles southwest of Angenrod, Jews were freed from paying a burial fee to the sovereigns von Solms. From 1553 until 1832, these feudal lords had imposed an interment charge on Jews living within their realm for burying their dead in their own Jewish cemetery.[28]

Beginning in 1816, all Jews in the Electorate of Hesse were permitted to become citizens if they were not engaged in *Nothandel*. *Nothandel* signified cattle-dealing or lending of money on a small scale, dealing in second-hand goods, and door-to-door selling. Jews with official permission to deal in *Nothandel*, were allowed to continue their occupation. However, if a Jew worked in *Nothandel* without permission, he was subject to a fine and could even go to jail. This group of Jews continued as *Schutzjuden* and were not permitted to marry. Since there were many *Nothändler* in the small villages in the Electorate of Hesse, this decree created a separate lower class of Jews who were forced to remain *Schutzjuden*. The impact of this ordinance was still apparent in the 1920s as rural Jews who were forced to practice *Nothandel* were generally poorer and considered less cultured.

Cattle dealing was very widespread and had always been uncontrolled and unrestricted. At that time, Jews paid neither toll fees nor other tax payments. From 1770 to 1780, trading in miscellaneous dry goods was restricted at the urgent request of the local merchants. Although in 1777 Jews were forbidden to peddle, this prohibition was lifted in 1784 for certain Jews who paid a yearly fee. Jewish traders who were caught peddling without official permission and payment had their merchandise confiscated. In 1787, Jews were obliged to pay ten *Kreuzer* per day while selling door-to-door in the landowner's territory. As proof of payment for the peddling permit, Jews were required to carry a printed document at all times. However, local merchants objected to even restricted commerce by the Jews and permits for Jewish peddlers were withdrawn the following year.[29]

In Lauterbach, records of my Great-Uncle Markus Strauss indicate that he dealt in flour. He avoided registering as a cattle dealer and part-time butcher lest the Lauterbach elders reject his application for residence on the grounds that too many already pursued this occupation. Sigmund Strauss of the Hintergasse sold insurance, feed, grocery items, and spirits. My Great-Uncle Samuel Strauss (I), a cattle dealer and part-time butcher, eventually invested in real estate and held mortgages.

Many of the Jews who settled in Lauterbach at the turn of the twentieth century embarked on various commercial pursuits, providing they could surmount the necessary license requirements which were jealously guarded by established townsmen. Nevertheless, by 1911, Joseph Herz of Giessen had a bank at Hintergasse 3. Most members of the Lauterbach Jewish congregation were unaware that the owner of this bank was a Jew. In the 1920s, during the galloping inflation in Germany, Mr. Hofstetter, a Catholic, directed that bank. His high ranking position, despite his religious persuasion in the predominantly Lutheran Lauterbach, can probably be ascribed to his Jewish employer, Mr. Joseph Herz. During the inflation of the 1920s, my father made daily inquiries at this bank about the status of the *Mark* versus the dollar.

ANTI-SEMITISM
IN HESSE

AN ORDINANCE OF 1816 decreed that all Jewish children were obliged to attend Christian public schools. Since the Christian schools in the Electorate of Hesse were denominational, this decree represented discrimination against the Jewish minority. But the ordinance stipulated that it was the duty of the Christian teachers not to tolerate any manifestations of unkind attitudes by either Jews or Christians. Prejudice against Jews remained strong in the masses and was intensified by an ordinance of February 12, 1819, which stated that only one son of a Jewish retail merchant was permitted to engage in the retail business and that the sons of Jewish merchants were not allowed to buy houses. An ordinance of December 24, 1821, directed that Jews could not marry unless they showed the capability to support a family by farming, by practicing an art or science, or by conducting a permissible trade.[30] On October 29, 1833, Jews were granted equal rights with Christians but were forbidden to acquire patronage over churches, and they were not permitted to teach the Christian religion.[31] (The last two restrictions appear to provide for unrealistic contingencies.)

In the late 1800s, the first great wave of modern anti-semitism occurred in Hesse. It was characterized by an economic bias against Jews. The Marburg librarian and explorer of folklore, Otto Böckel, carried on a fervent campaign against the Jewish minority. He demanded that equality of rights for Jews, obtained under Bismarck in 1872, be revoked and that Jews be treated in a class with foreigners. The anti-semitism in Upper Hesse and in the Electorate of Hesse brought a series of anti-semitic parliamentary representatives into the *Reichstag*. This development was a first indication that the relationship between the mostly poor rural population, the Jewish cattle dealers, and the Jewish grantors of credit could be manipulated for political purposes. Also at that time, Ludwig Werner, an anti-semitic parliamentary representative, became the forerunner of all the demagogues, including Hitler, who identified Jews with capitalism. Werner blamed Jews for the social tensions and conflicts of modern economic life.[32] In the 1920s, his notions were well established in Alsfeld, Lauterbach, and the surrounding rural areas.

In the 1930s, political conservatives began using the *Deutsche Landeszeitung* as their mouthpiece to call attention to the exploitation of rural Germans by

Jewish "fluid capital and middleman's trade."[33] These proclamations were intended to cause envy and instigate farmers and other rural people against Jews. The notion of the middleman who supposedly served no honest purpose damaged the reputation of Jews from then on. This view was the bane of my existence from the time I attended school, and it took years of living in the United States before I realized that middlemen are not parasites, but perform an essential service in a democracy where capitalism flourishes. In Angenrod, non-Jews coveted the fields and meadows that my grandfather gradually acquired for growing grains for bread and fodder for horses and cows.

In the villages of Upper Hesse, many rural non-Jews regularly visited the local saloons to partake of beer and wine. At the end of the month, this habit frequently robbed non-Jewish village families of savings and even necessities while most Jewish families generally advanced their economic status gradually. This circumstance, too, did not promote good feelings between Jews and their non-Jewish neighbors.

In 1988, Mrs. Dorothy Stausebach Tag, a native of Lauterbach whose husband was a highly respected land surveyor, mentioned how deeply the participation of the Protestant clergy had influenced her. It confirmed her favorable attitude toward Jews. However, to my knowledge the Protestant clergy of Lauterbach, before or after World War I and until 1934, never sermonized against anti-semitism or intervened whenever anti-semitism, a strictly un-Christian way of thinking, reared its ugly head. Nevertheless, between 1870 and the beginning of World War I, Jews felt comparatively more secure in the Hesse region than at any other time since the eleventh-century Crusades.

It is not without import that on October 14, 1922, an announcement appeared in the *Lauterbacher Anzeiger*, indicating that the lives of the Jews of Lauterbach were of interest to its non-Jewish citizens: "Our Israelite fellow-citizens celebrate holidays today and tomorrow. The eight days' festival of booths is observed in commemoration of the Israelites' dwelling in booths while passing through the desert. Tomorrow is the festival of Rejoicing over the *Torah*."

Endnotes

1. Dr. Ursula Wippich, *Memorbuch, 1981/82,* p. 19.

2. Daniel J. Cohen, *Neunhundert Jahre Geschichte der Juden in Hessen* (Wiesbaden: Kommission für die Geschichte der Juden in Hessen, 1983), p. 159.

3. Dr. Walter Gunzert, *Hessische Heimat #14*, July 14, 1965.

4. Wippich, *Memorbuch*, p. 110.

5. Ibid, p. 21.

6. Ibid, pp. 54-56.

7. Ibid, p. 19.

8. Ibid, p. 27.

9. Cohen, *Neunhundert Jahre Geschichte der Juden in Hessen*, p. 155.

10. *Juden in Preussen* (Dortmund: Druckerei Hitzegard, 1981), p. 82.

11. Friedrich Battenberg, *Neunhundert Jahre Geschichte der Juden in Hessen,* (Wiesbaden: Kommission für die Geschichte der Judem in Hessen, 1983), p. 84.

12. Ibid, p. 84.

13. Julius Carlebach, *The Jews in Nazi Germany, 1933-1945* (Tübingen, J.C.B. Mohr [Paul Siebeck], 1986), pp. 75-76.

14. Walter Grab, *Juden in Preussen* (Dortmund: Druckerei Hitzegrad, 1981), p. 25.

15. Ismar Elbogen, *Geschichte der Juden in Deutschland* (Berlin: Erich Lichtenstein Verlag, 1935), p. 173.

16. Leo Sievers, *Juden in Deutschland* (Hamburg: Verlag Gruner, 1977), p. 175.

17. Ibid, p. 179.

18. Ibid, pp. 181-182.

19. Geoffrey D. Wigodor, *Jewish Art and Civilization* (Jerusalem: Weidenfeld and Nicholson, 1972), pp. 266-269.

20. Sievers, *Juden in Deutschland*, pp. 139-140.

21. Hans Liebeschütz und Arnold Paucker, *Das Judentum in der deutschen Umwelt, 1800-1850* (Tübingen: J.C.B. Mohr, 1977), p. 141.

22. Wolf-Arno Kropat, *Neunhundert Jahre Geschichte der Juden in Hessen* (Wiesbaden: Kommission für die Geschichte der Juden in Hessen, 1983), p. 326.

23. Liebshutz and Paucker, *Das Judentum in der Deutschen Umwelt, 1800* (1 in chapter 3): p. 12.

24. Gunzert, *Hessische Heimat, #14,* July 14, 1965.

25. Peter Herde, *Neunhundert Jahre Geschichte der Juden in Hessen* (Wiesbaden: Kommission für die Geschichte der Juden in Hessen, 1983), pp. 13-14.

26. Peter Pulzer, *The Jews in Nazi Germany, 1933-1943* (Tübingen: J.C.B. Mohr, [Paul Siebeck], 1986), pp. 18-19.

27. Wippich, *Memorbuch, 1981/1982,* p. 143.

28. Ibid, p. 138.

29. Karl Maurer, *Freiensteinau vor 200 Jahren,* Heft 46 der "Lauterbacher Sammlungen" 1967 (Hessen: Bibliothek des Hohhausmuseums Lauterbach), pp. 31-32.

30. Kropat, *Neunhundert Jahre Geschichte der Juden in Hessen*, pp. 330-331.

31. Ibid, p. 335.

32. Wolf-Arno Kropat, *Kristallnacht in Hessen* (Wiesbaden: Kommission für die Geschichte der Juden in Hessen, 1988), p. 2.

33. Rüdiger Mack, *Neunhundert Jahre Geschichte der Juden in Hessen* (Wiesbaden: Kommission für die Geschichte der Juden in Hessen, 1983), p. 382.

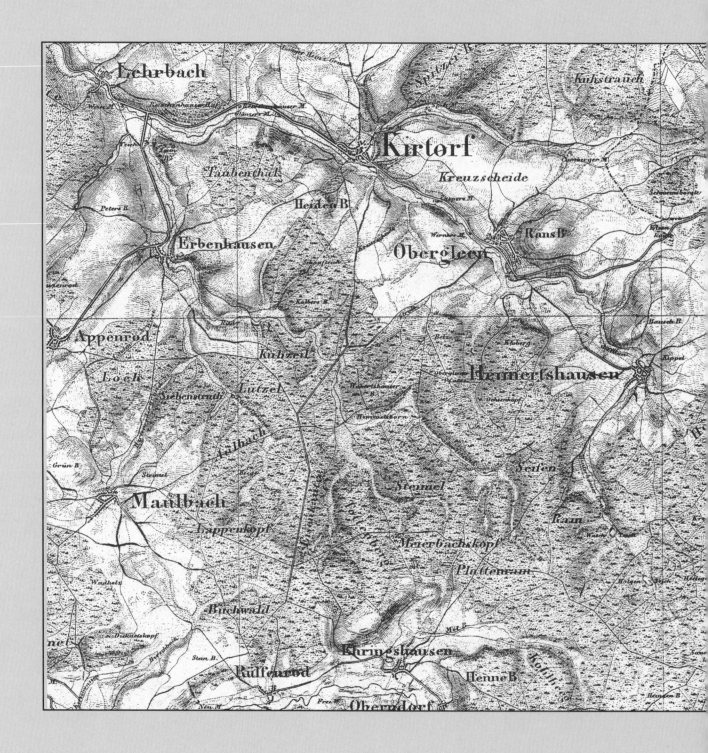

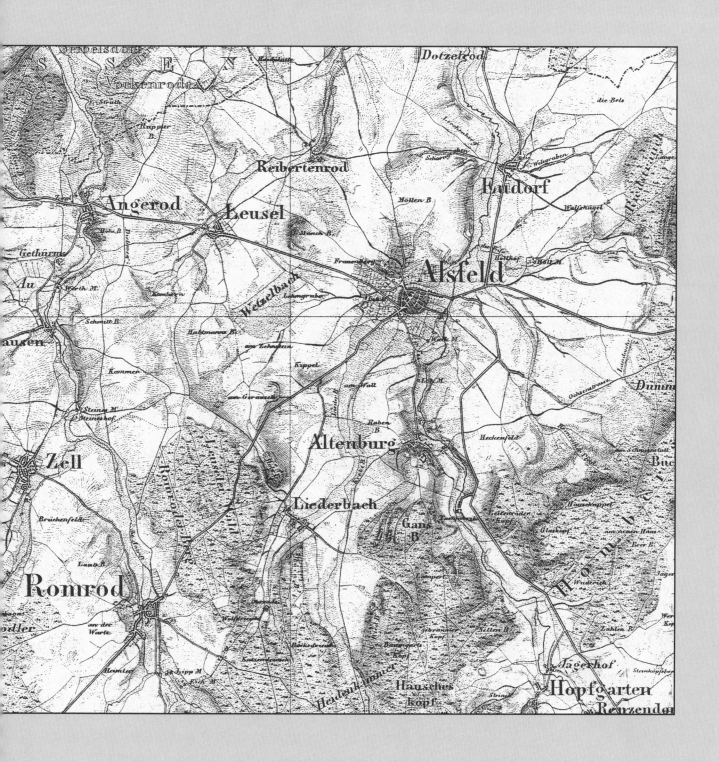

THE VILLAGE OF ANGENROD[a] in Hesse, Germany was already in existence in the year 1271.[1] This hamlet is situated on a brook, the Antreff, and lies approximately sixty miles north of the Limes, a fortification of castles, citadels, and watchtowers erected by the Roman emperors Domitian, Trajan, and Hadrian as a protection against the Germanic and Teutonic tribes. Angenrod lies fifteen miles northeast of Lauterbach and three miles west of Alsfeld, the nearest large town. Seven-and-a-half miles south of Alsfeld is the village of Storndorf, the birthplace of my maternal grandmother, Auguste Strauss Lamm.

In Angenrod in the fall, winter, and early spring, harsh winds and low temperatures prevail, which are typical of the climate in most parts of Upper Hesse and the rocky, hilly upland of the Vogelsberg region. Nevertheless, the climate tends to be less severe than in my birthplace, Lauterbach, which is located closer to the higher elevations of the Vogelsberg. It is often remarked that in the Vogelsberg region winter lasts for nine months and it is cold for the remainder of the year. A local saying declares that plums require two years for ripening. In the second year, the fruit had to be rehung in order to snatch enough sun to be harvested.

Angenrod was founded by the Fuldaic Feudal Knights of Romrod and was situated on a main thoroughfare where Jews had always found a livelihood, even if

Süsskind von Trimberg depicted in an early fourteenth century manuscript known as the *Manesse Codex*

it was a meager subsistence.[2] In l667, when the Angenrod Jewish community of modern times came into existence, the aristocratic landowner, Johann Heinrich Georg von Wehrda (called Nodung), was the sovereign. Wehrda is situated northeast of Angenrod near Hünfeld, where Jews had lived since the fourteenth century.

Süsskind von Trimberg, the only known Jewish lyricist between the twelfth and fourteenth centuries, was the son of a doctor from Wehrda. Süsskind was a common Jewish family name; 'von' in a German name designated aristocratic descent but, in this instance, it probably indicated the place of origin. Twelve verses composed by this traveling minstrel are known. In a picture painted after his death, Süsskind von Trimberg wears the dense beard of the Jews and the pointed hat with pommel.[3]

At certain times, the history of the Jews of Angenrod was linked to the history of the Jews of Alsfeld. According to the historian Paul Arnsberg, Jews already lived in Alsfeld before l359. He cites as evidence a house owned by a Jew named Kersancz,

---

[a] On an eighteenth-century map, Angenrod is recorded as 'Angerot.' An 'Angerot' is a village built around a village green, an appropriate description of Angenrod.

which was handed over to a Dr. Sibold in 1359. Despite the massacres of Jews during the Black Death (1348-1350), some Jews in this part of the Vogelsberg kept a slim hold on life in Angenrod and Storndorf.[4]

A now-demolished synagogue existed in Alsfeld as early as 1458. The vacated site of the synagogue was used for the construction of a castle. Between 1458 and the seventeenth century, Jews did not live in Alsfeld.[5] However, by 1933, Alsfeld possessed one hundred ninety Jews out of a total population of 7,500.[6]

In 1614, the anti-Jewish *Fettmilch* riots in Frankfurt am Main caused another dispersion of Jews in the region. Some Jews driven from Frankfurt may have settled in the Vogelsberg area and particularly in Angenrod, where sporadic settling of Jews had probably occurred even at an earlier time.[7] In addition, some of the last names of Jews in Angenrod (Bachrach, Höchster, Oppenheimer, Speyer, and Wertheim) indicate that they originated from these towns in the Main and Rhine regions of German lands where Jews came with the Romans and settled. Other Jews settled in Ulrichstein after expulsion from Spain and Portugal.

Although no Jews lived in Alsfeld in 1650, the Jews of Storndorf were compelled to go there annually in order to listen to the passion plays, which depicted Jews as the cause of Jesus' sufferingeather permitting, the passion plays took place on the Alsfeld market square. In 1511 and 1517, the passion plays lasted for three days during the week of Easter. This pageant invariably inflamed anti-Jewish sentiment and often led to physical attacks against the Jews from Storndorf.

From the sixteenth to the early part of the nineteenth century, a series of rulers held jurisdiction over Angenrod and the Vogelsberg region. Among them were the Landgrave of Hesse-Darmstadt, Emperor Josef, Napoleon, the King of Prussia, the Lords of Ehringshausen and the Sovereigns of Wehrda (called Nodung). Often several sovereigns made ordinances and statutes that applied to a single area. In a radius of twenty-five to thirty-seven miles from Angenrod there were eighty-four castles-each with a different lord.[8] The feudal rulers in Upper Hesse were empowered with authority over the courts: they levied taxes, recruited soldiers, and imposed fees on roads and bridges. The sovereigns decided where cattle could graze, who was permitted to hunt and catch fish, and who would be allowed to settle in their territory.[9]

In 1736, Squire Walter Rudolf von Wehrda had twelve houses built for Jews on his manorial grounds. Each of the twelve Jewish families lived in its own little home in the Judengasse (Jew Street) near the Antreff River, high above a wide valley. The first Wertheim families lived in Angenrod in the houses 42, 45, 46 and 63.[10] On my trip to Angenrod in 1984, Dr. Ursula Wippich showed me the area where this group of small Jewish homes had been built. These houses stood until 1942, the year the last Jews were compelled to leave Angenrod. The street name, Judengasse, has been preserved. A few blocks from the Judengasse, I found a street named Anne Frank Street.

Chapter One

The Judengasse in
Angenrod

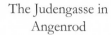

Between 1708 and 1712, a terrible famine occurred in the region of Angenrod. A second hunger period occurred again from 1739 to 1741. People collapsed in the streets from starvation and ate grass, thistles, stinging nettles, and other leaves.[11]

During the Seven Years War (1756-1763) troops were billeted in Angenrod. At that time, Kassel was loyal to Prussia and Darmstadt was on the side of Austria. Angenrod was located on the border of the conflict and suffered damage from both armies. Whenever the merchants could not obtain everything the troops demanded, the soldiers forced their way into the homes to rob, loot, and pillage. In these and other ways the troops behaved basely, wretchedly harassing and pestering the townspeople. In order to vent their anger, the Angenrod populace once again fell upon and attacked the Jewish population without warning.[12] In 1766, thousands of people from the Angenrod region followed the call to the east by Catherine the Great of Russia. The populace wanted to live in an area where they would not have to endure at least three sovereigns on each square meter of ground.[13]

In France in 1789, the masses stormed the palaces and monasteries to obtain food, while in the Angenrod area people did not know where to find food at all. Even in the woods there was scarcely a rabbit tail to spare. Robberies took place in broad daylight and included the theft of shoes and coats. No one trusted one another.[14] Meanwhile the army requested feed for their animals and food, wine, and other articles for themselves from the population. As is the case everywhere around armies, young girls had to be watched over.

Initially, the French Revolution had little impact on the lives of the Jews of Angenrod, but slowly significant changes did begin to occur that began to better the lives of the Jews of Hesse.

> *Moses Wertheim (I)—Born in 1742, died in 1829*
>
> *1742* Handel's *Messiah* was first performed at Fishamble Street Music Hall in Dublin.
> *1749* Johannn Wolfgang von Goethe, one of Germany's best-known poets, dramatists, novelists, and scientists, was born in Frankfurt.
> *1756* The Seven Years War breaks out in Europe.
> *1770* Ludwig von Beethoven was born.
> *1789* The French Revolution occurs in France.
> *1819* The 'Hep! Hep!' riots against Jews takes place in Angenrod.
> The lifetime of Moses Wertheim (I) also encompasses the Enlightenment, which emphasized the qualities shared by all mankind rather than those which called attention to individual differences spread across Europe. Its ideas rested on the philosophy of John Locke, Immanuel Kant, Gotthold Ephriam Lessing, and Moses Mendelssohn.

MOSES WERTHEIM (I)
AND HIS FAMILY

IT MAY BE THAT THE WERTHEIM family of Angenrod came from Borken near Gladenbach. Borken is situated in the hinterland of the Electorate of Hesse.[15] Moses Wertheim (I), the great-grandfather of my paternal grandfather, Herz Wertheim of Angenrod, was born in Angenrod in 1742. However, unlike the Moses of the Bible, Moses Wertheim (I) was not of the tribe of Levi. Evidently, the name of Moses was not used by Christians in Hesse, and Jew-haters demeaned and taunted anyone with the first name of Moses. Therefore, Jewish parents generally took care not to name a child Moses. Anti-semitic notions with regard to the name Moses were so unassailable in the late 1930s that there was no imperative for male Jews with the first name Moses to add Israel to their name, in contrast to the Nazi ordinance required for all other male Jews.

The name Moses appeared in succeeding generations of the Angenrod Wertheim family, but in the nineteenth and twentieth centuries the names Max and Marcus were used instead of Moses. A Marcus Wertheim, who was born in 1824 and who died in 1867, was the first Jew in Angenrod to be designated as a citizen.[16] Seventy-nine people in Angenrod had the name Wertheim. In 1981, members of the Angenrod populace could recall one hundred ten Jews from their town, thirty-two of whom had had the family name Wertheim and two of whom possessed the first name Vogel.[17]

The names of the parents of Moses Wertheim (I) are not recorded. Because his mother was pregnant during the period of famine from 1739 to 1741, doubtless the extreme scarcity of food kept her from obtaining enough to eat for herself and the child she carried. Nevertheless, Moses (I) lived to be eighty-six years old and died on January l, 1829, in Angenrod.[18]

During the lifetime of Moses (I), Jews in Angenrod and its environs spoke Hessian Yiddish, a local *patois* based largely on Hebrew. From its beginnings in the tenth century until the end of the eighteenth century, Yiddish was spoken from

Holland to the Ukraine and from Livonia to Rumania, as well as in the Ashkenazic colonies in Italy, the Balkans, and Palestine. Hessian Yiddish, locally called 'lashon hakodesh,' a mixture of early German and Hessian dialects, with some Hebrew-Aramaic words. It is considered to be 'Western Yiddish,' in contrast to the 'Eastern Yiddish' spoken by Polish and American Jews.[19] At late as 1933, Hessian Yiddish was still spoken in Lauterbach by cattle dealers and other Jews as a form of trade language.

My paternal grandfather, Herz Wertheim from Angenrod, and my maternal grandfather, Jakob Lamm from Kirtorf, frequently conversed in Hessian Yiddish. My father had a fair knowledge of this tongue and spoke it with my mother whenever they did not wish for their children to understand their conversation. In that manner, I mastered many Hebrew words which I might not have learned as readily through language drill. Moses Wertheim's writing was probably Hessian Yiddish in Hebrew letters. In 1959, Mr. Maurer, curator of the Lauterbach Museum, determined the date of my pewter *havdalah*[b] plate from Hesse to be of the early 1800s. The plate's inscription uses Hebrew characters to express German words, which was probably common practice in the eighteenth century in Hesse. But Jews had to communicate with the non-Jewish population in German as well. By 1782, the Jews of Angenrod had lived in their little homes by the Antreff River for forty-six years, and they began to consider whether they should speak modern German.[20]

I do not know how Moses Wertheim (I) and his family, who moved in 1736 into one of the twelve little Angenrod houses for Jews, supported themselves. Their ways of earning a living were very narrowly defined and circumscribed. Eventually in 1807, when Moses Wertheim (I) was sixty-five years old, the Jews of Angenrod were permitted to buy their small houses, the synagogue, and the bake house that made up an area of approximately one hundred and thirty feet by eighty feet.[21] It is not clear whether the twelve Jewish families were also allowed to acquire the land on which the houses stood.

In addition to the names of Oppenheim(er), Speyer, Höchst(er), and Bachrach, other Jewish surnames in Angenrod at the time of Moses Wertheim (I) were Ulmann, Haas, Steinberger, Minchrod, and Spier. During the last quarter of the eighteenth century, the surnames of Schaumberger, Rothschild, and Justus also appeared.[22] Names like Rothschild, Baum, and Lamm (my mother's maiden name) belong to the Jewish aristocracy of the Frankfurt am Main ghetto. To this day, inns located in this former ghetto bear those names.

Members of the Angenrod Jewish group used strict ritual during synagogue services and they employed melodies found in German folk songs. For instance, they sang the *Al-Cheth*[c] to the tune of *The Mill Clacks by the Rushing Brook*, and the *Musaf Kedusha*[d] was chanted according to the melody of *Henry Sleeps With His New Bride*.

---

[b] *Havdalah* means 'distinction' in Hebrew. It is the blessing recited at the termination of Sabbath and festivals to emphasize the distinction between the sacred Sabbath and ordinary weekdays.
[c] Prayer recited on the Day of Atonement (*Yom Kippur*).
[d] *Musaf* was the service in commemoration of the additional sacrifice offered at the Temple on the Sabbath, holidays, and new moon festivals.

Endnotes

1. Dr. Ursula Miriam Wippich, *Memorbuch 1981/82*, p. 31.

2. Ibid, p. 23.

3. Leo Sievers, *Juden in Deutschland* (Hamburg: Verlag Gruner, 1977), p. 35.

4. Wippich, *Memorbuch*, p. 19.

5. Paul Arnsberg, *Die jüdinschen Gemeinden in Hessen*, (Frankfurter Societäts-Druckerei, GmbH, 1971), Vol. 1, p. 31.

6. Wippich, *Memorbuch*, p. 31.

7. Arnsberg, *Die jüdischen Gemeinden in Hessen*, Vol. 1, p. 44.

8. Wippich, *Memorbuch*, p. 109.

9. Ibid, p. 29.

10. Ibid, p. 17.

11. Ibid, p. 13.

11. Ibid, p. 27.

13. Ibid, p. 26.

14. Ibid, p. 63.

15. Ibid, p. 17.

16. Ibid, p. 35.

17. Ibid, p. 36.

18. Ibid, pp. 17, 116.

19. Florence Guggenheim Grünberg, *Juden in der Schweiz* (Edition Kürz, Küsnacht/Zürich), p. 27.

20. Wippich, *Memorbuch*, p. 57.

21. Arnsberg, *Die jüdischen Gemeinden in Hessen*, p. 44.

22. Some of these names appear in Dr. Ursula Miriam Wippich's *Memorbuch 1981/82*, but are also based on my visits in Angenrod as a child and as a teenager.

Chapter Two
Urban and Court Jews
History of Angenrod and its Environs after 1789
Raphael Vogel Wertheim (I) and his Family
The Kalonymus Family and the Jews of Münzenberg

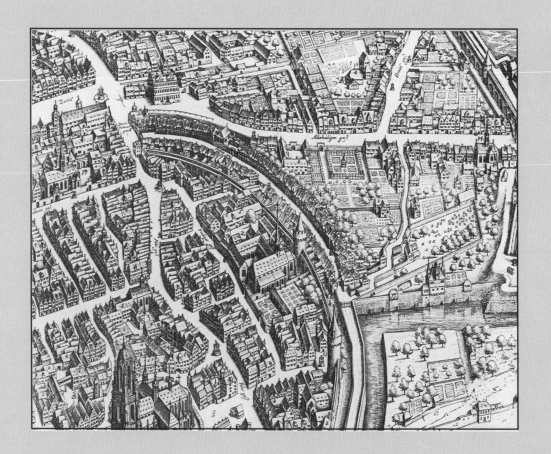

The Judengasse in Frankfurt am Main in 1646

URBAN AND
COURT JEWS

THOSE JEWS WHO LIVED IN CITIES also endured many restrictions. The overcrowded Frankfurt am Main ghetto had five hundred families and approximately three thousand people in 1709. Surrounded by high walls with three gates, the Frankfurt ghetto compared favorably to other ghettos that had only one or two gates. The Frankfurt ghetto gates were opened at sunrise and closed at sunset. However, the gates remained locked on Sundays, on church holidays, at coronations of emperors, and on days of public executions, because the Frankfurt townsmen did not wish to share the enjoyment of such festive occasions with Jews.

Jews were not permitted to walk on the banks of the Main River or to go to the food market after seven o'clock in the morning. They were forbidden to be seen in front of inns where important visitors might stay, lest the Jews ruin a guest's frame of mind. Jews were not allowed to appear in certain streets and locations. In the areas permitted to them, Jews were restricted to walking side-by-side in pairs, and they were required to make room for, salute, and remove their hats to Christians as a sign of deference. The Frankfurt governing body limited the ghetto inhabitants to twelve marriages and six newcomers, probably per year. Germany's great poet, dramatist, novelist, and scientist Johann Wolfgang von Goethe (1749-1832) became acquainted with the Frankfurt ghetto in his childhood and later described his visits there in *Dichtung und Wahrheit* (*Poetry and Truth*).

On May 24, 1786, Juda Löb Baruch was born in the Frankfurt am Main ghetto (on) am Wollgraben in the house #118. The work of Juda Löb Baruch's father involved the exchange of currency between German lands and other countries. In this environment, Juda Löb Baruch, who later called himself Ludwig Börne, grew up to become one of Germany's prominent journalists, a political columnist, and a brilliant reporter. Even his enemies affirmed that he was free of vanity, idealistic, honest, and absolutely incorruptible.[1] Although Ludwig Börne's father, Jakob Baruch, was not a court Jew, his financial status and his son's educational opportunities were far better than those of rural Jews such as Raphael Vogel Wertheim (I) in Angenrod, my great-great-grandfather.

The Hessian court Jew, Wolf Breidenbach (1751-1829), who was in the service of several German princes, doubtless had a benign influence upon the life of Raphael Vogel (I), the Jews of Angenrod, and many Jews in Hesse. Wolf used his connections to abolish the degrading body tax (*Leibzoll*) that Jews had to pay when going into a town or village where they had no rights of residence. When collecting the *Leibzoll*, principalities issued a ticket of passage for a limited stay, which enabled the authorities to oversee the coming and going of Jews and to generate a source of revenue. Wolf Breidenbach hailed from Breidenbach, a village fifty miles west of Angenrod.[a]

---

[a] My Great-Uncle Levi Stern was born in Breidenbach and lived there with his wife, Berta, and their children until the turn of the nineteenth century. Berta was the sister of my material grandmother, Auguste Strauss Lamm.

Chapter Two

AT FIRST, THE IMPACT OF THE FRENCH REVOLUTION and Napoleon's drive through Europe had little effect on the lives of the Jews of Angenrod. Although the Landgrave Ludwig the Tenth supported Napoleon by 1787, the military occupation of Angenrod and its environs left the general population impoverished and oppressed, and the drained populace frequently vented their frustration on the Jews. But by 1807, Napoleon's victorious armies had brought about the civic emancipation of the Jews in places where governments depended on the Emperor.

Every lord under Napoleon's jurisdiction was obligated—at least formally if not actually—to better the lives of his Jews. However, the Hessian Constitution of 1820 placed strict limitations on citizenship for Jews and they continued to be subjected to legal disabilities until the middle of the nineteenth century. Nevertheless the guiding principles of the French Revolution did leave their mark on Hesse and Angenrod. The example of equality in France and the ideal of the United States Constitution were highly regarded; henceforth emancipation became one of the central issues in Jewish life in German lands.

Undoubtedly, the presence of the French in Angenrod until 1813[2] facilitated the construction and dedication of the synagogue, which was collectively owned by

The Angenrod synagogue
in 1959

the twelve Jewish families.[3] This small group of Angenrod Jewish households must have endured many personal privations in order to meet the building expenses for their synagogue in the Judengasse. The synagogue was erected in the center of the ghetto where the twelve Jewish families lived. Attending the dedication were the local lord Carl Reinhard von Wehrda, his wife, Katharina, officers of the French army of occupation, and chairmen of the surrounding rural councils.[4] The rabbi who had jurisdiction over the Angenrod area came either from Fulda or Giessen.

In the eighteenth century, the general population in the Angenrod area included titled gentry and a moneyed patriciate. A kindred classification prevailed among the Jews. Most of the Ashkenazic Jews in the area lived in Treysa, approximately twenty miles north of Angenrod. Written accounts of those Jews have survived from as early as 1320 and can be traced back to the Jews who came with the Romans to the Limes as hired soldiers, merchants, artisans, and prisoners. Those Jewish families lived in the Rhine-Main area until the time of the Crusades, when they fled north, possibly to Angenrod.

In 1800, the Angenrod sovereign, von Nodung, who by then was approaching old age, began to institute ownership-by-possession of the little houses that had been built for the Jewish families.[5] Unlike other village dwellers, the Jews of Angenrod had not possessed real estate or a home for centuries. The possibility of ownership must have been an exciting prospect for the Angenrod Jews: they yearned to possess a house where the kosher laws could be effortlessly observed, where their children had space for studying, and where there was a meadow for their goat to graze.[6] Negotiations for the Jewish families to acquire the twelve modest houses they occupied in Angenrod lasted five years. Although the houses were finally purchased in 1807, it is probable that the Jews did not obtain the rights of ownership to the land on which they sat. Although the exact terms are unclear, it was stipulated that the Jewish families were responsible for the upkeep of the houses.[7]

In 1806, the Angenrod Jewish community was called 'New Jerusalem'[8] after the capital and religious center of Israel of yore. Such a designation shows that the Jews of Angenrod were committed to their study and practice of *Torah* and other Jews in Hesse looked up to the piety of the Jews of Angenrod. In 1818, the rabbis in the Angenrod area began an ongoing deliberation over whether the traditional tallow candles used on the Sabbath and on *Hanukkah* could henceforth be replaced by candles made of stearin. Although the candles made of stearin burned more efficiently, their use was continuously scrutinized because they were made of unkosher animal fats.[b]

The Angenrod Jewish community, which dedicated its synagogue in 1797, was of strictly orthodox persuasion until the 1930s. During and after the eighteenth century, Jewish communities such as Kestrich, Grebenau, Storndorf, and Angenrod offered a refuge against the assimilationist tendencies of the Enlightenment.[9] Some court Jews assumed some moral attitudes and manners of their Christian environment, but there were no incentives for ordinary Jews in the Vogelsberg region to assimilate with the local villagers, who were in many cases poorer than the Jews. From the Jews' point of view, the villagers did not lead exemplary lives in matters of morals and ethics. In 1981, thirty-nine years after the last Jews of Angenrod had been taken away by the Nazis, the local villagers listed the following traits of the erstwhile Jews who had impressed them most: diligence, knowledge, compassion, kindliness, abstinence from alcohol, the virtue of the women, familiarity with local social structure, hard work, modesty, and loyalty to the Jewish faith.[10] Another factor which discouraged assimilation was that Christian influence deprived the Jews of the deeply-felt joys of their singular Sabbath and holiday celebrations.

In 1807, serfdom was abrogated in Prussia and in 1813, the Jews were emancipated.[11] After 1807, some of the young Jewish men of Angenrod fought and died in the French Army, while some of their Jewish brothers were engaged in combat on the Prussian side. Many young Jews were proud to participate in military service because serving in the army and wearing a uniform were marks of distinction that had been forbidden to Jews for centuries. Jewish parents fretted about their sons' safe return from combat. In addition, there was envy, grief, and trouble if the Jewish soldiers returned and their non-Jewish neighbors perished in combat.[12] The same mind-set prevailed in Upper Hesse even after World War II. In several small towns, non-Jewish residents expressed distress about losses in their families and among their neighbors, but resented the fate of their former Jewish neighbors who survived after being driven from their native towns and villages.

---

[b] At that time, stearin was derived from the solid portion of animal fat.

In 1813, territories occupied by Napoleon revolted after the Corsican's unsuccessful campaign into Russia. An army of 137,400 men crossed the Vogelsberg where the Prussians suffered from an unspecified nervous fever. Sick people were billeted in houses and schools for weeks. In l814, Angenrod again became Prussian and compulsory military service was introduced for everyone, including Jews.[13]

For the Jews of Angenrod, 1819 was a particularly difficult year. The local population ran after the Jews in the streets shouting "Hep! Hep!," and when they caught them they knocked them down and roughed them up. Jewish homes were sacked and looted. It was forgotten that many Jews had been wounded and killed in the War of Liberation against Napoleon. Jews did not receive widow or orphan pensions and were also excluded from support payments for invalids. Although the Jews had fought for the common good, citizenship was still denied them.

Around 1800, there were twelve Jewish families in Angenrod. By 1837, there were thirty-nine Jewish fathers, whose wives presented them with a total of one hundred eighty children. If ninety of those children survived, there would have been two hundred people, including mothers and grandparents, to provide for them in thirty-one homes. Nearly everyone had to pay *Schutzgeld*. The amount due for the *Schutzgeld* was determined by the size of a place; in a larger town the dues were higher.[14]

Around 1826, the Jews of Angenrod generally dressed like other villagers, until the Grand Duke unexpectedly decreed that Jews must wear top hats on the Sabbath. The Jews looked so odd that even the barnyard chickens became transfixed with fear at such a sight. The wearing of that silk high hat was clearly inconsistent with the lifestyle of rural Jews. All week they walked from village to village, earning a living either as cattle dealers or peddlers. All week they wore practical headgear while battling the harsh elements of the Vogelsberg.

During the week, the Jews of Hesse looked forward to a sense of well-being on the Sabbath but, instead, while going to and from their house of worship, they had to endure the biting comments of their non-Jewish neighbors. What did the Grand Duke wish to achieve with this absurd decree? Doubtless, such an ordinance was not intended to promote goodwill among neighbors. The Jews of Angenrod would have preferred to dress normally in clean and simple clothing in order to praise the sanctity of the Sabbath. At synagogue it was customary to auction the honors connected with the *Torah* service and the reading of the sacred scrolls. The general membership would always strictly scrutinize the prayer leader's performance, zealously interrupting and correcting him in the event of an error. Throughout the service it was also customary to admonish the women for chatting too loudly.[15]

RAPHAEL VOGEL WERTHEIM (I) AND HIS FAMILY

IN 1774, RAPHAEL VOGEL WERTHEIM (I) was born in Angenrod. He was not named after a living relative. According to *minhag* ('custom' or 'usage' in Hebrew), the name 'Raphael' comes from the Hebrew verb 'to lead.' No newborn child was to stride in the steps of a living forebear—children were always named after a relative who had passed away. If a young child were very ill, it was considered prudent to give the sick youth a second name in order to bewilder the Angel of Death.

Raphael is one of the four archangels; the others are Michael, Gabriel, and Uriel. The angel Raphael is one of the four angels of the Presence, standing on the four sides of God. In reciting the bedtime prayer *K'riat Sh'ma*, one says: "To my right Michael and to my left Gabriel, in front of me Uriel and behind me Raphael and over my head God's *Shekinah*" ('the presence of God'). In the *Zohar*, the central work in the literature of the *Kabbalah*, Raphael dominated the morning hours that bring relief to the sick and suffering, and his main function was ministering to the ailing. The *Talmud* mentions Raphael as one of the three angels who came to visit Abraham after he had circumcised himself. As a planetary angel, Raphael governs the sun; in the division of the four corners of the world, he commands the west. Among the four elements, Raphael governs earth; in the colors of the rainbow, he represents green. Raphael is also ordained over one of the four rivers coming out of paradise. In Upper Hesse, the name Raphael was for some reason transformed into the name 'Vogel' and was also used as a girl's name. It was the only name where this cross-gender phenomenon occurred.[16]

In the name Raphael there is a commanding dignity, which may not have necessarily been outwardly reflected in the lives of the Upper Hesse Jews. In Angenrod, the career opportunities of Raphael Vogel (I) were limited and narrowly defined. Although his occupation is not known, it is certain that craft and trade guilds were closed to Jews in Hesse-Darmstadt. If a Jew had extra cash at his disposal, then he may have made small loans to villagers in Angenrod or nearby, a business transaction in which Jews were permitted to engage. More probably, if Raphael Vogel (I) had been a cattle dealer, then he may have also bought and sold animal hides or peddled small items in neighboring villages.

In Angenrod, Raphael Vogel Wertheim (I) was a *Schutzjude* like his father, Moses Wertheim (I), before him. Kaufmann Wertheim (I), the son of Raphael Vogel Wertheim (I), who was born in Angenrod in 1819, was also a *Schutzjude*. Herz Wertheim, the son of Kaufmann Wertheim (I) and my paternal grandfather, was the first member in our Wertheim family who did not have to endure the ignoble signification of *Schutzjude*. Born in Angenrod on March 29, 1851, Herz Wertheim was the first citizen of his line of the Wertheim family in Angenrod.

In the early 1800s, Raphael Vogel Wertheim (I) married Jüttel (maiden name unknown) from Münzenberg. In 1813, when Raphael Vogel (I) was thirty-nine years of age, his fifth child by Jüttel died at the circumcision ceremony before being named. Jüttel, too, passed away that day.[17] Two older sons of Raphael Vogel (I) and Jüttel were Liebman and Simon.[18] As late as the 1920s, a Liebmann Wertheim and a Simon Wertheim resided in Angenrod; they were most likely grandsons or great-grandsons of Raphael Vogel (I).

In 1815, Raphael Vogel Wertheim (I) married the widow Madel Höchster (née Strauss).[19] During his visit in Lauterbach, my maternal grandfather, Jakob Lamm, recounted that my parents, Berta Lamm Wertheim and Vogel (Frederick) Wertheim (III), were distantly related prior to their marriage. In that case, Madel Strauss Wertheim must have been a descendant of the Storndorf Strauss family of my maternal grandmother, Auguste Strauss Lamm. In 1817, Madel Wertheim gave birth to her first child,[20] which meant that Raphael Vogel (I) had sired six offspring by the age of forty-three.

On June 24, 1819, when Raphael Vogel Wertheim (I) was forty-five years of age, his wife, Madel, gave birth to her second and his seventh child, Kaufmann Wertheim (I), my paternal great-grandfather. The birth certificate states that Kaufmann (I) was born at five o'clock in the afternoon as the first son and the second child of Madel and Raphael Vogel (I) and that the child was named at the time of the circumcision. Although the name 'Kaufmann' translates to 'merchant' in German, the occupation of merchant was generally indicated as *Handelsmann* ('dealer' or 'trader') in the Angenrod documents. According to the Angenrod register, the birth certificate was signed by Mayor Bernhard and Raphael Vogel Wertheim (I).

Another son of Madel and Raphael Vogel Wertheim (I) was born on December 12, 1824, and their daughter, Blümchen, came into the world on February 6, 1826.[21] On May 5, 1831, Moses II (named after his departed grandfather who had died on January 28, 1829) was born to Madel and the fifty-seven-year-old Raphael Wertheim (I). This child died on January 1, 1832.[22] In Angenrod, the five children of Raphael Vogel (I) by Jüttel and his seven children by Madel lived in house #42.[23]

Raphael Vogel Wertheim (I) died on August 17, 1841, at the age of sixty-seven. My paternal great-great-grandparents, Madel and Raphael Vogel Wertheim (I), were buried in the Angenrod Jewish cemetery.

THE KALONYMUS
FAMILY AND THE
JEWS OF
MÜNZENBERG

SINCE 1806, MÜNZENBERG HAD belonged to Hesse-Darmstadt; prior to that it had been held jointly by the lords of von Solms-Braunfels, Solms Laubach, Stollberg-Rossla (Ortenberg), and Hanau. At the beginning of the eighteenth century, approximately one-third of the population of Münzenberg was Jewish. Although the first archival mention of Jews in Münzenberg was made in 1188, it is certain that Jews were residents there at an earlier time. The counts of Münzenberg had almost always been well-disposed toward Jews; Kuno I (1151-1212), in particular, protected and saved the Jews from persecution. For that reason, many refugees of the Jewish communities on the Rhine, especially from Mainz and Speyer, found refuge in Münzenberg.[24]

Among the group of refugees from Mainz and Speyer at the beginning of the thirteenth century were Judah ben Kalonymus, also called Judah of Mainz,

Tombstone of Madel Wertheim,
my father's great-grandmother, in
the Angenrod Jewish cemetery

and his son, Eleazar ben Judah, the pharmacist.[25] The Kalonymus name (meaning 'the one with the nice name' in Greek) derived from a Greek-Jewish family that had come from the Eastern Roman Empire (Byzantium). On July 13, 982, a Kalonymus saved the life of Emperor Otto II. As a result, before the Emperor's untimely death at the age of twenty-eight, he provided a house and citizenship for Kalonymus in Mainz. At that time, Mainz already had a Jewish community where a Jew could live safely under the protection of the local archbishop.[26] But even in Münzenberg there were uprisings against Jews. When a Christian girl fell into a well, the Jews were accused of having pushed her into the pit. In 1223, David ben Kalonymus of Münzenberg (originally from Speyer), one of the most distinguished rabbis of his day,[27] participated in the Rabbinical Synod in Mainz.

The Kalonymus families wielded decisive influence upon the religious, cultural, political, and economic life of the Jews in German lands from the ninth to the thirteenth centuries. More than a dozen *piyyutim*[d] describing the sufferings of

---

[d] A *piyyut* is a deeply-felt poem written to enhance a required prayer or religious ritual for a service that might be personal or shared with others. In ancient days, *piyyutim* often substituted for the prescribed rendition of prayers. Today, *piyyutim* are mostly set aside for the embellishment of religious services on New Years and the Day of Atonement.

Chapter Two

Jews in German lands were probably composed by members of the Kalonymus family.[28]

Endnotes

1. Leo Sievers, *Juden in Deutschland* (Hamburg: Verlag Gruner, 1977), pp. 151-152.

2 Dr. Ursula Miriam Wippich, *Memorbuch, 1981/82*, p. 79.

3. Paul Arnsberg, *Die jüdischen Gemeinden in Hessen* (Frankfurter Societäts-Druckerei, GmbH), Vol. 1, p. 44.

4. Wippich, *Memorbuch*, p. 67.

5. Ibid, p. 71.

6. Ibid, p. 74.

7. Arnsberg, *Die jüdischen Gemeinden in Hessen*, p. 44.

8. Wippich, *Memorbuch*, p. 20.

9. Ibid, p. 31.

10. Letter of May 15, 1984 from Dr. Ursula Miriam Wippich to Mathilda W. Stein.

11. George L. Mosse, *The Jewish Response to German Culture* (Hanover and London: University Press of New England, 1985), p. 2.

12. Wippich, *Memorbuch*, p. 75.

13. Ibid, p. 82.

14. Ibid, p. 25.

15. Ibid, pp. 125, 81, 88, 129.

16. Ibid, p. 52.

17. Ibid, p. 137.

18. Ibid.

19. Ibid, p. 84.

20. Ibid, p. 86.

21. Ibid, pp. 102, 104.

22. Ibid, p. 133.

23. Ibid, p. 139.

24 Arsnberg, *Die jüdischen Gemeinden in Hessen*, Vol 2, p. 299.

25. Ibid, p. 98.

26. Sievers, *Juden in Deutschland*, pp. 24-25.

27. Arnsberg, *Die jüdischen Gemeinden in Hessen*, Vol. 2, p. 98.

28. *Encyclopedia Judaica* (Jerusalem: Keter Publishing House, 1978), Vol. 10, pp. 718-721.

Chapter Three
The Schaumberger and Löb Levi Families of Angenrod
The Flörsheim Family of Romrod
Other Descendants of the Levi Family and Residents of Angenrod

Angenrod

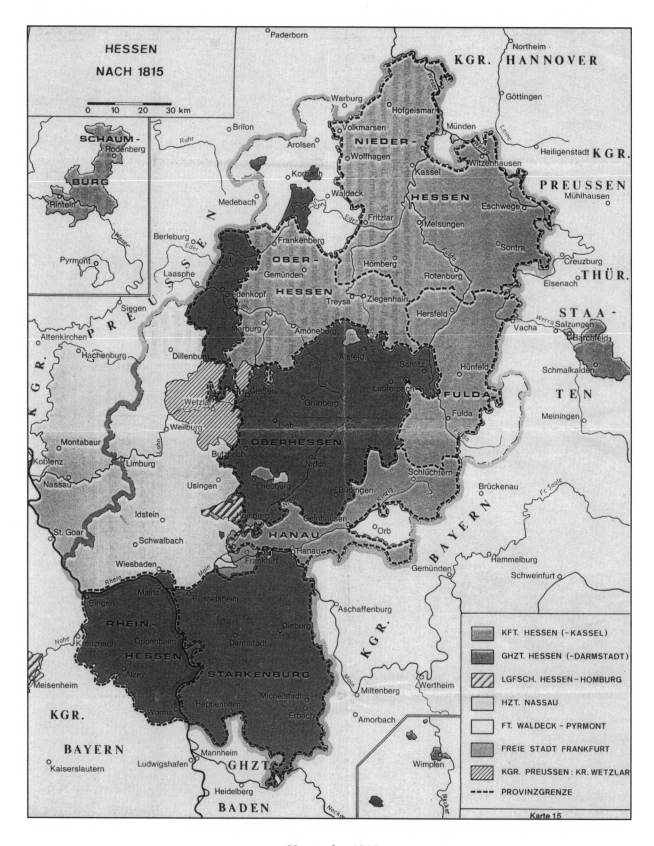

Hesse after 1815

The Way It Was: The Jewish World of Rural Hesse

THE SCHAUMBERGER
FAMILY OF
ANGENROD

*T*oward the end of 1813, Samuel Schaumberger of Angenrod died, having been married to Hennel Spier from Merzhausen since 1808. Michel Spier of Alsfeld, as Hennel's appointed guardian, looked after the pregnant widow. On July 27, 1814, Hennel Spier Schaumberger gave birth to a daughter who was named Samueline after her late father. Michel Spier tried to find a husband for the young widow, which was not an easy task in those times of constant war. In 1817, Löb Levi (I), thirty-five years old, went to Angenrod to marry Hennel and to be a father to the three-year-old Samueline. With a home of her own to take care of, Hennel was now a queen on the Sabbath.

Michel Spier, probably from Merzhausen, a village twelve miles north of Angenrod, was nine years older than Löb Levi (I). Michel Spier and his fourteen children were the first Jewish family recorded in the Alsfeld register. Michel Spier and Löb Levi (I) had a warm relationship that, according to the records, was one of the last important friendships between Jews from Angenrod and Jews from Alsfeld. Although Alsfeld and Angenrod were less than three miles apart, an invisible line of separation existed between Jews from those two communities. Until the early 1930s, the divisive issue was whether a Jew should assimilate to the world around him, and if so, then how much?[1]

I sensed the repercussions of this controversial issue when I attended the *Oberrealschule* in Alsfeld from 1931 to 1933. It was my impression that the Jews from Alsfeld regarded their Jewish brethren from Angenrod as rather insular. The Jews of Alsfeld certainly had accommodated themselves more to modernity, while the Jews of Angenrod, by now considerably diminished in numbers, had managed to hold on to their ways of yesteryear.[2] In 1933, the Jewish population of Alsfeld was one hundred ninety, while only sixty-five Jews resided in Angenrod.[3] The Angenrod Jews accepted the divergence of their Alsfeld brethren as a matter of fact, but they did not want their children to imitate the ways of the Alsfeld Jews.

LÖB LEVI (I)
IN ANGENROD

> ### *Löb Levi (I)—Born in 1782, Died in 1842*
>
> *1797* The Angenrod synagogue is dedicated.
>
> *1807* The Jews of Angenrod are allowed to own their own homes.
>
> *1816* Jews in Hesse are permitted to become citizens if they were not engaged in *Nothandel*, that is, cattle-dealing, lending of money, dealing in second hand goods, or peddling.
>
> *1819* The 'Hep! Hep!' riots against Jews takes place in Angenrod.
>
> The lifetime of Löb Levi (I) also encompasses the Enlightenment, which emphasized the qualities shared by all mankind rather than those which called attention to individual differences spread across Europe. Its ideas rested on the philosophy of John Locke, Immanuel Kant, Gotthold Ephriam Lessing, and Moses Mendelssohn.

Chapter Three

LÖB LEVI (I)
(MARRIED HENNEL
SPIER)

54]

IN OFFICIAL ANGENROD RECORDS, Löb Levi (I) was always registered as Lieb Löwi. Lieb means 'love' in German. In Angenrod, Löb Levi (I) was deemed the 'ice-breaker' because, it was said, he simply melted away prejudice. Even after two-hundred years, the last of his local heirs were still called 'the Löbches.' Reportedly, Löb (I) knew a story about each person and his remarks were always amusing, comical, and direct. He possessed a contagious laugh and sense of joy whenever he related witty stories. Löb (I) knew who was related to whom and how the relationship had come about. Reputed to have been a good friend to everyone, Löb (I) was always a gracious host and a favored guest.

Löb (I) knew all the roads and paths in the Angenrod area, especially the ones with which most people were less familiar. Everyone loved listening to his original travel reports. Christians and Jews alike were very fond of him and, without exception, he loved every living creature. Löb (I) was a person free from guile. Whatever he touched flourished. He performed all of his duties with love and devotion. In his presence no one behaved in a hateful manner.

At all times, Löb (I) liked his things in their proper place. He assumed, of course, that his Hennel would clean up after him, putting his things exactly where he wanted and needed them. The only fear with regard to Löb (I) was when he made the following statement: "We do not know him." Löb (I) would never tell a story about a person who had disqualified himself from Löb's world by a base reproach, a broken promise, or a petty betrayal. Löb (I) would turn away from such an individual and would not even dignify him by being his enemy. Löb's (I) most outstanding mark of character was his honor and integrity. Because his word was regarded like a sworn statement, no one cheated him.

Without ceremony, Löb (I) would put good things into the hands of the poor while remarking, "A thank you is not in order. Soon I will probably need something from you." He would feel sorry for a forlorn cat and in winter he never forgot to feed the birds. Whenever he would be called up to the *Torah* on the Sabbath, Löb (I) would return to his seat feeling like a king. Friend and foe alike came at the time of his death, everyone feeling that there would not be a man like him again, and that from then on the world would be diminished.

When Löb (I) came to Angenrod in 1817, the Jewish community there had been named 'New Jerusalem' for eleven years.[4] In biblical times, Jerusalem had been the place of assembly where the Hebrew tribes met to appear before God; similarly, in the nineteenth century, Jews of diverse backgrounds lived side-by-side in Angenrod.[5] In Angenrod, the male descendants of the Löb Levi (I) family lived consecutively in house #69 from the time Löb Levi (I) acquired the house in 1817, until Hermann Levi (I), the great-grandson of Herz Levi (I), and his family, left Angenrod for the United States in 1935. In 1990, Angenrod residents still designated house #69 as 'Löbches house.'

Löb Levi (I) was probably a cattle dealer. I cannot recall that my grandmother, Hannchen Levi Wertheim, ever mentioned another way of earning a livelihood in

The Way It Was: The Jewish World of Rural Hesse

her family in those days. The death certificate of Löb Levi (I) showed his occupation as *Handelsmann* (dealer) and described him as a *Schutzjude*. Löb (I) died in 1842 at half past nine at night in house #69. *Schutzjuden* Herz Speier and the teacher,

Meyer Bamberger, were recorded as trustworthy witnesses who testified about Löb's (I) death and who, together with Mayor Bernhard, signed the death certificate. As the law proscribed, the certificate included a postscript signed by Mayor Bernhard: "To the best of my knowledge this register contains the sum total of four deaths during the year 1842 occurring in the Angenrod Israelite community."

The tombstone of Löb Levi (I) in the Angenrod Jewish cemetery

Löb Levi (I) was buried in the Angenrod Jewish cemetery. On his tombstone, the date of his death was recorded in terms of the Hebrew calendar: the twenty-fifth day of the month of *Tishri* in the year 5603. The inscription on the tombstone reads: "There lived a man from the house of Levi who walked a straight path. He conducted his duties conscientiously, offered a helping hand to the poor, and prayed with fervor."

THE CHILDREN OF HENNEL AND LÖB LEVI (I)	LÖB (I) FATHERED SIX CHILDREN with Hennel: Herz (I) (born 1819); Sofia (born 1823, died 1824); Sofia (born 1825); Janette (sometimes called Shanette or Sheina) (born 1826); Rachel (born 1829); and Braunette (born 1832, died 1834).
Herz (I) (married Karoline Rosenberg)	HERZ (I)[a] WAS BORN IN ANGENROD on July 24, 1819, one month after Kaufmann Wertheim (I), my other paternal great-grandfather. Their birth certificates appeared on the same page of a municipal document, together with that of a Jewish boy with the surname 'Rothschild.' All three birth announcements recorded the year 'Christ 1819' and each of the boys was given his first name at the time of circumcision. The birth certificate of Herz Levi (I) showed that he was the second child and first son of Hennel, and the first child of her husband, Löb Löwi (I). Löb Levi (I) signed the document in German. Mayor Bernhard recorded and signed the three birth certificates.

---

[a] The name 'Herz' is probably derived from the Hebrew word '*chessed*' meaning 'grace' or 'mercy.'

Chapter Three

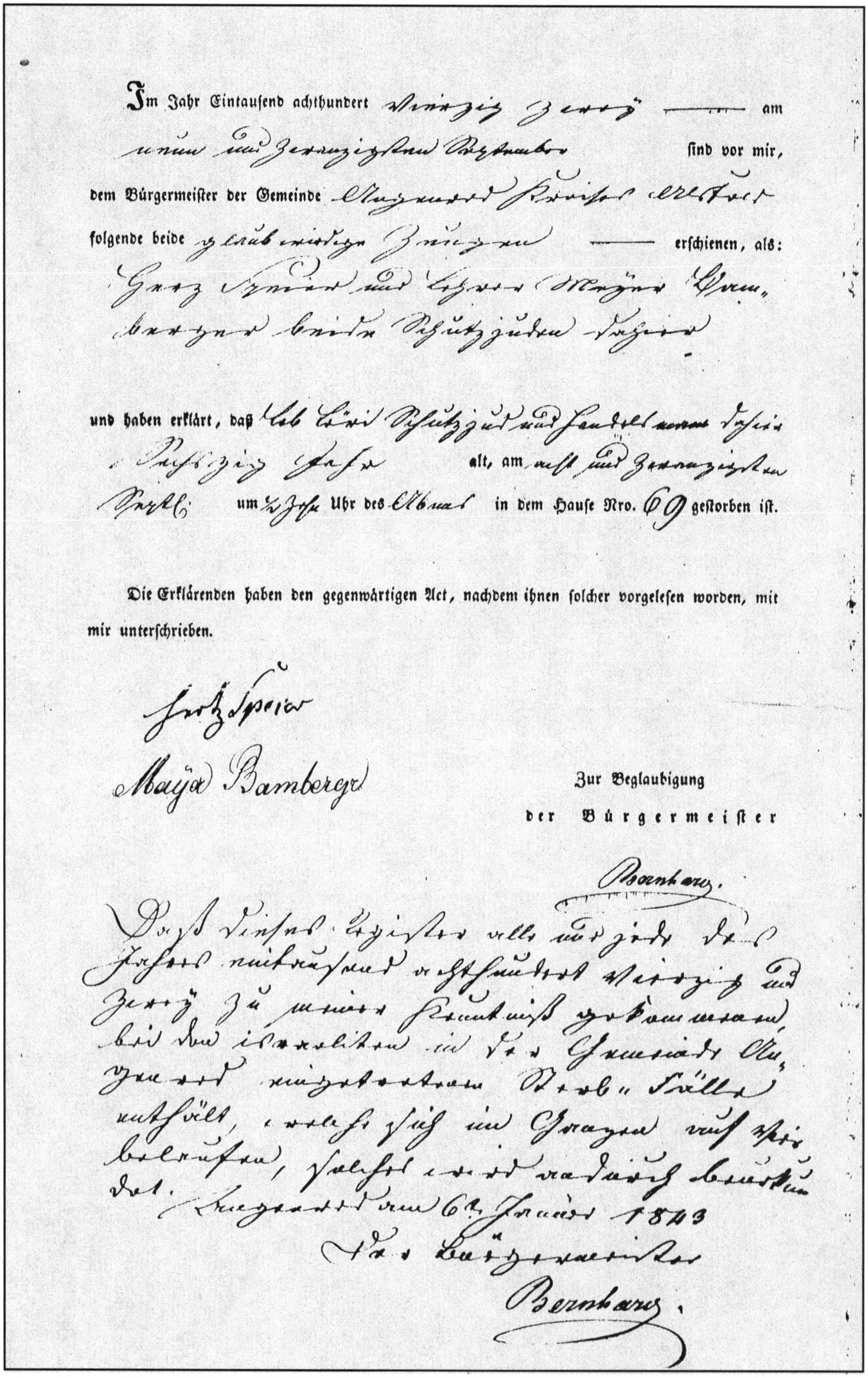

Im Jahr Eintausend achthundert vierzig zwey — am neun und zwanzigsten September sind vor mir, dem Bürgermeister der Gemeinde Angenrod Kreises Alsfeld folgende beide glaubwürdige Zeugen — erschienen, als: Hertz Speier und Lehrer Mayer Bamberger beide Schutzjuden dahier

und haben erklärt, daß Löb Levi Schutzjud und Handelsmann dahier Sechzig Jahre alt, am acht und zwanzigsten Septbr. um ½ zehn Uhr des Abends in dem Hause Nro. 69 gestorben ist.

Die Erklärenden haben den gegenwärtigen Act, nachdem ihnen solcher vorgelesen worden, mit mir unterschrieben.

Hertz Speier

Mayer Bamberger

Zur Beglaubigung
der Bürgermeister

Bernhard.

Daß dieses Register alle im Laufe des Jahres eintausend achthundert vierzig und zwey zu meiner Kenntniß gekommenen bei den Israeliten in der Gemeinde Angenrod eingetretenen Sterbe-Fälle enthält, welche sich im Ganzen auf [illegible] belaufen, solches wird dadurch beurkundet.
Angenrod den 6ten Januar 1843
Der Bürgermeister
Bernhard.

The death certificate of Löb Levi (I)

THE DAUGHTERS
OF HENNEL AND
LÖB LEVI (I)

Sofia

Sofia

Janette

Rachel

Braunette

IN 1823, SOFIA, Hennel and Löb Levi's (I) first daughter, was born, but grievously on September 28, 1824 the child passed on. That year many Jewish children in Angenrod died. It was a deeply distressing period: fear was constant because many children were ill and their helpless and piercing cries broke everyone's heart. In desperation, the Jewish families of Angenrod declared a fast. They opened the Ark of the Covenant so that God, the Judge, might recall the Angel of Death. After the Jews of Angenrod prayed fervently on *Yom Kippur*, fewer deaths befell the community. Then there followed the task of nursing the ill back to health, consoling the ailing, and teaching the disabled how to stand and walk. In 1824, five Jewish children were born in Angenrod and five Jewish children died.

Hennel Levi gave birth to another daughter on January 9, 1825, and named her Sofia after the departed infant.[6] Janette (sometimes called Sheina or Shanette) was born on December 14, 1826.[7] Rachel, the fourth daughter of Hennel and Löb Levi (I), was born on December 11, 1829. Braunette was born May 8, 1832, but died before she was two years old. The unusual names for women, such as Braunette, Fanne, Jette, Scheina, and Sowien, had been recorded in Frankfurt am Main before 1349, the time of the bubonic plague.[8]

THE FLÖRSHEIM
FAMILY OF
ROMROD

IN 1832, ISACK FLÖRSHEIM (I) OF ROMROD, which was five miles south of Angenrod, married the non-Jewess Frederika Stieler. At that time, intermarriage occurred very rarely among the Upper Hesse Jews in rural communities. Isack and Frederika Flörsheim lived in the house #131 in Romrod. According to the Flörsheim family, Frederika became a loyal member of the Romrod Jewish community.[9]

On January 10, 1849, Janette Levi of Angenrod married Isaac Flörsheim (II) of Romrod, the son of Isack (I) and Frederika Flörsheim. Rabbi D. Levi performed the wedding ceremony and the witnesses were Isaac Mayer and the teacher, Meyer Bamberger, from Angenrod. The Janette and Isaac Flörsheim (II) family lived in house #90 in Romrod. Janette Levi Flörsheim died on April 24, 1872, at the age of forty-seven. Of their children only Settchen, Salomon, and Joseph are known to me. Settchen Flörsheim, the daughter of Isaac (II) and Janette, married Sigmund Strauss of Grebenau and later this family resided in Lauterbach at Hintergasse 12.

The Jewish community of Romrod usually buried its members in the Angenrod Jewish cemetery, where several tombstones of the Flörsheim family were still legible in 1985. Joseph Flörsheim and his three sons, Jules, Isack, and Fritz fled to England at the beginning of the Hitler era. I can vividly recall Fritz as a tall, handsome individual who greatly impressed me when I was a young child. He was frequently a Sunday visitor at the Wertheim home in Lauterbach.

Salomon Flörsheim had four children. The oldest son, Emil, was killed in World War I fighting for Germany. The only daughter, Jenny, perished with her young teenage son, Manfred, in southern France. Salomon Flörsheim met his death in Theresienstadt. Moritz and his wife, Irma, survived by fleeing to the United

Chapter Three

Der

Großherzoglich Hessische Rabbiner zu Gießen

Daß heute, am 10ten Januar 1849, nach Einsicht Großh. Regierungsräthlichen Heirathsscheins und Großh. Landgerichtlicher Bescheinigung, daß dem Vollzuge der Ehe kein gesetzliches Hinderniß im Wege stehe, der Isaac Flörsheim II von Romrod mit Janette Levi von Angenrod daselbst zu Romrod, in Gegenwart der beiden Zeugen Isaac Mayer Schneidesohn und Lehrer Lamberger von Angenrod nach Vorschrift des israelitischen Ritus ehelich getraut wurde, darüber zur Urkunde gegenwärtige Bescheinigung ertheilt wird.

Romrod den 10ten Januar 1849.

Dr Levi.

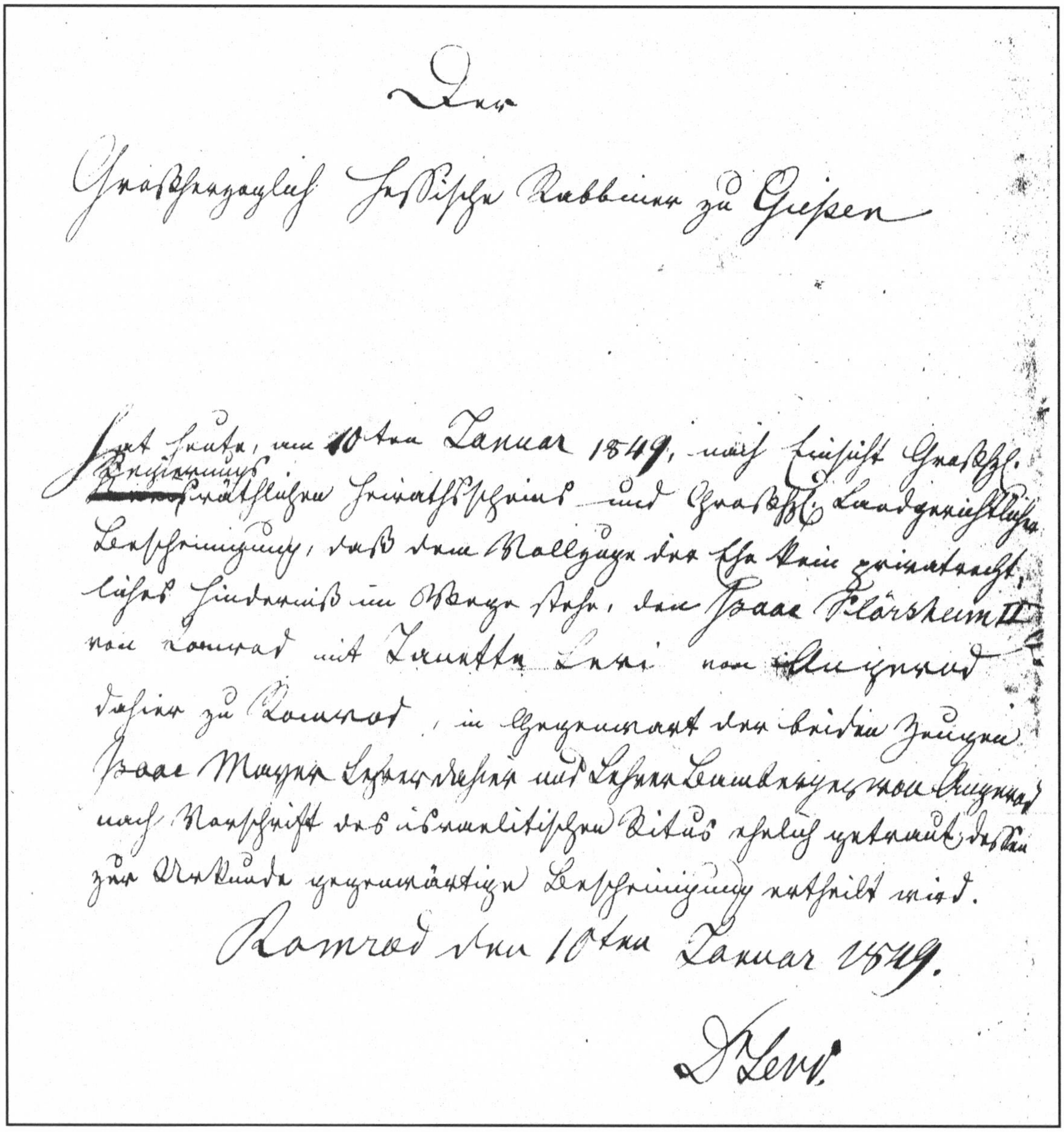

Marriage certificate of Isaac Flörsheim (II) of Romrod and Janette Levi Flörsheim of Angenrod

States. This childless couple was always very close to my aunt, Hilda Wertheim Herz, when the three of them lived in the same apartment house in New York.

The fourth son of Salomon Flörsheim was Ludwig; he, his wife, Kaethe, and their child, Renee, survived the Holocaust. At the outbreak of World War II, Kaethe was imprisoned in England as an enemy alien. The twenty-two-month old Renee was cared for by nuns and was delivered to a family friend in southern France. Eventually this family was reunited in the United States. In 1970, Ludwig died in Atlanta, where Kaethe and her daughter, Renee Rayel, still reside.

OTHER RESIDENTS OF ANGENROD

MICHEL SPIER IS BURIED in close proximity to Löb Levi (I) in the cemetery. As recorded on their almost identical tombstones, they died within three months of each other. The earliest tombstones in the Angenrod Jewish cemetery are dated 1842 and none had an effigy. Although Alsfeld had its own Jewish cemetery, some of its residents were laid to rest in the Angenrod Jewish cemetery. In all likelihood, members of the Levi family chose to rest with their forebears. Löb's (I) brother, Hirsch, was also buried in Angenrod. Hirsch was born in Birstein and died in Angenrod in April 1889 at the age of eighty. He married Samueline Schaumberger, the daughter of Samuel Schaumberger and Hennel Spier Levi (the widow Schaumberger). Samueline had been raised in the home of her mother and stepfather, Hennel and Löb Levi (I). Hirsch and Samueline were blessed with eight children. Samueline died on August 27, 1865 at the age of fifty-one.[10] Gabriel Levi, a son of Samueline and Hirsch Levi, was also buried in Angenrod.

On my visit to Capetown, South Africa in 1979, I met two of Gabriel's grandchildren, Thekla Sondheimer Levey and her brother Hermann Levi. Their widowed mother, Käthe Sondheimer, had died some years earlier in Capetown. In Alsfeld, Käthe had lived on a street near the railroad station. I had to pass her home daily on my way from the railroad station to the *Oberrealschule*. While in South Africa, I was not able to see Gabriel's grandchild, Seppel Levi. Seppel's brother, Hermann, formerly of South Africa, now lives in Indianapolis, Indiana. The other three siblings live in Israel. Benno Levi of Oak Park, Michigan is also a descendant of this Levi family.

Another member of the Levi family of Alsfeld was Dr. Gustav Levi, son of David, who had been given the nickname 'Wasserdavid' in Alsfeld because he sold water. In 1933, Gustav directed the Palestine Electric Company in Haifa.[11] Gustav frequently visited with my uncle, Carl Wertheim, and his wife, Irma Levi Wertheim, in Miami Beach, Florida. Both Irma and Carl hailed from Angenrod and were great-grandchildren of Löb Levi (I). All of these members of the Levi family had lived in Alsfeld before they were involuntarily scattered to foreign lands in the 1930s. It is doubtful whether Löb Levi (I), his brother, Hirsch Levi, or Michel Spier had even a reading acquaintance with some of the places their descendants would be dispersed abroad after Hitler took office on January 30, 1933.

Hirsch Levi's tombstone in the
Angenrod cemetery

While in Capetown, I also met by chance my school friend, Kurt Spier, formerly of Alsfeld. Kurt is a descendant of Michel Spier, Löb Levi's (I) close friend and Hennel's guardian before her marriage to Löb (I). Kurt Spier was one year ahead of me at the *Oberrealschule* in Alsfeld, which I attended from 1931 to 1933. Four generations after the deeply-felt friendship between Michel Spier of Alsfeld and Löb Levi (I) of Angenrod there exists much devotion between Thekla Sondheimer Levey's family and Kurt Spier in Capetown. In 1979, Thekla commented that in any family crisis she would be able to count on Kurt's complete loyalty.

All of the Jewish children in the three upper grades of the Alsfeld *Oberrealschule* received religious instruction by Herr Kahn. He was the spiritual leader of the Jews of Alsfeld, teaching the young of his flock as well as all the Jewish children who attended the various schools in Alsfeld. Our curriculum was post-biblical Jewish history. However, Herr Kahn spent many lessons discussing the currently rampant anti-semitism in Alsfeld and, in particular, the abusive language, physical maltreatment, and dirty pranks Jewish students were forced to endure daily by teachers and students. His sympathetic ear would often ease our heartache. In 1934, Herr Kahn, his wife, and their young daughter immigrated to the United States and lived in the Eighties on New York's East Side. That same year they invited me to spend *Yom Kippur* at their home so I would not have to travel to attend synagogue on the holiday. Shortly thereafter, the Kahn family immigrated to Israel, where they felt they could observe the commands of their religion more faithfully.

Endnotes

1. Dr. Ursula Miriam Wippich, *Memorbuch 1981/82*, p. 33.

2. Ibid, p. 106.

3. Paul Arnsberg, *Die jüdischen Gemeinden in Hessen* (Frankfurter Societäts-Druckerei, GmbH, Vol. I, pp. 31, 33.

4. Wippich, *Memorbuch*, p. 44.

5. Ibid, p. 57.

6. Ibid, pp. 102, 104.

7. Ibid, p. 66.

8. Letter from Dr. Ursula Miriam Wippich, June 1984.

9. Wippich, *Memorbuch*, p. 121.

10. Ibid, p. 84.

11. Arnsberg, *Die jüdischen Gemeinden in Hessen*, p. 32.

Essay
The Birstein Jewish Community
Jewish Education in Birstein

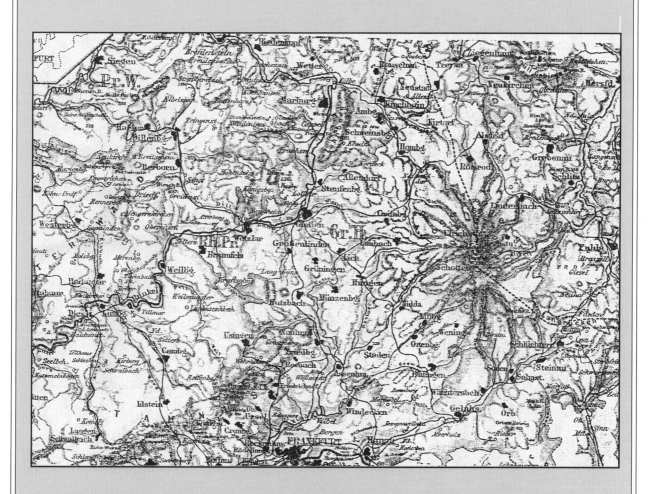

The Birstein region

ℒÖB LEVI (I), THE GRANDFATHER of my paternal grandmother, Hannchen Levi Wertheim, came to Angenrod in 1817 from Birstein. More-over, the information on Birstein mentions Wolf Kaufmann, a forebear of my husband, Max Kaufmann Stein. The town of Birstein in the Electorate of Hesse is situated on the southern edge of the Vogelsberg; in contrast, Angenrod and Lauterbach are located north of the Vogelsberg, where residents endure lower temperatures and harsher winds. During the Thirty Years War (1618-1648), a Levi family came to the Vogelsberg region from Italy.[1] In 1650, a Jew was mentioned in the Birstein records, but no name was cited for him. The practice of designating a person as "the Jew" without indicating his name evinced disrespect. The anonymous Jew had asked for permission to have his son circumcised; however, it is not clear whether the petition was granted. In 1754, the name Levi first appeared in the Birstein records when the widow of Mendele Abraham Levi petitioned that her son, Mayer Levi, a *Schutzjude* (protected Jew), who had been living in Birstein for one year, be given free wood. Her request was denied.[2] This Levi family was probably not forebears of mine, because the first names Mendele, Abraham, and Mayer subsequently did not appear in our Levi family, as *minhag* (custom) would have prescribed.

From 1786 to 1796, twenty Jewish families dwelt in Birstein. By the year 1806, Birstein recorded twenty-five families of *Schutzjuden*, all of whom existed in modest financial circumstances. In some cases, the sovereign could only obtain the *Schutzgeld* (protection fee) by force.[3]

ON DECEMBER 30, 1823, ELECTOR WILLIAM II issued a decree stating that: "Members of the Jewish faith are required to have their children attend the public schools of their place of residence." The District Council of Wächtersbach, the District Council of Gelnhausen (after 1830), the elders of the Jewish community, and the Provincial Government in Hanau were required to supervise the Jewish schools thereafter. From 1824 to 1827, three Jewish teachers served successively in Birstein: Samuel Schaaf, Moses Salomon, and Wolf Goldschmidt. Because these teachers had come from Bavaria, they were considered foreigners. The government of the Electorate of Hesse granted each of them a permit of residence for only one year. Because the Electorate of Hesse treated its Jews relatively favorably it therefore attracted Jews from all over. The Birstein Jewish community had to pay an annual fee of five *Gulden* to the provincial school treasury as dispensation money for using its own teacher.

1824-1827
Samuel Schaaf
Moses Salomon
Wolf Goldschmidt

1828
Elias Grünstein

In 1828, Elias Grünstein from Aschenhausen in the Spessart, a densely-forested upland between the Main and the Kinzig Rivers, was accepted as teacher in Birstein for three years. Mr. Grünstein taught twenty-six children (sixteen children from Birstein, eight from Untersotzbach, Obersotzbach, and Unterreichenbach; and two from Helfersdorf) and earned a yearly salary of one hundred thirty *Gulden*. In the Birstein Jewish community, a controversy developed about payment of that salary. Baruch Levi, Wolf Jonas, Heinemann Stern, Gonnebel Goldschmidt, and one woman, the widow of a man named Jessel, declared that because they had no children of school age, they refused to pay their share of the teacher's salary. After an exchange of opinions, the administration in Hanau decreed that two-thirds of the salary was to be paid by the members of the Birstein Jewish community and one-third was to be contributed by the parents of the students.

THE DISPUTE BETWEEN FISCHBORN AND BIRSTEIN

IN 1827 A DISPUTE AROSE between the communities of Fischborn and Birstein because Fischborn had its own Jewish teachers. The Fischborn community's first teacher was Löser Reis from Orb, followed successively by three teachers from Vollmerz; in 1830, the teacher from Vollmerz was Levi Hirsch. Although Fischborn belonged to the Jewish community of Birstein, Liebman Klein of Fischborn testified in Gelnhausen that for fifty years the community of Fischborn had conducted religious services in the room of a house that belonged to him. Furthermore, Mr. Klein declared that the Jews of Fischborn had attended worship services in Birstein only on *Yom Kippur* (the Day of Atonement) and *Rosh Ha-Shanah* (the Jewish New Year).

The Fischborn public school teacher, G. Reifschneider, confirmed that the Jewish children of his village had attended the Christian public school in summer and winter in addition to attending their own school. The Fischborn village mayor, Lutz, asserted that it was unreasonable to expect six- or seven-year-old children to go to Birstein for instruction during the frequently harsh weather of the Vogelsberg. Because children coming primarily from poor parents often had torn clothing and did not possess shoes, the mayor felt that they could not be expected to trudge along the wet and undeveloped road to Birstein.

Notwithstanding, the elder of the Birstein Jewish community, Abraham Katz, asked the members of the Fischborn Jewish community for a share of the salary of Birstein's teacher, Mr. Grünstein. Mr. Katz of Birstein remarked sarcastically that, for the cost of ten to fifteen *Gulden*, Fischborn had made use of uncertified teachers who would not be worthy to mime as teachers of religion. When the district council ordered the dissolution of the Hebrew school in Fischborn, Levi Hirsch went to Kirchbracht and the Jews of Fischborn sent their children there. However, on June 27, 1831, Gelnhausen decreed that the religious school in Kirchbracht be closed. The authorities referred to the law of 1823 that permitted religious services only in public places of worship.

THE BIRSTEIN JEWISH COMMUNITY ACQUIRES A CANTOR

IN ADDITION TO A RELIGIOUS TEACHER, the Jewish community of Birstein also obtained the services of a cantor who conducted worship in lieu of a rabbi on weekdays, the Sabbath, and holidays. The cantor had to read the prescribed portion from the Five Books of Moses in the requisite pattern of pitch. In Birstein, the cantor also slaughtered animals for the Jews according to the ordained ritual. Upon the death of their cantor and slaughterer ('*shohet*' in Hebrew) on October 20, 1830, the Birstein Jewish community looked for a successor.

1831 Isaak Bruck

On May 31, 1831, Seligmann Rosenthal and Heinemann Stern engaged Isaak Bruck of Gelnhausen for Birstein, Untersotzbach and Obersotzbach, Fischborn, Hitzkirchen, Helfersdorf, Hellstein, and Hedersroth. Mr. Bruck's yearly salary as cantor was ninety *Gulden*, and he received an additional five Gulden for accessorial services on holidays. Mr. Bruck had to defray his own expenses for room-and-board because he derived considerable income from the ritual slaughtering of animals. He received twenty *Kreuzer* for cattle and four *Kreuzer* each for a calf, mutton, or goat. On January 1, 1832, Liebmann Moses Löwenheim from Lissa in Posen was employed to fill the three positions of teacher, cantor, and ritual slaughterer. His salary was one hundred eighty-two *Gulden* and thirty *Kreuzer*, plus free lodging in the community house. But the following year, the Jewish community elder, Katz, prohibited Mr. Löwenheim from doing the ritual slaughtering. Juda Wolf from Sotzbach was then certified as ritual slaughterer by the rabbi in Gelnhausen. Mr. Wolf indicated that because of lack of funds and because he had been unable to pursue any other line of business, he was obliged to rely entirely on ritual slaughtering as an income.

1832 Liebmann Moses Löwenheim

As a teacher, Mr. Löwenheim had been engaged to work six hours daily in winter and eight hours daily in summer, but evidently he did not enforce regular school attendance strictly enough. Mr. Katz reproached the members of the Jewish community for taking their children to work to train them for business instead of sending them to school. Mr. Katz maintained that this lapse in education would be the undoing of the Birstein's Jewish youth, and would ultimately render the young people incapable of being trained for a trade or vocation.

1835 Menco Lion

The community elder, Katz, suggested that Menco Lion be hired as the new teacher, believing that Mr. Lion would be more capable of furthering the education of the Jewish young people. Moreover, as an actual inhabitant of the Electorate of Hesse (in the village of Zünterbach near the Bavarian border), Mr. Lion would be able to remain in Birstein without a special authorization and could therefore remain in the community for a longer period of time. Several members of the Birstein Jewish community would have preferred hiring their own—one Mr. Presburger. Marburg L. Kunreuther from

Gelnhausen, a son of the local rabbi, also applied for the position. But at the beginning of 1835, Mr. Lion was employed and a detailed statement of his income has been preserved. Mr. Lion's salary as teacher amounted to one hundred fifty *Gulden*, a free bed in the schoolroom, and two cords of wood. For heating the schoolroom, making the fire, and cleaning the schoolroom, Mr. Lion was paid eleven *Gulden*. He received fifty *Gulden* for his services as a cantor and an additional five *Gulden* and fifteen *Kreuzer* for special sermons on the Pilgrim Feasts (Passover, the Feast of Weeks, and the Feast of Booths). His services for blowing the *shofar* (ram's horn) on *Rosh Ha-Shanah* (New Year) and reading from the Book of Esther on *Purim* (Feast of Lots) earned him another three *Gulden* and thirty *Kreuzer*.

Menco Lion was especially qualified as a teacher. His school report was certified by Rabbi Gosen, the regional rabbi in Marburg and it attested to "very good" scholarship in Mosaic religious doctrine, Hebrew language, and the Old Testament. Mr. Lobenstern, of the commission for the examination of Jewish teachers in Hanau, gave Mr. Lion the overall grade of two. However, this certificate of second rank did not entitle Mr. Lion to teach in a public school. Evidently, Mr. Lion was highly respected by his co-religionists in Birstein because his employment contract was repeatedly renewed. Mr. Lion's instruction was considered preferable to the compulsory education in the public school.

In 1842, the local parson, Mr. Emmerich, reported in his capacity as school inspector that the Jewish children did not attend the public school. He stated that the Jewish children received daily lessons from their own teacher in five subjects: religion, Hebrew language, study of German, arithmetic, and penmanship. Mr. Emmerich also related that in the afternoon the Jewish children attended the local work-study school, where they obtained the necessary instruction for their advancement in the world. Mr. Emmerich advised that instruction for the Jewish children remain status quo, because irregular attendance in public school would only serve to disturb the lessons of the public school teacher, Mr. Schaubinger.

Following a long illness during the winter of 1843-44, Mr. Lion was granted a leave of absence by the Jewish community of Birstein; in July of 1844, he had to be discharged. In October of 1844, Salomon Adler from Burghaun became Mr. Lion's successor, having taught previously for twelve years at the Jewish school in Meerholz. Mr. Adler's yearly salary as teacher and cantor was one hundred seventy-five *Gulden*, free residence, and free wood for heating.

1844
Salomon Adler

On May 6, 1845, the Electoral government in Hanau licensed the religious school in Birstein as an 'integrated Israelite public school.' Mr. Adler gained a salary increase of twenty-five *Gulden*. On October 9, 1846, Mr. Adler was granted life tenure as cantor and Israelite public school teacher in Birstein. Thereafter, school-age children of the Birstein Jewish community and the Jewish children of the additionally authorized villages attended their own fully-equipped educational establishment, which existed until 1937.

There is a considerable amount of information about the circumstances of the Israelite school, because visitation reports by Mr. Emmerich, the local school inspector, and by Rabbi Felsenstein from Hanau have been preserved. Both of those reports were rendered in 1845, the year in which the school was established. Using his residence as a classroom, Mr. Adler taught three classes with a total of thirty-six children: fourteen children from Birstein, three from Obersotzbach, four from Untersotzbach, three from Helfersdorf, five from Hitzkirchen, and seven from Unterreichenbach. Mr. Adler instructed thirty-five hours during the week. Lessons were held in the morning from eight until twelve o'clock and in the afternoon from two until five o'clock.

Pewter oil lamp made in Birstein circa 1820

In 1843, the Jewish community bought Salomon Adler's house (on) am Riedbach. During instruction the pupils were seated facing each other around three tables and the only equipment was a blackboard. The first class succeeded in reading with "correct accentuation and with much expression," the second group read on an "inferior" level, and the first girl scholar of the third class recited the poem *Die Schuld* ('Obligation') by Gellert "rather well." Some samples of penmanship were rated "splendid," and in dictation some pupils made no mistakes. The students showed special skill in mental arithmetic, as well as the geography of the Electorate of Hesse. Both visiting examiners praised not only the teaching skills and the enthusiasm of Mr. Adler, but also the first-rate progress of his pupils.

The budget of the Birstein Jewish community indicated a surplus of seventy-three *Gulden*. The amount was set aside for the building of a *mikveh*, a pool or bath of clean water into which a ritually unclean person was immersed in order to become ritually clean. At that time, *mikvehs* were used primarily for post-menstruant women. In addition to two hundred *Gulden* for Mr. Adler's salary and five *Gulden* for the community attendant, twenty-five *Gulden* were allotted for wood, fifteen *Gulden* for tallow candles, and five *Gulden* for cleaning. The amount of tax imposed on the Jewish community members was twice the amount of the school tax, which was set at one hundred eighty-three *Gulden*. There was also an income of twenty-five *Gulden* from *Torah* money and occasionally thirty *Gulden* from school money or from synagogue chairs. It was not without cause that the Jewish community of Birstein was depicted as rather prosperous. Therefore, on October 9, 1846, the community granted Salomon Adler tenure at the independent Israelite school.

A DISPUTE BETWEEN BIRSTEIN AND HELLSTEIN

HOWEVER, SOON A CHANGE OCCURRED in the economic situation of Birstein. In addition to a general rise in the cost of living, the Jewish community of Hellstein seceded from Birstein on March 20, 1848. With Wolf Kaufmann as community elder, Hellstein employed its own teacher and cantor. Birstein community elders, Wolf Seelig and Samuel Katz, delayed beyond the time limit in paying Mr. Adler because the Jews from Hellstein no longer furnished contributions to the synagogue association. In March, 1852, the protracted legal battle between Birstein and Hellstein finally ended when the ministry of interior in Kassel terminated the independence of the Jewish community of Hellstein.

DIFFICULT TIMES IN BIRSTEIN

MR. ADLER COPED EFFECTIVELY with the delay of his salary payments. While his wife carried on a flourishing millinery business in the school building, he brokered the sum of three thousand *Gulden* by lending it out for interest. In other ways, too, Mr. Adler understood how to accomplish his own ends. During the difficult years of 1848 to 1849, when the community deducted the allowance for heating and cleaning the school room from his salary, he obtained the concession to use the community barn free of charge in order to keep a goat, geese, and animal feed. During the time when the Jewish community elders did not grant his request for additional heating material beyond the customary two cords of wood, Mr. Adler did not heat the schoolroom in the middle of the winter. In protest, the parents organized a school strike because the "little hands of the children had gone numb from the cold, and the children would not be able to either write or do arithmetic."

At times, Mr. Adler gave lessons for separate payment in Eckardroth and in Hellstein. Moreover, he was known for disciplining his students. A notice of 1854 from Romsthal stated that Mr. Adler had severely disciplined the headstrong and self-willed Elise Leopold, because "that youngster's achievements in the theatre arts had enabled her to simulate an epileptic attack." A notice of 1858 by the community elder, Jonas Hess, substantiated that Mr. Adler had beaten Mr. Hess's son with a bamboo stick.

In 1860, Mrs. Adler obtained the franchise for a dry-goods business and the family bought and moved into a house on Main Street. Meanwhile Mr. Adler negotiated with the Jewish community to lease the vacant apartment in the schoolhouse for seventeen *Gulden*. The Jewish community rented the teacher's vacant apartment for twenty-five *Gulden* to the shoemaker, Schneider. In 1858, the Birstein Jewish community moved to more spacious quarters in the house of Jacob Levi in the Schlossstrasse. In 1872, the school was returned to its earlier housing (on) am Riedbach.

On January 1, 1870, Salomon Adler voluntarily retired from his teaching position. He had taught for thirty-eight years in Meerholz and in Birstein. The Jewish children then had to attend the Christian public school in their respective villages until the teaching position could be filled. In May of 1871, twenty-five-year old Israel Schuster from Salmünster assumed the vacant post of teacher and cantor in Birstein. His annual salary was three hundred *Gulden* plus free living quarters and heating, which were evaluated at sixty-one *Gulden* and forty *Kreuzer*.

As school inspector, Parson Calaminus reported in 1873 that Mr. Schuster taught twenty-seven students divided into three groups in one room. Non-resident Jewish children attended their village public schools until their tenth year and then they transferred to the Jewish school in Birstein. The boys had to be present at two hours of gymnastics instruction per week in the Protestant public school, while the girls had to attend six hours of knitting and sewing at the same school. Mr. Calaminus praised the good condition of the schoolroom and the teaching aids as well as the "new spirit" prevailing in the school. Pastor Kausel even commented in his visitation report in 1877 that "achievements particularly in German, penmanship, and arithmetic had truly been exemplary." In the beginning of 1879, the Birstein Jewish community granted tenure to its teacher and cantor, providing an annual salary of seven hundred fifty *Mark* and an extra payment of two hundred *Mark* for his residence and heat.

Like his predecessor, Israel Schuster was a religious instructor in other villages. He gave lessons in Fischborn and Hellstein, where the poor Jewish congregations could not afford their own teacher. Also like his predecessor, Mr. Schuster was very efficient in business. His wife provided considerable supplementary income through sewing. In addition to owning his residence, Mr. Schuster was a partner in a profitable coal and wood business and in the liquor store of his brother-in-law Hess. However, the firm of Hess and Schuster was recorded in the trade registry under the names of Mr. Schuster's brother-in-law and sister. Upon an official inquiry as to whether Mr. Schuster's business enterprises would be detrimental to the school, Parson Kausel certified that the school would not suffer.

During Mr. Schuster's time of employment, the construction of the new community house took place next to the synagogue at the corner of Wächtersbacherstrasse and Reichenbacherstrasse. In 1904, Mr. Schuster's pupils were able to move into the upper quarters of the school building and thereafter worked under more favorable conditions. In that same year, while in the Fulda railroad station, Mr. Schuster suffered a severe accident that left him seriously handicapped in his walking. Nathan Adler from Kühlstein became the substitute teacher until Mr. Schuster was able to assume his duties on a reduced schedule. However, Mr. Schuster had to resign on January 1, 1907.

For a short time, the Christian teachers, Stein and Dauth, substituted at the Birstein Jewish school until Mr. Samuel Levi from Breitenbach in the Ziegenhaim district, was appointed to fill the vacant teaching post. One year later, Parson Hufnagel reported that "the high achievements of the formerly good school had gone down during the last year." Obviously Mr. Levi found it difficult to obtain the same esteemed position that his two ambitious predecessors had held in the community. Although Mr. Levi never attained the financial independence of the former teachers, he did earn some additional income by performing ritual slaughtering. In this capacity, Mr. Levi experienced difficulties with the law, because shortly after World War I ritual slaughtering at a residence could be performed only with a special permit and meat could be delivered to a customer only for the required stamps.

Samuel Levi remained faithful to his duty and to the Birstein Jewish school until the end. In spite of everything, there were still twenty-two students enrolled in the school in 1935. Mr. Levi taught thirty hours to the upper level, twenty-four hours to the middle level, and eighteen hours to the lower level. In the early part of 1937, the enrollment was seventeen pupils: three children from Birstein, two from Fischborn, five from Hellstein, two from Schlierbach, four from Wächtersbach, and one from Romsthal. In the meantime, because many Jewish families were leaving Germany, the school admitted Jewish children from more distant vicinities. In April 1937, the district education authority, Dr. Thaler, disbanded the Birstein Jewish school, assigned the Jewish children to the public schools in Birstein and Wächtersbach, and dismissed Mr. Levi. When he was sixty-two years old, Samuel Levi and his wife were deported and died in an extermination center.[4]

THE END OF THE JEWISH SCHOOL IN BIRSTEIN

TWO MONTHS LATER, THE EDUCATIONAL AUTHORITIES in Berlin reprimanded the termination of the Jewish school in Birstein "inasmuch as it had been the goal whenever possible to isolate Jewish children from children of German blood. Therefore, the reopening of the Birstein Jewish school should be brought about." On August 1, 1937, Dr. Thaler reported that Birstein no longer had Jewish children of public school age: the Jewish school's responsible body had been the Jewish community, which had been disbanded. After 1933, a number of Jews from Birstein settled in Hod Hascharon, Israel, where they founded their own synagogue.[5] The last Birstein Jewish community elder, Markus Neumark, moved to Frankfurt am Main on June 29, 1937. According to Dr. Thaler, the school's possessions, consisting of the building, six benches, a blackboard, a closet, a table and chair, an adding machine, and maps, should be sold. He also stated that the school register and chronicles had been left at the mayor's office.

Endnotes

1. Letter of December 12, 1987 from Dr. Ursula Miriam Wippich to Mathilda W. Stein.

2. Letter from Jürgen Ackermann, Wächtersbach of January 31, 1987.

3. Paul Arnsberg, *Die jüdischen Gemeinden in Hessen*, Societäts-Verlag, 1971, Vol. 1, p. 81.

4. Jürgen Ackerman, *Birstein Heimatbote*, #2, December 1983.

5. Jürgen Ackerman, *Birstein Heimatbote*, #1, December 1984.

Chapter Four
The Herz Levi (9) and Kaufmann Wertheim (9) Families
Cultural History of Rural Jews in Hesse
The Jewish Community in Lichenroth
The Marriage of Karoline Rosenberg and Herz Levi (9)
The Karoline and Herz Levi (9) Family in Angenrod
The Levi Home at #69

The Wertheim home in Angenrod

Birth Certificates of Herz Levi (I) and Kaufmann Wertheim (I)

THE HERZ LEVI (I)
AND KAUFMANN
WERTHEIM (I)
FAMILIES

*M*Y PATERNAL GREAT-GRANDFATHERS Kaufmann Wertheim (I) and Herz Levi (I) were born in Angenrod one month apart on or near the Judengasse ('Jew Street') in 1819 and in August of that year the "Hep! Hep!" riots against Jews broke out in German lands and spread to several neighboring countries. Both my paternal great-grandmothers, Karoline Rosenberg of Lichenroth and Sara Tannenbaum of Eiterfeld,[a] were born in the Electorate of Hesse in 1821. My paternal great-grandfathers, Kaufmann Wertheim (I) and Herz Levi (I), celebrated their *bar mitzvoth* (a ritual in which a thirteen-year-old boy agrees to observe the precepts of Judaism) in the synagogue dedicated in 1797 and located only a few steps from their respective residences.

Meyer Bamberger was the primary educator of Jewish children in Angenrod.[b] Mr. Bamberger taught the Hebrew language and *Talmud*, as well as arithmetic, German reading and writing, geography, and German history. His spirited penmanship is preserved in the marriage certificate of Matchen Flörsheim of the neighboring village of Kirtorf and Moses Wertheim (II) of Angenrod dated December 14, 1864, and the death certificate of Löb Levi (I) in 1842. On the death certificate of Löb Levi (I), Meyer Bamberger's handwriting was executed in well-shaped Latin characters rather than Gothic writing, while on the marriage certificate Mr. Bamberger wrote the proper names in Latin script and executed the body of the document in exquisite Gothic script. At that time, only educated Germans were taught and used Latin script, although I do not know where Mr. Bamberger had received his training. It is unlikely that the Angenrod synagogue elders would have chosen anyone who was not trained in, and conformed rigidly to, orthodox Judaism. The marriage certificate also indicated that Mr. Bamberger was invested with the power to perform marriages by the rabbinate of the Grand Duchy of Hesse in Giessen. The Angenrod Jewish teacher was reputed to have been a raconteur of witty tales. He married Fradchen Speier in 1830. Meyer Bamberger was the teacher of both Kaufmann Wertheim (I) and Herz Levi (I) and prepared them for their *bar mitzvot* in 1832.

CULTURAL
HISTORY OF
RURAL JEWS
IN HESSE

VERY FEW MARRIAGES AMONG THE RURAL Hesse Jews were the result of tender passion; usually a partner in marriage would be selected by one's parents. Early in a child's life, parents would look for a suitable mate for their son or daughter. Aunts and uncles from other towns helped to identify marriage prospects for their niece or nephew. If necessary, parents would also seek help from a reliable friend whose work regularly took him into a wider range of Jewish communities. Family background was a vital concern in choosing a partner for life.

---

[a] Eiterfeld is twenty-five miles east of Angenrod and approximately nineteen miles north of Fulda. Abbott Rabanus Maurus (822-842) of Fulda mentioned Jewish contemporaries. In 1235, the first blood libel in German lands occurred in Fulda, which resulted in the deaths of thirty-two Jewish men and women. Many feudal lords of the old northern Fuldaic domain facilitated settlement of Jews. The first Jews mentioned in Eiterfeld in 1701 were Hirz Möller and Jakob Katz. (Paul Arnsberg, *Die jüdischen Gemeinden in Hessen* [Frankfurter Societäts-Druckerei, GmBh], Vol. 1, p. 153.
[b] Subsequently there were several Jewish educators by the name of Bamberger.

In Angenrod, genealogy ('*yihus*' in Hebrew) was second in importance to a good name, manners, general conduct of the family members, and the relationships of family members within the community. Relatives living in other towns would also undergo close study and observation. Genetic diseases would often be a decisive factor in selecting a mate, so the newlyweds would not suffer the pain of a mentally or physically disabled child. In Hesse, that consideration weighed heavily, because for several generations Jews had intermarried, thus risking genetic defects. Another prerequisite for marriage was a similar orientation and devotion to Judaism, because too many differences might breed friction. A decisive element in determining a mate's suitability was the degree of emancipation of his or her family. More advanced stages of assimilation would definitely disqualify a prospective marriage candidate in Angenrod.

Parents of girls considered the prospective groom's competency to earn a living; they wanted to protect their hard-earned cash and other dowry possessions from being wasted by a squanderer. Conversely, the parents of a son judged the ability and willingness of a suitable marriage partner to perform and supervise household chores. Until the expulsion of Jews from Hesse began in 1933, it was common practice in that area for parents to furnish their daughter with a dowry. In olden days, the father had given a dowry ('*nedunyah*' in Hebrew) to the bride because a daughter was excluded from paternal inheritance. Often a wealthy man in a community would provide a poor or an orphan girl with a dowry. To do so was considered one of the highest *mitzvoth* (good deeds) a Jew could perform.

In the event of a father's death, the brothers of a girl usually provided the dowry for their sister. In many cases, brothers would postpone their own marriage date until their sisters were wedded. The rabbinic synods in Speyer, Worms, and Mainz ruled that if a woman died without children within the first year of her marriage, then her entire dowry should be returned to her father or his heirs, or if a woman died without children within two years of her marriage, then one-half of her dowry should revert to her father or his heirs.[1] The practice of dowry among the Jews of Hesse in the nineteenth and twentieth centuries was beset with flaws. Often Jewish girls felt like merchandise being sold to the highest bidder. Moreover, they did not wish to impose on their parents the task and duty of raising large amounts of money for a dowry.

Among rural Jews in Hesse, the eldest son inherited the family home and the father's business. Younger sons had the option of marrying into a family with only one daughter and no other children, therefore eventually inheriting the father-in-law's home and business. Moreover, parents in the Angenrod area did not permit their children to work on the Sabbath, which automatically excluded Jews from becoming apprenticed to a non-Jew. Therefore, it was rare for observant Jews to achieve the status of a master craftsman.

Most young Jewish men rarely married before the age of thirty. Intermarriage was rare and, when it did occur, traumatic for the entire family and community. In

1879, very few marriages between Jews and non-Jews took place in Hesse-Darmstadt. However, between 1885 and 1900, five percent of Jewish marriages were a union between Jews and others.[2]

THE JEWISH
COMMUNITY IN
LICHENROTH

LICHENROTH,[c] THE BIRTHPLACE of my paternal great-grandmother Karoline Rosenberg, is situated approximately forty miles south of Angenrod and six miles from Birstein. Fourteen miles southeast of Lichenroth is the infamous Steinau. During the bubonic plague of 1348 and 1349, so many Jews were murdered in Steinau that the few survivors swore that no Jew would ever return. At the time of the Holocaust, Steinau had no Jews to liquidate.[3]

Around 1699, according to the archival records of Birstein, Meier Lazarus was the first Jew mentioned in connection with Lichenroth. In 1835, there were fifty Jews in Lichenroth and in 1861 there were one hundred six. The cemetery for Jews in the area was in Birstein. Two Jews of Lichenroth who were killed in action in World War I were Isaak Levi and Max Rosenberg.[4] In all probability, both these men were related to my ancestors in Lichenroth and Birstein. In 1834, when Karoline Rosenberg, my paternal great-grandmother, was thirteen years of age, the Jews in her native village established a new synagogue that from the outside did not resemble a house of worship.[5] Many synagogues in rural areas and small towns in Hesse looked like a residence built in the half-timbered style. In this way, the synagogue could not be recognized as easily and be vandalized. Moreover, half-timbered structures were less costly.

In 1839, a Rosenberg was *parnas*, an elected head of the Jewish community of Lichenroth. From 1829 until 1933, when Hitler came to power, the following members of the Lichenroth Rosenberg family were members of the local municipal council: Aaron Rosenberg in 1829; Mordachai Isak Rosenberg in 1830; Benjamin Rosenberg in 1855; Joseph Rosenberg in 1872; J. Rosenberg in 1887; Isak Rosenberg (II) in 1899; a Rosenberg retired from his office and his son Felix took the position in 1924; and Salli Rosenberg in 1931 and 1933.[6] The law of 1816 in the Electorate of Hesse enabling Jews to become citizens undoubtedly facilitated the service of the Rosenberg families in the Lichenroth municipal council. Moreover, the Rosenberg families must have been held in high esteem by their fellow villagers in order to serve on the municipal council from 1829 to 1933.

THE MARRIAGE OF
KAROLINE
ROSENBERG AND
HERZ LEVI (I)

NEARLY TWO YEARS AFTER THE DEMISE of his father, Löb Levi (I), on September 28, 1842, my paternal great-grandfather Herz Levi (I) married at the age of twenty-five. His wife was the twenty-one-year-old Karoline Rosenberg (my paternal great-grandmother), who was born in 1821 in Lichenroth, forty miles south of Angenrod. I do not know the maiden name of Karoline's mother, because I was unable to obtain Karoline's birth certificate. At that time, statistics on women were recorded only in connection with deaths. Karoline was the daughter of

---

[c] Lichenroth is sometimes spelled 'Lichenrod' on maps.

Chapter Four

Im Jahr Eintausend achthundert *Vierzig und Eins* den

neunzehnten August sind vor mir,

dem Bürgermeister der Gemeinde *Nagmeet Kreises Alsfeld*

erschienen die Ehegatten: *Herz Löwenstein*

alt *dreißig fünf Jahre* und dessen Ehefrau *Michel*

alt *zwanzig vier Jahre* Tochter von *Seligmann Rosenberg*

und Löwenstein in Buchstein

sodann die beiden Zeugen: *Israel Löwenstein und Michel Rosenschild*

schild

und haben erklärt, daß sie Erstere, auf vorher von

Großherzoglichem *Kreis* rath zu *Alsfeld* ausgewirkten

Heirathsschein am *fünfzehnten August v. J.* laut

Bescheinigung der Rabbinen, welche sie hiermit vorzeigen, zu *Eisenbach*

kopulirt worden seien, worüber ich gegenwärtigen Act geführt habe, und welcher nach geschehener

Vorlesung mit den Erschienenen von mir unterschrieben worden ist.

Herz Löwi

M. Michel R. Rosenberg | Ehegatten.

Israel Löwi |
M. Rosschild | Zeugen.

Zur Beglaubigung

der Bürgermeister.

lauft Bernhard

Daß dieses Register alle und jede im Laufe des Jahres
eintausend achthundert vierzig und vier zu meiner Kenntniß
gekommen, bei den Israeliten in der Gemeinde Nagmeet
v. d. angestochenen Trauungen. Solle vollzieht, welche
sich im Ganzen auf eins belaufen, ein solches wird
beurkundet. N. Nagmeet 11. ter Januar 1845

Der Landgemeindes

Bernhard

Seligmann[d] Rosenberg (I) from Lichenroth, Electorate of Hesse. On Karoline's marriage certificate of August 15, 1844, Seligmann Rosenberg (I) was not designated as *Schutzjude* and therefore may well have been a citizen of the Electorate of Hesse.

On August 15, 1844, the civil marriage of Karoline Rosenberg and Herz Levi (I) was recorded in Eisenbach, the seat of the ancestral castle of the local feudal lords, the Barons of Riedesel, sovereigns of Eisenbach and Lauterbach. The choice of Eisenbach for their wedding was probably based on practicality. The groom would have traveled fourteen miles by horse-and-buggy to Eisenbach in order to meet his bride, who most likely had to rely on the same mode of transportation over an even longer distance. In 1844, railroads did not exist in the Vogelsberg region.[e]

My paternal great-grandparents, Karoline and Herz Levi (I), must have been guided by the Constitution of 1820 of the Hessian Dukedom, which in Title III mentions the general rights and duties of Hessians.[7] Despite curtailment of Riedesel sovereignty from 1806 on, Jews were not allowed to live in Lauterbach until the early 1860s. The late admission of Jews to Lauterbach was largely attributable to anti-semitism of the Riedesel families. No Jew ever lived in Eisenbach.

Herz and Karoline Levi (I) had a marriage license certified by the rabbi and signed by the Angenrod mayor, Bernhard, which stated that the Levi's wedding was the only Jewish marriage in the year 1844. In 1823, the Angenrod municipality had established special books for the recording of Jewish weddings and deaths, requiring payment for each entry from the respective Jewish family.[8] Israel Lorsch and Moses Rothschild, who signed the marriage certificate of Karoline and Herz Levi (I) as witnesses, were probably members of the Angenrod Jewish community (these names still appeared in the Angenrod Jewish community in the 1920s).

The signatures of Karoline and Herz (I) were in Gothic script, which usually indicated that the person's education terminated after the eight years of public school or its equivalent. By the time the Jewish primary school in Lichenroth was founded in 1869,[9] Karoline had left her native village. On her marriage certificate, Karoline signed her first name as 'Giedel,' although later her name always appeared as 'Karoline.' She probably changed her name, not to deny her Judaism, but so she would not be instantly identified as a Jewess.

THE FAMILY OF KAROLINE AND HERZ LEVI (I)

KAROLINE AND HERZ LEVI (I) had eight children: Löb (II) (born and died in 1845); Isaac (born 1847); Josef (born 1849); Hannchen (my paternal grandmother, born in 1852); Salomon (born in 1854); Fanne (born in 1857); Seligmann (born in 1860); and Jette (born in 1863).

Löb Levi (II)

LÖB (II), THE FIRST CHILD of Karoline and Herz Levi (I), was born in Angenrod in house #69 on October 17, 1845. Israel Lorsch and Moses Rothschild signed the

---

[d] Seligmann means 'blessed man.'
[e] In 1835, the first railroad in German lands went from Nuremberg to Fürth.

birth certificate as witnesses, and Elizabetha Schultz was the midwife. According to custom, the baby was named after his paternal grandfather, Löb Levi (I). To the best of my knowledge, Löb (II) died while he was very young.

ISAAC, THE LEVI'S SECOND SON, was born in Angenrod on July 1, 1847. Konrad Karnes (who, according to the name, was a non-Jewish villager) and Juda Steinberger signed as witnesses; Anna Elizabetha Solzer was certified as midwife

Isaac Levi and his wife, Klara Rosenthal Levi circa 1912

and Mayor Bernhard authenticated the document. Because Isaac was considered the senior member of the Levi family, he was always rendered the esteem and authority befitting the oldest son of a German-Jewish family of that era. A relatively short man, Isaac had a face that expressed kindness, goodness, and generosity. The mere allusion to his name among family members and others would spontaneously evoke high regard and admiration.

As a cattle dealer, Isaac was known for scrupulous conduct of his business affairs. But his greatest mark of distinction in the eyes of the community and his family was Isaac's *Torah* and *Talmud* scholarship. In approximately 1875, Iaaac married Klara Rosenthal of Bierstadt,[f] near Wiesbaden of Hesse-Nassau, about seventy miles southwest of Angenrod. When Isaac married Klara, he was the first member of the Angenrod Levi family to wed someone from that far away. Although complicated, railroad travel and connections were partially established in Germany by the time of Isaac's wedding. Even to this day, the village of Angenrod has never had a railroad stop.

My Great-Aunt Klara Levi fulfilled the criteria of an excellent wife for the Levi family of Angenrod. Klara was an educated person, observant of the tenets and customs of Judaism, a good cook and an excellent baker: her anise cookies were baked with an extra bottom layer ('*sie standen auf Füsschen*'), a sign of superior baking skills. As an orthodox Jewess, Klara wore a wig (*sheitel*) to cover her hair, which marked the distinction between a married and an unmarried woman.

Klara and Isaac Levi had one daughter, Hilda, born on September 4, 1883. She was in delicate health and was much pampered by her parents and friends in Angenrod. About 1905, Hilda married Moritz Katz from Hünfeld and they lived in Alsfeld at Untergasse ll with their son Manfred, who was born in 1908. In 1921,

---

[f] Around 1824, sixteen Jews lived in Bierstadt. Its synagogue was dedicated in 1827, and had a seating capacity for forty-eight men and twenty-five women. (Paul Arnsberg, *Die jüdischen Gemeinden in Hessen*, Vol. 1 (Frankfurter Societäts-Drukerei, GmbH, 1971): p. 74.

Hilda Katz and the thirteen-year-old Manfred were visitors at Bad Salzschlirf, where I also spent some weeks with my Great-Uncle Samuel. Although Isaac and Klara Levi had bestowed a large dowry upon their only child, their son-in-law managed to mishandle and squander it. Hilda Levi Katz died in the early 1930s of cancer.

After the advent of Hitler in 1933, which marked the legalization of persecution of Jews in Germany, many Jews of Alsfeld escaped to any country that would accept them. Moritz Katz and his son, Fred, sought refuge in Palestine. After the founding of the State of Israel in 1948, Manfred Katz became an Israeli policeman. On a visit to Jerusalem in 1966, we were gently and

Hilda Levi Katz and her husband,
Moritz Katz, circa 1905

sadly informed by the police department that Fred Katz, my cousin once removed, had died a short time before at the age of fifty-eight. His wife visited with us in Tel Aviv and proudly spoke of a grandchild.

Isaac Levi's cause of death at the age of eighty on April 23, 1927, was cancer of the throat or larynx. Like his grandfather, Löb Levi (I), and his father, Herz Levi, Isaac died in house #69 and was buried in the Angenrod Jewish cemetery. Klara Rosenthal Levi remained in her home in Angenrod until 1937, four years after the advent of Hitler in 1933. She then moved to a Jewish home for old people in Mainz, where she died in her eighties of natural causes.

Josef Levi
(married a non-Jewess in
England)

JOSEF, THE THIRD CHILD of Karoline and Herz Levi, was born in house #69 in Angenrod on October 25, 1849. The birth certificate was signed by Liebmann Wertheim, a relative of the Wertheim branch of our family, and Peter Dotzert, a non-Jewish villager. Mayor Bernhard authenticated Josef's birth record and midwife Anna Elisabetha Solzer signed the document.

When Josef and his siblings were growing up in Angenrod, the greater part of children's schooling and skills stemmed primarily from instruction by their communal teacher as well as from guidance and incidental learning from their parents. None of the children of Karoline and Herz Levi attended the high school in Alsfeld, which charged an expensive monthly tuition. Generally, children would begin attending high school at the age of ten—but how could a youngster of that age walk the three miles of muddy roads between Angenrod and Alsfeld twice a day? Although boarding in Alsfeld might have been a solution, it would have entailed

Josef Levi and his wife

additional expenses; it would also have involved finding a caring household with a similar religious outlook and observance where the needs of a young child could be met.

In the early nineteenth century, social mobility for Jews in Upper Hesse was severely limited, although it had been considerably more restrictive two generations earlier. In the 1890s, many Jews from Hesse had looked for better opportunities in the United States or other countries. It must have been difficult for Josef to leave the only world he had ever known and to grapple with uncertainty abroad. Nevertheless, he immigrated to England around 1868, where he married a non-Jewish woman. The mere mention of Uncle Josef's name, even as late as my father's generation, was considered tantamount to ungodliness in the family.

In 1986, I spent three weeks in Switzerland with my father's cousin, Hedwig Rosenthal Klaus. Hedwig, and most members of her family, had sought refuge in England after Hitler attained power in Germany. When I inquired about Uncle Josef and his family, Hedwig replied, "We never associated with him or members of his family because he married out." The ban imposed on Josef and his family because he had married a non-Jew remained in force by some members of the Levi family for a hundred years.

Josef's parents suffered severe pain at the time of his marriage to a non-Jew, but the perception of disgrace in Angenrod must have been even greater. Most likely Karoline and Herz lamented their son as being dead, rending their garments and reciting the mourner's *Kaddish*, a prayer of praise to God recited by mourners in synagogue. The world of Angenrod was a world of confined choices. It did not permit intermarriage or allow an empathetic reaction on the part of wronged parents. Josef had violated the well-defined forbiddance of the *Torah*: "You shall not intermarry with them: do not give your daughters to their sons or take their daughters for your sons. For they will turn your children away from Me to worship other gods" (*Deuteronomy 7:3-4*).

Josef demonstrated that the desires and passions of the heart, and perhaps of the body, were more important criteria to action than the rules and customs of his family. Certainly Josef must have known what the harsh consequences of his marriage would be. Nevertheless, he was not deterred by the prospect of being shut out by the family. Consciously or unconsciously, he may have wanted to distance himself from the Levi clan and from the narrow confines of its world. After his marriage to a non-Jew in England, Josef returned only once to his native village. Reports in the family claimed that Herz Levi violently rejected his third son.

The name of Josef's wife is not known. Her handwriting on the back of a photograph taken around 1910 of their daughter, Ludmila (Lula) Levi, shows that

Josef's wife must have been educated. But she was unmindful of the fact that my father's oldest brother, Carl, did not observe the Christmas holiday, because she wrote on the back of the photograph, "Mrs. Levi and Lula wish you a happy Xmas." Two photographs of Lula Levi were found among the belongings of Uncle Carl Wertheim, who as a young man went to live in England until the outbreak of World War I in Europe. Uncle Carl confessed to my mother that during his stay in England he had entertained a romantic interest in his cousin Lula, who is seen in the photographs as an attractive young woman. Thus, it would appear that not all of the descendants of Karoline and Herz Levi heeded the ban on Josef's family.

MY MUCH-BELOVED PATERNAL GRANDMOTHER, Hannchen Levi, the fourth child of Karoline and Herz Levi, was born on June 4, 1852. Gutkind Rotschild and Johannes Bernhard IV were witnesses and the midwife was Anna Elisabetha Solzer. Hannah means 'graciousness' in Hebrew, and the suffix '*chen*' in German indicates diminutive size. Both qualities were trademarks of my grandmother. Probably Hannchen was named after her paternal grandmother, Hennel (née Spier and widowed Schaumberger), who married Löb Levi (I).

Hannchen Levi Wertheim
circa 1930

My grandmother, Hannchen, expressed herself clearly in grammatically correct German. Her written German reflected the organized thoughts of an educated person and she was equally competent in Latin or Gothic script. My grandmother possessed many sterling traits and a deep insight into the human condition. She dealt leniently and compassionately with the shortcomings of others and generously overlooked peccable dealings. Expert in the social graces, she possessed an unmistakable sense of style and an appreciation for propriety. Certainly my grandmother managed her life as if her birth obligated her to responsible, honorable behavior coupled with generosity of thought and deed.

On May 20, 1878, Hannchen Levi married Herz Wertheim of Angenrod. At the time of their marriage, Hannchen and Herz were twenty-six and twenty-seven years old, respectively. They had grown up as neighbors and the Levi and Wertheim households shared a well with a hand pump which provided water for the two families, their horses, and their livestock. Herz Levi (I), the bride's father, and Isaac Levi, her older brother, were witnesses to the civil marriage. Herz Wertheim's father, Kaufmann Wertheim (I), had died by the time of Herz' betrothal to Hannchen.

SALOMON, THE FIFTH CHILD of Karoline and Herz Levi, was born on December 7, 1854, in Angenrod in house #69. Johannes Stiebig, a non-Jewish villager, and

Im Jahr Eintausend achthundert *[handwritten]* am *[handwritten]*

um *[handwritten]* Uhr des Morgens ist vor mir, dem Bürgermeister der Gemeinde *[handwritten]*

[handwritten] Regierungsbezirks Kassel, *[handwritten]*

[handwritten] erschienen, welcher mir erklärt hat, daß am *[handwritten]*

[handwritten] um *[handwritten]* Uhr des Morgens *[handwritten]*

[handwritten]

ein *[handwritten]* Kind *[handwritten]* Geschlechts geboren habe, welchem der Vornamen

[handwritten] gegeben worden; welches Kind in dem Hause Nro. 69 geboren worden

[handwritten] sei.

Diese Erklärung ist in Gegenwart der beiden Zeugen: *[handwritten]*

[handwritten] und der Hebamme *[handwritten]* geschehen,

und haben *[handwritten]* und die Zeugen mit mir gegenwärtigen Geburtsact,

nachdem ihnen derselbe vorgelesen worden ist, unterschrieben.

[signature: Herz Levin]

[signature: Guttind Rothschild]

Zeugen.

[signature: Johannes Leonhard 44]

Hebamme.

[signature: Anna Elisabetha Weber]

Zur Beglaubigung

der Bürgermeister.

[signature: Bernhard]

The birth certificate of Hannchen Levi

Meyer Bamberger, teacher of the Angenrod Jewish community, signed as witnesses on Salomon's birth certificate. Mayor Bernhard validated the document and Anna Elisabetha Solzer attested as midwife. Unlike the Hebrew midwives who ministered to Hebrew women in Egypt (*Exodus 1:15*) and delivered the child Moses from the tribe of Levi, a non-Jewish midwife assisted at the births of the Levi and Wertheim families and probably at the births of the other Jewish children in Angenrod.

Salomon Levi, like his older brother, Josef, immigrated to England as a young man. Salomon never married. In England, he was successfully engaged in the manufacture of tweeds and other woolens. He returned yearly to his native village to spend time with his sister, Hannchen, and to visit with his older brother, Isaac, and his younger brother, Seligmann. He was about five feet nine inches tall, with a slight build and delicate features.

Generally, Uncle Salomon did not go to the residences of his many nieces and nephews in Germany because an unwritten rule prescribed that every family member, and especially the younger children, call on him when he visited Angenrod. Rain or shine, punctually at five o'clock p.m., Uncle Salomon took his daily one-hour walk before dinner. Usually he would ask one of the visiting children to accompany him, during which he would engage his walking partner in a topic of conversation relating to the family. All their lives, Hannchen and her brother, Salomon, were exceedingly devoted to each other, probably because Hannchen was Salomon's senior by only two-and-a-half years. On his visit to Angenrod when I was about thirteen years old, Uncle Salomon told me about his heartfelt concern for the well-being and happiness of his sister, Hannchen. Uncle Salomon was exceedingly open-handed and kind-hearted toward his sister, Hannchen. He would often present his favorite sister with gifts of tasteful wool and silk intended to be made into blouses, skirts, and dresses.

Salomon Levi, son of Karoline Rosenberg and Herz Levi (I)

My grandmother, Hannchen, had very definite notions about how much clothing she actually needed. Therefore, I sometimes reaped the benefits of Great-Uncle Salomon's generosity when my grandmother presented me with material for skirts. Great-Uncle Salomon also bestowed gifts of money on his sister. Before I left Germany in 1934, my grandmother gave me an English twenty-pound gold piece as a farewell present. However, the currency regulations of Nazi Germany prohibited me from taking along this last remembrance of my dearly beloved grandmother.

Salomon stayed in close contact with his family until his death at age eighty-one in England in 1935. A few months after Salomon's death, Hannchen was the recipient of her brother's worn clothing. My father's oldest brother, Carl Wertheim, who was living in New York City, inherited Uncle Salomon's golden watch. Uncle Carl had lived in England as a young man until the outbreak of World War I. According to Uncle Carl, a warm-hearted relationship existed between Uncle Salomon and his nephew. Due to the perilous circumstances for Jews in Germany at the time of Salomon's death, my grandmother's branch of the Levi family was unable to properly look after its share of the inheritance from Uncle Salomon's estate.

84]

Fanne Levi

FANNE, THE SIXTH CHILD and second daughter of Karoline and Herz Levi, was born in house #69 in Angenrod on May 8, 1857. Anna Elisabetha Solzer was the midwife, Peter Dotzert and Zadok Lorsch attended as witnesses, and Mayor Bernhard authenticated the document. Fanne Levi died at an early age.

Seligmann Levi
(married Sara Plaut)

SELIGMANN LEVI, THE SEVENTH CHILD of Karoline and Herz Levi, was born on June 23, 1860. Seligmann's parents named him after his maternal grandfather, Seligmann Rosenberg from Lichenroth. Meyer Oppenheimer and Mendel Schaumberger signed his birth certificate as witnesses and Anna Elisabetha Solzer delivered him. At the time of his birth, Seligmann's mother and father were thirty-nine and forty-one years old, respectively. He, too, was born in house #69 in Angenrod.

My Great-Uncle Seligmann was five feet six inches tall and had a stocky build. He always lived in the shadow of his brother Isaac, who was thirteen years older and who was loved and favored by everyone. Seligmann married Sara Plaut (born May 22, 1866) in Frankenau around 1889, a town forty-five miles northwest of Angenrod.

The surname 'Plaut' appeared frequently among the Jews in Hesse. It may have been derived from the Hebrew '*palit*,' which means 'refugee,' or it may have originated from the Portuguese '*plato*.' Many of the Jews in Hesse came

Sara Plaut Levi,
wife of Seligmann Levi

from Spain, Portugal, France, and Italy, and were probably of Sephardic origin.[10]

Frankenau belonged to the administrative district of Kassel in the Electorate of Hesse. In Frankenau there were seven Jews in 1785, six *Schutzjuden* in Frankenau in 1824, and forty Jews in 1861. During the nineteenth century, the name 'Plaut' frequently could be found there among Jewish community elders. In 1874, when Sara was eight years old, the elementary Israelite school in Frankenau received public recognition and had twenty-four Jewish pupils. Most Jews in Frankenau earned their living as cattle dealers, dry-goods retailers, or grocers.[11]

Seligmann Levi and Sara Plaut had four children: Hermann (born November 2, 1890), Hugo (born January 30, 1893), Gisela (born December 22, 1893), and Irma (born April 3, 1899). I never knew Sara Plaut Levi. She died of complications of either pregnancy or childbirth on August 27, 1907 at the age of forty-one and was buried in the Angenrod Jewish cemetery. At the time of his wife's death,

Seligmann was forty-seven years old; he never remarried. By the early 1930s, Seligmann Levi had suffered a stroke that paralyzed one side of his body and affected his speech. Until his death at the age of seventy-five, Seligmann was cared for by a loyal non-Jewish domestic from one of the villages near Angenrod. Providentially, he died on June 16, 1935, three months before the September 15, 1935 Nuremberg Laws forbade Jews to employ females of German blood who were younger than forty-five. Seligmann Levi was buried in the Angenrod Jewish cemetery.

Hermann Levi in World War I
(Photograph by F. Kuno Borst,
Giessen)

Hermann, Seligmann and Sara's son, was a short stocky, but attractive man, who served his country in World War I. As the oldest son he inherited his father's half of the homestead as well as his share of the meadows and fields which had been owned conjointly by Isaac and Seligmann Levi. In contrast to American homesteads, meadows and fields were usually located outside of the villages in Hesse. During the early 1920s, Hermann married Marta Gross from Lasphe. Marta was a tall woman from a large family where she had acquired singular survival skills. Born with a twin brother, Marta was so weak in early infancy that her death appeared imminent. At that time, Marta's maternal grandmother tried to console her daughter by stating, "Even if you lose this daughter, you will have a son left." In fact, Marta Gross Levi outlived every family member of her generation, as well as both her children.

Erich and Sylvia, the children of Hermann and Marta Levi, were born in Angenrod in 1925 and 1926, respectively, where they attended public school. By then, the once flourishing Angenrod Jewish community was much smaller because Jews had fewer children. In addition, after approximately 1910, some young Jews went abroad or settled in larger towns in Germany. By the 1920s, Angenrod no longer had its own Jewish teacher and was forced to rely on the services of an itinerant Hebrew instructor.

Despite the fact that he clearly lacked the means, Hermann Levi attempted to emulate the lifestyle of a country squire. Eventually he was forced to sell his inherited meadows and fields. After those funds were spent, he relied on monetary assistance from his siblings and on my parents to help support his family and to subsidize their transportation to the United States. By the time the Hermann Levi family departed for the United States in 1936, there was nothing left of Seligmann Levi's inheritance from house #69 in Angenrod and from his share of the meadows and fields.

Chapter Four

Seligmann Levi (seated right)
Hermann Levi, his son,
(seated left)
Marta Levi, Hermann's wife,
(standing back)
and Erich Levi, their son

The effects of the Depression of 1929 were still significant in New York in 1936 and did not mitigate until after World War II. But Hermann Levi's sisters, Gisela and, and their husbands, who had emigrated to the United States in the early 1920s, provided as well as they could for shelter and sustenance of the Hermann Levi family. Moreover, at that time, political refugees seeking asylum in the United States were permitted to enter the country only if sponsors guaranteed the government that the refugees would not become a public charge.

In Angenrod, Hermann Levi had hired help for tasks involving toilsome labor, but in New York he butchered meat. His job involved standing in high rubber boots in water for extended periods of time and also enduring prolonged periods of work in refrigerators. Hermann had problems in adjusting emotionally, mentally, and physically to such tasks; he became ill and had to give up his job. Meanwhile, Marta rented a large apartment in Washington Heights, New York, where many refugees from Germany settled in the 1930s. She sublet rooms and frequently provided board to other newly-arrived refugees who, in some cases, were also relatives.

Additionally, Marta contributed to the support of her family by selling kosher sausages on Sunday to other German refugees in Washington Heights. However, she never made any attempt to repay my parents for the borrowed funds. After a prolonged illness of several years, Hermann Levi died in 1942 at the age of fifty-two. Marta remained a widow for at least ten years before marrying the widowed Mr. Isenberg, also a German-Jewish refugee. He died only a few years after their marriage. In 1991, Marta, well into her nineties, lived in a nursing home in Riverdale, New York, oblivious to people's identity and her surroundings.

Erich and Sylvia attended public school in Washington Heights. While still young, both children worked at sundry jobs in order to help support the family. They were eighteen and seventeen years old, respectively, when their father died. Although doubtless capable of completing a college education, Erich and Sylvia had to find jobs after finishing high school. Erich changed his last name from Levi to Gross (his mother's maiden name) and during the mid-1960s worked as a photographer. Against the wishes of his mother, he married a divorcée with a young son, and later Erich and his wife had one son. However, the marriage ended in divorce and left Erich estranged from his immediate family. He underwent open heart surgery and a few years later died of cancer when he was in his early fifties.

Sylvia remained in her mother's home and worked in a diamond factory where she met her future husband, Felix Berger, a concentration camp survivor. Felix became a highly respected cantor and religious schoolteacher in Plainview, Long Island, where they lived with their three sons in strict observance of the ordinances of Jewish orthodoxy. When Felix died from cancer, Sylvia was approximately forty-five years old and was left with three sons under fifteen years of age. In 1972, about a year after her husband's death, she visited her mother's home in Washington Heights during a Jewish holiday. Sylvia jumped off the roof of the apartment house and died instantly from the injuries she sustained. Shortly after his sister's death, Erich reflected on the possible underlying elements of her self-destruction. He believed that Sylvia felt unable to cope with life's exigencies without Felix.[12]

Hugo, Sara Plaut Levi and Seligmann Levi's second son, served in World War I as a German lance corporal in the infantry.[13] He was thirty-five when he died as a prisoner-of-war on September 24, 1918, less than two months before the Armistice on November 11, 1918. Since the marker on Hugo's grave is in English, it is to be presumed that he was taken prisoner by either Americans or the British.

Gisela, the third child and first daughter of Sara Plaut Levi and Seligmann Levi, was an attractive woman with beautiful brown eyes, light complexion, and dark hair. Her cheerful disposition and compassionate temperament made her generous, warm, and even-tempered. From the time of her mother's death in 1907,

Above: Gisela Levi Rosenbaum, 1931
Right: Hugo Rosenbaum in World War I. He served on the Russian Front.

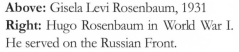

when Gisela was fourteen years old, until approximately 1920 when she married Hugo Rosenbaum (born May 28, 1891) in Hörnsheim, Gisela took over the management of the Seligmann Levi home. The household consisted of five family members and several people in steady help. As her cousin and neighbor, my father frequently spoke highly of Gisela's competence in carrying out the various duties of her father's household while still so young.

Chapter Four

Gisela's husband, Hugo Rosenbaum, was an expert tailor by trade. In the 1920s, this was an unusual occupation for Jews from rural areas and small towns in Hesse because of the many obstacles for a Jew to learn a trade in earlier days. Hugo fought for Germany in World War I and was a prisoner-of-war in Russia. Gisela and Hugo's decision to immigrate to the United States was probably motivated by financial factors.

During the galloping inflation in Germany in the early 1920s, paper money had a minimum amount of purchasing power and working men and women, who received wages in paper money, fared the worst. Payment for a custom-made suit on one day could only purchase half a loaf of bread on the next day. In 1924, when the United States was still enjoying a favorable economy, Irma Levi, immigrated to New York and she probably encouraged her sister, Gisela Levi, and other members of her family to join her.

Ernest, the oldest son of Hugo and Gisela Rosenbaum, was born on September 26, 1922 and Heinz, their second son, was born in 1924. In June 1926, Hugo, Gisela (who was seven months pregnant), Ernest, and Heinz left from Hamburg on the *S.S. Ballin*. During the crossing of the Atlantic, the two-year-old Heinz died on June 11, 1926 due to suspension of respiration attributable to poor blood supply. Heinz was buried at sea, thereby depriving his parents of being able to visit their son's grave. Although in later years, Gisela and Hugo always appeared in good spirits and never mentioned their loss, one sensed a certain resignation to unalterable destiny.

Upon their arrival in the United States, Hugo, Gisela, Ernest, and Ellen Rosenbaum (born on August 8, 1926) shared an apartment in Richmond Hill with Gisela's younger sister, Irma Levi Wertheim, and her husband, Carl Wertheim (my father's oldest brother). Irma was very fond of her niece, Ellen. She credited the child with the good judgment of being born on a Sunday because, since no one in the family had to go to work that day, Ellen lessened the task of caring for mother, newborn infant, and her four-year-old brother, Ernest.

After the ascension of Hitler to power in 1933, Gisela and Hugo Rosenbaum channeled much of their energy into sponsoring relatives from Germany so they could settle in the United States. In addition to providing financial guarantees (affidavits), Gisela and Hugo cared for and protected their immigrating relatives as best they could during a prolonged period of economic recession. As a nineteen-year-old refugee with limited command of the English language, I was transplanted into an unfamiliar world. Upon my arrival, Gisela spent the day with me in order to soften the initial distress of separation from close family and also to lessen the trauma of acclimation to new circumstances. Gisela and Hugo were always there when relatives needed them for advice or encouragement.

In approximately 1933, Irma and Carl took a three-room apartment in Flatbush, Brooklyn. The Hugo Rosenbaum family moved to Washington Heights to be near friends and distant relatives as well as to be in closer proximity to Hugo's tailor shop on West 83rd Street between Broadway and West End Avenue. There was always an exceptionally warm relationship between my parents and the Hugo Rosenbaum family, especially between my mother and Gisela, who visited often with each other. These two cousins-by-marriage had a kindred perspective on life that gave central importance to immediate family and distant relatives. When the vibrant Gisela died on June 29, 1964, in New York of a heart attack, she was the only one of her siblings who lived to the age of seventy. During the last years of his life, Hugo was ill from the complications of diabetes. He died on January 6, 1968, in Kew Gardens, New York, at the age of seventy-seven.

Ernest and Ellen Rosenbaum attended the College of the City of New York and Hunter College, respectively, where there was no charge for tuition. They were the first great-grandchildren of Karoline Rosenberg Levi and Herz Levi of Angenrod to have the privilege of attending and completing their American college education. In addition to attending Hunter College, the lovable and conscientious Ellen was also educated at the Bank Street School. Her entire teaching career was in the inner city of New York's public school system. Ellen married Murray Hausknecht, a sociologist at Hunter and Lehman Colleges of City University. Murray is the author of at least one book in his field as well as many scholarly articles. He is a contributing editor and a member of the editorial board of *Dissent* magazine.

In World War II, Ernest Rosenbaum served as a supply sergeant in the United States Air Force from December 1941 to August 1944. He was a printer by profession and on December 28, 1945, he married Suzanne Sussman (born September 9, 1922 in Great Neck, Long Island). Ernest was fifty-four when he died after a long period of illness in Northport, Long Island, perhaps due in part to his being overweight.

Laura, the oldest daughter of Ernest and Suzanne Rosenbaum (born March 20, 1947 in New York City), attended the United Nations School through high school and later graduated from Brandeis University. Like her first husband, Donald Davis, Laura became a teacher of Transcendental Meditation. During the 1960s, she divorced Donald and changed her name to Laura Rosetree. At the Maharishi University in Iowa she met David Ramsey, whom she married in a Presbyterian Church and from whom she was divorced three years later. In June 1990, Laura wedded Mitchell Weber. Laura is a free-lance writer for newspapers and has authored several books, including a cookbook, a typing manual, and a book about the form of New Age therapy that she practices.

Amy (born in New York City on May 25, 1952) is the second daughter of Ernest and Suzanne Sussman Rosenbaum. She went to the United Nations School, attended Middlebury College, and graduated from the University of Washington. She is a trained technical writer and lives with her husband, Douglas Patton, and her son, Thomas (born December 18, 1980), in Seattle, Washington.[14]

Ellen and Murray's children were both born in New York: David on April 20, 1961 and Gina on October 15, 1964. Some time during the late 1980s, David immigrated to Israel, where he lived and worked at *Kibbutz Keturah* in the Negev. As a youngster he did not celebrate a *bar mitzvah* and his parents were not affiliated with a synagogue or temple. David's enthusiasm for Israel appears self-directed and an outgrowth of Jewish youth movements.

After his marriage to Sue Brumer from South Bend, Indiana on October 8, 1991, David lived at *Kibbutz Keturah*. Named after her late maternal grandmother, Gina has eyes, hair, and coloring reminiscent of Gisela. The charming Gina is presently concluding her doctoral thesis on Milton at the University of Michigan in Ann Arbor. She will be the second great-great grandchild of Karoline Rosenberg Levi and Herz Levi from Angenrod to obtain this academic achievement from the University of Michigan. (Kenneth Ware Stein is the other descendant of the Herz Levi family.) Thus, the American descendants of Jews from Italy, Spain, and Portugal who settled in Hesse in the fifteenth and sixteenth centuries uphold the tradition of their forefathers by pursuing careers in science, diplomacy, and languages.

Irma Wertheim
(married Carl Wertheim)

IRMA, THE FOURTH CHILD of Sara Plaut Levi and Seligmann Levi of Angenrod, was born on April 3, 1899. One of my Aunt Irma's most impressive characteristics was the measured manner in which she handled people and problems. Irma was eight years old when her mother died and when her sister, Gisela, took over the management of the Seligmann Levi household. Irma had delicate features, a light complexion, dark-brown eyes, and a petite stature. In Angenrod, her bed and frilly dressing room impressed me as the latest feminine accouterments. I admired her warmly ingratiating manner and her expression of earnest attention and genuine affection.

In 1924, there was neither a role nor a prospect of income for Irma. Gisela had married Hugo Rosenbaum and moved to Hörnsheim and Hermann had married Marta Gross. The inflation had stabilized, although the economy was still depressed and many people were unemployed in Germany. Irma did not have money for her passage to the United States and no one in her immediate family could furnish the necessary funds. With a set of wineglasses as a farewell present from her Angenrod family, Irma entered into an agreement as an indentured servant in the United States. The arrangement was mediated through Mrs. Weisskopf, a distant relative who resided in Washington Heights, New York. It took Irma one year of hard work in the household of her sponsor to pay back the outlay for her transportation. After completing the work for her sponsor, Irma found employment as a filing clerk with the General Dyestuff Corporation.

At that time the General Dyestuff Corporation was controlled by German nationals who employed mainly German citizens or people of German origin. Probably Irma represented tokenism as the designated 'Jewish employee'; there were few if any other employees to demonstrate the company's lack of prejudice toward Jews. After nearly twenty-five years of service, Irma retired from the General Dyestuff Corporation and moved to Miami Beach. My aunt never rose to a position higher than filing clerk and ascribed her lack of advancement to her inability to type.

Before Irma's departure for the United States, an amorous bond bloomed between her and her cousin, Carl Wertheim (my father's oldest brother), who was eighteen years her senior. Carl was tall and slender with gently waved dark hair, brown eyes, and a capacity to captivate most women. At the time of Irma's farewell visit to my Aunt Katinka's (the third of my father's four sisters, who lived in Niederurff), Uncle Carl was also a houseguest. One evening, Irma and Carl volunteered to retrieve feathers from a pillow in a spare room. According to Aunt Kathinka, they worked at this chore into the morning hours—yet not all the feathers were in place the next morning. In 1925, one year after Irma's departure, Carl Wertheim immigrated to the United States when entry requirements were comparatively simple because of a thriving economy that needed more manpower. He and Irma were married that year.

Born January 14, 1881, Carl was named Kaufmann (II) on his birth certificate after his late grandfather, Kaufmann Wertheim (I). Carl was the only one of the seven living children of Hannchen and Herz Wertheim who was privileged to attend the high school in Alsfeld. At age fifteen, Carl did not pass the examinations for the lower school-leaving certificate and I do not know whether he took the examination a second time. Assuredly, Carl's life in high school and his grades were affected by the anti-semitism incited by Otto Böckel that was so widespread in Alsfeld at that time. Some teachers in the Alsfeld high school were readily inclined to fail a Jewish student. Perhaps it was because of

Irma Levi Wertheim, circa 1924

this situation that his parents had their other children educated under the auspices of the Jewish community in Angenrod.

After immigrating to Bradford in Yorkshire, England, Carl served an apprenticeship in the textile business. In England, Carl had a warm-hearted relationship with his uncle, Salomon Levi, my grandmother's youngest brother. Carl was also in contact with the family of his mother's brother, Josef, who was banned by most other family members because he had married a non-Jew. According to my mother, with whom Carl often spoke when he was in Lauterbach, he had an amorous relationship with his cousin, Ludmilla. Shown in photographs as a strikingly beautiful young woman, Ludmilla certainly had an excellent upbringing. In August 1914, violation of Belgian neutrality gave the British government the pretext and popular support necessary for entry into World

War I against Germany. Carl left England to be with his family and to serve Germany, his native country. I know neither the military branch and rank of my uncle nor whether he enlisted or was drafted.

Irma Levi Wertheim
and
Carl Wertheim, circa
1925

After the cessation of hostilities in 1918, Carl Wertheim did not return to England, although he was out of work in Germany for seven years until he immigrated to the United States in 1925. He continued to spend most of his time at his parents' home in Angenrod, but he also stayed for months at the homes of his other siblings. As a child, I got the impression that Uncle Carl, the textile expert, considered himself above the physical work required by cattle dealers and preferred chores which did not require that he soil his hands. Highly regarded for his advice, Carl was generally accepted as an authority because he was believed to possess a broader view of the world. In reality, his views were based on limited insight and an inability or unwillingness for discriminate reasoning. He had an unconscious desire to maintain the status quo because changes were too perplexing for him to contend with.

In New York, Uncle Carl worked as a salesman in a fabric store, the Haas Brothers, that specialized in high-priced silks. During the height of the Depression in 1933, his job was the first one in the firm to be terminated because, according to Irma, he made it known that his wife was also working. From the time Carl lost his sales job until he and Irma moved to Miami Beach, he worked for a trifling sum in the tailor shop of his brother-in-law, Hugo Rosenbaum. When Carl was first without a job, there was no unemployment insurance. He was too proud to mingle with other unemployed people, but he clearly lacked the enterprising spirit for having his own business.

As the sponsors for thirty to forty refugees, Irma and Carl Wertheim sent the necessary affidavits for Irma's brother, Hermann, and his family, several cousins of Irma related through her mother, Sara Plaut Levi, and all of Carl's siblings and their families (except his youngest brother, Salli, and wife and those members of the immediate Wertheim family who had found refuge in Switzerland). Although Irma and Carl saved the lives of many family members, their counsel to the young who had no other guidance was often short-sighted. During the mid-1930s, advice and assistance bore no resemblance to the ministration later offered to refugees in the 1980s and early 1990s. At that time, we were completely on our own and often had to rely on advice and advocacy from those who were willing to help but who were unschooled.

Irma and Carl's lifestyle in Miami Beach was uncommonly modest, as observed by their nieces and nephews who visited them. After diligently scrimping for most of her life in order to provide for her old age, Irma died of cancer in 1961 at the age of sixty-two after a long illness. Carl's death in 1965 when he was eighty-four was attributed to what was then termed the results of 'old age.' Both were buried in Miami Beach.

Jette (Hilda) Levi (married Siegmund Rosenthal)

JETTE, THE EIGHTH AND LAST CHILD of Karoline and Herz Levi, was born on February 12, 1863 in Angenrod in house #69. At the time of Jette's birth, her mother and father were forty-two and forty-four years old, respectively. Meyer Bamberger, the teacher, and Konrad Jung III, a non-Jewish villager, signed the birth certificate as witnesses; Anna Elisabetha Solzer served as midwife; the birth certificate was validated by Mayor Bernhard and signed by Herz Levi. There was a difference of eight years between Hannchen and Jette, the only two surviving daughters of Herz and Karoline Levi.

At some point in her life, Jette changed her name to Hilda, probably because her birth name was too reminiscent of the Jewish ghetto. A photograph of Hilda portrayed her as a very attractive young woman in a dress made of either heavy silk or light wool. The garment had controlled shirring below the elbow at the sleeves and lace trimming at the neckline and sleeves and the lower part of the skirt had horizontal pleating. Hilda's attire expressed a refinement of good taste and dainty elegance. The photograph was taken in Wiesbaden around 1886, near the time of Hilda's engagement to Siegmund Rosenthal of Bierstadt when she was twenty-three years old. According to the mores of the era, Hilda wore her engagement ring on the fourth finger of her right hand. Only upon marriage was the engagement ring moved to the left hand to be worn with the wedding ring.

Hilda Levi Rosenthal
circa 1886

Hilda's groom, Siegmund Rosenthal (born March 16, 1857), was a cattle dealer and was twenty-nine years old at the time of his engagement to Hilda. Siegmund was a brother of Klara Rosenthal Levi, whose husband was Isaac Levi, the oldest living brother of my paternal grandmother, Hannchen Levi Wertheim[g]

Hilda and Siegmund Rosenthal raised five children in Bierstadt and Wiesbaden: Klara, Fritz (born February 13, 1889), Hugo (born September 12, 1891), Rosel

---

[g] During Siegmund and Hilda Levi Rosenthal's life in Bierstadt, Mr. Rosenberg was a teacher of the Jewish community. He was known to be an active Zionist promoter and held office as a Zionist Commissioner as early as 1907. Mr. Rosenberg died in Auschwitz. (Paul Arnsberg, *Die jüdischen Gemeinden in Hessen*, Vol.1, p. 74.)

(born January 12, 1899), and Hedwig (born August 2, 1902). Fritz was the only one in the family who was favored to attend high school in Wiesbaden and obtain the *Einjährige*. The *Einjährige* was an educational standard, required before 1919 to serve in an army unit of one's choice. It was a prerequisite for becoming an army officer and necessitated one year of service in the army instead of three.

Siegmund Rosenthal
circa 1915

In about 1907, Fritz, like many other young Jewish men in Hesse, looked for a more promising future abroad. Since two of his mother's brothers had settled in England, he, too, chose to go there. At the outbreak of World War I, Fritz elected to return to Germany, probably because he feared being interned in England as an enemy alien. Fritz and Hugo Rosenthal served in the German army during World War I. I do not know whether Fritz attained the rank of a commissioned officer in the German army. After the war Fritz became a partner in the textile firm of Dick and Goldschmidt of Berlin and London and in the middle or late 1920s he settled in London with his Hungarian-born wife, Ilena (Lolo). There were two sons from this marriage.

In the summer of 1935, the number of '*Juden Verboten*' ('No Jews') signs increased outside of towns, villages, restaurants, and stores; in September 1935, the *Reichstag* passed the anti-semitic Nuremberg Laws. Fritz then arranged for his three sisters to go to London. While still in Germany, Klara Rosenthal married Joseph Schmidt of Limburg and they had one child, Inge. During their lifetime Fritz provided for Klara and Joseph Schmidt. (Siegmund and Hilda Rosenthal had died in Wiesbaden on May 22, 1929 and December 6, 1937, respectively.) In England, Inge married Jack Kreisler, who was also a refugee from Germany.

In 1959 or 1960, this family befriended our daughter, Judith, who was then studying at the London School of Economics. During the late 1960s, we met briefly with Inge and Jack while we were passing through London. Inge died of a heart attack in Switzerland on July 31, 1972 when her two children were still in their teens. Her son, a certified public accountant, moved to California. Inge's daughter, Susan, lives with her husband and two children in London, where she keeps in close touch with her great-aunt Hedwig Rosenthal Klaus. The widower, Jack Kreisler, moved to Germany and married a German national.

Hugo Rosenthal served in the German army in World War I and was a prisoner-of-war in France for four years. According to his sister, Hedwig Rosenthal Klaus, he always took exception to the fact that his older brother Fritz was favored with a better education, whereas he had to work as a cattle dealer in his father's business. Hugo emigrated with his wife, Selma, to the United States, where they resided in later years in Brooklyn with their daughter, Alice Kaufmann. Hugo died at the age of seventy-five on April 19, 1966. My parents saw this family from time to time in New York.

Rosel Rosenthal, the second daughter of Hilda and Siegmund Rosenthal, married Sidney Sternson and had no children. The third daughter, Hedwig, married Theo Klaus, who was born in Rülzheim, Palatinate, Germany. This marriage was also childless. Hedwig and Theo welcomed and cared for many refugees from Germany in the Klaus' London home during the late 1930s. As of 1991, Hedwig was eighty-nine years old and in relatively good health.

THE LEVI HOME AT #69 IN ANGENROD

UNTIL ISAAC LEVI'S DEATH OF CANCER of the throat in 1922, Seligmann and Isaac Levi were partners in their prospering cattle business. The Levi brothers also owned meadows in the out-lying area of Angenrod on which they grew hay to feed the cattle they bought and sold. Additionally, they possessed parcels of land for planting rye for the bread consumed in their households and they cultivated cow beets for their cattle. Their stable and barn were attached to house #69, where they both lived. A vegetable garden on the north side of the house was worked by both families, enabling them to enjoy fresh vegetables, apples, pears, and plums in season as well as to can foods and to dry fruits for wintertime. During those years, Jewish men did not usually engage in garden work. Such chores were left to women, either wives, daughters, or hired help.

The floor of the huge entrance hall of the Levi residence consisted of broad wooden planks painted a dark red. Although the floor always appeared scrupulously clean, as if no one ever stepped on it, it was actually a well-trodden surface. In the foyer, a door on the right hand side and three steps down led to the sunken living room of Klara and Isaac Levi; a door exactly opposite on the left side of the entrance hall led to the sun-flooded living room of Uncle Seligmann. Aunt Klara's rooms never received as much natural light, but the warmth of her person more than compensated for that deficiency. The tone was quite different on the left side of the double house. The kitchens were located in back of the large living rooms on both sides of the Levi residences, where there was also a second smaller sitting room. The upstairs of the house contained at least four bedrooms on each side.

Endnotes

1. *Encyclopedia Judaica*, Vol. 6 (Jerusalem: Keter Publishing House, 1978), p. 186.

2. Rüdiger Mack, *Neunhundert Jahre Geschichte der Juden in Hessen* (Wiesbaden: Kommission für die Geschichte der Juden in Hessen, 1983), p. 379.

3. Wippich, *Memorbuch, 1981/82*, p. 105.

4. Paul Arnsberg, *Die jüdischen Gemeinden in Hessen* (Frankfurter Societäts-Druckerei GmBh), Vol. 1, p. 489.

5. Ibid, p. 490.

6. Letter from Jürgen Ackermann of Wächtersbach of January 31, 1987. The information emanates from the archives in Marburg and Gelnhausen, Germany.

7. Letter from Dr. Karl August Helfenbein of January 17, 1985.

8. Wippich, *Memorbuch*, p. 100.

9. Arnsberg, *Die jüdischen Gemeinden in Hessen*, Vol. I, p. 489.

10. Ibid., p. 15.

11. Ibid, p. 189.

12. Telephone conversation with Ellen Rosenbaum Hausknecht on February 10, 1991.

13. *Die Jüdischen Gefallenen des deutschen Heeres, der deutschen Marine und der deutschen Schutztruppen, 1914-1918* (Der Schild: Reichsbund jüdischer Frontsoldaten, 1932).

14. Letter from Ellen Rosenbaum Hausknecht of March 4, 1991.

Chapter Five
The Marriage and Family of Sara Tannenbaum and Kaufmann Wertheim (9)

The Rabbi Performs a Wedding Ceremony under the Huppah (bridal canopy) by
Moritz Daniel Oppenheim

Marriage certificate of Kaufmann Wertheim (I) and Sara Tannenbaum

The Way It Was: The Jewish World of Rural Hesse

THE MARRIAGE OF
SARA TANNENBAUM
AND KAUFMANN
WERTHEIM (I)

*J*N 1847, THE ANGENROD REGISTRY recorded the marriage of my other paternal great-grandparents Kaufmann Wertheim (I) and Sara Tannenbaum of Eiterfeld, in the Electorate of Hesse. The biblical Sarah is the first of the four matriarchs. In *Genesis 11:30* Sarah is alluded to as "being barren-she had no child." Jewish parents bless their daughters with the words, "May you be like Sarah, Rebekah, Rachel, and Leah." Sara was also the name every Jewish woman was compelled to take during the later years of the Nazi era.

At the time of their marriage on February 17, 1847, Sara and Kaufmann Wertheim (I) were twenty-six and twenty-eight years old, respectively. The marriage certificate identified Sara's father as Herz Tannenbaum, merchant and *Schutzjude* from Eiterfeld. In May 1832, in the Electorate of Hesse, Representative Eberhard tried to promote the emancipation of Jews. He met with resistance from local sovereigns who threatened to veto the emancipation unless they received financial compensation for the loss of *Schutzgeld* from their Jews. Consequently, the local sovereigns in the Electorate of Hesse delayed the emancipation of Jews until October 29, 1833.[1] It was probably for that reason that Herz Tannenbaum was compelled to remain *Schutzjude*. Implementation for the betterment of Jews was at the mercy of local officials, who frequently engaged in delaying action.

The Tannenbaum-Wertheim marriage was officially witnessed by the *Schutzjuden* Israel Lorsch and Liebmann Wertheim from Angenrod. The signatures of the groom, Kaufmann Wertheim (I), and the witness, Liebmann Wertheim, were executed in Gothic letters, while Israel Lorsch employed Latin script. Sara, the bride, made three small circles in lieu of her signature. Some years after Sara had left her native village, the Jewish community of Eiterfeld obtained its own school.[2] When Sara was of school age, the edict of May 14, 1816, in the Electorate of Hesse directing Jewish children to attend Christian schools had most likely not yet been implemented. Even if it had, Sara's parents may have tried to avoid having their daughter attend a church school. Consequently, at the time of her wedding, Sara Tannenbaum was unable to write her name in either German or Hebrew. As attested by Mayor Bernhard, the marriage certificate stated that Sara's wedding was the only one that occurred in the Angenrod Israelite community in 1847.

THE CHILDREN OF
SARA
TANNENBAUM
AND KAUFMANN
WERTHEIM (I)

VOGEL (II), THE FIRST CHILD of Sara and Kaufmann Wertheim (I) was born on December 12, 1847, in house #49 in Angenrod but died in infancy. Herz, their second child, my paternal grandfather, was born on March 29, 1851, and named after Sara's father, Herz Tannenbaum of Eiterfeld. Moses (II), the third child of Sara and Kaufmann (I), was born on January 18, 1855 and died on September 24, 1855 when he was eight months old. Michnah, the fourth child and only daughter of this family, was born on November 1, 1859.

Vogel (II)

VOGEL WERTHEIM (II), the first child of Sara and Kaufmann Wertheim, was born on December 12, 1847 in house #49 in Angenrod. Vogel was named after his late paternal grandfather, Raphael (Vogel [I]) Wertheim, who had died on August 17, 1841. According to tradition, children were named after the father's family in order to memorialize the father's lineage. Witnesses to Vogel's birth certificate were Josef Wertheim and Nathan Oppenheimer and Anna Elisabetha Solzer signed the document as midwife. Mayor Bernhard testified at the bottom of the certificate on January 6, 1848 that, to the best of his knowledge, there had been eight Jewish births during the year 1847. The Angenrod registry indicates that Vogel died at an early age.

Herz Wertheim
(married Hanchen Levi

Herz Wertheim with
Hannchen, his wife,
circa 1928

HERZ WERTHEIM, MY PATERNAL grand-father and the second child of Sara and Kaufmann Wertheim (I), was born in house #39 in Angenrod on March 29, 1851 and was given the Hebrew name 'Naphtali.' In *Genesis 30:7* Naphtali[a] is introduced as the sixth son of Jacob and the second son of Bilhah, Rachel's maid. The biblical Naphtali had four sons and gave his name to one of the tribes of Israel; his shield displayed a stag. The biblical tribe of Naphtali, in contrast to some of the other tribes, continued to "dwell among the Canaanites" (*Judges 1:33*). Because the coat of arms of Naphtali is the hart ('Hirsch' in German), the name 'Herz' may also be derived from the word 'Hirsch.'

At the time of the birth of Herz Wertheim, Sara and Kaufmann Wertheim (I) were thirty and thirty-two years old respectively, and had moved from one of the little houses their forebears had lived in. My paternal grandfather's birth certificate designated Kaufmann Wertheim (I) as a *Schutzjude*. By contrast, documents from 1844 relating to the Levi family and executed by the same scribe in Angenrod termed Levi family members '*von hier*' ('from here'), but did not denote them as *Schutzjuden*. Herz Wertheim's birth certificate was signed in Gothic writing by his father and by witnesses Abraham Stern and Josef Wertheim. Anna Elisabetha Solzer affixed her signature as midwife and Mayor Bernhard authenticated the document.

Moses (II)

MOSES (II), THE THIRD CHILD of Sara and Kaufmann Wertheim, was born in Angenrod on January 15, 1855 in house #49. Anna Elisabetha Solzer served as midwife and Mayor Bernhard validated the certificate. Meyer Höchster (I) and Johannes Bernhard (IV) signed as witnesses. Generally, Jews in Hesse did not name their children after a living person. Therefore, the designation of the numeral one

[a] Napthali means 'to wrestle' in Hebrew, and indeed Herz Wertheim assertively came to grips with the trials and tribulations of the human condition.

after Meyer Höchster's name merely indicated that more than one Meyer Höchster resided in Angenrod. Among non-Jewish villagers, it was customary to name a son after a living father, thus distinguishing the elder from others by numbers. Moses Wertheim (II) died on September 24, 1855 at the age of nine months.

Michna Wertheim

SARA AND KAUFMANN WERTHEIM were thirty-eight and forty years old when their youngest child, a daughter named Michnah, was born in Angenrod on November 1, 1859 in house #49. Because Sara and Kaufmann Wertheim's four children were a consistent four years apart, the thought arises that birth control may have been practiced by some Jews. Martin Jung (II), a non-Jewish villager, and Mathes (probably short for Mattathias) Lorsch, a member of the Angenrod Jewish community, signed Michna's birth certificate. Like her three older siblings, Michnah was delivered by Anna Elisabetha Solzer, and her birth certificate was authenticated by Mayor Bernhard.

Michnah is probably a derivative of Michael, which means 'who is like God?' In *Samuel II, 7:16,* Michal, the daughter of King Saul and the wife of King David, despised her husband when he was leaping and dancing before God. The mere utterance of Michnah's name and reference to her family certainly evoked uneasiness in our home. While growing up, I sensed that Michnah was the skeleton in our family closet. Whenever my sister was not on her best behavior, my mother called her Michnah in a reproachful, belittling way. For whatever reason, Michnah and her family fell upon hard times. They lived near or in Frankfurt am Main and my father repeatedly gave them monetary assistance.

I do not know how Michnah became the 'black sheep' of the Wertheim family. She was spoken of only in whispers, lest the children unearth this blemish on the family or, worse yet, be tempted to emulate her. One of Michnah's children, and doubtless a contemporary of my father, lived in or near Frankfurt am Main in the early 1930s. On his frequent trips to the cattle market in Frankfurt am Main, my father regularly doled out money to this relative. I do not know whether anyone of this branch of the Wertheim family survived Hitler's 'Final Solution.' Poor people's attention to the future is only secondary in their lives while struggling for their daily bread.

Endnotes

1. Wolf-Arno Kropat, *Neunhundert Jahre Geschichte der Juden in Hessen* (Wiesbaden: Kommission für die Geschichte der Juden in Hessen, 1983), pp. 334-335.
2. Paul Arnsberg, *Die Jüdischen Gemeinden in Hessen,* (Franfurter Societäts Druckerei, GmbH, Vol. I, p. 154.

Chapter Six
The Hannchen and Herz Wertheim Family
The Herz Wertheim Residence in Angenrod
The Children of Hannchen and Herz Wertheim
The Herz Wertheim Family's Life in Angenrod

Residence of Hannchen Levi Wertheim and Herz Wertheim in Angenrod circa 1925.
In the foreground are (left to right) Walter Wertheim and Margot Wertheim.

THE HERZ AND
HANNCHEN
WERTHEIM FAMILY

*M*Y PATERNAL GRANDPARENTS, Hannchen Levi and Herz Wertheim, were united in wedlock in Angenrod on May 20, 1878, corresponding to the eighteenth of *Iyyar* 5639 of the Hebrew calendar and the minor holiday of *Lag Ba-Omer.*[a] At the time of their marriage, Hannchen and Herz were twenty-six and twenty-seven years old, respectively. The witnesses were Hannchen's fifty-nine year old father, Herz Levi (I), and her oldest living brother, Isaac Levi, who was thirty years old. By then Kaufmann Wertheim (I), the father of Herz (I), had passed on.

[103

According to my maternal grandfather, Jakob Lamm from Kirtorf (three miles from Angenrod), the parents of Herz (particularly his father, Kaufmann [I]) violently objected to their son's marriage to Hannchen Levi. This attitude is inexplicable because my grandmother, Hannchen, personified her name's Hebrew meaning of 'gracious' or 'forebearing,' while my grandfather Herz was not much disposed toward the Hebrew meanings of 'leniency' and 'compassion.'

Hannchen Levi and Herz Wertheim
circa 1920

My grandfather had broad shoulders, a light complexion, dark wavy hair, and dark brown eyes. Stocky and six feet tall, he dressed in quiet good taste and was very handsome. In his seventies, he suffered from frequent attacks of coughing and wheezing. He therefore made a particular effort to protect himself from the damp cold night air of the Vogelsberg region by wearing a peaked night cap. But otherwise he struck one as being in remarkably robust health.

Herz Wertheim presented so commanding an appearance that for as long as I knew him, and especially when I was a young child, I made myself scarce out of fear. He was unquestionably the absolute authority over his family, servants, and household. The only tender-heartedness I ever saw my grandfather Herz reveal was toward his beloved wife, Hannchen, and to his grandchildren. Although he functioned as the indisputable lord and master of his domain, he frequently entrusted major decisions to Hannchen. Whenever someone referred to the couple's prosperity and their accumulated wealth of fields and meadows, Herz would credit his wife. Without being scant in giving or spending, Hannchen prudently and masterfully managed their household of four daughters, three sons, and domestic help.

---

[a] This semi-holiday has been celebrated since the gaonic period and falls on the thirty-third day of the *Omer* (the counting of forty-nine days between the second night of Passover until *Shavuot*.) The thirty-third day of the *Omer* is the only day of this general mourning period when weddings are allowed to take place.

Chapter Six

At mealtime no one at the table spoke unless my grandfather commanded an answer. He was in charge of dispensing food, especially the highly-regarded portions of meat. My Aunt Hilda, Herz and Hannchen's second oldest daughter, related that in the event her father unintentionally neglected to serve meat to one of the children, everyone was afraid to call this omission to his attention. For weekday meals, the Wertheim family, as well as two female and two male servants, seated themselves on long wooden benches at the table in the large dining area next to the kitchen. During a midday meal in 1920, one of the male servants, either by an act of omission or commission that escaped me at age five, so vexed my grandfather that he pursued the servant around the *messuage*[b] and into the street with a long-handled broom. I do not know whether an actual beating was administered, but no one tried to hold him back.

My grandmother seemed to dread an intense display of the quick temper that her husband was generally unable to keep in check. However, Herz' vexations were usually of short duration and he did not harbor hard feelings. I concluded that such treatment of servants, even among rural Jews, was nothing out of the ordinary, because I had observed it to be common among non-Jews of the region and era. As a youngster I heard of peasants whipping their helpers and of masters of a trade pummeling an apprentice at will. By and large, rural Jews at that time adhered strictly to the precepts of *Torah*, but not infrequently they also adopted the mores of the neighboring non-Jewish peasantry, who were the majority of the population in Angenrod.

Herz Wertheim agonized considerably over the postulate in Judaism of the Inclination of Good (*yezer ha-tov*) and Inclination of Evil (*yezer ha-ra*). He subscribed to the notion in *Genesis 8:21* that "man's heart is evil from his youth" and must be controlled. He tried to control his zest for succulent foods and especially for meat, but he was not successful in resisting the sexual temptations of extramarital relations. A maid in the Wertheim household gave birth to a male child just about the same time (January, 1888) that Salli, the youngest son of Hannchen and Herz, came into the world. According to my aunt, Irma Levi Wertheim, Herz' offspring by the maid lived not far from the Wertheim residence in Angenrod, attended the public school, and bore a pronounced resemblance to Salli Wertheim.

My grandfather's views on child rearing were based on *Proverbs 13:24*, which states: "He that spares his rod hates his son, but he that loves him chastises him early." He also followed the teachings of *Proverbs 22*: "Bring up a child in the way he should go, and when he is old he will not depart from it." Herz Wertheim endorsed the prevailing notion that it is necessary for parents to break the will of their children in order to gain their respect and obedience. Even from his adult children he demanded unqualified obedience as a parental right. As a strictly orthodox Jew, my grandfather disapproved of the religious observances of the Jews of Alsfeld and other large towns in the area. He felt that they had forsaken Jewish orthodoxy for

---

[b] A dwelling house with its barn, stables, and adjacent land.

material gains and bodily comfort. My Aunt Frieda, Herz and Hannchen's young-est living daughter, stated that each Friday evening her father prepared himself diligently for reading the designated *Torah* portion. Because the *Torah* scroll has no punctuation and no vowels, reading it is a demanding task.

As children, Hannchen and Herz were neighbors. They attended the Angenrod congregational school in the synagogue for secular and religious instruction. The synagogue could be seen from the Herz Wertheim residence. My grandparents read, wrote, and spoke perfect German, which they regarded as their native tongue. They read and wrote Hebrew and they understood the daily, Sabbath, and holiday prayers in Hebrew. From an exhaustive understanding of Jewish history, they em-phasized the fifteenth-century Spanish Inquisition. Their mathematical skills were extraordinary and were usually executed orally. Hannchen and Herz also spoke Western Hessian Yiddish (called '*lashon hakodesh*' or 'holy tongue' in Hebrew). It consisted of a mixture of words from the Hebrew and Hessian dialects. In addition to German newspapers, they read a German-Jewish weekly that, to the best of my recollection, was called *Israelitisches Wochenblatt*. My grandfather read mostly from Hebrew biblical texts and their explanations.

The French occupation of Angenrod lasted fifteen years and ended more than thirty years before Herz Wertheim was born. But his speech pattern reflected a number of French expressions that came from either his parents or his duty as a guard of French prisoners-of-war in the Franco-Prussian War of 1870-71. Guard-ing French prisoners was an experience of import in his life that he alluded to with great pride. The years he spent in the German military undoubtedly accounted for his stiff-backed posture. My grandfather served between the ages of eighteen and twenty.

From cradle to grave, my grandparents' lives were guided by unceasingly strict faithfulness to the ordinances of orthodox Judaism. They kept holy the 613 biblical commandments made known to Moses at Sinai, including the 365 prohibitions (equal to the number of solar days) and the 248 dictates (equal to the number of bones in the human body.) Except on the Sabbath and holidays, Herz wore a small *tallit* (*arba kanfoth*) under his upper garment.[c]

My grandparents practiced strict observance of the dietary laws known as '*kashrut*.' These laws forbid the eating of meat from biblically 'unclean' animals and from those not ritually slaughtered (*shehitah*). Animals found defective in one of their vital organs and certain parts of the 'clean beasts' are also forbidden. Also prohibited is the combination or proximity of meat and milk foods, as well as fish

---

[c] A *tallit* is a four-cornered prayer shawl with fringe (*ziziyyot*) at each corner. It is usually made of cotton, silk, linen, or wool (fabrics may not be mixed). The *tallit* is worn by males during morning prayers except on *Av* 9, when it is worn at afternoon service as well as throughout Day of Atone-ment (*Yom Kippur*) services. The *tallit katan* is a small *tallit*, or *arba kanfot*, which is a rectangular garment of white cotton, linen or wool with *ziziyyot* on its four corners. On weekdays my grandfa-ther laid *tefillin* (phyllacteries). Phyllacteries are two black leather boxes fastened to leather straps and contain four portions of the *Pentateuch* written on parchment. *Tefillin* are affixed on the forehead and arm by adult male Jews during recital of morning prayers. They are not worn on the Sabbath and festivals and on *Av* 9 are worn during the afternoon service.

without fins or scales. My grandparents' lives centered around the solemnity of the Sabbath, major Jewish holidays, fast days, and the rituals and ceremonies pertaining to minor holidays. Hannchen and Herz observed the laws of family purity (*taharat ha-mishpahah*) pertaining to the sexual abstinence during the period of the wife's menstruation. In accordance with the law of *niddah* (meaning 'menstruous woman'), Hannchen submerged herself in the *mikveh*[d] after a minimum period of twelve days of separation from her husband.

THE WERTHEIM HOME IN ANGENROD

HANNCHEN AND HERZ WERTHEIM probably inherited their residence with the barn and stable from Herz' parents, Kaufmann (I) and Sara Tannenbaum Wertheim. Sara lived with the newlyweds until her death. The front of their house faced the back of the residence of Isaac and Seligmann Levi (Hannchen's brothers). This two-story home had high stone steps that converged from two sides to a large platform leading to the entrance. Underneath the platform was a wooden door leading to the cellar, where potatoes and root vegetables were kept in winter. The eating area on the first floor also had a door to the cellar.

The sides of the house were half-timbered, but the outside of the barn and stables (where each spring tiny swallows built their nest) matched the front of the house. The stables and barn also accommodated a carriage and one or two horses. As late as 1934, transportation from Alsfeld, the nearest railroad station, was either by foot, bicycle, or horse-and-carriage. The manure pile was beyond an eight-foot-wide strip paved with cobblestones along the outside cellar door. During the 1920s and 1930s, manure piles were generally in front of farmhouses in Upper-Hessian villages and this was still the case in 1959.

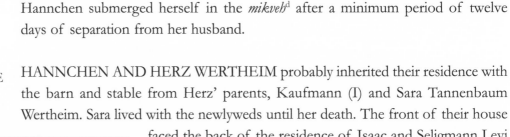

'The Herze,' village name of the Herz Wertheim residence in Angenrod in 1909. In the doorway of the house, from left to right: Irma Levi, Frieda Wertheim, Herz Wertheim, Gisela Levi, Katinka Wertheim, and Vogel Wertheim (III). In the foreground is Hermann Levi. Standing in the stable doorway are Abraham Herz and Alfred Mühlstein.

In addition to the kitchen and the dining area on the main floor of the Wertheim residence, there was a large living room with a sofa, chairs, a large desk, a square dining table, and a tiled stove. In this room, Sabbath and holiday meals were served. Behind the large living area was a small dark room called the '*Kämmerchen.*' A large bedroom on the other side was occupied in the 1920s and 1930s by the 'young couple'—my father's brother, Salli, and his wife, Minna. During that era, it was customary for three generations to live under the same roof. Upstairs there were at least four bedrooms, one of which was occupied by my grandparents, and a living room with furniture in my grandparents' quiet and exemplary taste, including a rococo love seat, a chest, and end tables. To the delight of young granddaughters, there was also a good-sized metal toy cooking stove with lidded cooking pans and pots.

---

[d] The *mikveh* is a pool of clear water used mainly for ritual cleanliness after menstruation.

As late as the early 1930s, my grandparents' residence in Angenrod had no indoor plumbing. All water was drawn off a hand pump in back of the residence and shared with the Isaac and Seligman Levi households. Between the Levi stable and the Wertheim house, on the same level as the platform in front of the house there was an outdoor toilet that in winter in the Vogelsberg region did not exactly effect a homelike ambiance.

A well-tended vegetable garden and an area of apple, pear, and plum trees were at the far edge in back of the residence, taking one-quarter of an acre. Chives growing in the herb garden were used as a border for the vegetable beds in an arrangement that is nowadays touted by adherents of companion planting. Other herbs were parsley, leek, dill, borage, and celeriac. Lettuce, spinach, carrots, beets, red, white and savoy cabbage, kale, and tomatoes flourished in the visibly fertile soil, augmented by generous amounts of manure. My grandparents' vegetable garden also had a device that used the rays of the sun for drying small pears and plums and peeled pieces of apple.

THE CHILDREN OF
HANNCHEN AND
HERZ WERTHEIM

IN THE INSIDE JACKET OF A PRAYER BOOK, my grandfather, Herz Wertheim, recorded the birth and death dates of his family. Mathilde, the oldest child of Hannchen and Herz, was born at 4:00 p.m. on January 22, 1879 (*Teveth* 27, 5639) and was named after her paternal grandmother, Madel Strauss widowed Höchster (Raphael Wertheim's [I] second wife). Kaufmann (II) (called Carl), the second child, was named after Herz' father, Kaufmann Wertheim (I), and was born on January 14, 1881 at 12:30 p.m. (*Shevat* 14, 5641). Leopold (a Teutonic version of 'Löb'), the third child, was born on Saturday, June 24, 1882 and named after Hannchen's oldest brother Löb (II), who had died young.

Vogel [III] (whose Hebrew name 'Raphael'), Hannchen's and Herz' fourth child was my father. He was born at 11:30 p.m. on October 4, 1883. His birthday was the third of *Tishri*, 5644, a fast day marking the slaying of Gedaliah, whom the Babylonians appointed as governor of Judah after the capture of Jerusalem in 586 B.C.E (Before Common Era). My father was named after Herz Wertheim's older brother Vogel (II) (born December 12, 1847), whose death as a young child made Herz the oldest living child of Sara and Kaufmann Wertheim (I).

Hilda, the fifth child of Hannchen and Herz Wertheim, was born at 3:30 a.m. on Friday, December 26, 1884 (*Teveth* 8, 5645), the second day of Christmas.[e] Minna, the sixth child, was born May 19, 1886 (*Iyyar* 14, 5647) and died on August 19, 1886 (*Elul* 19, 5646). Salli, the seventh child, was probably named after Hannchen's maternal grandfather, Seligmann Rosenberg of Lichenroth, Electorate of Hesse. Salli was born at 9:30 p.m. on Monday, January 30, 1888 (*Shevat* 17, 5648). Katinka, the eighth child, was born at 5:45 p.m. on August 27, 1889 (*Elul* 1, 5649). Frieda, the ninth child, came into the world on June 12, 1893. The tenth child was a girl born

---

[e] My orthodox grandfather's repeated allusions to the secular calendar are indeed thought-provoking. Despite every effort of not identifying with the ways of his non-Jewish neighbors, even my grandfather could not resist the local mores.

on November 21, 1894 at 8:30 p.m. who died shortly after birth. This infant lived too brief a time to receive a name.

AT THE TIME OF THE BIRTH of her youngest child, Hannchen was forty-two years old. My grandmother did not nurse any of her children, all of whom had wet nurses, except my father. In Angenrod and other Upper Hessian villages, non-Jewish peasant women, especially those who bore a child out of wedlock, performed this function for wages to provide the necessities of life for their own infant. Now and then a Jewish mother nursed another Jewish child, but I am not aware that Jewish mothers were wet nurses for peasant children.

When my grandmother referred to the loss of her three young children, she was not morose. Rather, she accepted without complaint that part of the human condition that she regarded beyond her control. My grandmother also pointed out that some pain from this bereavement remained. My grandparents named their sons at the time of circumcision; their daughters received names during the *holograsch* ceremony in the afternoon of a Sabbath several weeks after childbirth. Prior to Hannchen's first synagogue attendance after childbirth, she went to the *mikveh* in order to render her from *tomen* (unclean) to *tahor* (clean).

My grandmother told me how much she suffered with toothaches during her pregnancies and that she lost a tooth with each child. Frequently in the 1880s and early 1890s, dental care was crudely delivered in the home and consisted mostly of extractions. My grandmother related that once her dentist applied himself so vigorously to the task of extracting a tooth that she landed in a corner on the other side of the room. During her late forties and early fifties, Hannchen suffered frequent flu attacks that often rendered her gravely ill. She recounted how my father, then in his middle twenties, nursed her with much care and devotion.

My grandmother raised enough vegetables and fruits for her own household. In winter, the family slaughtered calves and heifers in accordance with the laws of *shehitah*. Family members did not consume large amounts of meat, but they seemed to relish the fat in goose and in smoked beef breast. My grandparent's own fields of rye at the village periphery provided the grain for the huge loaves of bread, each of which weighed about seven pounds. In Upper Hesse bread dough was also used for *Salzekuchen* (salt cake). This consisted of thinly-spread bread dough covered with a mixture of potcheese and sautéed parsley. In the 1920s, Jews and non-Jews alike used the Angenrod communal baking house.

In Angenrod, Hannchen and Herz Wertheim had many relatives. Two of Hannchen's brothers, Isaac and Seligmann, lived next door. The Schaumburgers were related through Hannchen's grandmother, Hennel. In Alsfeld, the Flörsheim, Levi, Sondheimer, and Rothschild families were all kin of Hannchen. Herz was related to the members of the many Wertheim families in Angenrod. Hannchen had warm, amiable relationships with everyone—family and friends, Jews and non-

Jews. Herz was much respected for his upstanding ways and his achievements in raising such a respected family.

As was common practice among Jews in Hesse, Herz gave each of his four daughters a sizable dowry ('*nedunyah*' in Hebrew) that consisted of house furnishings, a substantial amount of money intended to establish or enlarge the business of a future son-in-law, and linens embroidered and monogrammed by the bride. At the tender age of ten, young girls frequently began with needlework for their hope chest. During the early 1900s, family laundries were done only once a month, necessitating large quantities of linens.

In 1928, my grandparents celebrated their golden wedding anniversary, once more proclaiming their marriage vows in the Angenrod synagogue. They were surrounded by fourteen of their fifteen grandchildren and all their children except their oldest son, Carl, who had emigrated to America. During spring and summer, my grandparents visited for several weeks with one of their married children, but they always preferred to celebrate major Jewish holidays in Angenrod and they never traveled in winter. Until the ascension of Hitler to power on January 30, 1933, my grandparents often counted their blessings. But after they transferred Herz' thriving business, fields, meadows, and *messuage* to their son, Salli, and his wife, Minna Löwenthal Wertheim, my grandparents experienced much vexation and disappointment due to Salli's managerial shortcomings.

In my youth, the town of Alsfeld was always a stronghold of anti-semitism. In 1933, I was expelled from school there because anti-semitism had gained legiti-

The golden wedding anniversary in 1928 of Hannchen Levi Wertheim and Herz Wertheim (I). **Left to right, front row:** Edith Leiser, Betty Mühlstein, Margot Wertheim, Hannchen Wertheim, Friedel Leiser, Herz Wertheim (holding Karl Heinz Wertheim), Rut Herz. **Second row:** Meinhard Hammerschlag, Rut Mühlstein, Ruth Leiser, and Erna Wertheim. **Third row:** Tilli Wertheim, Kurt Herz, Lotti Mühlstein, and Walter Wertheim.

macy. Also in Alsfeld in March 1933, without a court order, the local Nazis arrested and jailed the Jew, Adolf Cahn.[f] Horror stories intended to scare other Jews and dissidents abounded. My grandmother opined that young people must forthwith leave Germany regardless of the heartache inflicted on those family members who had to remain behind. Hannchen was indeed a selfless interpreter of circumstances. She strengthened my already firm decision to immigrate to the United

[f] Around 1900 and later many Jewish parents in Upper Hesse named their sons Adolf.

Chapter Six

States even before my parents were ready to have me leave. I can still see my grandmother at our last farewell, standing on the platform atop the steps of her home, waving and wiping away tears until she could no longer hold in as the carriage took me away. Her premonition of not seeing me again came to pass.

Thereafter, though certainly not because of my departure, my grandmother's life took a turn for the worse. Partly because of the boycott the Nazis implemented against Jewish cattle dealers and partly because of financial mismanagement by my Uncle Salli, a cow from the Wertheim stables was scheduled to be auctioned by order of the court. This shame and dishonor caused my grandmother to suffer a fatal heart attack at 8:45 a.m. on January 13, 1936 (*Tevet* 18, 5696) at the age of eighty-three.[1]

Hannchen's daughter, Frieda Hammerschlag, who lived in Felsberg had to engage Hans Bodenheimer, the spiritual leader in that town, to perform the burial ritual, because there was no longer anyone left in Alsfeld and its vicinity who was officially empowered to perform the ritual of a Jewish funeral. Hannchen Levi Wertheim was buried in the Angenrod Jewish cemetery where her grandparents and parents had been laid to rest before her. As of May 1990, her tombstone had fallen and, according to the existing regulations in Germany regarding tombstones in Jewish cemeteries, it cannot be put in an erect position.

After the death of his wife of fifty-eight years, Herz lived for three more years in the home of his son, Salli, where one parcel of land after another of the Wertheim property was disposed of in public sale. During *Kristallnacht*[g] on November 10, 1938, my eighty-seven-year old grandfather had to look upon the destruction of the inside of the Angenrod synagogue, where *Torahs* and prayer books were burned and windows were shattered. He was also present when his son, Salli, was handcuffed and taken to the concentration camp in Buchenwald. Herz Wertheim was also at hand when his youngest grandson, Charles Wertheim, returned from the Jewish boarding school in Bad Nauheim because the Nazis had devastated the school and sent the students home.[2] However, the Nazi hordes did not beat my grandfather or otherwise harm him physically, unlike the brutality that was inflicted on German Jews in other villages in Upper Hesse.

In early February, 1939, Alfred Mühlstein, Herz' oldest grandson, and his wife, Edja, fetched Herz Wertheim from Angenrod to join his daughter, Mathilde, and her husband, Louis Mühlstein, in Geneva, Switzerland. Because of their Swiss citizenship, Alfred and Edja were permitted to return to Switzerland with their grandfather, Herz. On the train to Switzerland, but still under German jurisdiction, the eighty-eight-year-old Herz loudly voiced his bitterness against the Nazis. Above all he felt betrayed by his country because of his loyal service in the Franco-Prussian War of 1870-71.

[g] The "Night of Broken Glass." Nazi anti-Jewish outrage was perpetrated on November 9 and 10, 1938. Officially, this pogrom was provoked by the assassination of a German diplomat in Paris by the Polish refugee, Herschel Grynszpan. Widespread attacks on Jews, Jewish-owned property, and synagogues took place throughout Germany and Austria. Thirty thousand Jews were arrested and sent to concentration camps, one hundred ninety-one synagogues were set on fire and another seventy six were completely demolished.

In the French-speaking city of Geneva, in the home of his oldest daughter, Mathilde, Herz was distressed about the disarray of the household and he missed his Hannchen even more.[3] On May 11, 1940 (*Iyyar* 3, 5700), Herz Wertheim died in Geneva. On May 13, 1940, he was buried at #346 in Veyrier sur Saleve in Savoy, France. Herz' burial in France was necessitated by the fact that the Swiss canton of Geneva did not permit Jewish graveyards and Herz' family did not wish to lay him to rest in a non-Jewish cemetery. I visited my grandfather's grave in France in 1974.

Endnotes

1. Interview by Dr. Kenneth W. Stein with the Mühlstein family in Geneva, Switzerland, in January 1980.
2. Interview with Charlie Wertheim in Spring Valley, New York, September 13, 1989.
3. Interview by Dr. Kenneth W. Stein with the Mühlstein family in Geneva, Switzerland, in January 1980.

Chapter Seven
The Mühlstein Family and the Switzerland Connection
The Marriage and Family of Mathilde Wertheim and
Louis Mühlstein

The Army Reserve Battalion L.I.R. 80, Wiesbaden Company 2 during World War I
October 15, 1915.
Louis Mühlstein stands left of the tree on the right

MATHILDE WERTHEIM, BORN IN 1879, was the first child and first daughter of Hannchen and Herz Wertheim. When Mathilde Wertheim was twenty-six years old and considered passed her prime for matrimony, Mathilde married the twenty-nine-year-old Louis Mühlstein on February 15, 1905. Louis was born October 14, 1875 in Singhofen[a] near Nassau on the Lahn, the son of Moses Mühlstein (born 1840) and Babette Levita.

Mathilde and Louis Mühlstein

In Singhofen, Moses and Babette led an unpretentious life with their six children: Eva, Louis, Hermann, Johanna, Alfred, and Max. All of the children of Moses and Babette Mühlstein established themselves in Switzerland before World War I, except for Louis, the oldest son, and Eva, the oldest daughter, who married a Mr. Ahrens in 1904.

Eva Mühlstein
(married Mr. Ahrens)

The Ahrens family lived in Frankfurt am Main with their two children, Eric and Betty (doubtless named after her late grandmother, Babette Mühlstein). Shortly after the advent of Hitler in 1933, the Ahrens families came to the United States and settled in New York. Eva Ahrens suffered from diabetes and died in the early 1940s. In 1933, her daughter, Betty, married Henry Salfeld, an attorney from Wiesbaden. Eric Mühlstein and his wife, Thesy, had a son named Thomas, who married a non-Jewess. To the best of my knowledge, two of Eva Mühlstein Ahrens' grandchildren married non-Jews. Eric died in the 1970s; Betty Salfeld died in May 1991, when she was in her eighties.

During the late 1880s and 1890s, whenever a Jewish family in Hesse ran out of funds for dowries, younger daughters went abroad in order to find a husband. I saw that situation well substantiated in South Africa, where many young Jewish girls who emigrated from Hesse without dowries during the 1880s and 1890s found Jewish husbands from Lithuania and Latvia. In rural Hesse, Jewish younger brothers frequently left because the oldest son had inherited the parents' home. Younger siblings therefore had no place to stay, no business, and no job. This set of circumstances probably motivated Hermann, Alfred, and Max Mühlstein to immigrate to Switzerland in order to seek a livelihood. Their sister, Johanna, also went to Switzerland to find a husband. In the 1890s, the three Mühlstein brothers established a store in Geneva for men's clothing, haberdashery custom tailoring, and sporting goods.

---

[a] After the Nazis seized power in January 1933, the Jewish families of Goldschmidt and Hirschberg immigrated from Singhofen to settle in Columbus, Georgia. Later the only child of Hanna and Leo Hirschberg, Walter established himself with his own family in Atlanta, Georgia.

Chapter Seven

Hermann Mühlstein (married Binosa Böhler)

HERMANN MÜHLSTEIN MARRIED Binosa Böhler, a non-Jewess, whose sewing and tailoring skills were of prime importance for the Mühlstein store. Binosa and Hermann Mühlstein had a child in 1912 who died in 1918 and in 1920 their daughter Eva (Mimi) was born. Both in the United States and in Switzerland, where Mimi now lives, she and I have had several opportunities to renew our friendship that was first established when we were guests at my Aunt Mathilde's house in Nassau in 1930. Mimi keeps in close touch with her Mühlstein cousins and she has regularly rendered financial assistance to her father's branch of the Levita family in Israel.

Johanna Mühlstein (married Frederick Bunte)

IN GENEVA IN 1920, Johanna Mühlstein wedded Frederick Bunte, a non-Jew from Bremen, Germany. It is not known whether Johanna converted to Christianity; none of her descendants are Jewish or are married to Jews.

Alfred Mühlstein (married Marte Guggenheim)

IN 1922, ALFRED MÜHLSTEIN married Marte Guggenheim from Zofingen, Switzerland, where Jews had lived as early as the fourteenth century. Members of old Jewish communities generally held onto Judaism more tenaciously and this family remained faithful to Judaism. Their oldest daughter, Madeleine (born in 1923), married Werner Levita, a second cousin from Germany who immigrated to Switzerland during the late 1930s or early 1940s. Werner's brother was killed by the Germans during the time of the Nazis. Madeleine and Werner had two sons, both of whom live in Annacy, the capital of High Savoy. Marcel is an economic scientist and Maurice is an industrial consultant. Marcelle, the second daughter of Alfred and Marte, never married.

Max Mühlstein (married Marte Picard)

MAX MÜHLSTEIN, THE YOUNGEST SON of Babette and Moses Mühlstein, married Marte Picard. This Picard family had resided for at least several generations in Switzerland, was well-to-do and considerably represented in Lausanne in the 1970s. Marte and Max Mühlstein's daughter, Betty (born in 1924), married Fred Riesser. The families of both Betty and her brother, Philip, maintained their Jewish identity. During the time of the Nazis, the three Mühlstein brothers (Herman, Alfred, and Max) made every effort to snatch from the jaws of certain death by the Nazis as many members as possible of their family in Germany.

THE FAMILY OF MATHILDE WERTHEIM AND LOUIS MÜHLSTEIN

MY AUNT MATHILDE WERTHEIM MÜHLSTEIN'S features, coloring, and build bore much resemblance to her mother, but she lacked my grandmother's sagaciousness and vision in mastering human affairs. Aunt Mathilde was generally more self-absorbed and unmoved by her surroundings. Even in her function as mother, she seemed not to get too involved with her own children. Nevertheless, she kept up with girlhood friendships until the end and maintained contact even with distant relatives who were dispersed throughout the world. Educated at the Angenrod congregational school, her mathematical skills, penmanship, and letter writing were exemplary. But my Aunt Mathilde seemed to lack a drive for further education and upward mobility. After living twenty-five years in the French-speaking city of Geneva, Mathilde spoke little or no French and her contacts were restricted to family members and others who communicated in German.

Two days after Mathilde and Louis Mühlstein's wedding on February 15, 1905, Babette Mühlstein died of pneumonia. Mathilde and Louis moved to Obernhoferstrasse 10 in Nassau,[b] where Louis preferred to carry on his trade of being a butcher while his father, Moses, was primarily a cattle dealer. The prime reason for Mathilde and Louis Mühlstein's move to Nassau was for their children to benefit from better educational opportunities. Nassau had the advantage of having a Hebrew and Jewish history teacher, Samson Hanauer, who later died in 1918 in War I.

Louis Mühlstein, an orthodox Jew, kept his butcher shop closed on the Sabbath and uncompromisingly accepted the totality of historical Jewish religion as recorded in written and oral laws. Louis and Mathilde strictly observed the prescribed dietary laws and the laws of family purity.

During World War I, the forty-year-old Louis Mühlstein served Germany in the infantry in France after he received his training from July to October in Wiesbaden in 1915. He was a member of the army reserve, Battalion L.I.R. 80 of Company II. At that time, Mathilde and Louis had three children: Alfred (born November 22, 1906), Betty (born July 16, 1909), and Rut (born October 12, 1913). Louis' last army leave from Wiesbaden before going to the front in France was in October 1915, and their youngest daughter, Lotte, was born on July 3, 1916, nine months after Louis' leave. Before departing from Nassau on his last leave on October 15, Louis sent my parents a message on a photograph of members of his military outfit.

While Louis was off at war from 1915 to 1918, Mathilde and her four younger children were hurting from lack of food. Therefore, Betty was sent to Angenrod to live with her maternal grandparents, Hannchen and Herz Wertheim, who harvested vegetables from their garden, raised flour for bread from their fields of grain, and kept one or two cows for milk. Young Rut was sent to stay with her mother's sister, Katinka, in Niederurff, a small village near Kassel, where scarcity of food was not as widespread. Typical of wartime, individuals in rural communities had the advantage of growing most of the main ingredients for their own meals and bartering surplus foodstuffs for scarce goods.

After the cessation of hostilities in 1918 and upon the homecoming of their father, Betty and Rut returned to live with their parents in Nassau. Each child in this family eventually attended, either in Nassau or in nearby towns reached by railroad, an institution of learning ranked above public school and best suited to his or her aptitude. Among rural Jews, such a notion was unfamiliar and a child's ability and potential were not taken into consideration. Additionally, the monthly fee for high school attendance commencing at age ten was substantial. Nevertheless, Louis Mühlstein was determined that his chil-

---

[b] The small town of Nassau is situated on the Lahn River and had about thirty Jewish families, most of whom were cattle dealers and merchants.

dren be educated to their potential. He may well have arrived at this idea from his avid interest in newspapers and all other literature accessible to him. Louis characteristically escaped from background family noises by engulfing himself in reading material.

By 1931, Mathilde and Louis Mühlstein's son, Alfred, had finished his schooling and spent some time in Spain in order to improve his understanding of

Mathilde and Louis Mühlstein
in Nassau in 1931

commerce. Alfred then settled in Switzerland to work for his three uncles. Betty, too, left for Switzerland and for a while worked for her uncles in the Mühlstein store in Geneva. Shortly thereafter, Rut also went to live in Geneva. Lotte, who was then only fifteen years old, remained with her parents in Nassau. She was the baby of the family, and was much pampered by her mother. In 1922, when Lotte was six years old and I was seven, my Aunt Mathilde had a miscarriage during a visit to Angenrod. While Lotte and I were sitting on the steps, I overheard that the midwife had just arrived and my mother invited us to take a long walk. Afterwards, my mother stated that Aunt Mathilde was confined to bed because of a migraine headache. Although my aunt did indeed suffer from frequent migraines, at that particular time a headache may well not have been the worst part of her distress.

In 1932, as Hitler's dictatorship loomed on the horizon, Louis Mühlstein's business was in difficulty. Because three of their children lived in Switzerland, Louis and Mathilde sold their house and land in Nassau and moved to Geneva. In January, 1936, Mathilde returned to Germany for her mother's funeral in Angenrod. When traveling back to Geneva, she carried money sewn into a pillow. A Nazi injunction prohibited taking any currency out of Germany. In Frankfurt, Mathilde was taken, with her baggage and pillow, to the police station, but by good fortune the money was not discovered.

In Geneva, Louis worked as a maintenance man in the store of his three younger brothers. I do not know if Louis was proficient in French nor am I conversant with Switzerland's abundance of restrictive covenants with regard to Jewish immigrants that may have initially kept Louis from filling other than janitorial positions in his brother's store. My Uncle Louis was a highly intelligent man with a quick capacity for learning. Nevertheless, it appears as if all three brothers resolved that Louis eat humble pie because his rank as the oldest son of Babette and Moses entitled him to be the heir to his parents' home. Generally, in conjunction with this privilege, the oldest son had the same entitlement that parents had for free room, board, and care in case of illness. Correctly or not, Louis' brothers probably perceived their exclusion to be the reason for their emigration. Socially the Mühlstein brothers and their families mingled freely. I never detected any residual resentment on the part of Louis' children toward their uncles, or vice versa.

Louis Mühlstein died on April 28, 1956 (*Iyyar* 18, 5716). In Judaism, the manner in which a person dies and the day on which he dies are viewed to be consequential as a good or bad sign for the deceased. Therefore, Louis Mühlstein's death on the minor holiday of *Lag Ba-Omer* was fraught with positive meaning. Several years before Louis' death, he took ill with diabetes; he had severe problems of blood circulation and painful gangrene that made him cry out in pain and agony, especially during the night. After Louis' death, his children considered that their father's excessive consumption of meat and fat from beef may have exacerbated his illness. At that time, it was not customary to remove fat from meat, and in fact soups and vegetables were frequently prepared with rendered beef fat. After Louis' death, my Aunt Mathilde remained in the same apartment she had shared with her husband, but she visited more frequently for extended periods of time with her married daughters, Betty, in Lausanne and, Lotte, in Zürich.

During our 1959 visit to Switzerland, my eighty-year-old Aunt Mathilde was extremely hospitable and particularly open-hearted. Neither at that time nor during an earlier visit in Nassau was I aware of even a smidgen of the egotism for which she was known in the family. In fact, I discerned my Aunt Mathilde to be decidedly generous with regard to others. My Aunt Mathilde said that the migraine headaches, which had so severely beset her in earlier years, had lessened as she grew older. Nevertheless, she continued to be very careful about her diet and any excessive exertion. My Aunt Mathilde died in Geneva after a very brief illness at the age of eighty-nine in June of 1968 (*Sivan* 15, 5729).

Alfred Mühlstein
(married Esther Spiewak)

ALFRED, THE OLDEST CHILD and only son of Mathilde and Louis Mühlstein, remained with his parents in Nassau until 1923. He attended high school in Bad Ems, spent three months in Spain in order to perfect his knowledge of Spanish, and served a commercial apprenticeship for two years in Frankfurt am Main. His father's three brothers were eager for him to study French and join them to work in their store in Geneva, where he remained for thirty years. In 1939, in Geneva, at the age of thirty-three, Alfred married the twenty-four-year-old Esther (Edja) Spiewak. Born March 13, 1915, Edja was well-educated and engaging. Michel, Alfred and Edja's son and only child, was born June 15, 1947. I met Alfred for brief periods on my visits to Switzerland in 1959, 1974, and 1987. Each time I was struck by the similarity between my cousin and my father's oldest brother, Carl. Both favored the status quo because changes were too perplexing. Alfred also resembles Uncle Carl in stature, coloring, hair shades, and hair texture, but Alfred's features favor the Mühlstein family.

After his marriage to Edja, Alfred remained an employee in the business of his uncles until they liquidated their company in 1961. Then, at the age of fifty-five, Alfred and his wife opened their own clothing store. Their son, Michel, studied law in Geneva, where tuition for college and a professional education is well within the means of most families. While studying law, Michel met and married Sonja, a Sephardic Jewess whose family had fled from Egypt during the regime of Gamal Abdul Nasser (1918-1970), when life in Egypt for Jews was very difficult. Michel and Sonja both work in Geneva in their chosen field of law and have two sons. According to their grandfather, the boys have dark complexions and dark wavy hair. As of 1987, Alfred had sold his store and was fully retired.

Betty Mühlstein
(married Gaston Picard)

THE BIRTH OF BETTY, the second child of Mathilde and Louis Mühlstein, involved fewer complications than that of her youngest sister, Lotte. My dear cousin Betty is captivating, energetic, and vivacious. With dark black hair, dark eyes, and a very light olive complexion, she bears some resemblance to my late beloved grandmother, Hannchen. These similarities are apparent not only in Betty's stature, but also in her constant desire for study and betterment. Well into her seventies, Betty studied English with unflagging persistence, frequently attending lectures to broaden her horizons. Well into her eighties, she was an enthusiast of skiing. Upon daily rising she diligently performed the exercises necessary to keep her limber on the ski slope. Betty has always been thoughtful of others who are less fortunate. In 1974, she invited her late husband's relatives who had no other close family ties to attend her Passover holiday celebration.

In 1932, when she was twenty-three years old, Betty lived in Geneva and worked in her uncles' store. She met and married the thirty-five-year old Gaston Picard (born August 19, 1897) of Lausanne.[c] Gaston was the brother of Marte Picard Mühlstein, who was married to Betty's uncle Max, the youngest son of Babette and Moses Mühlstein. Betty's husband was attractive and charming, a well-bred man whose enjoyable sense of humor endeared him to all. Gaston's family was well-established in Lausanne. Their store and mail order business dealt mainly in fine linens, and the family possessed property in Bern, Switzer-

---

[c] In Lausanne, an organized Jewish community had been established in 1865, but Jews were admitted to full citizenship only in 1891.

land. Although the Picard family considered themselves orthodox Jews, their brand of orthodoxy was relatively less exacting than orthodoxy in rural Upper Hesse. In Lausanne, Jewish doctrine did not reach with such great precision into every facet of living.

From morning until night, Betty worked with boundless energy to sell, pack, and cart heavy packages in the linen store and mail order business, while Gaston

Betty Mühlstein Picard
circa 1931

traveled a great deal to obtain orders. Marlyse, their daughter, was born March 25, 1934 and Jean, their son, was born December 25, 1935. Notwithstanding Switzerland's neutrality during World War II, there was sufficient reason for Jews in Lausanne to fear invasion by the Nazis. During this time, Gaston made provisions to snuff out the lives of his wife and children and subsequently to kill himself to prevent their seizure by the Germans. Fortunately, the Nazis did not occupy Switzerland.

During World War II, the Jewish community of Lausanne was very active in aiding refugees from Nazism. For several years, Betty and Gaston took over the care of the young Inge Rosenbaum, the daughter of Betty's cousin, Ruth Herz Rosenbaum, and her husband, Max Rosenbaum of Haiger, Germany. Betty's task of caring for three young children was made somewhat easier by live-in household help. In Switzerland, young girls from German-speaking (*Schwyzerdütsch*) regions were eager to obtain knowledge of French; therefore they were very willing to work in homes where French was spoken. Gaston Picard died at the age of sixty-seven on July 9, 1964, of a heart attack. Several years earlier he had been ill with a cardiac illness that had weakened his heart.

In speaking with the Picard children in 1959, when they were in their mid-twenties, I sensed that their education in Judaism was without much substance even though they definitely regarded themselves as Jewish. Although the Swiss constitution provides for religious equality under the law, Betty related that, in 1959, young girls of Jewish faith rarely if ever could aspire to become public school or high school teachers. Therefore, Marlyse was educated in commercial subjects.

In the spring of 1955, Marlyse Picard married Michel Messmer (born March 12, 1930), a non-Jew who was then an employee of Philips and Company. Michel's parents, whom I met in 1974, were warm, kind-hearted individuals who lovingly accepted Marlyse; the Picard family, in turn, received Michel amiably. During my visit to Switzerland in 1974, Marlyse commented on the implication and undesirable aspects of a dowry for Jewish daughters which was still customary in Switzerland as late as the 1950s. As a devoted daughter she did not wish her parents to assume the burden of providing her with a dowry. Marlyse explained that this practice was followed only in Jewish circles in Switzerland.[2]

Marlyse and Michel Messmer had two children: Catherine (born April 10, 1956) and Patrick (born April 3, 1958). Because Marlyse did not change her religion, her children are regarded as Jewish. Marlyse, her husband, and their children celebrated some Jewish festivals in Betty's home. It seemed to me that religious persuasion was irrelevant in Marlyse's family, but she repeatedly referred to the fact that she, too, would have perished if the Nazis had reached Lausanne in World War II. In 1974, I met the parents of Catherine's fiancè, Marc Roulet, whose background seemed representative of Swiss middle-class. I do not know Marc's religion, but he is not Jewish. Catherine and Marc were married on April 18, 1980. They have three daughters who, according to Jewish law, are Jewish because they were born of a Jewish mother. During my visit to Switzerland, I met Marlyse and Michel Messmer's son, Patrick, who was then a student. By 1990, he had an electronics store in or near Gland, where his parents live.

Jean, Betty and Gaston Picard's son, is tall and slender. He completed his schooling in Switzerland and in 1959 or 1960 went to London in order to broaden his commercial horizons and improve his knowledge of the English language. He also visited us in the United States. Jean entered his parents' business and became its proprietor after his father's death. High above Lake Geneva, Jean built a beautiful home with a captivating view of the lake and its surroundings. He remained a bachelor until he was fifty-one years old and married Nicole in 1986, a non-Jewish lady from Bern. Nicole is twenty years younger than Jean. They have a son and a daughter who, according to orthodox and conservative Judaism, are not considered Jews unless they convert to Judaism.

Rut Mühlstein
(married Lucien Sigismond
Kohler)

RUT, THE THIRD CHILD of Mathilde and Louis Mühlstein, was born October 12, 1913 in Nassau. She is of slight stature and has black hair, dark eyes, and every appearance of delicate health. She inherited her mother's fragile digestive system and migraine headaches. Rut attended high school in or near Nassau and immigrated to Geneva prior to her parents' arrival there. She was an employee in her uncles' store and lived with her parents in Geneva until her marriage to Lucien Sigismond Kohler, a non-Jew (born May 5, 1900 in Etrembieres, France). Rut's marriage to Lucien was the first out-of-the-faith alliance of the fifteen grandchildren of Hannchen and Herz Wertheim. This marriage created much excitement among all the relatives and especially in Rut's immediate family. Indeed, during and after the first years of the Holocaust, Rut's aunts and uncles in the United States felt that she was joining with the enemy and that perhaps her non-Jewish husband's family had persecuted Jews.

Louis Mühlstein no longer regarded his daughter, Rut, as a living member of either his family or the Jewish community. Forbidding her to enter his home ever again, he observed the seven-day mourning period usually adhered to after the death of a close relative (*shivah*). My uncle probably pondered what he had done wrong that caused Rut to marry a non-Jew and now he felt right by disclaiming her. Moreover, at the time of the intermarriages of his younger siblings (Hermann and Johanna), he had felt powerless to raise any objections. Perhaps he was now secretly mourning for them also. Louis left a directive in his Last Will and Testament that Rut was not to follow his funeral procession. But at the time of Louis Mühlstein's death, the officiating rabbi ruled that Louis' edict was much too harsh and declared it null and void. Rut was permitted to be included in her father's funeral procession.

In Switzerland, the rate of intermarriage has always been high because Jews constitute only a small proportion of the total population. There were probably very few young Jewish men of Rut's age in Geneva and her attempt to enter Jewish community life must have been very difficult, as it has always been for outsiders. Furthermore, among Jews the dowry system was still prevalent; Rut was certainly aware that her family could not provide the required marriage portion. For this and other reasons, my cousin, Rut, wedded the suave Lucien Kohler, who had been recently divorced and was thirteen years her senior.

During her husband's lifetime, my Aunt Mathilde was not allowed to meet openly with her daughter, Rut. But behind Louis' back a loving relationship between mother and daughter secretly defied his severe dictum. Although outwardly conforming to her husband's will while he was alive, Mathilde told me in 1959 that Louis' conduct toward Rut had been much too strict. In retrospect, my aunt related that she was pleased that she had never severed the bond with this daughter who "is the comfort of my old age." Ironically, out of the four grandchildren of the strictly orthodox Mathilde and Louis Mühlstein, only Michel did not marry outside the Jewish faith.[3] By the time of the marriage of her granddaughter, Marlyse Picard, to a non-Jew, my Aunt Mathilde appeared as if she were resigned to an inescapable fate.

Rut and Lucien Kohler built a home in Geneva and spent their summers in a chalet in the Swiss Alps. My cousin, Rut, visited us in the United States and we saw her on our various visits to Switzerland. Lucien and Rut's son, Albert (born July 18, 1946), is a physician. When he graciously hosted me for dinner in Lausanne in 1974, I sensed that religious tenet was not a priority in Albert's life. As of 1991, Albert was not married.

Lotte Mühlstein
(married Kurt Ulmann)

MATHILDE AND LOUIS MÜHLSTEIN'S YOUNGEST CHILD was the gentle and lovable Lotte (born July 3, 1916). Because her birth was a very difficult one, she was especially pampered by my Aunt Mathilde and everyone else. Like her sister, Rut, Lotte is of slight build but she has a lighter complexion and lighter hair than her three siblings. Lotte appears more light-hearted than her sisters, but she has an inordinate concern about the cleanliness of her food and eating utensils. She remained with her parents until their emigration to Geneva in March 1932, where she worked in her uncles' store from 1936 to 1941.

On January 3, 1941 in the Schweizerhof in Bern, Switzerland, Lotte met Kurt Ulmann (born November 10, 1914 in Mulhouse, France) and they were

Lotte and Kurt Ulmann
in 1955

married on October 5, 1941. Kurt's father, a Swiss citizen, worked as a banker and stockbroker for an American firm in Frankfurt am Main, Germany. Kurt was brought up in Bad Homburg near Frankfurt am Main and from 1929 to 1934 he lived in Frankfurt an Main. After Hitler's seizure of power in 1933, when many Jews wanted to leave Germany, Kurt Ulmann was permitted to enter and remain in Switzerland because of his father's Swiss citizenship. Kurt sold suits in Zürich in order to earn a livelihood.

After his marriage to Lotte, Kurt worked in Geneva for Lotte's uncles from 1942 to 1947. Apparently Kurt was the first one to break away from employment 'by the uncles,' who considered his departure a lack of loyalty. In reality, the Mühlstein brothers as employers were loath to part with cheap help and Kurt was tired of earning low wages. Lotte and Kurt Ulmann moved to Zürich, where Kurt eventually established himself in a small business of his own that takes him traveling a good part of the week, while Lotte minds matters of business at home. Kurt and Lotte remained childless and both acquired diabetes as adults. They appear as a couple with unceasing devotion to each other. Each year they rent the same house for their vacation and they are intent on maintaining their physical well-being. Lotte and Kurt regularly attend services at an orthodox synagogue, which is probably the basis of their social contacts.

Reminiscing about her three daughters, my Aunt Mathilde characterized Betty as having a special passion for business, Rut as possessing a craze about spending time in her chalet, and Lotte as suffering from an obsession with bacteria.

Endnotes

1. Interview by Mathilda W. Stein with Marlyse Picard Messmer in Gland, Switzerland, in March 1974.

2. Ibid.

3. Information about the Mühlstein families is derived from Dr. Kenneth W. Stein's notes taken in Switzerland in December 1979 and from conversations of Mathilda W. Stein with members of the Mühlstein family.

Chapter Eight
Other Children of Hannchen and Herz Wertheim
Kaufmann (Carl) Wertheim (II)
Vogel Wertheim (III)
Hilda Wertheim Herz
Salli Wertheim
Katinka Wertheim Leiser
Frieda Wertheim Hammerschlag

Bert Mayer, husband of Margot Wertheim Mayer, served under General Patton at the liberation of Buchenwald in April 1945. He is walking at left wearing a helmet and sunglasses.

*B*ORN JANUARY 14, 1881, CARL WAS NAMED Kaufmann (II) on his birth certificate after his late grandfather, Kaufmann Wertheim (I). Carl was tall and slender with gently-waved dark hair, brown eyes, and a capacity to captivate most women. In 1925, Carl immigrated to the United States when entry requirements were comparatively simple because of a thriving economy that needed more manpower. He and Irma Levi, his first cousin, were married in the United States later that year.

Kaufmann (Carl) Wertheim (II)
and Irma Levi Werthem circa 1925

Carl was the only one of the seven living children of Hannchen and Herz Wertheim who was privileged to attend the high school in Alsfeld. After immigrating to Bradford in Yorkshire, England, Carl served an apprenticeship in the textile business. In England, Carl had a warm-hearted relationship with his uncle, Salomon Levi, my grandmother's younger brother. Carl was also in contact with the family of his mother's brother, Josef, who was banned by most other family members because he had married a non-Jewess. In August 1914, violation of Belgian neutrality gave the British government the pretext and popular support necessary for entry into World War I against Germany. Carl left England to be with his family and to serve Germany, his native country. I know neither the military branch and rank of my uncle nor whether he enlisted or was drafted.

After the cessation of hostilities in 1918, Carl Wertheim did not return to England, although he was out of work in Germany for seven years until he immigrated to the United States in 1925. He continued to spend most of his time at his parents' home in Angenrod, but he also stayed for months at the homes of his other siblings. As a child, I got the impression that Uncle Carl, the textile expert, considered himself above the physical work required by cattle dealers and preferred chores which did not require that he soil his hands. Highly regarded for his advice, Carl was generally accepted as an authority because he was believed to possess a broader view of the world. In reality, his views were based on limited insight and an inability or unwillingness for discriminate reasoning. He had an unconscious desire to maintain the status quo because changes were too perplexing for him to contend with.

In New York, Uncle Carl worked as a salesman in a fabric store, the Haas Brothers, which specialized in high-priced silks. During the height of the Depression in 1933, his job was the first one in the firm to be terminated because, according to Irma, he made it known that his wife was also working. From the time Carl lost his sales job until he and Irma moved to Miami Beach, he worked for a trifling sum in the tailor shop of his brother-in-law, Hugo Rosenbaum. When Carl was first without a job, there was no unemployment insurance. He was too proud to mingle with other unemployed people, but he clearly lacked the enterprising spirit for having his own business.

As the sponsors for thirty to forty refugees, Irma and Carl Wertheim sent the necessary affidavits for Irma's brother, Hermann, and his family, several cousins of Irma related through her mother, Sara Plaut Levi, and all of Carl's siblings and their families (except his youngest brother, Salli, and wife and those members of the immediate Wertheim family who had found refuge in Switzerland). Irma died of cancer in 1961 at the age of sixty-two after a long illness. Carl's death in 1965 when he was eighty-four was attributed to what was then termed the results of 'old age.' Both were buried in Miami Beach.

VOGEL (FREDERICK) WERTHEIM (III) (MARRIED BERTA LAMM)

VOGEL [III] (WHOSE HEBREW NAME OF RAPHAEL), my father, was the fourth child and second surviving son of Hannchen and Herz Wertheim. He was born on October 4, 1883. My father was five-feet-seven-inches tall and had a medium build. His shiny dark brown hair was slightly wavy; his complexion was light and his eyes nut-brown; his well-shaped features exuded candor, compassion, and sincerity.

Vogel (Frederick) Wertheim (III)

In the spring of 1891, at the age of thirteen-and-a-half, my father completed his formal education. In Angenrod, the young Vogel (III)[a] began to work in his father's cattle business and was inculcated with the notion that work is how a person makes sense of his or her place in nature. He worked many long hours during the day, late into the night, and early into the morning. My grandfather tutored his son, Vogel (III), well in every facet of the cattle business. For seventeen years, my father did not receive any pecuniary compensation for his work. He was allotted free room and board in his parents' home and money for necessary clothing.

When he was almost thirty, my father literally and bodily freed himself from the control and power of his father. On March 19, 1913, Vogel (III) moved to Lauterbach after he wedded my mother, Berta Lamm, who was born August 23,

---

[a] Vogel Wertheim (III) changed his first name to Frederick when he went to Lauterbach to be married to Berta Lamm.

1891 in Kirtorf (four miles west of Angenrod). In 1913, Samuel Strauss (I) and his wife, Johanna (Hannchen) Schloss Strauss, each transferred half a share of the residence of Cent 17, its adjacent buildings, *curtilage*, and adjoining lands to Vogel Wertheim (III) and his fiancée, Berta Lamm.

In May 1935, my father bade farewell to his daughter, Erna, in Hamburg. At that time, he was led away by Nazi police and interrogated on suspicion of not obeying foreign exchange regulations. However, he was set free within an hour because a careful Nazi search found no more than the lawful amount of currency on his person. In October, 1937, my fifty-four-year-old father and my forty-six-year-old mother arrived in New York. They chose an American ship because they did not wish to subsidize Hitler's economy through the variety of newly devised taxes and charges.

When my parents disembarked from the ship in New York, their examination by the Immigration and Naturalization Service and the customs check went smoothly. For the first two weeks, my father and mother stayed in our apartment in the West Bronx in New York. Their furniture and household items arrived at the end of that time, having been transported on a freighter. After the three-year separation, we had much to share and I wished to ease my parents' adjustment to the country of their refuge, where a refugee is confronted with a new language, a diverse culture, and unfamiliar mores. As newcomers, my parents suddenly had to cope with many changes in unfamiliar surroundings and also to adjust from a small town to a large metropolis.

Until the end of their days, my parents felt indebted to the United States for granting them asylum in their hour of distress and for saving them from cruel annihilation at the hands of the Nazis. Nevertheless, my mother and father smarted from the tribulations of adjusting to another culture and were tellingly depressed about the fate of their kin and friends still left in Germany. Remembering the traumas of the past, arduously establishing a new business, learning another language, adapting to a new culture, and adjusting to an unaccustomed climate after a lifetime in the temperate Vogelsberg region had a deleterious effect on the physical health of this formerly rugged individual. However, despite reversals and hard times, and in character with others who have been sorely tried, my father retained his sense of humor—the outward affirmation of spirit.

In a spirit of gratitude for having reached these shores, in 1953 they celebrated their Silver Wedding Anniversary in March 1938 by entertaining close relatives in their home. Until the end of his days, my father delighted in his marital bliss. Thanks to proximity in Washington Heights, my father also enjoyed the warm kinship, respect, and affection of his four siblings and their children. Above all, my father basked in the joy of his four grandchildren. All his life he was partial to children, understanding their needs in a time when this awareness was hardly commonplace. Moreover, in later life, Jewish children were living proof that Hitler's plan to eradicate all Jews was thwarted.

Chapter Eight

By late spring of 1953, my father's health had deteriorated visibly. By the middle of July 1953, he was diagnosed as suffering from a cancer of blood-forming tissues (lymphosarcoma). Although my father's body was wracked by much pain, he strove to live as usual by honoring his God and caring for his family. On August 8, 1953, a Sabbath, my father's condition worsened considerably. At the age of sixty-nine, my father died surrounded by his family in the late morning of August 10, 1953. On Wednesday, August 12, 1953, according to custom, my father was buried in a simple pine coffin in the loose white linen garment and corded belt that every married male donned in synagogue on the High Holidays in Upper Hesse. The spacious chapel was filled to capacity with family and friends (many from Lauterbach) who wanted to render the last honor to this unassuming man.

HILDA WERTHEIM HERZ (MARRIED ABRAHAM HERZ)

HILDA, HANNCHEN AND HERZ WERTHEIM'S FIFTH CHILD and second daughter, was born in Angenrod on December 26, 1884. On the Hebrew calendar, her day of birth was two days prior to the Tenth of *Tevet*, a fast day that commemorates the siege of Jerusalem by Nebuchadnezzar in 587-86 B.C.E. The page in my grandfather's prayer book that records his family's vital statistics shows a dual reference to the Hebrew date and the second day of Christmas. This confirms that even members of the orthodox community of Angenrod were mindful of the non-Jewish holidays observed by their neighbors. Although many Jews lived on, or contiguous to, 'Jew Street' in Angenrod, members of the Jewish community also lived among non-Jewish villagers.

My Aunt Hilda's resemblance to her mother was through her dark brown eyes, hair color, complexion, features, and height, but Hilda's broad build was inherited from her father. Similar to her older siblings, Mathilde and Vogel (III), Hilda was educated in the school of the Angenrod Jewish community. The core curriculum of the school was based on a thorough command of German reading and writing, basic arithmetic, in-depth knowledge of biblical Hebrew, and extensive facility in the Hebrew of daily and festival prayers. Parents closely supervised their children's progress and paid

Hilda Herz and her husband, Abraham Herz, with their granddaughter, Inge Rosenbaum, September 1938

scrupulous attention to all schoolwork. Poor conduct of students was not tolerated in school and was severely censured at home.

My Aunt Hilda possessed all the attributes and skills of an educated individual. She evidenced a well-honed sense of what was ethically and socially acceptable in human behavior. From her mother, Hilda probably learned her sterling judgment of the human condition as well as her considerable capacity for resigned acceptance of life's inherent foibles. My four aunts received instruction in cooking, baking, mending, darning, sewing, embroidering, and gardening from their mother, from incidental learning in the households of relatives, and from observing Jewish neighbors and friends. Rye dough, for example, was prepared in large amounts: the average loaf of bread was at least four pounds. It was customary to spread rye bread dough on large baking sheets and cover it with a mixture of pot cheese and sautéed parsley. All bread kneading and mixing were done manually and required considerable physical skill and energy. Ingredients for the Sabbath loaves (*hallah*) were unbleached white flour, baker's yeast, water, and sprinkled poppy seeds. Embroidery skills included monogramming and cutwork of linens for each daughter's hope chest and also for my father. Until he married at age thirty, my father diligently assisted his family in accumulating sufficient funds for his sisters' dowries.

I do not know how Hilda's marriage at age twenty-six to the thirty-five-year-old Abraham Herz (born in 1875), a cattle dealer from Haiger, was arranged in 1910; but young, impassioned love was probably not the paramount incentive. The notion prevailed that love would surely bloom as a by-product of marriage. I would surmise that this union was put together through the family of my aunt, Mathilde Wertheim Mühlstein of Nassau, because that town and Haiger belonged to the same rabbinical district of Bad Ems in Germany.

According to the existing mores, it was imperative that women marry before the age of thirty, lest they be considered spinsters. After the age of twenty-five, a girl's chances of finding a husband diminished rapidly. A groom much older than his bride was well-accepted and generally preferred. My Uncle Abraham was a broad-shouldered man of above medium height who always treated me with kindness and consideration. Nevertheless, I wanted nothing to do with him because of the harsh guidelines he applied to his own children and others. He was a professed follower of the orthodox Judaism of his day, but his personality also echoed the authoritarian traits of his predominantly German non-Jewish environment. Hilda and Abraham Herz had two children who were both born in Haiger: Rut on July 3, 1911 and Kurt on May 22, 1914.

Haiger, near the larger town of Dillenburg is situated in the Westerwald, a hilly region north of Frankfurt am Main and north of the Lahn River. In 1924, Haiger had a population of about three thousand inhabitants, including six Jewish families who interacted appreciably with each other daily and also with the rest of the local population. In 1924, when I spent my three-week summer vacation in Haiger, the Abraham Herz family owned an attractive large home in a very desirable part of town. As a nine-year-old, I considered life in Haiger rather pleasant. Both my aunt and uncle showered me with warm-heartedness and they treated their son, Kurt, adequately well. However, I was distressed by the way they acted toward their thirteen-year-old daughter, Rut. They humiliated her before my eyes by administering physical punishment for what seemed to me minor infractions and they spoke to her in a demeaning manner.

My Aunt Hilda, whose husband, Abramam Herz, obviously wielded total authority in the home, seemed outwardly relatively happy but her expectations were probably not too lofty after having lived in the authoritarian home of her father. The otherwise gruff Abraham Herz showed very tender feelings toward his wife's aged parents. Veneration of age was probably part of his early learning. While growing up, I had the impression that elders considered respect their entitlement, unmindful of whether in earlier years they had earned this privilege by imparting the milk of human kindness to others.

Abraham's brother, Hermann Herz, was president (*parnas*) of the Jewish community in Haiger. Although the two brothers were not on speaking terms, communication existed between their wives and their children. Disagreements between the Herz brothers in Haiger probably arose because of competition in the cattle business. Because of historical and economic developments in Hesse, too many Jews competed for a piece of a pie that was inherently too small. Such a configuration tends to bring out the worst, even in brothers. Since I recall attending Sabbath services in Haiger in a prayer hall with the Herz family, this community of six families must have numbered at least the ten males required for a public service (*minyan*).

Probably an itinerant Jewish teacher instructed Rut, Kurt, and other Jewish pupils in Haiger in Hebrew and Jewish history. Customs, ceremonies, and holiday celebrations were inculcated by parents. To the best of my recollection, Rut received training in business subjects and Kurt served an apprenticeship in a commercial house. During the late 1920s, the prevailing mind-set among rural Jews in Hesse and, in particular, my Uncle Abraham, was directed toward dealing in and with real objects such as furnishings, utensils, and tools. The notion of earning a living by poring over conceptional inferences and doctrines was considered too nebulous. There were, however, rare instances of wealthy rural Jews whose children studied medicine and even chemistry at the end of the nineteenth century and the beginning of the twentieth century. For example, there were Dr. Rothschild of Alsfeld, a physician and relative of my paternal grandmother; Dr. Gustav Levi, a chemist from Alsfeld and also a relative of my paternal grandmother; and my mother's cousin, Dr. Hugo Strauss, a chemist.

In 1936, a young local boy in Haiger arrested Abraham Herz and took him to jail in Wetzlar, a larger city nearby. Kurt Herz was able to secure his father's release by pleading with the wife of the *Gauleiter* (Nazi district manager) on behalf of his father. Unlike younger Jewish males, Abraham Herz was not taken into custody during *Kristallnacht* on November 10, 1938, probably because of his age (he was sixty-three years old). Not by choice, the Herz family sold their house in Haiger with the proviso that they be permitted to continue living in their home. However, the new and suddenly malevolent owner forced the Herz family out of their home. Abraham and Hilda Herz moved to Frankfurt am Main where so many other rural Hessian Jews sought refuge from their local Nazi tormentors, and later to the United States. Nevertheless, after the end of World War II, this owner had the unmitigated effrontery to ask for written certification of his benevolence toward the Herz family. Needless to say, no letter of recommendation was forthcoming and Kurt reported the accurate account to the authorities in Germany.[1]

Kurt Herz
(married Marian Andorn)

MY COUSIN KURT HERZ, who was a carefree, lively playmate during my stay in Haiger, has a short stocky build, dark brown eyes, and black wavy hair. As a child and adult, he has had an even temperament and a character that evinces high moral qualities. In May or June of 1927, the Abraham Herz family of Haiger celebrated Kurt's *bar mitzvah* with his maternal grandparents, Hannchen and Herz Wertheim, who considered this occasion one of the loftiest moments of their lives. All of Kurt's maternal aunts, uncles and their spouses were also in attendance, but I do not know how many members of Abraham's family were present. A sister of Abraham had immigrated at an earlier time to the United States, but Hermann Herz and his family were probably present for Kurt's *bar mitzvah* despite the dissension between the Herz brothers.

Before immigrating to the United States in 1936, Kurt Herz served a commercial apprenticeship in Germany. Kurt considered himself blessed with luck when, shortly after his arrival in the United States, he located a job with Child's Restaurant as an assistant waiter. Gradually the hard-working Kurt advanced himself to higher positions in the same firm. In fact, he remained with Child's until it went out of business almost simultaneously with his retirement age. Shortly after his arrival, Kurt Herz boarded with the Hermann Levi family in Washington Heights, New York. He was motivated in part to repay his aunt and uncle, Irma and Carl Wertheim, for sending him an affidavit. He also remained close to his mother's relatives who represented a known element in a world of so many new components.

After his arrival in New York in 1936 during the depths of the Great Depression, the twenty-four-year-old Kurt made his initial and primary objective the expeditious implementation of his sister's family and his parents' departure for the United States. American newspapers reported torments and persecutions that Jews were being subjected to in Germany, and prearranged code words incorporated in letters from family members in Germany told the rest of the story.

By the time Kurt Herz served in the United States' Army in World War II, he had married Marian Andorn from Gehaus, Germany. Marian's family was related to my father's sisters, Katinka Leiser and Frieda Hammerschlag, through marriage. Kurt's wife was also the beneficiary of the Butzel inheritance that was of great advantage to his Aunt Frieda, and Willi Hammerschlag, her husband, and their family.

Marian and Kurt had two daughters, Susanne (born June 7, 1943) and Jane (born April 21, 1948). Kurt is a devoted father and husband who puts his family's welfare before all else. Having always looked after his parents, Kurt assumed even greater responsibility for his mother after his father's death. Additionally he attended to the needs of his father's sister, who by then had lost her only son and was also bereft of her husband. Marian and Kurt have three grandchildren. Michael Fruchter is the son of Susanne, and Russ and Jill Hazelcorn are Jane's offspring. Both daughters live close by their parents' residence in Riverdale, New York.

132]

Rut Herz Rosenbaum (married Max Rosenbaum)

IN 1932, RUT HERZ MARRIED MAX ROSENBAUM, a cattle dealer from Sterbfritz, near the larger town of Fulda, who was a few years her senior. In Sterbfritz, which belonged to the rabbinate of Hanau, Max had attended the Jewish congregational school where he was taught Hebrew and religion. It is presumed that Max was instructed in the cattle dealing trade by his father. In Haiger, Max Rosenbaum entered his father-in-law's cattle business and moved into the Abraham Herz residence. Most often a young man entered his father-in-law's business after marriage, and frequently parents and newlyweds shared the same household. The young couple was intended to gradually take over the larger part of the duties and responsibilities of the business and household.

Rut and Max had been married only a short time when Hitler's rise to power was formalized on January 30, 1933. The first concentration camp, Dachau, was established on March 23, 1933. On April 1, 1933, the Nazis proclaimed a general boycott of all Jewish-owned businesses and on May 10, 1933, books written by Jews and opponents of Nazism were burned. Inge, Rut and Max Rosenbaum's daughter, was born on June 17, 1934. Two weeks later, after the death of Hindenburg, Hitler became Chancellor and Commander-in-Chief of Germany's armed forces on August 2, 1934.

For a Jew in Hesse, the urgency of leaving Germany grew with each passing day. Palestine was a realistic objective only if you were a qualified capitalist or an experienced agricultural worker. Entry into the United States required an affidavit, preferably from a close relative, stipulating that the applicant would not become a public charge. Immigrants to the United States also needed to pass a rigid medical examination by the consular physician. Rut and Max Rosenbaum obtained the necessary guarantees and passed the physical in order to enter the United States. I do not know if Abraham Herz' sister or Hilda's brother, Carl Wertheim, furnished the affidavits.

In the United States in the 1930s, the chances of finding gainful employment were bleak enough for citizens who spoke English, understood American methods, and were competent in a specific craft or some highly valued skill. But the opportunity to obtain work was even more unfavorable for the newly-arrived refugee. Kurt Herz had already arrived in the United States in 1936, having been sponsored by his uncle, Carl Wertheim. His sister, Rut, and her husband, Max Rosenbaum, left their three-year-old daughter, Inge, in the care of Rut's cousin, Betty Picard, of Lausanne, Switzerland and followed Kurt two years later. Rut and Max Rosenbaum arrived in the United States by the end of 1938, and were reunited with their daughter, Inge, just prior to the United States' entrance into World War II in 1941.

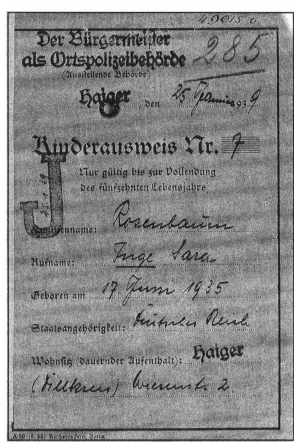

The four-year-old Inge Rosenbaum's identity paper shows the mandatory name 'Sara' which all Jewish women had to use.

Rut and Max Rosenbaum moved with their daughter, Inge, to Alexandria, Virginia, where Max started a floor-cleaning business that he later developed into a general building establishment. Max and Rut eventually changed their residence to Miami Beach, Florida, where Max died in the 1960s. Rut remained in touch with her parents and brother, Kurt Herz, but she had little contact with her aunts, uncles, and cousins. However, her cousin, Betty Picard, visited briefly with her in Miami Beach, Florida. Due to poor health, Rut was not able to be present at the funeral of either her father or her mother. By 1984, she had moved to San Rafael, California, where Inge lived, and was then looked after in a board-and-care home. My cousin, Rut's, final illness was short and immeasurably sad. Rut Herz Rosenbaum was seventy-five years old when she died in May 1986. In keeping with her wishes, her body was cremated and she was buried in Miami Beach, Florida next to her husband.[2]

Inge attended college and eventually became an eligibility worker for the county health department in San Rafael, California. During the late 1950s, she married

Chapter Eight

Donald Seabury Brower (born March 9, 1932 in New York), who is an auditor/appraiser for the state of California. Donald and Inge Brower had three children, who were born in San Rafael: Julie Hannah Brower (August 4, 1959), Anthony William Brower (December 25, 1960), and Patrick Jeff Brower (November 14, 1961). Among other favorable influences on Inge's life as an adult, the mild climate of California banished the effects of the harsh weather in Upper Hesse and the Westerwald regions of Germany. Moreover, there was apparently no lasting harm created by her separation from her parents for an extended period of time while she was quite young. Nor did the daily torments of the Nazis in Haiger, which affected her parents and grandparents, appear to have harmed Inge.

THE ARRIVAL OF HILDA AND ABRAHAM HERZ IN THE UNITED STATES

AMERICAN CONSULAR AUTHORITIES IN STUTTGART, Germany tended to embrace a milder stance on behalf of an applicant if a guarantor's affidavit was reinforced by an affidavit of newly-arrived children in the United States, even if the children were still aliens. Partly attributable to this special circumstance, Hilda and Abraham Herz, the parents of Kurt and Rut, arrived in the United States on a freighter from Spain in 1941. At that point in time, one of the few routes open for refugees from Western Europe to the Western Hemisphere was through Spain and Portugal. Francisco Franco, the Spanish dictator, although aided in his own political ambitions by Hitler and Mussolini, showed astounding forbearance toward Jewish refugees and it was rumored that on his mother's side there was a Jewish connection.

When they arrived in New York City, Abraham and Hilda Herz were sixty-six and fifty-seven-years-old, respectively. They were in good physical condition but penniless. Financial help to refugees was either unknown to members of my family or not taken advantage of if available. Moreover, the children of Hannchen and Herz Wertheim deemed financial aid by an organization as receiving charity, even if only temporarily rendered and repaid later. Their upbringing instilled the importance of giving generously to charity, but also fostered strong feelings against what they considered receiving alms.

Abraham and Hilda Herz settled in the Washington Heights section of New York, where most of their relatives lived. Abraham found odd jobs and Hilda supplemented the family income by sewing hems at home. During the early 1960s, when Abraham was in his eighties, he took ill with an incurable and painful type of cancer. He abruptly ended his life by jumping out of a window of his apartment. Probably severe pain and the prospect of long suffering moved him to knowingly destroy himself. Abraham's suicide discomfited his wife's siblings and their spouses, who deemed regard for human life (*pikkua'ah nefesh*), including one's own, as a major precept of Judaism. Abraham was not buried in a part of a cemetery reserved for people who took their own lives, as had been the prevailing custom in earlier days.

With her usual dignified and unassuming bearing, uncomplaining, and always reflecting credit upon others, my Aunt Hilda carried on life surrounded by friends and relatives. When her health deteriorated, she moved into Palisades Gardens, a German-Jewish retirement home north of New York, where Jewish holidays and dietary laws are strictly observed. My much beloved Aunt Hilda, in whose belief I could do no wrong, died September 15, 1971 at eighty-seven of a heart condition. Even during the last painful stages of her illness, she devotedly expressed gratitude for my visit.

SALLI WERTHEIM (MARRIED MINNA LÖWENTHAL)

SALLI, THE THIRD LIVING SON of Hannchen and Herz Wertheim, was born January 30, 1888 (the seventeenth day of Shevat, two days after the New Year for Trees called '*Tu bi-Shevat*'). The tallest member of the Wertheim siblings, young Salli had the stature of a tall, lanky tree. He had a light complexion, brown eyes, and wavy black hair. As a youngster he took ill with rheumatic fever that weakened his heart. Therefore, he had to repeatedly stay in a convalescent home for Jewish children in Bad Nauheim. After completing eight years at the Angenrod Jewish community school, Salli assisted in his father's cattle business. Herz Wertheim was a stern taskmaster who expected superior work, but everyone else in the family was very heedful of Salli's weakened heart.

Salli Wertheim circa 1919

Gradually, it became clear that Salli would take over his father's business, inheriting the Wertheim messuage and also the fields and meadows that had belonged to Herz Wertheim in Angenrod. Salli's older brother, Vogel (III), my father, had by marriage in 1913 to Berta Lamm, inherited a residence in Lauterbach. Vogel (III) also took over the cattle dealing business of Berta's uncle, Samuel Strauss (I) of Lauterbach. As the oldest of the Wertheim brothers, Carl would have been entitled to his parents' home and business, but he had pursued a career in textiles. Although unemployed in 1919, he did not wish to become a cattle dealer.

In Bad Nauheim in 1919, at the Hotel Flörsheim, Salli Wertheim married Minna Löwenthal from Hösbach (born September 4, 1892), whose parents were first cousins. Minna was nearly as tall as Salli but appreciably stouter. At first, the young Wertheim couple did not move into the Herz Wertheim residence, but rented rooms in a farmhouse about one city block away on the street toward Alsfeld. On August 25, 1920, Minna and Salli's winsome son, Walter Joseph, was born.

Around that time, Salli fathered another male offspring born to a non-Jewish woman of Angenrod. According to Walter Wertheim, the second child looked like Salli and these two boys sat next to each other in the Angenrod public school.[3] Somehow, Salli managed to persuade the local woodsman, Jung, by cash payment or, more likely, by transferring fields or meadows of the Herz Wertheim properties, to marry the young woman Salli had gotten with child. In due time, Salli's offspring was baptized and later became a Hitler Youth member. The Angenrod villagers were well-informed about this episode but kept it hushed up.[4]

A few months later, Minna, Salli, and Walter Joseph Wertheim moved into the Herz Wertheim residence, where they occupied the large downstairs bedroom. The interdependence, lack of privacy, differences in age, and disparity of life's objectives between parents and their married children inherently made for a living arrangement fraught with problems. Despite the near saint-like disposition of my grandmother, Hannchen, who tried to keep peace, there was constant friction between Herz Wertheim and his son, Salli.

Minna Löwenthal Wertheim
circa 1919

Margot, Salli and Minna's daughter, was born on December 19, 1921, and a second son, Carl Heinz, was born on May 5, 1926. On that day, Salli attended the annual fair in Lauterbach that had a lively trade in cattle. When my mother inquired about the due date of Minna's baby, Salli declared that his wife would be in for a hard time if this third child were not a boy. It is interesting to speculate how Salli might have reacted to the findings of some forty years later that a child's gender is determined by the father.

Walter, Margot, and Carl attended public school in Angenrod. An itinerant Hebrew teacher instructed them in religion once a week, which was supplemented by incidental learning about Judaism at home. Walter attended the *Oberrealschule* in Alsfeld in 1931 and 1932. He was an adequate student in mathematics but he had problems with French. By the time Margot was about to enter high school in Alsfeld, Jewish girls were already subjected to a more insidious and vicious anti-semitism in the Alsfeld *Oberrealschule* than was directed against Jewish boys.

Unlike his father, Herz Wertheim, Salli spent a lot of money, especially during his trips to the cattle market in Frankfurt am Main. His wife, Minna, with her frequent jaunts to the homes of other relatives, was no paradigm of frugality either. Nearly childlike, she seemed to fall short of a sense of realism. Moreover, after the inflation in Germany ended in 1923, anti-semitism increased in and around Alsfeld and many farmers were in economic straits. It became increasingly difficult for a Jewish cattle dealer in Upper Hesse to end a year with a profit.

By 1935, when the '*Juden Verboten*' ('No Jews Allowed') signs increased in number outside of the villages, Salli Wertheim's financial circumstances went from bad to worse. As a consequence, young Walter bicycled on Sundays from Angenrod to Lauterbach and back (a twenty-six mile round trip) in order to obtain money from my parents to cover weekly expenses for my grandparents and Salli's family.

Despite the ongoing generous help of my parents, by January 1936, Salli Wertheim's finances were so adverse that one of his cows had to be sold at public auction. My grandmother, Hannchen, apparently unable to endure this shame and degradation, died of shock.[5] My parents continued to support Herz Wertheim and the Salli Wertheim family until my parents departed for the United States in 1937.

In 1935, Salli Wertheim was accused of speaking offensively against Nazis and was taken to the jail in Giessen. His daughter, Margot, states that as she witnessed the arresting officer putting handcuffs on her father, she suffered her first attack of migraine headaches. During Salli's stay in prison, a relative on Hannchen's side who lived in Giessen took him food. During the trial, it was alleged that Salli's 'offense' had transpired on a bus on the Sabbath. Salli was set free because it was well-known that Jews did not travel on the Sabbath. During *Kristallnacht*, the Nazis took Salli to the Buchenwald concentration camp, where his hair was shaved off. Three weeks later he was released, and one night at 4 a.m. he returned home and knocked at his bedroom window. From the beginning of the early 1930s until his departure for Theresienstadt, Salli was the *parnas* of the Angenrod Jewish community. In Angenrod, several Jewish women, among them Minna Lowenthal Wertheim, were forced to pull wagons through the village on *Kristallnacht*. Minna's tormentor was one of the hired hands of the Wertheim house.[6]

In accordance with an official Nazi edict, Jewish children were expelled from German public schools and high schools on November 15, 1938. In Alsfeld, Angenrod, Kirtorf, and Lauterbach Jewish children were compelled to leave these institutions two years earlier. Consequently, Walter Wertheim served an apprenticeship as an electrician, Margot worked in a Jewish household in another town in Hesse, and Carl Heinz was sent to the hastily-established school for Jewish children in Bad Nauheim.

In 1939, Irma and Carl Wertheim sent an affidavit that pledged to the United States government that Minna and Salli Wertheim would not become public charges. My Aunt Irma, was not exactly a devotee of her brother-in-law, Salli, because in the past he had vexed her by mockery and derision. At the American consulate in Stuttgart, Minna was granted a visa to the United States, but Salli was not. His rheumatoid arthritis and resulting heart murmur were considered health risks for settling in the United States and becoming a public charge. Therefore, the American consular authorities wanted an extra surety bond. The amount for this bond was never raised because the newly arrived-refugee siblings of Salli had only limited liquid assets for a possible health emergency of their own. Although his sister, Frieda, and her husband, Willi Hammerschlag, had adequate funds, they were also disinclined to furnish the bond because Salli had not been a rock of trustworthiness in assuming previous financial obligations.

Moreover, in the eyes of Salli's siblings, Salli's son, young Walter Wertheim, (who was by then in New York and earning good money as an electrician), due to his spending habits, did not engender much trust in the event of a crisis resulting from Salli's precarious physical condition. Furthermore, the small income of Margot, who was working in New York as household help, was considered too inconsequential to be considered security in repaying the surety note.[7] Margot's efforts for her parents to escape to Cuba also failed.

In 1942, Salli Wertheim sent a card from Germany to his nephew, Alfred Mühlstein in Geneva, expressing his bitterness at being a scapegoat for the rest of the Wertheim family.[8] In Angenrod on November 16, 1942, Salli and Minna Wertheim and a family Speyer were picked up by truck and taken to Theresienstadt.[9] In Angenrod in May 1990, former neighbors of the Wertheims related that Minna and Salli waved to the townspeople, who watched as they were taken away. Apparently, Salli and Minna did not understand the perfidy of their Christian neighbors. In Jerusalem, their records state that they are missing and presumed dead in the east.

THE ARRIVAL OF MARGOT AND WALTER WERTHEIM IN THE UNITED STATES

IRMA AND CARL WERTHEIM SPONSORED Walter and Margot Wertheim, who arrived together in New York in 1938. Since the United States had need for electricians and household help, Walter and Margot obtained their American visas without difficulty. Walter secured a comparatively well-paying job in his field, as compared to other refugees who were not competent in an established trade. My cousin, Walter, spent his money freely—probably because, for the first time in his life, he was earning his own living and had control of his finances. His parents had borrowed from my parents, but Walter took responsibility neither for his parents' debts nor for their future well-being. Walter lived at Hermann and Martha Levi's home in Washington Heights, New York, where he paid for room-and-board.

Within a short time, Walter married Rose Fanto, a non-Jewess who was his senior by several years. His father's siblings were much distressed by what they considered Walter's lack of devotion to Judaism and by his lack of sympathetic regard for his parents, who were in such imminent danger. As time passed, Walter and Rose were accepted back into the family fold, although somewhat half-heartedly. Walter and Rose Wertheim lived for many years in Valley Stream, New York, and they remained childless. In the early 1980s, they moved to Florida, where Walter took ill with a sickness that manifests itself somewhat like muscular dystrophy and begins in later life.

Margot Wertheim (married Bert Mayer)

THROUGH HER COUSIN, KURT HERZ, Margot Wertheim, a sensible and realistic individual with prudent values, met Bert Mayer (born March 20, 1920) from Reichenbach near Darmstadt, Hesse. They were married during World War

II. At first, Bert served in a tank battalion and after a severe injury and subsequent recovery, he was transferred to an intelligence corps. Bert was easy-going and very pleasant. After the war, he operated a successful wholesale butcher business for many years while he and Margot lived in Yonkers, New York. Several years prior to Bert's death in 1984, he was ailing with a heart condition and retired from his business. After Bert's death, Margot remained in the home she had so happily shared with her husband.

Margot and Bert had two children, Linda and Scott. Scott was named after his late grandfather, Salli. Linda married Sheldon Mittelman, an electrical engineer, and they lived with their adopted daughter, Debora Rachel, in New England. In 1991, due to the recession, they moved to southern California, where Sheldon pursues his chosen career. This family remained faithful to the Jewish tenets of their fathers.

During Scott's service in the navy, he converted to Christianity. On Sunday, March 31, 1985, in San Diego, California, Scott Elliott Mayer married Tina Jean Parrish at the Clairmont Lutheran Church. The locale of Scott's wedding is incongruous. Since the end of the fifteenth century, Scott's forefathers in Germany, and particularly in Hesse, had endured endless suffering and torment attributable to the abiding influence of Luther and his church's continued condemnation of the Jews. Luther's detrimental influence definitely provided fertile soil for Nazi anti-Jewish propaganda. Unlike Catholics, Luther did not sanction any obligation to protect Jews and he retained all of the Catholic church's superstitious contempt for the Jews. Scott and Jean Mayer have two children—a son, James Elliot, and a daughter, Maryland.

Carl Heinz Wertheim (married Charlotte Bachrach)

CARL HEINZ, (who later assumed the name Charles Henry), the third and youngest child of Minna and Salli Wertheim, was much doted on by his parents and especially by his father. Similar to his older brother Walter, Charles possessed the comeliness of the Angenrod Wertheim men. He entered public school in Angenrod in 1932, a time when persecution of Jewish children by teachers and non-Jewish pupils was usual although not officially legalized until after January 30, 1933. In order for Charles to be even minimally educated, he was sent to Bad Nauheim in 1937 to the school for Jewish children. For a few months, Charles slept at the residence of his mother's uncle in the Hotel Flörsheim, and as soon as possible he joined his classmates at the Jewish boarding school until *Kristallnacht* on November 10, 1938.

Charles arose that morning to learn that only female teachers and one male teacher, who held Polish citizenship, remained at the school. All the other teachers had been taken away to concentration camps. The Nazis ordered that the student body be assembled to witness the destruction of the school's *Torahs* and Hebrew books. All the students were then given fifteen minutes to gather their possessions and march to the Bad Nauheim police station. Here they were directed to await further police instructions. After two hours, the Jewish children were told to return to their school, where the Nazis had wreaked utter havoc on the inside of the building, even damaging the water pipes.

For Charles and his fellow students, there was little choice but to go home. Near Alsfeld, a young fellow from a neighboring village boarded Charles' train, recognized him, and announced: "You are Salli's son—your father has been taken away and you are not going to see him again." As a Jew, Charles was not allowed to

Hermann Abt, the son of Joseph Abt

ride the bus in Alsfeld, and therefore the twelve-year-old walked with his small suitcase to Angenrod. At home he discovered that, in fact, his father had been taken away and his mother, Minna, had been forced to pull a wagon through the village in order for the Nazis to bestow upon her, as a Jewess, the rank of an animal. Charles also saw the inside of the Angenrod synagogue, which had been wrecked and desecrated. The elderly Joseph Abt (a member of a Jewish family that had lived in Angenrod for many genera-

tions) had been spared because he was too aged to be led away by the Nazis. He and Charles tried to clean up the synagogue and close what was left of its windows. After three weeks, Charles' anguish over his father's whereabouts was alleviated when Salli Wertheim returned to Angenrod from the Buchenwald concentration camp, with his hair shaven off.

I will never cease to marvel at the efficiency and determination with which Jews in Germany hastily organized and expedited the departure of their children despite the tremendous odds. In 1939, Charles left with a children's transport for Switzerland. Salli Wertheim escorted his thirteen-year-old son Charles to the train, because Minna Wertheim did not want to endure the pain of separation from the baby of her family in public.[10]

In Geneva, Switzerland, Charles lived in the home of Louis and Mathilde Mühlstein, where his grandfather, Herz Wertheim, also resided until his death in May 1940. To the disappointment of Louis Mühlstein, who believed profoundly in the importance of a good education, Charles was not a good student. Following his compulsory schooling, Charles worked on a farm in Switzerland. In 1946, at the age of twenty, Charles came to the United States and settled in New York. Until 1991, he worked as a butcher for Bloch and Falk, which specialized in kosher German-type sausages.

About 1950, Charles married Charlotte Bachrach (born October 8, 1931) from Kaltennordheim, Thuringia, Germany. Charlotte, a very attractive woman, was well-adjusted and rose to any occasion. Due to the outbreak of World War II in Europe, the ensuing complications of travel, and the difficulties of obtaining American visas, the eight-year-old Charlotte was separated from her parents for seven years.

From an orphanage in Frankfurt she was sent to France in 1939, where she lived in various children's homes operated by *Oeuvres de Secours aux Enfants* (Children's Welfare Organization). Because of the German occupation of France, these children were forced to go into hiding. For nearly two years, they lived in small groups in several farmhouses situated a few miles from each other. They were supervised by the same adults who had previously run the homes. Farmers in the vicinity provided food and other essentials. The children were always conscious of the fact that at any time a quisling might reveal their whereabouts to the Germans.

In April 1944, Charlotte's group, which was made up of children ranging from five to fourteen years of age, was selected to escape to Switzerland. With the help of the French underground and with the aid of an altruistic Swiss soldier on border patrol, the escape turned out well. In 1946, Charlotte was finally granted an American visa and she was able to join her parents in New York. A grandmother and grandfather of hers met death in Theresienstadt or Auschwitz, but her other grandmother survived, came to the United States, and lived to the age of eighty-nine.[11]

Charlotte and Charles Wertheim had two children: Steven Henry Wertheim (born August 18, 1951) and Maureen Lynn Wertheim (born April 23, 1955), who were named after their paternal grandparents, Salli and Minna Wertheim. As the only one of Hannchen and Herz' descendants who settled in Israel, Steven lives at *Kibbutz Kinneret* in the Galilee. In biblical days, the tribes Asher, Isaachar, Zebulun, and Naphatali dwelt in that region; the Hebrew name of Steven's great-grandfather, Herz Wertheim, was Naphtali. Steven married Adriana Silviani from Rome, Italy, and they have three children. Maureen married David Siporim and they live with their two children in Arvada, Colorado, where David is an employee of the Amoco Oil Company. In their fifties, Walter and Charles Wertheim encountered the onset of muscular dystrophy or a related disorder.

KATINKA WERTHEIM
(MARRIED LEVI
LEISER)

KATINKA, THE EIGHTH CHILD and third surviving daughter, of Hannchen and Herz Wertheim, was born August 27, 1889 (the first day of *Elul* of the Hebrew calendar, leap year 5649). She was the only one of the Wertheim sisters whose features, coloring, broad shoulders, and height bore much likeness to her father. My Aunt Katinka did not possess the earnest humility of her mother and sisters. However, during World War I, she generously opened her home to her young niece, Rut Mühlstein, lest she suffer from hunger. In later years, Katinka was more inclined to encourage generosity in others.

Until her marriage in 1912 to Levi Leiser (born January 16, 1884) of Niederurff near Kassel, Katinka remained at home assisting in her parents' household, much like her sisters had done before her. My Uncle Levi, was about five-feet eight-inches tall and of medium build. He had dark hair and light skin, and one of his eyes always seemed to turn independently of the other. As one relative said, Levi could probably see with his right eye into his left vest pocket. Much like my Aunt Katinka, Levi frequently spoke of rectitude and goodness.

Levi Leiser doubtless attended the Jewish elementary school in Zwesten, which was taught by Wolf Amram from Diemerode and by Simon Glauberg from Hochstadt.[12] As the only male sibling, my Uncle Levi took over his parents' grocery and provision store, which also stocked bedding and all manner of cloth and clothing used by the farmers in the area. In addition, the Levi Leiser family possessed a good-sized garden and some fields for growing grain. As a child, I visited them in rural Niederurff, where the family occupied two attached double houses. The grocery store was located on the lower floor of one house; the second house had several storage rooms, many bedrooms, and a privy. To my horror, under the loose wallpaper of the ceiling in the privy, rodents busily walked about in an undisturbed manner, which was not exactly an enticement for frequent visits there.

In 1925, approximately five or six Jewish families lived in Niederurff. For Sabbath services the Jews of Niederurff walked to Zwesten, where they had close social relationships with a few local Jewish families.

The first child of Katinka and Levi Leiser was a boy who lived only a short time. My Aunt Katinka attributed his death to her downhearted emotions about this unwanted pregnancy. She never absolved herself from the guilt that she believed was responsible for this child's death. Later Katinka and Levi Lesier were blessed with three daughters: Ruth (born May 30, 1914), Edith (born about 1921), and Friedel (born about 1923). For as long as I can remember, the members of this family were singularly inseparable, endlessly contending with an abundant measure of illness.

When it became increasingly difficult for Jews, especially in rural areas of Hesse, to remain in Germany after January 1933, Levi and Katinka Leiser, and their daughters, Edith and Friedel, obtained visas for the United States through an aunt and cousin of Levi Leiser and also through Katinka's brother, Carl Wertheim. In Washington Heights, New York, Levi Leiser supported his family by washing pots in a hospital kitchen, and my aunt rented out rooms in her large walk-up apartment.

Katinka and Levi Leiser carried on their lives in Washington Heights as if they were still living in Niederurff. They held fast to the same priorities of family and orthodox Judaism, in spite of financial hardships. On June 10, 1961, Levi Leiser died of cancer and was laid to rest in Cedar Park Cemetery in Paramus, New Jersey. In the course of time, my aunt moved to Palisades Gardens, New York to a German-Jewish retirement home. During a visit with her daughter, Ruth, she suffered a heart attack. My Aunt Katinka died shortly thereafter on October 28, 1973 at the age of eighty-four and was interred next to her husband.

Ruth Leiser
(married Simon Wolf
Edelman)

RUTH WAS A DARK-HAIRED, ATTRACTIVE, and rather tall individual. Even as a young girl she always walked somewhat stooped. She attended the village elementary school in Niederurff for eight years and then took some commercial training in Kassel. Subsequently, Ruth went to work for the Mühlstein brothers in Geneva. My Aunt Katinka was especially pleased that her daughter obtained work in Switzerland, ascribing this good fortune to her own acquaintance in earlier years with the Mühlstein brothers. It may be that she was not aware that the Mühlstein brothers were always looking for cheap labor,[13] especially if they could simultaneously contribute to another person's welfare.

In Geneva in about 1939, Ruth married the amiable watchmaker, Simon Wolf Edelman (born January 28, 1899 in Radzyn, Poland). Their son and only child, Henry Yves, came into the world in Geneva on May 9, 1941. Some time after the end of World War II in 1945, Ruth, Simon, and Henry immigrated to New York in order to be close to Ruth's family. Simon easily found employment as a watchmaker and Ruth worked as a saleslady in a department store in Washington Heights. In 1985, Simon died at the age of eighty-six. Henry, his wife (whose mother hails from Felsberg, a village nearby Niederurff), and his three daughters live in New Jersey, not far from Ruth's subsequent residence.

Edith Leiser
(married Benno Herz)

EDITH, THE SECOND DAUGHTER of Katinka and Levi Leiser, was a delicate-looking, very good-natured child who in earlier years seemed to suffer continuously from a distressing cough. She, too, attended the village elementary school in Niederurff, as did her attractive, much indulged younger sister, Friedel. The secular education of these two girls was interrupted after the Nazis attained power in 1933, and their formal education in Jewish history and Hebrew taught by Hermann Katzenstein came to an end on April 1, 1930.[14]

Edith, probably no more than eighteen years of age, came to the United States a brief time before the arrival of her parents and her younger sister. Edith worked as a mother's helper in New York, but after her parents' arrival she rejoined the Leiser household in Washington Heights. Shortly before the outbreak of World War II, Edith married Benno Herz from Frankfurt, who had traveled on the same ship as the Leiser family from Germany to the United States. Benno served in the American army and returned to civilian life after 1945.

Edith and Benno continued to live with Edith's parents, during which time their son, Jerry, was born. Several years later Edith took ill with influenza and shortly thereafter was diagnosed with muscular dystrophy. While valiantly battling this debilitating disease, she suffered very much and died in her early thirties in July 1953. At that time, her son, Jerry, was about five years old. Jerry's father remarried, and soon afterwards Jerry Herz went to live with his father and stepmother.

Shortly after her arrival in the United States, Friedel met and married Kurt Leopold. Like Benno Herz, Kurt Leopold also served in the United States Army. Friedel and Kurt Leopold had one son, Mark, whose mental development was retarded. In time, Mark was placed in an establishment for individuals of his maturation. Kurt took ill with a debilitating disease that prevented him from speaking, holding his head up, and performing other functions. In the summer of 1991, Kurt was hospitalized. Ruth was constantly very helpful in Friedel's life.

Chapter Eight

FRIEDA, THE NINTH CHILD of Hannchen and Herz Wertheim, was born June 12, 1893.[1] She was a very attractive and light-complected individual, with a slight build, wavy dark brown hair, and beautiful dark brown eyes. As the baby of the family, Frieda was pampered by her parents and siblings. This treatment was supported by her delicate skin and build and by the fact that she suffered from a stomach ulcer. Frieda's schooling was much like that of her older siblings. While being taught at home about domestic responsibilities, she generally assisted in the Wertheim household.

As long as Frieda was single she visited each year with her married siblings. She stayed in Lauterbach for several weeks during the very cold winter of 1914, when my sister, Erna, was born. At that time the easy-going, fun-loving Nathan Höchster courted Frieda devotedly. My mother discouraged this relationship because she was concerned whether Nathan was capable of assuming responsibility for a family. My Aunt Frieda compliantly accepted this decision; she did not act much on her own initiative, even later in her life. She relied to a large degree on my mother's counsel as long as my mother lived. Frieda punctiliously conformed to the rules of gentility, and her comportment expressed much modesty and self-effacing traits.

Frieda Wertheim
Hammerschlag circa 1922

In approximately 1920, Frieda Wertheim married Willi Hammerschlag (born October 26, 1885 in Felsberg near Kassel). At that time, after a formal betrothal, it was conventional for the engaged couple to exchange letters of love and courtship. This was considered a very private matter, yet my Aunt Frieda asked her cousin, Irma Levi, for assistance in formulating her letters of tender passion to her future husband. My Uncle Willi was a product of the Felsberg one-room Jewish elementary school, which at that time numbered approximately thirty-five children and was taught by Heinemann Neumark from Altenburg. In 1934, when I visited in Felsberg, I found that the Jews of this ancient town were generally rather prosperous. There were quite a few Jewish families in Felsberg with the name Hammerschlag. The young unmarried Hans Bodenheimer was then the spiritual leader of this orthodox Jewish congregation.

Willi Hammerschlag, like his father before him, conducted a cattle dealing business. My uncle was a light-complected, heavy-set, tall man, gifted with a droll sense of humor that rarely surfaced after the advent of Hitler. My Uncle Willi's family had lived in Felsberg for several generations and had accumulated wealth consist-

[1] After 1888, my grandfather's birth entries for his three youngest children did not indicate their birth dates based on the Hebrew calendar.

ing of fields for grain and meadows for feed. Additionally, the family received substantial financial assets from Willi's mother's sister in the United States. As was customary, my Aunt Frieda shared the home with her husband's parents and she tirelessly and gracefully took care of Willi's aged parents, who required frequent nursing care.

Meinhard Hammerschlag
(married Hilda Buchheim)

MEINHARD, FRIEDA AND WILLI'S HAMMERSCHLAG'S only child, was born April 12, 1922 in Felsberg. Except for his blond hair, Meinhard was a physical replica of his father, but he lacked his father's sense of humor and business initiative. His parents were vigilant about Meinhard's safety and well-being, most likely because they had already suffered the loss of a very young daughter. During the time of Hitler, peril laid in wait everywhere for a Jew in a small town in Hesse, which further caused Meinhard's parents to leave him little room for independence. His formal religious education was, at best, scanty, because the Jewish congregational school in Felsberg was terminated in 1931 when he was nine years old. Following other Jews from small towns or villages in Hesse, this family sold their home, fields, and meadows under duress and for considerably less than their true value. They moved to Frankfurt am Main, where Meinhard became a baker's apprentice.

Meanwhile, Willi's aunt in New York died and left a sizable share of her estate to him. It was no small feat for Uncle Carl to persuade the executors of this will to hold the Willi Hammerschlag inheritance in the United States instead of forwarding it to Germany. This stipulation qualified the Hammerschlag family to enter the United States in 1939 without an affidavit, because the immigration authorities deemed their funds an adequate guarantee that this family would not become a public charge.

The Hammerschlag family settled in Washington Heights, where their kin and friends lived. Willi and Frieda for some time performed piecework at home and Meinhard was employed as a baker. Despite their sizable inheritance, their lifestyle was simpler and more frugal than in Felsberg, where they had been affluent. The phenomenon of Hitler, with its numerous abasements, visibly took its toll on the Hammerschlag family, which was perceptibly more faint-hearted and uneasy than in their hometown.

In 1947, at the age of sixty-two, Willi Hammerschlag died suddenly of a heart attack and was laid to rest at Cedar Park Cemetery in Paramus, New Jersey. In approximately 1950, Meinhard, who continued his employment with the same baking firm, married Hilde Buchheim, who was also a refugee from the Hesse region in Germany. For some time after her marriage, Hilde worked as a beautician in Washington Heights. Vera, Hilde and Meinhard's daughter, was born February 9, 1952. The blond and comely Vera graduated from the City University of New York, majored in education, and adhered to the tenets of orthodox Judaism. Her parents were members of the orthodox Breuer congregation in Washington Heights, which is based on the teachings of Samson Raphael Hirsch (1808-1888). This rabbi's teachings had made Frankfurt am Main the center of German-Jewish orthodoxy.

My Aunt Frieda and her son and family occupied separate flats in an apartment house until she grew older and joined the household of her son. The problems associated with immediate proximity and generational differences particularly vexed and frustrated this household. Nevertheless, Frieda lacked the initiative to move to Palisades Gardens, a German-Jewish retirement home that greatly pleased her older sisters, Hilda and Katinka. Increasingly Frieda grieved for her late husband, complained of feeling useless, bereft of all her kin, and feeling that time went by too slowly. Although Frieda was considered to be of such delicate health in her youth, she would live longer than her parents and any of her siblings, some of whom struck one as being very robust. My Aunt Frieda was in good health until the last few days of her life. She died at the age of ninety-two on January 12, 1985, and was laid to rest next to her husband in Cedar Park Cemetery.

On November 19, 1972, my Aunt Frieda attended the wedding of her only granddaughter, Vera, to the accountant Milton Hamburger. Milton was one of three sons of a German-Jewish refugee family that matched the orthodoxy of the Meinhard Hammerschlag family. Having no children of their own, Milton and Vera adopted a young son and an infant daughter. Both children went through conversion in accordance with orthodox Judaism.

The marriages of the four daughters of Hannchen and Herz Wertheim were prearranged, and the brides received ample dowries consisting of generous sums of money, an extensive supply of linens, and personal and household furnishings. The four daughters settled in small towns or villages in the Hesse region, and only Katinka's husband was not a cattle dealer. All four husbands were strictly orthodox and, not unlike Hannchen and Herz, spoke some Western Hessian Yiddish. They spoke, read, and wrote fluently in German, which they considered their mother tongue. Except for Carl, who was a student at the Alsfeld high school, Hannchen and Herz' sons-in-law and daughters-in-law attended either small Jewish congregational schools or village schools. Those who came from small Jewish communities were taught Hebrew and Jewish history by an itinerant teacher. Before their marriage, a couple was carefully chaperoned; they married first and then lived together. Except for my Aunt Hilda, my father's sisters moved into the homes of their parents-in-law. As the parents-in-law grew old and feeble, it was taken for granted that their daughter-in-law would assume care for their total well-being.

The four daughters married men who were between four and nine years older than they. Carl's wife was his junior by eighteen years, my mother was eight years younger than my father, and Salli's wife was four years younger than her husband. Of the three sons of Hannchen and Herz, only Salli's marriage was prearranged. Carl followed his cousin and neighbor, Irma Levi, to the United States, where he married her. My father, Vogel Wertheim (III), married the love of his youth, Berta

Lamm, whom he had first met in the neighboring village of Kirtorf eight years earlier and with whom he had a long courtship.

Two of the fifteen grandchildren of Hannchen and Herz married non-Jews but did not convert to another religion. Out of the nineteen great-grandchildren of Hannchen and Herz, three married non-Jews. Two are somewhat mindful of Judaism and one converted to Christianity some years before his marriage to a Christian. My mother, father, his three sisters and their spouses who came to the United States were laid to rest at Cedar Park Cemetery in Paramus, New Jersey. Uncle Carl and Aunt Irma were buried in Miami Beach, Florida, and my Aunt Mathilde and her husband are buried near Geneva, Switzerland. My grandmother, Hannchen, rests in the Angenrod Jewish cemetery with her Levi forebears and her three children who died while still young.

Endnotes

1. Information obtained on June 23, 1991, in telephone conversation with Kurt Herz.

2. Information obtained from letters of June 30, 1984, and May 25, 1986, from Inge Rosenbaum Brower to Mathilda W. Stein.

3. Interview with Erna Wertheim Marx in Atlanta, Georgia, on January 18, 1991.

4. Letter from Linda Mittleman to Mathilda W. Stein, February 11, 1999.

5. Information obtained by Dr. Kenneth W. Stein from the Mühlstein family on December 30, 1979, in Geneva, Switzerland.

6. Interview with Charles Wertheim on September 13, 1989, in Spring Valley, New York.

7. Telephone conversation of Mathilda W. Stein with Margot Wertheim Mayer, January 17, 1991.

8. Interview on December 30, 1979, in Geneva, Switzerland, of Dr. Kenneth W. Stein with Alfred Mühlstein.

9. Dr. Ursula Miriam Wippich, *Memorbuch 1981/82*, p. 17.

10. Interview with Charles Wertheim in Spring Valley, New York, on September 13, 1989.

11. Information obtained from Charlotte Wertheim on November 7, 1988.

12. Paul Arnsberg, *Die jüdischen Gemeinden in Hessen, Vol II.* (Frankfurter Societäts-Druckerei, GmbH, 1971), p. 175.

13. Interview with Dr. Kenneth W. Stein with the Mühlstein siblings on December 30, 1979 in Switzerland.

14. Paul Arnsberg, *Die jüdischen Gemeinden in Hessen, Vol. 1* (Frankfurter Societäts-Druckerei, GmbH, 1971), p. 175.

Chapter Nine
History of Lauterbach
The Earliest Jewish Families in Lauterbach:
The Meyer Strauss Family
The Karl Strauss Family
The Sigmund Strauss Family

HISTORY OF
LAUTERBACH

*C*he scenic town of Lauterbach in Upper Hesse lies on the northeast slope of the hilly Vogelsberg upland, surrounded by wooded hills. In this region, the Grimm Brothers collected the background information for their generally cruel fairy tales. My Protestant teachers in the lower and upper school in Lauterbach made frequent references to Germanic forefathers, but neglected to point out that Lauterbach was founded by the Benedictines in the eighth century. From 1684 until 1806, the Barons of Riedesel were sovereigns over Lauterbach and some of its adjoining villages. During the lifetime of Martin Luther (1483-1546), the Riedesel converted to Protestantism and their subjects in Lauterbach had to convert or move. Catholics moved to Fulda, where an abbot was in charge and the adherents of Luther remained in Lauterbach. Tolerance was not known.[1] During the American War of Independence, the commanding officer of the Hessian mercenaries was a Baron von Riedesel from Lauterbach.

[149

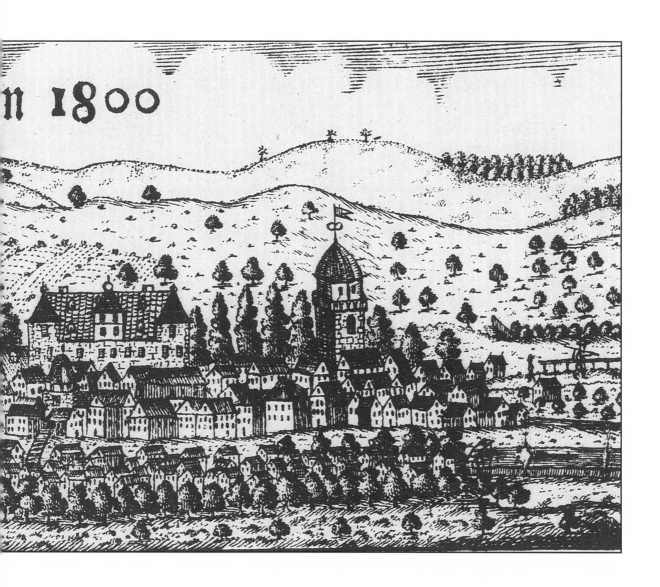

These feudal lords did not permit Jews to settle in their territory, although 'holding Jews' was a generally profitable business. However, some members of the Riedesel family had supposedly fallen victim to an immense fraud by a Jew from Frankfurt. Nevertheless, in 1571, Marshal Adolf Hermann Riedesel permitted a Jew to live in Stockhausen, but his cousins complained and brought about the Jew's departure.[2]

Jewish peddlers and traders who lived for centuries in the nearby villages of Crainfeld, Grebenau, Herbstein, Kestrich, and Storndorf conducted business in Lauterbach, where their industriousness elicited displeasure among the local merchants. Therefore, in May 1714, the sovereigns, at the direction of the merchants of Lauterbach, adopted a resolution banning Jews from any peddling and offering of wares at the annual country fairs. Violations were punished by confiscation of merchandise. For this ordinance the Lauterbach merchants paid the local sovereigns (*Zentgrafen*) a yearly fee of five *Gulden*.[3] Moreover, Jews were not allowed to enter Lauterbach before sunrise and had to leave town by sunset. So-called '*Judenpfädchen*' ('Jew paths') from Storndorf to Lauterbach were known as late as the 1920s.

In 1746, the sovereigns decreed that Jews could sell their wares at the markets, but that peddling was still forbidden. However, some exceptions were allowed. In April, 1748, at his request, the Jew Löw Gerson from Ulrichstein (the birthplace of my maternal grandmother Biena Reiss Strauss) was granted permission for a special fee to engage in peddling in Engelrod and Oberohmen.[4] In 1806, Lauterbach came under the jurisdiction of the Duchy of Hesse-Darmstadt; the Riedesel still participated in the provincial government, but these feudal lords were obliged to obey the laws of the Hessian Dukedom.

During the eighteenth century, the majority of the residents of Lauterbach were adherents of the Lutheran Church, but the town also numbered some Catholics and some members of the Reformed Church which had its ecclesiastical origin in the doctrine of Calvin. Although Jews were not permitted to reside in the town of Lauterbach, baptismal ceremonies of converting Jews to Christianity were celebrated with great flourish. During the office of Rector and Inspector Johann Daniel Bender two such baptisms took place.

On March 3, 1743, a seventeen-year-old Jew, son of Nathan and Freudge Löwe from Meiches (a village one-and-a-half miles south of Storndorf, the birthplace of my maternal grandmother, Auguste Strauss Lamm), was christened in the church in Lauterbach. The convert received the name Hermann (from the Saxon meaning 'man of the army' and a popular name with the house of Riedesel) Lauterbach. During Hermann Lauterbach's indoctrination period, barons and burghers provided him with free board and lodging. Magistrate Dr. Overlack and his assistant, Kanzau, were godfathers of the seventeen-year-old Hermann and they led him to the church. Inspector Bender preached to his assembled congregation about the word of Luther, "I love all

Jews for the sake of Christ, the Jew." Total offerings in Lauterbach and environs for the newly converted Jew amounted to seventy *Gulden*; the town itself raised twenty-six *Gulden*.[5]

About eighteen months later on October 11, 1744, a similar baptismal ceremony took place in Lauterbach. The prospective convert was Zippora ('bird' in Hebrew), a rabbi's daughter from Emden, East Friesland. The biblical Zippora, the wife of Moses, is praised for her piety, virtue, and beauty. Zippora from Emden was well educated in Hebrew, German, and French. She had learned that no Jews lived in Lauterbach, and therefore chose it for her conversion in order to avert persecution by her own people. All Riedesel ladies participated as godmothers in the baptismal ceremony. Total collections amounted to one hundred twenty-eight *Gulden* of which eighty three *Gulden* were collected separately in Lauterbach. The rabbi's daughter, Zippora, received the name 'Anna' after the wife of His Excellency, the property administrator of the house of Riedesel. She also received the name 'Christina,' as well as 'Heylin,' which means 'salvation.' Later, the new convert married the stocking weaver, Heinrich Scheffer, of Müs.[6] During the seventeenth and eighteenth centuries, more Jewish women than Jewish men converted to other religions because Jewish women felt second class and of lower rank.[7]

Although Jews were not permitted to live in Lauterbach, now and then there were contacts between Jews and the residents of the town. During January and April of 1795, imperial troops were billeted in Lauterbach. On January 20, Jews arrived as agents to purchase forage. The Jews were at variance with the citizens of Lauterbach, who asked two *Gulden* for a hundredweight of hay, while the Jews only offered 1.5 *Gulden* (one *Reichsthaler*).[8] In 1797, when a contagious disease struck the horses of Lauterbach, Jews who had contact in regions where the disease raged were dealt with outside of the city gates.[9]

The merchants of Lauterbach gave special attention to the issue of competition by Jews. In a petition during the early part of January 1823, the Lauterbach town council lodged a complaint against the nuisance of peddling by Jews that the Lauterbach merchants considered to be damaging. The townspeople were especially vexed by Clause 48 of the local by-laws that stipulated equality of Jews.[10]

In April 1898, twenty-two Jewish families in Lauterbach formed a Jewish religious community.[11] On September 8, 1900, the Lauterbach Jewish community bought the site for the Jewish cemetery in the old Leimkaute from Ferdinand Stichen-oth.[12] The date on the tombstone in Lauterbach of a Samuel Stein is November 8, 1899, which is inconsistent with the year of the acquisition of the cemetery but does not necessarily contradict it.

THE MEYER
STRAUSS FAMILY

AS LATE AS 1828, JEWS WERE NEITHER PERMITTED to reside in Lauterbach nor obtain citizenship in the town, but still Jewish dealers, traders,

The first prayer room of the fledgling Jewish community in Lauterbach by the Lauter brook from its inception until 1908, when the new synagogue was built

and peddlers who lived in nearby villages came to Lauterbach. On February 5, 1828, the Jewish merchant, Meyer Strauss from Grebenau, petitioned the Riedesel for permission to transfer his residence to Lauterbach, since by public edict door-to-door peddling was forbidden in that town. Mr. Strauss stated, "that his inventory was geared to suit his customers in Lauterbach." In answer to the petition, Georg Riedesel remarked, "that in his opinion there were compelling reasons not only to resist the settling of Jews in Lauterbach, but to engage actively in thwarting such a move." Georg Riedesel's brother-in-law, Johann Riedesel, declared that high-ranking civil servants in Darmstadt endorsed the position of the Riedesel toward Jews."

However, on August 28, 1828, Meyer Strauss was granted permission to open a store in Lauterbach, after repeated attempts and after receiving his citizenship in Grebenau. The baronial secretary, Mr. Hergert, facilitated Meyer Strauss' request. Presumably, Meyer Strauss did not write in German, because the records do not even show his signature. On August 29, 1828, in a complaint by the Lauterbach town council to the government authorities in Giessen, it was stated that admission of Jews and their accompanying corruption would undermine the integrity of local factory workers. However, Meyer Strauss' residence remained in Grebenau. Due to advanced age and poor health in July 1841, Mr. Strauss was permitted to turn over his business in Lauterbach to his son, Aron. By 1864, eleven Jews lived in Lauterbach.[13]

| THE KARL STRAUSS FAMILY | KARL STRAUSS WAS BORN AUGUST 21, 1860 in Grebenau and was of the lineage of Meyer Strauss. Karl married Therese Strauss (née Strauss and born in Storndorf on August 18, 1864). Therese, in contrast to other members of the Karl Strauss family, was of slight stature and she always looked as if she was harboring some secret sorrow. Her bearing cast an aspect of propriety without joy. Dorothee Tag in an interview in Lauterbach on July 28, 1988, referred to Therese Strauss as one of her 'good neighbors.' |

In keeping with the prevailing custom among the Jews of Upper Hesse of naming children, Karl called his oldest son 'Meyer' after his departed great-grandfather, Meyer Strauss, or his late brother, Meyer Strauss of Grebenau who died in 1881 at the age of twenty-seven. Two other children of Therese and Karl Strauss were Sara (born on October 10, 1892 in Grebenau) and Salomon [II] (born in Lauterbach on May 27, 1900).

The Karl Strauss family lived at Bahnhofstrasse 70, in a very attractive half-timbered building constructed in 1897. There was a small garden in front of the house, which in very early spring showed off the pink blossoms of a flowering almond tree. A garden behind the Strauss residence consisted of a good-sized vegetable patch and an orchard with sundry fruit trees. From January 1933 on, Jews in Lauterbach were increasingly compelled to sell their real estate and other possessions at much below market value. As a consequence, in

Lauterbach
Bahnhofstraße mit Postamt

154]

The post office of Lauterbach on the Bahnhofstrasse circa 1908

1938, Werner Opel, the owner of a local weaving-mill and father of my class-mate, Erich Opel, acquired the Karl Strauss residence at Bahnhofstrasse 70 at a cheap price.

When I knew Karl Strauss he was in his sixties and had grown hard of hearing. One was struck by his reluctant resignation at being excluded from life around him, which was dominated by the female members of the family: his wife, Therese, his daughter, Sara Strauss Spier, and his granddaughter, Ruth Gisela Spier. The Karl Strauss household also included Therese's maiden sister, the dainty, genteel, and soft-spoken Karoline Strauss, born in Storndorf on March 23, 1864. Karoline must have been well provided for financially; her bearing evinced refined upbringing transplanted into an unpredictable household. Karoline Strauss died at the age of seventy-four on January 21, 1938. She is buried in the Jewish cemetery in Lauterbach and was spared the turmoil of moving to Frankfurt am Main only to be blotted out in the east by the Nazis.

Karl's wife, Therese, and their daughter, Sara, had a small store at their residence that stocked non-perishable grocery items and Palmin, a popular kosher fat for cooking which was made of palm oil. Therese carefully observed the laws of orthodoxy as practiced by the Jews of Lauterbach. During the all-day services on the Day of Atonement (*Yom Kippur*) and the evening services on the previous night (*Kol Nidrei*), Therese and her daughter, Sara, remained standing continuously for about twelve hours.

Karl Strauss died February 8, 1937, and is buried in the Jewish cemetery in Lauterbach. On March 25, 1938, Therese, Sara, and Sara's son, Salomon (II), moved to Obere Mainanlage in Frankfurt am Main, because life in Lauterbach had grown intolerable. For the time being in Frankfurt, Jews felt comforted by the presence of other Jews.

The Way It Was: The Jewish World of Rural Hesse

Meyer Strauss

MEYER STRAUSS PURSUED A COMMERCIAL career and married the only child of a well-off banker in Kassel. For the Jewish holidays, Meyer, his wife, and their young son regularly visited at Bahnhofstrasse 70. Therese adored her oldest son and his family. Outstanding characteristics of Meyer's wife were her sympathetic interest in the portion of others and her treatment of children as equals. Meyer, his wife, and son perished in the Holocaust.

Sara Strauss Spier
(married Moritz Spier)

THE KARL STRAUSS HOUSEHOLD also included the widowed Sara Strauss Spier and her daughter, Ruth Gisela Spier, born on February 21, 1914 in Einbeck. Sara's late husband and Ruth's father, Moritz Spier, (according to his tombstone in the Lauterbach Jewish cemetery) was born in Momberg on October 25, 1886 and died on May 6, 1917, in the military hospital in Paderborn while serving his country in World War I. Moritz Spier may have been a public school teacher or he may have been employed by the Einbeck Jewish community.

The German government paid a monthly pension to Moritz' war widow and his daughter, who was also entitled to a free high school, college, and professional school education. Sara lavished much love on her only child, Ruth, who successfully completed high school in Lauterbach and Alsfeld, and to the best of my knowledge achieved her medical education in Germany on the strength of the prevailing statutes for the benefit of children of war veterans. Later on, the Nazis canceled this provision of the law for Jews.

Sara Strauss Spier and my mother remained close friends from the time my mother arrived in Lauterbach until the dispersion and deaths of the Jews of Lauterbach in the 1930s and 1940s. Moreover, Sara's daughter, Ruth, and my sister, Erna, were schoolmates in Lauterbach. According to my mother, because of the loss of her husband, Sara was easily frightened and depended on her mother, Therese, to lighten her burden as an adult. Salomon Strauss (I) saved his life by fleeing to England, but Therese and Sara Strauss could not effect their escape. Therese died in Theresienstadt and it is not known where the Nazis liquidated Sara. Ruth Gisela Spier fled to the United States with her husband, whom she later divorced. Ruth married a Dr. Levenbook with whom she had a daughter and a son. They lived in Brooklyn, New York, where Ruth practiced medicine for many years.

THE SIGMUND
STRAUSS FAMILY

SIGMUND STRAUSS WAS BORN on August 17, 1856. His wife, Settchen Flörsheim Strauss, was born on June 8, 1857 in Romrod. The surname 'Flörsheim' indicates that this family hailed from Flörsheim, a town near Frankfurt am Main. Settchen's parents were Isaac Flörsheim (II) (born September 20, 1822 in Romrod) and Janette Levi Flörsheim (born 1826 in Angenrod). The marriage license for Isaak (II) and Janette Levi Flörsheim states that no barrier for the union existed and that the ceremony was executed in accordance with the Israelite rites in the presence of the witnesses, Isaac Meyer of Romrod and the teacher, Mr. Meyer Bamberger of Angenrod.

Chapter Nine

Sigmund Strauss of
Lauterbach circa 1922

Isaak (II) and Janette Flörsheim died in Romrod on July 11, 1895 and on April 24, 1872, respectively, and are buried in the Jewish cemetery in Angenrod. Isaak Flörsheim's father, Michael Flörsheim, was born in 1793 in Fürth, Germany. His mother, Hendel Geiss Flörsheim, came into the world in Rhina (a district of Kassel) in 1795. Both parents died in Romrod: Michael on March 19, 1875 and Hendel Geiss Flörsheim on June 11, 1868 or 1869. Michael Flörsheim sent his brother Isaac, his wife, and nine children with a one-way ticket to Philadelphia in the United States, where Isaac Flörsheim founded the Flörsheim Shoe Factory.[14] In 1832, an Isaac Flörsheim (I) of Romrod (although probably there were several by that name) married Frederika Stieler, a non-Jew. This was an uncommon phenomenon in that region during that era.[15]

In Lauterbach, Settchen and Sigmund Strauss owned a half-timbered building at Hintergasse 12, where steps of stone from two sides led to a handsomely-carved old entrance door. One of the front windows of this house gave the appearance of a small store shop window without display in a room that in reality was a small grocer's shop with a dark wooden counter. It was from this room that members of the Sigmund Strauss family fetched one or two pieces of cube sugar for young visitors. Opposite this small store was what the Strauss family called the office (*Kontor*). Sigmund Strauss sold animal feed and flour to farmers in the area. This family's home at Hintergasse 12 had only limited storage facilities for their products. Therefore, they owned or leased a storehouse close by their home. In 1988, that street was renamed Landknechtsweg. The living room of the home was toward the back of the house, where a door led to a pleasant garden area.

At the dedication of the Lauterbach synagogue on August 14, 1908, Sigmund Strauss was president of the Lauterbach Jewish congregation. His signature appears on the synagogue architectural plans submitted by the architect, Mr. Reuter, and again on a document of October 20, 1911, pertaining to the hook-up of the synagogue to the Lauterbach town drainage system. In each case, Sigmund Strauss signed in the name of the Lauterbach Jewish congregation. The portly Sigmund Strauss possessed a dignified bearing and commanded respect. He was much admired by his family and highly thought of by members of the Jewish community. Toward the end of his life, Sigmund took ill with diabetes. His devoted family nursed him until his death at the age of seventy-eight on September 17, 1934. Sigmund is buried in the Lauterbach Jewish cemetery.

Settchen Flörsheim Strauss was a well-bred, warm, engaging individual who, at each meeting with her cousin, Hannchen Levi Wertheim, my paternal grandmother, took delight in their harmonious fellowship and devotion to each other. Settchen followed the rule of her era that women be well-rounded physically, and once remarked to my mother: "Berta, did you ever hear anyone refer to a slender woman as being attractive?" Settchen, like her husband, was deemed an especially faithful pillar of the Lauterbach Jewish community. She always showed great kindness toward children. Settchen died from a stroke on August 10, 1927, and is buried in the Lauterbach Jewish cemetery.

[157

THE CHILDREN OF SIGMUND AND SETTCHEN STRAUSS

SIGMUND AND SETTCHEN STRAUSS were the parents of four daughters: Jenny, Therese, Hedwig (born in 1890), and Anna Sara (born in 1892).

Anna Sara Strauss

ANNA SARA, THE FOURTH AND LAST daughter of Sigmund and Settchen Strauss, died in September 1892 when she was approximately one month old. I would surmise that Settchen and Sigmund gave their youngest daughter the name Sara after she took gravely ill. This custom was observed by some Jewish families at a time of grave illness in order to bewilder the Angel of Death.

Jenny Strauss (married Adolf Haas)

JENNY, THE ELDEST DAUGHTER of Sigmund and Settchen Strauss, married Adolf Haas and this family lived with their two sons, Kurt and Richard, in Frankfurt am Main. The two generations of the Haas family visited often in Lauterbach. With the advent of Hitler, the Haas family escaped to London, England, where Jenny and Adolf Haas remained until their deaths.

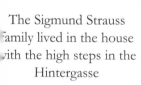

The Sigmund Strauss family lived in the house with the high steps in the Hintergasse

Chapter Nine

THERESE, THE SECOND DAUGHTER of Sigmund and Settchen Struass, (also called 'Resel'), was an individual with extraordinarily attractive features

158]

Left to right:
Hans Ehrman, Richard Ehrman, Hedwig Strauss Westerfeld, Therese Strauss Ehrman, Settchen Flörsheim Strauss, Jenny Haas, Adolf Haas, Richard Haas, Kurt Haas The group is at Bad Salzschlirf.

and down-home qualities, and was very well liked by all. On August 14, 1908, she was the only female participant of the official dedication of the Lauterbach synagogue on Hinter der Burg 17. The following evening, in a play celebrating the dedication of the synagogue, she played the part of Nettchen in a one-act comedy.[16] Therese married Sol Ehrman from Altenstadt in Upper Hesse, where most Jews hailed from Spain, France, and the Rhine region. Until the nineteenth century, the ancestors of the Ehrman family lived at Ronneburg near Altwiedermus where they served as treasurers for the local feudal lords.[17]

Sol and Therese Ehrman and their sons, Richard and John, lived in Frankfurt am Main. This family, and especially the children, spent some of their vacation time in Lauterbach, where they mingled in sports activities and social gatherings with their contemporaries in the Jewish community. Richard Ehrman obtained a doctorate in economics before he fled to the United States, where in the 1930s his parents and his brother, John, would also find refuge from Nazi persecution. Resel died in the early 1970s. Sol had already preceded her in death.

HEDWIG (BORN OCTOBER 18, 1890 IN LAUTERBACH), the third daughter of Settchen and Sigmund Strauss, in contrast to her two older sisters, Jenny and Therese (Resel), remained with her parents. In the 1920s and earlier, it was customary among Jewish and non-Jewish families of the Vogelsberg region for young married couples to join the household of their parents, and frequently three generations lived in one home.[a]

Hedwig Strauss was thirty years old when, on June 14, 1920, she wedded Hugo Friedrich Westerfeld (born October 5, 1888 in the Stockstadt district of Gross

---

[a] Among the Jews of Lauterbach, the only elderly parent with a married child in town who lived by herself was Mrs. Emma Rothschild, mother of Meta Rothschild Reiss.

Gerau in the governmental province of Darmstadt). In the eighteenth, nineteenth, and the beginning of the twentieth centuries, Stockstadt housed only a few Jewish families. Generally, members of the Lauterbach Jewish congregation took a dim view of someone who hailed from a Jewish community with only a few members, because they feared that at best such a person's knowledge of and loyalty to Judaism must be shallow. Nevertheless, Hugo Westerfeld with his humble, reserved, task-oriented manner, and decent traits gained much respect.

[159

Hugo Westerfeld was a tall, physically strong individual, and a hard, indefatigable worker in the Strauss feed-and-flour business. He carried heavy sacks of feed on his back or moved bags on a wheelbarrow to and from the business' storehouse at the Landknechtsweg to Hintergasse 12. During Hugo Westerfeld's time, farmers came to the store from all over the Vogelsberg region including Rudlos and Hopfmannsfeld. Other customers included the superintendents of the Riedesel estates at various locations in the vicinity of Lauterbach.

Hedwig Strauss Westerfeld was not as tall and as rounded as her sisters and, by the then existing standards of beauty, may not have been considered as attractive as her sisters, Jenny and Resel. Hedwig was invested with a singular sense of seemliness and decency, and even during that era, her tender devotion to her parents was considered to be exceptional. She considered the care of her family and the ad-

Map of Lauterbach

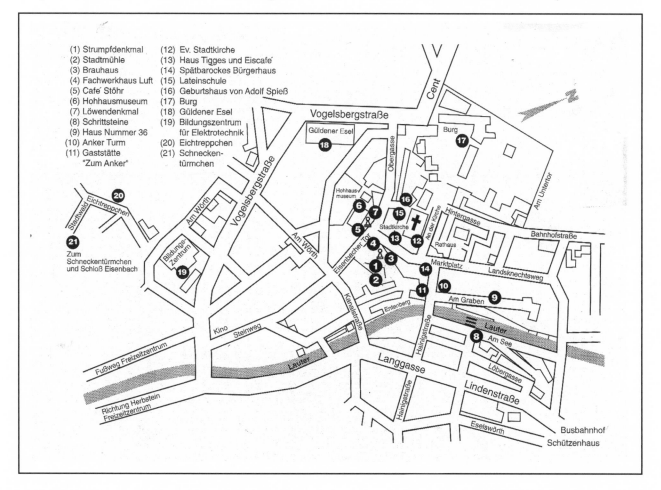

Hugo and Hedwig
Strauss Westerfeld,
April 8, 1955 in
Uruguay

vancement of her husband's business her primary duties. She probably did not socialize as much as other members of the Jewish community and did not participate in gossip.

Hedwig Westerfeld was a very hard-working individual, which is confirmed by Kätchen List from Frischborn, who worked for over two years for the Westerfeld family beginning in 1925. The former maid stated that Mrs. Westerfeld worked right along with her. To the best of Kätchen's recollection, the Westerfeld family had no parties and did not even go for a walk on the Sabbath. Also on the Sabbath, the maid, Kätchen, receipted the bills because the members of this family did not violate the Sabbath by writing. Kätchen considered the meals at the Westerfeld home unequaled, but made much of the hard work connected with Passover.[18]

On July 15, 1921, the twin children, Liesel and Ernst, were born to Hedwig and Hugo Westerfeld. I can recall Liesel's blond, slightly curly hair and her somewhat hoarse voice. Ernst was more delicate-looking and I can remember seeing them together in a perambulator. Liesel died at age three in Frankfurt am Main of a disease related to her throat and is buried in the Jewish cemetery in Frankfurt. Twice, after Liesel's death, in quick succession, members of this family came down with scarlet fever. At that time, this disease required an extended period of rigid isolation followed by sulfur fumigation of the home which the local health authorities carried out.

On March 13, 1926, Paul Meyer Westerfeld was born. From the beginning, his sunny, friendly temperament, beautiful lightly-curled hair, and pleasing features evoked fondness. In 1935, Paul was one of forty-five pupils at the Lauterbach public school at the *Goldene Esel* where, among the twenty-three boys, only Julius Baumann, Herbert Stern, Norbert Weinberg, and Paul Westerfeld were Jewish. Rita Jakob was the only Jewish girl among twenty-four non-Jewish girls. The four Jewish male pupils and Rita Jakob survived the Holocaust, while ten non-Jewish male students of this class died in World War II.

In 1934, Hugo Westerfeld threw water and bottles from a bedroom window at Nazis who were making a din in front of his residence. I do not know the details of his sentence by the Nazis. As a consequence of these events, and because young Ernst was forbidden to attend the *Realschule* (high school) in Lauterbach, the Westerfeld family moved, on June 29, 1936, to Bornheimerlandstrasse 55 II in Frankfurt am Main, where Ernst and Paul attended the *Philantropin*. This institution was originally intended for the education, board, and lodging of Jewish orphans. Later, it became an educational establishment for Jewish children after their exclusion from German educational facilities by the Nazis.

In 1936, before moving to Frankfurt, Hugo Westerfeld offered his household furniture without cost to their former household help, Kätchen List from Frischborn. She refused the furniture stating that she had no room. However, she named a prospect in Lauterbach who would accept furniture without cost. However, that person also rejected furniture from a Jewish household. According to Kätchen, at that time it was already dangerous to accept furniture from Jews, especially in Frischborn.[19]

During a general strike in Palestine in 1936 that evolved into outbreaks of violence, Hugo Westerfeld visited Palestine to explore the possibility of his family's immigration to that country. On the train from Frankfurt to Genoa, a German-Jewish family by the name of Speyer that was immigrating to Uruguay befriended him. The Speyers suggested that if the Westerfeld family encountered too many obstacles in immigrating to Palestine, they should contact them as an alternative for the purpose of going to Uruguay. The Westerfeld family did not wish to exchange one battleground with neighbors in Germany for another in Palestine, and therefore contacted Mr. Speyer to begin immigration proceedings to Uruguay.

In May 1937, the Westerfeld family, their furniture, household utensils, and equipment for opening a commercial laundry arrived in Uruguay. They also brought with them three *Torah* scrolls for the Jewish community in Uruguay, where Mr. Speyer was president. The *Torah* scrolls were probably from Lauterbach, where (to the best of my recollection) the congregation possessed at least five scrolls. Once Max Stern, the teacher, envisioned no hope for Jews to remain in Lauterbach or in Germany and practice their religion, he encouraged that some *Torahs* from Lauterbach be taken out of Germany.[20] This determination was in certain respects comparable to the decision of the Jewish elders of Danzig, who in the spring of 1939, with the assistance of the Joint Distribution Committee, shipped their most valued religious items to the Theological Seminary of America in New York.

In their new home in Montevideo, Uruguay, Hedwig and Hugo Westerfeld worked from sunrise to late at night in their commercial laundry. Their son, Ernst, studied to become a radio technician. In 1945, the Westerfelds bought their own home and in 1947 they purchased an apartment house with seven units. Unfortunately, that same year Ernst died of cancer at the age of twenty-six. In 1948, Hedwig Westerfeld traveled to New York to meet with her sister, Jenny Haas, from London and to visit her sister, Resel Ehrman. That was the first and only time the daughters of Settchen and Sigmund Strauss of Lauterbach saw each other after their immigration from Germany that had scattered them over three continents. In 1948, my parents visited with the three Strauss sisters in New York.

In 1953, Hugo Westerfeld suffered a heart attack and shortly thereafter turned his business over to his son, Paul. From that time on, Hugo pursued his hobby of collecting stamps and Hedwig became treasurer of WIZO (Women's International Zionist Organization). For the next twenty years, this couple was blessed with a good life. In

1974, after only four days of illness Hugo Westerfeld died at the age of eighty-six. Hedwig died in 1984 at the age of ninety-four, but during the last three years of her life she only recognized her son, Paul.

In 1954, Paul married a local girl who converted to Judaism; the wedding ceremony was performed by Rabbi Dr. Pinkus in São Paulo, because the local strictly orthodox rabbi in Montevideo refused to sanction the marriage. There are three sons of this union: Gustavo, Gabriel, and Fabian. In 1987, when Paul was sixty-one years old, his business celebrated its fiftieth anniversary. That same year, Paul visited Lauterbach for the first time, a visit that touched him deeply. In 1988, on the fiftieth anniversary of *Kristallnacht*, Kätchen List from Frischborn, the former household help in the Westerfeld home in Lauterbach reflected that after 1939 she knew nothing about the fate of the Jews in Lauterbach. However, she indicated that after the outbreak of World War II in Germany in 1939 she came to understand that the Westerfeld family had taken off in time before the war.[21] In the words of Richard Ehrman, Settchen and Sigmund Strauss' grandson: "Yesterday is not yet done with." This comment emphasizes that the past, in connection with the Holocaust, has yet to be resolved (*Vergangenheitsbewätigung*).

Endnotes

1. Lauterbach und Umgebung, *Herausgegeben vom Verkehrsverein Lauterbach 1913,* p. 17.

2. Dr. Eduard Edwin Becker, *Heimatblätter für den Kreis Lauterbach*, April 20, 1940.

3. Dr. Karl Siegmar Baron von Galera, *Lauterbach in Hessen II*, Neustadt an der Aisch: Verlag Degener and Company, 1965), p. 114.

4. Ibid, p. 115.

5. Ibid, p. 125.

6. Becker, *Heimatblätter für den Kreis Lauterbach*, October 15, 1932.

7. Dr. Ellen Umansky, "Women in Jewish Tradition," *Atlanta Jewish Times*, October 16, 1987.

8. von Galera, *Lauterbach in Hessen II*, p. 222.

9. Ibid, p. 228.

10. Ibid, Vol. III, p. 20.

11. *Lauterbacher Anzeiger*, September 7, 1984.

12. Letter from Mr. Gliss of Lauterbach of October 13, 1983.

13. Becker, *Heimatblätter für den Kreis Lauterbach*, April 20, 1940.

14. Letter of June 24, 1972, by John Ehrman of New York, New York, to Ludwig Flörsheim of Atlanta, Georgia.

15. Dr. Ursula Wippich, *Memorbuch, 1981/82*, p. 131.

16. *Lauterbacher Anzeiger*, August 15, 1908.

17. Paul Arnsberg, *Die jüdischen Gemeinden in Hessen, Vol. 1* (Frankfurter Societäts-Druckerei, GmbH), pp. 36-37.

18. *Lauterbacher Anzeiger*, November 10, 1988.

19. Ibid.

20. Interview with Dr. Naphtali Stern of Bar-Ilan University on January 28, 1988, in Atlanta, Georgia.

21. *Lauterbacher Anzeiger*, November 10, 1988.

Chapter Ten
Social Environment in Angenrod and Lauterbach,
1883-1933
Vogel Wertheim (999) and his Marriage
to Berta Lamm

Toward the Cent in Lauterbach

THE SOCIAL ENVIRONMENT IN ANGENROD AND LAUTERBACH, 1883-1933

Upper right:
Advertisement by Aron Stein in 1913 Tourist Information Booklet for 'Bleyle Boy's' suits

Lower left:
Advertisement of the Joseph Herz Bank on July 7, 1908 in the *Lauterbacher Anzeiger*

*I*n the fall of 1879, the term 'anti-semitism' was introduced in Germany by Wilhelm Marr (1818-1904), whose anti-Jewry crusade developed into a social-political movement. Marr replaced the religious issues against the Jews with racism; the terms 'Jew' and 'Judaism' by 'Semite' and 'Semitism.' Both these words—with the prefix 'anti' attached—attained common acceptance. In 1883, when my father was born, Richard Wagner (1813-1883), a German composer, titan of music, and anti-semitic writer died. He considered Jews villains who were causing mankind's downfall. Not only did his writings make anti-semitism culturally respectable in Germany, but his influence on Hitler was indelible.

In Upper Hesse, in 1913, the occupations of Jews were mostly limited to cattle dealing, butchering, and door-to-door peddling. However, there were some exceptions. The Lauterbach Tourist Information booklet of 1913 contained an advertisement by Aron Stein, one of the founders of the Lauterbach Jewish congregation, heralding 'Bleyle's Outfits' for boys and men, calling attention to the store's ready-made and fashionable articles, trousseau items, workmen's clothing and fine custom-made tailoring on site. Moreover, Sigmund Strauss sold insurance, groceries, seeds, and fertilizer from his shop in the Hintergasse. His clientele for seed and fertilizer even included the administrators of the Riedesel manors.

A striking departure from the common occupations of Lauterbach Jews was the Jewish banking house of Joseph Herz from Giessen, which established a branch office in Lauterbach. On July 7, 1908, this banking house, located at Bahnhofstrasse 5 in Lauterbach, advertised in the *Lauterbacher Anzeiger* regarding the investment of capital in German government bonds. On October 3 of the same year, this banking house advertised a variety of services: buying and selling of securities, redemption of coupons, procurement of new coupon sheets, redemption of domestic and foreign checks, safekeeping and management of securities and rental of safes in the fireproof and tamperproof money vault in Giessen.

In Upper Hesse, Jews were informally excluded from careers in education, the civil service, and the military. In addition, unofficial restrictive covenants also made it uncommon to find a Jewish doctor, lawyer, or architect in the region. Countries with democratic revolutions similar to the Netherlands in 1581, England in 1681,

Chapter Ten

the United States in 1776, and France in 1789, emancipated their Jews during or shortly after these epic events. However, *de facto* integration was not a reality in Germany and particularly not in Upper Hesse and Lauterbach. Until the official advent of Hitler on January 30, 1933, the upper-middle and lower classes of Lauterbach citizens rarely suffered themselves to extend any greater accommodation to a Jew other than a polite greeting in the street. There certainly was no visiting between Jews and non-Jews in each other's homes.

By 1913, the year my father moved to Lauterbach, the atmosphere of xenophobia became charged with a more aggressive organized spirit. In 1912, a local group called the '*Jungdeutschlandbund*'[a] (Young German Brotherhood) was founded.

German Empire, 1871-1918

Its aim was to inculcate fourteen to twenty-year-olds with pre-military experience. In the middle of 1914, there were one hundred members of the *Jungdeutschlandbund* in Lauterbach.[1] This group received its training on Sundays through maneuvers under the aegis of non-commissioned and commissioned army officers. The xenophobic, nationalistic *Jungdeutschlandbund* strongly influenced others in my native town and widely spread the notion that anti-semitism was part of patriotism. During my years in Lauterbach (1915-1934), this belief pervaded every circumstance of my life. However, because economic conditions were generally better in the years leading up to World War I, there was less

[a] Also known as the League for the Promotion of German Chauvinism.

scapegoating against Jews. My parents accepted anti-semitism as part of their everyday lives.

From 1906 to 1933, the social life of the members of the Lauterbach Jewish congregation met the needs of all its members. Hence no Jew was interested in belonging to a Lauterbach social club called the '*Kasinogesellschaft*.' This social club, which was composed of non-Jewish lawyers, rich manufacturers, merchants, teachers, and members of the bureaucracy, openly—as well as behind-the-scenes—directed the affairs of the town. The *Kasinogesellschaft* influenced every political, social, and economic decision in town.[2] Members of this club did not consider any Jew in town adequately enlightened, refined, and sufficiently well-bred to join their ranks. Further, many of the *Kasinogesellschaft* members were also members of the *Jungdeutschlandbund* or had an adherent of this group in their immediate family.

Nevertheless, I yearned to play on the lodge's tennis court, the only one in town, which was used by my non-Jewish schoolmates whose parents were members there. Moreover, ninety-eight percent of the Lauterbach Jews were orthodox and strictly observed the dietary laws (*kashrut*), so they could not dine with non-Jews, whose chief meat course was pork. Also, orthodox Jews were not permitted to drink wine that had been prepared by gentiles, although drinking of whiskey and beer prepared by gentiles was permitted.

Before World War I, and despite the threats and activities of the rabid anti-semites Stöcker and Böckel, Jews whose forebears had lived in Upper Hesse for centuries felt less burdened and less restricted than their forefathers in earlier days. Nevertheless, most Jews in Lauterbach lived in very modest circumstances. In Lauterbach, Jewish families expended little or no funds for alcoholic drinks that often impoverished non-Jewish families and seemingly managed their wherewithal better. Frequently, members of poor non-Jewish families performed in the Jewish homes the functions orthodox Jews were not allowed to discharge on Sabbath and holidays, such as stoking the fire and in some cases turning the lights on and off. Although Jewish families scrimped all week to be able to afford their Sabbath and holiday meals, non-Jews perceived these meals as daily fare in Jewish households and cast covetous glances. Until World War I, the Jews of Lauterbach, including my father, made remarkable cultural, intellectual, and financial strides. This fact is especially impressive because the Jews of Lauterbach, without exception, had hailed from rural environments and settled amidst mostly narrow-minded townsmen.

VOGEL WERTHEIM (III), HIS FAMILY, AND MARRIAGE TO BERTA LAMM

VOGEL WERTHEIM (III), MY FATHER, was born at 11:30 p.m. on October 4, 1883 in his parents' house in Angenrod, where he would live for the next thirty years. Herz and Hannchen named their fourth child after Herz' oldest brother, Vogel (II), who had died very young. My father's Hebrew date of birth was the

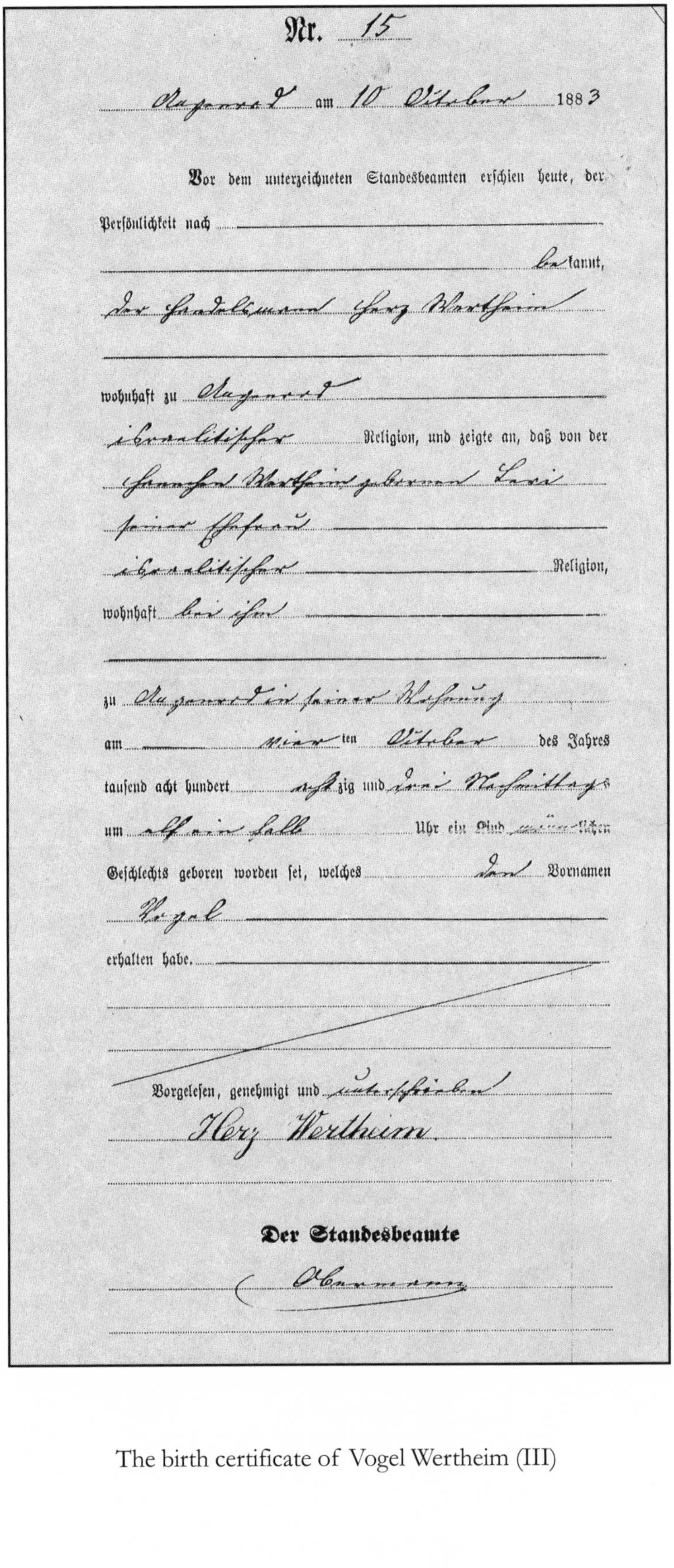

Nr. *15*

Regnrod am *10 Oktober* 188*3*

Vor dem unterzeichneten Standesbeamten erschien heute, der
Persönlichkeit nach _____
_____ be kannt,

Der Handelsmann Herz Wertheim _____

_____

wohnhaft zu *Regnrod* _____

israelitischer _____ Religion, und zeigte an, daß von der

Hannchen Wertheim geborene Levi

seiner Ehefrau

israelitischer _____ Religion,

wohnhaft *bei ihr* _____

_____

zu *Regnrod in seiner Wohnung*

am _____ *vier* ten *Oktober* des Jahres

tausend acht hundert *acht* zig und *drei Nachmittags*

um *ein halb* Uhr ein Kind *weiblichen*

Geschlechts geboren worden sei, welches *den* Vornamen

Vogel _____

erhalten habe. _____

_____

Vorgelesen, genehmigt und *unterschrieben*

Herz Wertheim

Der Standesbeamte

Obermann

The birth certificate of Vogel Wertheim (III)

third of *Tishri* (5644), a sad day in Jewish history. This fast day marks the murder of Gedaliah of Mizpah, governor of Judea. The Babylonians had appointed Gedaliah after the capture of Jerusalem in 586 B.C.E. (Before Common Era). After governing for only a short time, he and his associates were murdered during the days of the prophet Jeremiah.

My father was five-feet seven-inches tall and had a medium build. His shiny dark brown hair was slightly wavy; his complexion was light and his eyes nut-brown; his well-shaped features exuded candor, compassion, and sincerity.

My paternal grandfather was a rigid disciplinarian with his older children, but later he yielded to somewhat gentler treatment of his younger offspring, especially his daughters. My grandmother, although not openly disagreeing with her husband's stern measures, tried to mitigate his harsh treatment of children and servants. My father's character and disposition were much like my grandmother's and, until the Nazi revolution, his emotional tone and perspective were optimistic and untroubled. Although my father would hardly have won a prize for flawlessly carrying a melody, until the advent of Hitler he habitually sang to himself with lightness of heart and love of gaiety. One of his favorite songs was, *Ich bin der Doktor Eisenbarth, kurier die Leut auf meine Art* ('I am Dr. Eisenbarth and I cure people in my own way').[b]

During the Nazi period some of my father's former friends and neighbors changed overnight into his enemies, following the unjust accusation that he had tortured an animal and subsequent sentence of a year in prison. He courageously appealed this sentence, which was changed to appearing daily for four weeks before the local court officer. He never quite recaptured his earlier bright outlook of the human condition, even after his immigration to the United States. By then my father, who had earlier experienced each event of his life with great joy and gratitude as a special gift from his God, manifested dejection and disheartenment in his facial expression. However, his trust in his Creator seemingly did not waver, and to the end he maintained his belief that his cup was always half full rather than half empty.

Like his mother, my father possessed a patrician dignity. Both got along splendidly with people of all ages, social classes, and divergent religions. Both were slow to anger, and my father had a keen sense of humor that endeared him to all. His regard for and devotion to the interests of others were uncommon. Probably his greatest strength was his resourceful perseverance in steering a middle course of compromise in personal and business matters, and he manifested the meaning of his Hebrew name ('God is healing'). With heart and soul, and regardless of his own financial status, Vogel Wertheim (III) practiced philanthropy and openhandedness, even to a fault.

---

[b] Dr. Johann Andreas Eisenbarth (1661-1727) was born in Oberviechtach, Bavaria. He was reputed to be a healer who employed drastic remedies. However, research findings have lately indicated that Dr. Eisenbarth was a gifted surgeon with skills far in advance of his time. He was also a smart businessman. The Dr. Eisenbarth ditty was popular in Germany around the turn of the nineteenth century.

To my knowledge, my father was the only orthodox Jew among friends and relatives who championed women's liberation some fifty years before this movement gained a strong foothold in our country. Insightfully, he discerned that most orthodox women were disadvantaged by existing mores. My father imposed additional tasks on himself in order to ease the life of his mother, wife, and daughters.

He recounted that, as a young child during the harsh winters in Angenrod, he had shared a bed with three siblings in order to conserve warmth. At that time the upper floor of the Herz Wertheim residence had no heat. Because he and his siblings each possessed only one pair of leather boots each, in the winter each child washed and oiled his boots on Fridays before Sabbath as a protection against wetness and mud. He related that the Wertheim siblings were taught to lend a hand in caring for the younger children in order to lighten their mother's work load. Typical of their era and milieu, the Wertheim siblings were brought up with the expectation that children had the duty to ease the lives of their parents.

Unlike his older brother, Carl Wertheim, my father was not given the option by his parents to attend the high school (*Oberrealschule*) in Alsfeld, which had opened on January 7, 1861. My paternal grandparents probably arrived at this decision in 1890, when the voting district of Alsfeld-Lauterbach elected the anti-semitic candidate, Oswald Zimmermann, to the German Parliament.[3] In 1893, the year of my father's expected entry into high school, seventeen anti-semitic candidates were seated in the German Parliament. This situation doubtless emboldened local anti-semites in Alsfeld and dissuaded my grandparents from sending their son, Vogel (III), to school in Alsfeld.[c]

For as long as I can recall, the town and citizens of Alsfeld were deemed the stronghold of anti-semitism and Nazism among the Jews in the Vogelsberg region. Jewish children from Alsfeld frequently suffered at the hands of their classmates, but the Jewish children who entered high school from nearby villages and towns were even more ridiculed and were frequently slapped. High school teachers, who must have been aware of these confrontations, looked the other way and thereby tacitly agreed with the tormentors by not taking them to task. My grandmother, who was not given to hyperbole, felt that several teachers in the Alsfeld high school were also disposed to assigning lower grades to Jewish children than to others.

---

[c] After the emancipation of Jews in German lands (1833-1871), Jews generally made considerably more use of the facilities for higher education than their Christian neighbors. For instance, from 1816 to 1900 in nearby Fulda, the number of Jewish high school students rose substantially in schools that taught Latin, Greek, and Hebrew and in high schools with a curriculum of higher mathematics, French, and English. Toward the end of the 1880s, twenty-five percent of the high school students in Fulda were from Jewish homes, and in 1900 nearly one-third came from Jewish homes. A majority of the Jewish students were from nearby rural communities; they boarded in Fulda and frequently endured substandard living conditions. (Renate Chotjewitz-Häfner and Peter Chotjewitz, *Die Juden von Rhina, 1978* [Oberellenbach: Verlag Geisteswissenschaftliche Dokumentation, 1988], p. 22.) One of the nearby Jewish communities was Eiterfeld, where my paternal great-grandmother, Sara Tannenbaum Wertheim, was born in 1821. At the time, of her wedding on February 17, 1847, she was unable to write and thus marked three small circles in lieu of her signature.

My father was educated in the school of the Angenrod Jewish community that his older sister, Mathilde, and all his younger siblings attended. In 1889, my paternal grandfather, in keeping with his Jewish and village environment, never considered sending a daughter to high school in Alsfeld; his four daughters attended the Angenrod Jewish community school. In that society, daughters were looked upon exclusively as prospective homemakers, wives, and mothers who were required to garner the necessary expertise for their station in life from their mother, older sisters, or aunts. My grandfather viewed high school subjects such as French, English, Latin, physics, chemistry, and higher mathematics to be of little value in the morrow of his daughters' lives. However, it is to my grandfather's credit that he neither urged nor permitted his daughters to work as cooks or maidservants in wealthy urban Jewish homes, a common pursuit that young unmarried Jewish girls in Upper Hesse engaged in before marriage.

In the congregational school, there was only a single room and teacher for grades one through eight, for all secular subjects and for all instruction relating to Hebrew and the Jewish religion. The secular curriculum was based on thorough learning of reading, writing, penmanship, and basic arithmetic that emphasized mental computation. Later, my father's expertise in mental arithmetic became a critical element in his two successful business careers. His instantaneous and accurate computation of weight and price affected profit or loss in the cattle business. In the neighborhood of Upper Hesse, where the economic pie was too small and yielded only meager morsels, deft mental arithmetic made the difference in promptly closing a business transaction and therefore getting ahead of the competition. In his antique business in the United States, my father's sagacious evaluation of assorted merchandise was the sum and substance of his profitable business.

My father's penmanship was distinctive yet easy to read. He expressed himself clearly and grammatically correct in either oral or written German. Because he used an extraordinary amount of French terms, my father showed the influence either of his earlier forebears in Angenrod (which had been occupied by the French for fifteen years) or of the vocabulary his father had acquired during his duty as a guard of French enemy prisoners in the Franco-German War of 1870-71. As a child, I was troubled by my father's customary usage of French denotations, because students were inculcated that '*am deutschen Wesen soll die Welt genesen*,' ('the world shall be healed through the German essence'). Moreover, my secular teachers instructed me that anything foreign, and especially French, denoted decadence and was linked to Germany's hereditary foe, France.

My father was familiar with the fact that the French occupation of Angenrod had energized the dedication of the synagogue in 1797, and he believed that emancipatory progress in Western Europe had originated in France. He also opined that France was a better place for Jews to live, despite the Dreyfus Affair in which the Jewish French staff officer, Alfred Dreyfus, was framed on charges of espionage, accused, and then imprisoned on Devil's Island in 1894, pardoned in 1899, and finally cleared in 1906.

Vogel Wertheim (III) was knowledgeable about the history of Germany and well-informed about the history of the Jews. With great sorrow, and contrary to his generally cheerful emotional tone, he sometimes alluded to the Inquisition, persecution, and expulsion of Jews from Spain and Portugal that had occurred four-hundred years earlier. He spoke as if he had endured it in person. Although my father was not in command of a second language (other than biblical Hebrew), he was well tutored in all the skills and attributes of an educated person, which he exemplified by his consideration, kind-heartedness, and compassion for others. He was an affable, humble, winsome individual of breeding and cultivation.

My father possessed an inordinate appreciation of the fine arts, yet these disciplines were neither taught in his school nor in his home environment. His perception of good taste, faultless form, genuine style, and color was probably an inborn trait that received meager nurture during his boyhood. His deep-felt admiration for the universe, his harmony with nature's forces, and his veneration for the world around him probably nourished his discernment of artistic ability.

My father also spoke Western Hessian Yiddish (*lashon hakodesh* or 'holy tongue' in Hebrew) that consisted of a mixture of words from Hebrew and a Hessian dialect. In earlier days, when the use of Western Yiddish was more widespread in Upper Hesse, Hebrew letters were employed for writing down this language. In all probability, my father absorbed *lashon hakodesh* from his parents, aunts, and uncles who lived nearby. *Lashon hakodesh* was used by Jewish cattle dealers as a means of concealing a business tip from a prospective buyer or seller unfamiliar with this language.

The Angenrod community school also imparted a thorough knowledge of biblical Hebrew and extensive Hebrew facility in daily and festival prayers. My father performed his religious duties with great love and devotion. With his entire heart and soul, he bestowed the same fervor and single-heartedness upon daily religious duties and prayers that he employed in executing Sabbath and holiday precepts. In order to fulfill the commandment in *Numbers 15:39*, my father wore a *tallit katan* (small *tallit*, which was called '*arba kanfas*' by Jews in Upper Hesse) over his undershirt. Except for Sabbath and holidays, my father wore *tefillin*[d] before breakfast at home or during morning services. While uttering the appropriate prayers, he wound his *tefillah* of the hand clockwise, a practice followed by Sephardic Jews. He loved the celebration of the Sabbath and all Jewish holidays, and he particularly enjoyed the two *seder* nights on Passover that commemorate the Exodus of the Israelites from Egypt.

At the time of my departure from Lauterbach, my father was not yet considered an older man and was therefore not yet permitted to read from the *Torah*. Until the end of his days, Vogel Wertheim (III) practiced every precept and reli-

---

[d]*Tefillin* are phylacteries, two small square boxes containing four scriptural passages from *Exodus 13:1-10, 11-16; Deuteronomy 64-9* and *11:13-21.*

gious duty with devotion and humility. However, I do not know whether his narrow personal escape from the Nazi fangs, the loss of his brother and other relatives and friends, and the destruction of a way of life he held so dearly, clouded his faith in God or caused him to quarrel with his Creator.

In spring of 1891, at the age of thirteen-and-a-half, my father completed his formal education. In Angenrod, the young Vogel (III) began to work in his father's cattle business and was inculcated with the notion that work is how a person makes sense of his or her place in nature. He worked many long hours during the day, late into the night, and early into the morning. He gave an account of how he departed shortly after midnight from Angenrod, leading a cow or a heifer to market in Kirchhain, which was sixteen miles away. He would fall asleep while stepping along, awake quickly, and continue walking, all the while guiding the animal during the time he was asleep.

My grandfather tutored his son, Vogel (III), in every facet of the cattle business. For seventeen years, my father did not receive any pecuniary compensation for his work. He was allotted free room and board in his parents' home and money for necessary clothing. My grandfather held exclusive control of the family's purse strings. His immediate goal was to provide his four daughters with a dowry (*nedunyah*) lest they would not find suitable husbands or, even worse, remain unwed. Generally, a dowry consisted of a substantial amount of cash, furniture, house furnishings, and linens. In accordance with the prevailing mores, Vogel Wertheim (III) lent himself for seventeen years in order to help attain the dowries of his older sister, Mathilde, and two of his younger sisters, Hilda and Katinka. Doubtless at the time of my father's marriage, the dowry for his youngest sister, nineteen-year-old Frieda, also had been set aside. In return, during those years and under the direction of their mother, my father's sisters sewed and hand-initialed kitchen and bathroom towels, sheets, pillowcases, and duvet covers to be presented to their brother at the time of his marriage.

Despite his father's demanding personality, Vogel Wertheim (III) looked back warmly on his life as a bachelor in Angenrod. His sisters, for whom he labored so earnestly for so many years, admired and unceasingly revered him all his life, and he benefited from the spiritual-minded principles and guidance of his beloved mother. In later years, my father related, with a sense of fulfillment, that he had been able to apply himself to the care of his mother, as she frequently suffered from flu-type illnesses in the winter.

When he was almost thirty, my father literally and bodily freed himself from the control and power of his father. On March 19, 1913, Vogel (III) moved to Lauterbach after he wedded my mother, Berta Lamm, who was born August 23, 1891 in Kirtorf (four miles west of Angenrod). My mother's parents were Auguste Strauss Lamm from Storndorf and Jakob Lamm of Kirtorf. It is certain that the Herz Wertheim family of Angenrod and the Jacob Lamm family of Kirtorf were sociable with each other before their children fell in love.

Chapter Ten

My mother, Berta Lamm, in 1912, when she was engaged to Vogel (Frederick) Wertheim (III)

My mother's paternal grandfather was variously called Eliaeser, Löser, or Lazarus Lamm. He was born in Ober-Gleen (three miles from Angenrod and on the way to Kirtorf), lived in Kirtorf, died on February 27, 1904, and was laid to rest in the Angenrod Jewish cemetery. Several years later, the Jewish community of Kirtorf acquired its own cemetery located outside the village on a modest incline off the Marburgerstrasse toward Lehrbach. Doubtless both my parents attended Eliaeser Lamm's funeral. My mother was then thirteen years old and my father was twenty-one. At that time, whenever a Jewish burial took place, every member of the local and nearby Jewish communities attended. Not only was there an intense sense of cohesion among the Jews, who generally made up only a small percentage of a village's total population; but it is also a special good deed to serve the dead, who no longer are able to recompense.

Other family relationships between Angenrod and Kirtorf connected the Wertheim and Lamm households. Three generations earlier, Loeb Höchster from Kirtorf (my mother's great-grandfather) had wedded Rebecca Meyerfeld from Angenrod. Rebecca died young and Loeb married his first wife's sister, Lea Meyerfeld. She, too, died and Loeb wedded Hannchen Meier from Angenrod, my mother's great-grandmother. My parents' steadfast courtship endured for eight years and, contrary to the mores of most Jews of Upper Hesse of that era, their marriage was one of tender passion and affection. My mother recounted that when she was fourteen years old she joined her village friends, who were probably mostly not Jewish, for an afternoon at the local *Kermis.*[c] During her absence from home, my father arrived at the Jacob Lamm residence. Auguste Lamm admired my father and considered him a befitting suitor for her daughter.

In 1906, my mother permanently moved to Lauterbach in order to join the childless household of her aunt, Johanna (Hannchen) Schloss Strauss, and uncle, Samuel Strauss {I] (her mother's brother). This change of abode did not lessen my parents' understanding that Berta and Vogel (III) would eventually marry. Nevertheless, my mother enthusiastically joined in the social life of the comparatively

[c] A *Kermis* was a fair usually held for charitable purposes, and this particular occasion was for the benefit of the local Lutheran church. Even though Berta Lamm was probably aware of the religious implication of this fair, she may well have disregarded it since it was a rare opportunity for festivity. My grandmother, however, was rather piqued about her daughter's unseemly participation in such a frivolous fête.

large group of single people (approximately thirty-five) in the Lauterbach Jewish congregation. Well-accepted by her peers, Berta embodied the demanding work ethics that this group respected so highly. Also, the beauty of form and fullness of my strikingly beautiful mother bore a part in her unqualified acceptance by the group. In a culture where food was not as bountiful as in our society, the rounded female form was glorified as a symbol of security and affluence.[f] Later in my mother's life, she happily recounted that carefree stage of her life, before she was involved with the care of her own family and when she was totally free of pecuniary responsibilities. Moreover, her Aunt Johanna emphasized that my mother's wearing apparel should consist of the most tasteful, high quality, and low key garments, regardless of cost.

In 1912, my parents' engagement party was celebrated at the residence of her Aunt Johanna and Uncle Samuel at Cent 17 in Lauterbach. At long last, my father won the one and only love of his life. There was probably a large assemblage at the engagement party, since three married uncles and ten cousins lived in Lauterbach. In Geneva in 1986, my cousin Alfred Mühlstein recalled that at age six he had attended my parents' engagement party. He was very impressed by the much venerated and white-bearded Isaac Schloss (Hannchen Schloss Strauss' father). Alfred remembered seeing Isaac, who was in his nineties, drinking red wine. It was probably red currant wine, because red currants grew profusely in the gardens at Cent 17 and were made into wine each year.

The prevailing customs during the era of my parents' betrothal prescribed a formal engagement party in order to better acquaint all family members with each other. Prior to the party, my mother had received her engagement ring, a golden chain, and watch and slide (both imbedded with diamond chips). In keeping with current etiquette, my mother presented my father with a golden pocket watch and chain. At that time, the interval between the official engagement and the wedding date was usually at least one year; a briefer period may have been construed as a shotgun marriage. After his engagement and until the wedding, my father spent most Sabbaths in Lauterbach, where he was called up to the *Torah*. As a guest in the bride's home, a groom would be honored by being asked to recite the unabridged version of the grace after meals.

During these weekend visits, every effort was made to ensure that the engaged couple should not be unchaperoned. To this end, it was customary to invite female cousins of the bride and groom to visit for the weekend. In keeping with etiquette during her engagement, my mother also visited with my father's family in Angenrod. On this occasion, according to established conventions, my mother asked one of her favorite cousins, Bertel Strauss of Hinter Dem Spittel in Lauterbach, to be her chaperone (*Anstandsdame*). The seven-year-old companion entertained herself during this visit by sweeping the entrance hall, the high steps, and the large yard of the Herz Wertheim residence.

---

[f] Conversely, in a culture where food is abundant, the lean body is acclaimed for its discipline.

Chapter Ten

My parents' secular marriage certificate was dated March 19, 1913. My parents' marriage certificate stated that the bride had "no occupation by which one earns one's living (*gewerbelos*)" and that the groom's occupation was cattle dealer. Witnesses were my mother's sixty-five-year-old uncle, Samuel Strauss (I), and a long-time friend of the family, the sixty-four-year-old Moses Fröhlich of Bahnhofstrasse 34 in Lauterbach, who was also a cattle dealer.

My parents' religious wedding ceremony took place in Fulda on March 24, 1913. According to the Hebrew calendar, this was the fifteenth of *Adar* 5673, which commemorates the successful resistance of the Jews of Shushan (Persia) to Haman's plan to exterminate them. On the fifteenth of *Adar* the festival of *Purim* is celebrated in cities which have been walled since the time of Joshua (for example, Jerusalem); elsewhere *Purim* is celebrated on the fourteenth of *Adar*. My parents' wedding on Monday evening took place after three stars appeared in the sky and was, according to the Jewish calendar, the third day of the week. This day of the week is especially favored for marital union because in *Genesis 1:10* and *1:12* in which it is pronounced that "God saw that it was good."

I do not have my parents' *ketubah*, the marriage document which usually records the financial and personal obligations that a husband undertakes toward his wife in marriage and which is read as part of the wedding ceremony. Until the end of his days and with unconditional love, my father devotedly carried out his promises made to his cherished bride and assigned my mother's desires as his cardinal precedence in his life. In brotherly love, my mother's older brother, Siegfried Lamm, and my father's younger brother, Salli Wertheim, dedicated several popular songs to the newly-wedded couple. The songs were written in accordance with the humor of the day. One song was offered to mothers-in-law, another to the ladies, and another to the bridal couple. One was a clever dialogue between men and women, and another was a wedding medley with each verse sung to various cheerful, contemporary melodies.

My mother's high-necked wedding dress was custom-made of heavy white silk satin with modest overlays of lace at the front and at the lower part of the sleeves. I wore this dress for masquerade parties until I left Germany. My father's wedding raiment consisted of a heavily starched and pleated white dress shirt, gray bow tie, dark gray and black-striped trousers, a solid black coat that reached nearly to his knees, a black top hat, and white one-button kid gloves. When Jews in Lauterbach still felt moderately secure—that is, until the mid-1920s—my father and several other Jewish congregants wore this outfit (except for the gloves) for synagogue attendance on the Pilgrim Festivals of Passover (*Pesach*), *Shavuot*, and *Sukkot*.

Following their wedding, my parents did not take a trip or vacation during their honeymoon period. They went to their modern and well-appointed living quarters on the first floor of Cent 17 in Lauterbach. In my parents' light-oak bedroom, there was a large washstand with a white marble top, attached mirror, and four drawers. An armoire accommodated considerable quantities of bed and table lin-

Lieder zur Hochzeit

des

Fräulein **Bertha Lamm**

mit

Herrn **Friedrich Wertheim**

am Montag den 24. März 1913 in Fulda

Dem Brautpaare in brüderlicher Liebe gewidmet
von Sally Wertheim und Siegfried Lamm.

Wedding Songs and Poems for Berta Lamm and Vogel (Frederick) Wertheim (III)

Lobgesang zu Ehren der Schwiegermütter.

Mel.: Strömt herbei ihr Völkerscharen.

Als der Herr am siebten Tage
Mit der Erde fertig war,
Überblickte er das Ganze,
Ob auch alles klipp und klar,
Plötzlich kraut er sich das Öhrchen
Sprach nachdenklich, so aha
Bald vergass ich, welch' Malörchen,
:,: Eine Schwiegermamama. :,:

Sprach's und schuf aus bestem Stoffe
Ein'ge Dutzend also gleich
Schwarze, blonde und melierte,
An Gemüt und Schönheit reich.
Schickt sie aus nach allen Zonen.
Nach dem Nord. dem Ost, dem West
Ueberall wo Menschen wohnen,
:,: Bis ins allerkleinste Nest. :,:

Und sie gingen und sie taten
Nach des Schöpfers weisem Spruch,
Denn man findet allerorten
Schwiegermütter nun genug.
Und ein Glück ist es gewesen,
Dass der Herr sie nicht vergass,
Weil das Unglück, wenn sie fehlten
:,: Ueberstiege jedes Mass. :,:

Läg das Kindlein in der Wiege?
Säss der Kaiser auf dem Thron?
Fehlten uns die Schwiegermütter,
Gäb es dann 'nen Schwiegersohn?
Wärt Ihr hier, Ihr lieben Leutchen?
Tränket heut Ihr Hochzeitswein?
Küsste Friedrich die Bertha?
:,: Ohne alle Zweifel nein! :,:

Sie versüsst uns unser Leben,
Steht uns bei mit Rat und Tat.
Recht muss man ihr immer geben,
Weil sie mehr Erfahrung hat.
Hoch darum die Schwiegermutter,
Und zum Segen ist sie da,
Wer noch ledig, suche schleunigst
:,: Eine Schwiegermamama. :,:

Den Damen.

Mel.: Das schönste Mädel.

Als einst im Paradiese
Der Adam ganz allein,
Seufzt er vor Langeweile:
„Wär ich allein zu zwein!
Wie gerne würd ich geben
Vom eignen Fleisch ein Stück.
Erhör, o Herr mein Flehen,
Verschaff mir dieses Glück."
Der Herrgott hat' Erbarmen
Und schuf zum Zeitvertreib
Aus einer seiner Rippen
Das Gegenstück, das Weib.
Mit Staunen und mit Wonne
Betrachtet es der Mann,
Und hub in seiner Freude
Sogleich zu singen an:
:,: „Ist das ein süsses Mädel,
Das just so akkurat
In seiner schönsten Laune
Der Herrgott g'schaffen hat." :,:

Wie hat seit jenen Zeiten
Die Welt gedreht sich sehr,
Um eine Eva betet
Kein Adam heute mehr.
„Erhör, o Herr mein Flehen,
So hört man's allenfalls
Und schaff, statt aus ,ner Rippe
Sie lieber mir vom Hals.
Jetzt aber denkt der Meister,
Dein Wunsch ist rigoros
Dass nie du wieder klagest
Die du einst riefst, die Geister
Wirst Du nicht wiederlos.
Du wärst so ganz allein,
Soll sie für's ganze Leben
Sets Dein Begleiter sein.
:,: „denn solch ein süsses Mädel
Auf deinem Lebenspfad
Ist doch das allerschönste,
Was der Herrgott g'schaffen hat.":,:

Ihr Herren, der Schöpfung Krone,
Stimmt kräftig mit mir ein
Das Lied, zum Preis der Damen
Soll es gesungen sein.
Der Wahrheit gebt die Ehre,
Die Lüge sei uns fern;
Die Lieben, kleinen Mädchen
Haben wir doch alle gern.
Welch Herz hätt' nie geliebt
Und solchen Schatz begehrt.
Der machet unser Leben
Erst recht das Leben wert.
Erhebt drum Eure Gläser,
Stosst an, dass es nur kracht;
Es sei jetzt unseren Damen
Ein donnernd Hoch gebracht.
:,: „Ein Hoch den lieben Frauen,
Ein Hoch den Mägdelein,
Sie mögen ferner blühen
Und wachsen und gedeih'n." :,:

Dem Brautpaare
in brüderlicher Liebe gewidmet.

Mel.: Stimmt an mit hellem, hohen Klang.

So nehmt die Gläser in die Hand,
Gefüllt mit Rheinlands Reben,
Wir grüssen Dich, Du holde Braut,
Bertha, Du sollst leben!

Recht glücklich ist ja stets der Mann
Dem Frauenliebe lachet,
Dem Frauenliebe freudevoll
Das Leben stets ja machet.

Als Schwester sei willkommen uns
In unserm trauten Kreise,
Es tu' sich unsere Freude kund
In herzlich schöner Weise.

Mög' Gott Euch stets zur Seite sein
In gut' und bösen Zeiten.
Und immer Euch nur Glück verleih'n
Und Frohsinn Euch begleiten.

Dies ist der Wunsch, der allen uns
Wohl durch das Herze zog.
Dem Brautpaar nur zum Schlusse noch
Ein dreifach donnernd Hoch!

Tischlied.

Mel.: Studio auf einer Reis'.

Frauen sind des Lebens Zier, juchheidi heida!
Hast Du keine, nimm' sie Dir, juchheidi, heida!
Junggesellen allesamt
Marsch, sofort zum Standesamt
Juchheidi juchheida etc.

Frauen sind der Quelle gleich, juchheidi heida!
Die da sprudelt silberreich, juchheidi heida'
Kommt so eine Quell' in Lauf',
Hört das Sprudeln nimmer auf.
Juchheidi juchheida etc.

Jede Frau ist eine Ros', juchheidi heida!
Ist ein Veilchen in dem Moos,, juchheidi heida!
Mancher sieht vielleicht auch blos
Statt auf Veilchen, auf das Moos;
Juchheidi juchheida etc.

Frauen sind des Hauses Hort, juchheidi heida!
Trotzdem geh'n sie gerne fort, juchheidi heida!
Frauen sind des Staates Zier,
Doch den Staat bezahlen wir.
Juchheidi juchheida etc.

Darum Hoch den Frauen all', juchheidi heida!
Stosset an mit hellem Prall, juchheidi heida!
Mög' uns gnädig hinterdrein
Die Gardinenpredigt sein
Juchheidi juchheida etc.

Zwiegespräch
für Herren und Damen.

Mel.: Steh ich in finsterer Mitternacht.

Herren: Die Liebe ist ein komisch Ding;
Die macht den Menschen oft ganz blind,
„Wie mancher Herr hat sich vergafft
Und sich nur Elend angeschafft"

Damen: Darüber seid nur mäuschenstill,
Zwar geht's nicht immer, wie man will,
Doch wenn das Elend bricht herein,
Kanns nur die Schuld der Herren sein.

Herren: Ist so ein Mädchen 18 Jahr'
Und oft mit 17 schon sogar,
Tun sie wie Täubchen zärtlich fein,
Zieh'n schon die Herrn ins Netz hinein.

Damen: O bitte sehr, im Gegenteil,
Die Damen woll'n nur Glück und Heil;
Die Herrn verdrehen uns die Köpf
Und Damen sind ein schwach' Geschöpf.

Herren: Ja, auch die Herrn sind oft sehr schwach,
Es ist damit 'ne eigne Sach';
Durch Schönheit, Anmut, Frauenlist
Ein Herr zu leicht verführet ist.

Damen: Das geht zu weit, wir arm Geschlecht,
Wir sind wie Lämmer, schlicht und recht,
Mit Schöntun, Schmeicheln, Liebe schwör'n,
Sind viele Mädchen zu betör'n.

Herren: Nun ja, es mag wohl manchmal sein,
Es gibt auch Herrn, die sind nicht fein;
Doch, wer es treu und redlich meint,
Verdient, dass ihn das Glück vereint.

Damen: Das lässt sich hören immerhin;
Gibt's Damen auch mit falschem Sinn,
Sind doch die meisten ohne Tück'
Und bringen nur dem Ehstand Glück.

Zusammen:
Nun sind wir einig, bei den Eh'n
Muss Mann und Frau zusammengeh'n,
Und fängt das Glück zu weichen an,
Sind beide häufig Schuld daran.

Das Pärchen, das wir vor uns schau'n,
Beginnt den Eh'stand mit Vertrau'n,
Es ist von reiner Lieb' beseelt,
Drum sicher auch das Glück nicht fehlt.

Hochzeits-Potpourri.

Mel.: Es kann ja nicht immer so bleiben.

Es kann ja nicht immer so bleiben,
Das fühlet die Jungfrau, der Mann,
Bei dem sich Freund Amor im Herzen
Ein Nestchen zu bauen begann.

Mel.: Ein freies Leben führen wir.

Dein freies Leben hört nun auf,
Jetzt bist du verbunden,
Du hast zu Deinem Lebenslauf
Ein treues Herz gefunden;
Mag es Dich lieben immerdar,
Wir fragen nach im nächsten Jahr,
:,: Ob es wie jetzt geblieben. :,:

Mel.: Wohlauf noch getrunken.

Nun lasset ein Wörtchen uns weihen der Braut,
Der heutige Tag schon als Weibchen dich schaut,
Adieu nun, Du Jungfrau, nun richte Dich ein,
Denn morgen, dann musst Du die Hausfrau schon sein.

Mel: Ich bin ein Preusse.

Ja, rufet laut an diesem schönen Feste,
Erfüllet so der Freundschaft heil'ge Pflicht;
Dem Brautpaar wünschen wir das allerbeste,
Was uns die Erde immer nur verspricht.
Gesegnet sei ihr Leben,
Mag Frohsinn sie umschweben,
:,: Ja stosset an und rufet dreimal laut:
„Es leben hoch der Bräutigam, die Braut!" :,:

Mel.: Heil dir im Siegerkranz.

Heil nun dem jungen Paar,
Das sich für immerdar
Liebend umschlingt.
:,: Füllet das Glas mit Wein,
Stimmet von Herzen ein,
Dass es mit Jubelschall
Weithin erklingt! :,:

Mel.: Gaudeamus igitur.

Gäste hebt das Glas empor,
Lasst es voll Euch schenken,
Dass wir in dem Jubelchor
Des jungen Paars gedenken!
Liebe, Glück und Häuslichkeit,
Wohlergeh'n Zufriedenheit,
:,: Soll Euch blühen ewige Zeit. :,:

ens, because frequent washing of dirty clothes and linens betokened an absence of resources. The bedroom also had marble-topped night tables and twin beds. No home of our married relatives or Jewish friends had a double bed for a married

couple because of the laws of family purity (*taharat ha-mishpahah*). Statutes require a married couple to abstain from sexual relations during the period of menstruation until the wife's immersion in the *mikveh* (ritual bath). These regulations are considered by orthodox Jews to be basic to the Jewish way of life. From my Great-Uncle

Cent 17, residence of Samuel Strauss (I) and the Wertheim family in Lauterbach, circa 1910

Samuel and Great-Aunt Johanna (Hannchen) Strauss, my parents received furniture for the kitchen, bedroom, dining room, and living room, as well as all other home furnishings and implements. My paternal grandfather, Herz Wertheim, accommodated the newlyweds with additional linens, some silver flatware, a desk, and furniture for a second bedroom.

Conveniences to which they were unaccustomed from their parents' homes were indoor plumbing, running water, and a bathtub with heated water flowing into it. Few, if any, of their relatives and friends enjoyed such comforts. In earlier days, the Lauterbach water main had been controlled by the Riedesel (local feudal lords) in an arbitrary manner.[4] According to my mother, before running water in Lauterbach was supplied by the town, Cent 17 had had its own pump, which was situated approximately one-and-one-half meters south of an oak which is now legally protected. The sewage system on Cent 17 was installed in 1912.[5] By 1913, Cent 17 was equipped with electric lights, but the villages of Angenrod and Kirtorf probably did not have the convenience of this utility.

On March 13, 1913, as stated in the Lauterbach land register (Volume 18, Number 864), Samuel Strauss (I) and his wife, Johanna Strauss, each transferred half a share of the residence of Cent 17, its adjacent buildings, *curtilage*, and adjoining lands to Vogel Wertheim (III) and his fiancée, Berta Lamm. The document also stipulated entitlement of residence for Samuel and Johanna Strauss (thereafter they occupied the second floor of Cent 17), as well as other limited personal services to be rendered to them and lifetime benefit of the products of the gardens.

After my father's arrival in Lauterbach in 1913, my sixty-five year-old Great-Uncle Samuel, withdrew from active participation in the cattle business. Neverthe-

Samuel Strauss (I)

less, he continued to lay the groundwork for my father's business transactions, primarily in the communities of Angersbach and Landenhausen. Great-Uncle Samuel also looked after the payments due him on outstanding loans and mortgages. In addition to pruning trees and assisting in maintenance of the gardens of Cent 17, he carried on the major share of work whenever the family butchered a lamb, calf, or heifer. Until shortly before his death in 1924, Great-Uncle Samuel helped out at home and in the maintenance of the synagogue.

A very warm relationship existed between my Great-Uncle Samuel and my father, who was thirty-five years his junior. At age thirty, each of them had set off from his native village, both of which had old, tightly-knit Jewish communities. In Lauterbach in 1898, Great-Uncle Samuel was one of the founders of the Jewish congregation, which held religious services in a house (on) am Graben. Five years prior to my father's arrival in Lauterbach, the synagogue had been dedicated at considerable expense and great personal sacrifice by some members of this small Jewish congregation (about twenty families). Several members of the town's government and representatives of the local clergy attended the dedication ceremony.[6] In a town where the attitude of the local Protestant clergy was tantamount to the essence of a community's spiritual mold, their active participation greatly effected a more favorable attitude of its citizens toward Jews at that time.

My Great-Uncle Samuel and my father were humble individuals who enthusiastically shared the common goal of providing the best spiritual and physical conditions for their immediate family within the framework of Judaism and their duty as citizens of Germany. My Great-Uncle Samuel's devotion to Germany was stronger than my father's, probably because the former had to acquire his German citizenship in Storndorf in 1877 for a goodly sum, whereas the latter was a German citizen by birth. My father's forebear, Moses Wertheim (I) (a *Schutzjude*), was born in 1742 in Angenrod five generations earlier; however, in 1852 my father's grandfather, Kaufmann Wertheim (I), was still a *Schutzjude*.

Whenever my father chanced upon what he deemed utter hokum by Germans in authority, he politely consented while indistinctly uttering the word '*oser*,' meaning 'who will believe it' or 'this is no avowal.' In contrast to Jews in Hesse in earlier days, Great-Uncle Samuel and my father looked beyond the horizon of family, village or town, and traditions. Earlier generations of Jews in Upper Hesse had not been able to do anything but provide the scant necessities for their families, because of extra heavy taxation and restrictive economic covenants imposed on Jews. In view of the fact that my father was born a citizen of Germany and that his father served his country in the Franco-Prussian War (1870-71), Vogel (III) looked forward to a better life in Lauterbach than his forebears in Angenrod had been forced to endure.

Endnotes

1. Dr. Karl Siegmar Baron von Galera, *Lauterbach in Hessen III* (Neustadt an der Aisch: Verlag Degener and Company, 1965), p. 317.

2. Ibid, p. 306.

3. Rüdiger Mack, *Neunhundert Jahre Geschichte der Juden in Hessen* (Wiesbaden: Kommission für die Geschichte der Juden in Hessen, 1983), p. 394.

4. von Galera, *Lauterbach in Hessen III,* p. 275.

5. Ibid, p. 294.

6. Interview in Lauterbach in July 1988 with the then ninety-year-old Frau Tag.

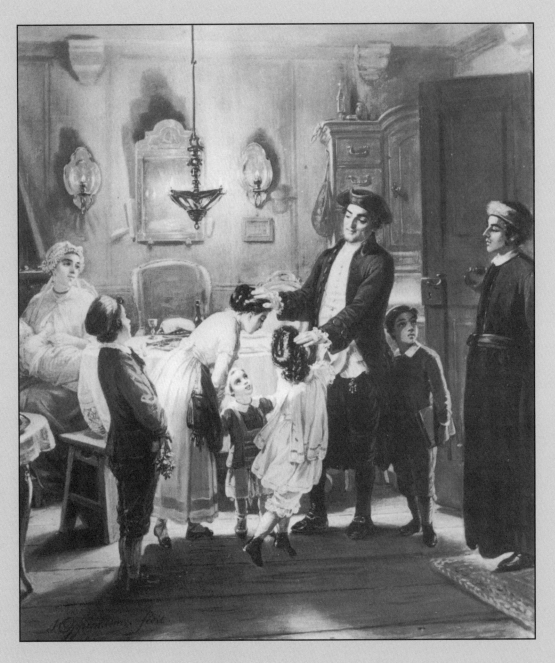

Sabbath Eve by Moritz Daniel Oppenheim, 1882

BLESSINGS $\mathcal{F}$rom cradle to grave, the life of a Jew in Lauterbach was explicitly guided by detailed religious ordinances, customs, and rituals. Virtually every circumstance in one's life prescribed a benediction. Each blessing contains the words '*Barukh Attah Adonai*' ('Blessed art Thou, O Lord'). One pronounced a blessing before drinking water and other drinks, a special blessing over wine, and before consuming fruits of the trees and the earth. There was a brief grace after eating fruits or drinking water as well. Grace after meals was said after any repast comprising bread. A blessing was recited over aromatic herbs, ambrosial fruits, condiments, fragrant wood, sweet-scented flowers, and sweet-smelling oil; at the sight of lightning, gigantic mountains, immense deserts, and at the time of stormy weather that included thunder or an earthquake.

A blessing was recited upon sighting the spectacle of a rainbow, at the first view of a blossoming tree in spring or at the sight of choice plants. Blessings were said whenever one spied an especially beautiful creature, or when glancing at a dwarf or a giant, at the time of a purchase of a house or a new dress, at receiving glad or even bad tidings, whenever meeting again with a friend after the space of a year, at the sight of a restored house of worship, when beholding a famous Jewish scholar, at the sight of a philosopher, looking at a sovereign, or seeing again a place where in the past one escaped a great peril.

Blessings were appropriate when catching sight of an ocean, when attaching a *mezuzah* (parchment scroll with selected *Torah* verses placed in a container and affixed to the doorpost or rooms where Jews reside), when installing a railing around a well, or a flat roof, or when redeeming a vineyard in the fourth year. Women pronounced a blessing at the time of removing a small part of the hallah dough. *Hallah* is the white bread over which the blessing was said on the Sabbath and which in Lauterbach was called '*berches*' after the Hebrew word '*berakhot*' ('benedictions').

CIRCUMCISION THE ONLY BIRTH AND CIRCUMCISION of a Jewish child of Lauterbach which I can recall is the one of Salochen Stern, son of Rosa Oppenheimer Stern and Max (Moses) Stern on January 22, 1922, because at that time the Stern family lived on the second floor of the Wertheim residence at Cent 17. Salo's circumcision[a] took place at his residence, because it would have been fraught with danger during the cold of January to take an infant who had barely survived the shock of birth to the synagogue. Among the forty Jewish families in Lauterbach during the 1920s and 1930s there was no resident *mohel*. I cannot remember that any circumcision (except possibly for the succeeding sons of the Max Stern family, who later on resided in an apartment in the synagogue building) ever took place anywhere but at the newborn male infant's residence, where at that time mothers gave birth.

---

[a] An operation removing part or all of the foreskin covering glans of penis performed on the eighth day after birth and called the covenant of Abraham, is discharged by a *mohel*.

In Lauterbach, the prompt consummation of circumcision on the eighth day after birth took precedence over laws of the Sabbath and other holidays. The term '*sandak*,' designating the one who holds the male child during circumcision, was not known in Lauterbach and immediate environs; instead that high honor was designated as '*Gevatter*,' which is an altered form of the German word 'godfather.' That term was used in the Christian community at the time of baptism and the naming ceremony of a Christian child.

NAMING

DURING A PRAYER FOR THE CHILD'S WELFARE, the *mohel* announced the newborn's name. Bestowing a name upon a newborn was a serious task for parents because a name was considered an influencing element for good or bad. The founders and early members of the Lauterbach Jewish congregation, for the most part born during the second part of the nineteenth century in Storndorf, Crainfeld, and Grebenau bore predominantly biblical first names. For example, Juda Baumann (I) and (II), Nathan Hess, Simon Höchster, Moses Jakob, Aron Stein, the brothers Salomon, Samuel, and Markus Strauss, and Abraham Weinberg.

Notwithstanding, Sigmund Strauss, born in Grebenau on August 17, 1856, who signed the plans for the accession of drainage installation on October 20, 1911 as chairman of the Lauterbach Jewish congregation, had a name of Teutonic origin meaning 'protecting conqueror.' Sigmund Strauss and his wife, Settchen (meaning 'little rose' from the French) from Romrod, named their children Therese (of Greek origin), Jenny (an abbreviation of Jennifer meaning 'graceful demeanor' in Hebrew), and Hedwig (probably from the Hebrew word for 'joy.') Sigmund's brother, who later also moved to Lauterbach, had the name Karl, a name not of biblical origin and meaning 'strong stalwart man.'[1] Among the generation following the founders of the Jewish congregation in Lauterbach, biblical names decreased and names of Teutonic origin occurred more frequently.

For example, Juda Baumann (I) from Storndorf and his wife, Karoline (née Hasenauer) from Wiesenfeld, named their sons Bernhard, Max, Siegfried, and Karl, and their daughters Mathilde and Jenny (all names of either Teutonic or Latin origin). Juda Baumann (II) and his wife, Elda (née Strauss), both from Storndorf, named their daughters Emma, Ida, Else, and Recha. The first three names are of Teutonic origin; Recha was a very popular name among the Jews of Hesse of the generation born toward the end of the nineteenth century and the beginning of the twentieth century. Nathan Hess from Crainfeld and his wife, Fanny (née Stern) from Hintersteinau, named their daughters Berta, Gidda and Jenny, and their sons Julius, Max, Samuel, and Salomon.

The name 'Berta' is of Teutonic origin, 'Gitta' probably stems from the Yiddish or German word '*gut*' ('good'). The name 'Julius' is of Greek origin meaning 'soft-haired' and has the symbolic meaning of 'youth.'[2] 'Max' is a Latin name—a short form of Maximilian—and means 'great' or 'famous.'[3] The names 'Samuel' and 'Salomon' emanate from the Bible. Aron Stein from Grebenau and his wife, Karoline, from Walldorf, Kreis Gross-Gerau, named their children Max, Settie (from the French 'little rose') and Toni (meaning 'revered' from the Greek and Latin).[4] Simon Höchster from Storndorf bestowed his daughter with the biblical name, Hannah (wife of the biblical Elkanah and mother of the Prophet Samuel).

My Great-Uncle Salomon Strauss from Storndorf and his wife, Jette Schloss Strauss from Allendorf, named their son 'Salli' after his great-grandfather, Samuel Hirsch Strauss (who was my great-great-grandfather), and their daughters Mathilde and Hannah. Mathilde is of Teutonic origin and means 'battlemaiden.' My Great-Uncle Markus Strauss (his family and close friends called him 'Mordche'—a diminutive form of Mordecai in Western Yiddish) from Storndorf and his wife, Lina Frank Strauss from Nieder-Ohnen, named their sons Siegfried, Hermann, Hugo, and Salli. The first three names are either of Teutonic or Saxon origin, whereas Salli may be an abbreviation of Saul, the first king of the Jews. My Great-Uncle Markus and his wife, Lina Strauss, called their daughters Minna (a short form of Wilhelmina after Kaiser Wilhelm, the then ruling monarch and meaning 'warrior') and Bertel (a term of endearment for Berta) and Selma (from the Celtic meaning 'fair.')[5]

Napoleon's occupation of Upper Hesse around the turn of the nineteenth century also influenced the naming of Jewish children, because the French army followed the principles of the French Revolution ('Equality, Brotherhood, and Liberty'), and generally ameliorated the lot of the local Jews. The French always received a goodly share of benevolent thoughts in the hearts and minds of my family. Whenever my parents wanted to signify that someone led a unqualified happy life, they said," he lives like God in France." During and after the French occupation of Hesse, names of French origin such as 'Jeanette' and 'Settie' became popular.

Generally the Jews of Lauterbach did not follow the Sephardic custom of naming a child after a living parent or grandparent. Usually the first daughter was named after a deceased grandmother, a great-grandmother, or a recently deceased sister or aunt. In naming a girl child, first consideration was conferred always upon the father's family. In the event of the arrival of a male child, too, the father's family was accorded first deference. Possibly with the event of a second or third child, a name from a deceased family member on the mother's side was bestowed upon the newborn.

In an effort to integrate more readily into the general society around the turn of the twentieth century and later, many Jews in Upper Hesse gave their children names that were neither of Western Yiddish extraction nor of biblical origin. Names of Teutonic and Latin origin such as Siegfried, Bernhard, Max, Julius, Mathilde, Selma, Recha, and Berta became very popular, as well as the name Minna. However, non-Jews rarely availed themselves of the names used by Jews—with the possible exception of Minna. Thus, these names made the Jews as conspicuous, as the names Moses, Samuel, Nathan, Seligmann, Rebecca, Sara, and Rachel of an earlier generation had before them. From approximately 1915 on, Jews in Lauterbach

Chapter Eleven

named their children much like those of the non-Jewish population: Erich, Erna, Kurt, Otto, Paul, and Herbert.

THE *GEVATTER* AND THE CIRCUMCISION CEREMONY

AS A RULE, THE HIGHLY-REGARDED HONOR of the *Gevatter*, who held the male child on his knees during the circumcision ceremony, was bestowed upon the paternal grandfather of a newborn male child. The next in line to enjoy this revered position for a second son of a family was the maternal grandfather. In Lauterbach, the *Gevatter* was looked upon as the person who, in the event of the death of the male child's father, would assume the moral and financial responsibility of a father. In particular, it was the duty of the *Gevatter* to be concerned with, and whenever possible, to be involved in the Jewish education of his charge. It was also the obligation of the *Gevatter* to pay for a new suit for the male child at his *bar mitzvah*.[b] Following the circumcision, the *Gevatter* and his family were responsible for providing and serving refreshments to at least ten male relatives or friends required to be present for a *minyan*.[c]

I clearly recall that on the first Sabbath eve after the birth of Salochen Stern on January 22, 1922, friends and relatives of the Stern family gathered on the second floor of our residence at Cent 17 in order to congratulate them and to partake of refreshments. This ceremony was called '*Sholem Zokher*' and means 'peace to the male child.' It was considered a good deed (*mitzvah*) to participate in this celebration. Only the father (Max Stern) of the infant, Salo, and the maternal grandmother, Frau Oppenheimer from Hanau, who had come to Lauterbach to be with her daughter during delivery, greeted the guests. In those days, even non-religious mores deemed it unseemly that Rosa Stern, the mother, six days after giving birth, was allowed to be up and about and to mingle with visitors. Moreover, six days after the birth of her son, Rosa was still considered unclean, because she had not yet immersed herself in the *mikveh* (ritual bath).

THE *HOLOGRASCH* CEREMONY

IN LAUTERBACH, THERE EXISTED NO CO-EQUAL ceremony to expressly ritualize the arrival of a female child. However, the Lauterbach Jewish children aged four to twelve greatly anticipated the festive event of the *holegrasch*, a ceremony that conferred a secular name on both female and male children. The term '*holegrasch*' may be derived from the Hebrew '*shem ha'arisah*' meaning 'cradle name.' The ritual was first alluded to in the fourteenth century in southern Germany, and additionally may relate to Frau Holle, a witch who descends upon infants.[6] The fable of Frau Holle is depicted in the fairy tales of the Grimm Brothers, whose stories were collected in regions of Upper Hesse and near Lauterbach.

Generally, on the fourth Sabbath after a child's birth, the newborn's mother attended Sabbath services for the first time. Prior to her synagogue attendance, the

---

[b] When a male Jew passes his thirteenth birthday, he publicly assumes religious responsibility and generally gives account by reading a section from the Five Books of Moses and from the Prophets.
[c] A quorum of ten male Jews above the age of thirteen necessary for services and certain religious ceremonies.

mother visited the *mikveh*, which rendered her from *tomen* (unclean) to *tahor* (clean). In order to honor the newborn, the child's father was called to the *Torah*. While the father was pronouncing the blessings and during the required *Torah* reading, the mother upstairs rose in her place and read *Tehinnah* (its subject is the relationship between God and the people of Israel). Besides that, there was a special prayer in the book authored by Mrs. Rothschild for women who attended synagogue services for the first time after a confinement. As a youngster during synagogue services, I hastily read the prayers pertaining to special matters of interest to women whenever my mother was not using her book and was not supervising me too carefully. As soon as the new father, who generally made a donation ('*schnodern*' in Hessian Yiddish) to the synagogue in honor of the newborn returned to his seat, synagogue etiquette permitted the mother, too, to be seated.

In Lauterbach, a *holograsch* alwasy took place at two o'clock in the afternoon on the same Sabbath the mother attended services for the first time after her confinement. All Jewish children old enough to eat by themselves and carry their own bag of goodies home were automatically invited to the house of the newborn. Usually the infant rested in a washbasket made of wicker (or of another small pliant twig), suitably equipped for the baby's comfort. The basket with the infant was kept on two chairs facing each other. Throughout the early 1920s, and possibly later, all babies were swaddled and for the first month or six weeks of a baby's life, the infant's arms also were snugly wrapped as with a wide bandage.

During the *holegrasch* ceremony all the children formed a large circle around the baby's basket. Max Stern, the teacher, designated several older children (generally boys) to lift the baby's basket three times, while the children forming the circle spoke the words "what shall the child be named," together with the infant's name.

After this ceremony, the twenty-five or thirty guests were seated in row upon rows of tables and served stewed prunes, pears, or other home-canned fruits. Cakes or cookies, which were usually prepared with butter during that era, could not be served, because the guests might have eaten meat less than four hours ago and in that event would have vio-

A *holograsch* ceremony

lated the dietary laws. During the meal, the children could not help but catch sight of and speculate upon the contents of bags of goodies, kept in a large basket nearby. After the meal, each guest was allowed to visit briefly with the infant, curtsy to every adult, and happily receive the bag of goodies on the way out.

RELIGIOUS
EDUCATION

IN LAUTERBACH, ALL JEWISH BOYS and girls upwards of six years of age received religious instruction from Max Stern. During my three years of compulsory attendance at the public school in the building of the *Goldene Esel*, Jewish children were not permitted to attend the five-days-a-week one-hour Christian catechism lessons (there was no catechism instruction on Saturday) offered by Mr. Meyer, the classroom teacher. After Mr. Meyer checked classroom attendance and assessed whether each pupil wore highly-shined shoes and that all boys and girls carried their own handkerchief, he opened the classroom door and announced "*Juden raus!*" ('Jews out!'). Mr. Meyer's class of approximately thirty pupils had three Jewish pupils: Erich Reiss, Lothar Schiff, and myself, Tilli Wertheim. For the duration of the one-hour catechism lesson, the three Jewish pupils were required to silently stand in the hallway without any materials for learning.

Moreover, this classroom teacher additionally singled out the three children by using the term '*Juden*,' which during those years denoted stigma and shame. During the 1920s, more thoughtful individuals used the term '*Israeliten*.' At the conclusion of Mr. Meyer's catechism lesson, he opened the door and commanded, "*Juden rein!*" ('Jews come in!'). For three years, from the age of six until I was nine years old, this vexatious routine was a habitual torment of my school life that I did not even communicate to my parents. To this day I turn scarlet whenever the agony of Mr. Meyer's subtly institutionalized anti-semitism visited upon helpless, young children comes to mind.

On Wednesdays from three to five o'clock in the afternoon and on Sundays from eight in the morning until twelve noon, all Jewish students of public and high school ages were obliged by law to attend Max Stern's classes in Hebrew and religion in a schoolroom on the second floor of the *Goldene Esel* building which remains today along the Rockelsgasse. To the best of my recollection, this classroom had windows that looked out over the Rockelsgasse and the schoolyard. The wall that faced the Rockelsgasse held a wooden closet for use solely by Max Stern, and for which he alone possessed a key.

During Max Stern's lessons of biblical history, Hebrew instruction, study, and the subjects of Jewish holidays and their observance, all pupils, regardless of age, were called upon to participate. Mr. Stern appointed two eighth-grade students, Selma Gottlieb of Am Wörth and Selma Strauss of Hinter Dem Spittel, my mother's first cousin, to instruct the three first graders, Erich Reiss, Lothar Schiff, and myself, Tilli Wertheim, in Hebrew reading. One weakness of Mr. Stern's methodology was that our fourteen-year old tutors were remiss in familiarizing our group with Hebrew writing.

In all other respects Max Stern's system was born of necessity and was of the first order. It was put to the test during periods of adversity and withstood the test of time: not one of Max Stern's students who attended classes with me followed any other belief, and no one married outside of Judaism. However, this phenomenon may also have come about because (especially for my age group) Christianity and its teachings epitomized enemy territory and who-beset by such inordinate fright, would dare to cross over of one's own accord into the perilous camp of the adversary?

Pupils attending religious school during my time were: Alfred Adler and Bertel Adler (both of Bahnhofstrasse 34); Emil Frank from Ober-Seemen who lived with his sister, Ricka Frank Strauss, and his brother-in-law, Siegfried Strauss (II) (my mother's cousin), in the Gartenstrasse in the house of Ida Mai; Selma Gottlieb and her brother, Siegfried Gottlieb (of) Am Wörth 16; Zilli Höchster of Rockelsgasse 54; Benno Jakob of Langgasse 19; Arthur Jakob of Bahnhofstrasse 103; Walter Kleeberg of Obergasse 24; Ludwig Marx, who lived with his uncle, Max Stern, in the synagogue building on Hinter Der Burg; the brothers Ernst, Otto and Richard Pfifferling of Bahnhofstrasse 18; and Elly Reiss and her brother, Erich, of Bahnhofstrasse 20; Ludwig and Lothar Schiff of Obergasse 27; Ruth Gisela Spier of Bahnhofstrasse 70; Irma and Kurt Stein of Eisenbacher Tor 7; Hermann Strauss of Rockelsgasse 10; Selma Strauss of Hinter Dem Spittel; Alfred Weinberg of Steinweg 11; and Erna, my sister, and myself, Tilli Wertheim.

Our black-and-white Hebrew primer, although meant for young children, contained no pictures or illustrations. By the third grade, Max Stern required that his pupils would have fluently mastered Hebrew reading of most daily, Sabbath, and holiday prayers. At best, there may have been three students whose Hebrew reading was deficient, and therefore were not able to carry out the required assignments, which included translations from the Daily and Holiday Prayer Book, selected translations from the Five Books of Moses ('*Humash*' in Hebrew and '*Pentateuch*' in Greek) and a biblical history written in German and intended for children. This book commenced with creation, included Jewish life in the Diaspora, and ended with the eventual emancipation of the Jews in all German lands in 1871. The biblical history was authored by a Max Stern and also contained all names in Hebrew printing.

The *Goldene Esel* (the public school in Lauterbach)

The Wertheim household possessed only one *Humash* with German translation, which resulted in a fierce competition by the Wertheim sisters for this book about half an hour before formal religious instruction. In class we were required to cover up the German translation, but tempted by the impulse to verify a word or sentence, most students peeked at the forbidden German translation that was supposed to be covered. The students of Max Stern's class absorbed with great enthusiasm those parts of the *Humash* which Max Stern passed over because he considered the contents inappropriate—for instance, those selections to which he decided had too much procreation mentioned in the text. In our translating assignment of the Daily and Holiday Prayer Book, Max Stern's students were not as easily tempted to cheat because we had a separate book of translation which was not for use during formal instruction. Generally, we read the newly-assigned chapter of biblical history in class, and as a result of this exercise I realized, too, that those students who were not fluent in Hebrew were also deficient in reading German.

Max Stern required his students to memorize the most frequently used benedictions, the entire grace after meals, and many daily and holiday prayers. About twice a year, Dr. Leo Hirschfeld, the regional rabbi, who resided in Giessen, came to our town in order to examine the pupils of Max Stern's classes. Whenever Rabbi Hirschfeld officiated at a funeral in Lauterbach during the morning, he arranged to remain in town in order to examine Max Stern's classes in the afternoon. The regional rabbi tested how much Jewish history Max Stern's students had committed to memory, how many blessings and prayers they knew by heart, and appraised the level of *Humash* translations.

At age eight, after I recited by heart the part of the grace after meals which is inserted on the Sabbath to Dr. Hirschfeld's satisfaction, he recommended, "have your mother reward you with the biggest apple in your cellar." In general, Dr. Hirschfeld tried to encourage stricter observance of Jewish laws and rituals during his visits in Lauterbach. He was definitely partial to my mother's homemade potcheese, because he always asked for a generous supply to take home. While my mother attended the funeral of a distant relative in Giessen where Rabbi Hirschfeld officiated, he expressed great disappointment for what he considered her oversight in not toting the runny potcheese to Giessen, which involved a mile-long walk to the railroad station and a two-hour trip by railroad with the prospect of standing room only. Rabbi Hirschfeld possessed a corpulent frame and an assertive personality. He was obviously accustomed to giving orders and having his way. In Upper Hesse; he was the final authority on all religious issues.

I do not remember whether my male contemporaries in Max Stern's classes wore the small *tallit* (*tallit katan*), which is a rectangular garment of white cotton, linen, or wool with fringes (*ziziyyot*) on its four corners. However, my grandfathers, my uncles in Kirtorf and Angenrod, and my father wore this garment faithfully.

The Lauterbach Jewish flock was indisputably an orthodox community. Max Stern was guided by the philosophy of Rabbi Samson Raphael Hirsch (1808-1888) and Max Stern labored untiringly to improve each member of his congregation in accordance with Rabbi Hirsch's beliefs of furthering secular education alongside orthodox Judaism. However, the notion of a *bat mitzvah*[d] was remote during the 1920s and early 1930s

---

[d] Meaning 'daughter of the commandment and religious duty.' It calls girls at age thirteen to read from the Five Books of Moses and from the Prophets.

in Lauterbach. At the same time, girls were encouraged to observe Jewish fast days commencing with their twelfth birthday.

THE *BAR MITZVAH* CEREMONY
THE *BAR MITZVAH* ('son of the commandment') ceremony, when a boy at thirteen years of age is called up to read from the *Torah* and from a prophetic reading, denotes his responsibility to observe the law. Subsequently, he counts for *minyan*. I came to know from my father, who was *bar mitzvah* in 1896, that henceforth his parents and his teacher in Angenrod considered him an adult responsible for his own decisions of right and wrong. However, I was unimpressed with the post-*bar mitzvah* seriousness of the religious responsibilities of my male contemporaries in the 1920s. Due to compulsory attendance of public school on the Sabbath, I was never privileged during my eighteen years in Lauterbach to be present at a *bar mitzvah* or to go to the *bar mitzvah* of a cousin.

However, my parents were present at the *bar mitzvah* of their nephew, my cousin, Kurt Herz of Haiger (in the Westerwald-Dill district), whose mother, Hilda Wertheim Herz, was my father's sister. My mother and father were impressed with Kurt's reverential attitude, but passed no judgment on his *Torah* reading or his chanting of the prophetic portion. The traditional *bar mitzvah* lunch menu included cold poached salmon—a food not available in Lauterbach. I recall that my paternal grandparents, Hannchen Levi Wertheim and Herz Wertheim, basked in the joy of the *bar mitzvah* of their grandson and in the deference and esteem accorded them at such a momentous occasion in their lives. My parents left on Friday by train for Haiger and returned on Sunday. At most, fifteen out-of-town guests attended Kurt's *bar mitzvah*, some of whom must have stayed overnight with the five or six Jewish families of Haiger.

CONFIRMATION
THE LAUTERBACH JEWISH CONGREGATION did not celebrate confirmations, and during my life in Lauterbach this term only emerged in connection with the church. However, my maternal grandmother, Auguste Strauss Lamm, who was born and raised in Storndorf, a village eight miles distant from Lauterbach, proudly explained to me that in 1875, at age sixteen, she was confirmed in the orthodox congregation of her native village. However, this happenstance was inconsistent with orthodox teachings of the era and the mind-set of the Storndorf Jewish community even fifty years later.

BETROTHAL AND MARRIAGE
IN LAUTERBACH AND AMONG THE JEWS of Upper Hesse at the turn of the nineteenth century and as late as the 1920s, there were few marriages because of tender-hearted love. Romance before marriage was not considered as important as lifelong devotion and affection after marriage. Generally, Jewish marriages were arranged by family members or close friends. It was deemed of primary merit for a girl at least to be engaged by age twenty. After the age of twenty-five the community regarded unwedded young ladies as a problem to themselves and their parents. My

mother often quoted her aunt, Johanna Schloss Strauss, with whom she lived in Lauterbach, as declaring, "young girls in full bloom should be unloaded quickly, much the same as freshly baked rolls." In 1877, at the time of my Great-Aunt Johanna's marriage to my Great-Uncle Samuel, they were twenty and twenty-nine years of age, respectively .

On the other hand, the older a young man was by the time he tied the nuptial knot, the better his chances of providing for a family were considered—especially in rural areas or small towns of Upper Hesse, where Jews had only begun to marginally penetrate economic and educational barriers. Young men less than thirty years of age were considered not 'dry behind the ears' and labeled '*datscher* boys' (another name for the Sabbath bread in some parts of Hesse). This indicated a lack of maturity, because freshly-baked bread is readily malleable, a quality which obviously was not much sought after in a prospective husband.

In keeping with the Rabbinic law of betrothal (*shiddukin*), the engagement period lasted for about a year. The notion of *shiddukin* involved a commitment by the intended bride and groom either by themselves, or their respective parents and other relatives. Parents or other older kinfolk negotiated and settled the cash amount of the dowry and the bride's trousseau. At the time of engagement, the groom presented his bride with an engagement ring and the bride's family gave a present of some monetary value to the groom. In Lauterbach, the engagement was regarded as an important step on the road to marriage. Any young Jew of either gender who had previously broken an engagement to be married thereafter had to demonstrate exemplary behavior because breaking an engagement was considered dishonorable and untrustworthy and left that individual with a blemish. After a broken engagement it was more difficult to find a mate, because some families were reluctant or excluded someone entirely who had experienced a broken engagement.

If a bride resided in another town, the groom periodically stayed at the home of the bride's parents for the Sabbath. He would arrive on Friday before the onset of Sabbath and depart on Sunday. Whenever a bridegroom visited his prospective bride's home, prevailing mores prescribed that a chaperone be present at all times. Either the bride invited a young female relative, or a girl friend, or the groom brought along his own escort—usually a young female relative. Therefore, my Uncle Leo from Kirtorf, the only living brother of my mother, invited me, at age nine, to accompany him as chaperone to Berleburg, Westphalia, where he visited his bride-to-be, Mathilde Krebs, for the Sabbath.

In retrospect, I question how effectually I carried out this assignment, since I was much encouraged by my hosts to retire at a very early hour. However, in Berleburg as my Uncle Leo and his new bride returned from the formalities of the civil marriage preceding their wedding on the twelfth of *Av* 5685 (1924), I and several neighbor children held a huge rope from one side of the street to the other, thus preventing the newly-wedded couple from entering the bride's home. We consented to their passing upon payment of a small sum of money.

In keeping with etiquette, some time after my mother's engagement party (that took place in Lauterbach at her home at Cent 17 in 1912), Berta Lamm journeyed to Angenrod in order to formally visit with the parents and family of her fiancé, Vogel (Frederick) Wertheim (III). For this occasion, my mother invited her then seven-year-old and beloved cousin, Bertel Strauss of Hinter Dem Spittel, in Lauterbach to escort her. Although the distance from Lauterbach to Angenrod is only fifteen miles, the journey was time-consuming and inconvenient. In mild weather, one could easily walk the mile-and-a-half distance to the railroad station in Lauterbach without luggage, but rain and heavy luggage necessitated the use of a wheelbarrow or a horse-drawn carriage. The railway trip to Alsfeld, the railroad station nearest to Angenrod, took at least fifty minutes because at the stops milk cans, either full or empty depending on the time of day, were removed or put on the train. Certainly, my father greeted his

Tilli Wertheim in Berleburg, Westphalia in 1924, purportedly acting as a chaperone

bride and her seven-year-old escort at the railroad station in Alsfeld while another member of the Wertheim family gently soothed the train-fearing horse. During this day's visit in Angenrod, Bertel, who must have been the only child present, entertained herself by sweeping the entrance hall, the high steps, and the big yard of the Wertheim residence.[7]

Among the generation of Jews who had moved from Storndorf to Lauterbach in the 1880s, there were two marriages between local Jews of their native village: Juda Baumann (II) and his wife, Elda Strauss Baumann, and Seligmann Jakob and his wife, Emma Baumann Jakob. The succeeding generation only included one marriage of Lauterbach Jews: Max Baumann and Jenny Hess Baumann. The only other marriage between Jews from Lauterbach took place in the United States: that of Arnold Weinberg, born on November 11, 1922, and Ruth Strauss Weinberg, born March 16, 1925.

I never saw my mother's *ketubah*,[e] however, the *ketubah* of my Aunt Mathilde Krebs Lamm written in the Hebrew month of *Av* ('month of consolation') states that her husband, Leo Lamm, will honor and support her in accordance with the custom of Moses and Israel. Furthermore, this *ketubah* states that inasmuch as Mathilde (Hebrew name 'Mela') was a virgin, she is given two hundred *Zuzim* (a monetary unit), which was due her according to the *Torah*. She was also en-

[e] Marriage document written in Aramaic which records the personal and financial obligations which a husband assumes in regard to his marriage.

titled to food, clothing and all her needs according to the prevailing mores of the country and to everything she had brought from her father's house: silver, gold, or jewelry, her clothes, and the use of the bed. Leo, her husband-to-be, gave her one hundred *Litrin* (a measure of volume) of money. Additionally Leo, who is called Rabbi Jehudah in the *ketubah*, takes on the responsibility of this *ketubah* and the additional gifts and pledges of all his belongings under the heavens and on earth and all that he will acquire in the future in accordance with the customs of the daughters of Israel and the changes made by the rabbinic forefathers.

In Lauterbach, furnishing a dowry (the property a wife brings to her husband at marriage) to a marriageable young lady whose parents are unable to furnish a dowry, was deemed one of the most notable good deeds a Jew could perform. Accordingly, my Great-Uncle Samuel Strauss (although he was not related to the Fröhlich family) furnished dowries for Julia and Gustel Fröhlich, daughters of Moses Fröhlich and Berta Rothenberg Fröhlich. Julia married Meyer Adler on May 5, 1911. Gustel never married, although she had a romantic relationship for several years with her neighbor, Siegfried Reiss, whose home was three houses away from her residence in the Bahnhofstrasse.

The majority of the Jewish families who, around the turn of the nineteenth century or shortly before, moved to Lauterbach from Storndorf, Crainfeld, Grebenau, and Ulrichstein usually had six or more children. Couples who married after 1910 rarely had more than two children. Apart from abstinence, I do not know what method of birth control the Jewish families of Lauterbach used.

VISITING THE SICK   MEMBERS OF THE LAUTERBACH JEWISH community deemed visiting the sick (*bikkur holim*) a fundamental religious duty. Shortly before the death of Rebekah Jakob, who was born on January 20, 1846 and who died on May 24, 1919, my mother invited me to accompany her to see Mrs. Jakob. At that time and probably throughout her entire residency in Lauterbach, Rebekah Jakob lived at the home of her older son, Seligmann Jakob, and his wife, Emma Baumann Jakob, at Alter Steinweg 7. Mrs. Rebekah Jakob's younger son, Moses Jakob, lived with his wife, Biena Jakob (née Jakob), and their four sons at Langgasse 19 in Lauterbach, which was but a stone's throw from Seligmann Jakob's home.

During those years, with rare exceptions, older parents and especially widowed spouses stayed at the home of a married daughter or son. Mrs. Jakob's bedroom was reached by negotiating a very steep staircase. I found out later that such steps were common in many older homes in Lauterbach, but at age four they represented a challenge and a new experience. No one else was present while my mother and I visited with Mrs. Jakob, who was resting in her bed on two high pillows with her eyes partially closed. The patient's features were thin and gaunt and her grayish hair had a red shimmer. Furnishings in the room consisted of her bed, a night stand, and a straight chair. No rug covered the well-worn wide floorboards. My mother greeted the seventy-three-year old Mrs.

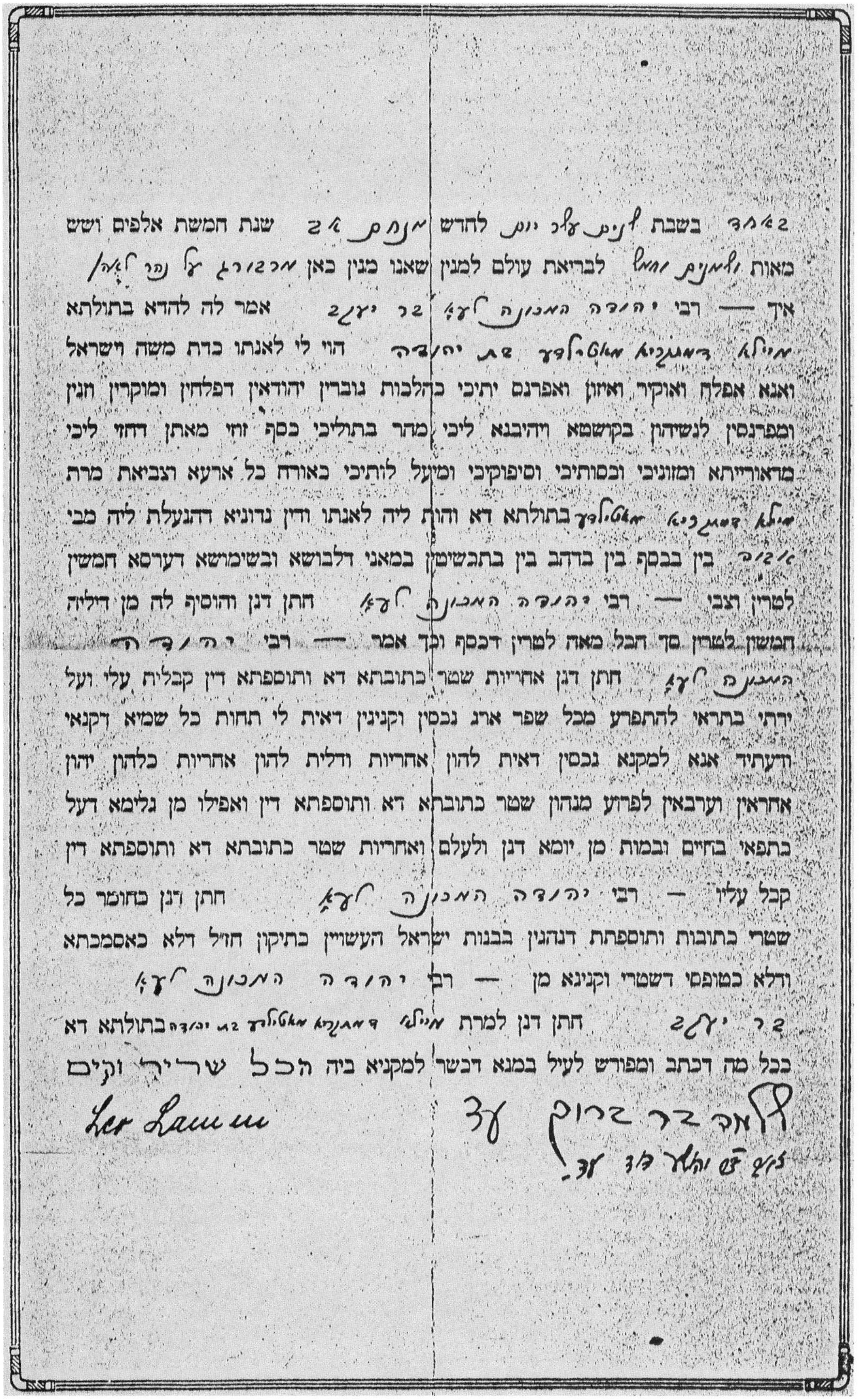

ב... בשבת ב... יום ... לחדש ... שנת חמשת אלפים ושש

מאות ו... ... לבריאת עולם למנין שאנו מנין כאן ... ...

איך — רבי יהודה ... ... אמר לה להדא בתולתא

... ... יהודה הוי לי לאנתו כדת משה וישראל

ואנא אפלח ואוקיר ואיזון ואפרנס יתיכי כהלכות גוברין יהודאין דפלחין ומוקרין וזנין

ומפרנסין לנשיהון בקושטא ויהיבנא ליכי מהר בתוליכי כסף זוזי מאתן דחזי ליכי

מדאורייתא ומזוניכי וכסותיכי וסיפוקיכי ומיעל לותיכי כאורח כל ארעא וצביאת מרת

... ... בתולתא דא והות ליה לאנתו ודין נדוניא דהנעלת ליה מבי

... בין בכסף בין בדהב בין בתכשיטין במאני דלבושא ובשימושא דערסא חמשין

לטרין וצבי — רבי יהודה ... חתן דנן והוסיף לה מן דיליה

חמשין לטרין סך הכל מאה לטרין דכסף וכך אמר — רבי יהודה

... חתן דנן אחריות שטר כתובתא דא ותוספתא דין קבלית עלי ועל

ירתי בתראי להתפרע מכל שפר ארג נכסין וקנינין דאית לי תחות כל שמיא דקנאי

ודעתיד אנא למקנא נכסין דאית להון אחריות ודלית להון אחריות כלהון יהון

אחראין וערבאין לפרוע מנהון שטר כתובתא דא ותוספתא דין ואפילו מן גלימא דעל

כתפאי בחיים ובמות מן יומא דנן ולעלם ואחריות שטר כתובתא דא ותוספתא דין

קבל עליו — רבי יהודה ... חתן דנן כחומר כל

שטרי כתובות ותוספתת דנהגין בבנות ישראל העשוין כתיקון חז"ל דלא כאסמכתא

ודלא כטופסי דשטרי וקנינא מן — רבי יהודה ...

... ... חתן דנן למרת ... ... בתולתא דא

בכל מה דכתב ומפורש לעיל במנא דכשר למקניא ביה הכל שריר וקים

<signatures — handwritten>

Ketubah (marriage contract) of Mathilde Krebs, witnessed by Shlomo Ben Baruch (Samuel
Sonneborn) and Dr. Joshuah David on Sunday, the 12th of *Av* 5685 (1924)

Jakob in a low tone of voice and then we sat quietly by her bedside for a short time. Contrary to her usual practice, my mother brought no food, because she knew that Mrs. Jakob was unable to eat anything. Less than a week after this visit, Mrs. Jakob died.

My mother commonly sent me with food to all members of the Lauterbach Jewish community and to non-Jewish neighbors as well who were ailing in body or soul. I frequently performed this task at the time of the illness of my mother's cousin, Salli Strauss (I), when I laboriously carried a black iron pot filled with noodle pudding for a mile-and-a-half to his residence. Briefly, I entered the upstairs sickroom of the fifty-five-year Salli, deposited the food courteously, and departed as quickly as possible. It would have been unseemly for a fifteen-year-old girl to remain in the sick room of an older male relative.

If a congregant—male or female—was not present at services on the Sabbath, inquiries were made and if the person were ill then some members visited the sick person immediately after services, believing it likely that a current report of synagogue affairs would cheer up the patient. Moreover, visiting the sick is deemed one of those obligations for which a reward is forthcoming in this world—in contrast to other commandments that are remembered in the hereafter. A confirmed illness prior to the Sabbath would require a community member to supply food to the home of the ailing person for the Sabbath. After the *Torah* reading, it was customary in Lauterbach to invoke a special blessing ('*Mi She-Berakh*' meaning 'He Who Blessed') for the ailing absent congregant. A *Mi She-Berakh* was also invoked by anyone called to the *Torah* and in Lauterbach a donation to the synagogue was customary.

Not only visiting of the sick but caring for an ill member of the Jewish congregation was a communal duty, coordinated by an unofficial network. In Lauterbach, established conventions recommended that in addition to physical care, a patient's mind must be disburdened of the care of his family in the event the family had suffered the loss of a housekeeper or a breadwinner. Even the rigid tenets of Sabbath devoutness were secondary to the welfare of a sick community member. Whenever reasonable, it was taken for granted that the closest relatives of an ailing community member accepted the lion's share for the care of an ill relative and his family. Most Jewish families of Lauterbach numbered at least one or two next of kin in town.

DEATH AND DYING

Generally, in Lauterbach, procedures connected with dying and burial were guided by the *Book of Life* (*Sefer ha-Hayyim*) which is an Ashkenazi-Hasidic discourse of mystical theology and ethical teaching. Meyer Höchster carried out the following episode in connection with death and dying in Lauterbach. According to my Great-Uncle Samuel, Meyer Höchster's wife was in poor health and unable to perform household chores, whereupon the husband hired a young housekeeper. Before long the housekeeper was pregnant, and eventually the ailing wife died. As Meyer grew older, he yearned to know how his peers would evaluate him upon his death. For that reason, he pretended to be drawing his last breath so that a *minyan* would be called at his home to recite the Affirmation of Faith ('Hear, O Israel: the Lord our God, the Lord is One') which is customarily recited at death's door. My Great-Uncle Samuel was one of the men at *minyan*. Meyer was in a recumbent position with his eyes tightly closed. The Affirmation of Faith was recited and then in hushed voices remarks about Meyer were made, which were overheard by the presumably dead Meyer. He suddenly opened his eyes and began breathing visibly. My Great-Uncle Samuel's opinion of Meyer Höchster was not especially enhanced by this episode.

In Lauterbach, there was a *chevra kaddisha* ('holy brotherhood' or 'holy sisterhood') which was organized solely for the reverential treatment of the dead. The most important task of the *chevra kaddisha* was to see that the preparation of the corpse (*mitassekin*), which in Upper Hesse was called '*metar sein*,' was performed in accordance with the stipulations of the *Sefer ha-Hayyim*. As a child, I overheard endless discussions of what was, and what was not, appropriate under certain circumstances. This was especially true since the Lauterbach Jewish community, despite its comparative homogeneity, also counted among its members some from other areas who wished to be heard as well, exert their influence, and show their knowledge. It was thought to be a singularly good deed and an honor to serve those who are no more. Such tasks were not performed in the spirit of reciprocity, because the dead can no longer reward the living. Following the attestation of death, close family members gently closed the eyes and mouth and extended arms and hands alongside the body of their departed relative. Also during the day, family members of the dead kept watch over the body.

When I was nine, at the time of my Great-Uncle

Book of Life (*Sefer ha-Hayyim*)

Chapter Eleven

Samuel's death in 1924, my mother invited me to watch over his body in an open pine coffin set upon two chairs in his living room on the second floor of Cent 17. I dutifully carried out my mother's order, because as my mother stated, "a mouse might otherwise come near the body." This notion is set down in the *Sefer ha-Hayyim* published in 1884 in Hanover, Germany in its sixth edition and revised by J. J. Krimke, the authorized rabbi.

From nightfall till dawn, the *chevra kaddisha*, serving in two shifts and consistent with gender, assumed watching over the body in the home of the dead person. My mother, despite her young age, was considered a master hand of the local *chevra kaddisha* and the preparation of the body for burial. In 1919, at the time of Rebekah Jakob's death, my mother's close friend and contemporary, Sara Strauss Spier, and my mother, who were then twenty-seven and twenty-six years of age, respectively, were elected to serve the first night watch until two o'clock in the morning. Sara, who only two years earlier had withstood the loss of her husband, Moritz Spier, in World War I as a front-line soldier, was understandably reluctant to perform this task. My mother conscientiously fulfilled her assignment alone and at two o'clock in the morning she walked home alone for about one mile through the utterly dark and deserted streets of Lauterbach.

The immediacy of burial on the day of death or the following day, which is practiced by orthodox Jews in the United States, was not prevalent in Lauterbach or nearby Jewish communities in Upper Hesse, because family members from even nearby towns and villages were restricted by slow modes of transportation. In some instances even notification of death could not be readily transmitted. Moreover, the tenor of the day was not geared to hurry and, among the Jews of Lauterbach and Upper Hesse, accounts circulated of those who had been consigned to the grave prematurely and alive.

Burial garments for both the husband and wife were usually part of their marriage portion and were also worn on *Rosh ha-Shanah* and *Yom Kippur*. For men they consisted of a loosely-fitting white garment of altar linen quality girded with an intricately-woven, narrow cotton belt and a hat comparable to a nightcap without a point. It was the wife's duty and responsibility to keep the burial garments in immaculate condition. After careful laundering, my mother bleached the garments on the lawn on a sunny day to ensure perfect whiteness and laboriously ironed the garment to perfection. Women were buried in a white dress and *Röckle*, a rectangular garment made of black silk and shaped like a *tallit katan* (small prayer shawl), which strictly observant male Jews wore under their upper clothing on weekdays. The headcovering for women was their *Häubchen* (an abbreviated *mantilla*), which may have had its inception in Spain or Portugal, where the forebears of so many Jews of Upper Hesse had lived.

The Lauterbach Jewish cemetery is situated in the old Leimenkaute and was obtained from Ferdinand Stichten-oth.[8] On July 25, 1988, the earliest still decipherable tombstone was that of one Samuel Stein, born on November 12, 1838. His death is recorded on the tombstone as November 8, 1899. Therefore, the

Lauterbach Jewish cemetery must have been acquired sometime prior to this date. Sigmund Strauss, Samuel Strauss (I), and Aron Stein signed as members of the board for the Lauterbach Jewish community at the time of the cemetery and synagogue grounds acquisition and documentation.[9] My mother repeated over and over that our Great-Uncle Samuel furnished the funds for the plot of ground for the Jewish cemetery site and as well as the funds for the site of the Lauterbach synagogue at Hinter der Burg 17.

My Great-Uncle Samuel's funeral in 1924 took place on the day before the Day of Atonement (*Erev Yom Kippur*). In Lauterbach, death or burial on this day denoted a lifetime of piety and rectitude to the ideals of Judaism. My parents commissioned a non-Jew in Lauterbach to transport his coffin by a coach solely intended for this purpose. Great-Uncle Samuel's coffin was covered with a heavy black cloth from Cent 17 to the Jewish cemetery at the end of the Kalkofenweg. The custom of covering a coffin in a black cloth on its way to the cemetery arose again in August of 1930 at the time of burial of my mother's cousin, Salli Strauss (I), (of) Am Eselswörth 6. At that time, a member of the local *chevra kaddisha* was responsible for the keeping of the black cloth. However, its whereabouts could not be ascertained, and as the funeral procession could no longer be delayed, the *cortège* advanced without a proper covering for the coffin. Such nakedness of the coffin betokened lack of dignity. Therefore my great-aunt, Lina Frank Strauss, the wife of my maternal grandmother's youngest brother, Markus Strauss, wryly commented: "*Wie gelebt, so gestorben.*" ("As one lives, so one dies"). Needless to say, Aunt Lina was not a devotee of her nephew-by-marriage, Salli Strauss.

Approximately in the center of the cemetery stood a small building that, to the best of my recollection, held some garden tools and was constructed after the manner of a half-timbered structure. This building may have been intended to serve members of the Jewish congregation as a shelter against the elements and, in the event of long harsh periods of frost, as a place of storage before burial could be facilitated. Additionally, this building contained running water, which enabled the mourners and others to have water poured over their hands from a pitcher before leaving the cemetery. This procedure was repeated at our home at Cent 17, before anyone coming from the cemetery was allowed to enter our living quarters. This custom reflected the notion that while honoring the dying and dead was looked upon as the most worthy of deeds, contact with the cemetery or dead also rendered one impure. In 1959, during my first brief sojourn in Lauterbach after the Holocaust, I saw this little building in the Jewish cemetery for the last time. Subsequently, the town fathers tore it down.

In Lauterbach and for some neighboring towns such as Herbstein, Bad Salzschlirf, Crainfeld, Gedern, and Schlitz, Max Stern, the teacher, delivered the eulogies; only in out-of-the-ordinary circumstances were the services of Dr. Leo Hirschfeld of Giessen, the duly authorized regional rabbi, requested. Mr. Stern's eulogies conveyed genuine true-heartedness that stemmed from his close contact with his fellow congregants. For this reason, the Jews of Lauterbach and the adjoining region preferred the services of Mr. Stern. Also, his fees were less than those of Dr. Hirschfeld whose charges included an additional payment for his railroad fare to Lauterbach and return to Giessen.

For many years, my mother kept the printed eulogy of Cilly Katz, the daughter of Hannchen Sonneborn Katz from Breidenbach and Joel Katz, who died some time after 1906 and before 1910. (In Lauterbach, this family lived near the *Elektrizitätswerk* and their home faced a little brook.) According to my mother who traveled in the same Jewish social circles of Lauterbach, Max Stern was romantically involved with Cilly Katz, whose young life was prematurely snuffed out by tuberculosis. It was rare during those years for a small Jewish congregation such as Lauterbach to print a eulogy and distribute it to those who were interested. The Jews of Lauterbach indicated in this manner how much they valued Max Stern's appropriate words at such a difficult time and also expressed that 'shared pain is half the pain' ('*Geteilter Schmerz ist halber Schmerz*').

In Lauterbach, rituals and prayers before and after burial took place in the house of the mourners and at the cemetery because funeral homes were unknown. The rending of garments (*keri'ah*) as a sign of grief at the time of death of parents, children, siblings, or a spouse was done at home by making a small tear in a garment which was worn frequently by the mourner. The local Jewish widow, Anna Adler Weinberg (of) Am Wörth 14, who, not usually in the foreground of sociability, suddenly and with great regularity appeared at times of grave illness and death when she unfailingly performed the task of *keri'ah*. Anna's mind-set in connection with illness and death earned her the name '*Todesvogel*' ('bird of death') among the Jews of Lauterbach. The Jewish bereaved did not usually wear black attire during their time of mourning as was the practice of non-Jews in town. Ordinarily, the wardrobe of Jews did not include the brightly-colored wearing apparel of non-Jews at any time, and certainly not during a period of bereavement. In a house of mourning, mirrors were covered up, because during *shivah* vanity is unbefitting.

Lamenting in public for a dear departed was expressed by gentle sobbing: anything louder was considered lack of restraint, and no burial hymn was sung at the grave. Upon returning from the cemetery, a period of seven days of mourning (*shivah*) commenced. The mourners sat on non-upholstered low chairs or stools and wore slippers of cloth or felt. For eleven months, a special light remained lit after the demise of a parent, child, or sibling. For a spouse, the special light remained lit for only thirty days (*sheloshim*). The first meal after the funeral contained no meat, but consisted of an egg to be consumed without salt. The shape of the egg expressed the abiding fellowship with God and the lack of salt indicated that this is no time to enhance the flavor of food for greater enjoyment.

Men observing *shivah* or *sheloshim* did not cut their hair or shave. In fact, even ordinarily very few men in Lauterbach used a razor in accordance with *Leviticus 19:27* which states, "Ye shall not round the corners of your heads, neither shalt thou mar the corners of thy beard." Most of the older men wore neatly-trimmed short beards and those younger men (including my father, who did not) burned off the growth of hair on their faces by applying an obnoxiously smelling paste that reeked of sulfur.

Often my mother took me along for *shivah* calls, in which a visitor sat close by the mourner, who generally initiated a conversation about the life and demise of the departed family member. Food or drink were never served during the *shivah* and frivolous topics of conversation were considered rude and in poor taste. Following the death of a wedded woman or man, the assigned synagogue seat was kept unoccupied for thirty days: after that period, the seat of the departed was reassigned.

In Lauterbach, close relatives of the deceased recited the mourner's prayer (*kaddish*) for eleven months—except for a spouse, who said *kaddish* for only thirty days. This mourner's prayer is for the most part written in Aramaic and extols God without reference to death. The practice of reciting the mourner's *kaddish* in the presence of ten adult males for eleven months and yearly thereafter on the date of death (*Yahrzeit*), when a candle is also lit in the home for twenty-four hours, probably originated in Germany in the thirteenth century at a time of the persecutions by the Crusaders.

Most of the Jews of Lauterbach discharged their ritual observances with great dignity and considered them to be an integral part of their lives. The *kaddish* prayer, other mourning rituals, and *yizkor*[f] constituted but one small segment of their religious faithfulness. An especially devout member of the Lauterbach Jewish congregation, Emma Baumann Jakob, many a time stressed that the day of death was to be favored over the day of birth (*Ecclesiastes 7:1*) The aged Emma Jakob, her husband, Seligmann Jakob, and two of her three sons, Julius and Max Jakob, fell victim to the mass destruction of the Nazis.

Endnotes

1. Alfred J. Kolatch, *The Name Dictionary,* (NY: Jonathan David Publishers), p. 28.

2. Ibid, p. 80.

3. Ibid, p. 97.

4. Ibid, p. 297.

5. Ibid, p. 287.

6. Leon Klenicki and Gabe Huck, *Spirituality and Prayer: Jewish and Christian Understanding,* (New York: Paulist Press, 1983), pp. 131, 132.

7. Letter from Bertel Strauss Nathan, March 8, 1989.

8. Letter from Hans Gliss, Municipal Officer of Lauterbach, dated October 13, 1983.

9. Ibid.

---

[f] Opening word of memorial prayer for the dead; also applied to memorial section of service on the eighth day of Passover, second day of the Feast of Weeks, on *Shemini Azeret* (the eighth day of *Sukkot*, and on the Day of Atonement (*Yom Kippur*).

Chapter Twelve
Lauterbach's Spiritual Leaders and Unmarrieds Establishing the Cemetery

The Jewish cemetery in Lauterbach

MAX STERN AND
RELIGIOUS EDUCATION
IN LAUTERBACH

*M*ax Stern was the spiritual leader of the Lauterbach Jewish community from 1906 until its destruction by the Nazis. His mother was Klara Weichselbaum from Dettelbach, Bavaria, and his father was Salomon Stern from Hintersteinau, where Max and his siblings were born and raised. Max Stern came into the world on July 21, 1885, the youngest of nine children. In 1754, thirteen Jews were mentioned in Hintersteinau, which at that time officially belonged to the territory of Hanau, Schlüchtern, and Steinau.[1]

Three miles west of Max Stern's hometown, Hintersteinau, lies the village of Freiensteinau. There, during the late eighteenth century, the Riedesel, the local agrarian elite sovereigns, did not permit Jews to settle in territories under their jurisdiction. As was the case in all other regions of the Riedesel domain, Jews were not allowed to acquire real estate. However, Jews who lived in almost every neighboring village within the jurisdiction of other sovereigns were considerably involved in court proceedings in Freiensteinau as cattle and horse dealers and as yard goods merchants.[2]

Max Stern, spiritual leader of the Lauterbach Jewish congregation from 1907 to 1935. He served in the German army from 1916 to 1918 and received the Iron Cross. In 1942 he was murdered by the Nazis.

Ten miles south of Hintersteinau is the village of Steinau. Prior to 1348 to 1349, the time of the bubonic plague, a great number of Jews had lived in Steinau. This Jewish community was annihilated during the years of the Black Death and few Jews survived. Two families of Sephardic lineage from Steinau fled to Schlüchtern. The Jewish remnant pronounced a ban that no Jew was ever to return to Steinau, which in fact they never did.[3]

In Fulda, Max Stern qualified for admission to a university (*Abitur*). He successfully completed his work at the teacher's seminary in Würzburg that licensed him to teach Hebrew and Jewish history as well as secular subjects in public school. At that time, Max Stern also passed the examination to be a *shohet* (ritual slaughterer). The test involved an oral examination on the law of *shehitah* (ritual slaughter) and the correct performance of the requisite skills at least three times in the presence of experts. After passing his examination, a *shohet* is obligated to go over the laws of ritual slaughter daily during the first thirty days, then once a month during the first year, and after that at least once in three months. In addition, a *shohet* is required to inspect the sharpness of his knives periodically and also to have them examined by rabbinic authorities.

Chapter Twelve

Like the majority of other Jews in Upper Hesse, the Lauterbach Jewish community was orthodox. Lauterbach was Max Stern's first assignment after finishing teachers' seminary in 1906, when he was twenty-one-years old. At about the same time, my mother, then age fifteen, went to live in Lauterbach. She often commented that Max Stern possessed a very jovial disposition and that he was an accomplished dancer. They moved in the same social circles although there was an age difference of six years.

UNMARRIED PEOPLE
IN LAUTERBACH

IN LAUTERBACH, THERE EXISTED an unwritten etiquette among young unattached Jews. Social interaction beyond formal greetings between Jews who were older than fourteen and non-Jews of the opposite sex was absolutely forbidden. The social etiquette of this orthodox congregation prescribed close friendships among Jews only. My mother often recounted the strong cohesion between the members of her Jewish circle in Lauterbach and their loyalty and good feelings toward every member. Naturally, there were some romantic interests within the group. The following persons belonged to the circle:

• the brothers Bernhard, Max, and Siegfried Baumann (children of Karoline Baumann [née Hasenauer] from Wiesenfeld and Juda Baumann (I) from Storndorf), who lived at Bleichstrasse 12 in Lauterbach;

• Emma, Ida, Else, and Recha Baumann (children of Elda Baumann [née Strauss] and Juda Baumann (II), both hailing from Storndorf), who lived at Bahnhofstrasse 66;

• Julia and Gustel Fröhlich (daughters of Berta Rothenberg Fröhlich from Gaukersweiler in the Pfalz and Moses Fröhlich from Ulrichstein), who lived at Bahnhofstrasse 34;

• Berta, Gidda, and Jenny Hess (daughters of Fanny Hess [née Stern] from Hintersteinau, Max Stern's sister, and Nathan Hess from Crainfeld), who lived at Langgasse 21;

• Kaufmann and Nathan Höchster (sons of Zippora and Meyer Höchster from Storndorf);

• Cilly, Meyer, and Moritz Katz (children of Hannchen Katz [née Sonneborn] from Breidenbach and Joel Katz from Storndorf), who lived behind the old electrical works near a tiny brook at Hinter dem Spittel;

• Berta Lamm, my mother, from Kirtorf (daughter of Auguste Lamm [née Strauss] from Storndorf and Jakob Lamm from Kirtorf), who lived with her aunt, Johanna (Hannchen) Schloss Strauss, and her uncle, Samuel Strauss (I), at Cent 17, which later became Cent 25;

• Auguste and Siegfried Reiss (children of Anna Reiss [née Gottlieb] from Neuhof-Flieden near Fulda and Mr. Reiss from Ulrichstein), who lived at Bahnhofstrasse 20;

• Jenny and Sophie Strauss (daughters of Helene Cahn Strauss of Rockelsgasse 41 and Kaufmann Strauss from Storndorf);

• Resl, Jenny, and Hedwig Strauss (daughters of Settchen Strauss [née Flörsheim] from Romrod and Sigmund Strauss from Grebenau), who lived at Hintergasse 12;

- Siegfried Strauss (II) and Minna Strauss (children of Lina Strauss [née Frank] from Nieder-Ohnen and Markus Strauss from Storndorf), who lived at Hinter dem Spittel 4;
- Max, Moritz, Settie, and Toni Stein (children of Karoline Stein from Walldorf county of Gross-Gerau and Aron Stein from Grebenau), who lived at Eisenbacher Tor 7;
- Sara Strauss (daughter of Therese [née Strauss] from Storndorf and Karl Strauss from Grebenau), who lived at Bahnhofstrasse 70; and
- David, Lina, and Rosalie Weinberg (children of Fanny Simon Weinberg and Abraham Weinberg from Storndorf).

[207

A sewing circle of twelve women (of which six were Jewish) in Lauterbach in 1920. The Jewish members are:

Front row:
Recha Baumann (center)
Selma Strauss (fifth from left)
Rosalie Weinberg (six from left)
Second row:
Emma Baumann (second from left)
Sophie Strauss (third from left)
Minna Strauss (fifth from left)

LIEBMAN
ROTHSCHILD

PRIOR TO THE APPOINTMENT of Max Stern, Liebman Rothschild had been the spiritual leader of the Lauterbach Jewish community, where he discharged the duties of teacher, *cantor*, and *shohet*. Before his coming to Lauterbach, Liebman Rothschild had pursued scientific and rabbinic studies in Breslau. In Lauterbach, he supplemented his salary from the Jewish community by tutoring students of the Kullmann Institute in classical languages. Mr. Rothschild lived (on) am Wörth and is reputed to have been a strict grammarian. He made it possible for his younger son, Adolf, to study at the university in Marburg. Later, Adolf became a pacifist. The older son, Leopold, was a classmate of Dorothy Stausebach Tag of Lauterbach. At age ninety-nine, Dorothy Stausebach Tag recalled that Leopold was seated in the last row in a schoolroom which housed two classes. Mrs. Tag emphasized that Leopold Rothschild was a very able student and much admired by others of his age group for his knowledge.[4]

THE OLD SYNAGOGUE
AND THE JEWISH
CEMETERY

FROM 1884 ON, THE FLEDGLING LAUTERBACH Jewish community held religious services (at) am Unteren Graben in the annex of a farm building, which until the 1980s belonged to the premises of Möller and Stöhr. In 1889, the thirteen Jews of Lauterbach, which included my Great-Uncles Samuel and Salomon Strauss

Chapter Twelve

(I), turned down a proposal for the establishment of a Jewish cemetery.[5] Based on *Job 30:23*, "For I know that thou wilt bring me to death, and to the house appointed for all living," Jews call a cemetery '*bet hayim*' (house of the living); in Lauterbach, as in most other Jewish communities in Hesse, the cemetery was called '*der gute Ort*' ('the good place'). The custom of a cemetery as a common burial ground is post-biblical and came into existence for practical reasons in connection with the purity laws. These laws forbid *kohanim* (descendants of the biblical Aaron) to touch a corpse or come within four cubits of a grave. *Kohanim* were not permitted to enter a cemetery except for the burial of a close relative—a parent, child, wife, brother, or unmarried sister. Therefore, it became customary to bury *kohanim* in a special section, which enabled relatives to visit the graves of *kohanim* without entering the cemetery.

In Lauterbach, Joel Katz was a descendant of Aaron, the high priest, because Jews with the surnames Cohen, Marx, and Katz generally fall into that category. He is buried in a special section of the cemetery set aside for *kohanim* along with members of the Nathan Hess family. Strict separation of *kohanim* was also maintained in Storndorf, where the Jewish cemetery was divided into three sections. One segment which can be entered without entering the cemetery was set apart for *kohanim*. Another parcel was assigned to Jews who had lived under the jurisdiction of the feudal lords, the Herren von Seebach. A third section was allocated to Jews who had lived under the sovereignty of other feudal lords, the Herren von Storndorf. Feudalism in Storndorf controlled its Jews even beyond life.

According to cemetery etiquette, a visitor is not allowed to wear a prayer shawl (*tallit*) or phylacteries (*tefillin*). Moreover, a visitor should not read from a *Torah* scroll, lest he shame the dead who no longer can carry out these religious duties. Eating or drinking are not allowed in a cemetery and the cemetery plot may not be used for worldly causes. In Lauterbach, from 1941 to 1959, the barber Helfenbein violated this reverence for the Jewish dead by planting a garden and sundry fruit trees in the Jewish cemetery (at) am Kalkofen.

THE NEW SYNAGOGUE (1908)

IN 1899, MY GREAT-UNCLE SAMUEL STRAUSS (I) was the *parnas* of the Lauterbach Jewish community. This title is used frequently by communities of Spanish or Portuguese origin to designate the elected head of the Jewish congregation. In 1900, ninety-five Jews lived in Lauterbach, most of who had moved there after the War of 1870 to 1871.[6] In 1908, two years after Mr. Stern's arrival, the Lauterbach Jewish community dedicated its synagogue at Hinter der Burg 17. In 1906, the Lauterbach Jewish community bought the property registered on Flur 2, Number 16 for its place of worship. The three congregational elders—my Great-Uncle Samuel Strauss [I] (Cent 17), Sigmund Strauss (Hintergasse 12), and Aron Stein (am Eisenbacher Tor 7)—initiated the purchase of land from Louise Engelmann.[7]

During the last quarter of the nineteenth century in Upper Hesse, a disproportionate number of Jews lived in small rural communities such as Angenrod, Crainfeld,

Grebenau, and Storndorf, where for centuries the local sovereigns had made capital out of the special taxes and tolls imposed upon their Jewish residents. In 1880, 25.5% of the total population of the village of Grebenau were Jews. This percentage marked the highest concentration of Jews in any village in Upper Hesse.[8] Around 1860, many Jews in the villages of Upper Hesse began to leave the small communities where they had found refuge earlier, settling in larger towns such as Lauterbach. Around 1890, Jews moved into Lauterbach because, among other reasons, it had become a railroad junction; routes were established from Frankfurt am Main to Lauterbach and from Giessen to Fulda. In addition, Lauterbach had been upgraded to a county town. Lauterbach had the newest Jewish community in Upper Hesse.

Until about 1900, many of the small Jewish congregations in Upper Hesse conducted religious services in a room set aside for this purpose or, if they could

A postcard issued in commemoration of the Lauterbach synagogue on August 14, 15 and 16, 1908

afford a more expensive option, they constructed a half-timbered building for their house of worship. In Hesse, the small Jewish communities generally were able to erect a house of worship only at great financial sacrifice to their members. The half-timbered synagogue building in Romrod stood as late as 1984. It eluded destruction during *Kristallnacht* (November 10, 1938) because for several years it had not been used for religious services.

During the first third of the nineteenth century, synagogues exhibited oriental characteristics, but after 1830, synagogues were designed in a Romanesque style that later resembled New Romanticism. An example was the 'New Synagogue,' built seventy-five miles from Lauterbach in Kassel in 1839. The architectural style of the Kassel synagogue symbolized the integration of Jews into the Christian milieu by indicating the German culture of the Jews. The Romanesque style echoed Romance and Byzantine motifs, which were rare in synagogue structures before 1840. While the revival of the Gothic style played a major part in the construction of churches of that era, it was of little importance in the building of synagogues.[9] First, throughout history the rabbis had discouraged or forbidden their flock to imitate the ways and mores of other religions and second, the Jews of Hesse had not forgotten the cruelties inflicted upon them by some of the princes of Gothic churches of the Middle Ages in France, the German lands, and Spain, that forced some Jews to flee to Hesse.

In early 1907, the Lauterbach synagogue elders, Samuel Strauss (I), Sigmund Strauss, and Aron Stein, enlisted the services of Mr. Reuter, the official architect of the dominant agrarian elite families of the Riedesel, to prepare plans for their synagogue at Hinter der Burg 17. There were as yet very few Jewish architects in Germany and most likely none in Hesse, therefore compelling the Lauterbach Jewish community elders to rely on Mr. Reuter. Because the aristocratic Riedesel landowners had always regarded Jews with disdain, Mr. Reuter's availability to the Jewish community was astonishing.

In 1985, I met with Mr. Reuter's grandson, Horst Reuter, who was then the Lauterbach town architect. When I asked him why his grandfather's employers allowed him to undertake the synagogue project, Horst Reuter stated that his grandfather, as well was one member of the Riedesel family, belonged to a freemason lodge. On December 6, 1738, the first freemason lodge had been established in Hamburg with the principles of freedom to state personal views, freedom of conscience, and freedom of assembly.[10] In 1907, was it perhaps the influence of the freemason lodge that guided Mr. Reuter and the Riedesel?

In April, 1907, Reuter signed the synagogue blueprint, whereon Sigmund Strauss' signature appeared for the Lauterbach Israelite congregation. An additional notation by Sigmund Strauss stated that the cost of the building without furnishings amounted to 18,000 *Mark*. The Lauterbach synagogue was situated behind the residence and offices of the Riedesel on a short side street. The property behind the synagogue belonged to the Peters family, who owned a bar parlor in Lauterbach. There the Stern family would drink cider on the Sabbath and pay their bill to Mr. Peters on Sunday. According to Jewish law, one was allowed to carry nothing on the Sabbath, especially not money.

Bordering the synagogue in the north lived the Georg family who, according to Dr. Naphtali (Herbert) Stern, was friendly with the Stern family. As stated in an interview on July 29, 1988, Florchen Georg Stiehler affirmed that her mother was a favorite person of Salochen Stern, the oldest and severely handicapped son of Rosa and Max Stern.

The Lauterbach synagogue was a composite of Art Nouveau and Moorish architecture. The latter was expressed by a cupola topped by a modestly sized Star of David. The six-pointed star was used for magic and decorative purposes in ancient times by Jews and non-Jews alike and by Christians in the Middle Ages. Mellow sandstone covered the walls and doors of the synagogue building. The humble dome and dark roof of the synagogue was in sharp contrast to those of the impressive Protestant church. This church was a pearl of high baroque architecture; its towering steeple was situated on Lauterbach's most important street,

Street view of the Lauterbach synagogue

View from the Bahnhofstrasse   View from the north

The Way It Was: The Jewish World of Rural Hesse

Interior view showing holy ark

the Marktplatz. The modest Catholic chapel, built after 1908 on the Rimloserstrasse, was also located on a more important street than Hinter der Burg.

The windows of the synagogue and a scalloped ornamental design at the edge of the roof showed the influence of Art Nouveau: an art movement called '*Jugendstil*' in Germany, and which was centered in Europe in the 1890s and in America was employed by Louis C. Tiffany. The Art Nouveau genre was used sparingly on the synagogue building, perhaps indicating that the synagogue elders were proceeding with measured guardedness. Nevertheless, as the human heart will, these community elders had faith in the decency of mankind and in the integrity of their non-Jewish neighbors. They had a stout-heartedness that was expressed in their synagogue building; and above all they had the vision for a better life for themselves and their children than they and their forefathers had endured in the communities of Crainfeld, Grebenau, and Storndorf.

A *mikveh*.
Johann Christoph Georg Bodenschatz, *Kirchliche Verfassung der heutigen Juden*, Leipzig and Frankfurt, 1749

The northern part of the synagogue cellar included a *mikveh* (a pool or bath of clear water). Immersion in a *mikveh* ritually cleanses a person who has become ritually contaminated. A *mikveh* must be built directly in the ground and contain at least one hundred twenty gallons of water. When a person immerses himself he momentarily enters the realm of the non-living, so that when he emerges he is like one reborn. The scriptures say, "And I will sprinkle clean water upon you and ye shall be clean; from all your idols will I cleanse you."

If a non-Jew desires to become a Jew, one of the requirements he or she must fulfill is to submerge in the *mikveh* for spiritual rebirth. To the best of my knowledge the *mikveh* in Lauterbach was never utilized for conversions, because there were none from 1906 until November 10, 1938, when the synagogue was destroyed.

In Lauterbach, the *mikveh* was used primarily by orthodox women after menstruation or childbirth. Ritual immersion in the *mikveh* was required before sexual intercourse could be resumed. Orthodox men who had no bathing facilities in their homes either bathed in the public baths behind the power plant (*Elektrizitätswerk*) or used the *mikveh* before the Sabbath and holidays. The Max Stern family also observed the dictum of immersing in the *mikveh* the vessels that they purchased from a non-Jew and which were made of metal and glass and intended for the preparation of food.[11] Others in the Jewish community used the water of the Lauter brook for observing this commandment, particularly the conscientiously orthodox Emma Jakob, who lived at Alter Steinweg 7 quite close by the brook.

My curiosity about the *mikveh* was aroused when my mother sent me at age seven

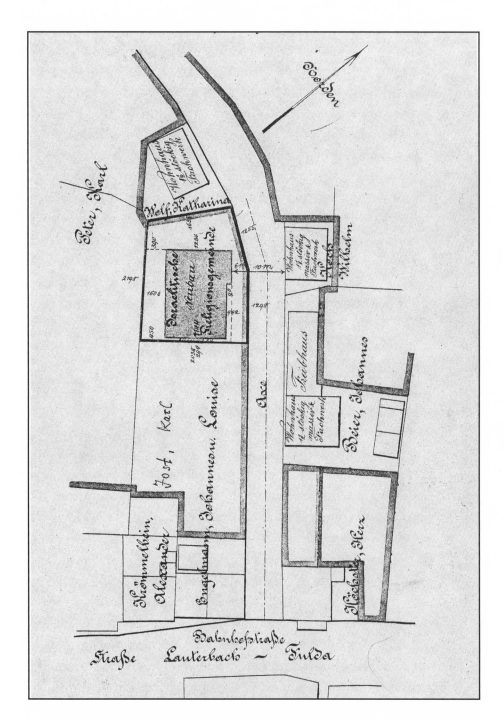

The new Lauterbach synagogue's location off the Bahnhofstrasse. The Bahnhofstrasse is the horizontal road at the bottom of the plan. The synagogue is located on the smaller sidestreet that runs vertically and is on the left near the top (*Israelitische Religionsgemeinde*)

or eight with a note to Anna Weinberg (at) am Wörth 14 requesting an appointment to the *mikveh*. I knew that the *mikveh* had something to do with taking a bath, but I could not understand why my mother bathed at home before going to the *mikveh*. Moreover, it is difficult for a young child to understand the concept of symbolic cleanliness. According to law, the *mikveh* in Lauterbach had separate bathing facilities for cleansing one's body, from whence seven steps led to the pool of water for immersion. The architectural drawing of the Lauterbach synagogue shows a waiting room and lavatory next to the *mi kveh* and an arched cellar took up the rest of this level.

On the main floor of the synagogue building was the sanctuary that housed the holy ark (*aron kodesh*). The ark faced toward the east because a Jew positions himself toward Jerusalem during prayer. The Lauterbach synagogue had seating facilities for one hundred men in the sanctuary downstairs and benches for seventy-four women upstairs. The medium-brown wooden seats for men were constructed so that the seats could be moved back noiselessly when the congregants stood to pray and would be pushed back down, when the men wanted to sit again. Every synagogue member was the owner of his own lockable bookstand where he kept his prayer books and prayer shawl. My father's bookstand also contained a tiny volume of the *Book of Psalms* (*Tehillim*), exactly 3½ by 2½ inches, with a cedarwood cover displaying multi-colored decorations and the word "Jerusalem." This tiny book delighted me during Sabbath *minhah* (afternoon) services as a young child.

The yellow, green, and blue windows pivoted horizontally toward the outside, when they were opened by a crank: the colors signified the sun, earth, and sky respectively. Benches for women, made of solid dark wood, were situated in the upstairs area on all sides except the east. The eternal light (*ner tamid*) hung above the holy ark where the sacred scrolls were kept. Above the holy ark was the eternal light. Max Stern's desk was installed immediately in front of the holy ark on an elevated area from which he delivered sermons on the high holidays, the pilgrim feasts, and on special sabbaths like the sabbath before Passover or other memorable occasions such as a *bar mitzvah*.

Max Stern had been instructed in oratory in the Würzburg Seminary and he discharged this duty well. Two seven-armed menorahs flanked Max Stern's desk and midway between his desk, and the seven-branched *menorahs* were several steps on each side that led down to the middle of the sanctuary where the *Torah* was read. Here was the *almemar*, or *bimah* (elevated place). In the Lauterbach synagogue, it was a platform with a railing, a bench, and a desk from where the *Torah* reading took place. A light on each corner of the *almemar* illuminated the area. The floor of the synagogue was covered with maroon runners and the walls were painted off-white.

Directly above the *almemar,* in the attic of the synagogue building, was located a window with the same design and colors as the horizontal pivoting windows. The attic window was reminiscent of an oriental style of building widespread in the first century. At that time, the scholar, Hillel the Elder, is said to have listened in on

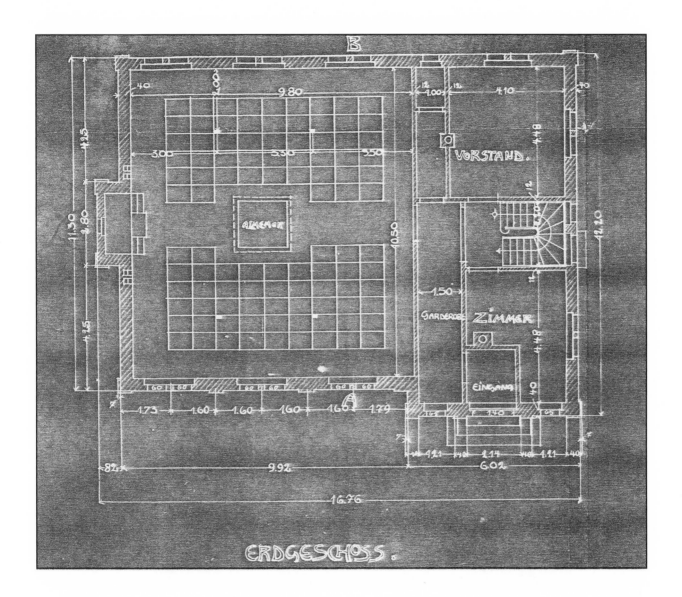

The first floor of the new Lauterbach synagogue. The holy ark is on the left wall, the *almenar* is in the middle of the floor in an open area surrounded by a balcony on the second floor. There is a cloak room (*Garderobe*). The *Vorstand* was the area from which the sermon was delivered.

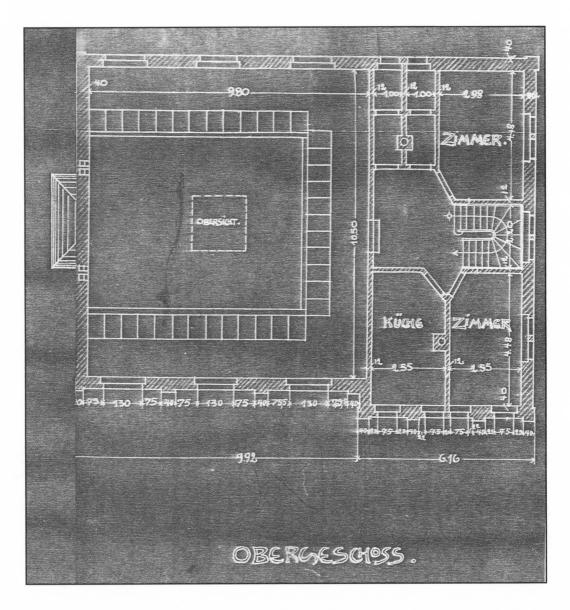

The second floor of the Lauterbach synagogue showing the women's balcony that overlooks the first floor (the *almenar* is in the middle of the opening). A kitchen (*Küche*) is one of the three rooms on this floor.

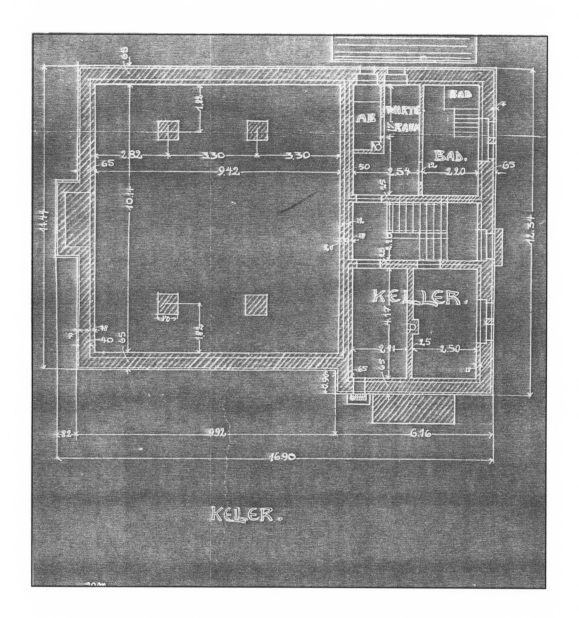

The cellar of the Lauterbach synagogue. The *mikveh* is in the upper right (*Bad*).

lessons and rabbinic discussions through the attic window, because he was too poor to pay tuition. In the synagogue attic, a brown wooden fence some thirty inches high surrounded the window. However, the fence was no deterrent to Ludwig Marx, Mr. Stern's nephew, who once wished to retrieve a ball that had fallen on the glass. Ludwig fell through the glass in the attic, picked himself up from the *almemar* and received considerable admonitions not to hop over the fence in the attic here-after. Ludwig Marx had come to live with his uncle and family in Lauterbach in order to avail himself of the opportunity of a high school education that he could not get in Rachtig where his parents lived.

The Jews of Lauterbach adhered to some Sephardic customs. Inside the almemar and bench were cabinets for storing *Wimpel*. A *Wimpel* was a banner made of a

The *Wimpel* of Max K. Stein-twentieth century

piece of linen or silk (in Lauterbach it was generally fashioned of linen) used to wrap up a male baby at the time of his circumcision. Afterwards, the cloth was thoroughly cleaned and cut into four equal pieces which were sewn together to create a long, narrow band to be used as a *Torah* binder. Generally, it was six to eight inches wide and nine to twelve feet long. The *Wimpel* was usually inscribed in painted letters with the name of the child, his parentage (indicating only the father's name), and his date of birth. Usually the Hebrew inscription would state that "God bless the boy child to grow up to study the *Torah* and perform good deeds. Amen."

A parent talented in art might make the *Wimpel,* creating fanciful Hebrew letters that were partially illuminated, or perhaps the local scribe or teacher would pro-duce the *Wimpel*, often emblazoning it with flowers. An observant German-Jewish mother had not a few tasks to perform before her son was eligible to present his *Wimpel* at the synagogue—preferably when the infant was fifty-two weeks old. It was the mother's task either to make the *Wimpel* herself or to find someone who would create one worthy enough for her son to donate to the synagogue. The mother also had to wean her infant, as Hannah in *Samuel I :22* said unto her hus-band: "Until the child be weaned, when I will bring him, that he may appear before the Lord."

Also, in keeping with the charge of the *Shulchan Arukh* (literally the 'prepared table,' the code of law arranged by Joseph Caro), the mother also had to toilet train the infant by the time he was fifty-two weeks old. Then the boy was taken to the synagogue by his father for the first time. After the *Torah* reading, the infant held onto the handles of the scroll while his father secured his son's *Wimpel* around the

Torah. The father's prayer included gratitude for the gift of his son and the petition to the Almighty, "Train up the boy in Thy way, and even when he is old he will not depart from Thee." Then the father pronounced the '*shehecheyanu*'—the blessing pronounced out of gratitude for the privilege of savoring a memorable event.

In the Lauterbach synagogue, young boys between the ages of six and eleven took turns in rolling up any *Wimpel,* which was not neatly wound. Two boys had to work simultaneously to accomplish this work neatly. Not infrequently on a holiday there were six boys busily engaged around the *Torah* and vying with each other to be extra neat and competent about rolling up the *Wimpel.* The *Wimpel* storage cabinet in Lauterbach was filled with the *Wimpel* of every boy born between 1908 and November 10, 1938. On that night, one night after the synagogues in other towns in Germany were burned in the Nazi pogrom called *Kristallnacht,* the local SS wearing stocking hats set fire to the synagogue at Hinter der Burg.[12] Any *Wimpel* not taken out of the synagogue by that day was destroyed, as was the case all over Germany. For that reason, a *Wimpel* from the twentieth century is a rare item.

Most of the Jewish families of Lauterbach had come from Storndorf: the families of Juda Baumann (I) and Juda Baumann (II); the Höchster families of Herz, Kaufmann, and Nathan; Simon Höchster in the Obergasse; the Moses and Seligmann Jakob families; the families of Kaufmann and Samuel Strauss (II); the families of Markus, Samuel (I), and Salomon Strauss (I); the Weinberg families of Josef, Rudolf, David, and Salli, the widow Anna Adler Weinberg; and the Moritz Weinberg family. For that reason, synagogue customs and etiquette were mostly patterned after established conventions in Storndorf.

Records of the Storndorf Jewish community evidence the following proclamation of August 1, 1856: "In accordance with a previously determined conviction that a member's standing in the synagogue is not his inherited entitlement, the board of directors of the Jewish congregation of Storndorf has resolved: Every member of the congregation shall be ranked for occupying one of the newly-built stands in accordance with the number of years of his marriage. Thus, number one will belong to Heskias Freund, married the longest. If there are sufficient vacant seats after the married men have been taken care of, then the bachelors will obtain their seats assigned according to age. In the event that a member will not conform to the determined sequence, or if any one is found responsible for a disturbance during synagogue services, the ordinance of December 29, 1845, paragraph 6, will apply. He will be reported forthwith to the Grand-Duke's District Office in Alsfeld for a fine." This document was signed by Löb Baumann and S. Freund on behalf of the executive committee.

Following the manner of their forebears, Jews in Lauterbach observed the law of *Genesis 2:24,* "Therefore shall a man leave his father and mother and cleave unto his wife, and they shall be one flesh." It was in the home where the essential celebrations and acts of observance took place. Although important, the synagogue was only a partner in fulfilling the commandments. Moreover, marriage perfects the individual as a person: "He who has no wife is not a proper man; he lives without joy, blessing, goodness and peace; he may not officiate as high priest on the Day of Atonement, and, ideally, not as *hazzan* (*cantor*) on holidays." Not unlike our sages of bygone days, Jews in Lauterbach believed that a woman would rather tolerate unhappy wedlock instead of remaining unmarried.

The seating sequence of women in the Lauterbach synagogue followed the same principle that governed the men downstairs. Upstairs, ladies who were married the longest filled the bench toward the southwest and the seniors were closest to the wall where the holy ark stood. The north side of the benches was occupied by women approximately in their forties and fifties, and on the southeast side women of forty and under were seated. On the southeast side, there was a bench placed behind the first one, to be used by unmarried women and girls.

Whenever my older sister attended services she was allowed to be seated next to my mother, probably because she was the first-born, while I was banished to the bench of the unmarried ladies. Here, even standing on my tiptoes, I could observe nothing of the service downstairs and additionally had no prayer book of my own. But my wounded ego mended when the forty-year-old and extremely near-sighted Recha Baumann, youngest daughter of Elda Strauss Baumann and Juda Baumann (II), befriended and treated me as her equal when I was only about ten years of age.

Heavy-arched oak portals graced the main entrance of the synagogue at Hinter der Burg; the floor of the vestibule was made of high-gloss terrazzo. The downstairs entrance into the sanctuary was from the southeast side of the foyer and facing the main doors was a wash room for *kohanim* (priests) and others. Also on the main floor was situated a sitting room with a piano, where on the Sabbath afternoons Max Stern instructed the young of his flock in *Torah*, *Talmud*, and the Ethics of the Fathers, in addition to regularly scheduled lessons during the week and on Sunday mornings.

On the north side of the synagogue was an entrance door that had solid wood on its bottom half and glass panes on its top half. Four steps led up to the level of the vestibule and from there a stairway went up to the second floor where the living quarters of the Stern family were located. On the Hinter der Burg side was the kitchen and a room with a couch for their disabled son. Across the foyer upstairs was situated the living room where my contemporaries and I spent many Friday nights during the winter receiving instruction in Jewish history, the poetry of our people, and general Jewish education, with an emphasis on Jewish morals and ethics. Also on the second floor was a long and narrow powder room. The bedrooms of the Stern family were on the third floor.

Five rows of sandstone formed the retaining wall that demarcated the frontal line of the synagogue property at Hinter der Burg, from which steps led to the level of the synagogue building. This additional elevation above the street formed an extra sense of security from sudden intruders. In the direction of the Georg family property stood a sycamore tree and two plum trees; one apple tree and a cherry tree were located toward the Peters' property. Beyond the synagogue building on the east the Stern family usually raised vegetables, and on the side nearer Hinter der Burg Max Stern discharged his task of *shohet* of poultry.

Frequently after school on Thursday it was my task, as early as age eight, to carry chickens in a sack tied with cord a quarter of a mile to the back of the synagogue. Here, obviously disgruntled about his work, Max Stern demonstrated great intensity as he executed his job of ritually killing poultry. He held onto a chicken while letting its blood run into ashes. He then threw the poultry a good way off toward the fence, as if to separate his person from this unpleasant but necessary chore, and quickly absented himself without a greeting.

Endnotes

1. Paul Arnsberg, *Die jüdischen Gemeinden in Hessen, Vol. 1* (Frankfurt Societäts-Druckerei GmbH, 1971), p. 369.

2. Karl Maurer, *Freiensteinau vor 200 Jahren, Heft 46 der "Lauterbacher Sammlungen,"* 1967 (Hessen: Bibliothek des Hohhausmuseums Lauterbach): pp. 31-32.

3. Arnsberg, *Die jüdischen Gemeinden in Hessen, Vol. 2,* p. 274.

4. Interview with Mrs. Dorothee Tag in Lauterbach on July 28, 1988.

5. *Lauterbacher Anzeiger*, September 7, 1984.

6. Dr. Karl Siegmar Baron von Galera, *Lauterbach in Hessen, Vol. 3* (Neustadt an der Aisch: Verlag Degener und Co., 1965), p. 393.

7. Letter of October 13, 1983, from Hans Gliss to Mathilda W. Stein.

8. *Heimatblätter für den Kreis Lauterbach, April 20, 1940, Der erste Jude in Lauterbach* by Dr. Eduard Becker, Darmstadt.

9. Annie Bardon, *Neunhundert Jahre Geschichte der Juden in Hessen* (Wiesbaden: Kommission für die Geschichte der Juden in Hessen, 1983), p. 352.

10. Anton Simons, *German Tribune*, January 3, 1988, p. 15.

11. Oral information obtained from Dr. Naphtali Stern in Atlanta on June 3, 1988.

12. Interview with Florchen Stiehler on July 29, 1988 in Lauterbach.

Chapter Twelve

Map of Lauterbach circa 1906

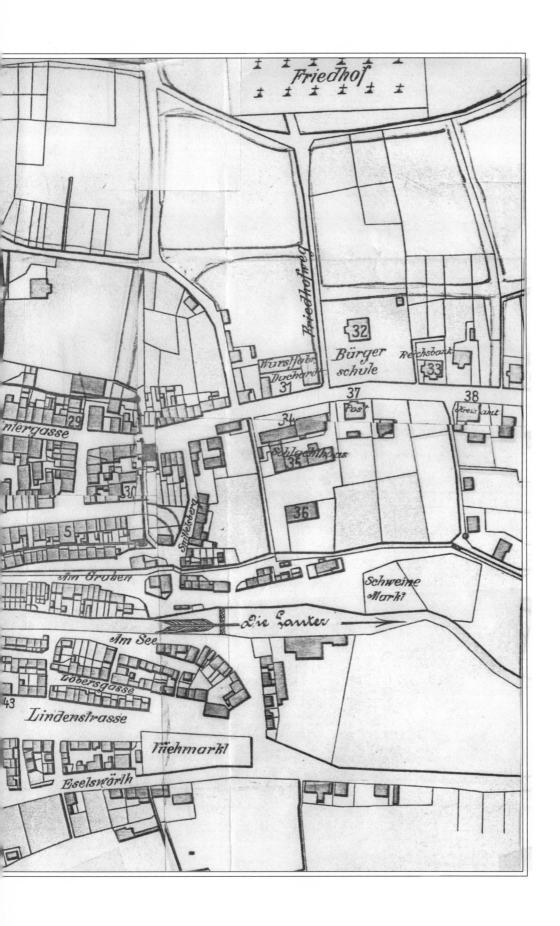

Friedhof

Friedhofweg

Würst.Fabr.
Ducharot
31

Bürger
schule
32

Reichsbank
33

37
Post

38
Kreisamt

34

Schlachthaus
35

36

intergasse
29

30

5

Schlossberg

Am Graben

Schweine
Markt

Die Lanter

Am See

Löbersgasse

43

Lindenstrasse

Viehmarkt

Eselswörth

Lauterbach
Synagoge

Lauterbach, 15. August 1908

□ Synagogen-Einweihung. Die Einweihungs-
feierlichkeit der Synagoge der hiesigen israelitischen Religionsgemeinde wurde am gestrigen Freitag nachmittag 1 Uhr unter
dem Beginn eines Abschiedsgottesdienstes in der alten Synagoge
vollzogen. Nach einem Festzug unter Vorantritt der Stumpf-
schen Kapelle von der alten nach der neuen Synagoge übergab
Frl. Resel Strauß in der Vorhalle im Auftrage des
Baumeisters (Herrn Reuter Lauterbach) mit einem sinnigen, der
Weihestunde angepaßten Prolog, den Schlüssel an den Vertreter der Großh. Regierung, Herrn Kreisrat v. Bechtold, dieser
übergab ihn mit einer Ansprache, in welcher er dem besonderen
Schutz der Regierung und der Opferwilligkeit der hiesigen Gemeinde Ausdruck gab, dem Gemeindevorstand, Herrn S. Strauß,
welcher ihn unter Dankesworten für das Wohlwollen Großh.

Regierung und für das zahlreiche Erscheinen der städt. und
geistlichen Behörden, und den Dank des Baumeisters an den
Provinzialrabbiner weitergab, der darauf unter dem üblichen
Spruch das Gotteshaus öffnete und es seiner Bestimmung
übergab. Nachdem die Weihegebete und die Chorgesänge ver-
klungen waren, betrat Herr Provinzialrabbiner Dr. Hirschfeld-
Gießen die Kanzel und hielt die Festpredigt verbunden mit
einem Gebet für das deutsche Kaiserhaus und unserem Landes-
fürsten Großherzog Ernst Ludwig. Er sprach in recht markigen
Worten über die Bedeutung des Tages und erläuterte seine
Worte im einzelnen über den Begriff Gotteshaus. Nach dem
üblichen Segen für unser Herrscherhaus sprach noch Herr
Rabbiner Dr. Kahn-Fulda. Den Schluß bildete der Ge-
sang des Psalm 150. Der Feier schloß sich gestern abend ein
Konzert an. Heute Samstag abend wird ein Theaterabend
und Sonntag ein Festball veranstaltet.

Announcement of the synagogue dedication on August 14, 1908 in the *Lauterbacher Anzeiger*

THE DEDICATION OF THE LAUTERBACH SYNAGOGUE

*A*t one o'clock in the afternoon of Friday August 14, 1908, the dedication festival of the local Israelite community commenced with a religious farewell service in the old building. From there a procession led by the Stumpf band made its way to the new synagogue. In the vestibule of the new building, Miss Resel Strauss (daughter of Settchen Flörsheim Strauss from Romrod and Sigmund Strauss from Grebenau) presented the key of the new synagogue on behalf of the architect of Lauterbach, Mr. Reuter. Receiving the key was Mr. von Bechtold who, as district alderman, was the representative of the Hessian Grand Duchy. In delivering a preamble appropriate to the occasion, the alderman gave expression to the special protection by the government and also to the sacrifices made by the Lauterbach Jewish community in establishing a new synagogue building.

As head of the Jewish community, Sigmund Strauss accepted the key from Mr. von Bechtold, thanked the government of the Grand Duchy for its benevolence, and also referred to the presence of numerous municipal and clerical authorities. Samuel Strauss (I) then extended gratitude to the architect, who in turn yielded to Dr. Hirschfeld of Giessen, the rabbi of the province. The rabbi pronounced the proper blessing for the occasion and consecrated the building. After the conclusion of the special prayers of dedication and the choral singing, Dr. Hirschfeld ascended the pulpit to sermonize about the festive occasion. He included a prayer for the German royalty and a plea for Grand-Duke Ernst Ludwig. Dr. Hirschfeld spoke in befittingly emphatic terms about the meaning of the day and rendered a sermon about the idea of a house of God. After the usual blessing for the governing authorities, Dr. Kahn (as Rabbi of Fulda) also preached. The dedication ended with the singing of *Psalm 150* and was followed by a concert. On Saturday evening a theater performance took place, and a ball was held on Sunday.[1]

On July 28, 1988, Dorothee StausebachTag recalled the synagogue dedication, making special mention of the number of participating clergy. She was aware that in 1908 (and most likely in 1988), the significant leadership of the Lutheran clergy in Lauterbach gave direction to the tenor and attitude toward Jews. The outlook of the Catholic Church and its supporters was of minimum consequence because there were fewer Catholics than Jews in Lauterbach at that time. Dorethee Tag reiterated at least twice that she could recall no distinction between Jews and others in Lauterbach at the time of the synagogue dedication. Her reflection may well be the consequence of the then-prevailing stance of the Lutheran Church in Lauterbach toward Jews.

Although some modern species of anti-semitism and racism had originated in France with Gobineau (1814-1882), and racial theories were popularized by the English son-in-law of Richard Wagner, Houston Stewart Chamberlain (1855-1927), these racist concepts fell on fertile soil in Germany. However, I learned from my mother that certainly between 1908 and the beginning of the World War I in 1914, the Jews of Lauterbach reached the zenith of their existence. For the first time in hundreds of years the human condition was more tolerable in Lauterbach than in

Chapter Thirteen

Grebenau, Crainfeld, and Storndorf. It is little wonder, then, that in deep piety and devotion they included *Psalm 150* in the dedication ceremony:

> *Hallelujah. Praise God in His sanctuary;*
> *Praise Him in the firmament of His power.*
> *Praise Him for his mighty acts;*
> *Praise Him according to His abundant greatness.*
> *Praise Him with the blast of the horn;*
> *Praise Him with the psaltry and harp.*
> *Praise him with the timbrel and dance;*
> *Praise Him with stringed instruments and the pipe.*
> *Praise Him with the loud-sounding cymbals;*
> *Praise Him with the clanging cymbals.*
> *Let every thing that hath breath praise the LORD. Hallelujah.*

The musical program included the *Cavalier*, a march by Lüdecke; *Love to the Fatherland*, an overture by Apitius; and *Songbirds: A Comedy in One Act* by E. Jacobson with music by Th. Hauptner. The cast of *Songbirds* was Nettchen acted by Miss Resel Strauss; Friedel was acted by Salli Kleeberg; and the servant of Box was acted by Max Stein. The play takes place in Nettchen's flower store. (One other person took part in this musical, but that name is no longer legible on the document). Other musical numbers included the *The Night's Quarters*, a fantasy by Kreutzer; *Song of the Angels* from the *Wedding of Figaro* as executed by Miss Alice Liseman; *The Clock of Corneville* by Metra; the couplet *Come my Chubby One* as executed by Mr. Otto Walter; and *Potpouri for Old and Young* by Stumpf.

The presentations of music and theater on August 15, 1908 included the *March of the Nibelungen*[a] by Sonntag; *La Frandre*, an overture by Bouillon; and *Leaps of a Ram!*, a farce in three acts by S. Hirschberger and Kraatz. Grünewald, a Gentleman with Independent Income, was played by Mr. Juda Baumann (II); Auguste, his Wife, was played by Miss Julia Fröhlich; Annie, her Daughter, was played by Miss Selma Jacob; Max Häser, Attorney, was played by Mr. Max Stein; Ella, his Wife, was played by Miss Tonie Jacob; Amalie Scheiblen, her Mother, was played by Mrs. Berta Weinberg; Professor Conrad, Son of the Public Executioner, was played by Mr. Salli Kleeberg; Felix, an Actor, was played by Mr. Rudolf Weinberg; Professor Löwenstrom, was played by Mr. Josef Weinberg; Ninette, Songstress of Comic Verses, was played by Miss Settie Stein; Arpad Vilagos was played by Mr. Ludwig Isenberg; Klettke, an Art Dealer, was played by Mr. Ludwig Isenberg; Mina, the Servant Girl at Häser, was played by Miss Ida Baumann; Opitz, a Hotel Proprietor, was played by Mr. Markus Strauss; Miezi, a Chambermaid at Ninette's, was played

[a] This march is part of the Middle High German epic, the *Nibelungen*, of the thirteenth century that incorporates pagan legends and also includes the Christian courtly world. The saga concludes with a slaughter and a holocaust. With the hindsight of fifty-five years after *Kristallnacht* and the Holocaust, one would question why the *March of the Nibelungen* was chosen for the synagogue dedication in Lauterbach. During my attendance at the *Oberrealschule* in Alsfeld, I saw plainly that the content of the legend of the *Nibelungen*, which was the substance of German studies for an entire school year inspired fellow students to ever greater hostility toward Jews.

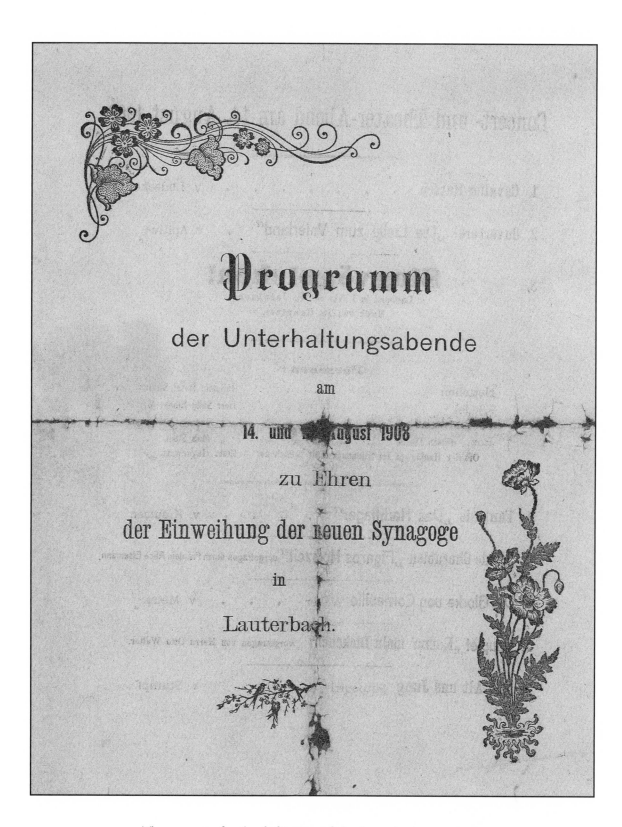

Programm

der Unterhaltungsabende

am

14. und 15. August 1903

zu Ehren

der Einweihung der neuen Synagoge

in

Lauterbach.

The program for the dedication of the Lauterbach synagogue

Concert- und Theater-Abend am 14. August 1908.

1. Cavalier-Marsch . . . . v. Lüdecke.

2. Ouverture: „Die Liebe zum Vaterland" . v. Apitius.

3. ## Singvögelchen!
Lustspiel in 1 Akt von E. Jacobson.
Musik von Th. Hauptner.

Personen:

Nettchen	Fräulein Resel Strauss.
Friedel	Herr Sally Kleeberg.
Box, dessen Diener	„ Max Stein.

Ort der Handlung: Im Blumengeschäft Nettchens. — Zeit: Gegenwart.

4. Fantasie „Das Nachtlager" . . . . v. Kreutzer.

5. Air de Chérubien „Figaros Hochzeit" vorgetragen durch Fräulein Alice Lisemann.

6. Die Glocke von Corneville Walzer . . . v. Metra.

7. Couplet „Komm' mein Dickchen" vorgetragen von Herrn Otto Walter.

8. Für Alt und Jung Potpourri . . . . v. Stumpf.

Concert und Theater-Abend am 15. August 1908.

1. Nibelungen-Marsch . . . . v. Sonntag.

2. Ouverture „La Flandre" . . . . . v. Bouillon.

3. ## Bocksprünge!

Schwank in 3 Akten von S. Hirschberger u. Kraatz.

Personen:

Grünewald, Rentier	Herr Juda Baumann
Auguste, seine Frau	Frl. Julia Fröhlich
Annie, deren Tochter	„ Selma Jacob
Max Häuser, Advokat	Herr Max Stein
Ella, seine Frau	Frl. Toni Jacob
Amalie Scheiblen, ihre Mutter	Frau Bertha Weinberg
Prof. Conrad, Freimann Sohn	Herr Sally Kleeberg
Felix, Schauspieler	„ Rudolf Weinberg
Prof. Löwenstrom	„ Joseph Weinberg
Ninette, Chausonettensängerin	Frl. Setty Stein
Arpad Vilagos	Herr Ludwig Isenberg
Klettke, Kunsthändler	„
Mina, Dienstmädchen bei Häuser	Frl. Ida Baumann
Opitz, Hotelbesitzer	Herr Marcus Strauss
Miezi, Kammermädchen b. Ninette	Frl. Aug. Fröhlich
Tapezierer	Herr David Weinberg
Stubenmädchen	Frl. Resel Strauss.

Ort der Handlung Berlin. 1. Akt Häusers Wohnung. 2. Akt bei Ninette.
3. Akt Opitz Hotel. — Zeit: Gegenwart.

4. Ich und Du. Concert Polka . . . . v. Gottlöber.

5. Finale aus Rienzi . . . . . . v. Wagner.

6. Ballsirenen. Walzer . . . . , . v. Lehar.

7. Aus dem Volke. Polka . . . . . v. Stumpf.

by Miss Auguste Fröhlich; the Paperhanger was played by Mr. David Weinberg; the Housemaid, was played by Miss Resel Strauss. The play is set in Berlin and the first act takes place in Häser's residence; the second act at Ninette's, and the third act at Opitz' hotel. The time is the present, meaning 1908.

Fourth on the program was *I and You*, a Polka concert by Gottlöber; fifth was the *Finale* from Rienzi by Wagner; the sixth was *Ballsirens*, a waltz by Lehar; and the seventh was *From the People*, a polka by Stumpf.[b]

SYNAGOGUE ETIQUETTE AND PROTOCOL

JEWISH LIFE CYCLE EVENTS, as well as fast and feast days, were celebrated in Lauterbach in keeping with the fundamental laws of *Torah* and also according to the customs which evolved because of the involuntary flight and plight withstood by most Hessian Jews from Spain and Portugal. Some customs in life cycle events can even be traced to heathen or Christian superstitions and beliefs.

On the high holidays in Lauterbach, married men were robed in their burial shrouds, consisting of a white ensemble of the quality of altar linen and comprising a loosely-fitting belted garment with long sleeves. They wore a hat made of the same white linen and fashioned similar to a nightcap without a point at the end. This manner of dress was of Ashkenazic origin. In keeping with *Isaiah 1:18,* "Come now, and let us reason together, Saith the Lord; Though your sins be as scarlet, They shall be white as snow." White was the mark of innocence and purity as well as a symbol of celebration and mourning. Underneath the shrouds, men wore their usual dark suits. A long, full woolen *tallit* (prayer shawl) was slipped over the shroud. Because no footgear of leather was permitted on the high holidays, men and women put on felt slippers in synagogue.

Typical bonnet as worn by my maternal great-grandmother, Biena Reiss Strauss (1821-1900)

Married women wore simple white dresses, indicating that everyone was equal and should wear the same color. Over the dress they slipped a *Röckle*, which means a 'small frock' in German. The *Röckle* was a rectangular garment made of black silk and was shaped like a *tallit* (small *tallit*, also called '*arba kanfoth*'), which strictly observant male Jews wear under their upper clothing on weekdays. The *Röckle* of a Jewish woman in Lauterbach was decorated in a soft color sewn upon the black cloth. My mother's *Röckle* was adorned by a pink rose in each corner and one small white silk scroll on each side.

Also on the high holidays, married women wore a small headcovering made of lace or ribbon, which was called a *Häubchen* (small bonnet). The *Häubchen* may have had its origin in Spain and may have represented an abbreviated *mantilla*. On the Sabbath and holidays other than the high holidays, from approximately 1900 until as late as 1920, Jewish married women in comfortable circumstances wore moderately elaborate black silk bonnets or hats while attending religious services. I can clearly recall that my grand-

---

[b] The program for the entertainment of the evening of August 14 and 15, 1908, in honor of the dedication of the new synagogue in Lauterbach was printed on paper of good quality by H. Domm of Lauterbach and was 11½ by 17 inches in size.

mother, Hannchen Wertheim of Angenrod, wore such a bonnet made of fine silk. On the holiest days of the year the prescribed simplicity of the *Häubchen* and *Röckle* strove toward equality and sameness of outer accouterments in order to allow for concentration on more meaningful bonds with one's neighbor and with God.

The shroud, the *Röckle,* and the *Häubchen* were part of every bride's dowry. Also included were a Sabbath prayer book (my mother's was bound in red leather); a set of prayer books consisting of at least one volume each for Passover, the Feast of Weeks, and the Feast of Booths; a book for the New Year; and a book for the Day of Atonement. A thin prayer book written in German by a lady member of the Rothschild family in Frankfurt, intended to be used for life cycle events as well as for holidays, was also included in this set of dowry items. My mother referred to this German volume as the *Tehinnah* book, and she made sure that I read the appropriate selections during the time of the *Torah* reading. My mother did not feel inclined to have her daughters read uncensored *Torah* text that might deal with a lot of begetting; she also wished her daughters to be inspired by Mrs. Rothschild's philosophy, which emphasized uttermost servility and self-effacement considered so befitting for young Jewish women of that day. Some married women of Lauterbach also possessed a *Zeenah U-Reenah Bible for Ladies* (from the Hebrew meaning 'Come and See').[c]

In Lauterbach, synagogue etiquette during the high holidays demanded that no one fix his gaze on the one who sounded the *shofar.* Women and children upstairs

were ordered to turn their back to the *shofar* blower, who was wrapped in his *tallit* with only the *shofar* visibly extending. In the sanctuary downstairs, young boys gathered together under a *tallit* lest they confuse the *shofar* blower, who had need of total concentration. By contrast, children in Eastern Europe were permitted to observe the *shofar* blower. Encountering the blast of the ram's horn as a young child in Lauterbach was not at all awe-inspiring; instead it brought on much anguish and anxiety because of the underlying element of the unexplored.

Until shortly before his death on October 5, 1924, my Great-Uncle Samuel Strauss (I) blew the *shofar* in Lauterbach. He was succeeded by Nathan Hess from Crainfeld. On *Kol Nidrei, Yom Kippur, Rosh Ha-Shanah* and on the first days of the Pilgrim Feasts (Passover, *Shavuot,* and *Sukkot*),

Shofar blower

an impressive men's choir strengthened and deepened worship in Lauterbach. To the best of my recollection, choir members included Bernhard, Max, and Siegfried Baumann, the sons of Karoline Hasenauer Baumann and Juda Baumann (I); Nathan Höchster, the son of Zippora and Meyer Höchster; Max Jakob, the son of Emma Baumann Jakob and Seligmann Jakob; Siegfried (II), Hermann, and Salli Strauss

---

[c] These writings were composed in the sixteenth century by Jakob ben Isaac of Janow and were used primarily by women as reading matter on the Sabbath. A 1906 Vilnius edition and commentary of this bible quotes the *Talmud* as saying that anyone who lights candles for the Sabbath will have scholarly sons, but that this duty falls to the woman "because she extinguished the light of the world when she made Adam sin by having him eat the fruit of the Tree of Knowledge."

Chapter Thirteen

(II), the sons of Lina Frank Strauss and Markus Strauss (cousins of my mother); and Salli Weinberg, the son of Fanny and Abraham Weinberg.

Although no one officiated as choir leader, the musically gifted individuals created a moving event. The remembrance of this choir's rendition of the *Yigdal* (a hymn based on the Thirteen Articles of Faith enumerated by Maimonides) still echoes from the past and moves me to tears. In Lauterbach, as was the practice in Sephardic congregations, this hymn was rendered only at the conclusion of festival evening worship. Siegfried Baumann was a uniquely talented prayer leader who regularly conducted services if Max Stern was absent. Mr. Baumann also assisted with cantorial services whenever necessary throughout the year, and I can still hear his impressive voice ringing out.

Also, in conjunction with a custom in Sephardic congregations, *selihot* services took place on Sunday morning at five o'clock or earlier, when stars were still visible in the sky. (*Selihot* prayers are recited during the Penitential season, which begins before *Rosh ha-Shanah*.) I am no longer certain whether in Lauterbach it was customary to recite *selihot* from the first day of *Elul* (the sixth month in the Jewish year) in anticipation of the Ten Days of Penitence (regarded as the month of repentance), which is the practice in Sephardic communities.

Custom in Lauterbach prescribed that adult males fast until after the sounding of the ram's horn on *Rosh ha-Shanah*. Therefore, some male members of the congregation brought to the synagogue building shoe boxes filled with generous supplies of plum or apple cake made of yeast dough. After the first blowing of the *shofar*, they consumed the food zestfully in the synagogue foyer or on the synagogue grounds, while ardently discussing the relative quality of the baked goods as well as the worthiness and competence of their wives or housekeepers.

As spiritual leader, Max Stern used to hold forth against this practice of noisily congregating because it was not at all helpful in maintaining dignified worship. Mr. Stern and others were fully aware that some non-Jewish neighbors of the synagogue objected to the noise. On the third of *Tishri* (the seventh month), which was my father's birthday in the Hebrew calendar, the Fast of Gedaliah was observed in our home by adults abstaining from food and drink until twelve o'clock. In this way they recalled the assassination of Gedaliah, the Babylonian-appointed governor of Judah in the sixth century B.C.E..

Erev Yom Kippur, the day before the Day of Atonement, was a most reverential day in Lauterbach and especially in our home. On regular workdays, my father usually went out of town, yet on this day he stayed at home in order to be able to perform strictly the prescribed religious obligations. My father was virtually unable to obtain kosher food away from home, except for bread and in some cases, cheese, which were not considered suitable fare for *Erev Yom Kippur*. Furthermore, most Jews of Lauterbach took very seriously the *Talmudic* instruction, "Everyone who eats and drinks on the ninth day of the month of *Tishri* is considered as having fasted on the ninth and tenth". An early midday meal consisted minimally of soup, several vegetables, a pasta or potato dish, and meat or fowl. Coffee and yeast cakes laden with fresh plums or apples would be offered in the afternoon. The meal before commencing the fast was the most elaborate consisting of soup, vegetables, salads, meat or chicken, noodle pudding, and fruit for desert.

As a young child, I accompanied my father after the midday meal to an early *minhah* service when most people made charitable contributions. In addition, my mother usually sent me to the widows Anna Weinberg and Biena Jakob with fruit or other eatables. I also had to take some prepared food to the family of my mother's cousin, Salli Strauss (I), who lived at the Wichhaus. Also, between midday and the last meal of this day, Jews in Lauterbach immersed either in the public baths, the *mikveh*, or their bathing facilities at home. From that practice I certainly drew the conclusion as a young child that cleanliness is next to godliness. Many Lauterbach Jews also got haircuts at that time. They made every effort to express outwardly that they were ready to spend a full day in prayer, fast, and supplication to avert the evil decree.

In the Max Stern household in Lauterbach, the memorial candle was placed in a dark corner, whereas other holiday candles could be sighted easily.[2] Before leaving for *Kol Nidrei* services, my father planted a candle deep into sand in a high metal pitcher so that the candle's glimmer could hardly be detected; he placed the pitcher on the floor of the dining room where the shutters remained tightly closed for *Yom Kippur* day. The banishment in both homes of the memorial candles to an area of diminished visibility makes one theorize whether such responses might not reflect on the lives of ancestral marranos, who were forced into such postures in order to secretly cling to their faith. Similar to the tradition of Sabbath and other holidays, my parents blessed their children before the *Kol Nidrei* service.

Our family also faithfully adhered to the custom of *kapparot*, either on *Erev* (the day before) *Rosh ha-Shanah*, on the day before *Yom Kippur*, or on *Hoshana Rabba* (the seventh day of *Sukkot*, which in post-talmudic times became a supplement to the Day of Atonement on which God's decrees for the coming year are finalized).

In observing the custom of *kapparot*, one aspect of making amends was the symbolic transfer of sins from a person to a fowl. Early in the morning of *Erev Yom Kippur*, my father tied the feet of a hen and swung it three times around my head while I repeated after him: "This is my substitute, my vicarious offering, my atonement; this hen shall meet death, but I shall find a long and pleasant life of peace." I always suffered a great deal of sadness and distress during and after this service. Usually, the hen had belonged to our own barnyard and it now helplessly blinked at me as if asking to be freed, a plea I was not allowed to fulfill. Symbolizing the scapegoat (*Azazel*), this bird met its fate at the hands of the *shohet* soon after this ceremony, and was oftentimes consumed at a holiday dinner. The hen's equivalent in money was given to the poor.

On *Sukkot* (the Feast of Booths and Tabernacles) nearly every Jewish household in Lauterbach purchased a *lulav* (palm branch) with *hadas* (myrtle), and *aravah* (willow), as well as an *etrog* (citrus fruit). It was customary to share these objects with those few who could not afford to buy them. The commandment of dwelling in a *sukkah* (booth) for seven days was strictly adhered to only by Max Stern, since Lauterbach was considered the Siberia of Germany, where frequent rainfalls and low temperatures in autumn were not conducive to eating and sleeping in an outdoors *sukkah*. Moreover, erecting a booth was a time-consuming task and many Jews in the town who eked out a minimal living as sole providers for their family could afford neither the time to build a hut nor the means to pay for this service. Also, some Jewish families occupied living quarters very close to non-

Synagogue service on
Sukkot

Jewish neighbors, but others resided in the middle of town in homes, which could not accommodate a *sukkah* because of lack of space.

However, the synagogue grounds were favorable for setting up a hut with an even wooden floor. The Stern family also acquired a watertight roof covering, operating it with ropes and large rings which impressed me greatly as a child. They strung roseships alternately with colored paper into attractive chains for decorating their sukkah and hung up fruit in their booth. To my great amazement, the Sterns also used the multi-colored balls that non-Jews in town used to decorate their Christmas trees.

Wooden *etrog* box from
Palestine circa 1900

My Great-Uncle Samuel and his family must have felt confident about their neighbors' amicability because the booth was some two hundred feet from the residence. Evidently not even the possible animosity of the brewery workers on the other side of the street, who doubtlessly hungered for the Jewish food and envied the holiday atmosphere of the Samuel Strauss family, had to be taken into account. In contrast, during the 1920s, the Wertheim family would not have chanced such actions for fear of arousing antisemitism. In later years, our *sukkah* was judged lacking (unkosher) by Dr. Hirschfeld of Giessen, the duly qualified rabbinic authority, because part of its roof was constructed of materials, which were considered too permanent. Ironically, that unkosher hexagon-shaped *sukkah* at the corner of the Gartenstrasse and the Cent splendidly withstood the ravages of time and, ever since the World War II, has effectively functioned as a kiosk.

Hoshana Rabba, the seventh day of *Sukkot*, was regarded as a distinctly holy day in Lauterbach, although work could be performed until sundown. As a young child, I enjoyed accompanying my father on the day before *Hoshana Rabba* to look for proper *aravot* (willows), by the small brook near the Steinmühle. My father instructed me to select only willows with perfect leaves. Five willow branches would be tied together and kept in water until the following day. During morning services they were beaten on the bench of the *bimah* after reciting the *hoshana* prayers ("Save, I Pray") for a good harvest.

On *Hoshanah Rabba*, corresponding to *Rosh Ha-Shanah* and *Yom Kippur*, the *parokhet* (curtains of the ark where the *Torah* scrolls were kept) were white, while on Passover, *Shavuoth*, and other *Sukkot* days blue curtains were hung. On Sabbaths not coinciding with another holiday the color of the curtains was wine red. Worshippers took special care to appear in formal attire whenever they anticipated being called up to the *Torah* (*aliyah le-Torah*).

On the Pilgrim Feasts, married men and congregational elders generally donned formal dress of tailcoat and top hat for services. The custom of wearing a silk top

Palm branch (*lulav*) with myrtle, willow, and critus fruit (*etrog*)

hat may have originated in 1826, when the Duke of Hesse arbitrarily decreed that Jews wear a top hat for worship.[3] A man did not wear a skullcap (*kippah*) for synagogue services, and I only learned the Yiddish word '*yarmulka*,' meaning 'skullcap,' in the United States. However, Jewish men unfailingly covered their heads, based on the biblical dictum not to emulate heathen custom; and in Lauterbach, Angenrod, and Kirtorf, bareheadedness was rejected because it was perceived as a condition of unbefitting levity (*kallut rosh*). Moreover, at that time, most Christians removed their headcovering upon entering church. Rabbis firmly directed that Jewish customs be different.

On the eve of the High Holidays and the Pilgrim Feasts, synagogue honors were auctioned off to the highest bidder. It was tacitly agreed not to outbid the community founders and leaders who had sacrificed so much already. In Lauterbach it was considered the highest token of esteem to pay tribute to a visiting elder relative by obtaining for him an honor connected with the *Torah* service on the High Holidays and the Pilgrim Feasts. Synagogue etiquette prescribed that on a regular Sabbath such honors were automatically conferred upon a visitor in accordance with *Genesis 18:2-8* concerning the paying of homage to strangers.

Chapter Thirteen

In my home town on *Hoshana Rabba*, devout Jewish households of means took turns in hosting the men of the community for evening prayer and study of the *Book of Deuteronomy*. On these occasions, our dining room table was extended with four auxiliary legs to accommodate twenty-eight guests. There was much ado in the Wertheim household about baking and setting the table whenever we hosted this party where refreshments of coffee and several kinds of home-baked cakes and cookies were set before the guests. This same custom endured also on the first night of *Shavuot* (Feast of Weeks or Pentecost) and, because of kabbalistic influence, readings from Jewish religious classics were chosen. Max Stern led these study groups, which women never attended because their participation would have been judged unbecoming. Either alone, or with the assistance of one maidservant, my mother waited upon the men. However, the bedroom my sister and I shared was located next to the dining room, and since one stove heated both rooms, the connecting wall had an opening that afforded me the enjoyment of secretly auditing these study sessions.

Shemini Azeret (the eighth day of *Sukkot*) stands out in my mind because of the prayer for rain. As a young child I could not comprehend why prayers for rain were still needed when it commonly rained a lot in Lauterbach already. The memorial services (*yizkor*) on the eighth day of the Feast of Booths, the Day of Atonement, the eighth day of Passover, and the second day of the Feast of Weeks were not treated as the special episode which I experienced in American conservative congregations, but were considered an essential component of worship. Moreover, young children or those who had not suffered a loss of near kin did not make an exit as if to separate themselves from those who mourned.

Simhat Torah (Rejoicing in the *Torah*), the last day of *Sukkot*, was a day of practical jokes and light-hearted fun-making among the otherwise staid and controlled members of the Lauterbach congregation. During the *Torah* reading, young unmarried men aimed to dislodge the top hats of older synagogue members by throwing paper balls. My mother's cousins, Siegfried (II), Hermann, and Salli Strauss (II), tended to be in the forefront of these activities. On *Simhat Torah*, an elder would occasionally distribute unwrapped hard candy to the children, who had to defer eating such a treat until after services.

It was not unknown during the *Torah* reading for someone clandestinely to hang a picture on another person's back which made the bearer the butt of a joke in a drawing or with words. My father's neighbor at synagogue was Siegfried Reiss of Bahnhofstrasse 20, who fostered an obsessive preoccupation with the acquisition of food, particularly fowl, for consumption on the holidays. At one time, there was a restrictive arrangement about buying chickens in the vicinity because of a pervading illness of some of the animals. Mr. Reiss, who had a high opinion of my father's sagacity, conferred with him about existing regulations and a possible infringement on Mr. Reiss' part. Based on my father's consultation, Mr. Reiss was anguished to realize he had left himself open to a violation of the law. Once and for all my father wished to put an end to the continual discussions about food and chickens. Therefore, during *Torah* reading time he adorned Mr. Reiss' back with a drawing and brief narrative of the chicken incident. After becoming the target of the congregation's humor, Mr. Reiss stopped his endless discussions of food in synagogue.

At the conclusion of this holiday, it was an established practice for the young unmarried people of the Jewish community either to hold a ball in their home town or to attend a dance sponsored by another Jewish community in the vicinity. Customarily, non-Jews were not invited to these dances, which were generally held at the *Gasthof Keutzer* in the Lindenstrasse or at the *Beilecke Gasthof* in the Bahnhofstrasse in Lauterbach. Nevertheless Emil Burkhardt, who in the early 1930s roomed with the Jewish family of Michel Jakob in the Bahnhofstrasse, recounted in 1985 that on the occasion of such a ball he danced the entire evening with my sister. When my sister and I grew up, it was regarded as a serious breach of etiquette for a lady to refuse to dance with any partner; in effect such a refusal was deemed a decided slight to the solicitant.

ENDNOTES

1. *Lauterbacher Anzeiger*, August 15, 1908.
2. Information obtained in Atlanta, Georgia, from Dr. Naphtali Stern of Bar Ilan University, Israel, on January 25, 1988.
3. Dr. Ursula Wippich, *Memorbuch 1981/82*, p. 109.

Havdalah ceremony recited at termination of Sabbaths and festivals
by Moritz Daniel Oppenheim, 1882

THE SABBATH

"*R*EMEMBER THE SABBATH DAY, to keep it holy. Six days shalt thou labor, and do all thy work; but the seventh day is a sabbath unto the Lord thy God, in it thou shalt not do any manner of work, thou, nor thy son, nor thy daughter, nor thy man-servant, nor thy maid-servant, nor thy cattle, nor thy stranger that is within thy gates." In the 1920s and 1930s, most of the members of the Lauterbach Jewish congregation devoutly and dogmatically observed this ordainment of the fourth commandment.

In our home, Sabbath preparations began on Thursday and involved extra house cleaning, shopping for fresh fish (carp, pike, or trout) from the Riedesel pond at the Burg, and taking fowl to be killed ritually by Max Stern, the Lauterbach teacher and *shohet*. The slaughtered poultry would be either an extra rooster from our home-stead (a thriving chicken colony needed only one rooster), a chicken which had ceased to lay an egg at least every other day, or any of our fowl that was more than three years old. In the event that a family member, especially a young child, had taken ill with a fever, it was deemed advisable to nourish the patient on the Sabbath with a pigeon purchased usually in Maar or Angersbach.

KOSHER
SLAUGHTERING

ON THURSDAYS IN THE 1920s, some of the Christian (Lutheran) butchers of Lauterbach, such as Mr. Duchardt in the Obergasse, would have a cow, heifer, or calf slaughtered by Max Stern at the Lauterbach slaughtering house in the Bahnhofstrasse. It was the butcher's intent to sell the forequarters of the animal to the Lauterbach Jews and the hindquarters, which Jews are not allowed to eat, to others. By slaughtering on Thursday, Mr. Duchardt was mindful of the regula-tion that for Jews meat is automatically prohibited unless it has been koshered within seventy-two hours. This process is founded in *Leviticus 7:26-27*, which states, "And ye shall eat no manner of blood, whether it be of fowl or of beast, in any of your dwellings. Whosoever it be that eateth any blood, that soul shall be cut off from his people." Accordingly, in our home all meat and fowl had to be immersed in a vessel used only for this purpose and soaked in cold, clean water for thirty minutes. Then the meat was laid on a perforated slanted board to provide for the blood to flow downward. Thereupon, the meat or fowl would be salted on all sides as well as inside the fowl. Afterwards, the meat and fowl were left to stand a minimum of one hour and then were washed at least twice in cold water.

Moreover, *Leviticus 3:17* states, "It shall be a perpetual statute throughout your generations in all your dwellings, that ye shall eat neither fat nor blood." In our household, my Great-Uncle Samuel Strauss (I) removed veins and fat before my mother koshered meat and fowl. The rooting out of proper veins and fat, a process known as '*proging*' in western Yiddish dialect was called '*borschen*' in Lauterbach and was often performed by Mr. Nathan Hess of the Langgasse 21 after my Great-Uncle Samuel's death in 1924. Whenever I watched the *borschen* process, I grew aware that precise knowledge of bovine anatomy and precise cutting skills were essential requisites for this procedure.

Chapter Fourteen

PREPARATION OF *HALLAH* FOR SABBATH

ON THURSDAY EVENING, my mother also prepared the starter for three loaves of white Sabbath bread (in contrast to the dark bread consumed on weekdays) because the blessings on Friday night and before the midday Sabbath meal should be pronounced over two whole loaves of bread in order to call to mind the double portion of the manna for the Sabbath. In Lauterbach and its immediate environs, the Sabbath bread was called '*berches*,' probably after the Hebrew word '*berakhot*,' meaning 'blessings.' On Friday morning after the bread dough had risen, my mother cast a small portion of dough into the fire of the cooking stove and pronounced the following blessing: "Blessed Art Thou, Lord our God, King of the Universe, who has commanded us to separate a portion from the dough." This blessing gives heed to the temple eras when prescribed sacrifices were practiced.

SABBATH SERVICES IN THE SYNAGOGUE

MY PARENTS, AND ESPECIALLY MY FATHER, enjoyed the conscientiously faithful observance of Sabbath in Lauterbach. As a young child, whenever I attended Sabbath morning services for two hours or longer, I felt bored because I could not yet read Hebrew. After I began Hebrew studies at age six, I was no longer free to attend Sabbath services because I had to be present at public school on Saturdays until twelve or one o'clock. Therefore, my knowledge of synagogue procedures and synagogue etiquette was limited to what I overheard at dinner conversations between Great-Uncle Samuel and my parents, and to my observations on high holidays and the pilgrim feasts, which were the only times we were excused from public school for religious celebration.

OBSERVING THE SABBATH

WHENEVER I HAD TO BE ABSENT from school due to religious holidays, I found it difficult to comprehend the concept that I had to make up the required assignments. From the beginning until the end of my secular education at age eighteen in Germany, I suffered through never-ending conflict. On the one hand was my desire to adhere strictly to the rigid laws of Judaism as taught by Max Stern, the religious instructor and leader of the community, and the observation of rituals caught from my parents. On the other hand was my earnest yearning for knowledge ignited by an innate curiosity and stoked by the certitude that learning could, in the course of time, be the tool of deliverance from the fate of a Jew in Hesse. Writing on Sabbath was strictly forbidden, as was carrying books, school equipment, or even a handkerchief. Therefore, on Friday afternoon I hastily completed my homework; then hoping that no one would see me, I secretly slipped into the side door of the *Realschule* to hurriedly deposit the required books and other paraphernalia for Saturday's lessons.

Most of my teachers were aware that I was forbidden to write on the Sabbath and, during my earlier years at the Lauterbach *Realschule*, were thoughtful enough not to ask me to write on the board. However, I often grappled with difficulties in carrying out homework assignments in mathematics because I lacked the written examples which explained the series of steps to be followed. Furthermore, convention demanded that Christian schoolmates not be disturbed on Sunday, their holy day. Often in history and geography I gave the appearance of having forgotten my textbooks, while actually I had needed the books at home in order to complete an oral assignment on Friday evening. Gym classes on Saturdays presented another predicament. Although Jewish law permitted calisthenics, exercises on the horse-and-bar and disk throwing were forbidden. My high school years in Lauterbach and Alsfeld were fraught with many conflicts created by trying to observe strictly every law of the Sabbath and also to produce my best school work. Moreover, tuition fees for high school attendance were expensive, and my parents clearly communicated that my efforts were certainly expected to be co-equal with their outlay.

On Friday there was considerable stress and strain to complete all necessary chores before the arrival of the Sabbath. The house was to look strikingly tidy and immaculate, and all foods that needed cooking or baking had to be prepared before the onset of Sabbath. The beginning of the Sabbath was as early as four o'clock Friday afternoon around the time of the winter solstice, and as late as eight o'clock during the middle of the summer. After my mother had kindled the white Sabbath candles, any work except reading and studying was strictly forbidden. Candles considered worthy of use on the Sabbath eve were the ones that lasted through *Psalm 124*, which was sung before the grace after meals. My mother's two-branched candelabrum was approximately fifteen inches tall; it was an Art Nouveau design and had been a wedding gift in 1913. On the Sabbath, the Wertheim household used a light blue silk *hallah* covering imprinted with the *kiddush* prayer and blessings, while on holidays a white cover with the appropriate prayers and blessings was utilized. While pronouncing the blessing over the Sabbath candles, my mother, grandmothers, or other female relatives did not use a headcovering. Warming-up of foods was to be performed only by non-Jewish household help in accordance with instructions rendered before the Sabbath.

Brass Sabbath lamp (oil), Germany, circa 1840

The large yard of Cent 17 had to be swept and raked in mild weather, which was a chore often assigned to me. Secretly, I would yearn for rain on Friday afternoon. But then I would fret about arriving dripping wet at school the next morning because opening and carrying an umbrella were forbidden. On the Pilgrim Feasts and on the Jewish New Year, providing these days did not fall on Sabbath, carrying an umbrella was allowed, but opening and closing one were prohibited.

KIDDUSH PRAYER   WHEN MY FATHER RETURNED FROM SYNAGOGUE, both parents blessed their daughters by placing their hands on our heads and pronouncing, "May the Lord bless you and keep you. May the Lord make His countenance to shine upon you and be gracious unto you. May the Lord turn His countenance unto you and give you peace. May God have you turn out to be like Sara, Rebekah, Rachel and Leah." My father would then recite the Sabbath *kiddush*, which is the prayer recited over a cup of wine on the eve of Sabbath or a festival and on a Sabbath or a festival morning before the first meal.

Chapter Fourteen

IN OUR HOME, GRAPE OR RAISIN WINE and two loaves of white bread were requisite for this prayer, because only the fruit of the grapevine was worthy of the blessing. Our own savory wines, made at home with other fruits such as gooseberries or currants from our gardens, were not acceptable, nor were wines produced commercially without rabbinical supervision appropriate for *kiddush*. In Lauterbach, a Jew was never allowed to consume wine in the company of a non-Jew and certainly wine without a rabbinical seal should never have passed a Jew's lips.

Notwithstanding the many bottles of berry wine available in our home, my mother would often prepare wine of raisins on Friday, which was acceptable for *kiddush*. During the *kiddush*, only my father or whoever performed this ceremony rose to stand. Others remained seated, in contrast to the manner in which this ritual is generally performed in the United States. No one in the Wertheim household spoke or whispered from the time we uttered the blessing over washing our hands before the meal, until after the *kiddush*[a] and the blessings over wine and bread. Although it contained salt, the bread was sprinkled with additional salt to indicate the high value placed on salt because of its relative scarcity. During the winter months, the Sabbath Eve meal usually consisted of chicken or beef soup with green rye (*Grünkern*) or home-made noodles, home-canned peas, small whole home-fried potatoes, boiled beef or roasted chicken. A chicken fricassee was prepared with the bird which had produced the chicken soup. Generally, dessert consisted of home-canned fruits from our gardens such as cherries, strawberries, pears, small yellow plums, and green gages.

We did not include our non-Jewish household help for the *kiddush*, because we thought it might offend her but she joined us immediately afterwards for *hallah*. She was in attire upgraded from her daily work clothing and in a discernibly subdued but festive mood. One reason the Christian village girls preferred working in Jewish homes was that the quality and quantity of food was generally better than the food in their own homes or in the households of a village farmer where they might have otherwise obtained employment. Moreover, if the Sabbath and other holidays were strictly observed in a Jewish home, the household help, too, enjoyed additional days of less toil.

In our home, festival and Sabbath meals were served one course at a time in the living room, which held a square dining table that seated eight. My Great-Uncle Samuel and my father were usually accommodated on the sofa, while the women occupied seats which readily enabled them to wait upon others. Should my father have to be absent, no other family member was allowed to occupy his seat, in accordance with Rashi's (a leading commentator on Bible and *Talmud*, [1040-1105]) admonition of fearing one's parents. After soup, a vegetable course was served that was followed by a meat dish. Whenever salad was available, it constituted the last course before dessert. In spring and early summer, Boston lettuce was the only attainable green salad, and in early fall, field (also called 'lamb') salad was traditional.

---

[a] *Kiddush* prayer recited over cup of wine in home and synagogue to consecrate Sabbath or festival.

On Friday evening or after the midday meal on the Sabbath, we rarely intoned *Psalm 126* before the grace after meals, probably because no one in the family was gifted with a singing voice. But my father or any male present chanted the full version of the grace after meals while the bread and salt stayed on the table. Our families in Lauterbach, Angenrod, and Kirtorf neither recognized nor appreciated an abbreviated version of the grace after meals. A recital of these lengthy blessings and prayers was often a criterion for considering if a groom who was sharing the Sabbath in his future in-laws' home for the first time was learned or uneducated. A visiting family member or a Jewish traveler, usually coming from Galicia or Poland, who was out of funds for lodging and who was eating in our home was accorded the honor of reciting the grace after meals.

ITINERANT JEWS THE TRAVELING POOR PEOPLE (*Schnorrer*) generally arrived in Lauterbach on Thursday. A Mr. Stern from Angenrod, who brought greetings from our folks of his village, probably had no intention of staying over for the Sabbath with his nephew, Moritz Stern, and wife, Rosa (née Gottlieb), of Am Wörth 16. He merely wanted to make sure that he and his brothers had sufficient funds to celebrate the Sabbath in a manner that they deemed proper. Whenever he reckoned the amount given by my mother and other Jewish families in Lauterbach and Alsfeld to be less than what he considered his due portion, he would quietly remain standing in the foyer until additional funds were forthcoming. Mr. Stern's solicitations for funds generally occurred monthly, and I recall vividly the dismay in my mother's voice whenever Mr. Stern appeared even more frequently.

During the 1920s and early 1930s, a considerable number of itinerant Jewish poor passed through Lauterbach. According to my parents, these poor women and men came from the east and especially from the Bukovina, that was a region of Eastern Europe in the West Ukraine and North East Rumania. Before World War II, many Jews had lived in towns of that region. In 1775, Bukovina, at first a district of Galicia, had been ceded to Austria by the Ottoman Empire. The suitcases of these itinerant poor exuded a characteristic aroma emanating from prayer books and candles for *Hanukkah*, the Sabbath, and *havdalah* (a ceremony that takes place at the termination of Sabbath and festivals, when a special braided candle is used). My parents observed the fundamental Jewish social virtue of *Gemilat Hasadim*, which stresses sympathetic consideration toward one's fellowmen by buying from the Jewish poor. Hence, it happened that the Wertheim household possessed a whole drawer full of *havdalah* candles that burn ceremonially only for a short period, and therefore last a long time.

I cannot recall that an itinerant poor Jewish woman ever remained in Lauterbach for the Sabbath. The social mores of the day surely would have frowned upon such a practice, because a woman was to be at home with her family for the Sabbath. Moreover, it was thought unbecoming for a female not related to a family to stay in a stranger's house overnight. My openhanded mother did not even invite poor Jewish women to stay for meals. Instead she wrapped up food for them to take along to fulfill what my mother deemed her charitable obligation. My mother's food packages were of superior quality, inordinately generous, and generally consisted of bread, homemade cheese, and fruit. Sandwiches *per se* were not a familiar item in Lauterbach. It always seemed to me that my mother did not want her daughters to be aware of the lifestyle of these poor itinerant Jewish women. They were supplied with food and were dismissed without ceremony.

The only poor Jewish itinerant who stands out in my mind was a Mr. Laufer, who came to Lauterbach approximately four times each year. He carried and sold the established assortment of ritual candles and prayer books, some with olivewood covers and imported from what was then Palestine. This traveler possessed all the earmarks of a highly-educated, well-informed, genteel person who was also a skilled calligrapher. With profound sincerity he regularly offered his services of elegant handwriting in return for our substantial hospitality. Mr. Laufer usually arrived for coffee on Thursday afternoon to make certain that our guest room was vacant. Soon afterward he left to collect money from other members of the Lauterbach Jewish community and returned to our house for Thursday evening dinner. He pursued his salesmanship from one Jewish home to another and his drive for funds lasted until just before the arrival of the Sabbath on Friday afternoon or evening. Thereafter he joined my father for services at synagogue, and then shared the pleasures of the Sabbath with our family. Mr. Laufer's manners were impeccable and he tactfully contributed to the conversation at the table, enlightening us about economic circumstances and anti-semitism in other regions of Germany.

During the 1920s, news from radio programs was constrained. Most Jewish households, including ours, were not equipped with a radio. Our only sources of information were the *Lauterbacher Anzeiger*, the *General Anzeiger* from Frankfurt, and *Das Israelitische Familienblatt* (a Jewish weekly newspaper). As a child in Lauterbach and its environs, I sensed that the terms 'Jew' and 'Jewish' were analogous to abasement and degradation. Therefore, tactful Christians, and Jews themselves, refrained from using this designation, as exemplified in the title of the Jewish weekly newspaper, which arrived on Friday to be read on the Sabbath. None of the newspapers we received provided what, by today's standards, would be designated as exemplary objective information intended for critical reading.

In Lauterbach, the indigent Jewish itinerants from far away and generally from regions east of Germany could always find free room and board for the Sabbath with members of the local Jewish community, who were inquisitive about information from travelers, which was not supplied through other sources. Moreover, most of the Jews of Lauterbach wished to fulfill one of the cardinal obligations of Judaism of helping the Jewish poor. Without previous announcement, my father frequently brought Jewish travelers, poor or otherwise, home for dinner. He considered it his responsibility to see that no traveling Jew be compelled to eat unkosher food at any time, and especially not on the Sabbath. Furthermore, my father wanted to observe the religious duty (*mitzvah*) of extending hospitality to a stranger.

Below: *Kiddush* cup, Germany, circa 1880

Below: *Kiddush* cup, Germany, circa 1900

Following grace after meals on Sabbath Eve, Great-Uncle Samuel meticulously prepared himself for chanting the *sidrah* (the section of the weekly *Torah* reading in synagogue). My Great-Uncle Samuel must have been mindful that several self-appointed overseers in synagogue were only too eager to catch him or any other *Torah* reader at even the slightest inaccuracy and to belabor the mistake vigorously, even while the supervisors themselves had the advantage of reading from a Hebrew text containing punctuation and vowels.

On Sabbath Eve, my mother and father read the newspapers, since both of them found very little time for reading on weekdays. Moreover, my parents, like many other Jews and non-Jews in Lauterbach, adamantly deemed reading for a purpose other than studying to be an occupation incompatible with their working ethics. My mother and father considered the devouring of novels to be downright frivolous and the least desirable form of reading. Therefore, even on the Sabbath, such a trifling occupation as absorbing oneself in a novel had to be achieved secretly or abstained from completely.

Like most members of the Lauterbach Jewish congregation, my parents regularly attended Sabbath morning services, which started at eight o'clock and ended at eleven o'clock. On an ordinary Sabbath, my father wore a dark suit, usually custom-tailored at the local Jewish establishment of Aron Stein. In winter he wore a dark felt hat and in summer he wore a light Panama hat, generally purchased from the Lauterbach hat firm of Groh. Headgear was never removed while saying one's prayers, or at any other time except when necessary. Observant Jews in Lauterbach did not appear anywhere with bare heads, and skullcaps (*kippahs*) were not popular. The ladies of the Lauterbach Jewish congregation dressed very conservatively and unobtrusively, lest they engender the open or concealed animosity of their Christian neighbors who, on the Sabbath, were strenuously preparing for their own day of rest. Ladies seldom, if ever, appeared in synagogue without a felt hat in winter and a straw hat during the other seasons, which they purchased from the local Jewish milliner, Julia Adler, of Bahnhofstrasse 34.

SABBATH MEALS

AT HOME, MY FATHER RECITED the *kiddush* over a cup of wine and two loaves of bread. During the summer, a favored appetizer was thinly-cut black radishes marinated in oil, vinegar, and salt. During our high school years in Lauterbach, my sister and I returned after one o'clock from school on Saturday. By that time, my parents and the household help had completed their noonday meal and, to my displeasure, we had to eat by ourselves.

According to the pattern of observing the Sabbath in Lauterbach, Jews were not allowed to kindle a fire, but could utilize an existing cooking fire for the warming up of foods, provided that no Jew had contact with the flame. In our home, only Christian household help was allowed to go near a stove, lest a family member inadvertently err by handling the actual flame. Sabbath meals had to be cooked on Friday and warmed up by the Christian household help, who received appropriate instructions before the Sabbath. Foods served in this manner were often hot baked puddings such as *Birnenkloss*, which was a huge dumpling surrounded by peeled and quartered juicy pears; *Zwetschgenkugel* was prepared with flour, beef-fat drippings, and stewed home-dried prunes; *Krautkopf* was a sizable cabbage roll, cooked in a large iron pot and made of white blanched cabbage leaves, soaked white bread (*hallah*), rendered beef-fat, a small amount of chopped beef, and chopped onions, and was generally served with apple sauce or other home-canned fruit.

During the winter months, several members of the Lauterbach Jewish congregation, and especially the families of cattle dealers, undertook to utilize the front quarters of a suitable heifer for their own households. It had been slaughtered by the *shohet*, Max Stern, at the local slaughtering house at the Bahnhofstrasse and additionally inspected by the authorized health authorities. Of course, this practice substantially increased the use of meat and meat products on the Sabbath. One such meat dish for the Sabbath was prepared by stuffing the spleen with soaked *hallah* from the previous week, mixed with onions and whatever sappy meat matter could be extracted from the inside of the uncooked spleen. After the stuffing was secured by needle and thread, this substance—which bore a resemblance to a sausage (2½ inches thick in diameter—would be baked in a heavy iron pot. Another fare of organ meats was stuffed stomach, which had ingredients and a baking process similar to the spleen. My mother would tirelessly scrape the stomach of the animal until all brown parts were completely removed. From early on I excluded both of these organ meat dishes from my list of edible foods.

On a Sabbath afternoon, most of the unmarried Jewish young of all ages, who were dressed better than their Christian neighbors in workaday clothing, walked with their friends and assembled in the *Eichküppel*, a nearby small stretch of woods with meadows and easy paths enclosed by beeches, oaks, spruces, and pines. Here in the clearings of the woods grew delicious, wild strawberries. From early on, we were taught at home and during formal religious instruction that picking fruit on the Sabbath, even if it should enhance the blessedness of the day, was forbidden. Most of the Jewish youth evaded this restriction by biting the strawberries off the stem, a task carried out with one's face close to the ground.

SABBATH ACTIVITIES   DURING THE SUMMER, many of the Jewish families enjoyed the last meal on Sabbath by picnicking in the *Eichküppel*. Observant families did not carry their food on the Sabbath, but had their non-Jewish household help perform this task. Our household help could not remain for the picnic because at that time of day the cows needed to be fed and milked, a chore which my father, if at all possible, preferred not to discharge on the Sabbath. On the *Eichküppel* grounds there was a refreshment restaurant where the Jewish families congregated. Upon the arrival there of several Jewish families, the non-Jewish customers promptly left the establishment, frequently without a hello and behaving as if they wished to avoid a displeasing circumstance. At other times the very same burgher of Lauterbach acted neighborly and well-disposed when meeting with a single Jew or a particular Jewish family.

When I was about ten I was permitted to join in these outings. I sensed the downright enmity of most of the local Christian population vis-à-vis the Jews, because the Christians coveted our day of leisure and also our clothing. Even on weekdays, most Jews dressed and ate better than Christians of similar social and economic level and income, a detail easily noticeable by non-Jews. The computable wealth of many Jewish families was, in fact, below the resources of their Christian neighbors. Nevertheless, the Christians perceived that the Jews had a higher standard of living because, dictated by dire circumstances for centuries, the Jewish families had learned to manage their resources with greater ingenuity. At other times (on Saturday afternoons during the summer), some of my contemporaries gathered after the *minhah* (afternoon service) in the room on the main floor of the synagogue building where the piano stood, and we studied *Pirkei Avot* (*Chapters of the Fathers*) with the assistance of Max Stern. These contain significant moral tenets and sayings of the sages of each generation, which have probably wielded appreciable influence all of my life.

Pewter *havdalah* plate with holder for twisted candle and spice box, circa 1800

AT THE END OF SABBATH

AT THE END OF THE SABBATH, whenever three stars were visible in the sky, we observed the separation ceremony (*havdalah*), which differentiated between Sabbath and weekdays. As the youngest member of the family, I was allowed to hold the braided candle. My father fixed his gaze upon his fingernails by the light of the candle and in this manner he reflected upon the difference between light and dark and between the Sabbath and weekdays. After the prayers and blessings, he extinguished the candle by pouring wine over it. Our silver spice box was filled with the pleasant fragrance of cloves, representing the wish for a good week.

Chapter Fourteen

Chapter Fifteen
Festival celebrations—Hanukkah, Purim, Passover, Shavuot, Lag Ba-Omer and Fast Days

Brass *Hanukkah* lamp from Germany, circa 1920

*H*ANUKKAH, AN ANNUAL EIGHT-DAY FESTIVAL during the time of the winter solstice-from the twenty-fifth of *Kislev* to the second of *Teveth* (the ninth and tenth months of the Hebrew calendar) commemorates a successful revolt in ancient times on behalf of religious freedom. This minor holiday also marks the

miracle of a cruse of oil for the eternal light in the holy temple. Although there was only enough for one day, this oil miraculously lasted for eight days. In our home we lit orange candles in a handsome copper *hanukkiah* (*Hanukkah menorah*) with its own music box, which played '*Ma'oz Zur Yeshu'ati*' ('*Mighty Rock of my Salvation*') composed by Mordecai. This *Hanukkah* hymn was composed in Germany during the thirteenth century by a poet named Mordecai. After the candle lighting ceremony our family lustily intoned all five verses of this song in Hebrew.

As a young child, I deemed the practice of lighting candles of only one color boring at best and I coveted the multi-colored tapers used on Christmas trees. However, in this instance, my parents staunchly followed the biblical injunction, "Do not imitate a heathen custom." While the

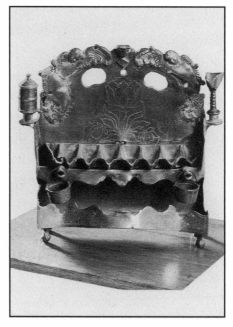

Pewter *Hanukkah* lamp from
Germany, eighteenth century

Hanukkah lights were burning, we were asked to reflect upon them. Because no work was permitted during that time, we played a game of *dredel* (a wooden top with the Hebrew initials of the saying, "A great miracle happened there"). The goal of this game was to garner an additional pile of walnuts. Gifts on *Hanukkah* consisted of oranges, apples, walnuts, filberts, and home-baked cookies. Generally, roasted goose was served on the Sabbath of *Hanukkah*—a custom that probably emulated the practice of local non-Jews who traditionally feasted on goose at Yuletide.

The Lauterbach Jewish congregation frequently marked the minor festivals of *Hanukkah* and *Purim* by a dance, a play, or both. On January 3, 1926, at three o'clock in the afternoon, a charity performance took place at the Johannesberg Hall in the Bahnhofstrasse. Max Stern, the congregation's spiritual leader, directed the choir and various theatrical performances, while Nathan Höchster arranged and rehearsed the several dances.

Brass *Hanukkah* lamp
from Hungary, circa 1900

Chapter Fifteen

The first part of the program contained the 'Baruch habah,' sung by a mixed choir. This verse is generally used during a Jewish wedding and reads: "Blessed be he that cometh in the name of the Lord, we bless you out of the house of the Lord. O come, let us worship and bow down; let us kneel before the Lord our Maker. Serve the Lord with joy; come before him with exulting."

There followed a prologue written by Nathan Höchster and delivered by Miss Irma Stein; an address by Max Stern, the spiritual leader; a march, *Hoch Heidecksburg* by V. Herzer. A play was also performed: *A Hanukkah Dream* by Frieda Mehler. The parts were: the Boy, played by Otto Pfifferling; the Father, played by Walter Kleeberg; an Angel, played by Zilli Höster; Antiochus, played by Benno Jakob; Nicanor, played by Ludwg Schiff; Eliezer, played by Alfred Adler; Hannah, played by Irma Stein; the First Son, played by Erna Wertheim; the Second Son, Tilli Wertheim; the Third Son, played by Richard Pfifferling; Leah, played by Ruth Spier; Nathan, played by Alfred Weinberg; John, played by Arthur Jakob; Judah, played by Ludwig Schiff; the Warriors, played by Hermann Strauss and Walter Kleeberg. An overture, the *Poet and the Peasant,* by Franz V. Suppe completed the first part.

The second part depicted a village concert and countrymen's dance. The parts were: the Organ-Grinder, played by Alfred Adler; the Drummers, played by Lothar Schiff and Kurt Stein; the Violinists, played by Arthur Jakob and Emil Frank; and the Trumpeter, played by Hermann Strauss. The Country Lassies were played by Irma Stein, Zilli Höchster, Tilli Wertheim, Ruth Spier, and Berta Adler. The Country Lads were played by Ludwig Schiff, Alfred Weinberg, Siegfried Gottlieb, Walter Kleeberg, Richard Pfifferling, and Erich Reiss. There followed a country waltz, the *Petite Grandmother*, by Langer.

Another play was also presented: *The Pearls of Judaism*, by Louis Böhm. The parts were: the Sage, played by Arthur Jakob; the Sinner, played by Emil Frank; the Simple-Minded, played by Siegfried Gottlieb; the Child, played by Fritz Jakob; the Sabbath, played by Erna Wertheim; *Purim*, played by Walter Kleeberg; *Passover*, played by Zilli Höchster; Feast of Weeks, played by Berta Adler; New Year's (*Rosh Ha-Shanah*), played by Ruth Spier; Day of Atonement, played by Alfred Adler; the Feast of Booths, played by Irma Stein; *Hanukkah*, played by Tilli Wertheim, and the Child, played by Lothar Schiff. The Mask Wearers were Richard Pfifferling, Erich Reiss, Lothar Schiff, and Kurt Stein. The round dances were performed by the Misses Jenny Baumann, Rosa Gottlieb, Frieda Stern, Ruth Weinberg, Berta Strauss, Paula Kleeberg, Lotte Kleeberg, Hilda Jakob, and Selma Strauss. The children who were members of the cast also participated in the round dances. The final piece was *Zion, Fantasy about Hebrew Vocal Music*, by M. Philippsohn.

A dance was held at eight o'clock in the evening, and the musical society of Lauterbach supplied the band. This may well have been the last time the Jews of Lauterbach dared to enlist the services of the local musical society for one of the Jewish communal functions.

Programm

für die am 3. Januar 1926, nachmittags 3 Uhr im Saalbau zum Johannesberg stattfindende

Wohltätigkeits=Veranstaltung.

Chor und Theaterleitung: Herr Lehrer Stern.
Tanz und Reigen verfaßt und einstudiert von Herrn N. Höchster.

1. Teil:

1. Boruch haboh (gemischter Chor)
2. Prolog (verfaßt von Herrn N. Höchster, gesprochen von Frl. Irma Stein)
3. Ansprache (Herr Lehrer Stern)
4. Marsch: Hoch Heidecksburg . . . . v. Herzer
5. Theater:

Ein Chanuka=Traum.
v. Frieda Mehler.
Personen:

Ein Knabe	Otto Pfifferling	Erster Sohn der Hanna	Erna Wertheim
Der Vater	Walter Kleeberg	Zweiter Sohn der Hanna	Tilli Wertheim
Ein Engel	Zilli Höchster	Dritter Sohn der Hanna	Rich. Pfifferling
Antiochus, König von Syrien	Benno Jakob	Lea	Ruth Spier
Nikanor, sein Feldherr	Ludwig Schiff	Nathan	Alfred Weinberg
Eleasar	Alfred Adler	Johannes	Arthur Jakob
Hanna	Irma Stein	Juda	Ludwig Schiff
		Krieger	Herm. Strauß u. Walt. Kleeberg

6. Ouverture (Dichter und Bauer) . . . . Franz v. Suppé

2. Teil:

Ein Dorfkonzert mit Bauerntanz.
Personen:

Leierkastenmann	Alfred Adler	Bauernmädchen:	Irma Stein	Bauernjungens:	Ludw. Schiff
Trommler	Lothar Schiff		Zilli Höchster		Alfr. Weinberg
"	Kurt Stein		Erna Wertheim		Siegfr. Gottlieb
Geiger	Arth. Jakob		Tilli Wertheim		Walter Kleeberg
"	Emil Frank		Ruth Spier		Rich. Pfifferling
Trompeter	H. Strauß		Berta Adler		Erich Reiß

8. Großmütterchen (Ländler) . . . . v. Langer
9. Theater:

Die Perlen des Judentums
v. Louis Böhm.
Personen:

Der Weise	Arthur Jakob	Masken:	Rich. Pfifferling	Jaum Kippur	Alfred Adler
Der Frevler	Emil Frank		Erich Reiß	Succoth	Irma Stein
Der Einfältige	Siegfr. Gottlieb		Lothar Schiff	Chanuka	Tilli Wertheim
Das Kind	Fritz Jakob		Kurt Stein	Vater	Herm. Strauß
Sabbat	Erna Wertheim	Pessach	Zilli Höchster	Mutter	Erna Wertheim
Purim	Walter Kleeberg	Schabuoth	Berta Adler	Kind	Lothar Schiff
Masken:	Tilli Wertheim	Rausch haschonoh	Ruth Spier		

Die Reigen werden ausgeführt von den Damen: Frl. Jenny Baumann, Frl. Rosa Gottlieb, Frl. Frieda Stern, Frl. Ruth Weinberg, Frl. Berta Strauß, Frl. Paula Kleeberg, Frl. Lotte Kleeberg, Frl. Hilde Jakobs, Frl. Selma Strauß, sowie von den mitwirkenden Kindern.

10. Zion, Fantasie über hebräische Gesänge . . . . M. Philippsohn

Abends 8 Uhr: Ball. / Die Musik wird von dem Musikverein Lauterbach ausgeführt.

Änderungen vorbehalten.

Hanukkah program of January 3, 1926 in Lauterbach

To the best of my recollection, the beginning passage of the play, *The Pearls of Judaism*, was: "I will show you images of renown—the treasures of Judaism." My sister, Erna Wertheim, who acted the part of Sabbath, wore a golden diadem, and carried two breads and a wine goblet on a silver tray. As the festival of *Hanukkah*, I donned on my head an electrically-lit *hanukkiyah* from which a cord led down in my back and into a silver basket, where a battery of not inconsiderable size and weight was hidden under gingerbread. In the play, *A Hanukkah Dream*, I was comforted to be on good terms with Benno Jakob as Antiochus and Ludwig Schiff as Nicanor, who impressed me with their fierce words, costumes, and large dimensions. After this benefit performance, actors and dancers enjoyed cakes and cookies obtained from a bake sale sponsored by the players' mothers.

TU BI-SHEVAT

THE OLDER GENERATION OF THE LAUTERBACH JEWS fasted a half-day on the tenth of *Tevet* (tenth month of the Jewish calendar, coinciding with December or January) in commemoration of the beginning of the siege of Jerusalem by Nebuchadnezzar in 587-86 B.C.E. *Tu bi-Shevat*, the festival of New Year for Trees and the beginning of tithes of fruit in Eretz Israel on the fifteenth day of the month of *Shevat*, generally occurred during the month of January. It was observed in Lauterbach by the Ashkenazic custom of eating fifteen diverse kinds of fruits. Fortunately, it was allowed to include sundry varieties of nuts in the count of fifteen, because the only available fruits in Lauterbach in January were apples stored from the previous year's harvest, dried pears, and prunes. Often my father brought Jaffa oranges from Frankfurt in order to fulfill the religious duty of eating a fruit from Israel on this day. My father also explained that the sap which circulates through a plant's system rises on *Tu bi-Shevat*—a perplexing notion for a young child to fathom while ice and snow still covered the ground in Lauterbach.

Notwithstanding the diaspora, my parents (and before them my Great-Aunt Johanna (Hannchen) Strauss and Great-Uncle Samuel Strauss [I]) observed the statute as stated in *Leviticus 27:30*, "And all the tithe of the land, whether of the seed of the land, or of the fruit of the tree, is the Lord's; it is holy unto the Lord." For that reason, my mother took fruit harvested from trees planted four years earlier and presented it to the Max Stern family who, in her mind, functioned as the Levites of old in accordance with *Numbers 18:21*, "And unto the children of Levi, behold, I have given all the tithe in Israel for an inheritance, in return for their service which they serve, even the service of the tent of meeting." Max Stern was not a descendant from the tribe of Levi.

PURIM
(FEAST OF LOTS)

IN LAUTERBACH THE DAY BEFORE *PURIM* (Feast of Lots) was marked as a fast day. *Aggadah* (the parts of the Bible which deal with narrative, history and ethical maxims) recounts that Esther, Mordecai, and the Jews of Shushan fasted prior to Esther's appearance before her husband, Ahasuerus, the King of Persia, in order to avert Haman's intended mass execution of Jews. On *Purim* Eve after the reading of the *Megillah* (Scroll of Esther), the Jewish youngsters of Lauterbach rushed home in order to put on a mask and a fancy dress which they themselves had devised, and then visited Jewish homes to recite the following verse:

> Good *Purim*, good *Purim* dear people.
> Do you know what *Purim* betokens?
> *Purim* stands for a long life,
> And you should put something into my purse.

> *Gut Purim, gut Purim Ihr liebe Leut,*
> *Wisst Ihr auch was Purim bedeut,*
> *Purim bedeut ein langes Leben,*
> *Und Ihr sollt mir auch etwas in mein Säckel geben.*

Money thus collected would be donated to a charity or given to an itinerant Jewish beggar, because the *Book of Esther* mentions "sending portions" (*shelakhmones*) to friends and of giving gifts to the poor. The formula directs the sending of least two portions of edibles to a friend and the giving of a present of money to at least two poor people. My mother fulfilled this pronouncement whole-heartedly and with innate generosity. Most Jews of Lauterbach attended two readings of the *Megillah* of Esther. On *Purim* during the reading of the *Megillah*, noises to drown out Haman's name were hardly audible at the Lauterbach synagogue, in contrast to the unrestrained and earsplitting clangor in many synagogues in the United States.

The *Purim* meal (*purim se'udah*) generally consisted of potato salad, a home-canned vegetable and fruit, and a tip of home-cured thinly-sliced smoked breast of beef. *Hamantaschen* (three cornered yeast cakes with a prune filling and generally eaten on *Purim* in the United States) were unknown in the Wertheim household, nor did I ever hear my grandparents of Angenrod or Kirtorf refer to this pastry. Nevertheless, during the time the Max Stern family resided at Cent 17, I was permitted to assist Rosa Oppenheimer Stern while she baked Haman pastry in the form of a gingerbread man. Mrs. Stern urged me first to bite off Haman's head in order to render the arch-enemy of the Jews powerless. In Lauterbach, I did not know about unadulterated exuberance customarily exhibited on *Purim* in the United States and Israel. One of the reasons for restraint may well have been the nearly simultaneous event of *Fasching* (a time of boisterous conduct in many German cities that ended with Ash Wednesday). Once again the Jewish elders of Lauterbach must have been inclined not to imitate a heathen custom. Besides, during my childhood and adolescence in Lauterbach, there were few, if any, grounds for mirth and hilarity.

PASSOVER (*PESAH*)   PASSOVER (*PESAH*), A SPRING FESTIVAL, recalls the Exodus of the Israelites from Egypt and God's liberation of his people from Egyptian slavery. Prayers, celebrations, and food are based on this historic event. The name 'Passover' stems from *Exodus 12:23* which states, "For the Lord will pass through to smite the Egyptians; and when he seeth the blood upon the lintel, and on the two side-posts, the Lord will pass over the door, and will not suffer the destroyer to come in unto your houses to smite you." Similar to the Pilgrim Feasts of *Sukkot* and *Shavuot*, Passover is also an agricultural festival, as *Leviticus 23:10* states, "When ye are come into the land which I give unto you, and shall reap the harvest thereof, then ye shall bring the sheaf (*omer*)[a] of the first fruits of your harvest unto the priest." Passover begins on the fifteenth of the Hebrew month of *Nisan* and lasts eight days in the diaspora. According to *Exodus 23:15*, "The feast of unleavened bread shalt thou keep; seven days thou shalt eat unleavened bread." *Exodus 39:12* declares, "And they baked unleavened cakes of the dough which they brought forth out of Egypt, for it was not leavened; because they were thrust out of Egypt, and could not tarry, neither had they prepared for themselves any victuals."

Therefore, toward the end of January, Jews in Lauterbach embarked on numerous conversations about ordering *mazzah* (unleavened bread). They recalled the quality of the *mazzah* of the previous year and debated whether or not to entrust the current year's order to the same supplier. Some *mazzah* suppliers in the area were Isaak Rosenberg of Grossen-Buseck, Halberstadt in Ober-Mockstadt, Naumann in Bisses (belonging to Echzell), and a *mazzah* bakery in Rhina.

The Wertheim household habitually ordered fifty pounds (fifty-five pounds in American equivalent) of *mazzah* for the eight days of Passover. This large order was partially determined by the paucity of many other foods that were permissible and/or available on Passover. A case in point is the conventional Passover breakfast in Lauterbach and vicinity that consisted of layers of *mazzah* broken into a cup, flavored with sugar, and softened with hot coffee and milk. This dish is called '*brocken*,' a name which is probably derived from the German word '*bröckeln*,' which means 'to break into small pieces.' Moreover, *mazzah* bakers did not produce *mazzah* again until the following year and my mother preferred to use *mazzah* for some menus after Passover.

Observant Jews of Lauterbach could obtain kosher foods for Passover only from Fulda or Frankfurt am Main, or by purchasing them locally from the impoverished widow Anna Adler Weinberg (of) Am Wörth 14. Whole almonds, the only available variety of nuts, but which were very expensive, had to be purchased in Fulda or Frankfurt am Main. An attachment on the meat grinder, cranked by hand and deemed an outright luxury, crushed almonds for baking. *Mazzah* meal (unavailable commercially) was obtained by pounding *mazzah* into a fine consistency with the help of an iron mortar and pestle.

Since food packaging did not exist in the twenties and thirties in Lauterbach, any grocery items permissible for Passover, such as coffee, salt, or granulated or cube sugar, had to be purchased from Anna Weinberg, lest these foods be rendered

[a] *Omer* is a barley offering brought to the temple on *Nisan* 16.

unkosher by contact with food items containing leaven. Mrs. Weinberg also provided the acknowledged treats of the day: rock candy and a sticky light yellow unwrapped candy called '*Glundchen.*' Kosher for Passover chocolate was not obtain-

Cross-stitch embroidery of a *mazzah* basket cover in Lauterbach, circa 1912

able. Fresh fruit was in meager supply and we had to rely on the shriveled apples from the previous harvest and stewed fruit derived from our home dried plums, pears, and apples which, when spread on *mazzah*, provided a snack or dessert.

Mazzah, the antithesis of fermented dough (leavened bread), was produced from the prescribed white flour and had an approximate diameter of thirteen inches (square *mazzah* was unheard of). Supervision of the flour for Passover *mazzah* began as early as the milling of the wheat in order to prevent fermentation. The Wertheim household also received as part of its seasonal *mazzah* shipment three *mazzahs*, which were used only for the *seder* service. This variety was baked with the most stringently supervised flour and was called '*mazzah shemurah.*'

Supervision of the wheat for this *mazzah* began at the time of its harvest. Three holes represented the priestly cast (*kohanim*), who descended from Aaron (the first high priest) and who were responsible for specified functions during the days of the First and Second Temple; two one-inch holes stood for the descendants of the tribe of Levi (Levites), who in biblical days served in the Tabernacle and later in the Temple; and a one-inch hole signified the Israelites, the most common and most numerous folk among Jews. This variety of *mazzah* was used during the *seder* (the order of religious service in the home on the first and second Passover nights) for the *Afikoman* (a Greek word referring to aftermeal refreshments or entertainment). During my youth in Lauterbach, there was no established practice of hiding the *Afikoman* for the children to find and to return for a specified compensation before the *seder* could be continued. That may have been one reason why I did not always gracefully endure the Wertheim home's three-hour *seder*, which included every word and song of our sixty-three page *Haggadah* (book of prescribed benedictions, prayers, and instructions for the Passover *seder*).

Whole-wheat *mazzah* was nonexistent, although the whole grain might have ameliorated the austere, unhealthy, and restricted Passover diet. However, the rather uncompromising mind set of the Rabbinates of Giessen and Fulda, as well as the inflexible views of the Lauterbach synagogue elders, would not have acceded to such an innovation if it had existed. An attitude prevailed among most Jews of Lauterbach, Angenrod, and Kirtorf that anything '*neu*' ('new ideas' or 'introductions') must be vigorously denounced in deference to strict adherence to the status quo. The concept of '*neu*' was fraught with the superstition that bad luck would strike those who followed new notions. Instead, my father purchased a small supply of the then highly regarded egg *mazzah* in a kosher for Passover store in Frankfurt am Main.

Exodus 12:19 directs: "Seven days there shall be no leaven found in your houses; for whosoever eateth that which is leavened, that soul shall be cut off from the congregation of Israel, whether he be a sojourner, or one that is born in the land." Hence, before or nearing the time of *Purim*, one month before Passover, my mother systematically embarked on cleaning every room, closet, drawer, and piece of furniture of the Wertheim residence. She took special care that individual items of clothing or laundry were carefully examined and shaken for fear that a crumb of bread might escape her painstaking scrutiny. (This tiresome process was called '*schütteln*,' or 'shaking.') The kitchen and pantry walls and closets were washed from top to bottom. For one month before Passover, the otherwise orderly Wertheim household endured an unpleasant state of unsettledness and derangement.

Rules of what and where to eat became more restrictive as the Passover holiday neared; hence I particularly rejoiced in the arrival of the first *seder*. The Wertheim household possessed sufficient sets of china, flatware, pots, pans, and linens for exclusive use on Passover. However, we rendered glasses for ordinary use permissible for Passover by filling them with water for seventy-two hours and changing the water every twelve hours. It was a laborious chore for women in a large household to remove everyday utensils and replace them with Passover cooking, baking, and serving implements. The routine had to be reversed at the conclusion of Passover in a single evening that we dubbed '*Rumpelnacht*' ('night of clatter').

The injunction of *Exodus 12:19* made it imperative that a Jew not consume the milk of cows whose fodder a few days before and during Passover might violate the edict. Moreover, many Jews in Lauterbach followed the regulation that observant Jews would drink milk acquired only from a Jew and under Jewish supervision. For that reason, some weeks before Passover my father bought several milk cows in order to provide kosher milk to those Jews in Lauterbach who had no other way of obtaining it. The cows whose milk was destined for Passover use could not be fed a by-product of the beer brewery from across the way, which my father ordinarily considered a healthful booster for milk production. For this holiday, only hay and other unfermented botanical products could be utilized as fodder. Consequently, during Passover some eight to ten customers would line up after the afternoon milking time for kosher-for-Passover milk. My mother preferred selling all available milk, because the production of cheese and butter was a prolonged process and impractical for only eight days. Moreover, it made little sense to invest in duplicate equipment used only for Passover. At that time, whole milk was the only available dairy product during Passover.

For the most part, *seder* gatherings in Lauterbach were celebrated within what we now designate as the nuclear family or with grandparents and single or widowed aunts and uncles who generally lived in the same household. My Great-Uncle Samuel, who resided in the same house, conducted our *seder* as long as he lived; my mother's uncles, Salomon (I) and Markus Strauss, who also lived in town, marked *seder* with their own families. Despite the fact that my grandparents lived only thirteen and fifteen miles away in Angenrod and Kirtorf respectively, they never celebrated Passover with us. They observed the holiday with the families of their sons, with whom they permanently resided. This circumstance was probably determined by both the

lack of spare household utensils for Passover and the cumbersomeness of the available travel modes.

Although Passover meant new clothing for the Wertheim sisters and although the holiday was considered a joyful one commemorating the liberation from Egyptian slavery and nature's awakening in the northern hemisphere from winter's slumber, I always had a feeling of downright austerity and never-ending toil-especially for women—and rigid rules too difficult to follow. Additionally, in our home, seating intended solely for men

Seder hanging depicting *The Four Sons*, taken from a *Haggadah* of 1711 in Sulzbach, Germany

was favored, with two white exquisitely embroidered pillows in order to fulfill the rule for reclining. I interpreted this female debarment to mean that, notwithstanding any attainment on my part, I would never be eligible for the distinction of reclining at the *seder* with two pillows.

Furthermore, in Lauterbach at the time of Maundy Thursday, Good Friday, and Easter, which often coincide with Passover, overt and covert sentiments toward Jews ran deeper among young and old. Instruction at home and in catechism taught children that all Jews were forever guilty of betraying and killing the Christian savior. Routinely, in grades one through three in Mr. Meyer's class, my public school peers accused me of perfidy toward Christ; but even they must have doubted that I was sufficiently powerful to kill their savior. All year long, throughout childhood and adolescence, I withstood inescapable denigration at school that invariably worsened at the time of Passover.

Atypical of my parents' and even of my grandparents' usual adamance against imitating heathen and Christian ways, we were allowed to hide and hunt eggs dyed with onion skins and coffee grinds. However, commercial Easter egg dyes of bright

Chapter Fifteen

colors, which I secretly preferred, were not permissible because the dyes might have contained leaven. Customarily, some six to eight religious school classmates joined in an egg hunt in the Wertheim gardens, where ingenious hiding places presented a creative challenge to adults hiding the eggs and to guests eager to find their prize.

One of the requisite components of the *seder* table is the horseradish herb (*maror*), symbolizing the bitter suffering of the Jews in Egypt. Horseradish, when eaten raw in even the smallest portions, induces the flow of tears. It grew vigorously in the Wertheim garden, as if to hint of bitter suffering and trials yet to be endured on this soil. A Passover *Haggadah* printed in 1906 in Rödelheim by S. Lehrberger and Company directed that the green crown of the horseradish as well as the white part be used for the *hillel* sandwich. Purportedly, this *mazzah* sandwich is the first traceable sandwich in history; it consisted of horseradish herb between two pieces of *mazzah*. Before eating it the following was recited: "In Memory of the Temple after Hillel: Thus did Hillel do when the Sacred Temple was standing: He used to combine *mazzah* and bitters and eat them together, in observance of what is said in the Writ: 'They shall eat it together with *mazzah* and bitter herbs.'" Several families of the Lauterbach Jewish community who were unable to grow their own horseradish received some from my mother so they could fulfill this religious duty properly. The main course of the Wertheim *seder* meal included roasted lamb, a custom generally observed among Sephardic Jews. Some Jews in Lauterbach viewed this practice with disfavor; according to their belief, this tradition should have been observed only in *Eretz Israel* (the land of Israel).

COUNTING OF
OMER TO
SHAVUOT

AN IMPORTANT PART OF THE SECOND *seder* night (the sixteenth of *Nisan*) service is the beginning of the Counting of the *Omer* for forty-nine days and terminating with *Shavuot* (Feast of Weeks). Time and again, we were instructed that the *Omer* counting represented a link between Passover and *Shavuot*, that is, liberty and freedom from slavery through obedience to *Torah*. In our home, the nightly counting of the *Omer* was considered a devotional ordinance. If the counting of the *Omer* in the evening is overlooked, it may be done the following day, but the blessing may not be vocalized. He who omits counting for even one day may not pronounce the blessing for the remainder of the *Omer* period. Furthermore, this lapse caused the transgressor to be excluded from partaking of cheesecake, a prescribed food of honor on *Shavuot* in Lauterbach.

Lag Ba-Omer, the thirty-third day in the counting of the *Omer* (the eighteenth day of the month of *Iyyar*), is the only day between Passover and *Shavuot* on which weddings or other joyous functions may take place. I cannot recall any light-heartedness or even a relaxed atmosphere in religious school on that day in Lauterbach. At no time did we celebrate this day with an outing. We were taught that in earlier times plagues and epidemics besetting Jews came to an end on *Lag Ba-Omer*, supposedly making us mindful of our more fortunate portion.

Shavuot, which is observed on the sixth as well as on the seventh of *Sivan* (the third month) in the diaspora, is also one of the Pilgrim Feasts. In biblical days, it earmarked the end of the barley and the beginning of the wheat harvest. Most Jews of Lauterbach gave expression to the agricultural aspect of Bible times of this holiday by serving meals consisting of vegetables, fruit, and dairy products. In the Wertheim household, the menu customarily included newly-picked Swiss chard ribs (either creamed or marinated), fresh or home-canned strawberries, and cheesecake prepared with a sweet yeast dough and topped with homemade pot cheese and sour cream.

On the eve of *Shavuot*, Lauterbach Jewish households alternately hosted meetings for *lernen* (study) lest congregants forget that on this holiday the *Torah* was bequeathed on Mount Sinai to the Jewish people. On *Shavuot*, the Lauterbach synagogue was adorned with Norwegian pines rented from a local nursery and by bouquets of lilacs and peonies from the Wertheim gardens. Max Stern delivered sermons on both days of *Shavuot*. Before the official advent of Hitler, his topic generally dealt with the spiritual aspect of *Shavuot* or of the appropriate holiday. However, beginning in 1933, Mr. Stern's preaching frequently touched upon the dark clouds on the horizon threatening his flock. With fewer and less stringent dictates, *Shavuot* was a more carefree and enjoyable holiday, particularly for women, which resulted in added happiness for the whole family.

Seder hanging called '*Sederhandtuch*' in Hesse

TISHA BE-AV   MANY MEMBERS OF THE LAUTERBACH JEWISH congregation fasted in observation of the seventeenth of *Tammuz* (the fourth month of the Jewish year), which commemorates the breaching of the walls of Jerusalem in 586 B.C.E. My father, and my Great-Uncle Samuel before him, faithfully adhered to this practice even while tending to demanding business and work schedules. They terminated the fast at about nine-thirty or ten o'clock at night. This fast marked the beginning of a mourning period of three weeks (*drei Wochen*), culminating in *Tisha be-Av*, also called Ninth of *Av* (the fifth month in the Jewish year), and designating the established day of mourning for the destruction of Temple in Jerusalem. My father and religious teachers made known that the expulsion of the Jews from Spain in 1492

Chapter Fifteen

German pewter Passover plate of 1877 by F. F. Altreuter

had also occurred on the Ninth of *Av*. As a youngster, I intuited from my father's exposition that some of our ancestors possibly had come from Spain, which I confirmed much later. Family members made no mention of this, but consistently referred to Spain and its history in a somewhat disparaging stance.

In Lauterbach, the Ninth of *Av* was also depicted as a symbol of Jewish suffering in the diaspora—especially in connection with the massacres in the nearby Jewish communities of Fulda, Frankfurt am Main, Speyer, and Worms at the time of the Crusades and the Black Death. From the 1920s until 1932, the Jews of Lauterbach lamented over the portion of their forefathers in earlier times; they would or could not understand that their own existence was no state of bliss, to say the least. The frame of reference of the Jews of Lauterbach was the lives of their fathers and grandfathers in Crainfeld, Grebenau, and Storndorf. Compared to that, the circumstances of the Jews of Lauterbach had indeed improved civically and economically. Upon reflecting during the 'three weeks,' with not much else to do in Lauterbach, I understood clearly that, despite some well-disposed Christians in town, Jews were removed from the mainstream of living. In school I felt all but cut off. Therefore, my thinking was dominated by a compelling desire to create the first possible opportunity to leave Lauterbach and Germany for Israel or the United States, even if it meant separating from my parents.

Although climatically late spring or early summer was the best season of the year, the three weeks between the seventeenth of *Tammuz* and the Ninth of *Av* were a period of little joy and laughter, but rather of much sadness and conditioned brooding. Swimming and boating were strictly prohibited. Accounts of those who had failed to heed this edict, and who had met with severe injuries or even death, were plentiful. Except for the Sabbaths between the seventeenth of *Tammuz* and the Ninth of *Av*, meat or meat products were forbidden, and most men refrained from shaving or cutting their beards.

Pewter Passover plate (1869) called '*Sederschüssel*' in Hesse

Dancing or listening to music were deemed unsuitable frivolities and were therefore not permissible during this period of traditional mourning. To the best of my recollection, only my father fasted all day on the Ninth of *Av*. The rest of the family broke their fast after one o'clock in the afternoon (so it would be considered at least a half day's fast) with a lunch consisting of boiled new potatoes and fresh cucumbers from our garden, which were marinated and served with sour cream. After the Ninth of *Av* a normative routine which lasted twenty days and had fewer restrictions was adopted until the first of *Elul* (the sixth month in the Jewish year) which, in anticipation of the Ten Days of Penitence, was considered a month of repentance and its attendant provisos.

The high school building (*Realschule*) in Lauterbach

THE MEYER
HÖCHSTER FAMILY

*T*he municipal Storndorf records of 1863 indicate that Meyer Höchster, a cattle dealer, obtained citizenship in Storndorf and later moved to Lauterbach. This took place after February 4, 1866, when Meyer Höchster, still in Storndorf, signed the birth certificate of my Great-Uncle Markus Strauss. Meyer Höchster (born July 18, 1839 in Storndorf) and his wife, Zippora Strauss Höchster (born November 18, 1848 in Storndorf, were among the early Jews who settled in Lauterbach.

Meyer's parents were Kaufmann Höchster and Giedel Herzberger Höchster both of Storndorf; Zippora's parents were Juda Strauss and Rebekah Strauss (née Strauss), also of Storndorf. In the mid-nineteenth century, numerous branches of Strauss families resided in that village and in the entire Vogelsberg region. I do not know the origin of this popular name among the Jews of Hesse except that 'Strauss' in German means 'ostrich' as well as 'bouquet.'

THE CHILDREN OF
MEYER AND
ZIPPORA
HÖCHSTER

ZIPPORA AND MEYER HÖCHSTER'S SON, Herz, was born May 13, 1867 in Storndorf and a second son, Kaufmann, named after his paternal grandfather, was born May 12, 1887 in Lauterbach. By 1887, the thirty-nine-year old Zippora was ailing and unable to perform necessary household chores. Meyer engaged a Jewish housekeeper, who on August 8, 1891, gave birth to Meyer's son, Nathan Höchster. Zippora died on September 6, 1904, and was buried in the Lauterbach Jewish cemetery. I do not know whether Meyer Höchster later married the mother of his son, Nathan.

On December 4, 1883, Meyer Höchster announced in the *Lauterbacher Anzeiger* that he moved from the house of Andreas Schmidt to the house of the widow, N. Neidhard in the Rockelsgasse. By 1887, he filed building plans for a stable at Langgasse 24. During the early 1880s, an account in the *Lauterbacher Anzeiger* explained the pricing system used by Meyer Höchster in his business: for white rags he paid the maximum price; for non-white rags he paid 6 to 8 *Pfennige* per pound; for bones he paid 3 *Pfennige* per pound.

According to a notice in the *Lauterbacher Anzeiger*, Meyer Höchster died at the age of seventy-seven on Wednesday, April 12, 1916, and his funeral was scheduled for Sunday, April 16, 1916. Perhaps the family

Obituary of Meyer Höchster in the
Lauterbacher Anzeiger

members wanted to be absolutely certain that Meyer had drawn his last breath, since some years earlier he had feigned death in order to find out how members of the Jewish community would regard him. Meyer's death notice was similar to those of non-Jews, especially since flowers and wreaths were not declined as they were in other Jewish obituaries of the era.

IN AUGUST 1893, MEYER HÖCHSTER'S OLDEST SON by Zippora, Herz, wedded Regine Eschwege (born in Fulda on February 26, 1869). In the 1920s, Herz sold stoves and fuel. During the early 1920s, Herz and Regine lived in Lauterbach on the ground floor of a duplex in the Bahnhofstrasse, only a few houses away from the synagogue building at Hinter der Burg 17. This location provided Herz and Regine with a vantage point from which they could closely observe the arrivals and departures of the congregants. As a childless couple, the Höchsters had free time to sit in surveillance, either openly by their window or hidden behind curtains. Regine and Herz Höchster spoke with young children to extract information from them about the food, finances, and modes of living of members of the Lauterbach Jewish congregation. Herz wanted to be equipped with disparaging information concerning a congregational member in the event that someone in the congregation refuted his notions.

My parents instructed their two daughters to avoid walking on the side of the street where the Herz Höchster family resided. If, by some unfortunate happenstance, we were to meet up with this family or, worse yet, to be invited into their home, we were to answer all questions with the words, "I do not know" or "I cannot remember." Not even a question about our lunch menu was to be honored with an informative answer. Behind their backs, Herz and Regine were nicknamed 'Herzchen' and 'Leberchen' (meaning 'diminutive heart' and 'small liver'). As a child, I viewed Herz and Regine as very unattractive individuals. Herz' eyes always looked as if he were permanently suffering from acute conjunctivitis. As a young child, I believed that the large golden ring on Herz' index finger was a mark of badness and wrongdoing, and I subsequently eyed with suspicion anyone wearing a ring on his index finger.

My Great-Uncles Samuel and Markus Strauss, who were highly respected and liked, avoided Herz Höchster like a communicable disease. Like many members of the Lauterbach Jewish congregation, Great-Uncle Samuel followed the admonition of the *Ethics of Fathers*, "Keep thee far from a bad neighbor, associate not with the wicked, and abandon not the belief in retribution." My father, Vogel (III), exchanged no more than greetings of the day with this family, while my mother tried to appear friendly from a distance and avoided any contact whenever possible. Herz Höchster and his family were also shunned by my maternal grandmother, Auguste Strauss Lamm, and her life-long friend, Elise Baumann Levi, who had known the Höchster family from their native village of Storndorf. The intense dislike of Herz was caused by some major strife pertaining to synagogue affairs either in Storndorf or in connection with the founding of the Jewish congregation in Lauterbach.[1] This family had no close friends among the members of the Lauterbach Jewish congregation and contacts came about only as required. Even the family of Herz' younger brother,

Kaufmann Höchster, was usually not on speaking terms with their oldest family member in town.

During his early years in Lauterbach, Herz Höchster engaged in the lucrative pursuit of collecting old rags and scrap metal. In 1896, he advertised in the

The Bahnhofstrasse in Lauterbach

Lauterbacher Anzeiger the sale of woolen and waterproof horse blankets, as well as fruit and potato sacks. He described his merchandise as a combination of high quality and low prices. By the early 1920s, Herz had bought a large tract of land in the Bahnhofstrasse, near today's Umgehungsstrasse, where he built several multi-family homes. Each unit had its own balcony, as was customary for the newer and better homes in that era. Soon the Herz Höchster family occupied the unit at Bahnhofstrasse 84 that bore the following inscription on the outside, "*Wir bauen hier so feste and sind doch fremde Gäste, und wo wir sollen ewig sein, da bauen wir so wenig ein.*" ("Stoutly we build here, although we are but alien guests, while into our eternal residence we build so little.") Herz' niece, Grete Höchster Ephraim of Nof Yam, Israel stated that Herz was rather wealthy because he held real estate in Frankfurt am Main. In the mid-1920s, Herz and Regine donated a *Torah* scroll to the Lauterbach Jewish community. This expenditure involved considerable capital due to the special parchment, the uncommon skill of the scribe, and the fact that it took one year to write a *Torah* scroll.

In Lauterbach, Herz Höchster was not known for his scholarly pursuit of *Torah* that was so common among other Jewish community elders from Storndorf, Grebenau, and Crainfeld. But he labored to enhance his status and respect in the community in order to contribute to the fulfillment of *Exodus 19:6*, "Ye shall be unto Me a kingdom of Priests, and a holy nation." Despite the generally low-key character of the Lauterbach Jewish community, dedication ceremonies involving the donation of this *Torah* scroll were elaborate. However, Herz' generosity did not elevate his position in the Lauterbach Jewish community.

After the deaths of the founders of the Lauterbach Jewish congregation (Aron Stein in 1918, Samuel Strauss (I) in 1924, and Sigmund Strauss in 1934), Josef

Weinberg was the *parnas*, the titular and elected head of the Jewish community, but Herz Höchster's voice was increasingly heard in communal affairs. In 1934, Herz disagreed with the spiritual leader, Max Stern's, Passover sermon recommending that his congregants leave Lauterbach and Germany as soon as they could to find a place of refuge abroad.[2] In 1936, Herz vociferously objected to Mr. Stern's stance in encouraging and entrusting Lauterbach Jewish families to take *Torahs* abroad. Mr. Stern's plan of action was formulated three years after Hitler had come to power and after more than twenty Jewish Lauterbach families had sought refuge from their local SS tormentors by emigrating or by moving to Frankfurt am Main or other German towns where they had relatives.[a]

When the childless Herz Höchster family became wealthy, they invited their nephew, Rolf Martin, born in Lauterbach on November 21, 1922, to live with them. Rolf was the oldest child of Herz' younger step-brother, Nathan Höchster, and Nathan's wife, Thea Schleicher Höchster. The Nathan Höchster family also had twins, Hans and Grete, who were born in Lauterbach on November 22, 1924. Among the Jews in Upper Hesse, it was not uncommon for a family coping with financial hardships or living in a town that lacked higher educational facilities to have the care of a child assumed by a close, often childless relative or by grandparents. Regine and Herz Höchster were ill-suited to handle the young Rolf, and educators would have recoiled at the way this elderly couple tried to guide the youngster. But the members of the Lauterbach Jewish community considered Rolf a lucky child because he obviously received more adult attention, better clothing, and more toys than his parents would have been able to afford. However, Rolf missed the close companionship of his younger sister and brother, Grete and Hans.

During the *Kristallnacht* on November 10, 1938, local Nazi perpetrators removed the aphorism on the Herz Höchster residence in Lauterbach, ravaged and pillaged their living quarters, and created a screaming clatter by throwing heavy items out of a second floor window.[3] Shortly thereafter, on November 21, 1938, Regine and Herz moved to Arndtstrasse 25 in Frankfurt am Main. On April 21, 1938, the sixteen-year-old Rolf Höchster left Lauterbach for Arndtstrasse 46 in Frankfurt.

As the last caretaker of the Lauterbach Jewish congregation, Herz Höchster sold its cemetery at the Kalkofen to the barber, Helfenbein. This transaction occurred prior to Herz' departure from Lauterbach and was probably done under duress. During our 1959 visit to Lauterbach, we saw Mr. Helfenbein's bill of sale that was signed by Herz Höchster. Only after extensive exhortation was Mr. Helfenbein willing to give us the key to the Lauterbach Jewish cemetery. He doubtless feared repercussions, because he had converted the vacant area of the cem-

---

[a] Mr. Stern's rationale was much like that of the Elders of Danzig in 1939, when they sent *Torahs*, Jewish ritual items, books, scrolls, tapestries, and memorabilia to the Jewish Theological Seminary in New York. In 1937, the Westerfeld family of Lauterbach took three *Torahs* with them to Montevideo, Uruguay.

etery into a fruit and vegetable garden for cabbages, cauliflower, and plum trees. At our request to the Jewish administrative authorities in Germany, the cemetery was then restored to its original purpose. Also at that time, the cemetery fence on the west side was taken down. On our subsequent visits in the 1970s and 1980s, it appeared that the reconstructed fence had been built ten feet closer to the graves and that the square footage of land outside the fence had been ceded to the neighboring property owners.

In 1936 or perhaps later, Herz Höchster sent a letter from either Lauterbach or Frankfurt am Main to the German Inland Revenue Office. The purpose of the letter was to inform against Max Stern for promoting the sending abroad of Lauterbach *Torahs* with departing members of the Jewish congregation. This disclosure by Herz interdicted the move from Germany to Israel of Max, Rosa, and the sixteen-year-old Arnold Stern. Two other sons, Manfred and Herbert, were already living in Palestine and had received a letter stating that their parents and brother would soon join them.[4]

Max and Rosa Stern, and their son, Arnold, perished in the Holocaust. Their fate had been foredoomed by Herz Höchster informing the authorities against Max Stern. Regine Höchster perished in Minsk, and Herz Höchster died of a kidney disease in Frankfurt am Main. This episode reveals the deep roots of evil and validates my Great-Uncle Samuel's faithfulness to the Jewish moralists of the thirteenth century: "Avoid, as much as may be, bad men, men of persistent angry feelings; thou canst get nothing from their company but shame."

Kaufmann Höchster
(married Blanka Wunsch)

KAUFMANN, MEYER HÖCHSTER'S SECOND SON by Zippora, was born on July 18, 1887, in Lauterbach. In German, 'Kaufmann' means 'merchant' or 'businessman.' In accordance with the prevailing customs among the Jews of Storndorf and its surroundings, this child was named after his late paternal grandfather, Kaufmann Höchster. On October 3, 1853, a Kaufmann Höchster, probably the grandfather of the one living in Lauterbach, signed the birth certificate of Jette Strauss, the fifth child of my maternal great-grandparents, Seligmann Strauss and Biena Reiss Strauss.

Kaufmann Höchster participated in World War I as a soldier for Germany. Throughout the early 1920s, he collected old metal and rags and he also sold coal and kerosene. During the late 1920s, he added an additional source of revenue to what seemed an already flourishing, diversified business: a single-pump filling station behind the family residence. The home was an older, half-timbered building with an ear-splitting bell that sounded whenever the front door was opened; and the home and furnishings were in a typical middle-class style, with a touch of costly *nouveau riche*. In addition to a record player and a collection of musical records, the Höchster family also owned a radio that was not affordable by even the middle class in Lauterbach and for which a monthly fee was due at the Lauterbach post office. Clearly this family's life style and consumption was more affluent than those of either their gentile or their Jewish neighbors in the Rockelsgasse.

Chapter Sixteen

Kaufmann Höchster, a light-complected redhead, was of short stature and was always extremely well-groomed, clearly attaching much importance to his appearance. In 1912, Kaufmann married Blanka Wunsch (born in Assenheim on May 2, 1886), who was a head taller and a year older.

Blanka Wunsch Höchster's mother, Jettchen Schiff Wunsch (born December 1, 1858 in Grosskarben, in the county of Friedberg), lived with the Kaufmann Höchster family in the Rockelsgasse. Jettchen Schiff Wunsch was an attractive, intelligent lady who, after she became a widow, joined her married daughter. One unmarried daughter of Blanka Wunsch immigrated to the United States before World War I and another daughter became a registered nurse. In the 1920s, the nurse spent most Jewish festivals with her mother and the Höchster family. I do not know of the fate of this Jewish nurse during the Nazi regime. However, Jettchen Schiff Wunsch moved on February 16, 1937, to Blücherstrasse in Mönchen-Gladbach with her daughter and son-in-law. From there she was shipped to Theresienstadt, and in her early eighties she disappeared into the night of Nazi extermination.

The Höchster family
Left: The sister of Blanka Höchster,
Right: Blanka Höchster, and Jettchen Schiff Wunsch (behind table)

Seated next to my mother in synagogue, Blanka Höchster dressed in contrast to the conservative Lauterbach standards. She showed off an extravagant wardrobe and flaunted an extensive collection of gold and diamond rings and bracelets. In 1930, hearsay in Lauterbach was that Kaufmann Höchster fathered a boy born to Kathrinchen, the household help at Rockelsgasse 54, and that this child, Hans, bore much resemblance to Manfred Richard Höchster. Shortly before her death, Kathrinchen acknowledged that Kaufmann Höchster was Hans' father.[5] It seemed that whenever Kaufmann committed a marital indiscretion, he strove to endear himself again to his wife by presenting her with a new bauble or piece of jewelry.

Some time after Hans' birth in 1930, Kathrinchen and Hans (later his surname would be Keller) moved to Rockelsgasse 41, the home of Kaufmann Strauss, his daughter, Sophie Strauss Oppenheimer, her husband, Jakob Oppenheimer, and their children, Helene and Ernst. Kathrinchen and her son, Hans, were on excellent terms with this Jewish family. Hans became heir to Manfred Höchster's splendid collection of well-preserved toys, but otherwise recalled an unhappy childhood.

Prior to the 'Night of the Broken Glass' (*Kristallnacht*) November 10, 1938, Kaufmann Höchster returned to Lauterbach to see Kathrinchen at Rockelsgasse 4l and was escorted to the train to Giessen by Wilhelm Eifert, in order to assure his safety.[8] Even in Lauterbach, where anti-semitism had been widespread before the Nazis legalized it and extolled it as a high virtue, there were always a small number of people who risked kind acts to Jews. These people defied the anti-semitic attitudes of the times in spite of danger and possible disgrace to themselves and to their families.

During the years 1947 to 1948, Hans Keller worked for the British Army in Bergen-Belsen, a Nazi concentration camp near Hanover, Germany. Bergen-Belsen had been established in 1943 as a prisoner-of-war camp for Jews whom the Nazis wished to exchange for Germans in allied territory and it functioned until 1945. Thirty-seven thousand people died in Bergen-Belsen before its liberation. It was here that Anne Frank fell ill and died in March 1945. The trauma of Bergen-Belsen overwhelmed Hans Keller, because he identified with his Jewish family members.[10]

Zilli Höchster
(married Mr. Sieger)

ON JANUARY 21, 1913, A DAUGHTER WAS born to Blanka and Kaufmann Höchster. They named her 'Zilli' after Kaufmann's mother, Zippora Höchster. 'Zilli' is an abbreviation of 'Zipporah' (the wife of Moses and daughter of Jethro, the Midianite Priest mentioned in *Exodus 18:20*), and means 'bird' in Hebrew. Zilli's small and delicate stature, her tiny brown eyes, and her diminutive features truly bore resemblance to a songbird. With a pleasant singing voice and a penchant for jest, Zilli was the most carefree and cheerful member of the young Jewish group. On June 6, 1935, Zilli Höchster married a Mr. Sieger of Mönchen-Gladbach, who lived at Blücherstrasse 18.

Zilli Höchster circa 1931

Manfred Richard Höchster

ON SEPTEMBER 2, 1922, A SON, Manfred Richard, was born to the then thirty-six and thirty-five-year-old Blanka and Kaufmann Höchster, who lived at Rockelsgasse 54. This couple struck one as being inordinately unsuited to train and guide a young child. However, Manfred's parents provided him with fine clothing and expensive toys in an effort to compensate for their parental unsuitability.

On November 10, 1936, approximately two months after the implementation of the Nuremberg Laws, the fourteen-year-old Manfred Richard Höchster left Lauterbach without his parents in order to join his sister, Zilli, in Mönchen-Gladbach. There he may have had the opportunity to attend a school already established for Jewish children or a school hastily created by larger Jewish communities as the need arose. By November, 1936, Jewish children in Lauterbach had been expelled from the *Realschule* (high school) and from the public school at the *Goldene Esel*.[7] The article of the Nuremberg Laws which forbade extramarital relations between Jews and citizens of "German blood" definitely hastened the departure of Kaufmann and Blanka Höchster on February 16, 1937. Lauterbach had a milieu where every-

Lauterbach high school class (probably Quarta) of 1924 with their classroom teacher, Mr. Benz. Seated in the front row second from the left is Irma Stein and third from the left is Zilli Höchster

one was well-apprised of his neighbor's circumstances and where forbearance—even without Nazi influence and laws—was hardly a widespread attribute.

As of 1940, Blanka and Kaufmann Höchster rest in a double grave in the Jewish cemetery in Mönchen-Gladbach.[9] Zilli and Manfred were able to escape to Colombia, where Zilli died in her thirties.

THE HITLER ERA AND THE HÖCHSTER FAMILY

THE ADVENT OF HITLER ON JANUARY 30, 1933, the creation of the first concentration camp in Dachau on March 23, 1933, the proclamation of the general boycott of all Jewish-owned businesses on April 1, 1933, and the burning of books authored by Jews and opponents of Nazism on May 10, 1933 went unheeded at the Kaufmann Höchster residence. In comparison, most of the other members of the Lauterbach Jewish congregation were significantly affected by these events. Kaufmann Höchster's gas pumping business was flourishing because it was the only one in that part of Lauterbach. As late as 1934 and 1935, the German Armed Forces obtained fuel for their vehicles from the gas pump owned by the Jew Höchster.[6] This circumstance, as well as Kaufmann's service in World War I, explain why the Höchsters felt no urgency about leaving Lauterbach and Germany. In fact, they berated other Jews for immigrating. I do not know if Kaufmann was eligible for the privileges of World War I soldiers who had been on the frontline or wounded in action. These entitlements lulled many German Jewish combat veterans of World War I into a mind-set of immunity from Nazi racist laws.

On September 15, 1935, the Nuremberg Laws were promulgated, which included the statement: "A citizen of the Reich is only that subject who is of German blood and who, through his conduct, shows that he is both desirous and fit to serve faithfully the German people and Reich." This law removed citizenship status for Jews. The second statute was the 'Law for the Protection of the German Blood and of the German Honor.' Among other things this law promulgated that marriages between Jews and citizens of German blood were forbidden; extramarital relations between

Jews and citizens of German blood were forbidden; and Jews could not employ in their households female citizens of German blood who were younger than forty-five. The first regulation of the Reich citizenship law, dated November 15, 1935, established the concept "non Aryan." From then on, Jews were barred from almost all positions and professions, and the letter "J" was printed on their identity cards

Nathen Höchster
(married Thea Schleicher)

MEYER HÖCHSTER'S SON by the Jewish housekeeper was Nathan Höchster, born on August 8, 1891. Named from the Hebrew word meaning 'he gave,' Nathan contributed a great deal indeed to his fellow men. Unlike the biblical Nathan who rebuked David about Bath-Sheba and the killing of Uriah, Nathan Höchster was not at all judgmental. As an outgoing and amiable person, Nathan appeared as if no adversity ever troubled him. He was a talented musician, a lyricist, and a competent choreographer; he was able to play any musical instrument, and if none could be found, he created cheerful tunes on a comb. Not only did he compose the prologue for the charity performance that took place in January 1926 at the Johannesberg Hall in the Bahnhofstrasse in Lauterbach, but he also arranged and rehearsed the dances for that production.

Nathan Höchster was one of four members of the Lauterbach First Aid Corps that volunteered as medical orderlies during World War I. The three other members of this corps were Friedrich Axthelm, Ernst Graulich, and Heinrich Weitzel.[11] An article in the *Lauterbacher Anzeiger* stated incorrectly that Nathan Höchster immigrated to the United States.

Nathan, the heart and soul of the Jewish non-married group of Lauterbach, courted, among many others, my father's sister, Frieda Wertheim, when she visited Lauterbach as a young woman during the years from 1918 to 1920. In 1921 or early 1922, Nathan married the attractive, cheerful Thea Schleicher, who was born on November 22, 1898, in Nonnenweiher in the Grand Duchy of Baden.

During their early years of marriage, Nathan and Thea lived on the ground floor of the splendidly-appointed patrician home of the three Diehm sisters at the Rimloser Strasse near the Catholic church. The Diehm residence was the epitome of sterling good taste: the entrance hall had a massive but well-proportioned staircase, handsome paneling, and an imposing light fixture. Bad times and galloping inflation obliged the elderly highborn Diehm sisters to rent out part of their ancestral home. As a child of seven or eight years of age, I frequently visited the Diehm residence, which was a block from my home. A cordial relationship and mutual respect prevailed between the Diehm sisters and this Höchster family.

THE CHILDREN OF NATHAN AND THEA HÖCHSTER

Rolf Martin Höchster

ROLF MARTIN, THE FIRST CHILD of Thea and Nathan Höchster, was born November 21, 1922 in Lauterbach. Thea and Nathan's twin children, Hans and Grete, were born on November 22, 1924, on their mother's twenty-sixth birthday. They were named after Hänsel and Gretel of *Grimm's Fairy Tales*, some of which were collected by Jacob and Wilhelm Grimm in the Lauterbach area. While the light-haired Rolf was a reserved youngster, his darker-haired brother and sister were definitely extroverted. However, Nathan's skills as a pleasant conversational-ist and a popular master of ceremonies did not earn too much hard currency for the family and it is not known how Nathan supported his wife and three children. Lack of means may have motivated Thea and Nathan to have their oldest son, Rolf, cared for by Nathan's half brother and his wife, the elderly Regine and Herz Höchster. Georg Vollmüller's mother, Katharina Vollmüller, worked for the Nathan Höchster family while Rolf and the twins were young children.[12]

On April 23, 1938, the sixteen-year-old Rolf Martin Höchster moved to Arndtstrasse 46 in Frankfurt am Main after the Jewish children had been expelled from the public school at the *Goldene Esel* and from the high school (*Realschule*) in Lauterbach. I do not know how Rolf's escape to Canada was accomplished. Rolf obtained a doctorate in biochemistry and later was in charge of a biochemical institute in Ottawa, Ontario. In 1971, Rolf died of a kidney ailment at the age of only forty-nine.

Beginning on April 23, 1938, Hans and Grete attended the Jewish school in Nauheim. Formerly a boarding school for convalescing Jewish children, the Nauheim school later enrolled Jewish youngsters from the Hesse area who had been forced to leave public municipal educational facilities. After 1935, the Nathan Höchster family was no longer permitted to live in the house of a non-Jew and was com-pelled to move into the home of Herz Höchster at Bahnhofstrasse 84. This law was proclaimed by the Nazis in order to facilitate attacks on Jews and also to clear the way for rounding up Jews for transport to extermination camps.

On December 21, 1938, the Nathan Höchster family departed hastily for Arndtstrasse 46 in Frankfurt am Main after the ill-treatment they endured at Bahnhofstrasse 84 at the hands of the Lauterbach SS during *Kristallnacht*. During this family's stay in Frankfurt, Thea accomplished the necessary studies for be-coming a registered nurse at the Jewish hospital at the Gagernstrasse. In the 1920s and early 1930s, among the Jewish women of Lauterbach there was only one other registered nurse, the oldest daughter of the late Herman Gottlieb from Grebenau and his wife, Jeanette, of Am Wörth 16. The female Jewish contemporaries of my mother and Thea Höchster, who were born around the turn of the twentieth cen-tury, were rarely prepared to enter a trade or profession. Young Jewish ladies of that era were taught at home, in a boarding school, or by an aunt in another town. In being prepared for managing a household, they learned how to cook, serve meals, and the art of needlework.

After *Kristallnacht*, the boarding school for Jewish children in Nauheim was dissolved and the students were sent home. Later, Grete and Hans reached Swit-zerland on a childrens' transport. By 1941, Thea and Nathan Höchster were shipped to Theresienstadt, where Nathan died on May 6, 1943, at the age of fifty-two of tuberculosis caused by hunger. After 1942, Theresienstadt received thousands of German deportees, who were Jews who had received decorations in World War I or who had some other privileged status. Theresienstadt was the concentration camp that was shown to the International Red Cross. Before scheduled inspections, thousands of camp inmates were shipped to annihilation camps in order for Theresienstadt to create a presentable impression.

Nathan Höchster was ordered several times to be shipped to Auschwitz, but his wife, Thea's, position as a nurse saved him from that horrible fate. Thea's nursing skills snatched her from the jaws of certain death as well because the Nazis needed nurses in order to preserve the necessary facade for the inspections of the International Red Cross. Dr. Naphtali (Herbert) Stern's grandmother, Hanna Steinhardter Oppenheimer, died in Theresienstadt in the arms of Thea Höchster.[13] After 1945, Thea reached Palestine to which Hans and Grete had effected their escape. The cheerful Grete lives with her husband and family in Herzelia, and Hans, too, made a successful life for himself and his family in Israel. Prior to her death at an advanced age, Thea related that Herz Höchster had denounced the spiritual leader, Max Stern, to the German Inland Revenue Office.[14]

In 1945, the attempts of Thea Höchster to locate Manfred Höchster in Colombia were unsuccessful and the investigations of Hans Keller from 1992 to 1994 found no trace of Manfred Höchster either.

THE SIMON
HÖCHSTER FAMILY

SIMON HÖCHSTER MOVED WITH HIS WIFE, Jeannette Reiss Höchster, and their family to Lauterbach in 1900. Until his death on January 31, 1927, the red-headed Simon (born in Storndorf in 1858) lived with his daughter, Hannchen Höchster Schiff (born in Storndorf on March 11, 1883), his son-in-law Bernhard Schiff (born in Karlsruhe January 18, 1879), his grandsons, Ludwig (born April 30, 1911 in Lauterbach), and Lothar Schiff (born June 18, 1915 in Lauterbach) at Obergasse 27 in Lauterbach. Hannchen Höchster Schiff possessed a no-nonsense air about her, had a shapely full-bosomed figure, a round face with very regular features, and red hair that lacked the intensity of her father's hair color.

Obituary of Simon Höchster in the *Lauterbacher Anzeiger*

In addition to their daughter, Hannchen, Jeanette and Simon Höchster had a son, Aron, who lived in Nuremberg with his family. Several times a year, and particularly on the Feast of Weeks (*Shavuot*) and the Feast of Booths, Aron visited his father. At these occasions, most members of the Lauterbach Jewish community called at the Schiff residence after religious services as a gesture of courtesy and respect to the family and their guest. My parents held Simon Höchster and his family in high regard and admired their unpretentious, reserved demeanor.

In the 1920s, Obergasse 27 also had a small grocery store, which Hannchen looked after and, like her father, she sold coffee and other grocery items from a

Gott dem Allmächtigen hat es gefallen, heute Nacht unsere
liebe Gattin, Mutter und Schwiegertochter

Jeanette Höchster

geb. Reiss

im Alter von 51 Jahren nach längerem, schweren Leiden in ein
besseres Jenseits abzurufen.

Im Namen der trauernden Hinterbliebenen

Simon Höchster.

Lauterbach, 4. September 1908   1746

Ihre Beerdigung findet Sonntag, nachmittags 3½, Uhr statt.
Für Kranz- und Blumenspenden wird bestens gedankt.

Obituary of Jeanette
Höchster in the
Lauterbacher Anzeiger

knapsack in Maar and other nearby villages. Simon Höchster was a polite, retiring gentleman whose interest centered totally on his family. Perhaps the premature demise of his wife, Jeanette Reiss Höchster, after much suffering in 1908 (at the age of only fifty-one) made him more withdrawn. Moreover, only one year later Simon's father, Löb Höchster (born in Storndorf in 1822), died after a long illness at the age of eighty-seven. Jeanette Reiss Höchster was related to Siegfried Reiss and his sister, Auguste Reiss Pfifferling (both of the Bahnhofstrasse in Lauterbach). This Reiss family hailed from Ulrichstein. I am not aware if, or how, these Reiss families were related to my maternal great-grandmother, Biena Reiss Strauss, whose birthplace was also Ulrichstein. Meyer Höchster probably was Simon's uncle. However, there appeared to be little friendship between Simon Höchster's family and the sons of Meyer Höchster.

Bernhard Schiff, the son-in-law of Simon Höchster and husband of Hannchen Höchster, was tall, slender, reserved and soft-spoken. An individual of few words, he earned a living as a traveling salesman. He concentrated on his family's welfare and particularly on his sons' education. Ludwig Schiff, like most boys of his age, was predisposed to mischief. He possessed an irrepressible sense of humor. On the other hand, Lothar Schiff, was a consistently earnest overachiever. Ludwig and Lothar did not mingle much with Jewish or other youths their age.

The idea that education was important was generally held by the Jews of Lauterbach and other rural Jews. For example, in the high school in Lauterbach that was founded in 1902 and among the thirty graduates in 1906, twelve were Jewish. Aron Höchster may well have been among these early graduates. The high value placed on education by Jews came from their cultural heritage as well as the experiences of their immediate past. Jews understood that while their non-Jewish neighbors might carry off their earthly holdings, nobody could rob them of schooling and knowledge.

In the 1920s and early 1930s, every Jewish parent in Lauterbach aspired to have his offspring attend the local high school. Jews residing in nearby towns with no high school sent their children to live away from home in order to receive a better education. Representative cases were Emil Frank from Ober-Seemen, who stayed with his sister, Ricka Frank Strauss of Gartenstrasse 13, and Ludwig Marx of Rachtig, County Bernkastel, who resided with his uncle, Max Stern, of Hinter der Burg 17. Due to a fall from a horse as a young child, Emil sustained a permanent injury which made him look like a humpback. His frail features and slender hands suggested a hypersensitive human being who, when he was away from his parents, seemed ill-equipped to manage his immediate environment at home and at school. Emil's deformity lessened his chances for immigration and he perished together with his parents, Simon and Rosa Frank, in Riga. Ludwig

276]

The Way It Was: The Jewish World of Rural Hesse

Marx immigrated in 1934 to Palestine, then went to the United States, but later settled permanently in Palestine.

One year after Simon's Höchster's death in 1927, the Hannchen and Bernhard Schiff family moved to Giessen where they envisioned better educational opportunities for their sons. In the late 1930s, Hannchen, Bernhard, and Ludwig Schiff immigrated to the United States. Lothar found refuge in England, where he studied dentistry.

Endnotes

1. Interview on April 17, 1988, in Forest Hills, New York, with Bertel Strauss Nathan, daughter of Markus Strauss.

2. Interview with Dr. Naphtali Stern in Atlanta on January 29, 1988.

3. Interview with Georg Vollmüller in Lauterbach on May 25, 1990.

4. Interview with Dr. Naphtali Stern in Atlanta on January 29, 1988.

5. Interview with Hans Keller in Lauterbach on May 25, 1990.

6. Interview with Georg Vollmüller in Lauterbach on May 25, 1990.

7. Interview with Dr. Naphtali Stern in Atlanta on January 15, 1988.

8. Interview with Hans Keller in Lauterbach on May 25, 1990.

9. Letter of September 11, 1992, from Denis Cummings, chairman of the Mönchen-Gladbach Jewish community, to the Jewish community of Fulda.

10. Ibid.

11. Karl Heinz Rühl, *Lauterbacher Anzeiger,* May 6, 1988, p. 16.

12. Interview with Georg Vollmüller in Lauterbach on May 25, 1990.

13. Interview with Dr. Naphtali Stern on January 30, 1988, in Atlanta, Georgia.

14. Ibid.

A Jewish cattle dealer

THE ABRAHAM
WEINBERG FAMILY

*A*s late as 1861, no Jew resided in Lauterbach.[1] However, the Lauterbach annals record that on June 30, 1875, the trader, Abraham Weinberg, born in Storndorf on June 19, 1844, and his wife Fanny, born on September 18, 1854, moved to Lauterbach. The first Hesse-Darmstadt Constitution of the autumn of 1820 and April, 1821 stipulated that Jewish householders of Hesse-Darmstadt be allowed to obtain citizenship for a fee. However, for most of the rural Jews in the Alsfeld-Storndorf area the fees for procuring citizenship were beyond their means.[2] In all likelihood, Abraham Weinberg attained citizenship in Storndorf, because neither the Riedesel (the local feudal lords of the Lauterbach area) nor the Lauterbach town fathers would have permitted Jews without citizenship to take up residence in their town.

Fanny and Abraham Weinberg had seven children: Josef, born March 4, 1876; Rudolf, born September 5, 1877; Berthold, birth date unknown; David, born August 6, 1886; the youngest son, Salli, born September 30, 1893; a daughter, Lina, born July 19, 1885; and daughter, Rosalie, birth date not known.

JOSEF WEINBERG
(married Berta
Bachenheimer Weinberg)

DURING MY CHILDHOOD IN LAUTERBACH, Josef Weinberg and his wife, Berta Bachenheimer Weinberg (born August 5, 1879, in Kirchhain, Hesse) lived at Steinweg ll in Lauterbach with their tall, blond, and very light-skinned daughter, Ruth, who was born August 28, 1905. Ruth mingled occasionally with her Jewish contemporaries, but generally remained distant and aloof from the Jewish societal mainstream. Ruth's mother, Berta, was a lady of manners and fine upbringing who was well liked by Jews and non-Jews alike.

Josef Weinberg and his brothers, Rudolf and David, were partners in a cattle dealing business and doubtless were initiated into this occupation by their father or another older relative, because this diverse business required extended periods of inculcation as well as incidental learning. Beginning with the turn-of-the-nineteenth century and ending with the Hitler era, Jewish cattle dealers in Hesse had to hold their own against a multitude of difficult circumstances. A cattle dealer in Upper Hesse, had to have sufficient capital, possess business astuteness and bookkeeping skills, the capacity to instantly assess by sight the correct weight of an animal, and above all, the ability to communicate with the peasants whose dialect varied from village to village.

Josef was manifestly the leader of the business partnership and the respected elder in his family. During the 1920s and probably until his death at age fifty-eight on September 9, 1934, Josef Weinberg held the elected position of *parnas* (head of the Jewish community) in Lauterbach. He was not considered one of the most learned Jews in Lauterbach or even one of the most observant Jews, but he valued his position as formal leader of the Jewish congregation exceedingly. Josef Weinberg's wife, Berta, died probably of cancer in a hospital in Frankfurt am Main on June 11, 1934, some two-and-a-half months before Josef's demise on September 24, 1934. At the time of his wife's funeral procession, Josef sat by the window of his home,

Chapter Seventeen

already shattered by a stroke, and asked whose funeral procession was passing. Josef and Berta Weinberg are buried in the Lauterbach Jewish cemetery.

Ruth Weinberg
(married Hugo
Schleicher)

ON OCTOBER 26, 1926, RUTH, the beautiful daughter of Josef and Berta Weinberg, married Hugo Schleicher, a tall, stately attorney from Nonnenweiher, Baden. The groom was the brother of Thea Schleicher Höchster, the wife of Nathan Höchster, of Lauterbach. Ruth and Hugo Schleicher's first child died at less than three years of age. During the Nazi era, this couple escaped with their second child, a daughter, to England, from whence they came to the United States. Here Hugo, unable to practice his profession as an attorney, earned a living by selling insurance to his refugee relatives and friends including my parents. He was probably seventy years of age at the time of his death.

Both my mother and Ruth Schleicher, before and after they were widowed, lived in Washington Heights in New York City, where in the 1930s and early 1940s many refugees from Hesse and other regions of Germany had settled. The two widows visited frequently with each other. At the time of my mother's death on September 5, 1966, Ruth affectionately reviewed their friendship and stated that no Jewish holiday ever passed without my generous mother sharing her home-baked cakes and other edibles. The Schleicher daughter, a practicing attorney, died of cancer in her mid-forties. As of 1989, Ruth Schleicher had reached the age of eighty-eight bereft of her husband, two children, and forcibly expatriated from her native country.

RUDOLF WEINBERG
(married Hilde Stiebel)

RUDOLF WEINBERG, BORN SEPTEMBER 25, 1877, was married on September 11, 1910, to Hilde Stiebel (born in Allendorf an der Lahn on April 4, 1889). To the best of my recollection, this family rented an apartment in the Blitzenröder Strasse in Lauterbach. Rudolf and his wife, Hilde, by the then existing standards, were rather tall, moderately attractive people, who seemed to lack friendliness, sociability, and congenial dispositions. Rudolf and Hilde Weinberg had one son, Alfred, born on February 18, 1912. Much like his parents, Alfred was not particularly outgoing or friendly: a feature probably compounded by his extremely frizzy hair and a somewhat protruding upper jaw, which among Max Stern's religious school students earned him the nickname 'Gorilla.' Alfred was a poor religious school student and he left Max Stern's classes as soon as he was legally permitted to do so. Alfred completed his compulsory eight-year formal education at the Lauterbach public school, in contrast to other Jewish contemporaries who at age ten or eleven entered the local high school.

After my parents' wedding and my father's arrival in Lauterbach, my father fell heir to the cattle business of my mother's uncle, Samuel Strauss (I), but he first had to establish himself in his own right. Prior to my father's arrival in Lauterbach, the Weinberg cattle dealing partnership exclusively dominated the area of Maar, Reuters, and others. The Weinberg partnership—and Rudolf Weinberg in particular—viewed the new competition with great dissatisfaction, and often conducted business to harm or shut out the newcomer. My father did not take kindly to these tactics and maintained a civil, but reserved, contact with Josef, Rudolf, and David Weinberg, while my mother continued a warmer relationship with these Weinberg families.

Shortly before Christmas 1937, Rudolf Weinberg's funeral procession along the Kalkofenweg to the Jewish cemetery was pelted with snow balls which Hilde Weinberg, already accustomed to much anguish and suffering, hardly noticed.[3] Hilde Weinberg, the last Jewish resident of Lauterbach, departed on July 26, 1940 for Frankfurt am Main, Sternstrasse 36. Hilde Weinberg perished in Riga. On July 14, 1938, Alfred Weinberg immigrated to the United States and in the 1980s he lived in Miami Beach, Florida.

[281

BERTHOLD
WEINBERG
(unmarried)

BERTHOLD WEINBERG, A TALL, KIND-LOOKING, friendly bachelor and successful businessman, lived in Frankfurt am Main. During the 1920s and early 1930s, he spent all Jewish holidays with his sister, Lina Jakob, his brother-in-law, Michel Jakob, and their two sons, Arthur and Siegfried Fritz, at Bahnhofstrasse 103 in Lauterbach. Custom among the Lauterbach Jews dictated that any visitor for a Sabbath or holidays be greeted at his host's home after the midday meal or subsequent to afternoon synagogue services. On such occasions, cookies or chocolate broken into small pieces from chocolate bars were offered. It was taken for granted that children up to the age of twelve accompanied their parents.

While girls silently had to endure arm pinching by elders, boys put up with their ears being pulled. Moreover, adults made little or no effort to converse with any child on his level. Luckily, most of the time these visits were of short duration. As the front door bell announced new visitors, seated guests cleared the room after a handshake and a curtsy by young girls. My parents were particularly fond of Lina and Michel Jakob, and before my mother's marriage the siblings, Lina and Berthold Weinberg, were part of the cohesive social circle of Jewish unmarrieds in Lauterbach. Berthold Weinberg immigrated to the United States before World War II, where he lived in Washington Heights in close proximity to his niece, Ruth Weinberg Schleicher. Berthold was at least seventy years of age at the time of his death.

DAVID WEINBERG
(married Gerda Stein)

IN 1921, AT AGE THIRTY-FIVE, DAVID WEINBERG, the youngest partner of the Weinberg cattle dealer partnership, married Gerda Stein (born on January 1, 1896 in Ruppertsburg), who was ten years younger than her husband. While living in Lauterbach, David Weinberg was a reserved individual and according to my father was overshadowed by his two older brothers and business partners, Josef and Rudolf, who habitually supervised him.

Gerda Stein Weinberg appeared to be the antithesis of her retiring husband; her friendly, outgoing manner was reflected in her wide, open face. David and Gerda's only child, Arnold, was born on November 12, 1922. The David Weinberg family lived at Langgasse 10, where their house also included facilities for feeding and sheltering cows and horses. Except for the Hess family of the Kanalstrasse and the family of Biena and Moses Jakob, most of Gerda and David Weinberg's neighbors were Lutherans. The

Chapter Seventeen

housing pattern of this Weinberg family was by and large the same as for most Jewish families in Lauterbach.

The greater number of Jewish households employed sleep-in girls from nearby villages to assist with the housework while other Jewish households only engaged day-help for cleaning, lighting and or stoking, cooking, and heating stoves as well as turning lights on and off on the Sabbath. Some Jewish families who could not afford either sleep-in help or help by the day, employed what was called a '*schabbas goy.*' Such a person generally resided close by the home of the Jewish family, and was happy to perform this task for a small amount of money and for a piece of *berches* (home-baked white Sabbath bread) and other tidbits from the Sabbath table. Among the working class as well as the middle class in Lauterbach, Jewish food preparation and quality was held in high esteem and much coveted. Moreover, during the 1920s and early 1930s widespread unemployment and poverty prevailed in Lauterbach and any extra food or additional income were highly valued.

Käthe Roth, an aunt of Elfriede Roth, (of) am See 2 in Lauterbach, assisted with cleaning in the homes of Josef, Rudolf, and Salli Weinberg. The Roth family also cleaned at the synagogue and, much the same as others in similar positions, remained loyal and steadfast friends of the Jewish families whom they knew well and worked for. For instance, Anna Bramm, who was employed in the home of Bertha Adler Flörsheim and Salli Flörsheim at Grünberger Strasse in Alsfeld, selflessly and at great peril to herself fixed up the graves of the Flörsheim family. These selfless deeds earned her the name '*Judensau*' ('Jew Pig') among her neighbors after the advent of Hitler on January 30, 1933.[4]

On April 21, 1936, at age fourteen, Arnold Weinberg moved to Mittelweg 16, in Frankfurt am Main. In May, 1939 (six months after *Kristallnacht)*, David and Gerda Weinberg and their son, Arnold, immigrated to Brooklyn, New York. David Weinberg died at age sixty-five while his wife, Gerda, maintained reasonably good health until her death at more than eighty-five years of age. In 1947, Arnold married Ruth Strauss (daughter of Ricka and Siegfried Strauss (II)) who, until the age of nine or ten years and before her immigration to the United States, lived with her parents in the Gartenstrasse in Lauterbach. Ruth Strauss' father, Siegfried Strauss, and my mother, Berta Lamm Wertheim, were first cousins: my mother's mother, Auguste Strauss Lamm, and Siegfried's father, Markus Strauss, were siblings from Storndorf. Arnold and Ruth Weinberg had two sons: Barry S. Weinberg born November 6, 1948, and David E. Weinberg, born April 22, 1952.

ROSALIE WEINBERG
(married, husband's name unknown)

SOME TIME AFTER 1920, ROSALIE WEINBERG moved away from Lauterbach to be married to a Jew in another town. On a photograph of the 'Students of the Sewing Needle Club of 1920,' Rosalie appears spirited and cheerfully wrapped in thought. Out of the twelve photographed members of the Club were six unmarried ladies of the Lauterbach Jewish congregation: Emma Baumann, Sophie Strauss, Minna Strauss, Recha Baumann, Selma Strauss, and Rosalie Weinberg. Among the six non-Jewish mem-

A sewing circle of twelve women (of which six were Jewish) in Lauterbach in 1920. The Jewish members are:
Front row:
Recha Baumann (center)
Selma Strauss (fourth from left)
Rosalie Weinberg (fifth from left)
Second row:
Emma Baumann (second from left)
Sophie Strauss (third from left)
Minna Strauss (fifth from left)

bers, the only one I can identify is Ida Holler, the daughter of Rektor Holler and Mrs. Otterbein Holler of a much-respected upper middle-class family in Lauterbach. Emma and Recha Baumann were sisters, Minna Strauss and Selma Strauss were sisters, and the sisters Emma and Recha Baumann were also cousins of Sophie Strauss. Apparently, there prevailed enough amiability and kind-heartedness in this group for the photograph to occur at all. I do not know whether Rosalie Weinberg survived the Holocaust.

LINA WEINBERG
(married Michel Jakob)

LINA WEINBERG, BORN JULY 10, 1885, married Michel Jakob, born October 10, 1882, in Grebenau, in Lauterbach on January 30, 1913. The name 'Jakob' in the Angenrod-Grebenau- Ulrichstein region relates to a few Sephardic families who arrived in the area as provisioners to the army during the Thirty Years War (1618-1648). These Sephardic families, as reward for their honest and loyal service, were permitted to settle in the Ulrichstein and Niedergemünden areas.[5] Prior to 1814, the Jews of Grebenau carried their dead for thirteen miles in order to bury them in the Angenrod Jewish cemetery.[6] Up to the time my father left Angenrod in 1913 and later, a strong bond endured between the Jews of Angenrod and the Jews of Grebenau.

Lina and Michel Jakob had two sons: Arthur (born June 27, 1914 in Grebenau) and Siegfried Fritz (born May 23, 1920 in Lauterbach). In Lauterbach, this family lived at Bahnhofstrasse 103, where they occupied one floor of a house that contained at least four separate apartments. Their dining room was furnished in dark wood in the Art Nouveau style, including a buffet with doors of leaded multi-colored glass. Like most middle-class Jews of Lauterbach, the dining room was the most important part in the house. It was the room in which guests were seated, but rarely invited to partake of food other than chocolate, cookies, hard candy, or water.

Lina was a competent housekeeper and hard-working helpmate of the always cheerful, good-natured Michel. During the late 1920s and until there was a ruling by the Nazis against living in the home of Jews in the 1930s, Emil Burkhardt, who became the owner of a respected automobile agency in Lauterbach, rented a room at the home of Lina and Michel Jakob. Emil credited his early success to Lina Jakob acting as his appointment secretary. Moreover, Emil stated that the Lauterbach Jewish cattle dealers, whom he taxied to outlying areas, were the principal reason for his early success.[7]

A warm friendship remained until death between the Michel Jakob family and my parents. Earlier, Lina Weinberg and my mother belonged to the same group of Jewish unmarrieds in Lauterbach. Michel and my father were both endowed with an irrepressible sense of humor and they arrived in Lauterbach at about the same time. Most likely, Michel Jakob and Vogel Wertheim (III) knew each other before their marriages to ladies from Lauterbach, where both were put to the test by the Weinberg brothers. Michel had to demonstrate that he was a worthy of being the husband of a Weinberg sister, and my father had to establish himself as a respectable competitor of the entrenched Weinberg cattle dealer partnership.

Michel Jakob and my father often undertook buying and selling cattle as partners. Also, not infrequently, my father obtained for a commission fee for cows he sold to Michel to be made into sausage meat by the Duchardt Sausage Company in the Bahnhofstrasse. Michel's mastery of bookkeeping was not of the highest grade. At times, entries in his book of memoranda progressed in the conventional method, but frequently Michel employed the same book of memoranda upside down, beginning with the back page, and he also commenced record keeping from the middle of the book. He was always at a loss in locating the desired entry, but somehow mastered the circumstance by frequently turning and reversing his book of memoranda as well as searching in the middle of the book, and eventually located the necessary information.

Due to poor economic conditions in Germany (and particularly in the Lauterbach region), and exacerbated by the harassment of Jews even before January 30, 1933, when Hitler officially took power, Michel, like many other cattle dealers in Hesse, fell on hard times. Repeatedly my father advanced money to Michel in return for promissory notes. Sometime after the advent of Hitler in 1933, the Michel Jakob family, while feeling particularly endangered by the local Nazis, took their valuables for temporary safekeeping to Dorothee Stausebach Tag, who resided in the Bahnhofstrasse near the home of the Michel Jakob family. A short time later, Dorothea Tag returned their valuables intact.[8]

Arthur Jakob, the eldest son of Lina and Michel Jakob, entered public school in Lauterbach with my sister into Mr. Dörr's class. One of Mr. Dörr's daughters attended the same class, and frequently called for my sister to walk with her down the Cent to school at the *Goldene Esel*. I never heard my sister complain about her teacher singling out Jewish children for ill treatment between 1920 and 1923. Arthur went to Max Stern's religious classes, where Max Stern did not display exceptional patience with respect to Arthur's limited predilection for the Hebrew language and with other minor failings of a child Arthur's age. After completing his schooling in Lauterbach, Arthur entered a commercial apprenticeship in Hersfeld. Few cattle dealer families wished their sons to enter their own arduous way of earning a living, and deemed another commercial field one step up on the ladder of social mobility.

Arthur Jakob immigrated to the United States prior to the arrival of his parents, Lina and Michel Jacob, and his brother, Siegfried Fritz Jakob, during November 1937 and lived at 1326 Halsey Street in Brooklyn. Michel's step-sister from Grebenau, who immigrated many years earlier to the United States and whose husband, Mr. Bachrach, was a cigar-maker, vouched through affidavits that the Michel Jakob family would not become public charges. During the later part of June 1934, and shortly after my arrival in the United States, I visited the sister and brother-in-law of Michel Jakob in Brooklyn, and found them both to be warm, kind, and intelligent individuals.

For some time after their arrival in the United States Michel, Arthur's mother, Lina Jakob, and his brother, Siegfried Fritz Jakob, continued to reside in the New York City area. The seventeen- or eighteen-year-old Siegfried Fritz managed to find employment, even though it was difficult to obtain for anyone during the depression of the 1930s and all the more so for new arrivals, who were uninitiated in the ways of the country and unpracticed in the English language. In small amounts each week, Fritz gradually paid off to my parents the promissory note his father had incurred some years earlier in Lauterbach before the family's immigration.

At the outbreak of World War II, Siegfried Fritz was drafted or volunteered for the United States Army. He made the ultimate sacrifice for the country which opened its door to his family, albeit grudgingly. After Siegfried Fritz' death, Lina and Michel Jakob moved to Cleveland, Ohio to be near their son, Arthur. Lina's and Michel's note of sympathy at the time of my father's death in August 1953, conveyed the mutual respect, great affection, and friendship of these two families. During a telephone conversation in October 1985, Arthur was unable to recognize me, and had died by 1989.

SALLI WEINBERG
(married Rosa Lamm)

SALLI WEINBERG, THE YOUNGEST SON of Abraham and Fanny Weinberg, was born September 30, 1893. On November 20, 1927, he married Rosa Lamm (born July 3, 1897 inOber-Gleen). Rosa's father, Hirsch Lamm, was a distant cousin of my maternal grandfather, Jakob Lamm of Kirtorf, which is two miles from Ober-Gleen. Hirsch Lamm was married to Gutta Levi from Gensungen. I can vividly recall the attractive, well-spoken, and much-respected Gutta, who presided over a well-arranged household. This Lamm Family had an older daughter, Johanna, who was married to Louis Stern in Diez on the River Lahn. Although Johanna Lamm was my mother's junior by four years, these girls must have attended the same religious school instruction, and they loyally visited with each other whenever Johanna was in Lauterbach.

Arthur, the only child of Rosa and Salli Weinberg, was born on October 26, 1929. He was regarded to be of delicate health because shortly after birth he underwent what was then considered extremely precarious surgery for bowel relocation. When I left Lauterbach on June 6, 1934, the Salli Weinberg family lived in their own house in the Bahnhofstrasse one or two houses distant from the Knoll butcher shop. Salli Weinberg, a tall, and a somewhat withdrawn individual, peddled sundry merchandise such as bedding and towels in nearby villages and also dealt in goat and other hides. Rosa's dowry, her thrifty, competent household management, and Salli's per-

Arthur Weinberg

Rosa Lamm Weinberg

severing diligence practiced by most all of the Lauterbach Jews enabled this family to own their own home within a comparatively short period despite the economic malaise of those years.

While on a visit in Lauterbach in 1985, the granddaughter of the cooper, Grau, at the Lauterbach Beer Brewery on the Cent stopped me across from the house of the Salli Weinberg family in the Bahnhofstrasse and expressed her disapproval with regard to the treatment of this family during *Kristallnacht*. She stated that "the Nazis pulled Rosa by her curly hair down the steps and the perpetrators of this will have to suffer for it." The Jew hater, Mr. Rockel, beat up Rosa Weinberg. That same night Salli Weinberg was beaten, the windows of his house were smashed, and the home furnishings were ruined.[9]

Käthe Roth, Elfriede Roth's aunt and an individual whom Captain Nickelsberg, an officer of the American occupation forces in spring of 1945, alluded to as the most worthwhile individual he had ever met, nightly brought soft cheese to this family when (after the summer of 1935) Jews were no longer permitted to set foot in stores or restaurants. As Käthe neared the Salli Weinberg residence on November 10, 1938, a multitude of bystanders had assembled in front of the Weinberg house, staring at the damage. Käthe tossed the package of soft cheese through the broken windows, to indicate to this family that at least this meager supply of food would remain constant. Elfriede, Käthe Roth's niece, stated on July 29, 1988, that the mutual devotion of Jewish family members touched her deeply, particularly that of the Salli Weinberg family. Elfriede empathized specifically with the eight- or nine-year-old Arthur, who could not play outdoors.[10]

On November 20, 1940, more than two years after the *Kristallnacht*, Salli Weinberg, his wife, Rosa, and his son, Arthur, moved to Röderbergweg 38 II in Frankfurt am Main, where so many Jews from villages and small towns of Upper Hesse sought refuge from the cruelties of the local SA and SS, who were so well informed of the personal circumstances of the Jews in towns such as Lauterbach.

In the late 1930s, Hirsch and Gutta Lamm moved from Ober-Gleen to a Jewish nursing home in Bad Nauheim. During the early 1940s, Hirsch died of pneumonia in a Jewish hospital in Frankfurt am Main, and his wife, Gutta, was brought to the same hospital with a broken hip. Her daughter, Rosa Weinberg, observed the mourning period for her father at her mother's bedside. Gutta died one week after her husband's demise: she never knew that Hirsch had preceded her in death.

Unfortunately, the plans of the Salli Weinberg family to flee to Chile never materialized. Salli and Rosa Weinberg and the then about eleven- or twelve-year-old Arthur was annihilated in Minsk. Their packed household goods remained in Holland at the end of World War II. Rosa's sister, Johanna Lamm Stern, grieved for her sister, brother-in-law, and nephew till her own death at age ninety on October 9, 1985, in the Bronx, New York.[11]

THE MARKUS AND ANNA WEINBERG FAMILY occupied one half of a two-story double house covered with bluish-gray painted scalloped shingles. The home also had a small vegetable garden where Anna grew parsley, leek, chives, and lettuce. The red-headed Anna Adler Weinberg, of am Wörth 14 in Lauterbach , was born in Storndorf on April 5, 1869. During those years, red hair was considered a detrimental characteristic for a woman in finding a husband. Anna, like many Jews of Upper Hesse villages, changed her name from 'Ester' meaning 'star' in Persian to 'Anna,' a Hellinized form of 'Hannah,' which appears in the New Testament. At that, time Anna was a name more favored by local non-Jews.

Anna's husband, Markus, died in 1912, and left her a childless widow at age forty-three. At about age nineteen, my mother, who arrived to collect the monthly interest on the mortgage held by my Great-Uncle Samuel Strauss (I) on the Weinberg residence (on) am Wörth 14, entered the Weinberg residence while Markus Weinberg was yelling and screaming at his wife, Anna. My mother admonished Markus Weinberg for speaking harshly to his wife, whereupon Anna reprimanded my mother for not minding her own business.

Anna proclaimed time and again how much she missed her husband after his death; she routinely bemoaned her state of widowhood, because she thought such conduct was expected of her. Anna knew that finding another husband was an unrealistic expectation, but at the same time, she was fully aware of the benefits widowhood granted her by the Jewish community elders and others who faithfully observed the biblical injunction of responsibility toward widows.

Almost exclusively, Anna Weinberg dominated the market for kosher for Passover foods. In addition, she obtained a fee from the Jewish congregation for preparing the *mikveh* for immersion for post-menstruant women of the congregation, as well as earned money by selling coffee in nearby villages to farmers who, during the harvest time, could not go to town. Whenever serious illness or death afflicted members of the Jewish congregation, Anna at once appeared at the scene, as if she were intent on being a spectator of sad episodes. She considered herself a specialist on death, dying, and *post mortem* procedures. In our family we called Anna behind her back '*Todesvogel*' ('bird of death'), as if she were hopping from one site of sadness to another.

After the death of my Great-Uncle Samuel Strauss (I) in 1924, and following the stabilization of the galloping inflation in Germany, my mother regularly had me collect payments on the mortgage of Anna's house, which had been willed to my parents. Anna Weinberg's brother, Löb Adler from Storndorf, was a *shohet* (he had passed the required examination for ritually killing permitted animals), who secretly and at great personal risk performed this chore in Lauterbach after the Nazis forbade the practice of *shehita* (the method of slaughtering for animals or birds for food). Anna Adler Weinberg moved to Frankfurt am Main on March 28, 1938. She did not survive the Holocaust.

In Lauterbach, on Hinter dem Spittel 12, situated near a little brook, lived the family of Markus Weinberg's step-brother, Nathan, and his family, which consisted of Nathan's second wife, Regina Katz Weinberg, who was born in Storndorf; their son, Moritz, who

288]

Lauterbach public school
class, 1935.
Among those pictured
are five Jewish students:
First row, first on left:
Rita Jakob
**Third row, third on
left:** Norbert Weinberg
**Third row, fourth from
the right:** Julius
Baumann
**Third row, third from
the right:** Herbert Stern
**Back row, sixth from
the left:** Paul Westerfeld

was born in Maar on October 6, 1894; Moritz' wife, Meta (née Marx), born in Mittelsinn on June 6, 1897, and married to Moritz in Fulda on May 13, 1925. This couple's son and only child, Norbert, was born on March 2, 1926 in Lauterbach. Between 1920 and 1922, this Weinberg family had acquired their residence consisting of one part of a double house from the Moritz Katz family (the parents of Moritz Katz were Hannchen Sonneborn Katz and Joel Katz). Nathan Weinberg died on October 17, 1907, and is buried in the Jewish cemetery in Lauterbach.

In 1934, the public school class at the *Goldene Esel* numbered forty-seven children, of which Julius Baumann, Rita Jakob, Herbert Stern, Paul Westerfeld, and Norbert Weinberg comprised the Jewish members of Frau Schad's class. As the Nazi laws against Jewish children attending public school intensified, this group of children was accordingly degraded and humiliated by classroom teachers.[12] On January 13, 1939, Norbert moved to Bad Nauheim, where the still remaining Jewish children of Upper Hesse attended a Jewish boarding school. On November 15, 1938, Jewish children were expelled from German schools.

On July 18, 1939, Regina Weinberg, her son, Moritz, and his wife and son, immigrated to New York. In 1948, Regina died in New York at age eighty-six; Meta Weinberg died after suffering a stroke in 1955. Moritz married again and (like his mother) died in 1980 in New York at eighty-six years of age.

Regina and Nathan Weinberg also had a daughter, Rosa, born during the 1890s, who was a contemporary of my mother in Lauterbach. Rosa Weinberg disavowed the biblical dictum: "You shall not intermarry with them: do not give your daughter to their sons or take their daughters for your sons. For they will turn your children away from Me to worship other gods." (*Deuteronomy 7:3-4*). In the milieu of Lauterbach, Rosa threw her lot in with a Lutheran. Rosa married the tailor Glitsch, who hailed from Landenhausen (a village three miles from Lauterbach) and they lived with their son, Kurt, on Hinter dem Spittel in Lauterbach only a few houses away from the residence of Rosa's mother.

Uncharacteristic of how relatives usually reacted to such an alliance, Regina Weinberg remained friendly with her daughter and her Lutheran son-in-law. On the Sabbath, generally at the time the Jewish families dressed in Sabbath clothing and went for their afternoon walk to the *Eichküppel,* they came upon Rosa Glitsch in work-a-day garb carrying a hoe or spade to tend her vegetable garden. Many Jews of Lauterbach despised Rosa Glitsch. They pretended not to see her and interpreted her carrying garden tools on the Sabbath as a premeditated personal insult.

Rosa appeared to be happy with her husband and her son and integrated well into her husband's family, while still managing to maintain the loyalty of her own mother against great odds. This bliss came to an abrupt end with the advent of Hitler. Her son, Kurt, was called to serve in the *Reichsarbeiterdienst* (RAD). In 1935, the Nüremberg Laws were promulgated, which deprived the German Jews of civic rights, forbade intermarriage between Jews and non-Jews, and deprived persons of partly Jewish descent of certain rights. As a consequence of the Nüremberg Laws, Kurt was dismissed from RAD.

According to Lauterbach town talk at the beginning of World War II, during an air raid precaution exercise at the lower Ritsch (a street in Lauterbach), this exercise was preceded by a vigorous address of the Nazi precinct leader, Alfred Zürtz, who suddenly, after being aware of Rosa's presence, interrupted his speech and exclaimed, "Jew, or Jewess, disappear!" Rosa rushed home crying.

Rosa was able to stay with her husband in Lauterbach until 1942 or 1943 when she was shipped to Theresienstadt, where her occupation as a seamstress helped her survive. After the end of World War II, she was returned by truck from Theresienstadt. When she arrived within view of the town of Lauterbach, she alighted from the vehicle and uttered a prayer of thanks. Shortly after World War II, Rosa's husband died of a blood clot in the brain. Kurt Glitsch lived in Karlsruhe, where his mother joined him after her husband's death. Rosa died, probably of cancer, about 1955. She was fond of reading the diaries of Jochen Klepper which, at that time, were popular with Protestant women.[13]

Endnotes

1. Dr. Karl Siegmar Baron von Galera, *Lauterbach in Hessen III, Neustadt an der Aisch 1965,* (Verlag Degener and Company), p. 21.
2. Letter of Helmut Riffer of Alsfeld of September 24, 1989.
3. *Lauterbacher Anzeiger,* September 7, 1984.
4. Interview with Kate Flörsheim in Atlanta, Georgia, on November 27, 1989.
5. Dr. Ursula Miriam Wippich, *Memorbuch 1981/82,* p. 54.
6. Interview with Helmut Riffer, Alsfeld archivist, on July 24, 1988, in Alsfeld.
7. Interview with Emil Burkhardt in Lauterbach on August 5, 1985.
8. Interview with Mrs. Tag in Lauterbach on July 28, 1988.
9. Interview with Georg Vollmüller in Lauterbach on May 25, 1990.
10. Interview on July 29, 1988, in Lauterbach with Elfriede Roth of Am See 2.
11. Letter of May 5, 1989, from Ruth S. Earnest of the Bronx, New York, Rosa Lamm Weinberg's niece.
12. Interview with Dr. Naphtali Stern in Atlanta, February 15, 1989.
13. Letter of November 25, 1985, from Dr. Karl August Helfenbein, Town Historian of Lauterbach.

Chapter Eighteen
The Seligmann Jakob and Moses Jakob Families

House of Seligmann, Emma and Max Jakob (Alter Steinweg 7) in Lauterbach

*I*n the Storndorf vicinity, Jakob was an old family name derived from several Sephardic families that moved with the army during the Thirty Years War (1618-1648). They took care of the food supply and clothing for the military. As recompense for honest and loyal service, the Jakob families were permitted to settle in Ulrichstein and Niedergemünden.[1]

THE SELIGMANN JAKOB FAMILY

SELIGMANN JAKOB WAS BORN IN STORNDORF on January 25, 1866, and his wife, Emma Baumann Jakob, was born in Storndorf on April 4, 1868. After their marriage in Lauterbach on December 6, 1893, they lived at Alter Steinweg 7. Seligmann's mother, Rebekah Jakob, was born on January 29, 1846; she died in Lauterbach at the home of her son on May 24, 1919. Seligmann's father, Josef Jakob, was born on February 20, 1840, and died on July 20, 1910. Jakob Seligmann's parents were buried in the Jewish cemetery in Lauterbach.

Feibel[a] Baumann of Storndorf was the father of Emma Baumann Jakob. According to official village documents of Storndorf, the merchant, Feibel Baumann, obtained citizenship on June 18, 1850, and some time later moved to Lauterbach. A Feibel Baumann who died on May 25, 1902, at the age of eighty-five was buried in the Lauterbach Jewish cemetery. A Löb Baumann was the first Jew who served in the Storndorf municipal council, notwithstanding the fact that in 1838 the village of Storndorf instituted legal proceedings against its Jews.[2] Löb Baumann and Associates were journalized in a financial record of the Storndorf Jewish congregation for the years 1842, 1843, and 1844, in connection with leased chairs that were projected to yield an income of twenty-two *Gulden* and twenty *Kreuzer* for the Storndorf Jewish community.

Josef Jakob

Rebeka Katz Jacob

When I knew him, Seligmann Jakob was a quiet individual in his late fifties. He eked out a meager living and conveyed a resignation to life's vicissitudes. Although Seligmann and Emma Jakob lived in outward cordiality in their modest home, it seemed as if they were not completely compatible. Their son, Louis, was born on October 13, 1893, two months prior to their wedding. Because Judaism bans sexual relations outside wedlock, Emma still seemed to be doing repeated penance for this transgression even many years later. Although my mother wanted to keep such background information from her daughters, I somehow came by this account. Emma and Seligmann Jakob had two more sons: Julius, born on January 27, 1896, and Max, born on September 28, 1900.

Emma Jakob was ardent and prayerful, trying to obey strictly each ordinance of Jewish law. While a youngster, I considered her a lay expert on moralist Jewish literature because she was able to quote verses applicable to life's perplexities. Emma washed her hands compulsively; she touched doorknobs only with her elbows for

---

[a] 'Feibel' is the western Yiddish form of 'Phoebus,' which is an epithet of Apollo, the sun god.

Chapter Eighteen

Seligmann and Julius Jakob

fear that using her hands might render her food unkosher. Apparently lacking confidence in her own work, she frequently asked my mother to tend to important cooking and baking in the Jakob household. Emma was afraid that if she canned food by herself the contents would spoil. The tasteful preparation of meals was especially important to Emma when her brother and his family, who had emigrated to the United States around the end of the nineteenth century, visited Lauterbach in the 1920s.

Her brother's sojourn in Lauterbach was a meaningful event in Emma's life. Not unlike many members of the Lauterbach Jewish congregation and other townspeople, Emma thought highly of the United States. In particular, she postulated from afar that the American system was conducive to bringing out the best in a community. In the minds of most, the disadvantages of going to the United States were the immense distance from Lauterbach and the fact that "water has no beams," a mind-set conditioned by people living in a country's interior region. Nevertheless, Emma Jakob's heartening utterances strengthened my desire to go to the United States.

After wearing her burial shrouds during the High Holidays in autumn, Emma laundered them in the spring. This routine was followed by other observant Jews in Lauterbach, since spring is a season better suited for drying garments outdoors. Every time that Mrs. Oppenheimer, a pious and observing Jewess from Hanau who was the mother of Rosa Stern (the teacher's wife), visited during the Passover season, Emma prevailed upon the visitor to put her shrouds to rights. During the High Holidays, Emma remained standing for the duration of the services and throughout the fast on *Yom Kippur*. She did not talk with fellow worshippers during services.

Emma Baumann Jakob

On November 9, 1938, during the 'Night of Broken Glass' in Germany and Austria, three SS men entered the home of the seventy-year-old Emma Jakob. Stricken by panic, Emma was forced to pack linens into a wash basket that was carried away and her flatware was stolen. Among the SS men of Lauterbach who were aggressively stealing Jewish property, destroying Jewish possessions, beating up Jews, and taking Jewish males to concentration camps were Bulle, Gittard, Rockel, Mehring, the brothers Böcher, and the brothers Kaiser.[3]

The Lauterbach SS robbers demanded the surrender of objects from this Jakob family, but they could not comply because Seligmann and Emma lived in very modest circumstances and did not possess valuable furnishings. During the 'Night of the Broken Glass,' either Julius or Max was taken to a concentration camp and was retained there for approximately one year.[4] Emma's faith in the decency of her non-Jewish neighbors was shattered simultaneously with the broken glass of *Kristallnacht*. What blows could be inflicted upon her by strangers if her own neighbors were so cruel? How could her agonizing fastidiousness about her burial shrouds and her devotion to Judaism have any redeeming function? Both Emma and Seligmann Jakob were victims of the 'Final Solution' of the Nazis: Seligmann died in Theresienstadt on January 22, 1943, and Emma perished in the East far from Lauterbach and Storndorf.

Louis Jacob (married Flora Stein)

LOUIS JAKOB, THE OLDEST SON of the Seligmann Jakob family, was a talkative individual who was disposed to quickly judge others. On August 21, 1924, he wedded Flora Stein, who was born in Storndorf on May 20, 1899. They lived in Lauterbach with their daughters, Rita (born on October 9, 1925), and Edith (born on October 29, 1929), on Hainigstrasse 25 in rented quarters in a multi-family home. Outward impressions indicated that Louis earned a modest living as a cattle dealer and that he resented people who were better off than he. But, rather than directing his energy into self-improvement, Louis seemed to make himself feel better by castigating others. His domineering demeanor was expressed even toward his parents.

After the summer of 1935, '*Juden Verboten*' ('Jews Forbidden') signs increased in number outside towns, villages, restaurants, and stores. After September 15, 1935, the Nuremberg Laws were implemented, which forbade Jewish children to attend public school. For these reasons, on November 29, 1937, Louis Jakob immigrated with his wife and daughters to New York. Prior to immigration, Rita Jakob attended the grade school in Bad Nauheim that was then sponsored by Jewish organizations. In New York, Louis Jakob provided modestly for his family but he did not become involved in bringing his

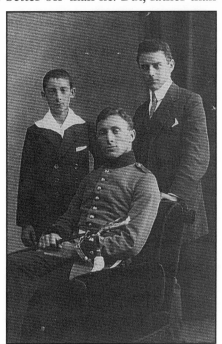

Standing left to right:
Max Jakob, Julius Jakob
Seated: Louis Jakob

parents to the United States. Although his cousin, Felix Levi, provided the necessary affidavit for guaranteeing to the United States government that the new arrivals would not become public charges, this undertaking lacked the active cooperation of Louis, the son, and therefore failed.[5]

Louis Jakob spent the last few years of his life with his wife, Flora, in a nursing home in upstate New York. He died at age ninety, and Flora passed away on October 18, 1987, at the age of eighty-eight. As of 1990, Rita Jakob Kahn resides in Teaneck, New Jersey, and her sister, Edith Jakob Heilbrunn, lives in New York.

Julius Jakob (unmarried)

JULIUS JAKOB WAS THE SECOND SON of Seligmann and Emma Jakob. During the late 1920s and until the advent of Hitler in 1933, Julius was a successful merchant in Regensburg and was highly respected by members of the Lauterbach Jewish community. In contrast to his talkative brother Louis, Julius was soft-spoken and calm. In World War I, he served as a front-line soldier for Germany. On a photograph of soldiers in uniform, Julius was pictured together with my father's older brother, Carl Wertheim. As of 1934, at the age of thirty-eight, Julius was a bachelor. He fell victim to the Nazi murderers in Piaski, Poland.

Max Jakob
(unmarried)

MAX JAKOB WAS THE YOUNGEST SON of the Seligmann Jakob family. He was an attractive man with a light-olive complexion and dark wavy hair. He commuted to Fulda, where he held a mid-level white-collar position. In 1931, Max favored the Second Spanish Republic, which was dominated by middle-class liberals and moderate socialists. An ardent soccer fan, he was a member of the executive committee of the *Lauterbach Association for Physical Exercise* in the 1920s. Max was romantically involved with Paula Kleeberg, who was the oldest daughter of Toni and Salli Kleeberg, a prosperous Jewish merchant family of Lauterbach. In a draining trench near our house on Cent 17, love letters were found that had been exchanged between Paula and Max affirming their everlasting love. The Kleeberg family did not approve of this courtship and sent Paula away. They successfully persuaded her to marry the wealthy merchant, Kugelmann of Witzenhausen, who was her senior by many years. On March 11, 1935, Max Jakob moved to Regensburg, where his brother Julius lived. Both Paula Kleeberg Kugelmann and Max Jakob were exterminated during the Holocaust: Paula was lost in Stutthof and Max perished in the East.

THE MOSES JAKOB
FAMILY

SELIGMANN JAKOB'S YOUNGER BROTHER, MOSES, was born in Storndorf on July 3, 1868. In Freienol on August 19, 1903, Moses married Biena Jakob (née Jakob), who was born in Öventrop on June 25, 1880. Moses and Biena Jakob had four sons: Ludwig, born July 4, 1904; Max, born August 29, 1905; Julius, born July 8, 1907; and Berthold (Benno), born July 7, 1909. Moses was an intelligent individual with a keen sense of humor who, at best, eked out a frugal living. This family lived in a modest home at Langgasse 19. Somehow, Moses always looked as if he were dislocated in Lauterbach, where his wit counted for little and where his sense of humor was hardly appreciated. In comparison with other Lauterbach Jews, he did not conform to the standard pattern of a successful trader or a businessman.

By age fifty, Moses walked in a stooped position, as if the responsibility of providing for so many mouths was wearing him away. Following a domestic squabble, Biena vexed Moses by remaining wordless and Moses was unsuccessful in coaxing his wife to converse. In a final effort to elicit the return of Biena's speech, Moses rummaged through every bureau drawer upstairs. Biena's tongue returned promptly with the words, "What are you looking for?" Moses quietly responded, "I am hunting for your voice." On September 18, 1926, at fifty-eight years of age, Moses Jakob died suddenly and was buried in the Lauterbach Jewish cemetery. At the time of their father's death, Ludwig was twenty-two, Max twenty-one, Julius nineteen, and Benno seventeen years of age.

Biena was a well-spoken and commonsensical individual who, after her husband's death, kept her family together and supported herself. Even during Moses' lifetime, Biena had been very involved in assisting her husband in his business and bolstering the family finances. One way she helped was to push a wheelbarrow with feed uphill and down. After Moses' death, Biena earned income by renting the cow shed attached to her house to the Weinberg cattle dealing partnership. In addition, upstairs in her house there was a facility for smoking liver sausages, beef sausages, and cured breasts of beef. During the winter months, some of the Lauterbach Jewish cattle dealers provided a less expensive meat supply for their families by taking charge of slaughtering instead of buying from butchers and availed themselves of the meat-smoking apparatus in Biena Jakob's house. In consideration for this service, Biena was presented with sausage and perhaps some smoked breast of beef. To assist the Jakob household, my mother arranged for Biena to receive a liberal supply of seasonal fruits and vegetables from the Wertheim gardens.

On October 19, 1927, Max, the second son of Biena and Moses Jakob, immigrated to the United States, where he wedded a non-Jewish woman. I do not know how Biena and her sons Ludwig, Julius, and Benno endured the *Kristallnacht*, which took place on November 9 and 10, 1938, in Lauterbach. On March 17, 1940, Biena Jakob moved to Goethepark 24, II in Berlin Charlottenburg, where she joined her oldest son, Ludwig, a commercial representative who had gone to live in Berlin on December 12, 1938, approximately one month after *Kristallnacht*.

Biena Jakob and her eldest son, Ludwig, effected their escape from Berlin to Switzerland by carrying falsified papers and traveling in separate compartments on the train. Biena and Ludwig's arrival in New York by way of Berlin and Switzerland was no small accomplishment at that time. Biena worked at nursing the elderly and died in a nursing home at an advanced age. Ludwig married Margaret Fuchs. He died at age seventy-eight in June 1982 in New York. His brother, Julius, a heavy-set individual who had worked for some time as a cattle dealer in Lauterbach, fled to Palestine on October 23, 1939. The youngest son of the family, Berthold (Benno), also escaped to Palestine.

Endnotes

1. Dr. Ursula Wippich, *Memorbuch, 1981/1982*, p. 54.
2. Alfred Deggau, Storndorf, February 1956, *Herausgegeben vom Geschichts-und Altertumsverein der Stadt Alsfeld*, p. 80.
3. Interview with Georg Vollmüller in Lauterbach on May 25, 1990.
4. Dr. Karl Siegmar Baron von Galera, *Lauterbach, in Hessen, Neustadt an der Aisch, 1965*, (Verlag Degener and Company, Volume III): p. 395.
5. Interview on September 18, 1987, in Atlanta with Rosi Levi Hess, Emma Jakob's niece.

Chapter Nineteen
Political and Social Conditions in Lauterbach During World War I

Vogel (Frederick) Wertheim (III) (seated first on the right) during World War I, 1914-1915,
14th Squad, Friedberg, Germany

*E*rna, the older daughter of Berta and Vogel Wertheim (III), was born at Cent 17 on January 8, 1914. According to custom, she should have been named after her paternal great-grandmother, Sara Tannenbaum, born in 1821 in Eiterfeld

However, my parents knew that in Upper Hesse the Old Testament name 'Sara' would certainly invite mockery of their daughter by her schoolmates. Lest their child become an object of ridicule, they gave her the Anglo-Saxon name 'Erna' (meaning 'retiring,' 'shy,' or 'peaceful') and designated the name 'Sara' for use in synagogue and ritual functions. During my time in Lauterbach (1915 to 1934), I remember that people with names such as Sara and Moses were addressed and spoken of with revulsion, which doubtless was inculcated by Christian parents, ministers, priests, and schoolteachers—people who were supposedly in charge of enlightenment and learning. None of our Lutheran or Catholic schoolmates possessed an Old Testament first name. One of the pleasant surprises in the United States was that not only that there was no disdain with regard to Old Testament names, but Americans proudly gave these names to their children.

Erna Wertheim, circa 1916-17

Jewish public school teachers could have done much to mitigate this attitude. However, there were no Jewish teachers in either public school or high school in Upper Hesse. Although young Jewish men attended Jewish teacher-training institutes that enabled them to pass the necessary examination for teaching in public schools, they were forced to find employment in Jewish community schools. Nevertheless, the Lauterbach public school journal of October 1914 indicated that Max Stern, a graduate from a teacher's institute, taught public school class VIa of the Lauterbach public school from 1914 to 1916, when there was a critical teacher shortage during World War I. This Jewish teacher's professional services were good enough when he served without compensation.

In Lauterbach, in accordance with the practice of the day, my parents kept their baby daughter, Erna, in swaddling bands for several weeks and laid her in a wicker basket placed on two chairs. It was customary to tightly wrap infants for the first six to eight months of their lives. After two months, their arms were no longer encased. From the wicker basket, Erna graduated to an iron mesh crib that later on became my Land of Nod.

Erna was nursed for about one year. She was four months old when my mother took her to Kirtorf where she was admired by her maternal grandparents, family, and friends and was photographed by the local photographer, I. G. Wig. Fauldrath. The serenity of the happy young Wertheim family was cut short on June 28, 1914, when the assassination of Archduke Francis Ferdinand at Sarajevo set in motion the diplomatic maneuvers that culminated in World War I. My mother's explanation for the cause of this war was that Emperor William II of Germany desired a separate empire for each one of his sons.

By the end of 1914, four hundred forty men in Lauterbach had been called up for military service. On August 22, 1914, the first four soldiers from Lauterbach died in Belgium. In the autumn of 1914, black marketers had already driven up the price of grain—in some cases fifty percent above the price before the war. The population was summoned to surrender gold. As a child I played with iron medals inscribed with "*Gold gab ich, Eisen nahm ich*" ('I gave gold and received iron') that dated from this period. Members of the *Jungdeutschland* (a far right wing association), together with other citizens, were assigned to guard the local railroads, because there was great fear about spies and demolition squads.

The first winter of the war was very trying. Unscrupulous black marketers continually escalated the price of foodstuffs. In the spring of 1915 there was a shortage of coal. The local dairy (a non-Jewish enterprise) sold no butter in Lauterbach. Instead, the dairy sent its cream to the parent firm in Fulda in order to force the Lauterbach town council to abandon the newly-introduced branch tax.[1] Doubtless. the Wertheim household kept one or two cows for its own use for milk, butter, and cheese.

My father was also drafted, and there are photographs of the handsome Vogel Wertheim (III) in military uniform. For a time he served in France, and later described the substandard sanitary facilities at the place of his military assignment. Unlike many of his Jewish and non-Jewish contemporaries, my father was not in favor of the war. To him, war equaled barbarity and brute force and always foremost in his thinking was the effect on his family and the aftermath on his people.

While in service, my father became infected with impetigo, an acute and conta-

Vogel (Frederick) Wertheim (III) in a World War I army hospital

gious skin disease that manifested itself with lesions in his face and lasted for several years after the war. As a young child, I was perturbed at the rule of not coming near my father's face. Prior to the infection, Vogel Wertheim (III) had obeyed the commandment in *Leviticus 19:27*: "Ye shall not round the corners of your heads, neither shalt thou mar the corners of your beard." According to the practice among Sephardic Jews in Western Europe since the second half of the seventeenth century, my father employed an obnoxious-smelling mixture of sulfur to remove his beard. But because of the impetigo, my father's doctors recommended that this routine come to an immediate end.

When nursing my sister Erna, my mother thought she could not become pregnant. This mistaken notion was, according to my mother, the reason that her children were not spaced further apart. Ten months after the beginning of World War

Mathilde Wertheim,
circa 1917-1918

I, I was born on Sunday evening, June 7, 1915 (the 25th of *Sivan*, the third month of the Jewish year 5675). While home alone with the fifteen-month-old Erna (the maid was on leave on Sundays), my mother was resting in bed when I appeared unaided and a few days early by her calculation. Unperturbed, my mother held a cover above the newborn infant and called me "inquisitive" for all time.

My mother tapped on the wall to enlist my Great-Uncle Samuel Strauss's help in calling the local midwife, Mrs. Lang, of the Kanalstrasse. There were no Jewish midwives in Upper Hesse in the early 1900s and none in Angenrod as far back as 1774. Even in the village of Rhina, where at times more Jews than non-Jews Jews lived, there was no Jewish midwife. However, during the early 1920s, the Jewish Dr. Rothschild, a relative of my paternal grandmother, Hannchen Levi Wertheim, practiced medicine in Alsfeld. From the late 1920s until his death by the Nazis in Maidenek in 1942, Gerson Friedländer was a Jewish dentist in Lauterbach. One trained Jewish nurse, Berta Gottlieb, whose family lived in Lauterbach, practiced her profession elsewhere. While I was growing up, the notion of a local Jewish nurse in a small town in Upper Hesse was not familiar. Generally, Jewish nurses practiced their profession in Jewish hospitals or performed nursing services in Jewish families.

According to custom, my parents named their second daughter 'Mathilde' after my mother's younger sister, who had died at the age of eleven on September 17, 1904. The name 'Mathilde' stems from the Teutonic and means 'battle maid.' 'Madel' is my Hebrew name and denotes 'young woman' as alluded to in *Isaiah 7:14*: "Therefore the Lord Himself shall give you a sign: behold the young woman shall conceive, and bear a son and shall call his name Immanuel." Immanuel is not a proper name, but a statement that "God is with us."

By the summer of 1915, there already existed a labor shortage in Lauterbach. After my father's contagious disease had made it imperative for him not to live in soldiers' barracks, Mr. Henkel of the local sawmill requested the services of Vogel (III) to cart critical supplies of wood from nearby areas to Lauterbach. My father's quiet facility for getting along well with people and his efficient

Left to right: Mathilde and Erna Wertheim, circa 1924

management of his horse and wagon were important factors in obtaining this much-coveted position. Vogel Wertheim (III) often commented on the virtues of all

Chapter Nineteen

members of the Henkel family. In general, Jews were rarely treated equitably and kindly in Lauterbach, which made the Henkel family all the more exceptional. Toward the end of the summer of 1915, the grain harvest was confiscated and shortly thereafter copper, brass, and nickel were seized as well. By the middle of November, the population was required to turn in any kind of old metal. Anyone not following this order was subject to penalty.[2]

On October 12, 1915, my mother's oldest brother, Siegfried Lamm, was hit by an enemy's shell while performing trench warfare near Ville Sur Turbe. He was twenty-five-years old and serving his country in the 10th Reserve Infantry Regiment Rank #81. The official death notice stated that Siegfried had died instantly.

Siegfried Lamm, my mother's oldest brother was killed in World War I near Ville Sur Turbe on October 12, 1915. He served in the 10th Reserve Infantry Regiment.

However, one of his comrades, Theodor Günther of the haulage business firm in Lauterbach, later reported that Siegfried's injuries were considerable while he was yet fully conscious. The wounded soldier was so severely crazed by pain that he begged his comrades to end his life by shooting him. Siegfried Lamm died after three days of torturous suffering. This loss deeply stirred every member of the Lamm and Wertheim families. My paternal grandmother, Hannchen Wertheim was chosen to shoulder the task of informing my maternal grandmother, Auguste Lamm, of the death of her oldest son. The demise of his brother-in-law, Siegfried, meant a further lessening of my father's enthusiasm for this war. He now appreciated even more his assignment of carting wood in and near Lauterbach, which made it possible to see his wife and children frequently.

Vogel Wertheim (III) frequently related that whenever Jews in Germany were successful in eliminating one particular prejudice the Christian population harbored against them, then countless new jaundiced notions against Jews would arise immediately. My father was of the opinion that Jews in Germany would never placate the German population, regardless of Jewish rightness and rectitude. Because of hard-core anti-semitism, he took a dim view of German army officers in general and General Ludendorff in particular.

In 1916, the German Officers Corps carried out a census of Jews at the front. Fourteen thousand Jewish servicemen from the Duchy of Hesse and from Hesse-Nassau served Germany in World War I. Of the one hundred thousand Jewish servicemen in total, ten thousand had volunteered.[3] Since the results of this count refuted the misconception that Jews were malingerers, the findings were never published. The percentage of Jews fighting for Germany was at least as large as that of the rest of the population.[4] Local Jews and their relatives frequently alluded to the fact that Jewish soldiers were sent to the front as cannon fodder without proper training.

The death notice of Siegfried Lamm, October 12, 1915.
It reads:
Mr. Jacob Lamm, Cattle Dealer Kirtorf,
I herewith fulfill the sad duty of informing you of the death of your son, Siegfried, last night. He died a hero's death for the Fatherland (October 13, 1915). You son was hit by an enemy grenade and died instantly. His grave is situated about 50 meters east of the street Cerney-Ville sur Turbe at [the] height of 150 [meters]. The company will erect a cross there. Be assured of my own as well as his comrades fervent expression of sympathy.
Signed Auhop
Lieutenant and Company Leader

To my knowledge, no local Jew served in the German navy or the fledgling German air force. In my father's time, the German navy was too exclusive an organization to recruit or accept Jews from Hesse in its ranks. To the best of my recollection, the following Jews from Lauterbach gave service in the German Army in World War I: Meyer Adler, Bernhard Baumann, Carl Baumann (I), Max Baumann, Siegfried Baumann, Samuel Hess, Aron Höchster, Nathan Höchster, Kaufmann Höchster, Louis Jakob, Moritz Katz, Siegfried Reiss, Moritz Spier, Max Stein, Max Stern, Siegfried Strauss (II), Moritz Weinberg, and Vogel Wertheim (III).

Moritz Spier died in line of duty for his country on May 9, 1917. His daughter, Ruth Gisela, escaped to the United States, but his widow, Sara Spier, was murdered by the Nazis. Carl Baumann (I) was also killed in action in World War I. His family later lost thirty-two members as a result of Nazi atrocities. Max Stern, his wife Rosa, and their second son, Arnold, also were killed by the Nazis.

Bernhard, Max, and Siegfried Baumann were prisoners-of-war in Russia, and returned from captivity in World War I several years after cessation of hostilities. I recall their synagogue attendance on the first Sabbath after their homecoming. In order to rejoice in the return of the three remaining Baumannn brothers, most members of the Jewish community called that afternoon at the Baumann home at the Bleichstrasse. During *Kristallnacht* in 1938, while the Nazis searched the home of the aged. Karoline Baumann and demanded valuables, she stoutly replied that she had already sacrificed her most valuable treasure, her son, Carl, for Germany. Several years later Karoline Baumann also suffered the loss of her daughter, Jenny, and her son-in-law, Mr. Hamburger, both of whom were murdered by the Nazis.

According to my mother, during World War I the church bells rang out every day to announce Germany's victories. But, as the war dragged on, foodstuff of all kinds became scarce. Roasted malted barley, for example, substituted for coffee in most Lauterbach households. This grain caused an illness of the eyes in some individuals. My Great-Uncle Samuel Strauss came down with this disease and had to wear blue eyeglasses for many years. My mother offered the fruit of our red beechnut tree to those in Lauterbach who collected it for the production of oil: indeed, all kinds of fruit stones and kernels were used for oil-making. Belt tightening became the order of the day. Some older inhabitants of Lauterbach later recalled that my generous mother had shared alike with Jews and others the fruits and vegetables of our gardens.

Folks from out of town came to Lauterbach in search of food. Profiteering was rampant, particularly in foodstuffs. Conrad List (a non-Jew), owner of a local linen store and father of a classmate and friend of mine, was reputedly indicted for earning large sums of money in connection with the war effort. There was talk in town of his serving time in jail. By the summer of 1918, extensive theft of food in gardens and fields persuaded the Lauterbach town council to pass an ordinance forbidding anyone, even owners, to be in the fields and gardens between seven at night and seven in the morning.[5] My mother bartered some fruits of our gardens for grain. Regularly she sent packages of home-baked cakes and chickens to her cousin, Minna Stern Strauss, in Giessen. The supply of food in larger cities was more limited than in Lauterbach.

During the autumn of 1918, a deadly influenza raged in Lauterbach and every member of the Wertheim family was ill. The sickness, combined with the bereavements suffered by many households in town due to war fatalities, lessened their earlier enthusiasm for the war. For example, two sisters, Stöhr from the metal factory and Duchardt from the sausage factory, each lamented the loss of two of their sons. It is noteworthy to mention that the immediate members of these families later did not engage in Nazism and took a dim view of the persecution of Jews.

On October 3, 1918, Germany formed a parliamentary government with Prince Max of Baden as its head. By October 9, 1918, the front had collapsed, there was mutiny in the German navy, and a revolution in Munich after which Emperor William II abdicated. Germany made peace overtures to President Wilson and on November 11, 1918, the German government signed the armistice treaty in a dining car in the forest at Compiegne.[a]

Germany was required to evacuate its army from France, Belgium, and the territory on the left side of the Rhine. Lauterbach was on the withdrawal route of the armed forces from Frankfurt am Main to Fulda. As a young child, I recall ongoing conversations among adults about the *Rückmarsch*, the withdrawal of the army. For my sister and me, this event constituted unique daily entertainment from our bedroom window that faced the street. I remember unceasing rows of loosely organized soldiers passing by, some clad in long field overcoats. Sometimes they led horses and occasionally other horses were pulling wagons.

Not infrequently, my family was required to provide lodging and food to soldiers who passed through Lauterbach. I recall one winter night when at least ten soldiers slept on our living room floor. In order to make them more comfortable, my father supplied additional horse-blankets from our stables. That night, Vogel Wertheim (III) kept inconspicuous vigil, because he was concerned that harm might come to his wife and children. Early the next morning the soldiers left with minimal commotion. On another occasion, two majors of the army were assigned to our home for lodging and meals. My parents cautioned their daughters, four and five years old, to mind their best manners and engage only in imperative conversation. Even at my young age, I was aware of my parents' distrust of German army officers, who were reputed to be chauvinistic and frequently anti-semitic. However, if these officers held xenophobic views, their mind-set was temporarily either well-concealed or mellowed by food and fellowship with their Jewish hosts.

---

[a] It is interesting to note that immediately after the war, anti-semitic principles pervaded the largest German veterans association, the *Stahlhelm*. The notion of a Jewish-Bolshevik conspiracy was adopted by this organization long before it was officially adopted by the Third Reich. In Lauterbach, the *Stahlhelm* was an active organization with many members. My English teacher, Mr. Koch, was a vocal follower of *Stahlhelm*.

Chapter Nineteen

Especially during the earlier years of the Weimar Republic (1919-1933), many members of the Jewish congregation, the local Protestant clergy, and the rural population in Hesse lamented the demise of the German monarchy. Sometimes, I heard a song that reflected the mindset: "*Kaiser Wilhelm der grosse Held zog mit der dicken, dicken Berta ins Feld. Kaiser Wilhelm, der liess sich nicht besiegen, liess mit Pulver und Kanonen schiessen, für das deutsche Reich, für das deutsche Reich, für das geliebte deutsche Reich*" ('Emperor William, the great hero, fielded the big, big Berta cannon. Emperor William who would not be defeated, ordered shooting with powder and cannon for the German Reich, for the German Reich, for the beloved German Reich.')

The Protestant rural population in the Lauterbach vicinity with whom the majority of the local Jewish cattle dealers conducted business belonged to the *Deutschnationale Partei*, a right-wing political party with fervent nationalist and anti-semitic views. In Catholic enclaves near Lauterbach, similar to Herbstein, the local farmers belonged to the *Zentrum Partei*, the Catholic Center party. Their views tended to be less anti-semitic, because Catholics in a predominantly Protestant environment were to a degree acquainted with the pain and prejudice of being a religious minority.

It will always be a wonder to me how, during the Weimar Republic, my father was able to conduct a flourishing one-man cattle dealing establishment. He succeeded despite being a comparative newcomer, the very adverse economic circumstances, the hostile attitude toward Jews often reinforced by officialdom in nearby villages and in Lauterbach, and the numerous and established Jewish and Christian competitors. Moreover, while self-help organizations for farmers with decidedly anti-semitic orientation were generally not too widespread in Upper Hesse, they had existed in the county of Lauterbach since 1890.[6] The anti-semitic farmers' cooperative, *Raiffeisengenossenschaft*, made every effort to prevent local farmers from trading with Jewish cattle dealers.

As a young child, I was very unsettled by the continuous and contemptible comments that I overheard in connection with the role of Jewish cattle dealers as evil middlemen who created nothing, and who depleted the farmers to the detriment of German society. In a community where little else but biased information was available, it was much easier to manipulate acceptance of untruths. That was the case in Lauterbach and its surroundings in the 1920s. However, despite all these negative views, one of my father's guiding principles always triumphed: work is how one makes sense of one's place in life and in nature.

In the 1920s, the cattle dealing business in Hesse was dominated by Jews. After rural Jews in Upper Hesse had obtained German citizenship in the 1870s, they frequently lacked the necessary financial resources required in large families to prepare their often-gifted children for professions or trades other than their father's cattle dealing business. Among the forty Jewish families in Lauterbach during the time of Vogel Wertheim (III), the following Jewish men contended for a finite share of the cattle dealing business: Meyer Adler and his elderly father-in-law, Moses

Fröhlich (who died in 1928) of Bahnhofstrasse 34; Juda Baumann (II) of Bahnhofstrasse 66 (who shipped sheep from northern Germany to other areas in Germany and who, therefore, did not generally compete with local cattle dealers); Julius Hess of Langgasse 21 and later of Rockelsgasse 10; Moses Jakob of Langgasse 19 (who died in 1926); Seligmann Jakob of Alter Steinweg 7; Louis Jakob of Hainigstrasse 25; Michel Jakob of Bahnhofstrasse 103; Jakob Oppenheimer of Rockelsgasse 41; Markus, Siegfried (II), Hermann, and Salli Strauss (II) of Hinter dem Spittel 4; Samuel Strauss (II) of Rockelsgasse 10; Josef and Rudolph Weinberg of Steinweg 11; David Weinberg of Langgasse 10; and Vogel Wertheim (III) of Cent 17. There was a tacit understanding that each cattle dealer would trade only with his own customers in a given village, and violations were looked upon with great disfavor. My father possessed a masterful facility for communicating with the populace of the surrounding villages, particularly in view of the fact that each village had a distinctly different dialect.

With few exceptions, the remainder of the Lauterbach Jewish families were, as newcomers, in more modest financial circumstances and were generally less well-educated than the Jews of Alsfeld. Alsfeld, ten miles from Lauterbach, had a larger Jewish population, where most industry was in Jewish hands until the advent of Hitler. The underlying reason for this discrepancy was that a few Jewish families had lived in Alsfeld in the seventeenth century and additional Jewish families had settled in Alsfeld beginning in the early 1800s. For instance, the descendants of Michel Spier from Merzhausen, who was laid to rest in the Angenrod Jewish cemetery in 1842, became the owners of a local Jewish bank. Moreover, in the 1830s and 1840s Jews from surrounding villages were permitted to move to Alsfeld. Conversely, Jews were kept out of Lauterbach by the maneuvers of the local town council and the local feudal lords (Riedesel) until the 1860s.

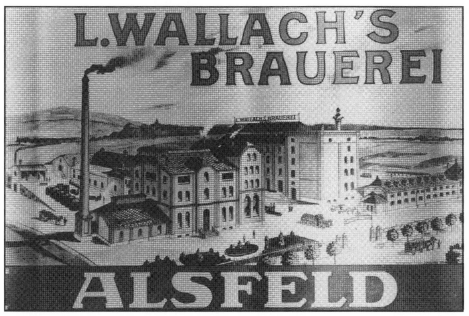

The Wallach Brewery in Alsfeld

Various occupations were represented by Jews in Alsfeld. There were several engineers, a banker, a doctor, a dentist, an owner of a large lumberyard, an owner of a liqueur factory, and several well-to-do retail merchants. In Alsfeld in the 1920s, there was a lower percentage of cattle dealers among the total Jewish population as compared to Lauterbach, but most of the recently-arrived Jewish families in Alsfeld from nearby villages were either cattle dealers or peddlers. When Jews were first allowed to settle in Lauterbach in 1861, the Jews of Alsfeld already could deliberate about having their children attend the newly-established high school that prepared them for entrance into professional schools at a university. In Lauterbach, the Jewish families who were already well-established in business by the beginning of World War I or earlier were also in better financial circumstances in the 1920s and 1930s.

In Wallenrod near Lauterbach, there was also the non-Jewish cattle dealer, Mr. Reibeling, who professed steadfast loyalty to Jews and particularly to our family. His positive attitude may have derived from the fact that during a critical housing shortage, his daughter, Anna Euler, and her husband found comparatively inexpensive living quarters in the second floor of our home at Cent 17. Mr. Reibling visited at our home and his daughter's apartment frequently. Many afternoons he stayed for coffee, as did several others of my father's non-Jewish friends, such as Mr. Listmann from Almenrod and Eckemüller-Heinrich Wahl (IV) from Angersbach. It always seemed unusual to me that, in a society where age is respected for knowledge and experience, the older Mr. Reibling wished to assimilate my father's methods of conducting business. Our frequent non-Jewish company stayed for hours. Notwithstanding the general ascendancy of anti-semitism in the 1920s and early 1930s and the strong influence of anti-semitic teachings in the Lutheran church (which most parishioners attended regularly), our regular non-Jewish visitors esteemed and plainly wished to assimilate our lifestyle and values.

Several years after the Nazi takeover, Mr. Reibeling cornered an exclusive margin of the cattle-dealing trade in the Lauterbach area. In the 1980s, we visited with Anna Euler, who made every effort to avoid analyses of Nazi days, but called attention to my father's industriousness. Mr. Listmann, a blacksmith, and the Eckemüller family of Angersbach remained loyal to our family. After the war, at a time when his income as a comparatively new immigrant to the United States was rather modest, my father sent food packages to both families. The demise of Mr. Listmann ended contact with that family. However, the loyalty of the descendants of the Eckemüller family in Angersbach and Grossenlüder endured, and friendship was renewed during our visit to Lauterbach in 1991.

My father's success in business was attributable to his indefatigable diligence, yet he always observed the Sabbath and all Jewish holidays assiduously by not conducting any business or engaging in any physical labor. Vogel Wertheim (III) was occupied in the various phases of cattle dealing from daybreak Sunday to sundown on Friday. Saturday evening after Sabbath he attended to bookkeeping chores and preparations for paying taxes. Of the many tax obligations during the Weimar Republic, he regarded the turnover tax (*Umsatzsteuer*) as the most onerous because he appreciated that turnover per se was no certainty for earnings. In summer on Sundays, my father used a scythe to mow the large meadows of Cent 17 and he used a sickle to cut the small grassy parcels. This was backbreaking labor because of the extensive size of the tracts and the crude nature of the implements. Labor-saving machinery such as lawn mowers was not available in Lauterbach, even as late as the 1920s. Menial work was carried out with the help of simple implements and human toil. Grass from our own meadows generally was fed green to the cows and very rarely was made into hay.

Frequently on Sunday afternoons, my father left by train for the cattle market in Frankfurt am Main (and sometimes for Leipzig in Saxony) in order to sell the calves, heifers, and cows that had been loaded into railroad stock cars on Friday afternoon. In Frankfurt am Main, my father's agent, Mr. Michel, supervised the unloading, shelter, and feeding of the animals until market time on Monday morning. Toward Monday evening, when Vogel Wertheim (III) returned by train from Frankfurt am Main, his small suitcase was usually filled with dark red Jaffa oranges (when in season) and other edibles that could not be obtained locally. On very rare occasions, when profits were exceptional, he brought perfume for my mother or a toy for his daughters.

At the end of World War I, my father used a horse-and-carriage for transportation. After the war, oats for horses were in short supply and consequently expensive. Beginning in the early 1920s, he walked or bicycled to the nearby villages of Maar, Wallenrod, Frischborn, Almenrod, Angersbach, Reuters, and Landenhausen. For greater distances such as Ulrichstein, Grebenhain, Crainfeld, and infrequently other villages in the higher Vogelsberg regions, my father engaged Emil Burkhardt's auto service. In the mid-1980s, Emil told me that his large automobile agency owed its initial success in the late 1920s to the loyal following of Lauterbach's Jewish cattle dealers. Vogel Wertheim (III) bought and sold cows, calves, heifers, and bulls. Not infrequently he was commissioned by the administration of a nearby town or hamlet to act as agent to obtain a suitable registered stud. My father secured such animals by collaborating with another Jewish cattle dealer, usually some distance away, whose specialty was registered purebred animals.

Every now and then, my father entered into a temporary partnership with a local cattle dealer (for example, Michel Jakob and Julius Hess) for the purpose of buying cows in northern Germany to be sold locally. Most of the time these undertakings were lucrative. However, I recall vividly one less successful project when the animals took ill with hoof-and-mouth disease shortly after their arrival. Official directives required that this highly contagious disorder be rigidly controlled by liquidating the affected animals. My father managed to elude this directive by successfully nursing the sick animals back to health without telltale signs.

The veterinarians in Lauterbach during the 1920s and early 1930s were Dr. Friedel and Dr. Kick. The latter was an elderly, rather corpulent gentleman whose golden watch chain bobbed up and down while he conversed. He breathed rather noisily as if he were suffering from asthma. It was common knowledge that the horse that pulled Dr. Kick's carriage knew intuitively where his master wanted to stop. Every now and again, the extremely pleasant Dr. Kick enjoyed sipping a glass of homemade currant wine at our house, especially after assisting in a difficult delivery of a calf.

A further element of my father's business success can be ascribed to his friendliness, his interest in the lives of his customers, his competence and timing for winning over a customer or trader, his quick ability for computing weight and price, and his mastery at negotiations. He listened to his disputant with attention, respect, and sensitivity. Purchase, sale, or exchange of livestock might last several hours. The buyer or seller often left, only to return at a later time, in order to create greater uncertainty and tension about the transaction and frequently offering half the asking price. Final confirmation of a deal was by handshake and reluctance to extend one's hand meant lack of good will. As a child, I failed to understand why several grown men would wear themselves out for hours before closing a transaction. I secretly wished for funds of my own in order to cover the difference between the bid and asked price, thereby enjoying my father's company on a weekday.

In 1919, the citizens of Lauterbach exercised their voting rights eight times within two hundred twenty-five days. They cast ballots for federal, state, provincial, county, and local governments. At that time the voting age was twenty and women were given the franchise.[7] Also by 1919, the German populace tasted the harsh consequences of defeat and in Lauterbach, outside of my family, no one, not even a schoolteacher, ever alluded to or admitted Germany's defeat in World War I. The majority of my teachers unfailingly portrayed Germany as an uncomplaining and constant sufferer that was subjected to great trials for the sake of its high principles. Also, in that year the economically devastating inflation began. As runaway prices climbed out of sight, old-age pensioners and senior citizens were often able to buy only one piece of bread or a potato for a whole month's pension or their entire savings. The inflation reached its zenith in the autumn of 1923. At that time, one dollar equaled 4.2 billion German *Mark*. The inflation was terminated by the introduction of the *Rentenmark*, which was later replaced by the *Reichsmark*.

My father immediately perceived the economic implications as they related to his business. He held onto his livestock and bartered foodstuffs with his farmer friends. At the time of the stabilization of the *Reichsmark*, my father's business capital consisted of his livestock. Despite the distressed economy, my father's income supported his family well and afforded his two daughters the tuition for high school and for private lessons (such as piano, handwork, sewing, and gymnastics). Moreover, there was always the ill will of most local bureaucrats, who tried hard to put any Jewish person at a disadvantage. Although anti-semitism was not yet officially mandated, every day life for a Jewish cattle dealer and his family in Lauterbach grew more trying. The greater part of the citizenry primarily and illogically blamed its own distress on the presence of Jews.

Endnotes

1. Dr. Karl Siegmar Baron von Galera, *Lauterbach in Hessen, III* (Neustadt an der Aisch: Verlag Degener and Company, 1965), pp. 340-341.

2. Ibid, p. 341.

3. Thomas W. Lummitsch, *Jüdisches Leben in Gedern* (Schotten: Gerhard W. Wenzel, August 1991), pp. 106-107.

4. Ingelborg Klein and Werner Licharz, *Juden und Christen in Deutschland* (Frankfurt am Main: Haag & Herchen, 1990), p. 14.

5. von Galera, *Lauterbach in Hessen, III*, p. 344.

6. Rüdiger Mack, *Neunhundert Jahre Geschichte der Juden in Hessen* (Wiesbaden: Kommission für die Geschichte der Juden in Hessen), pp. 392-393.

7. von Galera, *Lauterbach in Hessen, III*, p. 347.

Chapter Twenty
The Conditions Before and After January 30, 1933
Attacks on Jews in Lauterbach, Gedern, Kirtorf
and Crainfeld
Hitler in Lauterbach
Righteous Gentiles
The Jews of Lauterbach Flee Germany

In 1935, 'Jews Not Wanted' signs appeared in towns and villages in Germany and particularly in Hesse

THE POLITICAL
CLIMATE IN
LAUTERBACH IN
THE 1920S AND
EARLY 1930S

$\mathcal{P}$olitical events in Lauterbach clearly reflected the general developments in Germany in the period between 1924 and 1932. During the autumn of 1924, members of the Lauterbach Jewish congregation met to discuss a meeting of Nazis that had occurred several weeks earlier. On December 24, 1924, a meeting under Nazi sponsorship at the Johannesberg Hall (controlled by the local feudal lords, the Riedesel) stipulated *"Juden haben keinen Zutritt"* ('Jews are not admitted').[1] In 1928 and 1930, there were fourteen political parties. On August 23, 1924, the *Republikaner* of Lauterbach founded the '*Reichsbanner Schwarz-Rot-Gold*' ('the black, red, and gold of the Weimar Republic') under the auspices of the Social Democrats and labor unions and in cooperation with several members of the German Democratic party. This league was created to support the Weimar Republic openly. At the inception meeting at the *Keutzer* restaurant in Lauterbach, only one hundred twenty people attended and one hundred joined. Based on these numbers, the founders of the *Reichsbanner* doubtless assumed that the central tenets of the Weimar Republic were not being given much heed in Lauterbach and were therefore in compelling need of reinforcement.

Four weeks later, the newly-founded *Reichsbanner* publicly declared, "Never Again War." The *Reichsbanner* assumed the annual duty to celebrate 'Constitution Day' on August 11 with a torchlight procession, music, and songs about the struggle of the working man. On this occasion, many Lauterbach townsmen closed their windows and doors.[2] As a nine-year-old, I discerned—and my teacher and classmates clearly communicated—that few citizens of good repute would join the *Reichsbanner*. Most local Jews practiced their right to vote, but because of memories of earlier persecution, they rarely participated in political activities. In the November county election that year, the Nazis received 17 percent of the votes in Lauterbach and 14.5 percent of the votes in the town council election. For the first time, there were two Nazis among the fifteen town council members.[3]

On August 16, 1925, the *Stahlhelm* was formed. This organization had been founded in 1918 by German nationalistic anti-semitic front soldiers and it represented the antithesis of the *Reichsbanner*. My English teacher, Mr. Koch, was an active member of the *Stahlhelm*.[a] Whenever a procession of the *Stahlhelm* marched through town, members of the *Reichsbanner* closed their windows and doors.[4]

Beginning in the 1920s, a large sector of the Vogelsberg farming community near Lauterbach was in straitened circumstances, which in part were exacerbated by the protracted effects of the local feudal system and the rather limited opportunities for small farmers to sell farm products other than cattle. In an attempt to alleviate the plight of the small local peasants, an association was established under the stewardship of Karl Maurer, my biology teacher. He cooperated with the National Socialist veterinarain, Dr. Lang from Grebenhain. I recall persistent references, in the papers and in conversation, to the role of the Jewish cattle dealer as a non-productive member of society who ruined the valuable German farmer.

[a] In 1933, the *Stahlhelm* integrated itself into the Nazi party.

For the benefit of the local peasantry, the organization tried to obtain more favorable prices for all farming products, including cattle. In the course of this action, it shut out Jewish cattle dealers. The managing director of the regional cattle-dealers' association, my mother's cousin, Salli Strauss [I] (at) Am Eselswörth 6, responded in the *Lauterbacher Anzeiger* in January and February of 1929 by incriminating the general depression rather than local cattle dealers for the plight of the peasantry.[5] Under these difficult local circumstances and because of the catastrophic American stock market crash of October 29, 1929 and the ensuing Great Depression, 1929 was the last successful year of my father's cattle business.

In 1930, at the time of the parliamentary elections in September, thirty-seven percent of the Lauterbach electorate voted for the Nazis, and by November, 1931 there were nearly twice as many Nazi delegates as Social Democrats. The year 1931 was also a disturbing political time for Jews. During a mass meeting at the Lauterbach sports hall, Nazi speakers hurled impassioned accusations at Social Democrats, Communists, Freemasons, and Jews.[6] Zörner from Brunswick, Oberlindober from Munich, and Dr. Joseph Goebbels from Berlin addressed the local populace at a torchlight procession assisted by the town band. However, the main topic was hostility toward Jews.

Less than one month before, Hitler and Hermann Göring had addressed the regional populace at the Hoherodskopf (a highland in the Vogelsberg) during a celebration of the midsummer solstice.[7] This ceremony stressed Germanic traditions in order to estrange Lauterbach's faithful Lutherans from their accustomed ecclesiastical orientation. The Nazis wished to first weaken customs and then cast them aside. Also during the summer of 1932, anti-Jewish slogans and the swastika fluttered from the *Hohhaus*, an important building in the center of town that belonged to the Riedesel. In April of 1933, a strong faction within the Lutheran church of Lauterbach supported the Nazi regime. However, Pastor Schlösser resigned his post in 1935 and joined the German Confessional Church.[8] That community of worshippers did not distinguish itself by making a stand against Nazism. But Pastor Dotzert later refused to take orders from Nazis in connection with the funeral rites of the sister of a prominent Lauterbach citizen, Gustav Mandt.

In general, the Lauterbach Nazis took a somewhat uncompromising attitude toward Catholics. For instance, shortly after January 30, 1933, Mr. Höll, a court employee, was told in no uncertain terms that if his wife continued to attend Catholic services, his civil service position was in serious jeopardy.[9] According to my father, persecution of Jews in Lauterbach by Catholics was less widespread and not as fanatic as by Protestants.

PERSECUTION IN LAUTERBACH AND THE VICINTY

BEGINNING IN 1930, RELENTLESS CHARGES against Jews confirmed and energized the attitude of inveterate Jew-haters in Lauterbach, who constituted at least seventy percent of the total population. Because of Böckel's earlier anti-semitic campaigning, the harsh anti-Jewish agitation of the malicious Nazi propaganda fell onto the fertile soil that the Christian churches had carefully been preparing for centuries. The majority of the Christian population no longer simply refrained from nodding; they turned around and sneered if a Jewish person came into view. A small part of the local populace that had previously maintained business and limited social connections with Jews began to evince ambivalent conduct toward Jews. There was constant pounding about the evil of Jews, their unequivocal blame for Germany's political and economic undoing, and their responsibility for the many unemployed individuals in Lauterbach.

Within weeks, the harassment achieved its goal: there were more Jew-haters than ever before in my native town. In 1931, two years prior to President Hindenburg's appointment of Hitler as the Reich Chancellor (Prime Minister) on January 30, 1933, Jews were forbidden to enter the *Cafe Stöhr* at the Eisenbacher Tor, the Burghof restaurant, and the favored Nazi *Wachtel* restaurant. At this time, many civil servants, such as some schoolteachers, policemen, and petty officials, who had not previously exhibited open hostility toward Jews, began to harass Jews of all ages as if indulging in a long-repressed favorite sport.

According to my parents, from 1930 until 1936, there remained a tiny altruistic nucleus within the Christian populace of Lauterbach and its environs who contin-

Marie Hedrich in 1985

ued to associate openly with Jews. Moreover, these humane Christians secretly looked after Jews, frequently heedless of danger to themselves. With rare exceptions, the altruism bestowed upon my family and other Jewish families in Lauterbach generally emanated from individuals who, directly or indirectly, had had business dealings with Jews for many years (for example, household help or part-time employees). Sometimes, familiarity can breed tolerance rather than contempt. Marie Hedrich of Maar, who died in 1989, belonged to this class of righteous people. Marie came to us at the advice of Mrs. Feick, whose son would later marry Marie's oldest daughter, Lina. Marie and her family were disciples of the Krishona Protestant religious group. Nevertheless, one member of this group, Helmut Stöppler of Maar, a former schoolmate of mine who joined the SA in 1933, told me in 1959 that he had gathered Jews on trucks to be delivered to extermination camps.

My own situation worsened as well. From one day to another, none of my high school classmates spoke to me and my former friends suddenly hurled insults and mocked Jews in general whenever we came face-to-face. As a fifteen- or sixteen-year-old, I suddenly found myself in enemy territory in my native town. During high school classes in Lauterbach, Mr. Decker subtly berated me and all Jews. In the *Oberrealschule* in Alsfeld, Mr. Hainer, the school's principal and my history instructor, lost no opportunity, despite my good behavior and diligence, to scold me and rant against Jews in general. As a rule, I was compelled to listen in silent agony while other students and teachers openly uttered physical threats and made slanderous and abusive statements against me and other Jews. I was constantly warned that my blond hair would be cut off, because my Nazi classmates upheld the doctrine that blond hair was unbefitting a Jew.

I frequently withheld from my parents' accounts of hurtful and often cruel treatment by teachers and classmates. My parents, and especially my father, tried to mitigate my tribulations by assuring me that I was not to blame. My father felt compelled to accompany me daily at dawn for the twenty-minute walk to the railroad station, from where I commuted to school in Alsfeld. He feared that the ever-increasing threats of attack by Nazi hoodlums would be perpetrated on his younger daughter. At that time, Nazi rowdies chased my mother's cousin, Salli Strauss(II) of Hinter dem Spittel 6, who was then in his early twenties, down a high outdoor flight of stone steps (the *Portstreppe*). During this incident, he fell and sustained permanent leg injuries.

Members of the SA—armed men in brown uniforms who were trained by Nazis-regularly marched through Lauterbach and shouted "Germany awake!" and

Nazi assemblage in Lauterbach in 1933

"Jews should die a wretched death!" All demonstrations began or ended with the *Horst Wessel* song, that included the words, "When Jewish blood will splatter from the knife, all will be well with us." On January 15, 1933, a large deployment of SA gathered on the *Marktplatz*, the center of town in Lauterbach. Although Jews kept out of sight for fear of arrest, loudspeakers announced coming events. Terror held sway over most Jewish families in the Vogelsberg region. On January 30, 1933, a deployment of SA men and Nazis in civilian clothing marched through town for a demonstration in the *Marktplatz*. On an almost daily basis, the *swastika* and the black, white, and red flags fluttered from all public and many private buildings. My father considered this prodigious display of flags an attempt to cover up the Nazi regime's financial and social woes.

ON JANUARY 30, 1933, PRESIDENT HINDENBURG appointed Adolf Hitler as Reich Chancellor. From that time on, Germany's war against its Jewish citizens became official public policy and Nazi terrorists enjoyed the state's protection. My father was of the opinion that the Nazi movement was not a temporary episode, that it was a spreading disease among the German people. He took a dim view of the sentiment among local German-Jewish front line soldiers, who interpreted their present more favored status as a lasting circumstance.

On February 10, 1933, there was again a huge assembly on the *Marktplatz* to listen to the broadcast of a speech by Hitler. Local Nazis from Lauterbach and the surrounding villages marched through town on weekends and sometimes also on weekday evenings. On these occasions, it was necessary for all Jews to remain at home and indoors, lest they incur derision, mockery, or severe physical injury. Not infrequently, young Nazi hoodlums would insult or beat up a former Jewish class-mate or neighbor in order to manifest their zealous and recently-acquired loyalty to the Nazi cause.

In the unusual event that a non-Jew conversed with a Jewish citizen, it behooved the Jew to weigh his words prudently lest they be deemed an insult to the Führer. My father's good friend, Julius Hess of the Rockelsgasse, spent several weeks in the local jail because he did not speak in glowing terms of Hitler's economic accomplishments. Direct payments by Julius' father, Nathan Hess, to attorney Scheer of the *Marktplatz*, who acted as representative of the local Nazi party, effected his son's release. In those days, members of the Lauterbach Jewish congregation hurried to and from synagogue services, trying to avoid crowded areas and busy streets.

During the night of February 27, 1933, the *Reichstag* building in Berlin was, according to the Nazis, set on fire by communists, socialists, and Jews. My father perceived immediately that the Nazis themselves had set the *Reichstag* on fire, as was substantiated after World War II. At the *Reichstag* election on March 5, 1933, the Nazis obtained 63.6 percent of the votes in Lauterbach.[10] When returning from market in Frankfurt am Main or from a buying trip in the Vogelsberg, my father reported about other small towns in the Hesse area where Jewish homes were being searched for weapons and Jewish occupants were beaten up, mercilessly tormented, and sometimes taken away.

Compulsory incarceration in prisons or concentration camps was euphemistically termed 'protective custody.' Dachau was established on March 23, 1933, however I do not know of any Jews from the Vogelsberg region who were sent there. In the beginning of the Nazi regime, Vogelsberg Jews were usually assigned to Osthofen. My father's good friend, the cattle-dealer Elkan Sommer of Crainfeld, a kindly gentleman and a frequent visitor at our house, escaped from his local tormentors. He concealed himself from his Nazi pursuers in the crossbeams of another Jewish home in the area, and he later escaped to Palestine.

There were stories of horror about the treatment of Jews in Gersfeld in the Rhön region where a cousin of my mother, Mathilde Strauss Wahlhaus, lived. In

March 1933, in Gedern, which is about fifteen miles from Lauterbach, the SA beat the eighty-year-old Gabriel Blumenthal with a motorcycle chain. His screams of pain were heard on nearby premises. Berthold Simon was flogged with the same motorcycle chain until he sank to the ground. Among other Jews of Gedern who were badly beaten were Max Meier, the Vöhl family (friends of my father), Max and Julius Rothenberger, Max Oppenheimer, and the sixty-six-year-old watchmaker Michael Homburger.[11] The Gustav Blumenthal family sought refuge with Mrs. Blumenthal's father, Juda Baumann (II) of Bahnhofstrasse 66 in Lauterbach. Extreme and cruel excesses in Gedern may well have been the result of the anti-semitic mentality of the Lutheran ministries of the pastors Germer, Widman, and Saal, who had shepherded the local Lutheran church since 1900.[12]

Several young Jewish men from Lauterbach fled to relatives in larger towns where they were not so well-known. From these temporary abodes, these young Jewish men, and sometimes young women, accomplished the difficult task of finding asylum in a European country or perhaps even abroad. For instance, one such young man, Alfred Adler, lost no time escaping to Holland very early in 1933.

Beginning on January 30, 1933, the black, red and gold flag of the Weimar Republic suddenly vanished from Lauterbach. Thereafter, the majority of houses displayed *swastikas*, as well as black, white, and red flags (the colors of the German Empire). On March 13, 1933, Joseph Goebbels, who frequently spoke in the Lauterbach region, became Minister of Enlightenment and Propaganda. On March 23, 1933, barely two months after Hitler's seizure of power, the 'Law to Eliminate the Misery of People and the Reich,' the *Ermächtigungsgesetz*, was passed on March 23, 1933. From then on, legal ordinances were simply decreed by the government and were allowed to deviate from the constitution. Hitler's dictatorship was legally established. Exclusion of Jews from positions of commercial leadership and removal of Jewish doctors and lawyers were not applicable in Lauterbach because there were no such individuals. Now, the majority of the Lauterbach populace no longer needed to moderate its deep-seated anger against Jews, while other residents avoided contact with Jews out of fear.

On March 28, 1933, the National Socialist Party called upon the Lauterbach population to institute a boycott of all Jewish businesses on April 1, 1933. On that day, local SA men positioned themselves in front of Jewish stores and residences to prevent entrance by non-Jews. After one or two non-Jews were threatened and turned away from Jewish establishments, others no longer tried to gain entrance. Local SA men remained in front of Jewish stores until dark, bellowing anti-Jewish slogans.

On April 4, 1933, a faction of the Lutheran church openly came out in support of the new Nazi regime. Three days later, a law was promulgated that anyone not of Aryan descent or considered politically unreliable was to be dismissed from civil service. Among our acquaintances, this law applied to Mr. Ucko, a former member of the Lauterbach Jewish community, who had been a federal chief architect sta-

Nazi Brown Shirts prevent non-Jewish customers from entering stores owned by Jews

tioned in Lauterbach before his transfer to Kassel. The secret police, the *Gestapo*, was created on April 16 and Jews were at all times at its mercy. On May 10, 1933, our whole family and particularly my father, was much distressed about the public burning of books written by Jews and other authors who were not in full agreement with Nazi philosophy. On July 20, 1933, an agreement, the *Reichskonkordat*,

The burning of books
by the Nazis on May
10, 1933

was made between the Vatican (Pope Pius XI, 1857-1939) that assured that the Catholic Church would not work against the Nazis.

In the summer of 1933, my father declared that we would observe the Ninth of *Av* (the traditional day of mourning for the destruction of the Temples in Jerusalem) with regard not only to the past, but also to the present. His announcement aptly described our heaviness of mind and sentiments of impending doom. Additionally, the following public notice proclaimed by Dr. Mahr appeared in the *Lauterbacher Anzeiger* on August 31, 1933:

> Lately a large group of Jewish people was observed on Saturday afternoon, which creates rightful objections by the people of the national socialist persuasion. In conformity with the published decree of the police president in the *Darmstädter Zeitung* of August 29, 1933, public appearance of large groups of Jews must come to a halt in the district of Lauterbach.

Beginning in early 1933, the *Lauterbacher Anzeiger*, whose proprietors and editors were the Ehrenklau family, regularly published such announcements as, "Do Not Buy from Jews—Keep Your Hands Off Jewish Merchandise—and Avoid Jewish Stores." The Lauterbach press, not unlike the local Lutheran church, was predisposed to espouse Nazi doctrine and to function as Nazism's faithful tool and voice. A commanding Nazi power over Jews in Lauterbach was clearly and publicly established, and violators earned themselves ridicule and castigation. Strangling regulations and a reign of terror by Nazi rowdies dominated Jewish life. But even in the face of Nazi threats and appeals that farmers desist from engaging in business with Jewish cattle dealers, some of my father's customers in Almenrod, Angersbach, and Maar conducted business at night and visited our house secretly in 1933, 1934, and as late as 1935.

On October 14, 1933, Germany withdrew from the League of Nations. During the High Holy Days of 1933, at home and in synagogue, the mood of most Lauterbach Jews was that of hopelessness and despair. Our ranks were thinning and absences usually portended someone's imminent danger and the subsequent pain of permanent separation from close family members or dear friends. The same autumn, Hitler visited Lauterbach with much sound of horn and commotion. In the late afternoon, upon leaving town in the direction of Alsfeld, his entourage stopped in front of the gates of our *messuage* at Cent 17. When Hitler's automobile halted, the *Führer* stood with typically outstretched arm pointing toward our residence. The shutters of our residence were closed because we wanted to create the impression that no one was at home. I was aware that the poignant fear and trembling that had been haunting us in public would now beset us even within our own walls.

The Höll family.
Left to right: Irmgard Höll, Mrs. Höll, Erika Höll and Mr. Höll

Mr. Höll, a loyal non-Jewish court employee in Lauterbach and a longtime friend of our family, advised my father during a secret visit in the darkness of night that the Wertheim sisters had better leave town as soon as possible. In addition, he recommended that we not venture out during the day. His concern was based on his observation of the unrestrained behavior of the recruits of the newly-founded Nazi training camp in Sickendorf, who frequently visited Lauterbach and made a racket by shouting obscenities. Mr. Höll's counsel affirmed that our family should immediately pull up stakes from Lauterbach and Germany. My father's good friend, the master locksmith, Otterbein, of the Cent, also recommended that our family leave Germany as soon as possible.

THE FATE OF THE JEWISH COMMUNITY OF LAUTERBACH

THE PROBLEM OF FINDING EVEN TEMPORARY REFUGE from daily persecutions away from Lauterbach, and the far more difficult task of locating permanent asylum, beset every Jew in Upper Hesse. Moreover, even if a sanctuary could be located in another country, most Jewish families still had the problem of raising enough cash for moving relatives and necessary household goods, particularly during a severe economic depression coupled with stringent laws about conducting business with Jews. Most young Jews in their late teens or early twenties tried to arrange for a quick exit from Lauterbach or Alsfeld, with the ultimate aim that the older family members would join them as expeditiously as possible.

In many cases, older family members first had to dispose of their homes to raise the necessary cash for the cost of transportation. There were few purchasers of

Jewish property, even at debased prices. Nobody from Lauterbach emigrated to Rhodesia or South Africa, although young Jews from Alsfeld sought refuge there in 1933 and early 1934: Hermann and Josef (Seppel) Levi of Bahnhofstrasse 10, Bertha Lindenbaum of Marburger Strasse 1, Hermann and Thekla Sondheimer of Bahnhofstrasse 14, Kurt Spier of Grünbergerstrasse 19, and Hans and Curt Stern of Baugasse 6.[b] As soon as possible, the widowed mothers of Hermann and Thekla Sondheimer and of Hans and Curt Stern followed their children to South Africa.

Early in 1933, Mr. Kurtz of the Hintergasse pelted my sister's right eye with a snowball packed with pebbles. As a consequence, she lost sight out of that eye for several days. Thereafter, vision from her right eye was markedly impaired. My sister departed for Geneva, Switzerland, where my father's sister, Mathilde Mühlstein, and her family had resided since 1931. My sister could not obtain a work permit in Switzerland and she eventually found employment as a mother's helper in Paris. I was sent to Felsberg, where my father's sister, Frieda Hammerschlag, lived. Although my parents were not particularly pleased with my notion of immigrating alone at age eighteen to the United States, circumstances forced them into approval of my plan. My father obtained information on the status of immigration and existing quotas from the U.S. consular branch office in Frankfurt am Main.

My father was pleased that his oldest brother, Carl Wertheim, and his wife, Irma (my father's cousin from Angenrod), had sent an affidavit from the United States in which they guaranteed that his daughter, Mathilde, the prospective immigrant, would not become a public charge. What must my father's feelings have been on June 7, 1934, when he stood at the pier in Hamburg and watched the vessel with his younger child disappear over the horizon while the German ship's band lustily played the *Horst Wessel* song. In 1934, 23,000 Jews fled from Germany.[13]

Lauterbach's boycott against its Jewish citizens, in order to oust them economically, continued to cut increasingly deeper into the lives of the congregational members. Approximately thirteen Jews left Lauterbach in 1933 and forty Jews departed in 1934. In early 1934, Julius Hess advertised in the *Lauterbacher Anzeiger* that, on account of his moving away, he was selling a vestibule wardrobe, washstand, night table, bedstead, down quilt, and other items at bargain prices.

By early 1933, Jews were forbidden the use of the municipal swimming pool and by June 1934 the public baths near Hinter dem Spittel were off limits to Jews as well. Jews were also prohibited the use of the municipal hearse. Everywhere Jews evinced utter repugnance, as if they were leprous. The Nazis designated forced sales of Jewish properties and enterprises as 'voluntary aryanization.' For example, in the *Lauterbach Anzeiger* on October 1, 1934, an announcement read that Alex Pfifferling of Bahnhofstrasse 18 had handed over his shoe store, made-to-order establishment, and shoe repair shop to Fritz Brüggeman. Doubtless under much

The ad in the *Lauterbacher Anzeiger* advertising the sale of household goods of the Hess family

---

[b] Hermann and Seppel Levi and Hermann and Thekla Sondheimer are relatives of my father by virtue of the Angenrod Levi family.

Above:

Vogel Wertheim's official permission for his daugther, Mathilde, to emigrate to the United States. It was notarized on March 2, 1934. The text reads: "I hereby permit my daughter Tilli to emigrate to America. Vogel Wertheim. March 2, 1934."

Right:

Mathilde Wertheim prior to her departure for the United States on June 7, 1934. The object at right on the ground is our wooden butter churn.

duress, Mr. Pfifferling recommended that he confidence previously extended to him be passed on to his successor. The announcement further stated that this shoe specialty shop was absolutely Christian, offering highly competitive prices and quality because of bulk purchases made in cooperation with other similar Christian stores.

In 1933, 1934, and 1935, and until his departure for the United States in 1937, my father rendered considerable financial assistance to his parents and to the family of his brother, Salli Wertheim, in Angenrod. Weekly or bi-monthly, my cousin, Walter Wertheim, the oldest of the three children of Salli and Minna Wertheim, bicycled from Angenrod to Lauterbach to collect money purportedly for the subsistence of my paternal grandparents. Undoubtedly, some of these funds were also used for temporarily juggling Salli Wertheim's debts. Berta Wertheim ungrudgingly made many personal sacrifices for her much beloved mother-in-law, but grumbled that other family members benefited from the fruits of her own hard labor in conjunction with dairy products and garden produce. My Aunt Kathinka Wertheim Leiser from Niederurff, whose family was financially comfortable, initiated a campaign among the seven Wertheim siblings that my father and his immediate family be solely responsible for their parents.

In addition, Vogel Wertheim (III) contributed very generously to the immediate support and debt service of his cousin, Hermann Levi, and his family of Angenrod. My father also furnished considerable funds toward the transportation costs of Hermann, Martha, Erich, and Sylvia Levi. Beginning in 1933 and until his departure for the United States, my father financially assisted the family of his father's sister, Michnah, who lived in or near Frankfurt am Main.

On January 25, 1935, the *Lauterbacher Anzeiger* announced that it was solely committed to German craftsmen and German businessmen. As a matter of principle, it rejected announcements of Jewish businesses. The year 1935 began with an upsurge of terror and a wave of propaganda against Jews. In early 1935, one evening a stone was thrown through our living room window at Cent 17 and landed on my father's desk.[14]

During the summer of 1935, "No Jews" signs increased outside villages, restaurants, and stores in Lauterbach and its vicinity. According to my parents, the grocer Zinn in the Obergasse, was among those that publicized such placards. But Mr. Kullmann, owner of the Kullmann pharmacy on the *Marktplatz*, refused to post this placard; he considered it incompatible with the tenets of his profession. As far as I know, he suffered no repercussions by the Nazis, perhaps because his pharmacy was the only one in town. That year the tavern, *Wachtel am Marktplatz*, where Nazis had been regular customers since before 1933, displayed the large knife that Max Stern, the local *shohet*, had used for the ritual killing of large animals. The Nazis had seized the knife and stated that it was a weapon.[15]

In 1935, 21,000 Jews left Germany.[16] In the early summer of 1935, a tax officer on a mission of harassment arrived at our home. At that moment, a young local Jewish friend, Ernst Oppenheimer, was passing under the living room window at Cent 17. My mother threw the financial record books out of the window and asked Ernst to hide them in the woodshed. The tax officers left without examining the required books and, for the moment, without further investigation.

From 1935 on, the tenor toward Jews in Germany, and particularly in Hesse, can best be described by the words of Dr. Peltret in a medical journal: "Jews are identical to parasites and on par with the tuberculosis bacteria."[17] The museum in Alsfeld exhibits a placard that states, "Drive away Jews from judgeships, being attorneys, or physicians." From my father I heard that in Fulda, Nazi gangs armed with cudgels attacked Jewish cattle dealers and their livestock on July 11, 1935. Cattle that had been securely tied were let loose. Screaming multitudes of people and bellowing panic-stricken cattle surged through the marketplace and into the adjoining streets. Thereafter, the police suspended the cattle market.

Less than a year after my departure for the United States, my father's older brother, Carl Wertheim, and his wife, Irma, also furnished an affidavit for my sister, Erna, that enabled her to obtain a visa to the United States. Vogel Wertheim (III) traveled with his Erna to Hamburg and both boarded the *S.S. Manhattan*. Suddenly, while father and daughter were saying good-bye, SA troopers appeared from nowhere and requested that my father follow them instantly off the ship on charges of suspected currency smuggling. After a tense hour for both father and daughter, Vogel Wertheim (III) returned to the *S.S. Manhattan* somewhat shaken. But with his usual equanimity, he beheld the departure of his second daughter for the United States.

By the end of 1935, the following Jewish families of Lauterbach had left for Frankfurt am Main or other cities in Germany, where they joined family members in Holland, France, Switzerland, Palestine, Brazil, and the United States: Meyer, Julia, Alfred, and Bertel Adler; Max, Jenny, Julius, and Hans Baumann; Selma and Siegfried Gottlieb; Nathan, Julius,[c] Rosi, and Theo Hess; Arthur and Fritz Jakob; Salli, Toni, and Walter Kleeberg; Alex and Auguste Pfifferling; Irma Stein; Markus and Lina Strauss;[d] Bertel and Selma Strauss; and Erna and Mathilde Wertheim.

Nazis in Lauterbach worked zealously to drive the remaining Jewish citizens out of town as expeditiously as possible, anticipating the passage of the anti-semitic Nuremberg Laws that the *Reichstag* would pass on September 15, 1935. In Lauterbach, automobiles equipped with loudspeakers went through town urging the population to "spurn Jews" and the Nazis distributed inflammatory anti-semitic pamphlets. On July 19, 1935, the *Lauterbacher Anzeiger* stated that, at the request of the municipal administration, a sign had been affixed at the town park stating that Jews were not wanted and declaring that the town thereby initiated a first step toward earmarking its recreation centers for Germans only. The newspaper also reported that

---

[c] In 1933, Julius had been jailed in Lauterbach for allegedly denouncing Hitler.
[d] Markus and Lina Strauss had been advised by Mr. Otterbein to leave.

Chapter Twenty

other regulations would follow and asserted that local residents would surely be grateful for an abode that would be free of Jews. In addition, the newspaper stated that the German people were increasingly aware that Jewish characteristics were inimical and alien to Germans.

Increasingly, the small number of Lauterbach citizens who had previously only been spectators of Jewish persecution, were clearly being influenced by the unremitting Nazi propaganda and began to join the ranks of the Nazis. To help Jews was to risk harsh punishment: incarceration, removal to a concentration camp, or the infamy of being paraded as a '*Judensau*' ('Jew-pig'). Nevertheless, Anna Euler, a peasant woman from Maar, walked in the full darkness of night from the outskirts of her village across the meadows in order to bring eggs and other food to my parents. The Moeller family from Angersbach and the family of Heinrich Wahl (IV) (his village name was Eckemüller) from Angersbach also secretly supplied my parents with eggs and other edibles and in the process exposing themselves to considerable danger.

Anna Euler (center) of Maar, an altruistic individual who provided my parents with edibles

In 1935, non-Jewish female household help was forbidden to work in Jewish homes. This edict created a particular hardship for my parents because a Lauterbach ordinance further directed that all cultivable land must be utilized to the fullest extent lest the land be confiscated. It was beyond the bounds of possibility for my parents to cultivate and gather in fruits, vegetables, and hay on our large acreage without outside help.

FALSE CHARGES
AGAINST VOGEL
WERTHEIM (III)

A REVIEW OF THE ACQUISITION OF CENT 17 is of utmost importance for fully comprehending the episode of my father's court case in Lauterbach and his subsequent courageous appeal to the higher court in Giessen. In 1900, my Great-Uncle Samuel Strauss (I) bought Cent 17, including the dwelling with the adjacent buildings, *curtilage*, and land (four *Morgen*)ᶜ from Mr. Sommerlad, the local tax commissioner at that time. The tax offices, amazingly, took in only one floor (seven rooms) of Cent 17. There was no comparable property in the Lauterbach area with laid-out gardens, hardwood trees, several huge oaks, a mighty linden tree, two giant sycamores, and a towering read beech as well as fruit orchards with apples, pears, plums, cherries, many varieties of gooseberries, raspberries, and currants.

ᶜ Four *Morgen* are one hectare, a metric unit of land measure equal to 10,000 square meters or 100 *ares* (2.47 acres).

Cent 17 from the north
circa 1930

In the 1890s, the Riedesel obstructed Mr. Sommerlad's panoramic view by adding a malt house to their brewery. This so vexed Mr. Sommerlad that he vowed to sell his property to a Jew in order to rankle the Riedesel. On March 13, 1913, Samuel Strauss (I) transferred Cent 17 to my parents, Vogel Wertheim (III) and his wife, Berta Lamm Wertheim. It is important to point out that even after the termination of the German monarchy in November 1918, the Riedesel possessed the gold and the clout to make the rules in Lauterbach and its environs.

Moreover, after World War I, there was an acute housing shortage in Lauterbach and the Riedesel were landlords for many families who lived in the immediate vicinity of Cent 17.[f] During the 1920s and in the early 1930s, the Barons of Riedesel were uncomfortable about the proximity of the Jewish enclave at Cent 17 and they undoubtedly urged their already anti-semitic employees to take the lead in actions against the Wertheim family. Soon after January 30, 1933, for example, the family of the brewery manager, Mr. Obermayer (whose wife was the sister of Miss Friess, the Wertheim sisters' inept piano teacher), who had previously enjoyed considerable gifts of fruits from our gardens, ceased to greet us and spat when catching sight of a member of our family. Other brewery workers exceeded the example of the Obermayer family to gain favors and privileges from their employer.

On a Friday afternoon in July of 1935, my thirteen-year-old cousin, Meinhard Hammerschlag, was visiting from Felsberg, while Mr. Schuessler from Maar, who frequently assisted my father with work in the stable, was helping to expedite the transport of cattle. In front of Cent 17, a young calf jumped off a small wagon and was promptly retrieved by Meinhard while the openly anti-semitic brothers Böcher and other Riesedel-owned brewery employees stood by and watched. Because of this incident, the Lauterbach court found my father guilty of cruelty to animals, and sentenced him to a prison term of one year and the cost of the court proceedings. The counsel for the defense (certainly non-Jewish) was from Alsfeld, and he advocated a verdict of not guilty and assumption of court costs.

According to an article in the *Lauterbacher Anzeiger* of September 10, 1935, entitled "Hands off the Jew," the judge maintained that my father was nevertheless

---

[f] For example, the Horn family (whose daughters were Hanna and Marta) of the Gartenstrasse was beholden to the Riedesel for an apartment and a restaurant, which was housed in the building adjoining the Riedesel residence in the Burg). Similarly, the Scharmann family occupied an apartment nearby in the Riedesel-owned *Felsenkeller*. The granddaughter of the Scharmann family is Mrs. Falk, today's first lady of Lauterbach. In the 1920s, her grandmother, who was the mother of three daughters and one son, assisted in turning the ground in spring and autumn at Cent 17. In the early 1930s, Hans Scharmann and the Horn family were militant Nazis who became vicious anti-semites.

Chapter Twenty

Tierquälern zur Warnung.

Jüdischer Viehhändler vor dem Amtsgericht Lauterbach. — Gefängnisstrafe wegen Vergehens gegen das Tierschutzgesetz. — Hände weg vom Juden!

△ Lauterbach, 10. September. Das tägliche Leben bringt uns immer wieder Beispiele, wie das Verhalten des Juden auf allen Gebieten unserer Art, unserem sittlichen und damit auch unserem Rechtsempfinden zuwiderläuft. Am besten gewährt uns in das Leben und Treiben des Juden die Stunde Einblick, in der er, auf rechtswidrigen Wegen ertappt, vor die Schranken des Gerichts treten muß, wo der deutsche Richter den Tatbestand beleuchtet. Darum verdienen solche Verhandlungen auch des heimischen Gerichts Beachtung, um so mehr, als sie für den deutschen Volksgenossen wertvolle und ernste Lehren mit sich bringen.

Wir berichteten schon gestern kurz über die Verurteilung des Lauterbacher Juden Vogel Wertheim wegen Vergehens gegen das Tierschutzgesetz. Der gestrigen Verhandlung vor dem Amtsgericht Lauterbach lag folgender Tatbestand zugrunde: An einem Julitag dieses Jahres war der Angeklagte im Begriff, Vieh zur Bahn zu schaffen. Bei dem Transport befand sich auch ein kleiner Wagen, der mit drei Kälbern beladen war und von einem 13jährigen Jungen aus der Hausgemeinschaft des Juden beaufsichtigt wurde. Beim Abfahren von dem jüdischen Gehöft an der Cent ereignete es sich, daß eins der Kälber unruhig wurde und aus dem für drei Tiere reichlich engen, 60 cm breiten Wagen, der eine nur 40 cm hohe und zudem geneigte Umgatterung hatte, herauszuspringen versuchte. Das am Kopf am Wagen angebundene Tier blieb dabei natürlich an dem Strick freischwebend unter Qualen hängen, wurde wieder auf den Wagen geworfen, worauf sich das gleiche nochmals abspielte. Der Vorgang war von einer Reihe Zeugen beobachtet worden, die in der gestrigen Verhandlung fast durchweg übereinstimmend in obigem Sinne aussagten.

Der Vertreter der Staatsanwaltschaft führte aus, daß der Tatbestand des Tierschutzgesetzes erfüllt und erwiesen sei, daß das Tier roh mißhandelt worden ist, da diesem erhebliche Schmerzen verursacht wurden. Wenn auch als unmittelbarer Täter ein Jugendlicher gelten müsse, so sei doch der verantwortliche W. als eigentlicher, wenn auch mittelbarer Täter anzusehen. Ihm sei nach dem Ergebnis der Hauptverhandlung ein vorsätzliches Handeln nachzuweisen. Denn der Angeklagte habe es unterlassen, den Jugendlichen von der Zuwiderhandlung gegen die Gesetzesbestimmungen abzuhalten; seine Pflicht wäre es gewesen, als Viehhändler besser aufzupassen und für sorgfältige Verladung der Tiere zu sorgen. Der Strafantrag des Anklage-Vertreters stützte sich auf § 9 des Tierschutzgesetzes vom 24. 11. 1933. Er lautete wegen Vergehens gemäß Absatz 1 auf eine in ihrer Höhe dem Gericht zu überlassende Gefängnisstrafe; falls nur Uebertretung gemäß Abs. 3 Ziff. 1, 4 in Frage komme, beantrage er dann aber die Höchststrafe von sechs Wochen Haft sowie Auferlegung der Verfahrenskosten.

Der Alsfelder Verteidiger hingegen beantragte Freispruch für den Angeklagten und Uebernahme der Kosten des Verfahrens auf die Staatskasse. Er meinte, es habe sich um einen Zufall gehandelt und um kein böswilliges Verhalten des Angeklagten. — Daß indessen Tierquälerei, gleichgültig, ob vorsätzlich oder durch Nachlässigkeit gegeben, eine so milde Beurteilung nicht erfahren kann, zeigte der Urteilsspruch des Vorsitzenden und dessen Begründung.

Das Urteil gegen den Angeklagten Vogel Wertheim lautete, wie gemeldet, wegen Vergehens gegen § 1 und § 9 Abs. 1 des Tierschutzgesetzes auf eine Gefängnisstrafe von einem Jahr und auf Auferlegung der Kosten des Verfahrens.

In seiner Urteilsbegründung stellte der Richter zunächst fest, daß das Grundsätzliche der einschlägigen Strafbestimmungen, wonach ein Tier nicht unnötig zu quälen ist und ihm keine Schmerzen zu verursachen sind, gegeben sei. Er schilderte nochmals den Vorgang und betonte, daß der Angeklagte als Viehhändler die Schuld für den Viehtransport auf ungeeignetem Wagen nicht abschieben könne. Entsprechend der Rasseeigenart des Juden, der nach der Anschauung handelt: „Es ist ja nur ein Stück Vieh", müsse solche Roheit bestraft werden. Wir dürfen, so erklärte er mit Nachdruck, nicht dulden, daß dies weiterhin bei uns so geübt wird. Nicht nur das Tier, sondern auch das sittliche Empfinden der Nation müsse geschützt werden. Daher sei eine exemplarische Strafe hier am Platze.

*

Das ergangene Urteil sollte Lehre und Warnung zugleich sein. Die Ausschaltung des Juden aus dem Viehhandel ist nicht nur Notwendigkeit für saubere und reelle Gestaltung dieses Handels; sie ist auch, wie dieser Fall grausamer Tierquälerei beweist, vom Standpunkt sittlicher Betrachtung aus erforderlich. Denn dem Juden fehlt entsprechend seiner Rasseeigenschaft das Empfinden für die Kreatur; seine materialistische Einstellung ist einzig und allein auf möglichst hohen Profit gerichtet und fragt nicht nach den rücksichtslosesten Mitteln, die in den Dienst dieses „Handels" gestellt werden!

Wir sind aber offen genug, zu erklären, daß die Warnung vor Tierquälerei auch manchen deutschen Volksgenossen angeht. Das stete Umgehen mit lebenden Tieren auf handelsmäßige Art mag manchen in die Gefahr bringen, schlechter Gewohnheit zum Opfer zu fallen und mit den Strafbestimmungen des Tierschutzgesetzes in Konflikt zu kommen. Es kommt leider oft genug vor, daß namentlich zum Schlachten bestimmte Tiere roh behandelt werden. In bekannt werdenden Fällen wird auch hier die Polizei und gegebenenfalls das den Tierschutzgedanken achtende Publikum einschreiten und Bestrafung der Schuldigen veranlassen. Besonders muß bei dieser Gelegenheit einmal gesagt werden, daß die Beförderungsmittel für Vieh oft ganz ungeeigneter Art sind und das Fahren für die Tiere beispielsweise in nicht richtig geschlossenen, anstatt kastenartigen, womöglich überladenen Wagen zur Qual werden muß. — Das Kapitel Tierschutz ist damit nicht begrenzt. Verständnis und Empfinden für das Tier, wie es gerade im deutschen Menschen wesensbestimmt wurzelt, sollte nicht durch des Lebens oft harte Notwendigkeiten erstickt werden. Und wo das Töten erforderlich ist, sollte nicht nur auf das Tier selbst, sondern auch besonders auf junge Menschenseelen Bedacht genommen werden. Warum manchmal allzu unverhüllt all das zur Schau bieten oder gar Kinder beteiligen? So sollte es eigentlich nicht vorkommen und muß verurteilt werden, daß, wie dieser Tage aus einem Dorf des Schlitzerlandes berichtet wurde, ausgerechnet die Schuljugend einen „Spatzenkrieg" führen und Hunderte von Vögeln und Eiern vernichten muß!

Headlines from the September 10, 1935 *Lauterbacher Anzieger* which read: "A Warning to Those Who Torture Animals," describing court proceedings against the 'Jew Wertheim.'

Berufungsverhandlung gegen den Juden Wertheim in Gießen.

Vier Wochen Haft wegen fahrlässiger Tierquälerei für den jüdischen Lauterbacher Viehhändler

(Eigenbericht.)

Die Kleine Strafkammer Gießen verurteilte gestern in der Berufungsverhandlung den Lauterbacher jüdischen Viehhändler Vogel Wertheim unter Aufhebung des am 9. September vom Amtsgericht in Lauterbach ergangenen, auf ein Jahr Gefängnis lautenden Urteils wegen fahrlässiger Tierquälerei zu vier Wochen Haft und zur Tragung der Kosten des Verfahrens.

In der Berufungs-Verhandlung ergab sich auf Grund der Zeugenaussagen über den Tatbestand im wesentlichen das gleiche Bild wie in der Lauterbacher Hauptverhandlung. Wir berichteten seinerzeit eingehend darüber, wie bei einem Viehtransport, den Wertheim im Juli d. J. über die Umgehungsstraße nach dem Nordbahnhof vornehmen wollte, bei seinem Gehöft an der Cent aus einem hinter dem Großvieh von einem Neffen des Angeklagten gefahrenen „Lauterbacher Wägelchen" ein Kalb mehrmals übersprang und sich an dem Befestigungsstrick aufhängte. Einige aus der Brauerei kommende Herren wurden ebenso wie einige Insassen eines vorfahrenden Kraftwagens Zeugen dieser, wie sie betonten, empörenden Tierquälerei und veranlaßten Abhilfe.

Nach Schluß der Beweisaufnahme hob der Vertreter der Staatsanwaltschaft in seinen Ausführungen hervor, daß der Sachverhalt im wesentlichen geklärt sei. Entscheidend sei nun die Frage, ob durch diese Feststellungen ein vorsätzliches Handeln erwiesen sei oder ob fahrlässige Tierquälerei vorliege. Eine Vorsätzlichkeit sei nicht erwiesen, jedoch stelle ein Sprossenwagen der verwendeten Art keine genügende Sicherheit für einen Viehtransport dar. Das zweimalige Herabstürzen des Kalbes vom Wagen beweise, daß der Transport von dem Angeklagten nicht mit der genügenden Vorsicht vorgenommen wurde. Er habe sich vorher nicht davon überzeugt, ob der von einem Kind gelenkte Wagen ordnungsmäßig geladen war, habe also erwiesenermaßen grob fahrlässig gehandelt. Der Vertreter der Staatsanwaltschaft beantragte unter Zugrundelegung der einschlägigen Paragraphen des Reichstierschutzgesetzes gegen Wertheim wegen fahrlässiger Tierquälerei 4 Wochen Haft.

Diesem Antrag schloß sich dann auch das Gericht im Gegensatz zu der Auffassung des Verteidigers, der eine Geldstrafe gegen Wertheim für ausreichend hielt, an und fällte das oben bekanntgegebene Urteil. In der Urteilsbegründung wurde hervorgehoben, daß, auch wenn es sich nicht um vorsätzliche Tierquälerei handele, eine exemplarische Strafe Platz greifen müsse; daher sei eine Geldstrafe gegen Wertheim nicht ausreichend.

The appeal transaction against the 'Jew Wertheim' in Giessen

responsible for the transport of his animals, even in his absence. The judge remarked that the verdict was to serve as an example. As a result of this incident, my father endured feelings of much humiliation and shame, especially since one of his principle tenets of Judaism was the traditional crown of a good name.

Notwithstanding, my father dared to challenge the local verdict in Giessen, a town that in the 1920s and early 1930s was a stronghold of anti-semitism. During the preparation for his court appearance in Giessen, my father received much moral support from the court inspector, Mr. Kanngieser.[g] Vogel Wertheim (III) frequently praised Mr. Kanngieser's integrity and rectitude and intended to reward Mr. Kanngieser when settling his affairs after the war in Germany. Furthermore, my father intended to bring to justice the Böcher brothers, whom he accused of committing perjury.[h] Unfortunately, Vogel Wertheim (III) died before he was able to carry out these missions. By the time I ascertained the address of Mr. Kanngieser's daughter, Elly Wöhrm, she had already died in Darmstadt on September 4, 1992.

According to the *Lauterbacher Anzeiger*, the small criminal division in Giessen overturned the judgment rendered in Lauterbach and instead imposed on my father only the cost of the court proceedings and a four-week probation period. He was allowed to carry out the latter by appearing daily at the Lauterbach court. The

[g] In 1922, Mr. Kanngieser had been a candidate for mayor in Lauterbach.
[h] Karl Böcher did not return from World War II.

Chapter Twenty

Lauterbach court records of August 16, 1935, indicate that my father's offense was an infraction of the Reich's law to protect animals. Ironically, my father's love for and mastery of animals was much touted. On December 18, 1989, Eva Haberkorn of the *Hessiche Staatsarchiv* in Darmstadt stated that the Giessen court records prior to 1945 were no longer available.

THE WERTHEIMS LEAVE LAUTERBACH

AFTER THE COURT EPISODE, MY PARENTS felt compelled to conclude their affairs in Lauterbach as soon as possible. They were forced to expedite the disposal of their messuage, the equipment from the stables, and the contents of the residence (including antique furniture, valuable books, old-world furnishings, and household appointments from two kitchens, two dining rooms, two living rooms, and six bedrooms). Samuel Strauss' *Last Will and Testament* had designated Erna and Mathilde Wertheim the sole heirs of his antiques, furniture, household furnishings, and personal belongings.

Beginning in 1933, it became increasingly disadvantageous in Lauterbach for a Jew to sell real estate, goods, and furniture. Not only was there a large surplus of property put up for sale by Jews, but there was also a meager demand by non-Jewish buyers in a severely depressed local economy. Moreover, by September of 1935, the Nuremberg Laws were promulgated which, aside from other provisos, deprived German Jews of civic rights. In this environment and setting, my parents were compelled to sell their *messuage* to the only available buyer, the local Riedesel, for the sorry sum of thirty thousand *Mark*. My parents were also forced to give

Berta Lamm Wertheim and Vogel (Frederick) Wertheim (III) at Cent 17 in front of the stables in 1935

away or dispose of the furnishings of Cent 17 for a price far below cost or market value. On July 27, 1988, the ninety-eight-year-old Dorothee Tag (née Stausebach from the Entenberg in Lauterbach), whose husband was a close friend of Mr. Sommerlad, repeatedly spoke highly of the former residents of Cent 17 and their choice household appointments.

It came about that the sister of the Böcher brothers and her husband built a home on one parcel of land with frontage on the Ludwig Jahnstrasse that had belonged to Cent 17 prior to the sale. During my visit to Lauterbach in 1959, the then current owner, who was a member of the Böcher family (probably a brother-in-law), anxiously followed me all over town in order to find out how soon my mother would return to Lauterbach. It appeared that he feared retaliation, possible dispossession of his home, or payments for use of our property.

Unfortunately, after my father's death in 1953, my mother was not successful in coping with the complicated monetary compensation directives of the so-called reparation (*Wiedergutmachung*) procedures. Germany's distaste for compensating its former Jewish citizens for deprivation of civil rights

Vogel (Frederick) Werthem (III) leaving the Friedberger Anlage synagogue in Frankfurt am Main in 1936. He holds a *lulav* in his left hand, stepping into the street while looking over his left shoulder.

and monetary losses was evident through the numerous directives and statutes that were seemingly devised to impede reparation payments altogether.

My parents did not tell my sister and me of our father's episode at a Nazi court until after the judiciary in Giessen passed a more favorable verdict. In 1936, my parents moved to Hans Handwerkstrasse 39 in Frankfurt am Main to get away from the oppressive atmosphere in Lauterbach, where their neighbors alternated between waging open war against them and employing more subtle means to drive them away. In Frankfurt, my parents took up residence in an apartment house within walking distance of an orthodox synagogue and near the homes of Jewish friends and relatives.

In 1936, 25,000 Jews left Germany.[18] In the United States in 1936, we immediately undertook to forward the necessary affidavits for my parents' admittance under the quota system. An affidavit by my father's brother, Carl, and his wife, Irma, (both United States citizens), statements of gainful employment of the daughters, and bank statements persuaded the consular authorities in Stuttgart to grant immigration visas to my parents. Starting in 1937, there was an easing in entry requirements into the United States. Decisions regarding the granting of visas rested with the American consuls in Germany, who carried out orders from the State Department in Washington.

In early 1935, the Nazis had implemented strict laws that prohibited Jews from transferring their funds from Germany to another country. Therefore, my parents were obliged to invest cash derived from the sale of their *messuage*, securities, household furnishings, and my father's business into German-made consumer products, which they could take with them to the United States. These items included Leika cameras and binoculars. In addition, there were house furnishings, linens, and flatware for establishing three new households (for my parents and their daughters). Regrettably, Uncle Carl determined that furnishings of Cent 17 were unsuitable for America. In Frankfurt am Main, my parents had all of their effects packed into a massive wooden container called

Chapter Twenty

a '*Lift*,' which was shipped to Hamburg, and loaded for shipment by sea to New York.

On June 26, 1937, the *Lauterbacher Anzeiger* published a notice stating that the firm of Vogel Wertheim (III) was legally dissolved by order of the district court. On July 16, 1937, the Buchenwald concentration camp was opened only several miles from Weimar, one of Germany's most noted centers of culture. During *Kristallnacht*, most of the Jewish men from Upper Hesse, including those who had already moved to Frankfurt am Main, were sent to Buchenwald. One cannot fathom the measure of human depravity inflicted there on Jewish and other victims. Mercifully, my father was spared that disaster. However, his brother, Salli Wertheim, was taken to Buchenwald on November 9, 1938.

My parents were ordered to fill out a booklet designated "German Unity Family Documents." Although no mention was made of religion in these documents, the blank space designated for the date of baptism disclosed Jewish identity. My parents' wedding certificate and their daughters' birth certificates were entered in Lauterbach on February 2, 1937; my father's birth certificate was recorded in Angenrod on July 27, 1937; and my mother's birth certificate was registered in Kirtorf on July 23, 1937. All documents carried the Nazi seal and had to be obtained in person. This measure was intended to generate an accurate head count of Jews and to inconvenience and humiliate them.

On February 2, 1937, my parents returned for a few grievous hours for what would be their last visit to Lauterbach. They prudently avoided any main streets on their way to the Jewish cemetery (at) am Kalkofen. Here my mother's grandmother, Biena Reiss Strauss, who died in 1900, was laid to rest. Nearby were the three graves of her oldest son, Salomon Strauss (I), who died in 1923, his wife, Jettchen Schloss Strauss, who died in 1924, and their son, Salli Strauss(I), who died in 1930. My parents also paid their respects to my mother's relative, Hannchen Sonneborn Katz, her husband, Joel Katz, and their much-lamented daughter, my mother's friend, Cilly Katz, who passed on in 1910 of tuberculosis while in her early twenties.

Leave-taking from Johanna (Hannchen) Schloss Strauss, who had died in 1921, and from Samuel Strauss (I), who died in 1924, was the most heart-rending. The pain was all the more torturous because my parents had witnessed firsthand the destruction by Nazi forces of Samuel Strauss' untiring work, his aspiration for Jewish education of the young, financial sacrifices, his funding of the the Jewish cemetery at Am Kalkofen, and toil on behalf of the Lauterbach Jewish community. Although at that time the synagogue building still stood, its spiritual leader, Max Stern, was compelled to move to Frankfurt. By then, every local young Jew had fled to a large city in Germany or gone abroad wherever refuge could be found. Lauterbach Jews who were too old, sick, or poor to find a hiding place were ordered by Nazis to move into the synagogue building, which would later facilitate the roundup of Jews.

My parents cast a last brief glimpse at their *messuage*, where Else Reuel Glebe and Paula Pfeffer Ebel now lived as wives of brewery employees. Both Paula and

Else came from large families where there was frequently nothing to eat for the children and no money with which to buy food. In that rather persistent happenstance, the parents would counsel their children to ask for food at the Wertheim house. My generous parents fed the hungry children and sent them off with aliments for the rest of the family. In Lauterbach, it was Nazi rule of action to fill houses ignominiously vacated by Jews with a segment of the population that had previously never imagined occupying such quarters. All of a sudden, therefore, Paula and Else changed from begging for food at Cent 17 to occupants who would harvest the fruits of the former Wertheim manor house.

During 1937, 23,000 Jews fled from Germany. The 130,000 German Jews who immigrated from 1933 to 1938 were relatively affluent. Despite all the losses related to the forced liquidation of their households and real estate these Jews were able to salvage enough money to afford the substantial transportation charges for their family to another country.[19] In October of 1937, my parents arrived in New York, carrying the burden of the ceaseless pain and humiliation they had withstood since 1933. Nevertheless, they rejoiced to be with their children.

Endnotes

1. *Lauterbacher Anzeiger*, December 1924.

2. Dr. Karl Siegmar Baron von Galera, *Lauterbach in Hessen, III* (Neustadt an der Aisch: Verlag Degener and Company, 1965), pp. 377-378.

3. Ibid, p. 378.

4. Ibid.

5. Friedrich Schwarz and Karl Maurer, *Herausgeber Fotoclub Lauterbach, e.V 1990*, p. 74.

6. von Galera, *Lauterbach in Hessen, III*, pp. 378-379.

7. *Lauterbacher Anzeiger*, June and July 1931.

8. *Die Stadtkirche zu Lauterbach*, (Lauterbach Lutheran Church, 1981), p. 27.

9. Interview with Irmgard Höll Enders on July 29, 1987, in Lauterbach.

10. von Galera, *Lauterbach in Hessen, III*, p. 386.

11. Thomas W. Lummitsch, *Jüdisches Leben in Gedern* (Schotten: Gerhard W. Wenzel, August 1991), pp. 171-172.

12. Ibid, p. 170.

13. Leo Sievers, *Juden in Deutschland* (Hamburg: Verlag Gruner, 1977), p. 258.

14. Interview with Erna Wertheim Marx in Atlanta, Georgia, on November 6, 1992.

15. Interview with Dr. Napthali Stern in Atlanta, Georgia, on February 22, 1992.

16. Sievers, *Juden in Deutschland* (Hamburg: Verlag Gruner, 1977), p. 258.

17. Ibid.

18. Sievers, *Juden in Deutschland,* p. 258.

19. Ibid, pp. 258-259.

Unsere Geduld ist erschöpft.

Dr. Goebbels zum Pariser Attentat und seinen Folgen.

Reichsminister Dr. Goebbels nimmt unter der Ueberschrift „Der Fall Grünspan" in einem Artikel im „Völkischen Beobachter" zu dem jüdischen Mord an dem deutschen Diplomaten Stellung. Der Minister beschäftigt sich zunächst mit dem gemeinen Attentat in Paris und den Hintermännern und betont unter Hinweis auf den Ausbruch der Empörung in der Nacht vom 9. zum 10. November, daß die Geduld des deutschen Volkes nunmehr erschöpft ist. Dr. Goebbels gibt dem deutschfeindlichen Ausland, das die Vorgänge übertreibt und entstellt, den Rat, das Judenproblem und seine Lösung den Deutschen selbst zu überlassen. Die deutsche Regierung wird legal auf das Attentat des Judentums antworten.

In dem Artikel geht Dr. Goebbels von den Vorgängen am 7. November, als der 17jährige polnische Judenjunge in die Deutsche Botschaft in Paris eindrang und auf Ernst vom Rath mehrere Schüsse abgab, aus und zieht die Parallele zum Fall Gustloff. Der Minister stellt dann die Frage:

Wo sind die Hintermänner zu suchen?

und fährt fort: Seit Wochen und Monaten wird in den großen jüdischen Weltblättern gegen Deutschland als Nation zum Kriege und gegen einzelne prominente Vertreter des nationalsozialistischen Deutschlands zum Morde gehetzt. Besonders hervorgetan haben sich dabei die Juden Georg Bernhard und Emil Ludwig Cohn. In diesen Kreisen sind deshalb auch zweifellos die geistigen Inspiratoren des Attentats zu suchen. Es sind dieselben Kreise, die jetzt für den Mörder in der ganzen Welt eine nie dagewesene Stimmungspropaganda entfalten.

Die Gründe für den Mord liegen auf der Hand. Das Weltjudentum hat nach der fieberhaften Kriegshetze in den Sommermonaten dieses Jahres eine furchtbare Schlappe erlitten. Das Abkommen von München brachte seinen Vernichtungsplan gegen Deutschland zum Scheitern. Es hatte die Hoffnung gehegt, durch einen durch infame Hetze hervorgerufenen Weltkrieg Deutschland in die Knie zwingen und das verhaßte Naziregime zum Sturz bringen zu können. Nachdem in München dieser Plan zum Scheitern gebracht worden ist, wollten sie nun durch eine drastische und frivole Aktion die Friedensbemühungen zwischen den Großmächten Europas aufhalten und eine neue Hetze gegen Deutschland in Szene setzen.

Der Mord an dem Legationssekretär vom Rath sollte ein Fanal sein für das gesamte Judentum im Kampf gegen Deutschland. Der Mörder selbst hat gestanden, daß er damit ein Warnungssignal habe geben wollen. Allerdings ist dieser Schuß nach hinten losgegangen. Gewarnt worden ist weniger die Welt als das deutsche Volk.

Eruptiver Ausbruch der Empörung

Es liegt auf der Hand, daß eine Nation von 80 Millionen auf die Dauer derartige Provokationen nicht stillschweigend und wehrlos hinnehmen wird. Nach der Ermordung Gustloffs hat das deutsche Volk geschwiegen.

Nach dem Tode des Gesandtschaftsrats vom Rath ist es ganz spontan zu Vergeltungsaktionen gegen die Juden in Deutschland geschritten. Der eruptive Ausbruch der Empörung der Bevölkerung in der Nacht vom 9. zum 10. November ist daraus zu erklären und zeigt nur, daß die Geduld des deutschen Volkes nunmehr restlos erschöpft ist.

Wie aber reagiert nun die deutschfeindliche, zum großen Teil jüdische Auslandspresse auf die spontanen Folgen der Schüsse in Paris, die sich in Deutschland ergeben? Man versucht in diesem Teil der Auslandspresse, den Eindruck zu erwecken, als herrsche in Deutschland so eine Art von Bürgerkrieg. Greuelmärchen ohne Zahl werden erfunden, kolportiert und an den Mann gebracht. Man erklärt, die spontanen Reaktionen des deutschen Volkes seien durch „organisierte Mannschaften" durchgeführt worden. Wie wenig Ahnung doch diese Zeitenschinder von Deutschland haben! Wie erst hätten diese Reaktionen ausgesehen, wären sie organisiert gewesen!

Nirgendwo Plünderungen

Eines der hervorstechendsten Merkmale der in den vergangenen Tagen stattgefundenen Aktionen gegen das Judentum ist die Tatsache, daß es zwar zu Demolierungen, aber nirgendwo zu Plünderungen gekommen ist. Das benutzt natürlich diese deutschfeindliche Auslandspresse, um zu behaupten, daß es sich um rein kriminelle Vorgänge handele. Vor allem die jüdische Presse in Nordamerika tut sich in einer nie dagewesenen Hetze unrühmlich hervor, erinnert an das barbarische Mittelalter und erklärt, daß Berlin das Schauspiel des Bürgerkrieges biete. Es versteht sich am Rande, daß die gegen die Juden einschreitende Bevölkerung als „Nazimob" und „Gangsterbanden" bezeichnet wird. Leider aber passiert diesen Zeitungen das Mißgeschick, daß sie sich, wie immer in solchen Fällen, nicht vorher hinreichend verständigt haben und damit in offenbare Widersprüche verstricken. Ein Sammelsurium von Lügen, Verdächtigungen, Entstellungen und Verdrehungen.

Bewährte Disziplin

Wir stehen auf dem Standpunkt, daß die Reaktion des deutschen Volkes auf den feigen Meuchelmord in Paris eben durch die ruchlose Gemeinheit dieser Tat erklärt werden muß. Sie wurde weder organisiert noch vorbereitet, sie brach spontan aus der Nation heraus. Die Nation folgte dabei dem gesunden Instinkt, der ihr sagte, daß nun zum zweiten Male ein Vertreter Deutschlands im Auslande von einem Judenjungen niedergeknallt wurde, und daß, wenn man auch diese Untat schweigend und ohne Reaktion hinnehmen würde, deutsche diplomatische Vertreter in Zukunft im Auslande als vogelfrei zu gelten hätten.

Die deutsche Staatsführung hat nichts unversucht gelassen, die Reaktion im deutschen Volke auf das feige Attentat in kürzester Frist abzustellen. Das deutsche Volk hat dem Gebot der Regierung willig und diszipliniert

(Fortsetzung auf Seite 2)

Lauterbacher Anzeiger, November 12, 1938
The Nazi version (Dr. Goebbel's) of the events relating to *Kristallnacht*.
The headline reads: "Our Patience is at an End."

*T*he official Nazi edict of 'Aryanization' of Jewish-owned retail businesses was effective as of November 12, 1938. However, Lauterbach preceded this statute by four years when the Jewish firm of Pfifferling, among others, was forcibly transferred to the Fritz Brüggeman on October 1, 1934. According to the *Lauterbacher Anzeiger*, the firms of Vogel Wertheim (III) and Sigmund Strauss were dissolved as of June 26, 1937, and November 27, 1937, respectively. Both transactions took place well in advance of the official Nazi enactment of the law. Throughout Hesse,

beginning on January 30, 1933, the SA began to extort from Jewish merchants and cattle dealers statements which frequently compelled them to cancel in writing amounts owed by Germans to Jewish debtors.[1]

In January 1935, a German schoolgirl wrote: "Jews, like the rest of us are God's creatures, so they must be respected. But vermin are also animals, yet we still exterminate them." This letter was printed in the Nazi magazine *Der Stürmer*.[2] During formal instruction and so-called learning in the Lauterbach and Alsfeld schools in the period from

Announcement in the *Lauterbacher Anzeiger* on January 25, 1935 regarding the dissolution of the Pfifferling family business and its subsequent forced sale to Fritz Brüggemann

1921 to 1933, teachers and students habitually equated Jews with 'vermin' and 'parasites.' Jews in Germany, and particularly in Hesse, where Jews had always been sorely tried, could hardly fathom that the stripping of rights could still be escalated.

By 1936, all Jewish children were expelled from public and high schools in Lauterbach, although official Nazi forbiddance of attendance was duly authorized only as of November 15, 1938. In this instance, the high school in Alsfeld even surpassed anti-semitic measures. Early in 1933, Jewish students in the Alsfeld high school were either expelled outright or subjected to continual harassment by most teachers and classmates, making school attendance a ceaselessly painful ordeal. For those reasons, the high school in Alsfeld was quickly transformed into a '*judenrein*' ('Jew free') system by the end of 1933.

On August 4, 1936, the *Lauterbacher Anzeiger* depicted a snapshot of a Theodor Günther moving van captioned as follows:

> It steers our thoughts that in our day of significant
> radical changes all that matters should be returned
> to its inmost substance: we Germans must proceed in
> our anti-semitic path and give expression that solely
> German spirit should determine our course. For that
> reason those who came here as foreign guests no
> longer feel at home in this place. They are at lib-
> erty to go where they may feel more in their proper

element. As we see on the photo, the shipment of the
furniture crate will be looked after properly and
without delay. This load will proceed to Haifa, Palestine. The cargo is loaded in a simple, strong box
which saves excessive transportation costs while serving the purpose. We are not at all averse to these
transports if only on account of the employment pos-
sibilities in the shipping industry.

On October 25, 1936, Hitler and Mussolini concluded the Rome-Berlin Axis and on November 25, 1936, Germany and Japan signed a military pact. That same year, Hitler re-militarized the Rhineland. Although German Jews for the most part were increasingly deprived of civil rights by 1936, the Nazi government tended to permit continuance of Jewish firms in the export businesses. A sudden liquidation of all Jewish firms would have had catastrophic repercussions on the domestic economy and the labor market, as well as on the mortgage and real estate businesses.[3] None of these phenomena was a significant factor in Lauterbach. In 1931, the Hessian Felt Industry of Katz and Strauss of the Rockelsgasse, which employed local workers, had already moved to Luckenwalde near Berlin. The Aron Stein firm at Eisenbacher Tor, which also employed local workers, was absorbed by the competitive firm of H. Luft, then of the Steinweg, for the insignificant sum of 3,800 *Reichsmark*.[4]

Announcement in the *Lauterbacher Anzeiger* regarding the dissolution of the firm of Aron Stein

On August 30, 1938, the *Lauterbacher Anzeiger* reported that the firm of Aron Stein had ceased to exist.

During 1936, the economic situation of the Jews deteriorated. As the negative consequences of the worldwide depression were generally being overcome, the Nazi government pushed forward with the Four-Year Plan that promoted the quick conversion to an armament-based war economy. Economic dependency on Jewish firms no longer existed in view of almost full employment. Therefore, pressure to liquidate Jewish firms increased considerably in 1937 and 1938.

The following account appeared in the *Lauterbacher Anzeiger* during the summer of 1937:

Constantly more Jews emigrate. Even in our town that
was rather richly blessed with Jews (in 1933 Lauterbach
had a population of 5000 and the approximately 150
Jews amounted to 3.2 percent, migration is strongly
noticeable. Numerous Jewish families have moved--
some relocated in larger cities of our country and
others proceeded abroad. Of late a double transport
left for America where two local Jewish families
intend to settle. We do not grieve that these foreign
guests no longer care to be here. Perhaps quicker
than one envisages the day may come when the synagogue will have terminated its purpose.

On April 14, 1934, the widow of Salli Strauss [I] (my mother's cousin), Martha Strauss, and the Strauss children, Siegfried (III) and Blanka, moved from Lauterbach (on) Am Eselswörth 6 to Sturmiusstrasse 5 in Fulda. The late Salli's sister, Mathilde, and her husband, Juda Wahlhaus, also relocated to Fulda, where they sought refuge from the ceaseless and cruel torment in their town of Gersfeld, a Nazi hotbed in the Rhön. Since 1933, Gersfeld had proudly named itself an 'Adolf Hitler town,' like Zierenberg near Kassel.

In 1937, the authorities in charge of the Fulda phone book published a separate edition for Jews only, as if it were an unwarranted expectation for Christians to be listed in the same book as Jews.[6] It is interesting that in Fulda, which is primarily a Catholic community, the term 'Christian' was more persuasive than the term 'Aryan.' 'Aryan' was more effective in Lauterbach, essentially a Lutheran town, where racial postulates rather than religious ones proved more convincing to the populace. In 1966, the Jewish neighborhoods of Judenberg and Judengasse ceased to exist in the Fulda street register.[7]

From 1933, until early autumn of 1938, twenty-eight Jewish families out of approximately forty had left Lauterbach. In 1937, the town of Gedern levied a special municipal fee of one thousand *Reichsmark* on the sale of property of the family of Hermann and Jettchen Frank.[8] I am not certain if the town of Lauterbach levied a special municipal tax on its Jews on the sale of Jewish property, above and beyond the taxes imposed by the state of Hesse and Germany. In Gedern, early in 1933, local Nazis brutally attacked Jews, including Berthold Simon, Julius Blumenthal, Gustav Blumenthal (the husband of Emma Baumann Blumenthal from Lauterbach), Max Meier, and members of the Vöhl families. Primarily, harsh excesses against Jews generally occurred in Upper Hessian towns and villages where Lutheran ministers were anti-semitic, such as in Gedern. Here Protestant men of the cloth had practiced anti-semitism since 1911.[9]

PERSECUTION IN KIRTORF

KIRTORF IN UPPER HESSE, my mother's birthplace, was another town that was fervently anti-semitic, which was probably attributable to the town's intellectual leaders, the Lutheran clergy. Already in 1932 and in early January of 1933, local Nazi hordes recurrently awakened and frightened my maternal grandmother, Auguste Strauss Lamm. When she was home alone at night, Nazi hoodlums smashed the window panes on the first floor of her home and simultaneously pounded on the house doors. On February 19, 1933, my timorous, frail grandmother died on her seventy-fifth birthday. She had suffered the loss of her twelve-year-old daughter, Mathilde, through illness and had sacrificed her oldest son, Siegfried, for Germany in World War I. Her sudden demise was hastened by her constant fear and dread of local Nazis. However, it is to the credit of the Kirtorf populace that they hurled neither snowballs nor stones at her funeral procession. One week later, on February 26, 1933, Hitler had the *Reichstag* set on fire. A few days earlier, when the Zionist student convention in Leipzig ended with the traditional ball, everyone was unaware of the impending crisis. Even political organizations did not comprehend the gravity of what was to come.

After 1933, my maternal grandfather, Jakob Lamm, whose forebears had lived in Kirtorf for more than a century, was severely beaten on his head, face, and

Chapter Twenty-One

shoulders for walking in town. He would have succumbed to his injuries if the local physician, Dr. Engländer, acting against the regulation not to treat a Jew, had not violated the Nazi ordinance and treated his wounds. Moreover, the Nazis of Kirtorf so frightened my Uncle Leo Lamm that he temporarily fled to Lauterbach, which was hardly a paradise for Jews at that time.

PERSECUTION IN GELNHAUSEN

I DO NOT KNOW WHY ANOTHER HESSIAN TOWN, Gelnhausen, pursued persecution and banishment of its Jews sooner and with greater fervor than Lauterbach and Alsfeld. In December, 1932, the local SA actuated a boycott of Jewish stores and the local police did not intercede. In the spring of 1938, the people of Gelnhausen walled up the synagogue portals, closed the entrance to the house of a local Jew named Scheuer, devastated the Jewish cemetery, arrested young Jewish men for no reason, and threw stones into the synagogue during services. As the remaining members of the Gelnhausen Jewish community (founded eight hundred years earlier) carried the coffin of one of their members to the cemetery (they were forbidden the use of the municipal hearse), stones descended upon the pallbearers and the person who delivered the funeral rites. In September of 1938, the Nazis affixed a sign at the railroad station that read, "*Gelnhausen ist judenrein*" ('Gelnhausen is free of Jews'). By that time, all Jews had left Gelnhausen—except for one who committed suicide.[10] I do not know the fate of Mr. Heilmann of Gelnhausen, one of my father's good friends.

PERSECUTION IN KASSEL

ON MARCH 10, 1933, VIRULENT ANTI-SEMITIC rabble-rousing occurred on the *Spohrplatz* in the much larger city of Kassel (Hesse-Nassau), the birthplace of the noted Jewish theologian Franz Rosenzweig (1886-1929). The Nazis hurled cobblestones at Jewish stores and drove an aged Jewish attorney, Plaut, through the streets with a sign, "I am a Jewish pig." As a result, Mr. Plaut died of a heart attack. In April of 1933, the Kassel Nazis set up a cage near the Spohr Memorial, wherein they confined a donkey together with prominent members of the Kassel Jewish community.[11] From 1920 to 1930, extreme anti-semitic excesses also occurred in the schools in the large Upper Hesse town of Giessen. Early lashing out against Jews was as intensive and extensive in large cities as in small towns and villages of Upper Hesse and Hesse-Nassau.

IMMIGRATION OF JEWS AND 'ARYANIZATION' IN LAUTERBACH

ON MARCH 13, 1938, HITLER ANNEXED his native country of Austria, which welcomed him with great enthusiasm. In Vienna, strict application of Nazi statutes was practiced with extreme severity that not infrequently compelled Jews from Vienna to seek temporary refuge in Berlin.[12] Pressure on Jews to liquidate their businesses increased in 1937 and 1938, well ahead of *Kristallnacht*. Approximately forty percent of German Jews left Germany before the *Kristallnacht*.[13] Hermann Goering was primarily interested in the financial pillage of the German Jews in order to finance the Four-Year Plan and Germany's rearmament.[14] On May 20, 1938, the *Lauterbacher Anzeiger* printed the following notice:

> Jewish Emigrants-the family of the Jew Bernhard Baumann who until now lived (at) Am See is moving in order to live in America (New York). Emigration of local Jews who were formerly so numerous here (3.2 percent) is proceeding and will soon continue.

When Mayor Falk invited former Lauterbach Jews to visit in 1991, Carl and Rut, the children of Bernhard Baumann, who in 1938 were twelve and ten years old, respectively, did not go. Carl (II) and Rut decided not to return to Lauterbach because of the base and vile conduct of their former classmates and grief over the loss of family members (such as their Aunt Jenny Baumann from Lauterbach). They did not wish to rend anew the scarred over, yet still deeply felt wounds.

The first official census pertaining to race was taken on May 17, 1938, and Jews were ordered to take on the first name 'Sara' for women and 'Israel' for men on August 17, 1938. In the case of the Lauterbach Jewish teacher Max (Moses) Stern (who by then had moved to Frankfurt with his family), the Nazi authorities sarcastically declared that his first name (Moses) was adequate for identification. In addition, the letter 'J' was stamped on Jewish passports in conformity with the decree of October 5, 1938, and in response to a suggestion by Swiss authorities.[15]

On July 6, 1938, the International Refugee Conference at Evian-les-Bains on the French shore of Lake Geneva convened with representatives from thirty-one countries in order to discuss asylum for refugees from Hitler's persecution. But because the conference had very limited results, the Nazis were further emboldened to think that no one was really concerned about persecuted Jews from Germany and Austria. The outcome surely ranks as one of the great failures of the western powers to deal firmly with Hitler. Nevertheless, the United States government resumed admission of refugees from Germany, Austria, and Czechoslovakia. Australia also agreed to take in fifteen thousand refugees for the next three years.

In New York, the Dominican Republic Settlement Association, under the stewardship of James N. Rosenberg, was established. Generalissimo Trujillo's government offered to establish an agricultural settlement of one hundred thousand refugees on twenty-two thousand acres of land in Sosua, east of Puerto Plata in the Dominican Republic. Approximately seven hundred refugees eventually established themselves in Sosua, but five thousand refugees used Dominican visas to escape the Holocaust. Two members of Lauterbach Jewish families tried to save their relatives through this organization. Ruth Gisela Spier wished to save her grandmother, Therese Strauss, and her mother, Sara Strauss Spier. Otto Pfifferling wanted to rescue his parents, Auguste and Alex Pfifferling. Ruth Spier's family moved to Frankfurt am Main before *Kristallnacht*, and the Pfifferling family left Lauterbach for Dresden in 1934. Both families had resided in the Bahnhofstrasse in Lauterbach, and both families were put to death by the Nazis.

Chapter Twenty-One

ON SEPTEMBER 29, 1938, BRITAIN AND FRANCE accepted the German occupation of the *Sudetenland* of Czechoslovakia, and Neville Chamberlain returned to England announcing that he had secured "peace in our time." On November 7, 1938, a young Polish Jew, Herschel Grynszpan, assassinated a German diplomat, Ernst vom Rath, a second secretary of the German Embassy in Paris. Grynszpan's aim was to draw attention to what had happened to approximately seventeen thousand Polish Jews of German origin, including his own family, who had been forcibly and barbarously expelled across the Polish border.[a] The Nazi propaganda machine instantly falsified this act of an individual into an anti-German plot by 'International Jewry.' In retaliation, Reinhard Heydrich, a senior Nazi official, ordered the destruction of all synagogues in Germany and Austria. Those few that remained standing owed their survival to the fact that they adjoined residences or other important buildings which the Nazis had decided not to put into the fire's path.

Squads of Nazis, mostly SA thugs, stormed through villages and towns throughout the country armed with clubs and other weapons. They laid waste to Jewish property and roughed up Jewish citizens. Obeying orders, the police paid no attention to such excesses. The police intervened only in acts of violence against Jews that either damaged the Nazi party or attracted detrimental publicity abroad.[16] In Kassel, on November 10, 1938, thirty SA men burned *Torahs* and other ritual items and also destroyed twenty Jewish stores and *Cafe Heinemann*, the Jewish community building in the Grosse Rosenstrasse. Nazi leaders claimed that the pogrom was a spontaneous expression of popular anger, but even in Lauterbach only a few believed that account. To the best of my knowledge, most Jewish men of Upper Hesse under sixty-five years of age were taken to Buchenwald on the evening of November 9, 1938. In Hesse alone, one hundred forty-five synagogues were destroyed.[17]

In 1938, the Jewish population in Lauterbach represented less than one percent of a population of five thousand and consisted mostly of older people who, for financial reasons, could not leave or were unable to find a place of refuge. On November 11, 1938, the *Lauterbacher Anzeiger* gave the following account of the previous night:

> Lauterbach's Settlement with the Jews: The intense indignation in all of Germany that was brought about by the cowardly Jewish assassination yesterday gave vent to its righteous anger in our town. The population of Lauterbach retaliated for the assassination in Paris by a show of force against the Jewish rabble. Everywhere vengeance and punishment were inflicted. All window-panes and household appointments in Jewish homes and in the synagogue were left in ruins. Nothing was stolen. It did not come to greater excesses, since the police took the Jews into protective custody.

Eyewitness descriptions and other portrayals differ substantially from the above report. The torture of Lauterbach Jews, arrests of Jewish men under sixty-five

---

[a] The late Abraham Joshua Heschel, the great Jewish philosopher and theologian, was in this group.

years of age and their subsequent incarceration in Buchenwald, the devastation of Jewish homes, and destruction of the interior of the Lauterbach synagogue took place during the day and night of November 9 and 10. Since 1923, the Lauterbach Nazis had annually celebrated November 9 as Hitler's 'Beer Hall Putsch' (his first, and unsuccessful, attempt at armed insurrection in Munich). As was customary since 1923, the local Nazis (in this case, local youthful derelicts) lined up at the Lion Memorial and marched a short distance to the local Nazi tavern, *Wachtel*. There—before rounding up Jews for Buchenwald, destroying Jewish homes, stealing, and extorting money and other valuable items from Jews—the Nazis swilled down considerable amounts of alcoholic drinks and blackened their faces with soot.

THE LOOTING OF THE LAUTERBACH SYNAGOGUE

THROUGHOUT THE DAY ON NOVEMBER 9, 1938, many adults, juveniles, and children wreaked havoc upon the interior of the synagogue. Ironically, in the forefront of this group was the oldest grandson of Mr. Reuter, the synagogue's architect, who had been present at the synagogue's dedication in 1908 and who had previously been well-disposed toward the founders of the Lauterbach Jewish congregation. Perched high on a ladder with a hammer and chisel, the oldest Reuter grandson zealously removed the golden inscription above the synagogue's portals.[b] During the destruction, costly ritual items such as the silver *Torah* breastplates and the silver *Torah* finials (*rimmonim*) were stolen. During my visits to Lauterbach in the early 1980s, my classmates claimed that *Kristallnacht* perpetrators at the synagogue and Jewish homes came from nearby towns and villages and took the stolen items away with them. I have since learned that these items were allegedly still in the possession of local citizens as of 1991.

THE NAZIS IN LAUTERBACH

Former Wertheim property at Cent 17. The *sukkah* is now the kiosk in the foreground.

MEMBERS OF THE LAUTERBACH POPULATION who were willing to attack, torture, profiteer, and steal from their Jewish neighbors fell upon their victims under cover of night. Among many other local perpetrators of crimes during *Kristallnacht* were the brothers, Hans Georg Kayser and Horst Kayser, whose father worked at the Lauterbach power station. Hans Georg Kayser, who was nicknamed 'Kleinauto,' was killed in World War II. In 1953, Horst Kayser, a member of the SS, found refuge in Argentina with the help of the Vatican. Until his mother's death in 1991, Horst brazenly visited her regularly each summer in Lauterbach.[18]

At the time of *Kristallnacht*, Alfred Zürtz was Nazi district administrator. In 1945, as the Americans approached Lauterbach, he went into hiding in our former *sukkah*. However, a neighbor reported his whereabouts to the American command. Mr. Fickgeiss was a chief of the SA and reportedly was disinclined to destroy the synagogue by fire: he wished to convert the sanctuary into a gymnasium. A short

---

[b] Mr. Reuter's grandson was killed in World War II.

Chapter Twenty-One

time after *Kristallnacht*, Mr. Fickgeiss committed suicide. Participants in the pogrom and arson of the Lauterbach synagogue included the Böcher brothers, employees of the Riedesel at the brewery who rendered false testimony at court and brought great harm to my father.

Another Nazi participant was the cutler Gürtler of the Bahnhofstrasse. On April 1, 1933, during the boycott of Jewish stores in Lauterbach, he diligently guarded the stores of Siegfried Reiss and Alex Pfifferling (he was their neighbor across the street) and zealously prevented non-Jewish customers from entering the store. Sometime after the November pogrom, Mr. Gürtler committed suicide because, according to town rumor, he was distraught over his share of the devastation during the pogrom. A third suicide was that the daughter of the respected bookseller, Gustav Mandt, and the wife of a regional Nazi administrator.

I am not aware of any suicides in Lauterbach between 1923 and January 30, 1933. To the best of my knowledge, no Jew from Lauterbach committed suicide while still in town, during flight, at a place of refuge, or even in a concentration camp. It may be that centuries of suffering of Jewish forebears in Hesse and Judaism's regard for human life (*pikkuah'ah nefesh*) ruled out such an act. However, after 1933 there were two suicides in our family: my uncle, Abraham Herz on December 11, 1961, at the age of eighty-seven in New York after he was diagnosed with incurable cancer, and my mother's cousin, Claire Stern Hermann, at the time of the Nazi occupation of Luxembourg.

Another Nazi participant was Fritz Reuel, who in 1933 and 1934 was already deeply committed to the Nazis. His sister, Else Reuel Glebe, was allocated an apartment, probably as a reward, in our home on Cent 17 shortly after my parents left Lauterbach. Also Mr. Bully, Mr. Gittard, Mr. Rockel, Mr. Wagner, Mr. Mehring, Carl Heinz Schnegelberger, and Kurt Peter took part in the November pogrom. Mr. Bully and Mr. Gittard were punished after 1945, especially since they had beaten up Mr. Boos, a prominent local Social Democrat who was jailed merely on account of his party affiliation. After 1945, other active Nazis, such as Mr. Neidhart and Dr. Clarence Wagner, were not disciplined,[19] leading one to conclude that the more educated and the economically more powerful were spared penalty and punishment.

According to Karl H. Gorsler,[c] the windows of the David Weinberg house in the Langgasse were shattered, the house door smashed, and the inside and exterior of the residence were splattered with raw eggs and ink while neighbors and other citizens of Lauterbach helped themselves to household items and furniture. This scenario was repeated at other Jewish homes. According to the *Lauterbacher Anzeiger* of November 10, 1988, pilfered furnishings and furniture from Jewish residences survived in town to that date. Guilt and fear of being discovered as a town of thieves may well have been the reason for Lauterbach's extended reluctance to invite the return of its Jewish citizens and for the lukewarm and extremely limited

[c] Then nine years old and in 1991 a member of the Lauterbach town council.

participation of Lauterbach citizenry during public functions at the time of the visit. David, Gerda, and Arnold Weinberg survived the Holocaust, and in 1991 Arnold declined Lauterbach's invitation to return.

At the home of Emma and Seligmann Jakob of Alter Steinweg 7, three SS men forced the frightened Emma to pack linens in a wash basket that they carried away. The hoodlums also stole silver flatware and demanded the surrender of valuables that this family did not possess. Although Emma Jakob and her husband lived in very modest circumstances, the Nazi thieves stole whatever they could lay their hands on.[20] One of the Jakob sons (probably Max, because Julius lived in Regensburg and was unlikely to be in Lauterbach during the November pogrom) was taken to a concentration camp for one year.[21] Seligmann Jakob's house was eventually razed, but the terror inflicted on its occupants will be more difficult to erase. In 1991, Rita Jakob Kahn, the daughter of the only surviving son of Seligmann and Emma Jakob, explained that she shrank from returning to Germany and Lauterbach because two of her uncles and her grandparents had been victims of the Holocaust and because of mental and emotional cruelties inflicted in school in her native town.

During my visit to Lauterbach in 1985, the granddaughter of the late cooper, Grau, expressed her disapproval of the shameless treatment of the Salli Weinberg family of the Bahnhofstrasse during *Kristallnacht*. That night, the Nazis grabbed Rosa Weinberg's curly hair and pulled her down the steps, Mr. Rockel beat up Salli Weinberg, and other Nazis smashed the windows and ruined the house furnishings. Salli Weinberg was taken into 'protective custody' in Buchenwald.

On the other hand, Käthe Roth, an altruistic Lauterbach citizen, continued to supply the Weinberg family with food and refused to conform to Nazi regulations. On the night the Weinberg family was attacked, she tossed a package of soft cheese through the broken windows in the presence of a multitude of bystanders.[22] Salli, Rosa, and Arthur Weinberg left Lauterbach on November 20, 1940 for Frankfurt am Main. All three were murdered in Minsk.

Gretel Dillmann Stöhr was a neighbor and eyewitness to the demolition and the attending welter of discordant sounds at the Bahnhofstrasse 66 home of Juda Baumann (II). By Lauterbach standards, Mr. Baumann was considered well-to-do. A sewing machine was heaved out of a window and a piano, sullied with the contents of home-canned fruits and vegetables, was thrown into the street outside the house.[23] For Lise Hammerstett of Angersbach, who worked for the Wertheim family in 1935, this was a night of devastation and utter despoliation of Jewish homes.[24]

In 1949, Recha Baumann, one of the surviving daughters of Juda Baumann (II), told me that furniture, pictures, a typewriter, and a radio were destroyed in her father's home. Linens, rugs, and bedding that were not stolen were splattered with oil and flatware, clothing, and linens were carried off. Florchen Stiehler of Friedhofstrasse 12 mentioned that, although she was not an eyewitness to the event, she had heard considerable talk about the Baumann's dog being put to death and hung upside down.[25] The Nazis yanked the telephone off the wall and demanded that Juda Baumann (II) pay repair costs to the post office. In a completely perverse twist, the entire German-Jewish community was fined one billion *Mark* for having 'provoked' the destruction of the November pogrom, and six billion *Mark* in insurance money was seized by the Reich. Juda Baumann (II) was therefore obliged to pay for the damage inflicted on his own property.

On November 10, 1938, the Höchster family (Nathan, Thea, Rolf, Grete, and Hans) and the Friedländer family (Gerson, Bertha, and their sons) had already been commanded by the Nazis to evacuate rented quarters in non-Jewish property and had moved into houses owned by Herz Höchster at Bahnhofstrasse 84 and 86. On November 9, 1938, a repeat of the events at the Baumann house took place at the Herz Höchster house, where the Nazi hoodlums heaved heavy home furnishings through windows and where masked civilians who coveted Jewish property stole flatware and other valuables.[26] Moreover, the Nazi hordes removed the inscription on the Herz Höchster house which read, "Stoutly we build here, although we are but alien guests, while into our eternal residence we build so little." The Nazis predicated their action on the popular Nazi notion that Jewish parasites could lay no claim to this German maxim.[27]

The *Lauterbacher Anzeiger* of May 6, 1988, reported Nathan Höchster's army medical services in World War I and also stated that he left for the United States in the 1930s. Germans, particularly from small towns like Lauterbach, are unwilling to accept responsibility for the deaths of their Jewish neighbors. This denial and distortion of facts stung Grete bitterly. In 1992, she related a more accurate account to the *Lauterbacher Anzeiger*.

On December 16, 1938, the *Lauterbacher Anzeiger* reported the end of the Jewish cemetery: "The Jewish cemetery situated near the Gartenstrasse has changed hands to the barber Helfenbein as a real estate acquisition." During our visit to Lauterbach in 1959, Mr. Helfenbein produced the bill of sale signed by Herz Höchster on behalf of the Lauterbach Jewish congregation. The cemetery transfer occurred prior to Herz Höchster's departure on November 21, 1938, from Lauterbach to Arndtstrasse 25 in Frankfurt am Main. Mr. Helfenbein's plans to transform the Lauterbach Jewish cemetery into a real estate development were frustrated by Germany's entrance into World War II on September 1, 1939, and the penetration of American troops into Lauterbach on March 29, 1945. In 1959, the portion of the cemetery without tombstones had been planted with plum trees of several varieties, together with white and red cabbages. Since the 1970s, the cemetery has been restored. However, an area on its west side appears to have been truncated.

The Lauterbach Nazis[d] also dispensed harsh treatment on Gerson Friedländer, his wife Bertha, and their sons, even though in World War I Gerson had been the recipient of Germany's Iron Cross.[28] Mr. Friedländer had been a popular dentist in Lauterbach who served many non-Jewish patients and had an office on the

---

[d] I estimate that in 1934, ninety-five percent of the Lauterbach population were dedicated Nazis.

Marktplatz. An onlooker observed the Friedländer telephone being pulled out of the wall and also watched how public school pupils contributed their share to the devastation during recess. Boys and girls of the public school went on a rampage, stealing money and jewelry and throwing bed linens, dishes, and broken furniture into the street. Only one person, a simple working man, refused to take part in setting fire to the synagogue.[29] With hardly an exception, every witness whom I interviewed about in *Kristallnacht* in Lauterbach concentrated on the destruction of property and possessions, and manifested minimal thought about the suffering of Jewish individuals.

Sometime in the late 1920s or early 1930s, the Friedländer family lost an infant who was less than one month old. To my mother's consternation, he was buried in the Lauterbach Christian cemetery. Otherwise, Gerson and Bertha seemed to adhere to the mores of the local Jewish community.[e] As late as 1938, the Friedländer family had a non-Jewish maid who, despite Nazi regulations, remained loyal to the family. This maid asked Gretel Dillmann Stöhr for money in order to buy milk and other foodstuffs for the Friedländer children. In the early 1930s, Gretel Dillmann was employed as an assistant in Mr. Friedländer's dental office. On March 1, 1939, this family moved to Rossdorfstrasse 23 in Frankfurt am Main. Gerson Friedländer, his wife Bertha, and their young sons fell victim to Nazi annihilation.

Also during the night of November 9, 1938, a Nazi shot to death the sixteen-year-old Herbert Stein (son of Laura Kugelmann Stein and Max Stein) of Eisenbacher Tor 2. In Bornsdorf in the county of Bitterfeld, Herbert Stein was a member of the agricultural program of *Youth Aliyah*, a branch of the Zionist Movement that was founded in 1932 by Recha Freier and which rescued and educated Jewish children. In later years, the identity and address of Herbert's murderer became known to the Stein family. However, the family's petitions to the authorities in the DDR (East Germany), where he lived, remained unanswered. Max and Laura Stein moved to Palestine on July 31, 1939. Their daughter, Irma, and their son, Kurt, had left Lauterbach for Palestine earlier, having departed on April 26, 1934 and January 1, 1936, respectively. Irma did not come to Lauterbach in 1991 at Mayor Falk's invitation. Since the 1950s, Kurt Stein has lived in Hanover, Germany; he joined the invited group of former Lauterbach Jews in 1991, although bitterness about his brother's early death and failure to charge or punish the assassin remained uppermost in Kurt's mind.

I do not know what fate befell the Moritz Stern family (wife, Rosa, and daughters, Beate and Susi Sylvia) (at) Am Wörth 16 during the pogrom in Lauterbach on November 9, 1938. However, the close proximity of their residence to Heinrich Schrimpf, a tailor who lived (at) Am Wörth 32, and other dedicated Nazis was an ill-omen in itself. Thirteen days later, this family left their home and moved to Karlsruhe. At the tender ages of six and three, Beate and Susi came to the United States with a children's transport to be near their mother's sisters, Bertha Gottlieb

---

[e] In the *Pentateuch*, Gerson was a son of Moses by a Midianite woman and in Hebrew 'Gerson' means 'stranger.'

Chapter Twenty-One

and Flora Gottlieb Schmidt. At that time, many Jewish parents opted for painful separation from young children to spare them from the greater tragedy that they perceived looming on the horizon. Moritz and Rosa Stern are reported to have died in Auschwitz. In 1991, Beate and Susi rejected Mayor Falk's invitation to Lauterbach's erstwhile Jewish citizens.

THE DESTRUCTION OF THE LAUTERBACH SYNAGOGUE

DURING THE DAY OF NOVEMBER 9, 1938, local adults, adolescents, and children took part in the destruction of the Lauterbach synagogue. On November 10, after everything had been ruined and knocked to pieces in the Lauterbach synagogue and before the building was set ablaze, hordes of people went to look at the destruction. Although it was officially forbidden to photograph buildings ravaged by the Nazis, Hans Curt Scheer of Bahnhofstrasse 82 took a picture of the synagogue, which was still standing but with its interior despoiled.[f]

Mrs. Georg, whose house was near the synagogue on Hinter der Burg, was home alone during the early part of the evening of November 10, 1938. At that time, she observed three men coming out of the private entrance on the north side of the synagogue. They were dressed in coats and wore hats pulled over their faces so that it was impossible to recognize them. One of the men called to her, "Get away from the window, you lily-livered bunch!" Toward midnight of November 10, 1938, Mrs. Georg noticed flames and heard a crackle. As she pulled aside the curtains, she noticed many onlookers in the street. The butcher, Knoll, and his wife, who were returning to their home at the Bahnhofstrasse, thoughtfully knocked on their door to alert the Georg family to the fire within close range of their house.

The synagogue in Lauterbach as of November 9, 1938

At first it was forbidden to call the fire department. Finally, at the urgent request of Mr. Georg and other neighbors, the fire department arrived to hose down the Georg house lest it catch fire. But the synagogue was passed up and it burned down to the foundation walls. In 1941, the Georg family purchased the property from the town of Lauterbach.[30] Mr. Rockel, a Nazi official dressed in civilian clothing, took part in setting fire to the synagogue building.[31] As the flames from the synagogue fire illuminated the sky, the fourteen-year-old Mechtild Kullmann asked her father why the fire department did not promptly put it out. Her father answered that the firemen were not permitted to extinguish the synagogue blaze.[32] As Mr. Gorsler's mother watched the synagogue being consumed by flames, she an-

---

[f] In Alsfeld, members of the History and Antiquity Association somehow took nearly all synagogue items to safety. After World War II, this Association shipped the salvaged ritual items to Haifa, where many Alsfeld Jews had settled. One *Torah* is on permanent exhibit in the Alsfeld museum.

nounced that Germany was readying itself for war.[33] Scarcely nine months later, World War II began on September 1, 1939 when Germany invaded Poland. On the day after the synagogue went up in flames, fourteen-year-old Ernst Oppenheimer and twelve-year-old Norbert Weinberg turned over the earth around the synagogue in a childlike endeavor to recover some of the sacred ritual items.[34]

By November 11, 1938, the Jakob Oppenheimer and Kaufmann Strauss families had already been dispossessed of their homes by the government. Kaspar Kircher acquired the Oppenheimer family residence for little or no money.[g] In later years, this house was demolished, as was the Seligmann Jakob house at Alter Steinweg 7. The razing of Jewish homes in less-imposing neighborhoods may have been ordered to prevent restitution payments.

During the summer of 1938, the Oppenheimers and other Jewish families (such as Samuel Strauss (II) and his wife, Minna Bechtold Strauss of Rockelsgasse 10) were compelled to move into the synagogue building in order to facilitate the round up of Jewish males to be shipped to Buchenwald or other concentration camps. By six a.m. on November 11, 1938, Sophie Oppenheimer escaped from the smoldering synagogue clad only in her nightclothes and coat. She ran to the Keller residence at the Kanalstrasse, and begged for help from Hans Keller's mother.[h] Within a day after leaving the burning synagogue, Sophie made her way to her sister-in-law, Martha Oppenheimer Strauss of Alsfeld. Jakob, Sophie, and their two children, Helene and Ernst, reached New York sometime in 1939. According to Helen Oppenheimer Katz, her grandfather died in Frankfurt am Main but did not commit suicide, as was erroneously reported. I do not know where or when Samuel Strauss (II) and his wife, Minna Bechtold Strauss, met their death at Nazi hands. But I do know that Mrs. Georg shared eggs from her chickens with this family and also provided them with food from stores that Jews were forbidden to enter.

As a result of the November pogrom, most Jewish males from Upper Hesse and Lauterbach who were under sixty-five years of age were confined to the Buchenwald concentration camp atop the wooded Ettersberg near Weimar. The Nazis cynically termed these arrests 'protective custody.'[i] On November 10, 1988, the eighty-two-year-old Morris Herbert of Frankfurt am Main, before the Congregation Ohav Shalom in Manhattan, recounted that during *Kristallnacht*, he, together with fifty other Jews, was lined up before machine guns when the Nazi commander

---

[g] Kasper was nicknamed 'Geisskaspchen,' meaning 'goat,' probably because he or someone in his family raised or herded goats.

[h] For some period during the mid-1930s, Hans Keller and his mother lived at the Oppenheimer house at Rockelsgasse 41. However, at the time the Oppenheimers were forced to turn their home over to Kaspar Kircher, Hans Keller and his mother had to move. (Interview with Hans Keller in Lauterbach on May 25, 1990.)

[i] Buchenwald was liberated on April 11, 1945, by the Fourth Armored Division of General George S. Patton's Third United States Army. The lives of twenty thousand inmates were saved, but only after sixty-five thousand souls had perished. Seventeen-year-old Elie Wiesel was liberated by an American soldier who cried like a child. (Henry Kamm, *New York Times*, March 25, 1989.) As General Patton, a seasoned warrior, entered Buchenwald, he was so shocked by what he saw that he ordered the military police to bring a thousand citizens from Weimar, a center of German culture, to make them aware of the horrors that had been perpetrated in their neighborhood. (Leo Sievers, *Juden in Deutschland* (Hamburg: Verlag Gruner, 1977): p. 268.

Chapter Twenty-One

was called away to take a phone call. Upon the commander's return, this group of Jews was sent away and Mr. Herbert was shipped to Buchenwald.

KRISTALLNACHT NEAR GIESSEN

BEFORE THE SAME CONGREGATION in Manhattan, Mrs. Fannie Joelson of Grossen-Buseck (Hesse) near Giessen related that her father and her husband were taken away by the SA and she "never heard from them again. Never." She also stated, "In my town, Grossen-Buseck, they did not burn the synagogue because it was too close to the houses owned by Germans. The Nazis were ordered not to destroy German property. However, they took the *Torahs* and *tefillin* from the synagogue and made a fire of them in the street. They took us to the school to show us. And I said to my friend, 'When they shoot us, don't cry. Don't cry. Stand proud!'" But Fannie and her friend were not shot. They and the other women were ordered to go home and clean up the shattered glass, the smashed doors, and the broken furniture. Three years later, despite desperate attempts to emigrate, Fannie was still in Germany and was taken to the concentration camp in Theresienstadt. She survived there until it was liberated by the Allies in 1945. At the same gathering in Manhattan, Norbert Lowenstein, an eighty-year-old man from the town of Giessen in Upper Hesse, said: "I lost thirty-five members of my family. Thirty-five. I am the only one left."[35]

KRISTALLNACHT IN CRAINFELD

IN NEARBY CRAINFELD, THE HISTORY of the Jews goes back to 1626. The Jews of Bermutshain, Grebenhain, and Nieder-Moos worshipped with the Crainfeld Jews and buried their dead in the Crainfeld Jewish cemetery. In 1933, Crainfeld had a Jewish population of sixty (eighteen families). Early in 1933, Elkan Sommer escaped to Palestine after much ill-treatment in his native village. My mother's cousin, Minna Strauss Sommer, her husband, Leo, and their son, Kurt, were forced to leave Grebenhain early in 1934 for the United States. In World War I, Leo Sommer had lost his brothers, Albert and Gustav. At the time of the November pogrom, the only Jews remaining in Crainfeld were the widow of Hermann Lind (called 'Izig's Guste'), Salli Weinberg, his wife, Flora, and their two children. Following the November 1938 pogrom, Crainfeld's last Jews fled to Frankfurt am Main. At least twenty-four Jews from this village met their death at Nazi hands.

KRISTALLNACHT IN STORNDORF

IN JULY OF 1987, IRENE GLATZEL of Storndorf stated that, during the November pogrom, a Jewish neighbor woman implored Irene and her mother to rescue her from the hands of the Nazi hoodlums. Herself a member of a minority group (Jehovah's Witnesses), Irene was still haunted by her Jewish neighbor's call for help to which she had not responded courageously and with more compassion. A wealthy farmer of Storndorf took the terrified Jewess into his home for a short time. However, she eventually fell into the Nazi's clutches and disappeared.

The Way It Was: The Jewish World of Rural Hesse

AFTER *KRISTALLNACHT*, APPROXIMATELY ONE-QUARTER of the Lauterbach Jewish population had been so severely afflicted by their neighbors and townsmen that they left within one month even though they were almost completely destitute. Before their departure, they were forced to sell the remainder of their belongings at ridiculous prices, and the Nazis took part of their money as a 'Jew tribute.'[36] In Atlanta, Georgia, on January 20, 1993, Elise Eichenauer Rücker, formerly of Bergstrasse 14 in Lauterbach, (her sister, Marie Eichenauer, had worked in our household in the early 1930s) showed me a ring with diamonds and rubies that she had purchased from a Lauterbach Jewess after the November 1938 pogrom. The buyer had undoubtedly paid but a fraction of the market price for the ring. Jews were forced by decree to sell any gold, silver, precious stones, and works of art, and to deposit the proceeds in a blocked account.

The following Jews left Lauterbach with all deliberate speed after *Kristallnacht*: Juda Baumann (II), Recha Baumann, Trude Blumenthal, Ida Baumann Cussel (on November 28, 1938, to Frankfurt am Main); Gerson Friedländer, Bertha Friedländer, and their two sons, Ernst and Herbert (on March 1, 1939, to Frankfurt am Main); Herz and Regine Höchster (on November 21, 1938, to Frankfurt am Main); Nathan and Thea Höchster and their children, Rolf, Hans, and Grete (on December 21, 1938, to Frankfurt am Main); Seligmann and Emma Jakob and their son, Max (in November 1938, to Regensburg, where their son Julius lived); Jakob and Sophie Oppenheimer and their children, Helen and Ernst (on November 11, 1938, to Alsfeld); Sophie Oppenheimer's father, Kaufmann Strauss (on July 7, 1939, to Frankfurt am Main); Max and Laura Stein (on July 31, 1939, to Palestine); Moritz and Rosa Stern and their daughters, Beate and Susi Sylvia (on November 22, 1938, to Karlsruhe); Samuel Strauss (II) and his wife, Minna (on November 17, 1938, to Nieder-Weisel, Hesse to join their family because of a lack of funds for an apartment in Frankfurt am Main); David, Gerda, and Arnold Weinberg (on May 8, 1939, to the United States); Moritz, Meta, and Norbert Weinberg (on July 18, 1939, to the United States); Salli, Rosa, and Arthur Weinberg (on February 22, 1940, to Frankfurt am Main)[i]; Biena Jakob (on March 17, 1940, to Berlin-Charlottenburg). The last Jew to leave Lauterbach was Hilde Weinberg on July 26, 1940. At the time of her husband's death in 1937, his funeral procession was pelted with snowballs. For many of the above, the worst was yet to come.

I am not aware if after 1945 the inhabitants of Lauterbach, Storndorf, Crainfeld, Giessen, Grossen-Buseck, or any of the other communities in Hesse (except for Gedern and Langen) openly perpetrated hostile acts toward foreigners and Jews. However, my mother's native town of Kirtorf unrelentingly held on to its anti-semitic notions. Even in the 1980s and early 1990s, its citizens glowingly spoke of the exemplary times of Hitler. During the late 1980s, a practic-

---

[i] David and Salli Weinberg's parents, Fanny and Abraham Weinberg, had been among the earlier Jewish families to move from Storndorf to Lauterbach in 1875.

Chapter Twenty-One

ing Israeli physician settled in Gedern and the people of Gedern promptly ran him out of town. Just as in October 1938 in Langen, when Hitler Youth prematurely had partially destroyed the interior of the synagogue,[37] in November 1992, xenophobic individuals of Langen committed excesses against foreigners in their town. *Kristallnacht* was a misnomer that more correctly should be spoken of as the 'night of zealous destruction of German Jews.' However, in the overall course of events, the shattered glass of their homes was of minor import.

Following *Kristallnacht*, articles in the *Lauterbacher Anzeiger* indicated that those Jews still remaining in town were subjected to constant abasement and peril. Moreover, Jews were dependent on the good will and courage of non-Jewish neighbors to provide them with food and other meager essentials for living. A spate of laws had increasingly restricted the lives of Jews. They were not allowed to use streetcars and were forbidden to enter a park. They were forced to turn in their bicycles and all electrical equipment. They were not allowed to own furs or objects made of wool; nor were they permitted to own dogs, cats, or canaries. Their food stamps did not entitle them to receive milk, fish, meat, fruit, tobacco products, and soap for shaving. They had to leave their apartments and were not permitted to take along any possessions.

Moreover, whenever bombs fell, Jews were excluded from entering bomb shelters. But worst of all, there was the ever-present threat that they would be picked up by men with hobnailed boots for forced labor. In that event, they were allowed to take along one suitcase, one bundle of hand luggage, one cover, and one piece of bed clothing. Some Jews found a hideout with friends who shared their food rations with them. Sometimes, total strangers took in a Jew. In this way, approximately three thousand German Jews survived. In the Upper Hesse area, Hermann Abt of Kirchhain, whose kin had lived in Angenrod for several generations, survived although he endured visible physical injuries. Liselotte Bruck, who lived in Frankfurt am Main in the 1930s (her father was Mr. Loewenstein from Gedern) also managed to go into hiding.

On November 11, 1938 the *Lauterbacher Anzeiger* stated:

> [O]n the preceding day, as soon as it became known in Frankfurt that Ernst von Rath succumbed to the injuries inflicted by Jewish hoodlums, a spontaneous attack in all parts of the city took place against Jews who had incited the whole world against Germany. The masses demanded retaliation for the assassination in Paris.

According to the newspaper report, the agitated multitudes attacked Jewish stores, but there was no looting. It also stated that all synagogues in Frankfurt am Main were destroyed. In the same edition, the *Lauterbacher Anzeiger* reported that, in Giessen, the masses burned down two synagogues and demolished Jewish stores and when the Jews of Giessen asked for protective custody, it was granted them magnanimously. However, this report does not corroborate the account of Mr. Norbert Lowenstein, a survivor of Giessen who lost thirty-five members of his family and who is now the sole survivor.[38]

Krokodilstränen!

Wieder einmal die „armen verfolgten Juden".

Zu einer Londoner Nachricht des „Oeuvre", derzufolge die in Deutschland an den Juden durchgeführten Vergeltungsmaßnahmen für den Mord an dem Legationsrat vom Rath in der englischen Oeffentlichkeit „mit Entsetzen" zur Kenntnis genommen worden seien und in einer der nächsten Unterhaussitzungen den Gegenstand zu einer Aussprache über die Juden in Deutschland bilden sollen, schreibt der „Deutsche Dienst":

Daß bei dieser Meldung des berüchtigten französischen Hetzblattes der Wunsch der Vater des Gedankens ist, braucht wohl nicht erst gesagt zu werden. Man möchte, wie es so oft geschehen ist, wieder einmal der Opposition im englischen Unterhaus die Bälle zuwerfen, um eine große Debatte über die „armen verfolgten Juden in Deutschland" in Szene zu setzen. Oder sollte man sich in gewissen englischen Kreisen wirklich mit dem Gedanken tragen, eine Debatte über eine Angelegenheit anzuzetteln, die nicht nur eine rein innerdeutsche Angelegenheit ist, sondern bei der auch der Gegenstand selbst so gelagert ist, daß für irgendeine moralische Entrüstung wirklich nichts übrig bleibt.

Nicht nur in Deutschland, sondern auch im Ausland ist der Mord an dem deutschen Diplomaten als ein gemeines und hinterhältiges Verbrechen gebührend gekennzeichnet worden. Trotzdem hat sich die Vergeltungsaktion gegen die Juden in einer äußerst disziplinierten Form vollzogen, und Reichsminister Dr. Goebbels hat noch am gleichen Tage an die Bevölkerung die strenge Aufforderung erlassen, von allen weiteren Demonstrationen und Vergeltungsakten gegen das Judentum sofort abzusehen. In Paris ist Blut geflossen, und ein junger Deutscher liegt auf der Totenbahre. In Deutschland aber wurde nicht einem Juden ein Haar gekrümmt. Wir meinen, die Kreise, die durchaus eine Aussprache über die deutsche Aktion gegen die Juden im englischen Unterhaus veranlassen wollen, hätten allen Anlaß, den Strom ihrer Krokodilstränen einzudämmen, um so mehr, als es in der Welt genug andere Vorgänge gibt, die wirklich Anlaß „zum Entsetzen" bieten.

Da liest man von massenhaft gefallenen und hingerichteten Arabern, von gesprengten Häusern, von Luftangriffen durch Flieger und vom Einsatz motorisierter Truppen. Man ist so gewöhnt an diese Meldungen, daß sich mit ihnen kaum mehr eine klare Vorstellung von blutigem Elend und grausamer Verzweiflung derer verbindet, die davon betroffen wurden.

Erst wenn man diese Vorgänge mit eingeschlagenen Schaufensterscheiben vergleicht, kann man sich so richtig vorstellen, was Häuser bedeuten, die mit Ekrasit in die Luft gesprengt worden sind. Häuser von Arabern, die nichts getan haben, als daß sie einen heroischen Freiheitskampf um ihre Heimat führen. Man wird auch Massenhinrichtungen wieder richtiger bewerten können. Ebenso Massaker von der Luft aus.

So wurden z. B. in der vierten Oktoberwoche in der Nähe von Nablus durch eine Aktion der britischen Luftwaffe 60 Araber getötet. In der ersten Oktoberwoche kam es um den See von Galiläa ebenfalls zu einer blutigen Aktion englischer Flugzeuge gegen Araber, die es ablehnten, sich den jüdischen Eindringlingen zu unterwerfen: Ueber 90 Tote waren die Folge dieser Aktion. Aber nicht nur Flugzeuge, sondern auch motorisierte Einheiten wurden gegen die Freiheitskämpfer vorgeschickt. Im ganzen gab es in den letzten vier Monaten rund 2500 Tote und Verwundete in Palästina, von denen selbstverständlich der erdrückende Teil auf die Araber entfällt, die sich in der Verteidigung befinden!

Aber die Geiferer, die in den westlichen Hauptstädten hinter der Weltpresse stehen und die Oeffentlichkeit verhetzen, haben für diese Schrecken kein Wort des Bedauerns gefunden. Das ist auch anderen aufgefallen: Heuchler kann man nicht überzeugen!

Die nationalspanische Zeitung „Correo Espaniol" wurde erst vor wenigen Tagen vor die Notwendigkeit gestellt, diesen Satz auszusprechen. Es handelte sich in diesem Falle um ein furchtbares Bombardement bolschewistischer Flieger, das im Ort Cabra, dem keinerlei militärische Bedeutung zukommt, unter der friedlichen Zivilbevölkerung ein wahres Blutbad angerichtet hatte. 100 Tote waren als Folge der unter dem Schutz der scheindemokratischen Blätter arbeitenden Bolschewistenmeute zu beklagen. Wären die Zeitungen in den westlichen Ländern wirklich objektiv gewesen, dann hätte sich ihnen, wie „Correo Espaniol" sehr richtig bemerkte, die schönste Gelegenheit zu einer geradezu ungeheuren Empörung geboten. Aber leider wußte man schon im voraus, so mußte das nationalspanische Blatt erklären, daß die sogenannten liberalen und demokratischen Zeitungen kein Wort über die unbeschreiblichen kommunistischen Greuel verlieren würden.

Wenn es englische Oppositionskreise laut dem Pariser „Oeuvre" für richtig halten, das deutsche Vorgehen gegen die Juden im Unterhaus zur Sprache zu bringen, dann wäre man in Berlin ebenso gut berechtigt, eine Debatte im Deutschen Reichstag über das englische Vorgehen in Palästina in Gang zu setzen. Nur mit dem Unterschied, daß dann im Deutschen Reichstag genug Stoff vorhanden wäre, um wochenlang über das englische Zerstörungswerk und die englischen Greueltaten zu sprechen, während im englischen Unterhaus die Debatte sehr schnell nach der Behandlung einiger zerbrochener Schaufensterscheiben und in Brand geratener Synagogen im Sande versickern müßte.

Rom. Mit kurzen Ansprachen des Ministers für Volksbildung, Alfieri, des deutschen Botschafters von Mackensen und des Reichsintendanten des deutschen Rundfunks, Dr. Glasmeier, haben am Donnerstag tägliche Sondersendungen des italienischen Rundfunks für Deutschland begonnen.

The *Lauterbacher Anzeiger,* November 13, 1938 The article is entitled "Crocodile Tears!"

In the *Lauterbacher Anzeiger* of November 12, 1938, Goebbels declared "that enemy countries exaggerate events in Germany." He advised them to leave the solution of the 'Jewish problem' to the German people. On November 13, 1938, the *Lauterbacher Anzeiger*, in an article headed "Crocodile Tears," referred to a forthcoming debate in the English Parliament's Lower House regarding the events of the November pogrom in Germany. This newspaper article also alluded to the alleged fact that only German blood flowed on *Kristallnacht*: "A German lies in his bier, and no hair was hurt on a Jewish head." The article further stated that if the English Parliament's Lower House saw fit to discuss action against Jews in Germany, then the *Reichstag* should initiate a debate on the British in Palestine. According to the article, the only difference would be that the *Reichstag* had enough material for weeks of discussion about atrocities by the Jews towards the Arabs in Palestine, whereas debates in the Lower House would be quickly depleted after conferring about a few broken windows and some burnt synagogues.

In reality, during *Kristallnacht*, the police and the auxiliary police arrested more than twenty-five thousand Jews and carried them off to the Buchenwald, Dachau, and Sachsenhausen concentration camps. Immediately thereafter, Jews were forbidden to go to the theater or to the movies and their drivers' licenses and motor vehicles were seized. Furthermore, the government imposed a fine of a thousand million *Mark* on Jews and held them responsible for the repair of any damages to their own property. By edict they were forced to sell all precious metals, jewels, and works of art, and they were ordered to put the proceeds into a blocked account.[j39]

On November 17, 1938, the *Lauterbacher Anzeiger* carried an article titled, "No One Wants Anything To Do With Jews," which stated that the international press in the United States and England was agitating against Germany's position in relation to its 'Jewish parasites.' Accordingly, the American and English press were advised to note that, in addition to Germany and Italy, many other countries wanted no part of the Jews. In this same newspaper article, the Belgian government was accused of taking increased measures against the immigration of Jews by housing them in the former penal colony of Merrplas near Antwerp. The article stated that, in the future, Jewish inmates would be increased to several thousand and they would be obligated to work. Additional concentration camps would be established shortly. The newspaper further maintained that in Amsterdam, Holland, an enthusiastic audience of ten thousand demanded that all Jewish judges and Jewish teachers be removed and that all Jews who immigrated after 1914 be expelled, because the only goal of international Judaism was the enslavement of the Dutch people. The article also noted that Ecuador was bent upon protecting its population against 'Jew-

---

[j] The Nazis, however, did not invent levying fines on Jews in Germany and certainly not in Hesse. As far back as 1697, for example, Ernst Ludwig, Landgrave of Hesse, imposed a body toll on Jews that endured until 1805. During the early 1800s, the local Lutheran church in Storndorf (a village of approximately five hundred inhabitants) annually each December assessed a tax of a silver spoon weighing three *lot* (a measure for silver alloy) on its small Jewish community. (Alfred Deggau, *Storndorf* (Giessen: Geschichts-und Altertumsverlag der Stadt Alsfeld, 1956): p. 76.

ish hyenas,' Uruguay had halted immigration of Jews, Costa Rica needed no part of 'Jewish parasites,' and Australia had refused the entrance of Jewish immigrants.

On November 19, 1938, the *Lauterbacher Anzeiger* reported that the citizenry of the Bukovina had banded together, made its way into Jewish stores and factories, and set them on fire. At that time, the Bukovina was part of Romania and ten percent of its population consisted of ethnic Germans. From the day I entered Mr. Meyer's public school class in Lauterbach in 1921 until I had to leave the *Oberrealschule* in Alsfeld in 1933 because I was Jewish, I was compelled to make generous weekly contributions for the benefit of the '*Auslandsdeutsche*,' of which the ethnic Germans of the Bukovina were among the beneficiaries. Even at age six, I was fully aware that this mandatory donation was for the promotion of Nazism and was to the detriment of Jews.

The *Lauterbacher Anzeiger* also stated that Belgium had protected itself against Jewish intruders by expulsion to prevent Jews from becoming a threat to public security. Moreover, according to the article, Switzerland had informed the Dutch Embassy in Bern that its resources were not unlimited with regard to the ever-increasing Jewish immigration from other European countries and, in view of the current unemployment situation, Switzerland could only be a country-in-transit for Jews. Even as early as 1934, my sister had been unable to obtain a work permit in Switzerland, where we had relatives, and she had been obliged to find employment as a domestic in Paris, where she had no kin.

The *Lauterbacher Anzeiger* faithfully upheld the Nazi principle of isolation of Jews—the first step toward implementing the deportation and extermination of the Jewish people. By specifying that other nations had also erected barriers against Jews, the *Lauterbacher Anzeiger* emphasized that Lauterbach's attitude toward Jews was analogous to others abroad.

Isolation of Jews was also achieved by permitting Aryan homeowners to serve Jews notice of termination of their lease. Jews were summarily assigned to live in other Jewish homes. For instance, in Lauterbach, the Gerson Friedländer family was obliged to move into a house owned by Herz Höchster in the Bahnhofstrasse, and the seventy-seven-year old Kaufmann Strauss was assigned to the home of Biena Jakob of Langgasse 19. This measure was also instituted in order to simplify the later rounding up of Jews for shipment to the East.

On November 29, 1938, the *Lauterbacher Anzeiger* made reference to Father Charles Edward Coughlin, a Roman Catholic priest in America who, in 1934, on his Sunday morning radio program, regularly preached anti-semitism. His messages engendered in me the horrible dread that Nazism was imminent in America. Father Coughlin's speeches echoed precisely the same invectives against the Jews that I had been compelled to listen to since age six in Lauterbach and Alsfeld. Father Coughlin referred to a carefully guarded document that had originated with the American Secret Service that dealt with the alleged Jewish financing of the Russian Revolution. According to Father Coughlin, this document detailed how

Chapter Twenty-One

the *coup d'etat* of 1916 had been staged primarily by Guggenheim, Max Breitung, and the directors of the Jewish bank Kuhn Loeb and Company: Jacob Schiff, Felix Warburg, Otto Kahn, Mortimer Schiff, and Hanauer.

At the end of December, 1939, the following Jews were still in Lauterbach: Biena Jakob of Langgasse 19;[k] Salli Weinberg, his wife, Rosa (née Lamm) from Ober-Gleen, and their son, Arthur[l] (born October 26, 1929). The last Jew to leave Lauterbach was Hilde Weinberg. It is astounding that these people were able to survive in Lauterbach after the beginning of World War II. Their survival is probably attributable to several altruistic individuals in town: among them the members of the Roth family (of) Am See, who were of much service to the various Weinberg families and the parents of Wilhelm Euler of Ensertweg 3. By 1939, approximately half of the five hundred thousand German Jews had emigrated from Germany; of the seventy thousand Jews of Hesse, roughly thirty-five thousand had departed.[40] In the *Reichstag* in January 1939, nine months prior to his attack on Poland, Hitler predicted the annihilation of the Jewish race in Europe. On October 12, 1939, the first deportation of Jews from Austria and Moravia to Poland took place.

On November 23, 1939, approximately one year after *Kristallnacht* in Germany, the wearing of the *Judenstern* (Jewish six-pointed Star of David) was made compulsory throughout occupied Poland.[m] In the spring of 1940, the Jews of Denmark, Norway, Holland, Belgium, and France came under Nazi rule. Notwithstanding German occupation, the Danes and their government did not cast their lot with the Germans regarding Jewish persecution. Instead, when it became known that deportation of Jews was imminent, a rescue operation to Sweden was successfully executed.

---

[k] She moved to Berlin-Charlottenburg on March 17, 1940 and reached the United States with her son, Ludwig, before America's entry into World War II in 1941.

[l] They all moved to Frankfurt am Main on February 27, 1940.

[m] Badges or distinctive clothing in order to identify Jews was not a Nazi invention. In Spain, France, and the Holy Roman Empire, Jews had been required to wear badges. When Napoleon outlawed ghettos in 1797, the last badges were abolished.

Endnotes

1. *Lauterbacher Anzeiger,* November 8, 1988.

2. *German Tribute*, September 29, 1985.

3. Wolf-Arno Kropat, *Kristallnacht in Hessen* (Wiesbaden: Kommission für dis Geschichte der Juden in Hessen, 1988), p. 10.

4. Interview with Mr. Gorsler, a member of the Lauterbach Town Council on October 14, 1991.

5. Renate Chotjewitz-Häfner and Peter Chotjewitz, *Die Juden von Rhina* (Oberellenbach: Verlag Geisteswissentschaftliche Dokumentation GmbH, 1988), p. 42.

6. Ibid.

7. Ibid, p. 11.

8. Thomas W. Lummitsch, *Jüdisches Leben in Gedern* (Schotten: AS-Druck und Verlag GmbH, August 1991), p. 199.

9. Ibid, p. 170.

10. *Aufbau*, November 7, 1986, p. 9.

11. Renate Chotjewitz-Häfner and Peter Chotjewitz, *Die Juden von Rhina*, p. 41.

12. Interview with Fred Bohm, a Viennese Jew, on January 4, 1988.

13. Kropat, *Kristallnacht in Hessen*, p. 11.

14. Ibid, p. 12.

15. *Encyclopedia Judaica,* Vol. 8, (Jerusalem: Keter Publishing House, 1978), p. 839.

16. Kropat, *Neunhundert Jahre Geschichte der Juden in Hessen* (Wiesbaden: Kommission für die Geschichte der Juden in Hessen, 1983), p. 435.

17. Thea Altaras, *Synagogen in Hessen* (Königstein im Taunus: Verlag Karl Robert Langewiesche Nachfolder Hans Köster), p. 26.

18. Interview with Georg Vollmüller in Lauterbach, October 10, 1991.

19. Information regarding the 1938 pogrom was obtained on October 14, 1991, from Karl H. Gorsler; Hans Keller, on May 25, 1990; Georg Vollmüller, on May 25, 1990; and Gretel Dillmann Stöhr, on August 8, 1988.

20. Dr. Karl Siegmar Baron von Galera, *Lauterbach in Hessen,* Vol. III (Neustadt an der Aisch: Verlag Degener and Company, 1965), p. 395.

21. Ibid..

22. Interview with Elfriede Roth in Lauterbach on July 29, 1988.

23. Interview with Gretel Dillmann Stöhr in Lauterbach in July 1985.

24. Interview with Lise Hammerstett in Angersbach on October 12, 1992.

25. Interview with Florchen Stiehler on July 28, 1988.

26. von Galera, *Lauterbach in Hessen*, Vol. III, p. 395.

27. Interview with Georg Vollmüller in Lauterbach on May 25, 1990.

28. Interview with Florchen Stiehler on July 28, 1988, in Lauterbach.

29. von Galera, *Lauterbach in Hessen*, Vol. III, p. 395.

30. *Lauterbacher Anzeiger*, November 10, 1988, and personal interview with Florchen Stiehler on July 28, 1988.

31. Interview in Lauterbach with Mr. Georg Vollmüller on May 25, 1990.

32. Interview with Mechtild Kullman Moliter, in Lauterbach, on July 28, 1988.

33. Interview with Mr. Gorsler in Lauterbach on October 14, 1991.

34. Interview with Hans Keller in Lauterbach on May 25, 1990.

35. Ari L. Goldman, *New York Times*, November 10, 1988.

36. von Galera, *Lauterbach in Hessen*, Vol. III, p. 395, 396.

37. Kropat, *Kristallnacht in Hessen,* p. 25.

38. Goldman, *New York Times*, November 10, 1988.

39. Sievers, *Juden in Deutschland*, p. 261.

40. Kropat, *Neunhundert Jahre Geschichte der Juden in Hessen*, p. 440.

Arnold Stern
Born 12.15.1923 in Lauterbach
Deported from Frankfurt am Main
Murdered in an unknown place

Max (Moses) Stern
Born 7.21.1885 in Hintersteinau
Deported from Frankfurt am Main
Murdered in an unknown place

**THE MAX
STERN FAMILY**

Rosa Oppenheimer Stern
Born 4.22.1893 in Hanau
Deported from Frankfurt am Main
Murdered in an unknown place

Chapter Twenty-Two
The 'Final Solution' and the Lauterbach Jews

THE KUGELMANN FAMILY

Paula Kleeberg Kugelmann
Born 10.16.1903 in Lauterbach
Deported from Witzenhausen
Murdered in Stutthof

Husband of Paula Kleeberg
Kugelmann
Presumed deported from Witzenhausen
Presumed murdered in Stutthof

Daughter of Paula Kleeberg Kugelmann
Presumed deported from Witzenhausen
Presumed murdered in Stutthof

THE MORITZ
STERN FAMILY

Rosa Gottlieb Stern
Born 12.13.1900 in Grebenau
Deported from Karlsruhe
Murdered in Auschwitz

Moritz Stern
Born 10.24.1900 in Ober-Breidenbach
Deported from Karlsruhe
Murdered in Auschwitz

THE HÖCHSTER FAMILY

Regine Höchster
Born 2.26.1869 in Fulda
Deported from Frankfurt am Main
Murdered in Minsk

Jettchen Schiff Wunsch
(Mother of Blanka Höchster)
Born 12.12.1858 in Grosskarben
Deported from Mönchen-Gladbach
Murdered in Theresienstadt 9.21.1942

Emma Baumann Jakob
Born 4.10.1868 in Storndorf
Deported from Regensburg
Murdered in Theresienstadt 1.29.1943

Seligmann Jakob
Born 1.25.1866 in Storndorf
Deported from Regensburg
Murdered in Theresienstadt
1.22.1943

Julius Jakob
Born 1.27.1896
Deported from Regensburg
Murdered in Piaski, Poland

THE JACOB FAMILY

THE KATZ FAMILY

Max Jakob (I)
Born 9.28.1900
Deported from Regensburg
Murdered in an unknown place

Martha Stern Katz
Born 8.31.1891in Giessen
Deported from Berlin
Murdered in Auschwitz

Hannelore Katz
Born 4.14.1933 in Berlin
Deported from Berlin
Murdered in Auschwitz

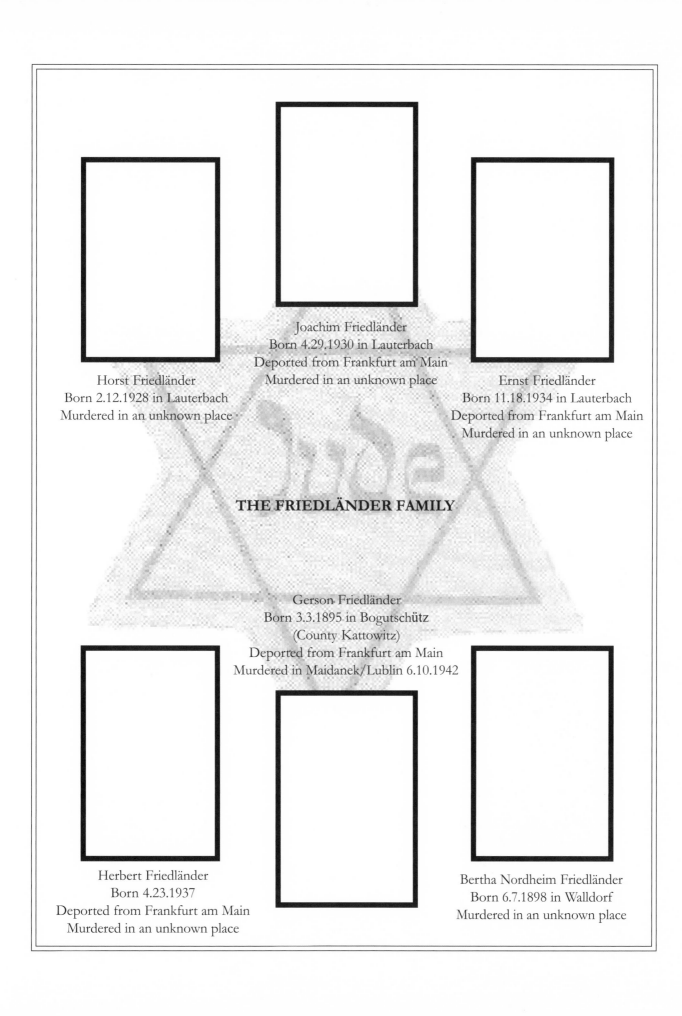

Joachim Friedländer
Born 4.29.1930 in Lauterbach
Deported from Frankfurt am Main
Murdered in an unknown place

Horst Friedländer
Born 2.12.1928 in Lauterbach
Murdered in an unknown place

Ernst Friedländer
Born 11.18.1934 in Lauterbach
Deported from Frankfurt am Main
Murdered in an unknown place

THE FRIEDLÄNDER FAMILY

Gerson Friedländer
Born 3.3.1895 in Bogutschütz
(County Kattowitz)
Deported from Frankfurt am Main
Murdered in Maidanek/Lublin 6.10.1942

Herbert Friedländer
Born 4.23.1937
Deported from Frankfurt am Main
Murdered in an unknown place

Bertha Nordheim Friedländer
Born 6.7.1898 in Walldorf
Murdered in an unknown place

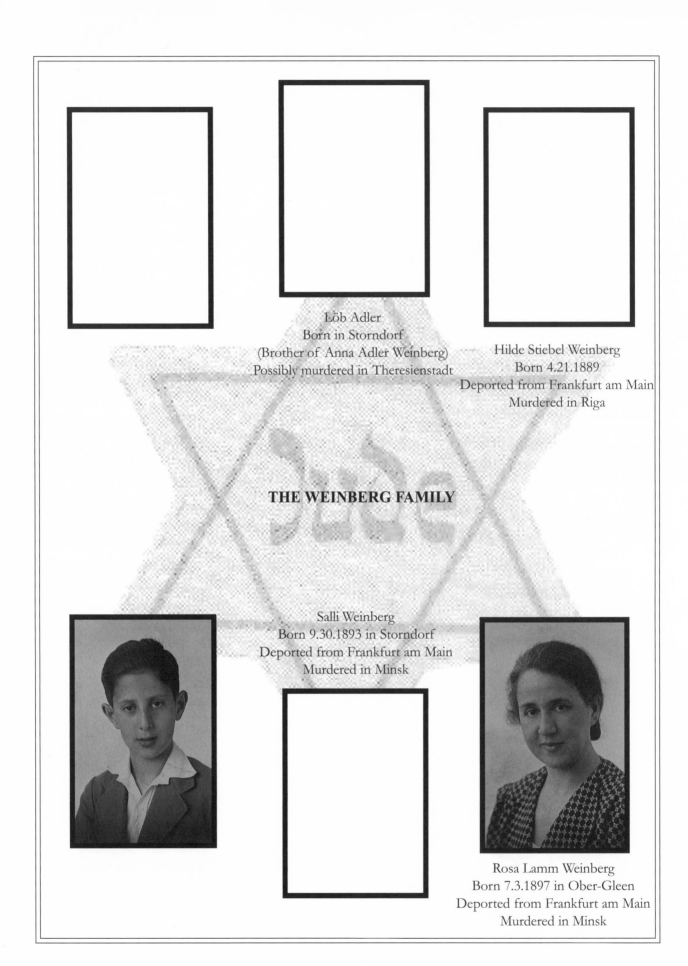

Löb Adler
Born in Storndorf
(Brother of Anna Adler Weinberg)
Possibly murdered in Theresienstadt

Hilde Stiebel Weinberg
Born 4.21.1889
Deported from Frankfurt am Main
Murdered in Riga

THE WEINBERG FAMILY

Salli Weinberg
Born 9.30.1893 in Storndorf
Deported from Frankfurt am Main
Murdered in Minsk

Rosa Lamm Weinberg
Born 7.3.1897 in Ober-Gleen
Deported from Frankfurt am Main
Murdered in Minsk

THE SELIGMANN FAMILY

Johanna Strauss Seligmann
Born 5.21.1881 in Lauterbach
Deported from Oberndorf
Murdered in an unknown place

Anna Gottlieb Reiss
(The mother of Auguste Pfifferling)
Born 3.27.1858 in Neuhof
Deported from Dresden
Murdered in Theresienstadt 9.5.1942

**THE PFIFFERLING
FAMILY**

Alex Pfifferling
Born 5.17.1878 in Datterode
Deported from Dresden
Murdered in an unknown place

Auguste Pfifferling
Born 9.8.1882 in Ulrichstein
Deported from Dresden
Murdered in an unknown place

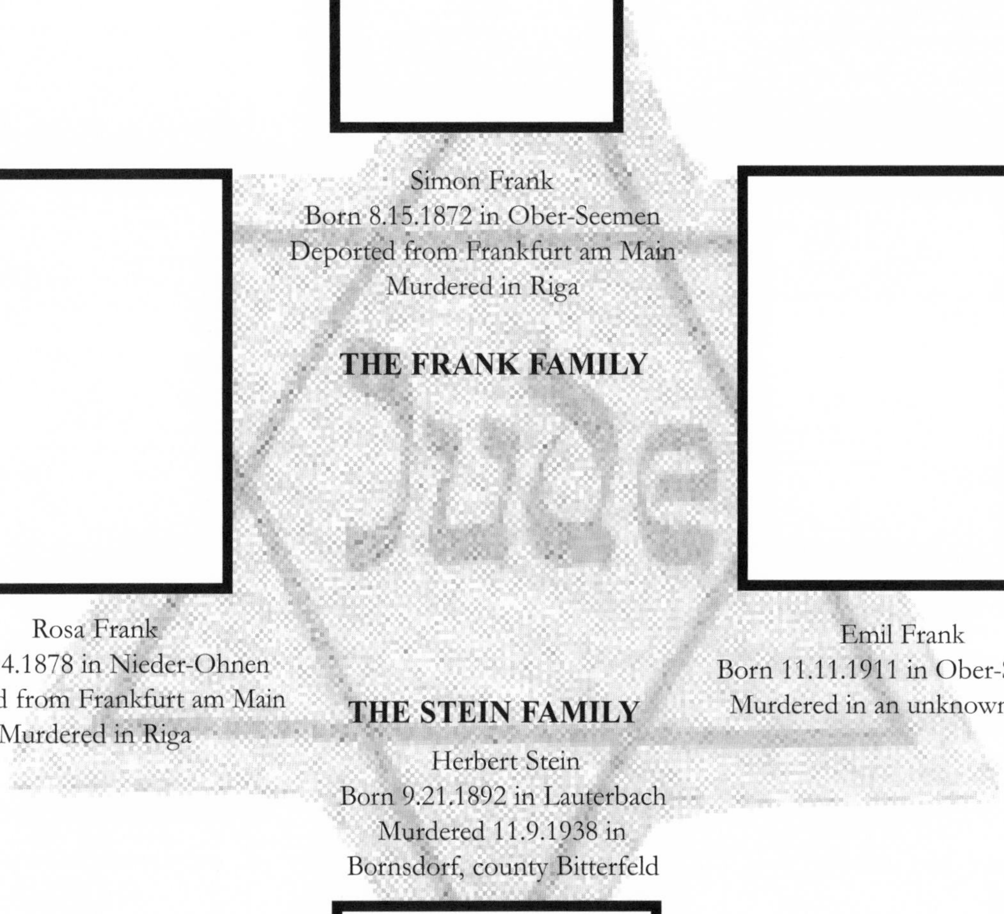

Simon Frank
Born 8.15.1872 in Ober-Seemen
Deported from Frankfurt am Main
Murdered in Riga

THE FRANK FAMILY

Rosa Frank
Born 2.4.1878 in Nieder-Ohnen
Deported from Frankfurt am Main
Murdered in Riga

Emil Frank
Born 11.11.1911 in Ober-Seemen
Murdered in an unknown place

THE STEIN FAMILY

Herbert Stein
Born 9.21.1892 in Lauterbach
Murdered 11.9.1938 in
Bornsdorf, county Bitterfeld

Blanka Strauss
Born 1.7.1924 in Lauterbach
Deported from Fulda
Murdered in Riga

Martha Amalia Meyer Strauss
(Mother of Blanka Strauss)
Born 1.7.1887 in Beerfelden
Deported from Fulda
Murdered in Zamosc, Poland

Minna Bechthold Strauss
Born 1.3.1878 in Bechhofen
Deported from Frankfurt am Main
Murdered in an unknown place

THE STRAUSS FAMILIES

Samuel Strauss (II)
Born 7.14.1875 in Storndorf
Deported from Frankfurt am Main
Murdered in an unknown place

Therese Strauss
(Mother of Sara Strauss Spier)
Born 8.18.1864 in Storndorf
Deported from Frankfurt am Main
Murdered in Theresienstadt 6.2.1943

Sara Strauss Spier
Born 10.20.1892
Deported from Frankfurt am Main
Murdered in an unknown place

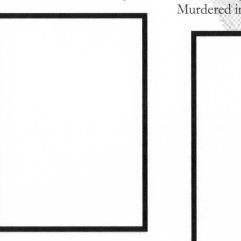

Else Baumann
Born in Storndorf
Murdered in an unknown place

Juda Baumann (II)
Born 7.15.1864 in Storndorf
Deported from Frankfurt am Main
Murdered in Theresienstadt 11.15.1942

THE BAUMANN FAMILY

Trude Blumenthal
Born 11.23.1925 in Gedern
Deported from Frankfurt am Main
Murdered in an unknown place

Jenny Baumann
Born 6.29.1900 in Lauterbach
Murdered in an unknown place

Ida Baumann Cussel
Born in Storndorf
Murdered in an unknown place

THE
'FINAL SOLUTION'

*O*n July 31, 1941, Reinhard Heydrich was appointed to carry out the 'Final Solution.' On September 23, 1941, the first experiments with gassing were made at Auschwitz. From May 1, 1941 until October 1, 1941, the number of Jews in Germany diminished from 168,972 to 163,696; by January 1, 1942 the number of German Jews was reduced to 131,823.[1] On January 20, 1942, the Nazis called the Wannsee Conference in Berlin to plan the implementation of the 'Final Solution.' Details of this conference became known through the Eichmann trial in Israel in May, 1962. After the Wannsee Conference, deportations commenced on a large scale. On January 1, 1943, only 51,257 Jews still lived in Germany, which was about one-tenth of the Jews who resided in Germany before Hitler's ascent to power.

During the Nuremberg trials in 1945 and 1946, the SS group leader Otto Ohlendorf, who was responsible for the murder of tens of thousands of Jews, reported that "in the spring of 1942 the chief of the security police had gas vans delivered with the order to use them for the killing of women and children. The victims were informed that they were being resettled and for this purpose they had to climb into the cars. Thereafter the doors were closed and the gas streamed in— it was activated by motion. Then the cars were taken to the place of burial." The commandant of Treblinka and later Auschwitz, Rudolf Höss recalled: "The commanding officer of Treblinka told me that he liquidated 80,000 in the course of half a year. He used [carbon] monoxide and in his opinion his methods were not very effective. As he set up the extermination building in Auschwitz he also used Zyklon B, a crystallized hydrocyanic acid, which we threw into the death chamber through a small opening. It lasted three to fifteen minutes—we knew at what point they were dead because their screaming came to an end."

The deportations of the German Jews '*nach dem Osten*' ('to the East') began in the fall of 1941. In Hesse, thousands of Jews were taken from their homes and were carted off to concentration and extermination camps. From Frankfurt am Main (where so many Jews from Lauterbach and the vicinity sought refuge) and its surroundings, 9,145 Jews were deported. At first they were shipped to Lodz, Minsk, and Riga; later they were sent either to Auschwitz or Theresienstadt, which was established in 1941 in Czechoslovakia. Originally intended for only seven thousand people, more than one hundred fifty thousand were squeezed together until the end of the war in 1945.

An additional 34,000 perished from hunger and illness, more than eighty-eight thousand were ultimately sent to extermination camps, and 30,400 lived to see the day of liberation. Most of the Jews of Hesse were liquidated in extermination camps, primarily Auschwitz.[2] On January 12, 1943, Else Ury from Berlin, author of the well-known ten-part series called 'Baby In The Family' ('*Nesthäkchen*') and many other books, was given number 638 on the deportation list to Auschwitz, where she was murdered.[3] In the 1920s, the young girls of Lauterbach enthusiastically devoured her books unaware, as was I, that their favorite author was Jewish.

Chapter Twenty-Two

Many Jews still in physical good health worked in armament factories and were also used in medical experiments conducted by physicians in the camps. These doctors infected the Jewish inmates with pathogens (disease-causing agents) in order to try out various methods of treatment. A medical team in Dachau researched malaria, a group in Buchenwald explored typhus fever, and a team of physicians in Ravensbrück investigated gangrene and tetanus.

The largest medical group in Auschwitz worked on sterilization procedures, with the objective of sterilizing Jewish men and women without costly operative measures. The Nazi doctors at Auschwitz proceeded from the notion that the ability of Jews to work was to be preserved, but their propagation was to be prevented forcibly.[a] The gynecologist, Klaus Clauberg, worked on a method of sterilizing women by injecting a caustic substance into their uterus. Dr. Schumann, a radiologist, x-rayed for fifteen minutes the testicles of Jewish men who were twenty to twenty-four years old. Two weeks later, he removed their testicles and forwarded the organs onto the doctor in charge of histological examinations. Whenever the work output of these guinea pigs lessened, Dr. Schumann released them for gassing.

Although some concentration camps kept careful accounts, the number of people who perished can only be estimated: 1,000,000 were liquidated in Auschwitz; 700,000 in Treblinka; 600,000 in Belzec; 300,000 in Chelmno; 250,000 in Sobibor; and 200,000 in Maidanek. On April 1, 1943, there were still 31,807 Jews in Germany, but on September 1, 1944 there were 14,574.[4] The detection, gathering, deportation, and liquidation of Jews comprised the entire area of Europe occupied by the Nazis: from Norway to Rhodes and from the Atlantic to the Caucasus.

After the Nazi occupation of France, my mother's cousin, Selma Strauss, formerly of Hinter dem Spittel 4 in Lauterbach, was living with her husband in Paris. In the middle of the night, when her husband answered a knock at the door, he was carried off and was never heard from again. The number of Germans facilitating the Nazi program in occupied Europe was astoundingly small. In all of France there were only two to three thousand men designated for this purpose.[5] The Nazis were able to make arrests in the occupied countries only with the aid of local authorities and others who willingly cooperated and informed against Jews.

Selma Strauss

Selma Strauss was interned in Gurs, a refugee camp in southern France. There she encountered my mother's cousin, Bertel Strauss Wolf of Bruchsal, and Bertel's husband, Ferdinand Wolf. Each day in Gurs, Ferdinand announced the amount of capital Germany owed him after the defeat of the Nazis. He based his computations on the losses accrued by his enforced absence from his business. In 1941, Ferdinand Wolf and his wife, Bertel Strauss Wolf, were liquidated by the Nazis in Poland. In her youth, Bertel, the only daughter of the four children of Rosalie Stern Strauss (born April 5, 1867 in Pflaumloch) and Leopold Strauss, my maternal

[a] In the early 1930s, my classmates in Alsfeld were already enthusiastic advocates of this notion.

grandmother's brother (born November 30, 1861 in Storndorf), had led a very pampered and protected life. Her youngest brother, Richard Strauss, was killed on December 15, 1916 in World War I while fighting for Germany. Rosalie and Leopold Strauss' twin sons, Siegfried (I) and Alfred, born on April 24, 1891 in Battenfeld, Hesse; Siegfried's wife, Regina Rosenberg Strauss, born January 13, 1898 in Ahlen, Westphalia; their son, Richard, born October 10, 1926 in Essen; and Alfred and his wife, Lore Dahl Strauss, were shipped from Essen/Düsseldorf to Theresienstadt on September 10, 1943. On December 18, 1943, these families were deported and murdered in Auschwitz.[6b] Selma Strauss was able to obtain an entrance visa after World War II to the United States.

THE CHILDREN OF LAUTERBACH WHO PERISHED IN THE 'FINAL SOLUTION'

ONLY ELEVEN PERCENT OF ALL JEWISH CHILDREN under fourteen survived the war.[7] The following children from Lauterbach perished: Trude Blumenthal,[c] Horst Friedländer, Joachim Friedländer, Ernst Friedländer, Herbert Friedländer, and Arthur Weinberg. At the time of his assassination in 1938, Herbert Stein was sixteen years old. The Lauterbach public school classmates Arnold Stern (Hinter der Burg 17) and Blanka Strauss (am Eselswörth 6) were liquidated while still in their teens. I do not know where the handicapped child, Trude Blumenthal, was murdered; nor do I know where the four Friedländer children were killed. Arthur Weinberg was lost without trace in Minsk. Herbert Stein was slain in Bornsdorf in the county of Bitterfeld. I do not know where Arnold Stern was killed, but Blanka Strauss was liquidated in Riga. This camp was liberated by Soviet troops on July 24, 1944, one month after the beginning of the Soviet offensive on June 23, 1944.

TWO SURVIVORS OF THERESIENSTADT

ONLY TWO JEWS FROM LAUTERBACH SURVIVED their incarceration in Theresienstadt. In general, older Jews were transported there, as well as Jews who were war-disabled ex-servicemen from World War I or Jews married to a Christian. In August 1942, Nathan Höchster and his wife, Thea, were hauled off to Theresienstadt. In May 1943, Nathan Höchster died of tuberculosis caused by starvation, but before he died he was twice taken out of groups headed for Auschwitz. Because of her profession as a trained nurse, Thea was essential to the Nazis because they wanted to pass health inspections for Theresienstadt by the International Red Cross. She was a gentle but resolute individual who doubtless rendered much comfort to the elderly. The aged Mrs. Oppenheimer of Hanau, mother of Rosa Stern (the teacher's wife in Lauterbach) died in Thea's arms. In 1945, Thea went with a transport from Theresienstadt to Switzerland to be with her children, Grete and Hans, after having been separated from them for seven years. In September, 1945, this family went to Palestine, where they found a new home.[8]

[b] In order to reduce overcrowding, transfers from Theresienstadt generally occurred just prior to scheduled visits of the International Red Cross
[c] Born in Gedern, she moved to Lauterbach to live were her aunt, Ida Baumann Cussel of Bahnhofstrasse 66.

The second survivor of Theresienstadt from Lauterbach was Rosa Weinberg Glitsch, the daughter of Regina and Nathan Weinberg. Rosa had married the non-Jewish tailor, Glitsch, from Landenhausen and converted to Lutheranism. She was permitted to stay with her husband in Lauterbach at Hinter dem Spittel until 1942 or 1943. Thereafter she was shipped to Theresienstadt, where her occupation of seamstress helped her survive. After the end of World War II, she was returned by truck from Theresienstadt. Within view of the town of Lauterbach, she alighted from the vehicle and uttered a prayer of thanks.[9]

THE BAUMANN
FAMILY

THE NAZIS LIQUIDATED MOST MEMBERS of the Baumann families who had lived for many years in Lauterbach and, in a number of instances, for two generations. On November 28, 1938, the seventy-four-year old Juda Baumann (II) moved with his daughters, Ida Baumann Cussel and Recha Baumann, and his retarded granddaughter, Trude Blumenthal, to Friedrichstrasse 48 in Frankfurt am Main. On November 15, 1942, Juda Baumann (II) died in Theresienstadt. It is not known where Juda Baumann's daughters, Ida Baumann Cussel and Else, who lived with her husband in Nuremberg, were liquidated by the Nazis.

When Emma Baumann Blumenthal, the oldest daughter of Juda Baumann (II), immigrated to the United States, Emma and Gustav's handicapped daughter, Trude, was refused an American visa. Emma departed with her son, Werner, and her husband, Gustav Blumenthal, who already had suffered much at the hands of the Nazis in Gedern. The parents left the care of their disabled daughter in Lauterbach to Ida Baumann Cussel, Emma's sister. Could Trude Blumenthal have been the one who was sent to death by Dr. Hans-Joachim Sewering[d] when he directed a disabled girl to a euthanasia site. Gustav Blumenthal died shortly after he came to the United States, probably due to physical injuries that the Nazis had inflicted on him in Gedern and the anguish about his daughter, whom he had to leave behind. Emma outlived her husband by some years. One of her granddaughters is a practicing physician in Utah, and another granddaughter practices law in Atlanta.

Juda Baumann (II).
He perished in
Theresienstadt

Altogether, the Baumann family of Lauterbach lost thirty-three of their immediate relatives, among them: Else Baumann (daughter of Juda Baumann (II) and Elda Baumann of Bahnhofstrasse 66), who lived with her husband in Nuremberg; Ida Baumann Cussel; and Jenny Baumann, the daughter of Juda Baumann (I) and Karoline Hasenauer Baumann of Bleichstrasse 12.[10]

THE FRIEDLÄNDER
FAMILY

I DO NOT KNOW WHERE THE NAZIS wiped out Bertha Nordheim Friedländer. Gerson Friedländer perished in Maidanek.

---

[d] Ironically, Dr. Sewering was elected president of the World Medical Association on October 1, 1992, although *Der Spiegel* had disclosed information about his past in 1978. However, early in 1993, Dr. Sewering was forced to resign from his post. (Jennifer Learning, *New York Times*, January 6, 1993.)

Trude Blumenthal and her brother, Werner Blumenthal

REGINE HÖCHSTER WAS MURDERED IN MINSK; her husband, Herz Höchster, died in Frankfurt am Main of a kidney ailment, which is believed to be an inherited disorder of the Höchster families.[11] Herz Höchster's brother, Kaufmann Höchster, and his wife, Blanka Wunsch Höchster, repose in Mönchengladbach in a double grave inscribed with their names, the years of their birth (1887 and 1888, respectively), and 1940 as their date of death.[12] Blanka Höchster's mother, the widowed Jettchen Wunsch [née Schiff] (born December 12, 1858 in Grosskarben) had, for as long as I can recall, resided with the Kaufmann Höchster family in the Rockelsgasse. On February 16, 1937, she moved with her family to Mönchengladbach. Jettchen Wunsch was probably still in town at the time of the deaths of her son-in-law and daughter and was probably instrumental in erecting a tombstone for them. Jettchen Wunsch was an individual of considerable sincerity, goodness, and strength. What thoughts must have crossed her mind when, older than eighty and bereft of her family, she was hauled off to Theresienstadt by the Nazis? Jettchen Wunsch was lost without trace in Theresienstadt.

ANNA REISS (NÉE GOTTLIEB) OF BAHNHOFSTRASSE 20, (from Neuhof), and the mother of Siegfried Reiss and Auguste Reiss Pfifferling, also met death in Theresienstadt. Anna's son, Siegfried Reiss, her daughter-in-law, Meta Rothschild Reiss, and her two grandchildren, Erich and Elly Reiss, managed to come to the United States. However, I do not know where the Nazis and their willing helpers dealt the death blow to Auguste Pfifferling, Anna Reiss' daughter, and her husband, Alex Pfifferling, of Bahnhofstrasse 18. Beginning in March 1933, local Nazis tyrannized this family relentlessly and in October, 1934, they were compelled to move to Dresden, where their oldest son, Ernst Pfifferling, resided. In May 1936, Anna Reiss also moved to Dresden in order to escape the ill-treatment of Lauterbach Nazis.

I DO NOT KNOW WHERE THE NAZIS ANNIHILATED the teacher Max Moses Stern (born July 21, 1885 in Hintersteinau), his wife Rosa Oppenheimer Stern (born April 22, 1893 in Hanau), and their teenage son, Arnold (born December 16, 1923 in Lauterbach). On January 1, 1936, Max and Rosa Stern, together with their children, Salochen (afflicted with spastic paralysis since birth), Arnold, Manfred, and Herbert, left Lauterbach for Frankfurt am Main (Obermainanlage 22). Providentially, Salo died a natural death in Frankfurt am Main and was laid to rest in the Jewish cemetery. In the late 1980s, Dr. Naphtali (Herbert) Stern found his oldest brother's grave.

The Stern family was persuaded to leave Lauterbach because the local school authorities forbade Jewish children to attend classes, whereas in Frankfurt am Main the Stern children were able to go to a Jewish school. Ironically, during World War I, Max Stern had taught for two years (1914-1916) in the Lauterbach public school system without monetary compensation. Thereafter, he volunteered for military service and was awarded the Iron Cross. With the official advent of Hitler in 1933,

Left: Max and Rosa Stern. Date and place of death unknown.
Above: Arnold Stern, the son of Max and Rosa Stern, was murdered by the Nazis and lost without a trace.

Passport of Manfred Stern dated December 7, 1939. Manfred is thirteen years of age. Manfred escaped to Palestine on a childrens' transport.

Chapter Twenty-Two

the lives of the Stern family were considerably embittered by the inveterate Nazi family Beyer (owners of a nursery across the way); in contrast, the neighboring principled Georg family strove to make the existence of the Stern family less painful.

On November 22, 1938, Moritz Stern (born October 24, 1900 in Oberbreidenbach near Alsfeld) and his wife, Rosa Gottlieb Stern (born December 23, 1900 in Grebenau near Alsfeld), hastily moved their family from Am Wörth 16 to Karlsruhe after the Lauterbach Nazis wreaked great damage on them and their property. From Karlsruhe, the Nazis hauled Rosa and Moritz off to Auschwitz, where they were liquidated. Providentially, Moritz and Rosa Stern possessed the fortitude to part with their young daughters, Beate and Susi Sylvia, and had them join a children's transport to the United States.

THE KUGELMANN FAMILY

THE NAZIS ALSO LIQUIDATED Paula Kleeberg Kugelmann (born October 16, 1903 in Lauterbach), her husband, and their young teenage daughter, all of whom lived in Witzenhausen. Paula was the daughter of Salli Kleeberg and Toni Stein Kleeberg of Obergasse 24 in Lauterbach.

THE SALLI STRAUSS FAMILY

THE NAZIS ALSO LIQUIDATED Amalie Martha Meyer Strauss (born January 7, 1887 in Beerfelden), widow of the late Salli Strauss (I), my mother's cousin, who

Left to right, first row: Carola Strauss, Ludwig Jakob, Lotte Kleeberg
Left to right, second row: Bertel Strauss, Max Jakob (II), Rosa Gottlieb, Max Jacob (I)
Left to right, third row (standing): Ruth Weinberg, Hermann Strauss, Jenny Baumann, Paula Kleeberg, Salli Strauss (II), and Siegfried Baumann.
Circa 1926 or 1927.

The Nazis murdered Jenny Baumann, Rosa Gottlieb, Max Jakob (I) and Paula Kleeberg of these thirteen young Lauterbach Jews.

lived at Am Eselswörth 6 in Lauterbach with her two children, Siegfried (born September 3, 1921 in Lauterbach) and Blanka (born January 7, 1924 in Lauterbach). On April 4, 1934, Martha moved with her son and daughter to Sturmiusstrasse 5 in Fulda, from whence the Nazis shipped her to the East. She died in Zamosc, Poland. Siegfried [III] (Steven) fled to England from whence he reached Australia. The Nazis also murdered Sara Strauss Spier of Bahnhofstrasse 70, the widow of Moritz Spier of Momberg, who had sacrificed his life for Germany in World War I. The Nazis shipped Sara's mother, Therese Strauss (born in Storndorf, who lived at Bahnhofstrasse 70) from her residence in Frankfurt am Main (Obere Mainanlage 20) to Theresienstadt, where she died.

Left: Martha Amalie Strauss, widow of Salli Strauss (I). She was murdered by the Nazis in Zamosc, Poland. (Also pictured is Salli Strauss (I) and their son, Siegfried [Steven] Strauss.)

Below: The young Blanka Strauss' verse in her friend's album. It reads:
"I will love you forever dear friend. Think of me even though I am no longer here. At least I wrote into your album. In fond memory, Blanka Strauss.
Lauterbach: April 4, 1934."

Blanka Strauss. She was murdered in Riga.

Samuel Strauss (II) (born July 14, 1875 in Storndorf) and his wife, Minna Bechthold Strauss (born January 3, 1878 in Bechhofen), lived in the Rockelsgasse in Lauterbach. At the time of the November 10, 1938 pogrom, this Strauss family resided with other Jewish families in the synagogue building on Hinter der Burg. By then the Stern family had already moved to Frankfurt am Main. The destruction by fire of the synagogue building made Minna and Samuel Strauss homeless. On November 17, 1938, this family moved to Nieder-Weisel, where they were taken in by family members. I do not know where the Nazis murdered Minna and Samuel Strauss (II).

Siegfried (III), the son of Martha and Salli Strauss (I), successfully withstood the rigors of immigration and internment, and eventually became the first judge in Melbourne who was not Australian by birth. Salli Strauss' sister, Mathilde Wahlhaus, who was in her late fifties at the time of her immigration, survived the long trip to South Africa by ship in order to join her only child, Friedel Wahlhaus Nussbaum; her husband, Juda Wahlhaus, died en route.

THE SELIGMANN FAMILY

JOHANNA STRAUSS SELIGMANN (born May 21, 1881 in Lauterbach) disappeared into the night and fog of Nazi extermination. Johanna was the daughter of Salomon Strauss (I) and Jettchen Schloss Strauss and was Salli Strauss' sister. Since 1878, this family had lived at Am Eselswörth 6. Circa 1908, Johanna married Isack Seligmann of Oberndorf near Braunfels. In the early 1930s, Johanna was afflicted with deep grief over the loss of her husband and her two teenage daughters, Selma and Toni. By the late 1930s, Johanna's sons, Fritz and Herbert, and her daughter, Trude, fled to the United States, which was evidently not within Johanna's reach. The place of Johanna's murder is not known.

Johanna Strauss Seligmann. The place of her murder by the Nazis is unknown.

THE WEINBERG FAMILY

THE NAZIS ANNIHILATED Salli Weinberg, his wife, Rosa Lamm Weinberg from Ober-Gleen, and their young son, Arthur. They lived in the Bahnhofstrasse, a few houses away from the butcher, Knoll. During *Kristallnacht*, the Lauterbach Nazis grabbed Rosa's curly hair and pulled her down the steps while Mr. Rockel beat up Salli Weinberg. Subsequently, Salli was taken 'into protective custody' for a stay in Buchenwald. Salli and Rosa Weinberg and their son, Arthur, perished in Minsk. This family had been unable to materialize their plan to flee to Chile. Their packed household goods remained in Holland at the end of World War II.

I do not know where the Nazis killed Hilde Stiebel Weinberg (born April 21, 1889 in Allendorf an der Lahn), widow of Rudolf Weinberg. Since 1910, Hilde had lived with her husband and son, Alfred, in a rented flat in the Vogelsbergstrasse in Lauterbach. In 1935, Hilde Weinberg moved into the residence of her late brother-in-law, Josef Weinberg, at Steinweg 11 in Lauterbach. She left Lauterbach for Frankfurt am Main on July 26, 1940. Alfred Weinberg escaped to the United States on July 14, 1938.

I am not informed of the fate of Anna Adler Weinberg, widow of Markus Weinberg (born April 5, 1869 in Storndorf), who resided (at) Am Wörth 14 in Lauterbach. She moved to Frankfurt am Main on March 28, 1938. Moreover, I do not know what happened to her brother, Löb Adler (born November 17, 1865 in Storndorf), who lived with his sister in Lauterbach until July 19, 1937, when he moved to Ellar, Kreis Limburg.

THE JAKOB FAMILY

SELIGMANN JAKOB DIED IN THERESIENSTADT on January 22, 1943. Emma Baumann Jakob died in Theresienstadt one day before Seligmann (January 21, 1943). Julius Jakob was murdered in Piaski, Poland and Max Jakob met his death in an unknown place.

THE KATZ FAMILY

I AM INFORMED OF THE UNDOING OF THE MORITZ KATZ FAMILY, who in the 1920s lived Hinter dem Spittel 12 prior to the time Moritz Weinberg acquired this residence. Moritz Katz and his sons, Horst and Herbert, were able to flee from Berlin to South America. However, the Nazis liquidated Moritz' wife, Martha Stern Katz (born in Giessen), and their young daughter, Hannelore in Auschwitz. In the early 1920s, Moritz' felt factory in the Rockelsgasse put a number of local unemployed people to work. In the mid-1920s, Moritz moved his business and his family to Luckenwalde near Berlin. In 1924, Hannchen Sonneborn Katz, wife of Joel Katz and Moritz and Meyer Katz' mother, was laid to rest in the Lauterbach Jewish cemetery.

OTHER VICTIMS OF THE 'FINAL SOLUTION' FROM LAUTERBACH

IN ADDITION TO THE LONG-TIME JEWISH RESIDENTS of Lauterbach whom the Nazis liquidated, there were also Jewish victims who had lived in my native town for several years. For example, Emil Frank resided with his sister, Ricka Frank Strauss, at Gartenstrasse 13. Emil was crippled due to a fall from a horse. He attended the *Realschule* in Lauterbach, because his native Ober-Seemen had no high school. His parents, Rosa and Simon Frank, refused to go abroad without Emil. The Nazis subsequently annihilated Simon and Rosa in Riga. Emil Frank was murdered in an unknown place.

THE END OF THE WAR IN LAUTERBACH

BEGINNING IN JULY 1944, the Lauterbach area endured occasional air attacks and the bombs that landed on Giessen on December 6, 1944 disquieted the Lauterbach populace considerably. American troops reached the Rhine River on March 5, 1945. On March 7, 1945, the United States First Army seized the bridge at Remagen and crossed the Rhine. On March 29, 1945 the United States Army Corps reached Lauterbach by way of the Dirlammer Strasse on *Gründonnerstag*, (a day before Good Friday, on the semi-holiday named after the green mass garments worn by priests at the Lord's Supper).

By an irony of fate, as the Americans entered Lauterbach on March 29, 1945, some of the twenty-four casualties were those who imprudently remained outdoors. For example, Helga Meyer, the granddaughter of my anti-semitic public school teacher, succumbed to a shot in the stomach, and four other individuals were hit by an explosion set off in the Lauterstrasse by retreating German soldiers. Lauterbach's casualties of World War II (incited by Germany) were three hundred eighty-five, or approximately seven percent.[13] In the war against its Jews, Lauterbach annihilated approximately twenty-six percent of its Jewish citizens. This number does not take into account the Jews who died prematurely due to physical, mental, and emotional injuries. Certainly my parents' tribulations contributed to and hastened the onset of their poor health and early deaths. Additionally, immigrants were forced by necessity to cope with the unaccustomed hardships of a different climate, poverty, and adjustment to another culture and language. These transitions were, of course, more difficult for immigrants who were in mid-life or older.

Why did the Nazis' ruthless persecution and murder of Jews in Hesse not cause any obvious disquiet among the burghers of my native town? During my visit to Lauterbach in 1959, the townspeople evaded conversation in connection with the persecution or murder of the Jews except to state that the ill-treatment of the Jews was not right-minded. Everyone I spoke to claimed to have had nothing to do with *Kristallnacht* nor were they friends with anyone who engaged in hostile actions toward Jews or their property. I could not detect any sense of accountability. For centuries in Lauterbach, the mind-set of the burghers had been conditioned by the Catholic and Protestant clergy, who railed against Jews for having killed Christ and for Jewish stiffneckedness in not recognizing the "truth" of Christianity. Generally, the local Christian clergy disregarded the emancipation of the Jews that had been half-heartedly granted by the secular state sixty years earlier in Hesse. During the Hitler era, among the younger people in Lauterbach, the Nazi racial doctrines gained a strong foothold; in comparison, the older burghers generally embraced the bigoted creed of the Lauterbach churches.

Many of my contemporaries in Lauterbach still claim that they were uninformed about the abominable brutalities masterminded and executed by Germans—perhaps a next door neighbor. This is hardly fathomable. How can a crime of such immensity that involved the concerted action and effort of so many be kept secret? Although there were no direct deportations from Lauterbach, some of the town's burghers surely were familiar with the herding together of the Jews from Giessen. Because local Nazis, like my classmate Helmut Stöppler from Maar, performed the task of rounding up Jews, relatives and other townspeople knew of their activities. Moreover, a neighbor of the Wertheim family of Angenrod gave a detailed account of the rounding up of village Jews in broad daylight. Certainly the soldiers and officers on the eastern front heard of and saw transports of humans in cattle cars. At least two of my classmates were stationed on the eastern front. Did they not discuss those events while at home on furlough? What about the huge number of Germans involved in the industry of annihilating Jews?

Endnotes

1. Leo Sievers, *Juden in Deutschland* (Hamburg: Verlag Gruner, 1977), p. 266.

2. Wolf-Arno Kropat, *Neunhundert Jahre Geschichte der Juden in Hessen* (Wiesbaden: Kommission für die Geschichte der Juden in Hessen, 1983), p. 440-441.

3. Barbara Asper, *Aufbau*, January 29, 1993, p. 4.

4. Sievers, *Juden in Deutschland*, pp. 266-269.

5. Theodore S. Hamerow, *Commentary Magazine*, March 1985, p. 33.

6. Letter from Marianne Ellenbogen of Liverpool, England, to Mathilda W. Stein of November 1984.

7. Saul Friedländer, "Juden und Deutsche," *Spiegel Spezial Nr. 2*/1992, p. 30.

8. Letter from Grete Höchster Ephraim to Mathilda W. Stein of September 24, 1991.

9. Letter of November 25, 1985, from Dr. Karl August Helfenbein, Town Historian of Lauterbach.

10. Interview with Julius Baumann of Porto Alegre, Brazil, in Lauterbach on October 7, 1991.

11. Interview with Grete Höchster Ephraim in Tel Aviv, Israel, in March 1992.

12. Letter of September 11, 1992, of Denis Cummings of Mönchengladbach to Mrs. Weiland of the Jewish Community of Fulda.

13. *Lauterbacher Anzeiger,* June 27, 1953 and March 29, 1985.

Chapter Twenty-Three
Demography of Jews in Hesse before 1933
and after 1945
Post-War 'Reparations'
The Jews of Fulda
Jews in post-war Lauterbach

The Angenrod synagogue in 1959

THE SITUATION OF THE JEWS IN GERMANY AND HESSE AFTER THE WAR

*B*efore 1933, 75,000 Jews lived in the Hesse, including Rhine-Hesse. By January 1, 1980, the number was 6,558. Because this count included 4,931 Jews residing in Frankfurt am Main,[1] only 1,527 Jews lived in the remainder of Hesse. By the end of 1932, there was a total of 401 Jewish congregations, exclusive of Frankfurt am Main; 198 of these Jewish communities were located in Upper Hesse.[2] As of October 1992, only a nominal number of Jews lived in a sprinkling of small towns and villages in Upper Hesse. After the end of World War II, not only did the number of Jews in Hesse diminish considerably, but the nature of the group had changed fundamentally.

After the end of World War II, the Jewish population of Germany consisted mainly of displaced persons from Eastern European countries who stayed in camps which were situated primarily in the American zone. In 1947, there were fifty-four German Jews in an UNRRA camp in Bad Salzschlirf (nine miles south of Lauterbach).[3] During the 1920s and early 1930s, only two or three Jewish families (one of which was Weihl) lived in Bad Salzschlirf; the remainder of the Bad Salzschlirf population was devoutly Catholic. Max Stern, the teacher of the Lauterbach Jewish congregation, instructed eligible Jewish children of Bad Salzschlirf on Sunday afternoons. To the best of my knowledge, the Jews of Bad Salzschlirf buried their dead at the Schlitz Jewish cemetery.

Because Jewish displaced persons had lost family members and endured much suffering themselves, most were determined to leave the loathsome soil of Germany with alacrity. Many went to Israel subsequent to the State's establishment in May, 1948, while others opted for Canada, Australia, and the United States. As of March, 1949, almost seventy-four percent of the Jewish communities in Hesse were composed of displaced persons (1,479 of 2,005 members). Jewish congregations were increasingly composed of a disproportionate number of older people. (In the summer of 1959, we witnessed this phenomenon while attending religious services in Frankfurt am Main in the Westend synagogue.) During the first quarter of 1963, the Jewish congregations in West Germany reported one hundred forty-two deaths and only nine births.[4]

In 1980, the average age of a Jewish person in West Germany was 44.6 years. It is estimated that by 1982 there were approximately 35,000 Jews in West Germany and 8,000 to 9,000 resided in Hesse. Until 1982, most Jewish residents of West Germany had come from Hungary, Poland, and Czechoslovakia; eighty percent had come from Eastern European countries, mostly Poland.[5] By 1992, about 30,000 Jews were members of approximately seventy Jewish congregations in Germany. As of May 1992, more than half of West Germany's Jewish population was located in Berlin (9,394), Frankfurt am Main (5,322), and Munich (4,095).[6]

A significant difference between the Jews of Germany before 1933 and those of the post-World War II area was that the former had regarded themselves as German citizens of Jewish faith ('*deutsche Staatsbürger jüdischen Glaubens*'). After 1945, the Jews residing in Germany considered themselves first and foremost as Jews.

Chapter Twenty-Three

They rejected applying for German passports, preferring a passport from another country or even carrying a passport of a stateless person. Before World War II, being stateless was disadvantageous because the individual was deprived of legal rights and protection by any government. In addition, being stateless at that time foiled entry into the United States under the quota system. In the 1920s in Lauterbach, I frequently overheard the sentiment expressed by itinerant Jews from Eastern Europe that life for Jews in Germany appeared, in comparison to Eastern Europe, like living in the Promised Land.[a]

In 1980, the 6,522 members of Jewish communities in Hesse represented an increase of two hundred fifty-six percent since 1955, as compared to a growth of only eighty percent for the remainder of West Germany.[7] Before 1933, more Jews had lived in Hesse than in other German provinces: for centuries a very high percentage of the Jews of Upper Hesse resided in many small rural communities (in Angenrod since 1667,[8] in Storndorf since the end of the sixteenth century,[9] and in Ulrichstein since 1347).[10] In these and many other Hessian villages, Jews were very deeply rooted despite the often inimical treatment by fellow villagers and German officialdom. My mother frequently referred to this circumstance by saying that if 'a man is used to hanging, his neck will not puff out.'

Before 1933, the Jewish population of most villages in Hesse usually represented an insignificant minority of the total population. However, the December 1, 1875 census of the village of Rhina recorded the rare proportion of 337 Jewish and 263 Christian inhabitants.[11] Not far from Rhina is the town of Fulda, where in the eighth century Abbott Rabanus Maurus referred to Jewish contemporaries. In 1933, the Fulda Jewish community had approximately 1,000 people; by 1942 it had dwindled to 243 members.[12] As of October 1947, thirty-six Jews of German ancestry again lived in Fulda.[13] As of 1993, there was a small Jewish congregation in Fulda comprised of four or five German Jews who had remained hidden in Germany, Jews from Eastern European lands, and recent arrivals from the republics of the former Soviet Union. In October 1991, the Fulda Jewish community graciously invited Lauterbach's official Jewish guests to attend its Friday night services. Although the Lauterbach group included five males, it was not possible to arrange for a *minyan* (a quorum of ten male Jews older than thirteen necessary for services).

Jews from the republics of the former Soviet Union are treated as 'tolerated foreigners' in Germany, which permits these immigrants to circumvent the slow application procedure that asylum-seekers normally have to undergo. They are granted social security benefits when they arrive and they also receive a limited work permit. In March, 1992, the Central Welfare Office of Jews in Germany reported that during the previous year about 8,000 Russian Jews had sought to make a new home in Germany. The small Jewish community of Essen with barely

---

[a] Before 1933, this notion likely motivated the three notable Jewish scholars and philosophers Leo Baeck, Martin Buber, and Abraham Joshua Heschel, who hailed from Eastern Europe, to settle in Germany.

one hundred residents doubled its membership within a few months; in Düsseldorf, the fourth largest Jewish community in Germany, membership grew by forty percent (from 1,500 to 2,100) during the same period of time.[14] In Fulda, a comparable situation exists. The Jews from the former Soviet Union, due to the repression of all religions by the Communist regime, do not now know what it means to be Jewish—they have to learn the essentials of Judaism.[15]

The present Jewish community of Fulda is housed in the former Jewish grammar school and draws its membership from the town of Fulda and the surrounding areas (such as Lauterbach). The large presence of American military forces was doubtless one reason for choosing the area of Hesse in general, and Fulda in particular, as the location for a Jewish community. In May 1987, approximately three hundred Jews visited Fulda, composed of one hundred seventy who were former residents. One woman had returned to Fulda several years earlier, but she had departed hastily after spending half a day in the park in severe emotional distress. Because the other Jewish visitors had experienced similar feelings, they found that being together lessened their pain.[16] Prior to the visit, anti-semitic slogans appeared on walls of houses. Although the visit of Fulda's former Jews passed without a major anti-semitic incident, the Jewish guests were frequently accompanied by police in civilian clothing.[17]

On August 14, 1993, five hundred neo-Nazis marched in a parade in Fulda on the occasion of the fourth anniversary of the death of Rudolf Hess, Hitler's deputy. When the Fulda police did not initially intervene, the neo-Nazis loudly proclaimed their slogans and unfurled flags and banners of the neo-Nazi movement. Eventually, in the course of the day, the Fulda police checked this neo-Nazi exhibition.[18] After World War II, two Jewish families, Dyrenfurth and Bruck, moved to Lauterbach. Following the cessation of hostilities in 1945 and the dismissal of some Nazi-oriented teachers, Mrs. Dyrenfurth was invited to serve as Latin teacher at the Lauterbach high school, a position she held for many years. Mrs. Dyrenfurth was so admired by her students and the Lauterbach community that, after her death, her former students and others cared for her aged husband.

While Mr. Dyrenfurth had been imprisoned by Nazis in a concentration camp, the Dyrenfurth daughters managed to flee from Germany. They eventually settled in Canada, where the younger daughter married Mr. Bilek. The older daughter, Inge, obtained a doctorate in chemistry and practiced her profession in Canada until her retirement in upstate New York in an anthroposophical community. Inge became an impassioned follower of Rudolf Steiner. After being severely handicapped in her sixties by a stroke, Inge was cared for in the anthroposophical community in Spring Valley. Mr. Dyrenfurth died at the age of nearly ninety-nine in December, 1990.

Before World War II, Lilo Bruck, was a warm, outgoing, well-educated woman who lived with her family in Frankfurt am Main. From her accounts it is not entirely clear whether those who concealed her from the Nazis acted out of altruism or were persuaded by large sums of money. After the war, Lilo was nearly paralyzed by the fear of having to master a new language and culture shock. Therefore, despite her past tribulations in Germany, she settled with her son, Hannes, in Frischborn (now a part of Lauterbach). Lilo was not a complete newcomer to the Vogelsberg region, since her uncle, Mr. Löwenstein, was one of several butchers who had provided the Jewish community of Gedern with kosher meat before 1933.

In Frischborn, some of the local citizenry objected to any Jewish presence on the basis that no Jews had lived in that village before World War II. In the late 1980s, Lilo's cleaning lady from Lauterbach stated that, out of fear of unpleasant repercussions, she had not told her children that she was working in a Jewish household. In the 1980s, Lilo's social contacts were primarily with members of the Jewish community in Fulda. She was also friends with a few non-Jews who genuinely wished to make amends for past injustices and who were drawn to this big-hearted altruistic woman. By 1992, the infirmities of age impelled Lilo to check into the possibility of accommodations in a personal care home in Alsfeld. Ultimately, however, she decided against that particular home because below her proposed quarters, an elderly resident habitually goose-stepped around clad in the uniform of a Nazi officer. Lilo eventually moved into a personal care home in Bad Salzschlirf.

During the early and mid-1980s, two Jewish women resided in or near Alsfeld. One, an Edith Marx, was the widow of the manager of the local Wallach Lumber Yard and a returnee to Germany who had not lived in Upper Hesse prior to 1933. The second, Dr. Ursula Miriam Wippich, was born in 1945 in Königsberg. Her father, a captain in the German medical corps, was killed in World War II before her birth. She was formerly a Catholic and had practiced medicine in Romrod. In her own words, at the age of twenty-one she had read the entire Bible and had mastered Hebrew by age thirty-three. She had a very impressive knowledge of *Torah* and *Talmud* and she has recorded detailed accounts of Jews in the Vogelsberg region until 1870. For several years prior to Miriam's formal conversion to orthodox Judaism, she was a faithful member of the Jewish congregation in Giessen. In 1987, she left Romrod for Schöppingen in order to be with her aged mother.

In 1991, Rita Malcomes and her husband, both Catholics from Queck-Schlitz near Lauterbach, decided to convert to orthodox Judaism. Mr. Malcomes underwent circumcision at age sixty, and husband and wife immersed themselves in the study of Judaism for five years. However, the orthodox Jewish communities of Frankfurt am Main and Fulda would not receive the Malcomes couple into their fold.

An account recently published by the German Ministry of the Interior ascertained that, from 1991 to 1992, there was a fifty-four percent increase in violent activities by the extreme right. Violence on the whole was directed against 'foreigners.' However, in 1992 there were incidents of vandalism against Jewish sites and facilities. Acts of desecration of cemeteries and memorials and incitement by right extremists did not diminish in the first quarter of 1993. The German Ministry of the Interior disclosed that thousands of Germans continued to be active in the extreme rightist organizations. In 1993, in Hesse, the *Republikaner* party—led by Franz Schoenhuber, a former SS officer—obtained 8.1 percent of the vote, thereby gaining representation in the state legislature. In Frankfurt am Main, support for the *Republikaner* was 9.3 percent.[19]

In 1971, during a visit to Lauterbach and the region of Hesse, I heard some unsavory remarks about Jewish displaced persons. In Limburg, a bookstore proprietor stated "that having gotten rid of the Jews in World War II was useless because there are just as many of them around now and they are up to their old tricks." In Lauterbach, Mr. Sedelmayer, an optician at the *Marktplatz*, stated that the Jewish displaced persons who lived in the area were guilty of all the scandals that the Nazis had ascribed to the native Jews of yesteryear. It is true that former concentration inmates, who for years had been cruelly mistreated, were not in a particularly tolerant frame of mind. Because the Jewish displaced persons were a daily reminder of German wrongdoing, the victims did not elicit compassion from the perpetrators. Nevertheless, the presence of the Allies after World War II made it easier for Jews to reside in Germany.

By 1953, some Jews had begun to return to Germany and as a result Jewish congregations had 21,775 members in 1960 and 25,757 in 1965.[20] No member of my father's immediate family (seven siblings and their offspring) or any of his many cousins or their children permanently returned to Germany. Nor did any of my mother's family, including her many cousins from Giessen or any of the seven children of Markus Strauss (Hinter dem Spittel 4 in Lauterbach) return permanently to Germany. In fact, among my parents' many relatives, friends, neighbors, and acquaintances in Washington Heights (upper Manhattan, New York) who hailed from all parts of Germany not a single individual returned. Mention should be made that no high German public official explicitly invited Jews to return to the country of their birth and citizenship. Neither did the German government appeal for forgiveness for the Nazi atrocities.

Of about 200,000 refugees of the Nazi era, only a few thousand returned to Germany. Nevertheless, Kurt Stein (formerly of Eisenbacher Tor 7), who left Lauterbach in 1936 for what was then Palestine, returned for a brief visit to his native town in the early 1950s and subsequently settled in Hanover, Germany, where he resided with a non-Jewish woman. Kurt did not return to Lauterbach again until 1990. Older German Jewish returnees were perhaps persuaded by the hardship of adjusting to another culture, the difficulty of mastering a new language at an advanced age, and in anticipation of reparations (*Wiedergutmachung*). Among the older generation of Germans, I observed a more tolerant mind-set toward Jews during the early 1980s. Of the people under eighteen whom I met in the Hesse area, the majority rarely held a position on Jews because they had never met any.

REPARATIONS (*WIEDERGUTMACHUNG*) TO GERMAN JEWS AFTER WORLD WAR II	*WIEDERGUTMACHUNG* PUT A RIGHTFUL CLAIMANT into the demeaning predicament of being a supplicant. Former members of the Nazi party, the SS, and the SA were appointed to take charge of reparations. In a few cases were applicants able to identify their former oppressors.[21] For this reason, I recoiled from

Chapter Twenty-Three

yet another humiliation at the hands of Germans and only at my mother's repeated exhortations did I finally apply for my *Wiedergutmachung*. The total in my case amounted to the token payment of $2,500, which was intended to make up for the involuntary interruption and loss of my college education. This amount was inadequate for a college education in the United States at that time and did not account for my loss of earnings due to a lack of completed higher education over a period of twenty-five years.

I received no indemnification for the harsh pain and the constant feeling of anxiety I had relentlessly been subjected to at school and in public in Lauterbach and in Alsfeld. Being constantly referred to as a 'parasite' had not enhanced my self-image and has caused me to apologize for my very existence throughout life. My recurrent and frightening dreams, accompanied by sensations of oppression and helplessness, were signs of my psychic pain, but they were dismissed with the explanation that I was susceptible to these illnesses beforehand.

My parents' *Wiedergutmachung* was even more paltry. Because of the onset of my father's illness in the spring of 1953, he was unable to travel to Germany to collect damages in the fabricated court case in which he had been falsely accused of animal torture. My father had intended to bring Karl Böcher to justice for the perjury he had committed during the trial and to prefer charges against Mr. Burg and Mr. Ruhl. All three individuals were employees of the Riedesel brewery and all three had terrorized my father and our family. My father was always of the opinion that this triumvirate had performed in accordance with their employer's tacit approval—indeed even at their employer's express instigation—and with an understanding of special employee benefits.

My father also planned to appeal the sale of our *messuage* at Cent 17 because it was a compulsory transaction. Prior to its sale on January 11, 1937, Mr. Klippert, the administrator of the Riedesel in Lauterbach, had repeatedly urged him to give first preference to the Riedesel as buyers. In addition, Mr. Klippert had promised that at any time the property would be returned for thirty thousand *Mark*, the 1937 purchase price. Probably because they may have had to return the *messuage* after World War II, the Riedesel made only the most necessary repairs on the residence and the stable buildings and carved up our living quarters to be occupied by six families. They took down many fruit trees, several huge oaks, an enormous linden tree, a large sycamore, and a mighty red beech tree. The Riedesel converted our stately lower gardens into a parking lot and demolished all existing landscaping.

Within several years, seven of the sixteen Riedesel partners who had attained ownership

The *messuage* at Cent 17 circa 1910

of Cent 17 lost their lives in traffic accidents or as war casualties. In November, 1937, Joachim von Riedesel died over Ostend, Belgium while on a Sabena flight from Munich to London when the plane exploded and went down in flames.[22] During the early 1930s, Joachim von Riesedel had been a weekly Friday afternoon guest at the home of the Jewish family Hess in the Rockelsgasse. Here he engaged in long conversations with the sharp-witted elderly Nathan Hess and his son, Julius. Von Riedesel shared newly-brewed coffee and freshly-baked white Sabbath bread (*'Berches'* in Lauterbach). Shortly after Hitler's rise to power, Joachim von Riedesel made it known to the Hess family that, if he were a Jew, he would depart from Germany.

Reparations would have offered my parents more favorable financial arrangements if they were residents of Germany. They never considered returning permanently because they were not confident that the majority of Germans were willing to tolerate Jews in their midst. To my parents, Auschwitz was the disheartening testimony that the Christian world in Germany could not be trusted. In fact, Pastor Meyer of the Lauterbach Lutheran Church did not advance the October, 1991 invitation to Lauterbach's formerly Jewish citizens. He and his colleague, Pastor Hoffmann, participated only perfunctorily in the interactions with former Lauterbach Jews. Furthermore, because only a few Jews had returned to live in Hesse, Jewish communal life no longer existed. Even in the 1990s, Jewish communal life in Hesse (except for Frankfurt am Main) remains negligible.

Of the three hundred sixty-three synagogues in Hesse, one hundred forty-five (forty percent) were destroyed during *Kristallnacht* and fifty-nine (sixteen percent) were destroyed after May 8, 1945.[23] The synagogue in Angenrod, which had been dedicated in 1797, endured the ravages of *Kristallnacht* only because of its close proximity to other village buildings that would have also been swallowed by flames. In 1959, the Angenrod synagogue building appeared structurally unscathed and sturdy, except for broken windows and a devastated interior. However, in the early 1970s, even that synagogue was gone and the last glimmer of Angenrod's Jewish past was thereby erased. The fact that Angenrod designated a street 'Anne Frank Street' was probably meant to mitigate guilt connected with the fate of its own Jews. Doubtless, the local villagers found it simpler to come to terms with the fate of this young Jewish girl rather than the memory of their own neighbors.

My parents' first request for restitution was dated December 1, 1949, but the matter had not been settled to my father's satisfaction when, on August 10, 1953, he died at age sixty-nine of lymphosarcoma. At that time, my mother was sixty-two-years old and possessed limited financial resources. Although my father's illness had lasted only a few months, it had considerably depleted my parents' sparse financial reserves. Over the next twelve years, my mother pursued the matter with an unwavering resolve but she never achieved resolution because, from the beginning, the scales of *Wiedergutmachung* were balanced against the claimant.

Chapter Twenty-Three

The German government consented to *Wiedergutmachung* primarily as a political decision in order to facilitate Germany's reentry into the family of nations. Restitution did not originate from a deep yearning on the part of Germany's populace to atone for the violent assault, dispossession, and inhuman slaughter of its own Jewish citizens and all Jews within its range of action during World War II. On the occasion of Konrad Adenauer's ninetieth birthday in January, 1966, the then-German chancellor earmarked peacemaking with France and reconciliation between the German people and Jews as the main goals of his political activity. He said that he was motivated from a sense of justice because the crimes against the Jews had to be atoned for so that his country could gain esteem among the nations of the world.

In 1952, an opinion poll by the Allensbach Institute showed that forty-four percent of Germans believed that payment of three billion *Mark* to *Wiedergutmachung* to Israel was "superfluous."[24] Restitution to victims of Nazi persecution was further encumbered when, on June 18, 1957, the German finance minister, Schäffer, stated in a speech in Frankfurt am Main that Parliament had not adequately thought out the *Wiedergutmachung* law and had therefore put the *Mark* in jeopardy.[25] It took seven years before a lawful arrangement of restitution was formally presented.

This delay created a great deal of hardship for the elderly applicants in my family, whose physical and mental health had deteriorated due to their ill-treatment in Germany, the unaccustomed climate at the place of their asylum, and the unpracticed and frequently arduous manner of earning a living. Conversely, in Germany the costly reinstatement of civil servants who had been dismissed during the denazification process was settled in 1951.[26] My parents conjectured that the majority of reinstated former Nazis missed no opportunity to impede and to prevent the whole process of restitution for Jews.

On July 11, 1951, my parents received 14,815.59 *Mark*, which included twenty thousand *Mark* from the Riedesel (diminished by legal expenses) for our *messuage* at Cent 17. At that time, that compensation totaled $1,140.34 in American dollars. On April 23, 1956, my mother received $1,800 for the loss of my parents' business. Additionally, there was a goodwill payment of $50 for my father's business and the settlement for forced sales amounted to just under $400. In the aggregate, these trifling amounts were hardly representative of my parents' huge financial losses or of their agony, humiliation, and anguish under the Nazis from 1933 to 1937.

My parents' first request for restitution was dated December 1, 1949. Until shortly before my mother's death on September 1, 1966, she was engaged in a paper war with the bureaucracy in Hesse, which she could hardly budge despite her undaunted efforts. Whenever my mother furnished the required documents, the German bureaucracy came up with another stumbling block she had to overcome. For example, my mother should have been entitled to a small widow's pension at age sixty-five. However, for nine years the German authorities decided that she was ineligible for this pension because my father died fifty-two days earlier than the qualifying date. Finally, because of hardship and illness, my mother was granted an old age pension of about $50 per month in late 1965—six months before her death.

Of Lauterbach's former Jews with whom I consulted, none fared any better than my parents in connection with German restitution. For example, Kurt Stein of the prosperous clothing and carpet establishment (at) Am Eisenbacher Tor affirmed that his parents, Laura and Max Stein, who immigrated to Israel, received only a trifling compensation for their flourishing business and imposing building on a main commercial street in Lauterbach. Julia and Meyer Adler received no financial compensation from Germany at all.

How did the German government square itself with people such as Max Stein and his wife, who suffered the loss of their young son, Herbert? What amends would be equitable for Siegfried (Steven) Strauss (III) of Eselswörth 6 for the killing of his mother, Martha Meyer Strauss, and the murder of his young sister, Blanka Strauss? By what means could a government, even if a high-principled bureaucracy had been in place, compensate Manfred and Herbert Stern for the loss of their parents, Rosa Oppenheimer Stern and Max Stern, and for the murder of their young brother, Arnold Stern? How could restitution be made to Beate and Susi Sylvia Stern for the killing of their parents, Rosa Gottlieb Stern and Moritz Stern?

Some buyers who acquired the former property of Lauterbach Jews at bargain rates, resented making compensatory payments. In July of 1987, when I discussed the situation with my former classmate Erich Opel, he told me that his father took exception to paying an additional amount for Bahnhofstrasse 70, but was obliged by government regulation to comply. In March 1938, Mr. Opel had acquired the beautiful half-timbered family residence and large grounds for much less than the market value from Therese Strauss, her daughter, Sara Strauss Spier, and her son, Salomon Strauss (I), prior to their departure for Obere Mainanlage 20 in Frankfurt am Main. In the early 1990s, the stately building was still owned by the Opel family and was occupied by two ophthalmologists.

In August 1987, Gertrud Knapp Hoos of Steinweg 23 voiced unmitigated disapproval that her father-in-law, the late Mr. Hoos, was mandated to make compensatory payments for the land and stable buildings he had bought from my Great-Uncle Markus Strauss of Hinter dem Spittel 4. Before immigrating to the United States in 1937, my uncle had sold the property to Mr. Hoos under duress and below market value. The Opel and Hoos families were not the only ones who had expected to acquire booty from Jews without redress.[b] In addition, Jewish forced laborers or foreigners who did not live within German borders during the time of the Nazis or who did not come to Germany within narrowly prescribed time limits were also completely excluded from German restitution payments.[27]

---

[b] For example, in 1349, at the time of the Black Death, Emperor Charles IV permitted the inhabitants of the city of Speyer to keep confiscated Jewish property and he also annulled all debts owed to the Jews. Around the same time in Deggendorf, Jews were attacked and killed and the town council collected their assets. Toward the end of the fourteenth century, Jews in Nuremberg were spared upon receipt of money. (Edward H. Flannery, *The Anguish of the Jews* [New York: Paulist Press, 1985]: pp. 109, 111.)

It is necessary to point out that looking after restitution was inherently and virtually a full-time occupation. In addition to their own endeavors, my parents engaged Mr. L. Sondheim, whose specific competency was restitution. He, in turn, employed Dr. Kinzenbach of Giessen, who commanded an additional fee. The Giessen lawyer was entitled to retain as his payment my mother's pension for five years ($3,000), but he waived this arrangement in favor of six months ($150). My mother did not live long enough to receive her small pension for even one year. Regardless of legal representation, it was incumbent upon my parents to keep abreast of any change in an existing law or any additional decree that might work in their favor. Generally, they gleaned the latest facts and developments about restitution from the *Aufbau*, a German-Jewish newspaper founded in 1934.

The worst part of the *Wiedergutmachung* process was that the applicant who requested rightful return or adequate compensation for his lost property or deprivation of his civil rights was assigned the role of petitioner. *Wiedergutmachung* was a demeaning and, for the most part, futile exercise that was programmed by Germans to produce heaps of paper. In the end, Jews who had been forced to sell or abandon their property recouped ludicrously meager amounts.

DENAZIFICATION IN GERMANY AFTER WORLD WAR II

IN JULY, 1993, THE GERMAN AUTHORITIES revealed that Kurt Franz had been released from prison in May. Franz had been deputy commander and then commander of Treblinka where approximately 900,000 Jews had been murdered. In 1965, a German court sentenced Kurt Franz to life imprisonment for the murder of at least 300,000 people, of whom the greater part were Jewish, and for personally killing one hundred thirty-nine individuals. The court determination stated that "a large part of the streams of blood and tears that flowed in Treblinka can be attributed to him alone." Franz had beaten Jews mercilessly and then revived them with water to extend their torment and prolong his enjoyment. Once he took target practice by shooting prisoners between the legs as they sat on the latrine.

When Franz was arrested in 1959, the authorities found in his apartment an album of photographs from Treblinka with the inscription, "The Best Years of My Life." Kurt Franz was set free under Article 57a of the Criminal Code, which allows for a life prisoner to be discharged after fifteen years unless "the particular gravity of the guilt of the convicted prisoner mandates the further execution" of the sentence. Citing this provision, the state prosecutor argued against his release. However, two courts invoked Franz's failing health and argued that his crimes were not sufficiently severe to justify his serving the full sentence. The seventy-nine-year old Franz spent thirty-four years in prison, which is approximately equal to one hour in jail for each of the 300,000 people he killed.[28]

Endnotes

1. Wolf-Arno Kropat, *Neunhundert Jahre Geschichte der Juden in Hessen* (Wiesbaden, 1983, Kommission für die Geschichte der Juden in Hessen), p. 448.

2. Paul Arnsberg, *Die jüdischen Gemeinden in Hessen* (Frankfurter Societäts-Druckerei, GmbH, Volume 1, p. 10.

3. Kropat, *Neunhundert Jahre Geschichte der Juden in Hessen*, p. 449.

4. Ibid, p. 456.

5. Ibid, pp. 456-457.

6. Wolfgang Benz, "Juden im Nachkriegsdeutschland" *Spiegel Spezial*, Nr. 2/1992, p. 49.

7. Kropat, *Neunhundert Jahre Geschichte der Juden in Hessen*, p. 457.

8. Dr. Ursula Miriam Wippich, *Memorbuch 1981/82*, p. 13.

9. Alfred Deggau, Storndorf, *Geschichts-und Altertumsverein der Stadt Alsfeld*, February 1956, p. 73.

10. Ibid.

11. Renate Chotjewitz Häfner and Peter Chojewitz, *Die Juden von Rhina*, Verlag Geisteswissenschaftliche Dokumentation GmbH, Oberellenbach 1988, p. 5.

12. *Fuldaer Zeitung*, May 29, 1987.

13. Kropat, *Neunhundert Jahre Geschichte der Juden in Hessen*, p. 449.

14. Boike Jacobs, *German Tribune*, March 6, 1992.

15. Letter of July 8, 1992, by Mrs. Wieland of Fulda to Mathilda W. Stein.

16. Bertram Lenz, *Fuldaer Zeitung*, May 27, 1987, p. 9.

17. Elke Hoesmann, *Lauterbacher Anzeiger*, June 1, 1987, p. 3.

18. *Aufbau*, September 10, 1993.

19. Roni Stauber, "Anti-Semitism in Europe in the First Quarter of 1993," *Wiener Library*, Tel Aviv University, Ramat Aviv, pp. 4-5.

20. Kropat, *Neunhundert Jahre Geschichte der Juden in Hessen*, p. 453.

21. Irene Meichsner, *German Tribute*, November 5, 1989, p. 13.

22. *Lauterbacher Anzeiger*, November 18, 1937.

23. Thea Altaras, *Synagogen in Hessen*, Verlag Karl Robert Langewiesche Nachfolger Hans Köster Königstein in Taunus, p. 231.

24. Meichsner, *German Tribute*, November 5, 1989, p. 13.

25. Kropat, *Neunhundert Jahre Geschichte der Juden in Hessen*, p. 476.

26. Ibid.

27. Benz, "Juden im Nachkriegsdeutschland" *Spiegel Spezial*, p. 53.

28. Daniel Jonah Goldhagen, *New York Times*, August 21, 1993.

Chapter Twenty-Four
Emigration to the United States
The Wertheim Family in their New Country

Berta Lamm Wertheim and Vogel (Frederick) Wertheim (III) circa 1933

For German-Jewish refugees, entry to the United States was based on the quota laws of 1921 and 1924. This arrangement limited immigration from individual countries. In addition, the immigration laws stipulated that an applicant for permanent residence in the United States be evaluated by the American consul and also present a birth certificate, passport, marriage certificate, army records, and police records. For Julius Hess of Lauterbach, a motorcycle speeding citation temporarily prohibited his entry into the United States. At that time in Hesse, minor traffic offenses became part of an individual's police record.

The American Consulate officials in Stuttgart were hardly expeditious in aiding Jews in getting out of Germany, although I never heard of anyone being treated disrespectfully. Consular officials carried out orders from the State Department in Washington. In the 1930s, Germans of international eminence gained admission to the United States more easily than other refugees. Included in this group of prominent immigrants were physicist Albert Einstein, author Erich Maria Remarque, composer Kurt Weill, psychologist Erich Fromm, and sociologist Max Horkheimer. Moreover, these famous newcomers found employment with no trouble at all. For that reason, many Americans mistakenly assumed that all political refugees from Germany —Jewish or otherwise—were famous and did not need financial or other assistance. In reality, a great proportion of nameless exiles encountered hard rows to hoe.

In 1937, my parents were invited to the American consulate in Stuttgart at the same time as my Great-Uncle Markus Strauss and his wife, Lina Strauss (of Hinter dem Spittel in Lauterbach). Both these families had children in the United States, which generally eased the granting of visas. Because my Great-Uncle Markus Strauss was anxious that his wife's hearing problem not deter her entry into the United States, he admonished her not to act so deaf. (*"Lina, stell Dich nicht so taub an!"*) Although Lina's hearing problem was not discovered, her husband's visa was delayed several hours, until

Markus Strauss

a thorough medical examination diagnosed a leg rash of his as psoriasis rather than a contagious disease.

THE ARRIVAL OF BERTA AND VOGEL (FREDERICK) WERTHEIM (III) IN AMERICA

IN OCTOBER, 1937, MY FIFTY-FOUR-YEAR-OLD FATHER and my forty-six-year-old mother arrived in New York. They chose an American ship because they did not wish to subsidize Hitler's economy through the variety of newly-devised taxes and charges. In May 1935, my father had bid farewell to his daughter, Erna, in Hamburg. At that time, he was led away by Nazi police and interrogated on suspicion of not obeying foreign exchange regulations. However, he was set free within an hour because a careful Nazi search found no more than the lawful amount of currency on his person.

Chapter Twenty-Four

When my parents disembarked from the ship in New York, their examination by the Immigration and Naturalization Service and by the customs check went smoothly. By comparison, when I arrived in June 1934, I had a strange encounter with a customs officer. As I opened my cabin trunk on the pier at the duty officer's request, the full aroma of well-ripened handcheese so completely overwhelmed the officer that he suspended any further customs examinations. The dozen home-made handcheeses (*Handkäse*) had been requested by my relatives in New York. Dutifully packed by my mother, they had been in the ship's hold for the duration of my sea journey. My trunk and suitcase contained only clothing, books, and several smoked sausages to be given to relatives.

For the first two weeks, my father and mother stayed in our apartment in the West Bronx in New York. Their furniture and household items arrived at the end of that time, having been transported on a freighter. After the three-year separation, we had much to share and I wished to ease my parents' adjustment to the country of their refuge, where a refugee is confronted with a new language, a diverse culture, and unfamiliar mores. As newcomers, my parents suddenly had to cope with many changes in unfamiliar surroundings and also to adjust from a small town to a large metropolis. It must also have been difficult to be shown the way by their daughters, since heretofore it solely had been their role to guide. The notion of unconditional leadership of family elders was deeply embedded.

The difficulty of my parents' acclimation was intensified because they had to unlearn many essential aspects of surviving as Jews in Germany even before Hitler had come to power. Frequently, these same characteristics were a definite encumbrance to living in the United States. After midlife, it is difficult to shed values and practices lived by since early childhood. Furthermore, my mother and father were debilitated by the daily debasing treatment in Nazi Germany and particularly by my father's narrow escape from a Nazi jail for twelve months.

Until the end of their days, my parents felt indebted to the United States for granting them asylum in their hour of distress and for saving them from cruel annihilation at the hands of the Nazis. Although they venerated President Roosevelt, my father criticized the Department of State for not attempting to intervene more effectively on behalf of Jews in Europe. During World War II, my mother and father enthusiastically invested in War Bonds and readily subjected themselves to any inconvenience or personal deprivation, which would advance the war effort. My parents were eager to love America wisely, but not too deeply, lest they suffer another emotional blow.

Similar sentiments prevailed among other refugee relatives. My husband's brother, Fred Stein, a civilian, delightedly furnished the American army with details of a strategic installation relating to the Mensfelder Kopf situated close by his native village (Mensfelden) near Limburg an der Lahn. All of my refugee cousins were drafted and they eagerly served their new country. Meinhard Hammerschlag was stationed in Hawaii; Kurt Herz was assigned to an army post in Alabama, as was Kurt Leopold, the husband of my cousin, Friedel Leiser Leopold; Walter Wertheim served on the Navy repair ship *S.S. Hamilton* in the Pacific; and Benno Herz, the husband of my cousin, Edith Leiser Herz, served in the European field of operations.

Bert Mayer, husband of my cousin, Margot Wertheim Mayer, was a staff sergeant with General Patton in the Seventh Armored Division. Bert was wounded in the Battle of the Bulge, and he fought at Remagen, where American troops crossed the Rhine in March 1945. When Bert entered Buchenwald with General Patton's army, he was horrified by the diabolic barbarity masterminded by the Nazis. He vowed that, after his army duty, he would never again set foot on German soil.

The only cousin on my mother's side, Walter Lamm of Baltimore, served in the army in Europe and was stationed in Germany in 1945 after Germany's surrender. Walter's commanding officer persuaded him not to return to his native town, Kirtorf, lest with the hot-headedness of a nineteen-year-old he would settle accounts with local Nazi villagers, who had so severely tormented his paternal grandparents, his parents, and all the Jews of Kirtorf. In the late 1980s, some Kirtorf townspeople bemoaned Hitler's demise because he had kept law and order among young Germans; other residents of Kirtorf equated America's war in Vietnam with Germany's treatment of the Jews.

As late as the 1980s, some older citizens of Lauterbach were still afraid of retaliation. They were haunted by the notion that former local Jews, clad in the victor's uniform, might have entered their town with the American occupying forces on March 29, 1945. Would these Jews seek revenge, measure for measure, from those who had mocked and tortured their people, and from others who had stood idly by? Many Lauterbach citizens noticeably breathed a sigh of relief that they were spared such a fate.

A few months after armistice, a young American soldier named Ernst Oppenheimer (formerly Rockelsgasse) peaceably and briefly visited his native town. The unexpected appearance of a former local Jew in uniform filled the populace with considerable unease, disquieting those who were old enough to have witnessed *Kristallnacht*. Ernst Oppenheimer had escaped with his family to the United States after enduring the November pogrom at the Jewish boarding school in Bad Nauheim and then in Lauterbach. In 1991, he did not accept Mayor Falk's invitation to Lauterbach's former Jews.

In Lauterbach, only the presence of black American soldiers as members of the occupying forces moved some citizens to even greater fear and trembling than a native Jew clad in the uniform of Germany's victor. During the period of American occupation of Lauterbach, two American officers of Jewish faith took local brides. One of these women came from a family who was much in the foreground of the local Nazi movement (*Rast*).[1]

In connection with America's war effort, the following achievement should be called to mind. Walter Strauss, son of Ricka Frank Strauss and my mother's cousin,

Siegfried Strauss (II), distinguished himself while serving with the 634th Field Artillery Battalion of the Seventh Army. Until his emigration to the United States in November 1937 at the age of fourteen, Walter lived in Lauterbach at Gartenstrasse 16 and consequently spoke German fluently. In 1944, as a twenty-one year old private in the U.S. army, he resourcefully enticed forty-nine German soldiers to surrender. In 1991, Walter Strauss did not return to Lauterbach at Mayor Falk's invitation. As a matter of record, none of the participants of the 1991 reunion either served in the American Armed Forces during World War II or had witnessed the horrors of Germany's pogrom against its Jews on November 9 and 10, 1938.

By the time of the arrival of my parents' household goods, they had located a spacious six room apartment at 935 St. Nicholas Avenue (157th Street) in Washington Heights, which is situated in the upper section of Manhattan in New York. Washington Heights extended roughly from Harlem to beyond Inwood Park. At that time, St. Nicholas Avenue and other nearby streets still retained some attractive private residences. Various considerations persuaded my parents to locate in the Washington Heights area. Transportation was served by the nearby subway stations at Seventh Avenue and Eighth Avenue; streetcars and buses traversed the area, some connecting to downtown New York and to other boroughs.

Moreover, there were several newly-established German-Jewish congregations in the immediate area and many members hailed from towns in Hesse. It was a gratifying experience for my parents and other refugees to be able to discuss at great length the shortcomings of these synagogues they did not wish to join, whereas in a small town in Hesse there had been no choices. For the first time since living under a dictatorship, there was also the joy of indulging in critical judgment without unpleasant consequences. My parents did not immediately commit themselves to a German-Jewish congregation. But in visiting other congregations, they were uncomfortable with the lack of solemnity. At first my parents preferred that the synagogue sermon be delivered in German. German-Jewish refugees founded more than a dozen congregations where the delivery of sermons was in their mother tongue.[2] In synagogue and at home, my parents were inclined to the accustomed manner of practicing rituals. However, my father no longer wore a tailcoat and a top hat, which he had traditionally donned during services on the Pilgrim Feasts in Lauterbach. My parents preferred silent prayer; they did not favor cantorial repetitions and emotional presentations. They were somewhat disquieted with the uncontrolled swaying (*shokeling*) of other congregants.

During my own visits to German-Jewish congregations in Washington Heights, I did not observe unusually devotional characteristics. In fact, a male monitor repeatedly admonished ladies in their assigned section to refrain from conversing loudly. The undue obsession with quiet and solemnity has historic origins. For centuries in the Vogelsberg region, silence and what Christians deemed appropriate conduct during religious services and near the synagogue were imperative. If non-Jewish neighbors detected a lack of discipline, they derisively labeled synagogue behavior as '*Judeschul.*' This term was even used by Jews to describe a lack of order and decorum. It is probably for this reason that noisemaking during the Book of Esther (*megillah*) reading on *Purim* was not practiced in Hesse; non-Jewish neighbors would have regarded such a din unsuitable for a house of worship.

Around 1700, a complaint was launched against the Jews Abraham and Israel of Kirtorf (my mother's native town), who allegedly prayed loudly on Sunday and caused the church-attending Christian populace much annoyance.[3] Moreover, in Hesse the authorities withheld German citizenship until Jews learned to act like Christians: synagogue behavior was expected to be much the same as conduct in church. This fixation on seemly synagogue decorum influenced synagogue policy. When their synagogue building was enlarged in 1823, the elders of Storndorf decreed that unruly behavior during assignment of new seats would not be tolerated. Violators were subject to arrest and would be led away for detainment in Romrod.[4]

In 1938, as my parents' first Passover in New York approached, my father searched in vain in the Jewish section of the lower east side of Manhattan for *mazzah shemura.*[a] Throughout his life, my father had joyously performed every religious duty and good deed. Thus, he could hardly fathom that, in this affluent society with no restrictions on religious observances, *mazzah shemura* was unavailable. In Germany, *mazzah shemura* had been an integral component of the *seder* and had always been included in our *mazzah* shipment. Stringent and continual supervision of the wheat and baking of these three *mazzahs* (approximately thirteen inches in diameter) began at harvest. Three holes in the *mazzah* represented the priestly caste (*kohanim*), which descended from Aaron (the first high priest) and which were responsible for specified functions during the days of the First and Second Temple. Two one-inch holes stood for the descendants of the tribe of Levi ('Levites'), which in biblical days served in the Tabernacle and later in the Temple. A one-inch hole in the *mazzah shemura* signified the most common and the most numerous folk among Jews.

My parents felt uncomfortable when a congregational member addressed them in Yiddish and they could reply only in German or broken English. My own inability to speak fluent Yiddish piqued a professional social worker at the Brooklyn office of the Council of Jewish Women. Instead of offering me encouragement after my browbeating by the Nazis, Miss Neuman seemed somewhat resentful that my lot was not worse. Although, as a social worker, she surely must have been aware of the exploitation of young girls working in households, she recommended that I seek domestic employment. In 1934, I worked as a nursemaid in Stamford, Connecticut, and was at the complete mercy of the Inselbuch family who were summering there. Mrs. Inselbuch's humanity toward a nineteen-year-old refugee can best be epitomized by her frequent pronouncements that the fate that had befallen the German Jews was well deserved.

---

[a] *Mazzah shemur*a is guarded *mazzah*, specially prepared from wheat watched from the moment of harvesting so that no moisture should touch it. For the *mazzah shemura*, every process must be under strict supervision of observant Jews.

Chapter Twenty-Four

In the late 1930s, my fellow workers at the United Jewish Appeal seriously questioned my Jewishness because I was not in fluent command of Yiddish. They accepted me into the fold only after I recited blessings in Hebrew and read from the *siddur* (prayer book). Moreover, my fellow workers at the American Jewish Joint Distribution Committee could hardly accept the notion that in Germany, where they perceived every Jew to be reform, even a young girl was so thoroughly initiated into the teachings of orthodox Judaism. My female co-workers coveted my education in Hebrew, Jewish history, customs, and ceremonies. In their *milieu*, such schooling was offered only to males.

The German Jews of the 1930s were a minority within a minority. It is estimated that from 1933 to 1943 the United States opened the door to approximately 97,374 Jews born in Germany.[5] From my own observation, disapproval of German Jews existed because this group possessed a better formal education than earlier waves of immigrants from Eastern Europe. In the 1930s, this phenomenon applied equally to the German Jews of Washington Heights (approximately twenty thousand)[6] who seemed to have benefitted from more secular and religious schooling than their Jewish neighbors from Eastern Europe. Among Jews from Eastern European countries who immigrated around the turn-of-the-century, there was displeasure that the German Jews arriving before *Kristallnacht* were, in general, not completely destitute.

The tree-lined streets of Washington Heights reminded my parents of their home in Lauterbach. To the delight of my parents, they were surrounded by three rivers (the Hudson, the Harlem, and the East River) and several parks. On Saturday and Sunday afternoons they frequently walked to their favorite park by the Hudson River and met with relatives, friends, and acquaintances, who also lived nearby. By contrast, long before 1933 in Lauterbach, it was tacitly understood that Christians did not wish to share recreational areas with Jews; and certainly by the end of 1933, Jews were absolutely forbidden to enter the *Eichküppel*, the local recreational area. My personal inclination was to live away from the German-Jewish section of Washington Heights because I wished to adapt as quickly as possible to the patterns of Jewish culture in America and grasp the American way of life. In this connection, it is astonishing that as of 1991 in West Hartford, Connecticut, an orthodox German-Jewish congregation (comparable to the orthodox German-Jewish congregations in Washington Heights) matched the national average of 51 percent for intermarriages. Moreover, this congregation had remained under the stewardship of its original spiritual leader from Germany, Hans Bodenheimer.

In the 1930s, landlords in Washington Heights offered a new occupant one or two months free rent for the first year's lease. This was not a minor consideration for my parents and other refugees in favoring the neighborhood. Until World War II, many of my parents' friends and some of our relatives shared an apartment with their children and grandchildren. Typically, the grandmother was responsible for the household and the grandchildren because every other family member worked outside of the home in order to make ends meet.

My parents chose a large apartment to accommodate the considerable quantity of household furnishings and goods they had brought. Because the Nazis frequently did not permit currency to leave Germany, even before 1937, my parents were forced to invest their remaining liquid assets in house furnishings, cameras, and binoculars. Their objective was to convert some of these items into cash once in the United States. By selecting a large apartment, my parents were able to have a room for my sister and an additional room to sublet.

Another reason for renting a large apartment was to provide housing for my maternal grandfather, Jakob Lamm, my mother's brother, Leo Lamm, his wife, Mathilde, and their son, Walter, all of whom arrived from Kirtorf in the summer of 1938. As a twenty-two year old, I provided an affidavit for my seventy-seven-year-old grandfather and assumed responsibility that he would not become a public charge. My Uncle Leo's cousin, Fritz Stern, who had gone to the United States from Giessen before World War II, provided the affidavit for the three members of the younger Lamm family.

At that time Fritz Stern and his family lived on West End Avenue. At best, Fritz manifested passing interest in the welfare of the Lamm family. There were recurring discussions between my mother and her brother about the letdown they experienced because of the emotional distance of their three Stern cousins. The disappointment was especially significant because their parents had lavished so much thoughtful consideration and affection on these nieces and nephews. After arriving in the United States, my grandfather stayed at my parents' home for several months while my aunt, uncle, and Walter lodged with the refugee family of her sister, Rosa Hess from Lasphe. The entire Lamm family took their meals at my parents' home.

Later in 1938, Jakob Lamm and the Leo Lamm family settled permanently in Baltimore, Maryland because it was extremely difficult for a middle-aged male to find any kind of work in New York unless he was well connected. Moreover, the quest for a job was even more trying for recently-arrived refugees with limited knowledge of English, lack of familiarity with local practices and customs, and no specific skill in a trade or craft. Among our friends, more refugees were employed toward the end of the 1930s than in 1934, 1935, and 1936.

As a beginning, my Uncle Leo took a job as a night watchman in the Baltimore clothing factory of his cousin, Jack Lamm. In 1938, Jack Lamm recounted how, when his parents arrived in Baltimore at the turn of the century, the non-Jewish Ruppert family of Ober-Gleen (near Kirtorf) befriended and aided the newly arrived Jewish immigrants from Kirtorf. This Ruppert family from Ober-Gleen was the original producer of Ruppert Beer.

In the New York City area, a large number of male refugees of all ages worked as sweepers, stock boys, or assistants arranging merchandise at Hearns, a department store on Fourteenth Street, and at Klein's, a specialty store for ladies apparel at Union Square. Some earned their livelihood by selling merchandise door-to-door to refugee friends. It was less of a problem for female refugees to find employment as cooks, nursemaids, or general houseworkers. Doctors' wives, who had been addressed as *Frau Doktor* in Germany, were now employed cleaning floors and performing kitchen work. Female refugees also seemed to find jobs more readily in factories because women generally commanded lower wages than men. For a rural German Jew, having his wife become the family's main breadwinner, exacerbated by his lesser prospect of finding a job, was doubtless an irksome experience.

My Uncle Abraham Herz had previously let no chance pass in declaring himself the breadwinner and the absolute head of his household; now he had to make the best of his wife, Hilda Herz, supplementing the family income at home by altering clothes. My uncle, Levi Leiser, whose involvement in household chores had been decidedly limited, was engaged in the not particularly ego-enhancing occupation of scrubbing pots in a hospital kitchen, with limited outlook for the future; his wife, my aunt, Kathinka Leiser, rented out rooms. My aunt, Frieda Hammerschlag and her husband, Willi, did piece work at home; their son, Meinhard, found employment as a baker, his chosen trade. Based on their training and unmindful of need, the children of Hannchen and Herz Wertheim—without exception—neither relied on their sponsor nor accepted financial aid. They staunchly upheld the precept inculcated in their youth that, even in hard times, one must always contribute to charity and must never accept alms.

By this time, my father's cousin, Hermann Levi, was permanently disabled by a heart condition. His wife, Marta Gross Levi from Angenrod, rented out rooms with board to some of our male cousins sponsored by Irma and Carl Wertheim. On Sunday mornings, Marta supplemented her family's income by selling smoked and uncooked kosher sausages to relatives and friends. My mother usually purchased only half of her requirements from Marta because another refugee friend regularly supplied the balance. The sausage was part of the standard Sunday night evening fare that also included potato salad, fetticus salad (*Rapunzel*), and tea.

Most of my kin in Washington Heights, as well as my refugee relatives in the West Bronx (the Markus Strauss family from Lauterbach), and in Forest Hills (the Sonneborn family from Marburg and the Stern family from Mannheim) generally remained faithful to the food they were accustomed to from Germany. Soups made from potatoes, lentils, and beans were popular on weekdays, and the Sabbath soup contained *Grünkern* (a species of unripe wheat with grains that do not thresh free from the chaff). Another traditional food was *Apfelschalet* made of thinly-cut apples enclosed in pastry dough and baked in a high iron pot; *Kartoffelschalet* was prepared with grated potatoes and soaked left-over *challah*, and was baked in a heavy iron pot. Characteristic foods of Germany, such as yeast cakes with crumble topping, plum topping, goose, celeriac, and white asparagus, remained popular. Dishes prepared from the organ meats were gradually discontinued, except for liver. (In Upper Hesse, eating organ meats had been traditional because in winter many Jewish households butchered for their own use.)

A tacit understanding prescribed that, for all purchases or services, close relatives were to be given first consideration, followed by former townspeople, acquaintances, and others who were expected to reciprocate. My parents placed their insurance with Hugo Schleicher, who had been a successful attorney in Germany but his inexperience with American law prevented him from practicing here. His wife was Ruth Weinberg from Lauterbach. By the late 1930s, some German Jewish doctors who had passed the requisite tests practiced medicine in Washington Heights.

Many immigrants entered the United States with the assistance of a sponsor who guaranteed that the applicant would not become a public charge. Others came here as capitalists, which meant that the visa applicants would have a substantial sum of money at their disposal in the United States. My mother's cousin, Hugo Strauss from Lauterbach, who had lived in Krefeld after his marriage to Grete Gompertz, was probably granted a capitalist visa. In all likelihood, my mother's Stern cousins (Beate and Fritz) and her Sonneborn cousins from Marburg also entered the United States under this classification. Hugo Strauss, who had a doctorate in chemistry, later participated in the cattle business owned by his brothers (Siegfried (II), Hermann, and Salli [II]). Comparable to their occupation in Mannheim, members of the Stern family pursued work in connection with the commodity exchange. Samuel Sonneborn, who was older and perhaps freer of pecuniary responsibilities, assembled a family tree.

Hedwig Stern Rollmann, my mother's cousin from Cologne, founded a successful health food store on 34th Street in Manhattan. My female Strauss cousins from Lauterbach worked as specialists in stringing pearls. My sister sewed furs at Brenner Brothers on Madison Avenue. Among our acquaintances, young girls only rarely found employment as clerical workers. In our family, young girls who came here without their parents at age sixteen or so were, without regard to intellect or potential, expected to work as sleep-in help in households, thereby accumulating funds to assist parents, grandparents and other relatives.

Understandably, many refugees settled near their sponsors, who frequently provided friendship and moral support. Who were the sponsors of the refugees of the 1930s? They were those who had already come to the United States for personal or economic reasons. Around the turn of the century, many young marriageable Jewish women of families with several daughters went abroad because their parents were unable to provide the large amounts required for dowries (*nedunyah*). Before World War I, my husband's aunt, Ricka Kaufmann Lammel from Hellstein, chose to immigrate because her parents could not provide a dowry to a prospective husband. Later, during the 1930s, Ricka Lammel provided several affidavits for both close and distant relatives from Hesse.

In 1923, my Aunt Irma Levi Wertheim came to the United States because her impoverished family could not gift her with a dowry. The Levis of Angenrod were not even able to pay for her crossing. For almost a year, Irma was bound by contract as a domestic in New York City to work off the costs of her transportation.

Shortly after Hitler came to power, Irma's vision about the future of German Jews and her steadfast sponsorship facilitated her brother's family of four, nine nieces and nephews, three sisters-in-law and their husbands, and numerous cousins to come to the United States (a total of thirty-nine refugees). Most of the family members of the older generation established themselves in Washington Heights. None of our family members and refugee friends relied for financial support on those who furnished affidavits. On the contrary, sponsors were regarded as individuals who had rendered aid in times of extreme need. Their acts of rescue were henceforth reflected in unremitting beholdenness. Those who had benefited from pecuniary advantages of age, making it necessary for younger siblings to immigrate, now felt guilty that these younger siblings were helping them out. In the 1930s, in contrast to subsequent immigration statutes, organizations were not allowed to serve as guarantors for refugees.

It was for need of a dowry that several daughters of the Adler family of Neuhof-Flieden near Fulda emigrated to South Africa; their brother, Meyer Adler, lived in Lauterbach with his family at Bahnhofstrasse 34. Among South African Jews, marriage portions were no longer in favor. Rather, young unmarried Jewish women from rural Germany were valued because of their religiosity, competence, and willingness to work hard. They were held in the highest regard by Jews from Lithuania who had established themselves in South Africa at the turn of the century. The Adler sisters from Neuhof-Flieden married immigrant Jews from Lithuania. A generation or two later, these families aided their refugee kin from Germany. While visiting in Johannesburg and Capetown in the late 1970s, I met a large group of Jews from Alsfeld and from other towns in or near the Vogelsberg region who, based on contacts with earlier immigrants, had found refuge in South Africa in the 1930s. My mother's cousins, the Juda Wahlhaus family from Gersfeld, were able to immigrate to South Africa because they had kept in touch for many years with a long-time friend from the Hesse region.

In Washington Heights, education of Jewish immigrants who had come from Hesse before World War I and during the 1920s was virtually the same as that of my parents and most other refugees of the 1930s. Generally, formal education consisted of graduation from public school or its equivalent in a Jewish congregational school, excellent mastery of reading, writing, and arithmetic, and a fair reading knowledge of Hebrew. Three of my mother's nine Stern cousins from Giessen who came to these shores before World War I had been educated in a larger city, where higher education was within easier reach. They lived on West End Avenue and Central Park West in New York and in Buffalo, New York. In the 1930s, these families did not adhere to orthodox Judaism. In fact, Jack Stern's first marriage was to a non-Jew who, to the best of my knowledge, did not convert to Judaism. Jack's second wife was a Jewess. Fritz Stern and his sister, Gustl Stern Sonneborn, were members of Reform congregations.

My father's brother, Carl Wertheim, Carl's wife, Irma Levi Wertheim, and Irma's sister, Gisela Levi Rosenbaum, came from Angenrod in the 1920s. Although they were not affiliated with any Jewish congregation, they were strongly-oriented ethnic Jews. Of my father's four sisters, three of them came to the United States in the 1930s and joined orthodox German Jewish congregations. The fourth sister, Mathilde, lived and died in Switzerland. In the early 1990s, my father's grandniece, Vera Hammerschlag Hamburger, was principal of the secular section of the Orthodox Breuer congregational school in Washington Heights.

Relatives who resided in affluent areas tended to be more reluctant to send affidavits and render assistance to refugees, particularly in connection with employment. These relatives endlessly discoursed about the difficulties American citizens encountered in looking for work and about the meager prospects for employment for a refugee. Based on my own experience and the encounters of my parents, our more affluent relatives who had come here before World War I seemed to keep their distance. A cousin of my mother was curious enough to greet her four cousins from Lauterbach at the pier but failed to involve herself in finding shelter for this family. Although she was my kin, she introduced me to her friends at a social function at Central Synagogue in New York City as "a refugee from Germany."

However, there were many amenable guarantors of affidavits who spared no effort in enthusiastically assisting refugees and also finding jobs for them. One such person was Carl Laemmle, who was born in 1867 in Laupheim (between Ulm and Bieberach in southern Germany). Mrs. Laemmle's maiden name was Stern, and she hailed from Hintersteinau in the Vogelsberg region. Carl Laemmle not only sponsored close relatives and others, but he also secured employment for many refugees at Universal Studios, which he founded.

My parents' first apartment was on St. Nicholas Avenue. One year later they moved to a similar apartment on 162nd Street, between Fort Washington Avenue and Riverside Drive. During that time, my father began liquidating photographic paraphernalia, optical equipment, and other items that they had brought for converting to cash. My father discovered a flourishing market in these and other items brought by refugees from Germany with the objective of selling. After my father's forty-year commitment to animals—the continual demands of feeding, milking, and providing clean habitats—he now felt liberated and consequently lavished all the more care on his family.

Unlike most German Jewish refugees of the 1930s who fled to Palestine (*jekkes*) and to the United States, my father had a warm and relaxed manner with people. Moreover, a vital element of his business success was his acumen for instantaneously appraising assortments of vendibles in days when calculators were not generally at hand. Moreover, his remarkable adjustment to unfamiliar work at his age was in essence attributable to his penetrating grasp, his pleasant and friendly disposition without deceit or pretense, his calmness and utter self-control, and his genuine regard for the lives he touched. Above all, my father's achievement in all

Chapter Twenty-Four

things can largely be attributed to his expertise in the art of compromise in business as well as in personal contacts.

Within a short time, my father readily adapted to market changes in the refugee district and had also mastered enough English to get along in a non-German speaking environment. After *Kristallnacht*, trade in optical and photographic equipment lessened because the German Jews who could still reach these shores had been forced to pay for the damages the Nazis had perpetrated on Jewish properties. In addition, the Nazis systematically deprived Jews of any assets and generally reduced them to pauperism. From that time on, refugees from Germany arrived without any belongings except the clothing on their backs; an example was the Jakob Oppenheimer family from Lauterbach.

By this time, some refugees who had arrived earlier were devoid of liquid assets. They were frequently compelled to dispose of paintings, objects of art and Judaica, valuable Oriental rugs, old books, fine linens, china, crystal, flatware, and furniture. Despite his imperfect fluency in English, my father soon absorbed enough requisite information from books and trade magazines to carry on an adequately thriving business until his death. His instinctive devotion to handsome form and seemly craftsmanship was reflected in his cherishing handling of treasured articles. I will never cease to wonder at his broad and expert knowledge in the field of antiques. In case of incertitude about an object, my father was unselfishly guided by loyal friends in the trade. Among other reasons why he treasured America so highly were his many friends who readily accepted him as a member of humankind, regardless of his Jewishness. Although his merchandise came mainly from refugees, my father's clientele was not restricted to Jews; many buyers were German Christians of Yorkville, New York City, and Valley Stream, Long Island.

Although my father was usually silent in discussions about God's part in the Holocaust, the Holocaust seemed to diminish neither his heartfelt belief in God nor his deep devotion to Judaism. Therefore, the most compelling reason for owning a business was his determination to observe the Sabbath and all Jewish festivals as he had done in the past. In the 1930s, the majority of commercial enterprises required at least half a day of work on Saturday. There would also have been the matter of an early dismissal on Friday afternoons during the winter months, when Sabbath commenced shortly after four o'clock. In addition, my father strictly observed the High Holy Days, Passover, the Feast of Weeks, and the Feast of Booths. Except for the seventeen-year stint in his father's business, when his father controlled funds, Vogel Wertheim (III) had never worked for anyone. At the age of fifty-four, he was not much disposed toward earning a living as an employee.

During a wave of anti-semitism in the 1930s, leaders of Jewish immigration and welfare agencies were concerned that a large concentration of refugees in the New York area might provoke anti-refugee interest groups to press for even more restrictive entry regulations. Refugee organizations therefore proposed that my parents and other exiles leave the New York area and settle in midwestern areas, where they would be less conspicuous. For my parents, the idea of relocation was problematical and unappealing; they wished to live near their children, who were gainfully employed in New York.

Moreover, my parents' proximity to other Jewish refugees enhanced their confidence in their immediate surroundings, and they dreaded a third adjustment within three years. My parent's social life was dominated by their family members, other refugees, and their synagogue; they rarely went to the theater or saw motion pictures. Not wanting to settle in a community with only a handful of Jews, my parents were anxious to avoid possible restrictions on their activities on Sunday and other Christian holidays.

My mother and father smarted from the tribulations of adjusting to another culture and were tellingly depressed about the fate of their kin and friends still left in Germany. But in a spirit of gratitude for having reached these shores, they celebrated their Silver Wedding Anniversary in March 1938 by entertaining close relatives in their home. Until the 1960s, our family always celebrated weddings, bar mitzvahs, anniversaries, and birthdays at home. Several kinds of homemade cakes were regularly prepared for birthday celebrations, which my father's siblings and their spouses faithfully attended. In March 1953, my parents observed their fortieth wedding anniversary in their apartment with a full-course dinner for about thirty close relatives and a few friends. On this occasion, a relative recited a poem that was intended to wittily depict my parents' life. This exercise in occasion poetry was a traditional ingredient of all joyous German-Jewish family gatherings. It was, at best, a rendition of bland and largely humorless rhyme.

From the time of his arrival in the United States until his death, my father's eyes reflected the pain, degradation, and agony of spirit he had been forced to endure for four years under the Nazis in Germany. His eyes also mirrored the disillusionment of trying to understand how humankind could descend to such heretofore unimaginable depths of wickedness. Why should the reparations process (*Wiedergutmachung*) be so demeaning, apparently designed to reduce Jewish victims to the role of petitioners? Remembering the traumas of the past, arduously establishing a new business, learning another language, adapting to a new culture, and adjusting to an unaccustomed climate after a lifetime in the temperate Vogelsberg region had a deleterious effect on the physical health of this formerly rugged individual. However, despite reversals and hard times, and in character with others who have been sorely tried, my father retained his sense of humor—the outward affirmation of spirit.

Until the end of his days, my father delighted in his marital bliss. Unfailingly and joyfully, he upheld the Jewish precept that a man shall honor his wife more than his own self, shall love her as he loves himself, and shall constantly seek to benefit her according to his means. He lived by the *Talmudic* injunction: "A man should spend less than his means on food, up to his means on clothes, but beyond his means in honoring his wife and children, because they are dependent on him."

Chapter Twenty-Four

Thanks to proximity in Washington Heights, my father also enjoyed the warm kinship, respect, and affection of his four siblings and their children. Above all, my father basked in the joy of his four grandchildren. All his life he was partial to children, understanding their needs in a time when this awareness was hardly commonplace. Moreover, in later life, Jewish children were living proof that Hitler's plan to eradicate all Jews was thwarted.

By late spring of 1953, my father's health had deteriorated visibly. In addition to weight loss, he complained of pain in his joints and bones and he experienced severe gastrointestinal problems. By the middle of July 1953, Dr. Isidor Kross diagnosed him as suffering from a cancer of blood-forming tissues (lymphosarcoma). Dr. Kross ruled out surgery because the illness was already too far advanced. My mother linked the origin of my father's illness to contagion from an infected cow years earlier. Although my father lost strength rapidly and his body was wracked by much pain, he strove to live as usual by honoring his God and caring for his family. On August 8, 1953, a Sabbath, my father's condition worsened considerably. The attending neighborhood physician, Dr. Wertheimer, advised that we gather a minyan in order to recite the *Shema*, the outstanding prayer in Judaism and a declaration of God's unity. The *Shema* was traditionally recited on a deathbed by Jews in Upper Hesse and also in some other parts of Germany. My father joined in a clear voice in this affirmation of faith, discharging this religious custom naturally and without personal concern.

Thereafter, for two more days, his bodily suffering seemingly lessened, his mind was most discerning, and as always he was extremely thoughtful of others. At the age of sixty-nine, my father died surrounded by his family in the late morning of August 10, 1953, the first day of *Elul*, the sixth month in the Jewish year. The first of *Elul* is the *Rosh ha-Shanah* (beginning of a new year) with regard to the tithing of cattle (ma'aser). Certainly, cattle had been a significant factor in my father's life. According to legend, the forty days of Moses' stay on Mount Sinai commenced on the first day of *Elul*. Befitting my father's life, an allusion to the initial letters of *Elul* are, "I am my beloved's and my beloved is mine" (*Song of Songs*: 6:3).

On Wednesday, August 12, 1953, according to custom, my father was buried in a simple pine coffin in the loose white linen garment and corded belt that every married male donned in synagogue on the High Holidays in Upper Hesse. This white garment and accessories, a new *talith* (prayer shawl), *tefillin* (phylacteries), a set of *mahzorim* (festival prayer books), and a *siddur* (prayer book containing daily and weekly prayers) constituted an integral part of a man's possessions at marriage. My mother directed that a set of my father's *tefillin*, which were no longer ritually faultless (*posul*) be placed in his grave. The spacious chapel at Hirsch and Sons in the Bronx was filled to capacity with family and friends (many from Lauterbach) who wanted to render the last honor to this unassuming man.

My father was laid to rest at Block Nine in Cedar Park Cemetery in Paramus, New Jersey. We commenced the seven days of mourning (*shivah*) in my mother's home immediately after burial, and we observed *minyan* in the morning at six o'clock and at nightfall, except on the Sabbath. On Monday and Thursday we followed the regular *Torah* portion and read Psalm 49. My father's congregation supplied the *Torah* scroll for the duration of the *shivah*. From early morning until well into the night, a steady stream of relatives, friends, and acquaintances visited to offer condolences. Expressions of sympathy poured in from all parts of the world, where so many of my father's family and friends had been dispersed.

My mother grieved deeply for the remainder of her days. She was laid to rest next to him in 1966, and three of his sisters were interred nearby.

Endnotes

1. Interview with Elfriede Roth in Atlanta, Georgia, on November 20, 1993.

2. Henry Marx, *Aufbau*, January 7, 1994, p. 1.

3. Otto Christ, *Aus Kirtorfs Vergangenheit*, 1932, p. 130.

4. Alfred Deggau, Storndorf, *Geschichts-und Altertumsverein der Stadt Alsfeld*, February 1956, p. 81.

5. Steven M. Lowenstein, *Frankfurt on the Hudson* (Detroit: Wayne State University Press, 1989), p. 270.

6. Ibid, p. 22.

Epilogue

"May the God who is always present comfort you together with the other mourners for Zion and Jerusalem."
Taken from the desecrated Angenrod synagogue in 1959.

When I visited the Angenrod synagogue in 1959, the sanctuary was littered with bicycles and agricultural machines, which defiled the sanctity of the building. Although some of the Angenrod population were certainly aware of our displeasure with this state of affairs, they proudly emphasized that the synagogue in their village had survived the pogrom of *Kristallnacht* in Germany on November 10, 1938. However, the synagogue of 1797 endured for practical rather than ideological reasons: it was a wooden structure that had been built about nine feet away from other buildings. If the Nazis had set fire to the Angenrod synagogue, then adjacent houses would also have gone up in flames.

I can vividly recall the interior of the synagogue before its defilement during and after the Nazi era. The walls were painted off-white and women sat upstairs on dark wooden benches. To the best of my recollection, there was no partition screen (*mehizah*) between the space reserved for men and the space, generally in the rear or upstairs, reserved for women. The holy ark was made of dark wood and the *bimah* (the platform for the desk from which the *Torah* is read) was located approximately in the center of the sanctuary.

During my visit in 1959, I took from the synagogue any books I could find with Hebrew writing. Although no sacred books or scrolls of the Angenrod congregation had survived, one segment of Hebrew writing remained on the wall. Ironically it read, "May the God who is always present comfort you together with the other mourners for Zion and Jerusalem." The salvaged books had been used and left during World War II by members of the American armed forces who had conducted religious services in the synagogue while they were stationed in the region. No Jews have lived in Angenrod since 1942.

412]

[415

The Way It Was: The Jewish World of Rural Hesse

424]

List of Maps

List of Art Works